At War's Summit

This is the story of the highest battlefield of World War II, which brings to life the extremes endured during this harsh mountain warfare. When the German war machine began faltering from a shortage of oil after the failed Blitzkrieg against the Soviet Union, the Wehrmacht launched Operation Edelweiss in the summer of 1942, a bold attempt to capture the Soviet oilfields of Grozny and Baku and open the way to securing the vast reserves of Middle Eastern oil. Hitler viewed this campaign as the key to victory in World War II. Operation Edelweiss presumed the crossing of the Caucasus Mountains. Mountain warfare requires unique skills: climbing and survival techniques, unconventional logistical and medical arrangements, and knowledge of ballistics at high altitudes. The Main Caucasus Ridge became the battleground that saw the elite German mountain divisions clash with the untrained soldiers of the Red Army, as they fought each other, the weather, and the terrain.

Alexander Statiev is Associate Professor of History at the University of Waterloo, Canada. His extensive experience in mountain trekking, white-water rafting, and ski expeditions across five continents helped him assess the challenges to military actions in the mountains described in this book.

Cambridge Military Histories

Edited by

HEW STRACHAN,
Professor of International Relations, University of St Andrews and Emeritus Fellow of All Souls College, Oxford

GEOFFREY WAWRO,
Professor of Military History, and Director of the Military History Center, University of North Texas

The aim of this series is to publish outstanding works of research on warfare throughout the ages and throughout the world. Books in the series take a broad approach to military history, examining war in all its military, strategic, political, and economic aspects. The series complements Studies in the Social and Cultural History of Modern Warfare by focusing on the 'hard' military history of armies, tactics, strategy, and warfare. Books in the series consist mainly of single author works – academically rigorous and groundbreaking – which are accessible to both academics and the interested general reader.

A full list of titles in the series can be found at:
www.cambridge.org/militaryhistories

At War's Summit

The Red Army and the Struggle for the Caucasus Mountains in World War II

Alexander Statiev
University of Waterloo, Ontario

CAMBRIDGE
UNIVERSITY PRESS

CAMBRIDGE
UNIVERSITY PRESS

University Printing House, Cambridge CB2 8BS, United Kingdom

One Liberty Plaza, 20th Floor, New York, NY 10006, USA

477 Williamstown Road, Port Melbourne, VIC 3207, Australia

314–321, 3rd Floor, Plot 3, Splendor Forum, Jasola District Centre, New Delhi – 110025, India

79 Anson Road, #06–04/06, Singapore 079906

Cambridge University Press is part of the University of Cambridge.

It furthers the University's mission by disseminating knowledge in the pursuit of education, learning, and research at the highest international levels of excellence.

www.cambridge.org
Information on this title: www.cambridge.org/9781108424622
DOI: 10.1017/9781108341158

First published 2018

Printed in the United Kingdom by TJ International Ltd. Padstow Cornwall

A catalogue record for this publication is available from the British Library.

Library of Congress Cataloging-in-Publication Data
NAMES: Statiev, Alexander, 1956– author.
TITLE: At war's summit : the Red Army and the struggle for the Caucasus Mountains in World War II / Alexander Statiev, University of Waterloo, Ontario.
OTHER TITLES: Red Army and the struggle for the Caucasus Mountains in World War II
DESCRIPTION: Cambridge ; New York, NY : Cambridge University Press, [2018] | Series: Cambridge military histories | Includes bibliographical references and index.
IDENTIFIERS: LCCN 2017053771 | ISBN 9781108424622
SUBJECTS: LCSH: World War, 1939–1945 – Campaigns – Caucasus. | Operation Edelweiss. | Soviet Union. Raboche – Krest'ianskaia Krasnaia Armiia – Mountain troops. | Germany. Heer – Mountain troops. | World War, 1939–1945 – Mountain warfare. | Caucasus – History, Military – 20th century.
CLASSIFICATION: LCC D764.7.C3 P67 1995 | DDC 940.54/2175–dc23
LC record available at https://lccn.loc.gov/2017053771

ISBN 978-1-108-42462-2 Hardback

To Grisha Don, my partner in mountaineering

CONTENTS

FIGURES

MAPS

TABLES

ABBREVIATIONS

Abwehr	German military intelligence
MCR	Main Caucasus Ridge
NKVD	Narodnyi komissariat vnutrennikh del SSSR (USSR People's Commissariat of Internal Affairs)
OG	Operations Group for the Defence of the Main Caucasus Ridge Passes
OKH	Oberkommando des Heeres
OKW	Oberkommando der Wehrmacht
OPT	Obshchestvo proletarskogo turizma (Association for Proletarian Tourism)
OPTE	Obshchestvo proletarskogo turizma i ekskursii (Association for Proletarian Tourism and Excursions)
OSOAVIAKHIM	Obshchestvo sodeistviia oborone, aviatsionnomu i khimicheskomu stroitel'stvu (Association for Assistance to Defence, Aviation, and Chemistry)
SMERSh	Smert' shpionam (Soviet Military Counterintelligence Service)
TCF	Transcaucasian Front

INTRODUCTION: THE PATH TOWARDS THE TOP SUMMITS OF WORLD WAR II

Gde snega tropinki zametaiut,
Gde lavinvy groznye gremiat,
Etu pesn' slozhil i raspevaet
Al'pinistov boevoi otriad.

[A unit of military mountaineers
Wrote this song and sang it
While climbing under the roar of terrifying avalanches
Along snow-covered paths.]

Andrei Griaznov, Liubov' Korotaeva, and Nikolai Persiianov, 'Baksanskaia' (1942)[1]

When I started to participate in sport expeditions in the early 1970s, I heard the 'Baksanskaia' and other wartime songs[2] telling the story of Soviet climbers who had defended the Caucasus during World War II. These songs, written by military mountaineers, were enormously popular among Soviet climbers, rafters, skiers, and trekkers who wandered across remote Soviet regions after the war. The wartime songs triggered a folklore that glorified Soviet mountaineers as a vital component of the formations that fought the Germans in the high Caucasus. In 1966, Vladimir Vysotskii, the most popular Russian bard ever, visited a mountaineering camp in the Caucasus. After he heard wartime songs and stories about the battle of the Caucasus, he added another dramatic and emotional spin to the Soviet narrative: his 'Edelweiss Troops' song described Soviet and German climbers who had been partners in joint Soviet–German expeditions before the war and had developed strong personal bonds but were pitted against each other by war in a bitter, almost fratricidal fight:

A do voiny vot etot sklon
Nemetskii paren' bral s toboiu.
On padal vniz no byl spasen.
A vot seichas byt' mozhet on
Svoi avtomat gotovit k boiu.

[Before the war, you climbed this slope
With a German partner.
He fell down but you saved him;
And now he is probably loading his submachine-gun
Getting ready for battle.][3]

Vysotskii popularised the feat of Soviet mountaineers far beyond the circles of sport tourists. Today, the songs and stories about climbers' endeavours in World War II are as popular in the post-Soviet outdoor community as they were in the Soviet Union. In the absence of scholarly studies, the breathtaking and tragic mountaineering folklore shaped the Russian collective memory about this little-known episode of World War II, and most Russians who have been exposed to it believe that it relays historical facts.[4] This enduring perception stirred my interest in the battle on the Main Caucasus Ridge (MCR), which became the highest battlefield of the two world wars, reaching, at times, an altitude of more than 4,000 metres.

The major focus of this study is on the actions in the high Caucasus in the late summer and autumn of 1942. After the Wehrmacht recovered from the defeat at Moscow during the previous winter, the High Command of the German Armed Forces (Oberkommando der Wehrmacht, OKW) chose southern Russia as its main operational region for the 1942 campaign. In the summer, it launched two strategic offensives that were expected to decide the fate of the war. The first offensive, code-named Operation Blau, presumed that Army Group B would advance towards Stalingrad and take it, thus destroying a major industrial centre and intercepting a vital supply artery along the Volga River used by the Soviets to transport oil from the Baku region to central Russia. The second simultaneous strategic offensive, codenamed Operation Edelweiss, had higher stakes than Operation Blau. With the failure of the Blitzkrieg against the Soviet Union, the German war machine began faltering from the shortage of oil, which was delivered in insufficient quantities by Romania, its only oil supplier. Hitler calculated that without abundant oil reserves the German war economy was doomed to steady attrition and eventual collapse. In order to solve this problem once and for all, the OKW launched a two-pronged offensive by Army Group A: one major attack was to proceed towards the Grozny and Baku oilfields via the steppes of the Northern Caucasus and the other was to go along the Black Sea coast via Tuapse and Sukhumi to Transcaucasia and then to the Middle Eastern oilfields. In addition to these two major strikes, the 49th Mountain Corps was to advance across the Main Caucasus Ridge to the Black Sea into the rear of the Soviet 18th Army, which defended the Tuapse region; this would facilitate the advance of the German 17th Army along the Black Sea coast. This study focuses on this last component of Operation Edelweiss – a minor offensive meant to pave the way to the main campaign of 1942, a campaign perceived by the OKW as a key to victory in World War II.

At the turn of the twentieth century, the armies of several European states came to the conclusion that only a special force with mission-tailored skills, gear, and structure would be able to operate effectively in the mountains. However, as with any other special forces, the concept of mountain formations suffers from the internal contradiction between their ability to perform certain missions more effectively than regular infantry and their usefulness beyond these missions. It takes much time and effort to train the personnel of such formations, but the skills they acquire after lengthy training, their weapons, and the structure of their units are too mission-specific to secure an advantage in other conditions. A state expecting future wars to unfold mainly on the plains, with actions in the mountains occurring only on rare occasions, needs only a small mountain force, because such a force excels only in mountains or other terrain inaccessible to motor transport and heavy weapons. It makes no sense to deploy this force on plains with a decent road network, because its weak firepower and primitive logistics make it inferior to regular infantry, whose personnel require less individual training and can be easily replaced. Special forces, including mountain formations, must be few but well trained for their specific missions. This was the approach chosen by the Wehrmacht. In contrast, the Red Army raised many 'mountain' divisions but did not train them for mountain warfare. Since these formations differed from regular rifle divisions only in structure and not in skills, this designation can be used only in quotation marks.

The outcome of battles in the mountains often turns on the ability of the protagonists to cope with unique challenges unknown on the plains: narrow, steep trails accessible only on foot; limited opportunities for manoeuvre across broken landscape outside these trails; the impact of weather, soil conditions, snow cover, and winds above the treeline; the scarcity of population and, concomitantly, the shortage of shelters and food supply; the absence of vegetation or, by contrast, its exceptional thickness; and severe fatigue. Only those trained and equipped to operate in such conditions could be effective in the mountains.

However, the Stalinist state scoffed at the very notion of specialisation. The tendency to 'think big' while ignoring the details, even vital ones, surged during the Soviet modernisation rush of the 1930s and became a key component of Stalinist culture. The implications, in both the civilian and the military spheres, were a preference for quantity over quality, uniformity over specialisation, collectivism over individualism, and improvisation over professionalism. The Stalinist perception of people as mere cogs in the Soviet state machine[5] prompted communist leaders to ignore individual skills in the belief that the massive collective endeavour that inevitably had to be undertaken while performing any mission set by the state would make these skills unimportant. Such a mentality led to a series of strenuous but ineffective efforts in addressing problems that could have been solved more easily by smaller numbers of skilled manpower. The dismissive attitude of Soviet generals to military specialists was a repercussion of this tendency.

My father's war experience can serve as an example. He grew up in Baku, a city on the Caspian Sea with a warm, semi-arid climate, where even the lowest winter temperatures are well above freezing. When the government began allowing university students to volunteer for the Red Army in the autumn of 1941, he joined up and was sent to an officer school in Tashkent, a city with an even warmer climate. Upon graduation and with the rank of lieutenant, he was assigned to a ski brigade that fought on the Northwestern Front. Ski brigades conducted raids into the flanks and rear of immobilised Germans and also provided manpower to support armour in winter offensives, when they had to follow the rushing tanks closely. Such endeavours were torment for a person who had never skied before but who was expected, as a platoon commander, to be an example to his men. He dreaded the exhausting ski marches and his subordinates' mockery more than enemy fire. It would have been easy to find enough good skiers in Russia to field as many ski brigades as necessary, yet those in charge of recruitment enlisted a junior officer who had hardly ever seen snow. A key argument of this study is that such incidents were not bizarre aberrations but the rule, stemming from the general contempt for professionalism pervading the Red Army. The discussion of military professionalism in the context of mountain warfare is the core theme of this book.

The Caucasus is the highest mountain ridge in Europe; eleven of its peaks are higher than Mont Blanc, the top summit of the Alps. The climate of the region changes dramatically with elevation from the subtropical resorts dotting the Black Sea shore and surrounded by mandarin groves and tea plantations to the windy mountain passes well above the treeline that are free of snow for only two months a year. During the first winter of the war between the Soviet Union and Germany, the Red Army knew what battle environment to anticipate, while the Wehrmacht did not; this knowledge helped the Soviets to inflict the first strategic defeat on the German land forces in World War II. In contrast, the vertical dimension of warfare in the Caucasus furnished great surprises for both sides. When the Soviet and German general headquarters planned actions in the high Caucasus, none of them understood what atrocious conditions their soldiers would face there. Although the well-trained German mountain divisions sent across the Caucasus had gained a wealth of combat experience in the lower Carpathians, Norway, and Yugoslavia, all these regions were accessible to regular infantry. Only in the high Caucasus did they have to employ the full extent of their special skills in mountain warfare, and these skills enabled them to cope with the severe battle environment much better than Soviet regular infantry, some of which had the misleading designation of 'mountain troops'. The higher the elevations in which the battles occurred, the greater the imbalance of casualties in favour of the Germans. The Red Army's preference for uniformity and disregard of mission-tailored skills resulted in the unprecedented misery experienced by the Soviet soldiers sent to defend the high Caucasus. The Caucasus separates Europe and Asia; by crossing the MCR, the 49th Mountain Corps became the only Wehrmacht formation that reached Asia in World War II.

In order to better understand the environment in which the battles studied here occurred, I retraced the footsteps of the armies in the campaigns examined in detail or surveyed in this book: I walked along Suvorov's entire route across the Swiss Alps, crossed the Balkans via the Shipka pass, the MCR via the Marukh pass, and the Carpathians along the route of the Soviet 3rd Mountain Corps, and followed the trails chosen by the Lanz Division during its trek towards Tuapse. This field research allowed me to grasp some of the challenges experienced by soldiers, often imperceptible in combat records; it also helped me to assess the credibility of these records.

While the two major German strikes presumed by Operation Edelweiss have received sufficient coverage in histories of World War II, its most spectacular component – the bold attempt to break through the MCR – has attracted little scholarly attention. The German and the Russian narratives on the battle in the high Caucasus exist in parallel, and neither Russian nor German authors cross-reference their sources. German writings on this episode are limited to several brief memoirs,[6] a study of relations between the Wehrmacht and the local population,[7] and popular histories, the latter based on unidentified German sources.[8] All Western interpretations rest on these writings. Russian historiography on the battle in the high Caucasus consists mostly of memoirs of dubious credibility;[9] pseudo-scholarly, ideology-tainted writings that contain more misinformation than facts;[10] unreferenced popular histories;[11] and summaries of these popular histories.[12] The three trustworthy memoirs[13] and an unpublished PhD dissertation[14] of the Soviet period were thoroughly sanitised by censors and suffer as well from self-censorship. The post-Soviet, multi-volume official history of the Great Patriotic War devotes less than one page to the actions on the MCR, and most of the information it provides on this subject is false.[15] The post-communist scholarly contributions to this historiography are thus limited to one chapter in a monograph devoted to the entire 1942 campaign in the Caucasus that describes some events at the MCR but does not analyse them[16] and two valuable document collections.[17] This study is the first attempt to integrate data from Russian and German military archives and analyse the Soviet war effort in the high Caucasus.

The book starts with a discussion of the knowledge about mountain warfare that the Red Army had before it embarked on the campaign in the Caucasus in 1942. Military academies all over the world study historical experience in order to draw lessons for the future and avoid the disasters suffered by their predecessors.[18] And so did the Russian Imperial Military Academy, which thoroughly analysed the campaigns in which Russia participated. Since most lands of European

Russia and the adjacent lands of its western neighbours are plains, the Russian Army rarely fought in the mountains, and when it did these were minor episodes in Russian military history. However, they still demonstrated what the Red Army, the successor to the imperial army, should have anticipated in the next major war to operate successfully in the mountains. The Russian Imperial General Staff accumulated and processed a large volume of information on those experiences, sufficient for the Red Army to prepare itself for similar challenges in the future and train its soldiers to cope with them.

Having realised in the interwar period that mountains would likely be among the battle environments in which the Red Army would have to operate in the next war, its General Staff restructured several infantry formations as mountain divisions and undertook vigorous steps to create a pool of potential recruits with intimate knowledge of mountaineering. By the mid 1930s, this well-focused effort, supplemented with field experiments and conceptual research, had created a solid basis for raising a force able to match the elite German mountain divisions. However, the Soviet state wasted this impressive potential during the Great Terror of 1937–8, during which it destroyed not only the major proponents of mountain formations but the entire concept of such a force before it had taken its first steps towards professionalism. A host of problems, real and imagined, prevented the Red Army from following the Wehrmacht's example in recruiting local highlanders into mountain divisions. As a result, the Soviet 'mountain' divisions barely differed from regular rifle formations. After a series of embarrassing defeats suffered against the small, poorly armed Finnish Army during the Winter War demonstrated the simple fact that tactics, training, weapons, and uniforms must be adapted to the conditions of the potential military theatre, the Red Army made a consistent effort to prepare for winter warfare; however, it failed to extrapolate the conclusions it drew from the Winter War to actions in the mountains and entered the war against Germany having no units trained to operate in the mountains.

Although both Soviets and Germans made many grave strategic errors on the Eastern Front, Operation Edelweiss set a record in the number of blunders. The offensive of the German 49th Mountain Corps across the Caucasus was a wild gamble marked by thoughtless strategy, poor intelligence about the terrain and enemy forces, and the hubristic belief that the racial superiority of the *Herrenvolk* would secure an easy victory over numerous *Untermenschen*. As for the Red Army, its generals, none of whom had ever visited the high Caucasus, persuaded themselves that the ridge was impassable and failed to occupy mountain passes with the large forces they possessed. They squandered all but two 'mountain' divisions in actions on the plains long before the Germans approached the Caucasus and then had to rely mainly on regular infantry and cavalry to defend the MCR. Yet, despite the remarkable victories the German mountain troops won in the high mountains, the Red Army successfully countered their superior skills with far greater numbers and stopped the Germans as soon as they reached lower elevations at the southern slopes of the Caucasus, where their lack of alpine skills mattered less.

After that, the Soviets launched a counteroffensive that was to push the Germans back across the ridge and throw them down its northern slopes. However, the Germans regained their skill advantage at the high elevations and terminated the Soviet attack with small forces. Despite vigorous assaults, the Soviets failed to reconquer a single pass across the MCR and continued to keep numerous formations in the mountains, thus playing into the hands of the Germans, who were seeking to pin down as large a Soviet force as possible in order to frustrate the transfer of Soviet divisions to the area of the major offensive towards the Black Sea coast. Thus, the Germans snatched the victory from Soviet hands and turned the battle in the high Caucasus into a stalemate.

The combat effectiveness of the opposing forces depended on factors such as firepower, command-and-control systems, logistics, food supply, gear, uniforms, the ability to withstand atrocious weather and assist wounded men, relations with local people, and the morale of soldiers. Skill in mountain warfare enabled the Germans to outperform the Soviets in most regards, which resulted in a great disproportion of casualties being suffered by the opponents. After the Headquarters of the Transcaucasian Front (TCF) realised, belatedly, that, instead of regular infantry, they needed a special force able to operate effectively in the mountains, they scrambled together a handful of climbers, ordering them to help local commanders in raising genuine mountain units. The Mountaineering Section organised within the TCF quickly established a training infrastructure modelled on the one that had existed in civilian mountaineering before the war and trained thousands of soldiers within a tight timeframe, thus creating the potential to approach mountain warfare professionally. However, the elite mountain units raised as a result of these strenuous efforts emerged too late to affect the battle of the Caucasus.

The Red Army fought two more battles in the mountains on the Eastern Front. In the autumn of 1942, it faced a major German offensive across the wooded foothills of the Caucasus towards the Black Sea coast in the Tuapse region. It beat off this attack by deploying the same type of manpower that it had used in the high mountains: regular riflemen untrained for mountain warfare. Yet since their numbers were far superior to the grossly overstretched Germans and since the lower mountains offered fewer advantages than the high Caucasus to the skilled German mountain troops, the Red Army won a strategic victory, which contributed to the decisive failure of the Wehrmacht's campaign in the Caucasus. The Soviet soldiers who fought in the Caucasus drew many correct conclusions from their endeavour, and several senior officers promptly analysed the actions there and issued valuable recommendations on mountain warfare. However, the Soviet High Command (Stavka) ignored, for the most part, the grim experience of the Red Army in the Caucasus; it dismantled the sound training infrastructure established by the TCF in the wake of the battle and dissolved the elite mountain units that had been raised with such great effort. When the Stavka decided to exploit the September 1944 uprising in Slovakia in order to break into the rear of the German Army Group South across the Carpathians, it again planned this strategic offensive in the way it planned offensives on the plains. This last operation in the mountains on the Eastern Front, conducted by formations with a wealth of combat experience but without training in mountain warfare, ended in a bloody stalemate, with two Soviet armies pinned down by much smaller German forces.

The unimpressive performance of the Red Army in the mountains stemmed mainly from the absence of appropriate training. Was, then, its failure to organise a force able to operate effectively in the mountains a unique misstep or a typical undervaluation of mission-tailored skills? I argue that the basic training of Soviet soldiers serving in 'mountain' divisions was as inadequate as that of their counterparts elsewhere. The habit of sending untrained soldiers into battle with the idea that they would gain the necessary skills in combat had the effect of turning only those who survived the long and costly trial-and-error learning process into an effective force. Despite grave attrition, the large numbers of enlisted personnel eventually provided enough skilled survivors to match their German counterparts. However, the brief and casual mountain campaigns produced few trained soldiers, and most of those fell in subsequent battles on the plains before they could apply their skill to the next action in the mountains. In the absence of a training infrastructure, most participants in that next action were, again, soldiers untrained for mountain warfare. Without the scores of heavy weapons that were the major trump card of the Red Army, the enormous gap in skills resulted in a huge disproportion of casualties during every campaign in the mountains throughout World War II. The universal Stalinist disdain for professionalism was at the root of such an outcome.

1 RUSSIA'S HISTORICAL EXPERIENCE IN MOUNTAIN WARFARE

The knowledge basic to the art of war is empirical.

Carl von Clausewitz[1]

The French victories in the Italian Alps in 1796–7 that paved the way for the defeat of the First Coalition against the French Republic, and the Swiss campaign of 1799 that provoked the disintegration of the Second Coalition, showed that armies able to extend the theatre of war to the mountains could gain a strategic advantage over their enemies. The General Staffs of the Alpine countries began to implement special training for mountain warfare in the late nineteenth century, and soon thereafter the Austrian and Italian mountain troops proved their worth during actions in the Alps in World War I. Russia's traditional theatre of war – its European portion and the lands of its western neighbours – consists mostly of plains. Since the Russian Army had rarely fought in the mountains, its generals came to the idea of special mountain forces only in the late 1920s, and even then this urge was a response to trends in Western armies rather than a product of their own original strategic thought. Once the Red Army General Staff decided to address this issue, they had to learn the strategies, tactics, and logistics of mountain warfare and raise divisions with special structure, training, and gear. As Clausewitz argues, 'Historical examples ... provide the best kind of proof in the empirical sciences', which 'is particularly true about the art of war'; therefore, 'the detailed presentation of a historical event, and the combination of several events, make it possible to deduce a doctrine'.[2] In searching for a doctrine of mountain warfare, the Red Army could lean on the historical experience of the imperial army in the mountains. Although limited, it had the potential to provide valuable lessons for future wars. Russian imperial military history includes five important episodes related to mountain warfare: the campaign against revolutionary France in the Swiss Alps in 1799, the counterinsurgency in the Caucasus in 1817–64, the war against the Ottoman Empire in 1877–8 in the Balkans, and the actions in Transcaucasia and the Carpathians during World War I. These campaigns demonstrated the scope of the strategic, tactical, and logistical challenges presented by mountain warfare. The following survey of Russian military endeavours in the mountains shows the extent of knowledge about mountain warfare available to the Red Army on which it could lean while preparing for actions during the interwar period.

The Swiss Campaign (1799)

In the summer of 1799, Russia and Austria, members of the Second Coalition against revolutionary France, planned to counter the French invasion of Switzerland. Alexander Suvorov, arguably the best Russian general ever, led his corps of 21,286 men on an impromptu 270-kilometre trek from Italy across the Swiss Alps, planning to join another Russian corps stationed near Zurich and his Austrian allies deployed to the north of the Alps; together they aimed to expel the French Army from Switzerland.[3] He started the trek on 21 September without detailed maps or knowledge of the region. He planned to reach Zurich by the shortest route: via the St Gotthard pass (2,106 m) and along the Reuss valley to Lake Lucerne, and then, he thought, a shortcut along the lake's bank would lead to Schwyz and to a good road to Zurich. His force consisted of professional and battle-hardened soldiers who, however, had never fought in the mountains. Armed with the four-page *Manual on Mountain Warfare*, hastily written by Suvorov, his corps confidently headed towards the Alps, which were higher than any terrain the Russian Army had ever visited. Suvorov did not anticipate serious problems along his route in September but soon learned that the 'fog of uncertainty' was thicker and the 'friction of war'[4] more severe in the mountains than on the plains.

The chosen shortcut route along Lake Lucerne turned out to be impassable, which forced Suvorov to march through three additional mountain passes, two of them higher than 2,000 metres (Map 1.1).

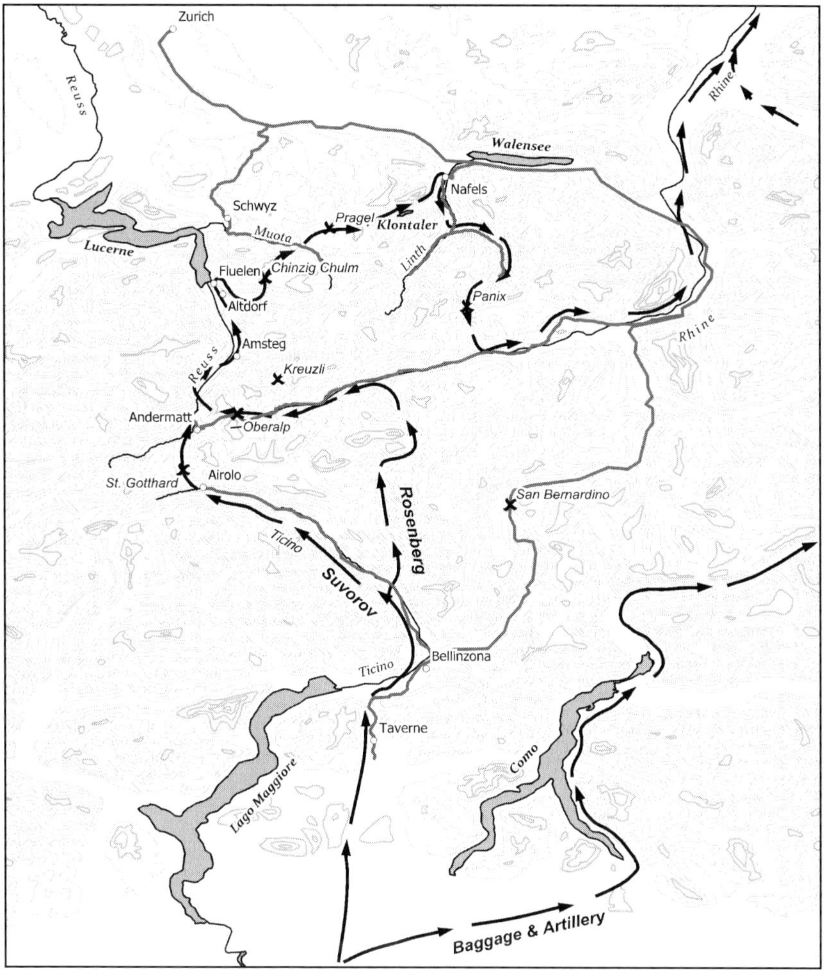

Map 1.1 The routes taken by Suvorov and his baggage train, September–October 1799

Exposed to icy wind and rain at high altitudes and shivering in their summer uniforms, the only ones they had on the hot Italian plains, his men suffered also from malnourishment because they could not live off the land in the sparsely populated highlands, while animals of the supply train suffered great attrition on rocky mountain trails, and those that were left could not keep up with the soldiers. Within two weeks, the boots of most soldiers became so worn down that their officers referred to Suvorov's army as 'mostly barefoot'.[5] Cavalry was useless in the high mountains; the greatest service that cavalrymen provided to Suvorov was compensating for the fallen mules by carrying supplies with their horses. Suvorov's corps experienced enormous attrition both from 'the elements, the most terrifying and merciless enemy',[6] and from the staunch resistance offered by much smaller French forces that had, however, experience of mountain warfare and occupied good defensive positions. Suvorov could break repeatedly through the French lines only because he always attempted to outflank these positions and most often succeeded. However, Russian soldiers became increasingly demoralised by hunger and fatigue. Being unable to carry hundreds of wounded men across high mountains, Suvorov abandoned them to the mercy of the French.[7]

By the end of the seventeen-day trek on 7 October, Suvorov had lost half of his soldiers, killed, wounded, sick from hypothermia, frostbitten, or taken prisoner,[8] many more than the French had, and all the artillery with which he had started the march.[9] The trek across the Alps did not attain its goals because Suvorov could not link with the other Russian corps or his Austrian allies before the French crushed them. Suvorov escaped annihilation but suffered so many casualties that, in the words of Clausewitz, they 'equalled those in a lost battle'.[10] Russia left the coalition as a result of the Swiss campaign and tensions with its allies, thus vitally undermining the cohesion of the alliance; the subsequent actions ended with a French victory and the disintegration of the coalition.

The Dargo Expedition (1845)

The Russian Army faced its next mountain endeavour during the Caucasus War. Russia's expansion to the mountain regions of Dagestan and Chechnya caused fierce resistance from the local tribes that began in 1817 and lasted for half a century until the Russians captured Imam Shamil, the rebels' last important military and religious leader. The Caucasus War was a long series of predominantly small-scale unconventional actions that could hardly provide valuable lessons for future campaigns against a regular enemy army. The exceptions were several large punitive expeditions intended to decisively defeat the rebels, the most dramatic of which was an expedition in the summer of 1845 launched by General Mikhail Vorontsov against Dagestani and Chechen rebellious tribes. A competent commander, Vorontsov had arrived in the Caucasus only a month before the raid; he had never

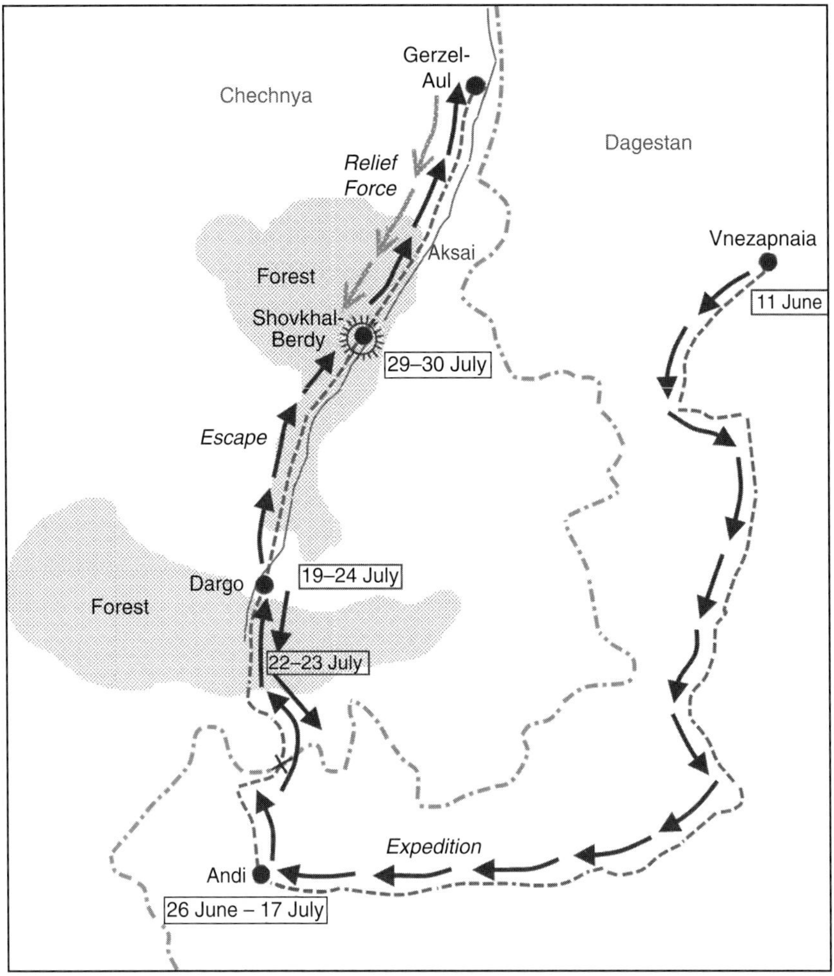

Map 1.2 The Dargo expedition, June–August 1845

fought in mountains elsewhere.[11] The Vorontsov force consisted of 10,616 professional soldiers with an impressive military record, most of whom, however, had no experience of action in the mountains.[12] The daring raid into the depths of the territory controlled by insurgents targeted Dargo village, the residence of Imam Shamil (Map 1.2). Vorontsov believed that the destruction of Dargo would terrify the rebels, ruin their morale, and thus end the decades-long insurgency with a single decisive blow.[13]

The expedition departed from the Vnezapnaia Fortress on 31 May 1845. The first misfortune came in early June when a vanguard regiment, advancing without tents, blankets, or food, was hit by a blizzard at a mountain summit well above the treeline and lost 200 men frostbitten and many more sick.[14] Poor weather, insufficient forage, and attacks by small insurgent bands aggravated the numerous logistical problems that inevitably occurred on the long, steep mountain trails. At the approach to Dargo, the expedition ran into a long series of barricades blocking the trail. The rebels, whose number was fifteen times smaller than the Russian force,[15] stubbornly defended the barricades made of huge trees, which were hard to bypass because of dense vegetation. The expedition found itself under fire from the barricades, from ravines above and below the trail, and from trees. Firing long muzzle-loading rifles, slow to load but more accurate and with a greater range than Russian muskets, the rebels devastated the Russian column from a distance. Demoralised by their impotence, and occasionally succumbing to panic, members of the expedition struggled through knee-deep mud from one barricade to another, increasingly losing tempo.[16] They reached Dargo and destroyed it but this action did not affect the rebels' determination. The expedition could not live off the land because the local population had fled their homes, while re-supply across the mountains teeming with rebels was extremely difficult. Having exhausted their supplies, the Russians had to retreat along another road.

During the retreat, the rebels, poorly armed but familiar with the mountain terrain, inflicted a decisive defeat on the expedition and surrounded it at Shovkhal-Berdy village, intending to destroy it to the last man. Only mountain artillery kept them at bay. Vorontsov began planning a breakthrough but it was possible only if the Russians abandoned their wounded men to certain death at the hands of the rebels.[17] In the end, a Russian relief force lifted the siege and allowed the expedition to escape. The expedition lost one-third of its manpower. Its participants perceived the Dargo raid as a strategic defeat which 'boosted the morale of mountaineers, who saw that large military formations with a proven record of courage, well armed, well trained, and well supplied, those who had scored many glorious victories in Europe, could do almost nothing against their disorganised hordes'.[18]

War in the Balkans (1877–1878)

In June 1877, the Russian Army invaded Bulgaria with the goal of crushing the Ottoman Empire, setting up, in its European portion, several independent states dominated by Russia, and obtaining leverage on the Ottomans sufficient to keep the Bosporus and Dardanelles Straits permanently open to the Russian merchant marine and the navy. The Russians planned to quickly cross the Balkan Mountains via the Shipka pass (1,150 m) and then march along the Maritsa River to Constantinople. The whole campaign was to take about a month (Map 1.3).[19]

The Russians took Shipka in mid July by outflanking its defenders through a neighbouring pass but postponed their march to Constantinople until the fall of Pleven, whose 40,000-strong garrison[20] could potentially threaten the right flank of the main forces if they advanced to Constantinople. The Shipka garrison received an order to hold the pass at any cost[21] but was slow to fortify its positions because its officers believed that the rugged terrain provided cover in itself. Instead of digging in, engineers set seven 'stone-throwers' (*kamnemety*) – mines filled with gunpowder and stones – around the major positions.[22] When it became clear that the Ottomans planned to retake Shipka, the Russians began building trenches in earnest, but, as it turned out, it was hard to dig the rocky soil; the standard quantity of spades and picks per unit was insufficient, and the work proceeded slowly. When the Turks attacked on 21 August, the fortifications were still embryonic.[23] In the face of the charging Turks, the nervous engineers exploded only two 'stone-throwers ', and both were released too early to inflict any harm on the enemy.[24] The Russians beat off the assault in a six-day battle, although they suffered heavy casualties that could easily have been avoided had they made an effort to dig in earlier. Pleven turned out to be a hard nut to crack, which led to a stalemate at Shipka. The Russians had arrived at Shipka mostly with field guns but discovered that they also needed mortars because field guns could not hit the Ottoman living quarters and the large-calibre mortars located on the opposite slopes. After they brought several mortars and developed correction tables for firing at targets located at high angles, they began matching the Turks in the effectiveness of artillery fire.[25]

However, they faced the rapid advance of the cold season. This part of the front remained uneventful but, despite the absence of action, in late autumn the Russians began suffering daily non-combat casualties equal to those occurring in bitter battles. These casualties stemmed from cold weather, miserable living conditions, and the inability of Russian commanders to foresee these problems and address them promptly. Since the

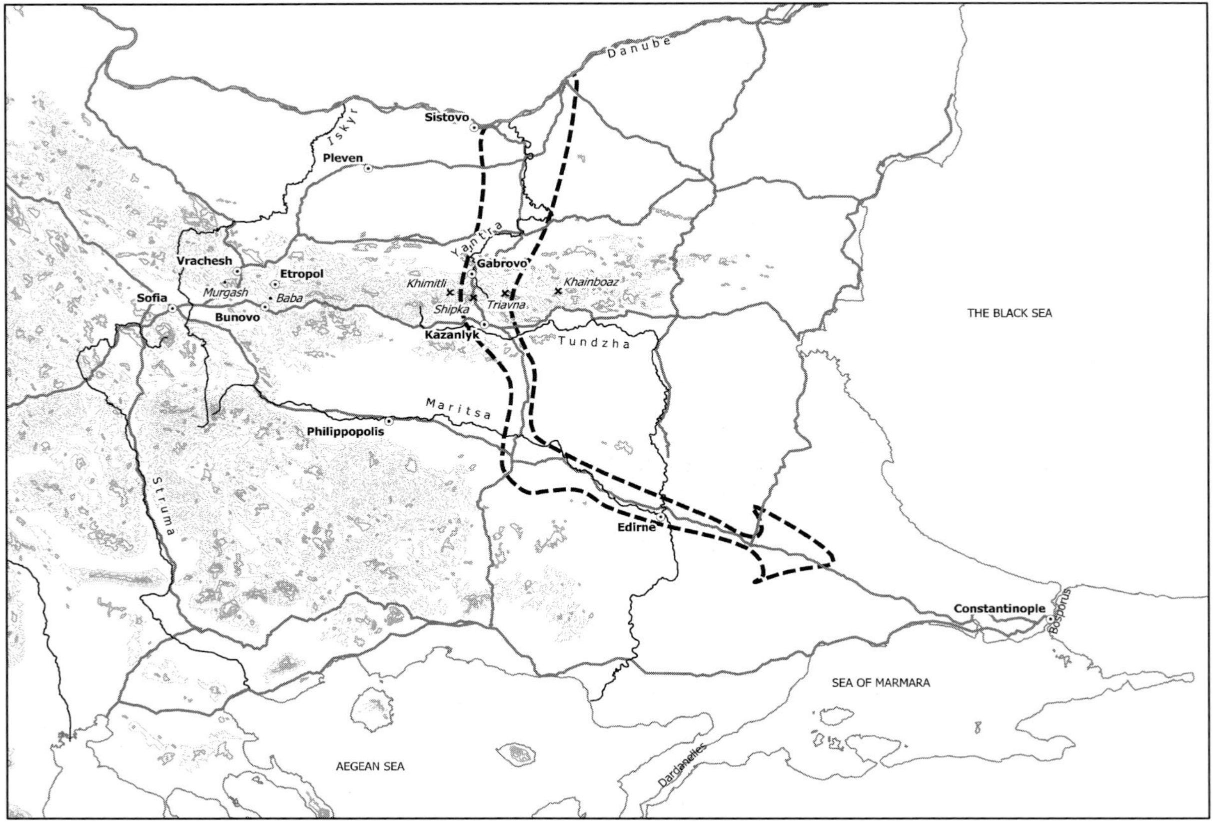

Map 1.3 Russian plans for the campaign against the Ottoman Empire, 1877

Russian General Staff had initially planned to finish the campaign in summer, the army had no winter uniforms, and it took a long time to deliver them from Russia. Firewood had to be brought from the valley below the pass along a road that the Turks kept under fire, so it was always scarce. Standard field kitchens were too bulky and could not surmount the steep trails leading from the main road to the highest positions located above the pass; soldiers defending them received no hot meals.[26] Although the average temperature in the Balkan highlands was not that low – between −5 °C and −12 °C, even in December and January – it dropped to −20 °C during snowstorms;[27] extreme humidity created what felt like bone-penetrating cold, and the strong winds made the wind-chill temperatures much lower. Once ice had covered the Shipka positions, the evacuation of the wounded and the sick became a grave problem; some soldiers froze to death at the front-line dressing station while waiting for evacuation.[28] In November and December, the average daily casualties from disease and frostbite among the regiments deployed in the Balkan Mountains were ten times as great as the average for the entire army. From 22 November to 25 December, the defenders of Shipka lost 12 men killed and 122 wounded by enemy fire and 6,563 frostbitten and sick.[29] The stalemate at Shipka ended when, soon after the surrender of Pleven on 10 December, the Russian Army began crossing the Balkan Mountains through several passes simultaneously. The Ottomans did not expect such a daring manoeuvre in the midst of winter. Although some regiments lost up to 15 per cent of their personnel due to exposure during this offensive,[30] the Russians successfully crossed the Balkan Mountains and surrounded the Ottoman forces at Shipka, which surrendered after a two-day battle on 9 January 1878. The following swift march towards Constantinople ended with a decisive Russian victory which brought the end of the war.

The Russians had not anticipated serious action in the mountains when they initiated this campaign. Indeed, having easily conquered the Shipka pass, they could have exited the mountains within two hours; the good road descending from the pass was free of Turks. However, the stubborn defence of Pleven forced them to interrupt their march to Constantinople and engage in mountain warfare. Since such a course of events was unplanned, it caught the Russians unprepared. Their endeavours at Shipka and during the crossing of the Balkans were the logical outcome of their ignorance in this type of action.

World War I (1914–1915)

The experiences of the Russian Army in the mountains during World War I were limited to two winter campaigns: one was a series of brief mobile actions in the Sarikamis region at the frontier between Russia and the Ottoman Empire from late December 1914 to mid January 1915, and the other, much larger in scale, occurred in the Beskids, the lowest northern part of the Carpathians, between mid January and April 1915, when the Austrian and Russian armies launched simultaneous offensives against each other. By the beginning of the war, more than a dozen military studies had already examined in detail the Swiss campaign, the Caucasus War, and the actions in the Balkans, and their participants had left many more descriptions of these campaigns. World War I provided the first occasion when the Russian Army could have utilised this limited knowledge. To what extent did it help the Russians to operate in the mountains during the war?

Sarikamis (1914)

As soon as the Ottoman Empire entered World War I in November 1914, Enver Pasha, the Ottoman war minister, began planning a major campaign against the Russian Army in Transcaucasia, intending to rout it as swiftly and decisively as the Germans had done at Tannenberg in August of that year. The Ottoman strategic offensive was the outcome of this ill-thought-out plan, which presumed a swift march by the 9th and 10th Army Corps against the Sarikamis Formation, a part of the Russian Caucasus Army, and its total destruction. The march was to proceed across the Sarikamis plateau, which was 1,500–2,000 metres high (Map 1.4). In summer, the region could be crossed in most places, even without a trail. However, in winter, the hills and the cart road network were under snow. Enver planned this offensive under the palms of Constantinople, 1,200 kilometres away from the battlefield; he arrived only nine days before the beginning of the operation.[31] Ottoman maps showed goat paths as roads. To secure a fast-paced advance along these 'roads', Enver ordered his soldiers to leave their supply wagons behind and to reckon on living off the land. However, few people lived in the region and the advancing army, dressed in thin tunics and having no tents, had to spend the nights in the open in subzero temperatures.[32]

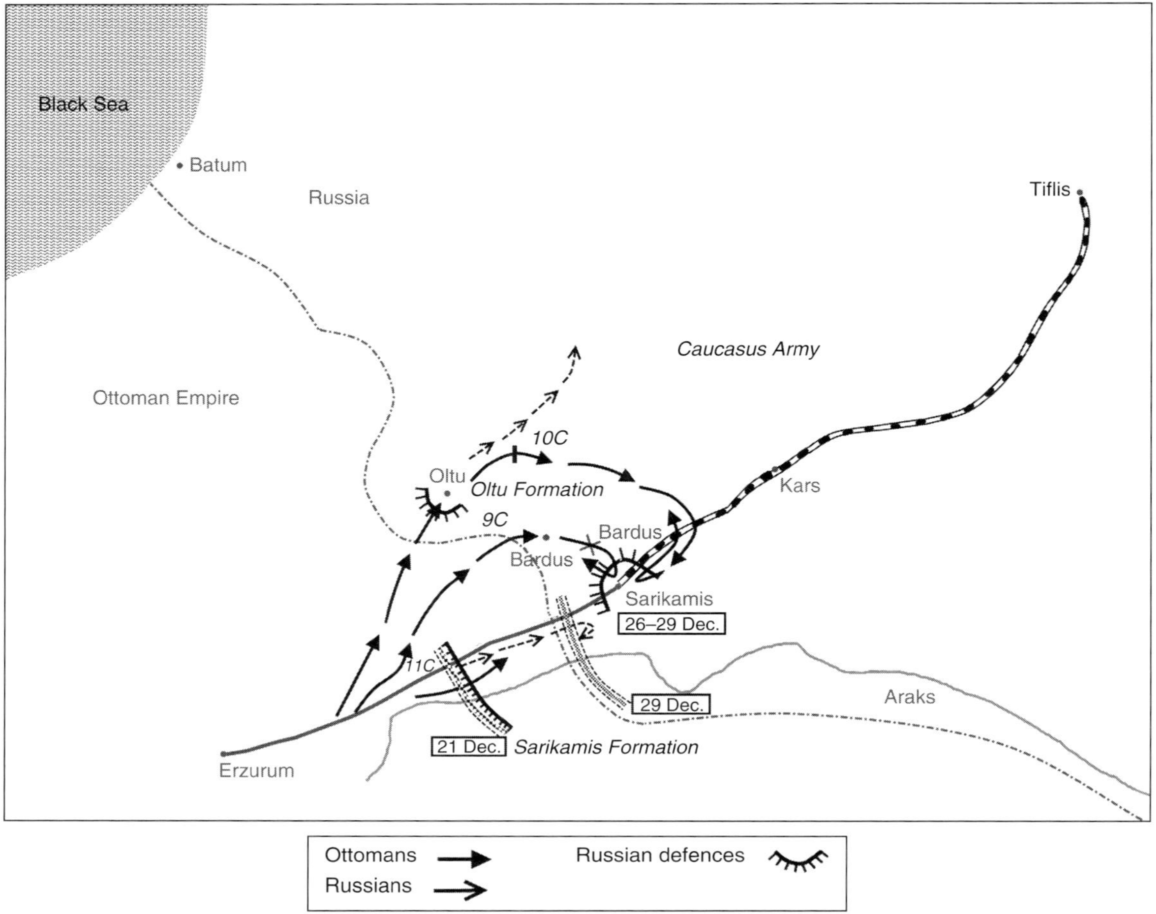

Map 1.4 The Ottoman assault on Sarikamis, December 1914

The Ottoman offensive began on 22 December 1915, and on the night of 25 December the Turks approached Sarikamis town, where Russian regional headquarters were located, but the defenders beat off the assault.[33] The Russians had their quarters in the immediate rear, whereas the Turks found themselves in sparsely populated hills, exposed to bitter cold. By the time the Ottoman 9th Corps arrived at Sarikamis, its soldiers had already eaten all their food, and the draught animals of their meagre supply columns had been quickly depleted because of the cold and the absence of forage.[34] The starving soldiers easily succumbed to cold. The temperature plummeted to −20 °C,[35] and by 26 December the 9th Corps had lost half of their manpower as stragglers, sick, frostbitten, and frozen to death.[36] The Russians launched a counteroffensive on 30 December, planning to destroy completely the two Ottoman corps. However, during the counteroffensive, the Russians suffered from the same problems that had plagued the Ottoman attack. They had to advance without artillery because it was impossible to move it across the snow, which increased their casualties during assaults on the Ottoman positions. The co-ordination between units separated by ridges was poor; it took messengers six or seven hours, one way, to deliver information.[37] The Russians lost few men to frostbite while they were in positions around Sarikamis with a well-maintained rear, but during the counteroffensive frostbite knocked out 10 per cent of their manpower within three weeks.[38] Yet their casualties did not match those of the Ottomans, who lost 78,000 of the 90,000 men who had begun the offensive on 22 December[39] – killed, frostbitten, frozen or starved to death, sick with typhus, or taken prisoner. The remnants of the Ottoman 9th Corps, demoralised by their ordeal, surrendered, along with their entire headquarters, while the 10th Corps escaped with only a fraction of its manpower.[40] The battle of Sarikamis thus ended on 18 January in the rout of the Ottomans. Yet the experience Russians had gained in earlier campaigns in the mountains played no role in this outcome. Despite the fact that the Caucasus Army was deployed in a mountainous region, it had no knowledge of mountain warfare, nor did it have any special equipment. The Russians merely reacted to circumstances; it was Enver's bungles rather than the skills of his adversaries that brought them a decisive victory.

The Carpathians (1915)

The battle of the Carpathians was a long, bloody, and messy static campaign with action at a depth of about 30 kilometres. In early January 1915, the front line followed the Beskids – a series of parallel, gently sloped, forested ridges (Map 1.5). The Russian and Austrian armies both planned offensives in directions perpendicular to the ridges, which meant that the attacking army had to cross all the ridges before it could get to the plains on the other side. The Austrian offensive, launched by General Franz Conrad von Hötzendorf, chief of the Austria-Hungary General Staff, pursued the relief of Przemysl, a fortress besieged by the Russians about 90 kilometres from the front line. Nikolai Ivanov, commander of the Russian Southwestern Front, planned an offensive across the Beskids that would open perspectives for a future advance towards the Hungarian plains.[41] Neither the Austrian nor the Russian General Staff took into account the terrain or the weather conditions.

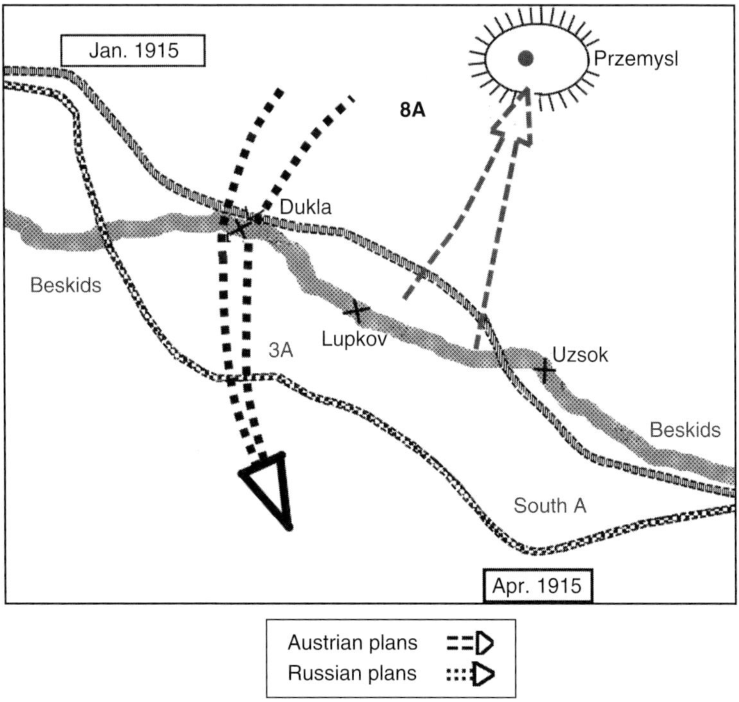

Map 1.5 The battle of the Carpathians, January–April 1915

The campaign in the Carpathians earned, in the words of Graydon Tunstall, 'the dubious title of Stalingrad of World War I', and it 'could hardly have been conducted under worse conditions', with temperatures at times plummeting to –20 °C.[42] The Russian 8th Army attacked the Austrians on 20 January, and the Austrian 3rd Army launched its offensive two days later. The action was inevitably slow because soldiers, according to Aleksei Brusilov, commander of the 8th Army, had to fight in snow 'up to their necks'.[43] Neither side had warm uniforms. Boots that served fairly well on the plains fell apart within several days in the mountains. The absence of white camouflage provided for good targets in the snow. It was extremely hard to pull the guns and the ammunition wagons to new positions through the snow, which was 1 to 2 metres deep. Thaws turned the Beskids' soil, infamous for its heavy clay even in summer, into impassable mud. Draught animals died in droves, both from exposure and from lack of fodder. The Beskids offered good defensive positions but the logistical difficulties led to attacks without artillery support and to the slaughter of the attackers by machinegun fire, which was hard to suppress without artillery. The Austrians suffered from lack of artillery support more than the Russians did, because they had few mountain artillery pieces,[44] whereas about a quarter of the Russians' artillery comprised mountain guns.[45] However, many Russian commanders believed that mountain terrain itself provided sufficient cover[46] and failed to fortify their positions, which led to unnecessary casualties. Supply to the front-line units disintegrated. Field kitchens got stuck in the snow far away from the front line, and food carried on soldiers' backs arrived frozen solid. The soldiers frequently found themselves without food for several days at a time. Evacuation of the wounded required enormous effort; they often froze to death before they were transported to dressing stations or died during wrenching cart rides down mountain slopes.

The combined impact of the severe environment and heavy battle produced horrendous casualties on both sides that rivalled those sustained at Verdun and the Somme.[47] Non-combat casualties from frostbite, lung and respiratory diseases caused by hypothermia, and typhus far outnumbered the casualties inflicted in battle. In early February 1915, the 3rd Austrian Army was losing an average of 500 men a day to frostbite and death by freezing. The enormous fatigue caused by such unbearable conditions ruined morale. Entire battalions surrendered to the enemy, unable to withstand the privations any longer.[48] In the end, the Russians repelled the Austrians and then crossed the Beskids, but the Russian offensive did not achieve its goal: although Przemysl surrendered and the Russians created a large bridgehead for further advance to the south of the Beskids, their divisions – plagued by enormous casualties, insurmountable logistical problems, and the exhaustion of the demoralised soldiers – could not use this bridgehead to develop their offensive.[49] The Austrian and German reinforcements pinned down the Russians when they had already exited the Beskids. When the action stopped in mid April, the total Russian casualties equalled about 1 million men, including those sustained during the siege of Przemysl, whereas the Austrian and the German armies lost about 800,000 men.[50] Nikolai Ivanov attributed this failure to turn a tactical success, attained at an enormous cost, into a strategic one to fatigue from the severe battle environment and logistical problems. However, as Mikhail Bonch-Bruevich remarks, the Russian offensive was doomed primarily because Ivanov ignored

> the local conditions in the mountains, whereas ... the difficulty of action in the mountains in winter is the most important factor that must be taken into account during operational planning ... The formations entering the mountains ... broke down in their vain efforts to overcome the resistance of the elements, which was insurmountable in the absence of painstaking preliminary calculations.[51]

Unlike the actions at Shipka or Sarikamis, the winter offensive across the Carpathians was an operation planned by the Russian General Staff. However, there is no evidence that the masterminds behind this offensive had studied past campaigns in the mountains or undertaken any steps facilitating action in such an environment, except that they supplied this section of the front with mountain artillery. Ivanov had no knowledge of the operational terrain; his divisions had a standard infantry structure; his officers were ignorant of mountain warfare and his soldiers had only standard equipment, continued to wear standard uniforms, and ate standard low-calorie rations. To be fair, the Austrians showed even less competence in the Carpathians than the Russians did.

Lessons of Past Campaigns in the Mountains

By the end of World War I, the Russian Army had accumulated some experience in mountain warfare. While not extensive, it still offered many lessons, demonstrated specific risks and challenges, and illuminated possible ways to mitigate the risks and meet the challenges. This experience suggested strategies and tactics suitable for mountain warfare, principles of fortification, and emphases in the training of units operating in the mountains. It helped to identify necessary items of soldiers' equipment, rations, and weapons and revealed the peculiarities of logistics and medical service. The imperial Russian General Staff spared no effort in examining in detail Russian military history, including campaigns in the mountains. Its high-profile publications intended to enlighten the officer corps about various aspects of these campaigns, such as strategic planning in the mountains; tactics in mountain terrain; possible solutions to inevitable and formidable logistical problems; and specific training, gear, and composition of the units expected to operate in the mountains. These deliberations were spread across a broad range of studies that included chapters on action in the mountains. If distilled from a plethora of publications printed during the imperial period,[52] these ideas would have read as follows.

In terms of strategy, the campaigns conducted by the imperial Russian Army implied that the margin of error is inevitably narrower in the mountains than on the plains and that impromptu actions would most likely end in failure. Mountain warfare defies amateurism, dilettantism, and spontaneity. An army planning a campaign in the mountains must invest extra effort in preparations for it during peacetime. It should acquire comprehensive information on the potential operational region and take into account the limitations imposed by terrain, high altitude, and seasonal weather variations. Strategy should be simple in the mountains, because grave communication and logistical problems frustrate the coherent actions of large formations scattered at great distances, but it is hard to make it simple because the landscape inevitably splits the armies. It is easier to surprise and be surprised in the mountains than on the plains because the landscape impedes intelligence acquisition and conceals manoeuvres, and the weather complicates things by piling surprises on top of those prepared by the enemy; it can disable more men than enemy actions and often becomes a factor directing strategy. Meticulous study of the terrain during the operational planning can thin 'the fog of uncertainty'; therefore topographers should provide accurate large-scale maps and detailed descriptions of the potential mountainous theatre of operation well before the war, not only to facilitate operational planning but also to familiarise commanders with this theatre during exercises in peacetime. It is difficult to calculate many factors involved in mountain warfare while planning a campaign. Such planning, therefore, has to be flexible, and commanders should pursue alternative solutions if unforeseen circumstances bring the operation to a halt.

As for tactical lessons, the past campaigns showed that numerical superiority brings fewer benefits in the mountains than on the plains because the mountain landscape often prohibits the concentration of the available units at a certain point and may help a handful of soldiers to pin down a far superior force through thoughtful defence. Since both sides understand it, they should race against the enemy for better positions. The defender, rather than relying on the mountain landscape for personnel protection, should fortify not only the main position but also the neighbouring heights dominating it, and cover all the minor trails in the proximity with strongholds to block the enemy's infiltration along these trails. Strongholds and artificial obstacles built at the right place can be more effective in the mountains than on the plains; this means that engineers should learn fortification techniques constrained by rocky terrain and test a variety of obstacles to find out which ones would be optimal in different landscapes. It is hard to dig the rocky soil; therefore, units fighting in the mountains must have extra spades, picks, and crowbars.

However, even if the fortifications are perfect, 'the defender cannot count on pinning down a courageous and resolute enemy' who can bypass these fortifications.[53] Envelopment of a well-entrenched enemy rather than frontal assaults should be the main tactic of mountain warfare, notwithstanding the frequent failures of such manoeuvres due to impassable terrain. Such envelopments can be conducted by small units. As Clausewitz observed, 'Mountain warfare leads to atomisation of military formations; their various elements often fight on their own, which means they have to take initiative. This is true for both ... generals and ... every private.'[54] The atomisation poses additional challenges for command and control, especially in conditions of limited visibility. This implies that formations deployed in the mountains should have more signals personnel and signalling equipment than those operating on the plains. Since 'the efficiency of riding messengers is low, or it may be impossible to use them',[55] alternative means of communication must be developed. The rough terrain makes it hard to quickly close in on the enemy; this means that long-range infantry weapons and skilled marksmanship are crucial in mountain warfare. Infantry should be backed by mountain artillery, which, although inevitably inferior to regular field guns, is still able to provide adequate support in a terrain prohibitive for regular cannons. Mortars and howitzers should be a part of the arsenal in the mountains because they can hit enemy positions on the opposite slopes. Artillery crews need to introduce corrections while firing at targets located at high angles; therefore, correction tables with range/elevation ratios should be developed during peacetime exercises in mountain terrain. Cavalry, however, has 'very limited use'[56] in the mountains, especially in winter.

Logistics is often the *Schwerpunkt* of mountain warfare, and logistical miscalculations are deadlier in the mountains than on the plains. Logistical problems are enormous: marches are slow and exhausting; a shorter but steeper trail often takes more time than a longer but gently sloped one. The scarcity of population in the mountains makes it difficult to live off the land or find accommodation. Soldiers are exposed to cold, bitter winds, and possibly blizzards even in summer; consequently, they must carry the most essential supplies, such as reserves of food, ammunition, warmer uniforms, and tents. However, every additional kilogram in the knapsack enhances fatigue, and the quick attrition of supply trains increases the loads carried by soldiers. Subsequently, commanders must be able to foresee what soldiers can and cannot do in a certain season, given the topography on which they operate and calculate the smallest details of logistics, such as the option of living off the land; the maximum capacity of the supply routes in certain seasons, as well as the supply priorities; the number of pack animals and local civilians that the army needs and can mobilise to secure an uninterrupted flow of supplies; and the reserves of harnesses, horseshoes, and packs. Only elaborate preparations can secure a constant flow of supplies in the mountains, preparations that would include the formation of pack animal columns, the establishment of shelters and forage depots for these columns, the deployment of numerous engineering units to maintain the trails, and the transfer of considerable manpower from the front line to logistics.

The mountain environment alone, even in the absence of enemies, distresses soldiers unaccustomed to such an environment. Since operations in the mountains presume more physical discomfort than those on the plains, and poor weather has graver consequences, a special effort must be made to maintain soldiers' morale and health, such as the prompt building of decent shelters, regular delivery of hot meals and firewood, and frequent rotation between the front line and the close rear. Since standard field kitchens cannot surmount steep and narrow trails, smaller portable kitchens and stoves have to be designed, and enough pack animals allocated to transport a steady stream of firewood from lower valleys. Given the likely interruptions in the delivery of hot meals to positions in the high mountains, soldiers deployed there should have tinned food as a substitute for regular meals. Soldiers need warmer uniforms to survive in the mountains, especially those deployed above the treeline – where winds are much stronger, temperatures are lower, and no firewood is available. They also need sturdier boots than usual. Even if soldiers are dressed appropriately, the mountain environment guarantees that casualties from non-combat causes – disease, frostbite, and injury – will be considerably higher per capita in the mountains than on the plains and, while the number of casualties inflicted by enemy fire will likely be smaller, the transportation of the wounded and sick is a thorny problem that requires special attention but offers no easy solutions; their abandonment at the mercy of the enemy can ruin the morale of able-bodied soldiers. Failure to anticipate all these problems and find viable solutions may cause far graver repercussions in the mountains than on the plains.

The mountain campaigns of the imperial army showed that an admirable past record on the plains cannot guarantee similar performance in the mountains, while the experience of the Italian Front in World War I suggested that special forces organised and trained for mountain warfare were particularly effective in the highlands. The structure of these forces – raised, preferably, from physically robust residents of mountain regions – should be adjusted to the terrain in which they are expected to operate, with a higher proportion of signals, engineering, medical, and logistical personnel than are necessary on the plains as well as reconnaissance parties able to access the most difficult sections of such terrain. Their equipment should be light because it must often be carried on horseback or on the backs of soldiers, and it should include a variety of items different from those used on the plains:

long-range infantry weapons and mountain artillery, warmer uniforms, sturdier boots, small tents and portable field kitchens, warm blankets, extra digging tools, special means for transportation of the wounded, and possibly skis and climbing gear, depending on the terrain. The individual training of a soldier fighting in the mountains must be more diverse than that of his counterpart operating on the plains. In order to acquire the expertise needed for war in the mountains and to smooth the anticipated 'friction of war', these special units should invest much time in exercises on terrain similar to that on which they are expected to fight and should learn the tactics of mountain warfare with an emphasis on the training of junior officers and individual soldiers in the development of initiative, climbing, and marksmanship skills.

All of these ideas were either expressed explicitly or were implied by imperial military scholars. However, no one summarised them in a single succinct manual. Despite impressive analyses of the past campaigns, the conclusions made by military academics had a minimal effect on how the Russian Army fought in the mountains because institutional inertia made the generals ignore the peculiarities of mountain warfare and prompted them to fight in the mountains in the same way that they fought on the plains, which resulted in costly errors.

The Intellectual Impact of Past Campaigns on Soviet Military Thought

A new approach to mountain warfare became possible only after the Red Army General Staff, impressed by the actions of mountain units in the Alps during World War I, decided to organise mountain divisions in 1929. The experience of the past, accumulated through trial and error, gave Soviet senior officers ample information to prepare the Red Army for action in the mountains, or at least for avoiding the pitfalls suffered by its imperial predecessor. In 1937, Nikolai Korsun, a professor at the Soviet Frunze Military Academy, published a detailed study of the Sarikamis operation and offered a number of ideas regarding war in the mountains. Some of those ideas repeated earlier observations made by the imperial General Staff, others developed those observations in depth, and some were advanced for the first time. Korsun's thoughts, expressed five years before the battle of the Caucasus and during a quickly deteriorating international situation, could have given the Red Army General Staff at least a rough outline of the action needed to prepare for operations in mountain regions. He argued against an impromptu approach to mountain warfare: 'Any improvisation replacing painstaking calculations can ruin the operation. In short, two factors are most important for operational planning: precise calculations and expertise in mountain warfare among all commanders.' The troops operating in the mountains have to be able to move across rugged terrain, 'which requires the organisation of mountain units in peacetime'. These units are to be 'supplied with appropriate uniforms, including white camouflage and sunglasses, and climbing gear'.[57] Most importantly, the mountain divisions had to learn new skills that would turn them into a force able to operate in highlands far more effectively than conventional infantry.

However, while the emergence of mountain divisions as a separate army branch reduced institutional inertia, ideological constraints limited generals' ability to learn from the past. Although Suvorov's essay 'The Science of Victory' was a part of the curriculum in the Military Academy of the Red Army General Staff, and some of its ideas were even incorporated in soldiers' identification cards,[58] party leaders pointed to the fact that Suvorov was 'a devout monarchist' whose 'activities strengthened the feudal-absolutist state'.[59] Furthermore, in 1774, Suvorov marched to suppress Pugachev's Rebellion, wrongly interpreted by Soviet leaders as the greatest peasant uprising against the monarchy. That is why the Soviet interwar studies of Suvorov's heritage were limited to a small chapter in a single book and a one-page article.[60] The earlier excellent studies of the Swiss and the Balkan campaigns were kept in research libraries, but it is unknown how many Soviet officers read them. The imperial General Staff had no opportunity to study the mountain campaigns of World War I, and these campaigns received little coverage after the Bolshevik Revolution because the Bolshevik Party condemned the war as a quarrel 'between two packs of imperialist predators'.[61] It was unpopular in the Red Army to study the Sarikamis operation because its main hero, General Nikolai Yudenich, later became an enemy, and the fact that Lavr Kornilov, another bitter opponent of the Bolsheviks, advanced farther than other generals during the campaign in the Beskids discouraged its study.[62] In 1940, after his excellent monograph on the Sarikamis operation, Korsun submitted a manuscript analysing the nineteenth-century wars in the Caucasus, but the military press Voenizdat refused to publish it.[63] Foreign publications that covered the campaign of

1915–17 in the Alps were available to students at the General Staff Academy, but probably few of them wanted to read such publications in the thickening atmosphere of spy-mania in the 1930s. Yet the decision to raise mountain units proved that some ideas expressed in imperial Russian and foreign publications on mountain warfare had penetrated the Red Army, and some of its officers, perhaps those who had participated in World War I mountain campaigns, understood that special skills, equipment, unit structure, and logistical arrangements often made the difference between sound success and catastrophic failure in mountain warfare.

After Vladimir Lenin called Clausewitz 'the most insightful military author',[64] the Red Army General Staff had to acknowledge his credibility and lecture students at the Soviet General Staff Military Academy on his ideas, and Soviet military theoreticians cited *On War* to add weight to their own conclusions.[65] Clausewitz devoted four chapters of his masterpiece to mountain warfare. He made several curious observations that would not be obvious to a layperson. He warned about the tendency to inflate the strength of defensive positions in the mountains: although, indeed, 'a unit that on open ground can be dispersed by a couple of cavalry squadrons ... can face an army in the mountains', the idea of creating an 'impenetrable front'[66] along a mountain ridge by relying on the advantages offered by mountain landscape is a delusion. Strategists who try this confuse the difficulty of manoeuvre in the mountains with the impassability of mountainous terrain: 'where one is not able to march in a column, or with artillery or cavalry, one can, in most cases, still advance with infantry, or make some use of artillery'.[67] Well-trained attackers can outflank strong defensive positions built by the enemy and get into the rear, cutting enemy forces off from their supplies and provoking panic disproportionate to the strength of the enveloping units. These enveloping units, even if weak, can exploit the advantages of the mountainous terrain and prevent the attempts of the surrounded enemy to break out. Fear of such envelopment 'weakens the contestant's every fiber. His flanks become abnormally sensitive; indeed, every handful of soldiers that the attacker deploys ... in the rear provides new leverage towards his victory'.[68] Clausewitz came to a paradoxical conclusion regarding mountain warfare: while the defender can easily hold the enemy temporarily, 'in a decisive battle, mountainous terrain is of no help to the defender; on the contrary ... it favours the attacker'. The attempt to create a mountain version of the Maginot Line with the hope that sheer defence would make the mountains an impregnable fortress is 'so dangerous that the theorist cannot overstate his warnings'.[69] The conclusions on the tactics of mountain warfare made by Clausewitz were valid only if the formations operating in the mountains could manoeuvre across a rugged terrain and fight on it, for which they had to be well trained.

This was the key point of contention within the Red Army General Staff regarding mountain warfare: how much time and effort is it worth investing in the narrow specialisation of the divisions to be deployed in the mountains? While some senior officers believed that such an investment was fully justified, others supported the view expressed by a military scholar who stated in reference to mountain warfare: 'The only innovation of the West European bourgeois-aristocratic military thought in the nineteenth century was the organisation of special mountain units that allegedly were the only ones able to operate in the mountains. Suvorov's experience – crossing the Alpine ridges without special gear or training – refuted this idea.'[70] Such a stunning conclusion, ignoring the enormous casualties suffered by Suvorov's army precisely because it had no experience in mountain warfare, questioned the entire concept of special units trained, structured, and equipped for operations in a mountain environment. The Red Army policy on mountain divisions fluctuated depending on the outcomes of the struggle between a small vociferous minority who viewed this force as highly trained professionals and the large passive majority who questioned the need for a narrow military specialisation of the units operating in the mountains.

2 SOVIET PREPARATIONS FOR WAR IN THE MOUNTAINS

Fix your sledge in summer and your cart in winter.
Russian proverb

Once the Red Army General Staff decided to raise mountain divisions in 1929, the Soviet state undertook a concerted effort to provide proper manpower, a training infrastructure, and instructors for them. As a first step in this direction, the party leaders decided to transplant the culture of sport tourism from Western Europe to the Soviet Union but to 'turn tourism from a tool of the bourgeoisie into a tool of the proletariat':[1] that is, to create a Soviet version of this recreation tailored to the strategic priorities of the state. Soviet sport tourism was to facilitate the ideological indoctrination of the younger generation; strengthen the health of the nation; foster its unity by building intercultural bridges among Soviet ethnic groups; and, most importantly, provide outdoor skills to prospective recruits and to soldiers already serving in the Red Army, thus enhancing their ability to fight in an unconventional environment. Sponsored and promoted by the government, sport tourism made stunning progress within a decade, attaining most of the desired objectives. Meanwhile, the Red Army began formulating its concept of mountain warfare, and enthusiasts among the senior officers launched field experiments in the mountains to test the new manuals, military equipment, climbing gear, and logistics. Soviet administrators and generals created considerable potential for raising effective mountain units on the eve of the battle of the Caucasus. However, Bolshevik culture, ideology-based military doctrine, and the Great Purge of 1936–8 frustrated this gallant effort to prepare the Red Army for action in the mountains, an effort that, in the end, produced negligible results.

Efforts to Create a Pool of Recruits for Special Forces

Sport tourism and, in particular, mountaineering developed rapidly in Western Europe after its origin in the mid nineteenth century. Beginning in the 1860s, members of numerous alpine clubs engaged in treks and climbs in the Alps. West European military strategists realised that they could exploit this outdoor culture to extend the theatre of war to the high mountains, thus gaining a sound advantage over their enemies who still perceived such mountains as impregnable. These strategists viewed the residents of mountain regions who engaged in trekking and climbing as the best recruits for military units raised specifically for mountain warfare.

Mountaineering began developing in Russia much later than in Western Europe: several outdoor associations emerged in the last years of the nineteenth century, but no more than a dozen of their members engaged in serious climbs.[2] After the Bolshevik Revolution of 1917, Russian sport tourism, including mountaineering, continued in its pre-revolutionary form throughout most of the 1920s; this type of recreation attracted only a handful of intellectuals.[3] However, having received vigorous state support, Soviet mountaineering made a giant leap forward in the late 1920s and the 1930s.

After the Rapallo Treaty of 1922 normalised Soviet–German relations, scores of German mountaineers came to try their luck in the Caucasus and in Central Asia. The top Bolsheviks perceived Germany as a model of modernity; some of them viewed the sport of German climbers as a component of modern culture, especially those who had engaged in mountaineering while being in exile in the Alpine countries before the Revolution, such as Nikolai Krylenko, the first commander-in-chief of the Red Army and later the people's commissar for justice of the USSR; and Vasilii Semenovskii, a diplomat.[4] These Bolsheviks began promoting a Soviet version of sport tourism: 'a tool of the cultural revolution that ... elevates socialist mass culture and thus accelerates the involvement of the masses in building socialism, infusing them with the qualities necessary to defend socialism from external and internal class enemies'.[5]

This rhetoric found a favourable response among most senior Bolsheviks who believed that the USSR could survive the next major war only if it had, in addition to modern industry, a unified nation standing behind the government and a modern army able to operate in any terrain, including the mountains. The enthusiasts of sport tourism persuaded the government that a small investment in the endeavour would initiate a self-sustaining impetus, turning this recreational pursuit into an effective tool of social engineering and paramilitary training that would provide a large pool of patriotic, motivated, and healthy recruits with outdoor skills useful for military service. After the government began sponsoring sport tourism in 1929, the pace of its development suddenly and greatly accelerated.

Since Soviet sport tourism was to fulfil multiple 'socio-political, military, and economic missions ... set by the party and the state', 'promote the values of a socialism builder and a soldier of the revolution, and ... [secure] a collectivist mentality and discipline',[6] it needed an agency that would 'harness the spontaneous movement, organise it, and channel it' towards these goals.[7] Such an agency, the Association for Proletarian Tourism (Obshchestvo proletarskogo turizma, OPT), emerged on 30 November 1929 and was renamed the Association for Proletarian Tourism and Excursions (Obshchestvo proletarskogo turizma i ekskursii, OPTE) in March 1930.[8]

The three most important leaders of OPTE were prominent communist functionaries: Krylenko, its chair; Lev Gurvich, secretary of the Komsomol Central Committee and Krylenko's deputy; and Vladimir Antonov-Saratovskii, deputy chair of the Minor Council of People's Commissars. Although OPTE was a non-governmental organisation, they administered the association in accordance with the guidelines received through party channels and sought to turn it into an obedient tool of the emerging totalitarianism. Russian authors correctly call OPTE 'a socio-political, paramilitary, and sport association'.[9] OPTE viewed as its main mission that set by the 1st All-Union Congress of Paramilitary and Scientific Associations, which occurred in December 1924: 'the training of hardy, fearless, physically strong people inspired by the ideas of the global socialist revolution'.[10] Despite OPTE's claim to be a proletarian agency, those who engaged in sport expeditions were overwhelmingly members of the intelligentsia or white-collar workers.

In the framework of its leaders' philosophy, 'proletarian tourism' pursued three major goals. First, it was to be a tool of social engineering. Mikhail Pogrebetskii, a famous Soviet climber, argued that 'mountaineering develops the qualities needed to overcome the elements – courage, dexterity, stamina, discipline, a sense of collective responsibility, fitness and an iron will for victory – and thus moulds the builders of socialism'.[11] When the hopes for a global communist revolution faded away in the mid 1920s, and official ideology shifted from proletarian internationalism to Soviet nationalism, OPTE adopted the philosophy expressed by Aleko Konstantinov, a major Bulgarian advocate of tourism: 'Get to know your motherland and you will fall in love with it!'[12] Tourism, in this view, was a means to stir nationalist sentiments. The ideologically committed, mission-oriented, and patriotic culture imposed on sport tourists shaped their views.

The second goal of 'proletarian tourism' was to spread the party message to 'the remotest and wildest regions of the Union',[13] where government institutions were weak and the values of 'primitive [*malokul'turnye*]' ethnic minorities conflicted with those promoted by Moscow. Indoctrinated sport tourists had to help the party to unify the Soviet nation in the face of the imminent attack of world capitalism, and mobilise it for work towards party goals.[14]

Finally, OPTE stated that 'proletarian tourism' 'provides motivated and tough soldiers' and 'trains reservists able to defend the Soviet Union from anyone who would dare to attack it'.[15] The idea of using sport tourism for military purposes far overshadowed all other objectives pursued by the state through its sponsorship. The 1st OPTE Congress, which gathered in April 1932, promised 'to shape all methods and types of our work towards the increase of Soviet military might'.[16] As a sport tourist periodical maintained, by 'nourishing love for the motherland and Soviet patriotism, developing endurance and providing marching, topography, and navigation training, and instilling collectivism, [sport] tourism becomes the perfect preliminary school for a future soldier'.[17]

The major features that distinguished Soviet sport tourism from its Western counterparts were the power of the team leader, strict discipline, and a collectivist stance. In tune with the mounting authoritarianism in the USSR, Soviet team leaders enjoyed nearly absolute power while on the tour. In the words of Lev Barkhash, a prominent mountaineer and journalist, 'Tourism is a means to develop collectivism … In difficult situations demanding quick decisions, his [the leader's] orders are followed [as strictly] as the orders of a military superior.'[18] Young people with an education level far above average and trained to act as a team, to follow the orders of the leader, and to suppress personal desires in favour of the ultimate goal were good potential recruits for military service – in particular, the special forces that operate in small groups whose survival depends on the coherent actions of all group members.

OPTE made a sustained effort to collect information from various itineraries. Every team had to write a detailed report on their travel that included a route description, maps and sketches of its most complicated parts, lists of necessary gear, and references to settlements and supply opportunities. The OPTE library accumulated such reports.[19] By the end of the 1930s, the association had data on many passes in the Caucasus: elevation, prominence, height of treeline, approaches to the pass, location and quality of the trails, seasonal weather patterns and snow cover, advice on crossing the pass, and alternative routes. OPTE always kept the military implications of such information in mind: these data would be invaluable for mountain warfare. The association also supervised the printing of travel guides and textbooks, articles, and manuals on climbing techniques, mountaineering expeditions, and basic meteorology, which could be used for soldier training.[20]

Keeping in mind that Soviet-produced outdoor gear was primitive, expensive, heavy, and of poor quality,[21] OPTE began publishing manuals teaching members how to make gear with their own hands: tents, sleeping bags, rain capes, light portable stoves for multi-week winter tours, and even boots, ski bindings, ski wax, and water-resistant chemicals.[22] Many sport tourists used the manuals to produce high-quality gear. The ability of these potential recruits to special forces to improvise gear from makeshift materials gave them an edge over their Western counterparts if supply of the standard gear was interrupted for whatever reason, as often happens in war. Furthermore, the superior self-made gear could serve as a prototype for the mass production of items needed in but absent from the Red Army.[23]

The aggressive promotion of sport tourism, its growing infrastructure, and the emergence of outdoor gear, travel guides, and textbooks led to a great surge of outdoor culture. In 1928, only 500 sport tourists were registered in the USSR.[24] In 1935, OPTE expected that, by the end of the year, the number of its members participating in sport expeditions would have grown to 38,000.[25] The number of sport treks and climbs, and their degree of difficulty, grew exponentially during the 1930s.

Numerous Soviet teams began climbing Kazbek (5,047 m), the seventh-highest peak in the Caucasus, and then proceeded to the more difficult Elbrus (5,642 m), the highest peak in Europe. Before World War I only 59 persons had made their way to the top of Elbrus, whereas in 1935 alone a total of 2,016 persons climbed it. By 1935, 20,000 persons had participated regularly in trekking and climbing, and many more were engaged in other types of sport tourism.[26] Hundreds of teams undertook mountaineering, trekking, white-water rafting, and ski touring expeditions annually in Karelia, the Caucasus, the Urals, the Altai, Pamir, and Tian Shan.[27]

Soviet mountaineers soon engaged in climbs that rivalled or even eclipsed the most difficult ones undertaken by their foreign colleagues. In 1931–8, they climbed four of the five Soviet peaks above 7,000 metres: Khan-Tengri (7,010 m), Lenin (7,134 m), Pobeda (7,439 m), and Stalin (7,495 m), the highest Soviet peak.[28] Few foreign mountaineers were conquering such high peaks at that time; Mont Blanc (4,478 m), the highest Alpine peak and the target of European mountaineers, is a dwarf compared to the peaks climbed by the Soviets in the 1930s. By 1937, the Soviet Union had more men who had climbed peaks over 7,000 metres than any other country.[29] The best Soviet climbers were awarded the title Master of Sport. The record climbs, like the records of industrialisation and the record flights, received broad media coverage, which prompted Soviet youth to flock into mountaineering.

The dramatic progress of Soviet mountaineering in the 1930s and the increasing complexity of the expeditions undertaken by Soviet teams dictated the opening of special training schools. OPTE maintained two types of training facilities: schools where novices could acquire basic skills in various types of tourism, and guide schools for tourists who had already participated in several difficult expeditions but sought advanced sport education and a commercial mountain guide licence. A basic mountaineering training course, after which the trainees received the Alpinist of the USSR 1st Class badge, lasted fifteen days and included 'familiarisation with climbing gear; cutting steps in ice and walking in crampons; belaying; traversing of rocks, scree, and ice- and snow-covered slopes; ... basic knowledge of tempo regime, food rationing, water balance, and methods of protection from the cold, wind, snow glare and acute mountain sickness … and first aid; and … the ability to read and correct maps'.[30] The course ended with a climb of Elbrus or a peak of similar difficulty.

The commercial guide candidates were taught how to organise and lead an expedition. In June 1929, Vasilii Semenovskii, who possessed a Swiss commercial mountain guide licence,[31] organised the first Soviet climbing guide school at Bezengi in the Caucasus; in 1936, eleven such schools operated in the Soviet Union.[32] The best Soviet mountaineers – Evgenii and Vitalii Abalakov, Daniil Gushchin, Stanislav Ganetskii, Arii Poliakov, Lev Barkhash, and dozens of others – worked in the schools as instructors.[33] Between 1929 and 1933, 180 persons received mountain guide licences; in 1935 alone, the number of graduates surged to 1,279, and in 1936 to 2,000.[34] It was easy to copy such established training facilities and procedures in the Soviet mountain divisions.

The boom in sport tourism and the increasing difficulty of the tour itineraries resulted in frequent accidents. The idea of a professional rescue service emerged in the Soviet Union in 1936, when OPTE published a translation of a German manual on rescue work.[35] OPTE began insisting that every mountaineer learn the basics of rescue operations. The first school to train professional mountain rescue staff began operating in 1938.[36] Although the Soviet rescue service was only in an embryonic state when World War II began, even its limited experience provided enough background to establish safety standards and procedures and introduce them to mountain divisions.

Militarisation of Soviet Sport Tourism

Following the proclamation in 1925 by the 3rd Congress of the Soviets that the 'universal militarisation' of Soviet society was a primary means to counter the imminent joint invasion of capitalist states,[37] OPTE made a valiant effort to contribute to this programme. Soviet observers examined reports about multi-week marches across Sicily, South Tyrol, Sardinia, and Libya that involved up to 12,000 blackshirts; long cross-country ski expeditions conducted by the Suojeluskunta national guards in Finland; annual treks launched by the Polish rifle associations in the Carpathians; the vigorous development of military mountaineering in the Alpine countries; and the mass pilgrimages of French youth to Verdun. Based on these reports, they concluded that in the West 'tourist and sport associations have turned into a sort of producer of physically strong people with special skills. Only brief military training is sufficient to turn a [sport] tourist into a good soldier.'[38]

OPTE decided to follow these Western examples; it introduced into its charter a promise to 'facilitate the defence of the USSR through the militarisation of tourism'[39] and assured the authorities that

> the goals of the Soviet proletarian tourist movement fit in with our country's defence priorities ... Tourism [will] enhance the Red Army's reserves by elevating the political education and culture of proletarian youth, familiarising them with various regions of our country, training their willpower and initiative, [providing them with] outdoor skills and the ability to navigate using a map and a compass, and strengthening them physically and mentally.[40]

The 1st All-Union OPTE Congress, which took place in April 1932, set the following guidelines for the militarisation of tourism:

> a. in-depth learning of certain military skills (signals, topographic, and endurance training and terrain studies) during tourist trips; b. intensive promotion of militarised trips, especially to the battlefields of the civil war; c. methodical training of specialists (guides, mountaineers, scouts, mountain troops, etc.); d. intensive development of [sport] tourism in the Red Army as a method of combat and political training.[41]

OPTE functionaries proposed two avenues towards raising the manpower able to operate in an unconventional battle environment: first, 'introduction of military elements in tourism' and, second, involvement of serving officers in sport tourism.[42] Moving along the first of these two avenues, OPTE pressed civilian sport tourists to 'develop military and political skills needed by a Red Army soldier'.[43] Its slogan, 'Tourism trains staunch and hardy soldiers',[44] was well founded. Expeditions in the wilderness inevitably introduced young men and women to discipline, comradeship, and élan and provided them with scores of skills invaluable for military personnel, especially those enlisted in various types of unconventional forces, like mountain, ski, guerrilla, or commando units. Such expeditions developed stamina and taught youth how to move across mountains, taiga, swamps, and snowfields deemed impassable by laypeople. Sport tourists learned how to pack a backpack; repair and produce gear with their own hands; keep an optimal walking tempo at various altitudes; maintain a comfortable psychological climate in a small team during multi-week treks; avoid and treat injuries, frostbite, and acute mountain sickness; transport injured comrades; ford rivers with a strong current and build river crossings in the absence of fords; cut trees to fall in the desired direction; construct wooden rafts and manoeuvre them across or down rivers; organise camps; survive outdoors in poor weather or in winter; read topographic maps; and navigate with a compass or with a watch and the sun during the day and by the stars at night. Sport tourists knew safety standards and basic rescue techniques and could identify mountain hazards. They learned all these skills even without OPTE's intervention.

However, OPTE made a concerted effort to 'impregnate [*propitat'*] all types of tourism with a military content',[45] promote military rituals, hierarchy, and discipline, and also provide the young people with skills they would not have acquired independently. OPTE's periodical described the effort of Italian blackshirts to impose military values on civilians as a model to emulate.[46] OPTE functionaries pressed tourists to introduce elements of military training into their expeditions, such as familiarisation with patrols, Morse code, light signals and flag semaphore, and communications via radio, as well as exercises in shooting and bayonet fighting, throwing hand-grenade dummies, crawling, marching for long distances in gas masks, and pulling sledges during ski expeditions, thus practising the transportation of heavy machineguns and wounded personnel.[47] Officers from the OSOAVIAKHIM[48] paramilitary association sometimes accompanied sport expeditions and supervised the military games.[49] The aura of romantic heroics surrounding such tours facilitated the indoctrination of young people. Militaristic values quickly proliferated among sport tourists, shaping their mentality and easing their adaptation to military service when they were drafted into the Red Army.

In the framework of militarisation, OPTE promoted travel to the borderlands, arguing that, in the next war, the Red Army would 'have many soldiers who have already visited the frontier regions, who have learned their peculiarities, who know their terrain well, and who have already established bonds with the local population'.[50] According to Pavel Sudoplatov, head of the NKVD Special Task Force, mountaineers drafted into the Red Army established rapport more easily with the locals than the average Soviet soldier did.[51]

Efforts to spread military culture among sport tourists, the encouragement of paramilitary activities, ideological indoctrination, the study of the terrain in potential operational theatres, and the attempts to establish rapport with ethnic minorities living there – all of these were rational steps towards the goal of creating a large pool of reservists who possessed special skills and were familiar with the social environment of frontier regions. Along with these general steps towards militarisation, OPTE made a concerted effort to prepare sufficient potential manpower for mountain divisions, which quickly multiplied in the 1930s. The Plenum of the OPTE Mountaineering Section held in May 1932 maintained that this agency had 'to turn mountaineering into a school for mountain troops' training' and demanded from the section's regional branches 'a decisive shift towards the militarisation of mountaineering' and the organisation of 'militarised expeditions and the establishment of militarised camps' in the high mountains.[52] The section leaders argued that 'the soldier of a mountain unit must know mountaineering technique as well as he knows marksmanship ... The most important OPTE duty is to provide at least a basic knowledge of mountaineering to Soviet soldiers who will probably fight in the mountains, and also to potential recruits.'[53] The Plenum suggested that mountaineers be registered with conscription offices so that they could be drafted into mountain divisions in case of war.[54]

After the opening of its first alpine camp in the Adyl-su gorge near Elbrus in 1931, OPTE began the construction of militarised alpine camp networks in the Caucasus, Central Asia, and the Altai. The explicit goal of this investment was to 'train highly skilled mountaineers. The campers will receive military training sufficient to use them in future as military climbing instructors.'[55] The selection of trainees for the camps was competitive; passing a firearms course increased the chance of being accepted.[56] While in the camp, the trainees were subject to military discipline. The campers followed a rigid schedule: they woke up and went to bed upon a signal; stood at attention in formations called 'platoons' during morning roll calls, flag raising, and instructors' announcements of the day's agenda; and afterwards participated in intensive daily climbing exercises. They also had to attend political lectures.

When mountaineers applied for financial sponsorship of their expeditions, the extent of the expedition's militarisation was among the criteria upon which support was granted.[57] Such pressure forced mountaineers to introduce paramilitary elements into their trips, even if they disliked them. However, most of them did not mind the militaristic flavour of their recreation. In fact, OPTE's motto, 'Those confident in snowy mountains will be courageous in combat',[58] struck a chord in the hearts of climbers, as reflected in the 'Baksanskaia' song:

> Our camps are not for jerks.
> If it comes to a fight in the mountains,
> We will take submachine-guns along with our ice axes
> And hold them as tenaciously as we hold the ropes while belaying.[59]

OPTE's slogan, 'Tourists are the skilled reserve of the Red Army',[60] reflected reality. Outdoor skills, physical fitness, a high level of education, patriotic and ideological indoctrination, and a militaristic culture elevated sport tourists well above the average Red Army recruit.

The Development of Sport Tourism in the Red Army: A First Step Towards Professionalism in Mountain Warfare

Along with the promotion of military values among civilians, OPTE sought to involve Red Army officers in sport tourism. Association leaders presented this recreation in the same way that medieval knights had perceived hunting: as a peacetime activity that provided training useful in combat.[61] They referred to the Turkish casualties in the Sarikamis operation, arguing that, in order to avoid similar disasters in the future, soldiers should be trained to operate in an unconventional battle environment.[62] This initiative received the enthusiastic support of the Red Army General Headquarters. Sergei Kamenev, deputy people's commissar of the Red Army and Navy, thought that 'any type of [sport] tourist travel – mountain, boat, bicycle, horseback riding, or ski tours – serves to train soldiers, develop their resourcefulness and courage, and strengthen their health'.[63] Marshal Aleksandr Egorov believed that sport tourism helped the Red Army to study tactics in all kinds of rugged terrain and to train mountain guides, scouts, commandos, and guerrilla experts.[64] Aleksandr Sediakin, deputy chief of the General Staff of the Red Army, maintained that 'mountaineering toughens men and makes them perceptive, staunch, courageous, resolute, and smart; they develop qualities ... precious in combat'.[65] Brigade Commander Maksimov, the head of the Military Topography Section of the General Staff, observed that during the civil war the Red Army had 'sustained unnecessary casualties when treacherous guides took entire [military] units to a murderous terrain'.[66] To avoid this in the war to come, soldiers had to master navigation, and the easiest way to do this would be to engage in mountain trekking.[67] Iosif Nemerzelli, the deputy head of the Political Section of the Caucasus Army, sought to organise an officer sport section that would run trekking expeditions studying prospective battlefields,[68] whereas Konstantin Avksent'evskii, the commander of the Caucasus Army, argued that such expeditions would help build inter-ethnic bonds between Soviet soldiers recruited all over the USSR and the local populations.[69] Rapport with local civilians would secure their co-operation during the looming apocalyptic war, as well as their assistance with logistics, guidance, reconnaissance, intelligence acquisition, and information about the terrain and seasonal weather patterns.

In early 1928, a year before OPT was launched, the Red Army organised the Military Tourist Bureau, which was to develop sport tourism within the army's ranks.[70] In 1930, after the General Staff began raising mountain divisions, the 1st Conference of Military Tourists in the Caucasus stated that 'the development of mountaineering is among the priorities of tourists in the Caucasus Red Banner Army. Any trips to the mountains and climbs of snow-covered peaks will provide enormous benefits to commanders and soldiers. We must learn how to act effectively in the mountains. Tourism will help us to train specialists who know the mountain terrain and can operate there.'[71] The conference decided to organise one mountaineering expedition per division of the Caucasus Army. In July 1934, Kliment Voroshilov, the people's commissar for defence, signed an order commanding the intensive development of military tourism.[72] Krylenko backed this decision with enormous enthusiasm, arguing: 'Bourgeois armies have special mountain units trained to operate at an altitude of several thousand metres. It is extremely important [to develop] mountain trekking in the Red Army', which would allow its special forces 'to surmount impassable abysses, steep slopes, and mountain peaks. This will ensure the reliable protection of our borders.'[73] Officers engaged in sport tourism were expected to become mountain guides able to pass on their outdoor skills to their soldiers.

Sport tourism had a vigorous start in the Red Army. In 1928, only a few teams of three to five officers engaged in sport tourism, but in the next year, after military tourist bureaus emerged in major cities, the number of participants in military sport expeditions surged.[74] They covered hundreds of kilometres across mountains, down rivers, or on skis in European Russia, remote regions of the Caucasus, and even the Altai.[75] In 1931, officer teams made 39 long treks of 100 to 400 kilometres in the high Caucasus; they crossed 32 passes and climbed 7 peaks.[76] By 1936, 4,000 officers and cadets had taken part in at least 1 mountain trek or climb.[77] Their teams had political, topographic, meteorological, tactical, medical, veterinary, signals, and logistics sections responsible for various experiments and for the accumulation, processing, and systematisation of information acquired during the expeditions. Doctors accompanied the military climbers and studied acute mountain sickness and methods of avoiding it.[78] The officers compiled detailed descriptions of their itineraries, corrected existing maps, and drew sketches of mountain passes.[79] They sought to intermingle with the local population, trying to bridge the wide culture gap, and gave numerous shooting lessons and political lectures to the locals. In order to study the possibilities and the limitations of logistics in rugged terrain, the officers launched several horse expeditions in mountain regions.[80]

Brigade Commander Vasilii Klement'ev, the head of the Infantry Cadet School in Tbilisi, was the most enthusiastic proponent of mountaineering in the Red Army. He did not pursue sport records but maintained that soldiers serving in mountain regions had to be trained in the environment in which they were expected to fight. As a first step to such training, he led volunteer officers and cadets on several multi-week treks through high passes in Georgia, Dagestan, and Chechnya[81] and organised several climbs to the highest peaks of the Caucasus. In August 1927, twelve of his cadets, led by two Georgian guides, reached the top of Kazbek after a four-day climb, and the following year seventeen cadets climbed Elbrus after trekking 400 kilometres to reach it.[82] From 1933 to 1940, the Red Army practised mass climbing of various peaks on an annual basis: 58 and 278 officers climbed to the top of Elbrus in 1933 and 1934, respectively, while in 1935 a team of officers accomplished the first winter mass climb of the peak.[83] In February 1936, about 400 soldiers and officers claimed to have reached the Kazbek summit, carrying with them rifles, machineguns, and even a mountain gun.[84]

Klement'ev's goal was 'to train experienced mountaineer commanders', 'to familiarise officers with logistics, topography, the terrain, and local customs',[85] and to test command and communications, uniforms, and gear during long treks at high altitudes; he also conducted shooting exercises during these treks. He uncovered numerous problems that had to be solved before Soviet divisions labelled 'mountain' could effectively operate in the mountains. Klement'ev found that 'navigation skill in a complicated mountain landscape can only be attained via systematic training' in the mountains,[86] which the Red Army did not provide. He taught soldiers how to build shelters in the snow and pointed to frequent exercises in the high mountains as the main means of coping with acute mountain sickness. He explained how to breathe at high altitude, walk across glaciers and steep slopes, set an appropriate march tempo, maintain a hydration balance, and determine the degree of fatigue of pack animals.[87]

Klement'ev offered a number of suggestions regarding the improvement of soldiers' equipment in the high mountains. Since mountain troops carried on their backs more supplies than regular infantry, every soldier had to have a backpack instead of the standard Soviet shapeless infantry sack with thin shoulder straps. Soldiers also had to be supplied with individual alcohol burners to warm up their food and individual small heaters, the size of a cigarette case, with special slow-burning coal. He found the quality of Soviet climbing gear unacceptable: ice axes and crampons were 'totally useless'; their tips bent and broke; and the crampon strap clips were in the wrong place. The soles of the mountain boots fell off quickly.[88] The poor design of pack boxes caused injury to the horses. The pack items had to be such that they could be easily loaded and unloaded, because if loading required a great effort soldiers would not unload the packs during the hourly break stops, and the horses would quickly become exhausted. After Klement'ev discovered that the standard pack kitchen did not fit the narrow mountain trails, he designed a light and compact kitchen, as well as light oblong cooking pots that were easier to mount on horseback than the standard round ones. Mountain troops needed hooded, water-resistant sleeping bags instead of the standard blankets, as well as small tents accommodating three or four persons rather than the standard large tents, which were too heavy, could not withstand strong winds, and required a large flat spot, difficult to find in the mountains.[89] Mountain troops had to be supplied with special food rations: light but calorie-rich, providing no fewer than 4,500 calories per day. Such rations had to contain high proportions of sugar and fat, as well as dried fruit and currant syrup to stir appetite, which was usually poor at high altitudes, and to prevent scurvy in the absence of fresh vegetables.[90]

Klement'ev was the only Soviet senior officer who discussed evacuation of the wounded in mountain conditions and came up with valuable proposals. First, since such transport would inevitably be slow and difficult, a paramedic had to be attached to every platoon. Second, the standard stretchers were too heavy and too long to be carried along narrow mountain paths with sharp turns; they had to be replaced with folding light bamboo stretchers.[91] Third, the number of stretcher bearers in mountain units had to be doubled because it was harder to carry a wounded man along a mountain path than across fields. Fourth, after stretcher bearers took a wounded soldier from the front line to a dressing station, he had to be evacuated, usually along a better trail, to a hospital on a stretcher fixed between two donkeys, and the donkeys had to be specially trained for the job. Finally, heated medical tents with a stock of warm clothes should be set up on the trail between the front line and the rear.[92]

Meanwhile, signals officers, helped by civilian climbers, began conducting important experiments with radio communications in the mountains. They even attempted to take radios to the top of Elbrus in 1932, Stalin Peak in 1933, and Belukha, the highest peak in the Altai, in 1936, although in all these cases they had to abandon them before they reached the summit because of their prohibitive weight. They discovered that the maximum communication range was only 15 kilometres; interference allowed them to communicate only for two hours in the morning.[93] These experiments revealed the problems of wireless communications in the mountains that had to be urgently addressed. It is hard to overestimate the value of the experiments conducted by Klement'ev and several other military enthusiasts for turning the nominal 'mountain' divisions into real ones.

The military mountaineers followed the example of their civilian counterparts in establishing permanent training facilities. In 1935, a military mountaineering school was launched in Terskol village near Elbrus. From 1934 to 1936, 120 to 150 officers enrolled in the school on an annual basis.[94] The graduates were qualified as mountain guides and could pass on their expertise to their soldiers. They also launched multi-week treks across mountain regions of the Caucasus, the Urals, the Altai, and Central Asia.[95] Dozens of officers participated in extremely complicated climbs. In 1934, a team of twenty officers led by Vitalii Abalakov undertook a climb of Lenin Peak. Only two of them, along with Abalakov, reached the summit, but few foreign expeditions, military or civilian, could boast a group of twenty-one men reaching an elevation of 7,000 metres, which shows that Soviet military mountaineering had gained a respectable place in world climbing.[96] That year Voroshilov summarised the achievements in this area, stating that

> the mountain treks of Red Army officers to Pamir, Elbrus ... Tian Shan, and Altai brought excellent results. They broke the world records in the number of mountaineers to climb Elbrus (5,595 m) and Zailiiskii Alatau (above 7,000 m). They conducted bold and valuable experiments in radio communications and studied [the particularities of] trekking on foot and on horseback in the high mountains. About 350 officers received good mountaineering training. Despite the extremely challenging tasks and obstacles, these results were attained without a single accident.[97]

What was the outcome of the effort invested in sport tourism as a means to secure a recruitment pool for Soviet mountain units, identify their proper equipment, and build their training infrastructure? Dozens of top world-class climbers existed in the Soviet Union, hundreds participated in complicated climbs, and, reportedly, by 1940 about 50,000 persons had earned the Alpinist of the USSR 1st Class badge, which means that they had received basic mountaineering training and had climbed above 5,000 metres.[98] This figure cannot be taken at face value because, being under severe pressure to increase the number of badge holders, the administrators of alpine camps handed them out to those who did not deserve them.[99] Nonetheless, even if reduced by one-third, this number was sufficient to raise six full-strength mountain divisions – as many as the Wehrmacht had by 1941.[100] OPTE and the Red Army enthusiasts took most of the necessary preliminary steps for organising proper mountain units: they involved hundreds of officers in outdoor sports and secured a large number of reservists with outdoor skills; established civilian and military climbing schools and trained enough civilian and military climbing instructors to pass on their skills to mountain troops; collected topographic and meteorological data in potential theatres of war; tested uniforms, weapons, gear, wireless communications, and logistics in the anticipated combat environment; and attempted to build bridges with borderland communities. Although the Red Army still had no trained mountain units by the mid 1930s, it seemed to be on the right track in its preparation for mountain warfare. The next and decisive step for organising effective mountain forces would be to begin routine, standardised training of the existing mountain divisions in the environment in which they would presumably be operating. However, the Red Army never took this crucial step because of the chaos produced by the Great Purge, Stalinist contempt for professionalism, and a switch to an ideology-based military doctrine.

With the opening salvos of the Great Purge in 1936, the state began a crackdown on non-governmental organisations. OPTE, dominated by the intelligentsia and white-collar workers, caused grave suspicion during the brewing witch-hunt.[101] On 17 April 1936, the Central Executive Committee of the USSR dissolved OPTE[102] and passed all its assets to the All-Union Trade Union Council, which had never run sport tourism and quickly ruined it.[103] The reputation of mountain climbers suffered a severe blow after the NKVD, in July 1937, opened a criminal case against twelve mountain guides working for the Adyl-su alpine camp; the investigation revealed an alleged 'fascist-terrorist group existing among mountaineers and tourists'. This was followed in November by the arrest of Vasilii Semenovskii, the founder of the camp and the former head of the OPTE Mountaineering Section, who was accused of 'organising accidents in the mountains' and planning to throw Lazar Kaganovich, the people's commissar for the railways, into an abyss when the latter visited the Caucasus.[104] A year later, Krylenko, the former OPTE chair and people's commissar for justice of the USSR, shared Semenovskii's plight, as did most members of the presidium of the OPTE Central Council and the top Soviet mountaineers associated with Semenovskii and Krylenko. Dozens of climbers found themselves either in front of the firing squad or in the Gulag, including Lev Gurvich, Krylenko's deputy in OPTE; Vitalii Abalakov, the leader of the first Soviet team to climb Lenin Peak, in 1934; Nikolai Gorbunov, secretary of the Council of People's Commissars of the USSR and the leader of the expedition that reached the Stalin Peak summit for the first time in history in 1933; Aleksandr Get'e, who came close to the summit during the latter expedition; Lev Barkhash, a major promoter of the militarisation of mountaineering and the leader of the expedition that made the second Soviet climb of Lenin Peak in 1937; Stanislav Ganetskii, Grigorii Rozentsveig, and Arii Poliakov, team members of the latter expedition who reached the summit; Avgust Glantsberg, head of the Terskol school of military mountaineering; Georgii Kharlampiev, the first Soviet climber who made the extremely difficult traverse of both Ushba summits; and Solomon Slutskii, a founder of the OPTE Moscow Mountaineering Section. These climbers, whom Voroshilov had eulogised three years earlier, were accused of espionage and of 'having compiled tourist-fascist plans of tourist bases, alpine camps, and refuges' and 'having betrayed the location of the Soviet frontier guard outpost at the Khan-Tengri Peak to German spies'.[105] These arrests, followed by ridiculous accusations, targeted the cream of the climbers, and they ruined the prestige of Soviet mountaineering as a whole. No senior officer dared to refer positively to mountaineering after its high-ranking promoters were executed for alleged treason, among them Aleksandr Egorov, one of the five Soviet marshals; Aleksandr Sediakin, head of the Anti-Aircraft Defence Directorate of the Red Army; and Iosif Nemerzelli, deputy head of the Political Directorate of the Leningrad Military District.[106] Survivors of the purge among civilian and military mountaineers preferred to keep a low profile and were reluctant to advertise their expertise, let alone fill the mountain guide vacancies created by the purge.

Theory and Practice of Mountain Warfare in the Soviet Union During the Interwar Period: Developing the Concept

Those few Soviet officers who had studied actions in Western Europe during World War I claimed to have found that 'the best soldiers [on the Western Front] were the alpine troops and the Scottish Highlanders – that is, people accustomed to climbing rocky cliffs and walking dozens of kilometres daily along mountain trails'.[107] They pointed to the fact that the southern borders of the Soviet Union followed the Caucasus, Pamir, and Tian Shan and maintained that, 'without knowledge of mountain warfare, the Red Army would inevitably sustain heavy and unnecessary casualties, as happened to the Arakan formation ... We should keep in mind that capitalists dream of the Baku and Grozny' oilfields, and on the way to these strategic targets they would have to cross the mountains at the Soviet Union's southern borders, where the Red Army, having skilled mountain divisions, would be able to pin them down.[108]

However, although Soviet civilian and military mountaineering, sponsored by the state with the idea of utilising it in mountain warfare, made a stunning leap after the late 1920s, the Red Army was slow to formulate the concept of mountain units. Although many senior officers promoted sport tourism among soldiers in order to improve their outdoor skills, only a handful understood that the army needed a professional force with special tactical training, gear, and logistical and communications means to operate effectively in the mountains. From 1929 to 1931, the Red Army attached the label 'mountain' to several rifle divisions in the Caucasus and Central Asia that did not differ from regular rifle divisions except in terms of structure, showing that the General Staff had no clear concept of what a mountain division was supposed to be. The top commanders of the Transcaucasian Military District frequently wrote critical reports about the state of combat training in their 'mountain' divisions, listing a great number of flaws. However, until 1936, they did not write a single line related to mountain warfare, simply because they had never conducted any exercises in the mountains.[109] In order to turn the regular infantry enlisted in what were called 'mountain' divisions into a force able to operate effectively in the mountains, the Red Army General Staff had to proceed through several steps: first, accumulate and process information on Russian experience in past campaigns and on mountain formations elsewhere; second, compile a manual on mountain warfare – that is, on the ideal to be pursued; third, test the validity of the manual's assumptions during persistent field exercises; and, finally, refine the manual and the mountain formations on the basis of the experience gained. The goal of this section is to outline the theoretical knowledge that the Red Army General Staff had about mountain warfare and to show how the Soviet commanders applied this knowledge to practice.

Having examined the Russian military experience in the mountains, the General Staff could proceed to the next step: the development of a manual for its mountain formations. Every army manual should explain the role of a certain arm of the military in the overall doctrine; describe the tactics this arm must employ; and outline the formations' structure, training procedures, and equipment required to meet the expected challenges. Since after 1933 Soviet leaders perceived

Germany as the most probable adversary, the Red Army acquired for its mountain force two German manuals as examples to follow. One manual addressed mountain warfare, and the second instructed on mountaineering at altitudes above 2,000 metres.

The first manual, marked ‘obtained via unofficial channels’, most likely arrived in the hands of the Red Army via Comintern spies in the mid 1930s. Written by a Captain Wagner, who had served for two years in a German mountain unit during World War I, the manual summarised the experience gained by the Austrian and German armies. It contained many valuable observations on the tactics of mountain units, as well as on their personnel, equipment, and structure.

Wagner briefly outlined the basic strategic tenet of mountain warfare: ‘The enemy must be pinned down in the mountains, but the main strike should be delivered on the plains.’[110] He thus implied that actions in the mountains are inevitably only an auxiliary component of major operations. However, in order to make a valuable contribution to a campaign, those engaged in such auxiliary actions must know the peculiarities of mountain warfare. Wagner’s observations on tactics in the mountains mirrored some of the thoughts of Russian theoreticians, although he articulated his ideas more clearly and in far greater detail. He pointed out that mountain units should display initiative, imagination, and flexibility. Since the mountain landscape divides large formations along a broad front and rugged terrain, which makes close command and control extremely difficult, senior commanders can give general directives only once every several days, and junior officers in charge of small units should act on their own in the spirit of these directives.[111] Frontal attacks in the mountains are always costly and often futile, which makes it necessary to search for ways around enemy strongholds. Envelopments ‘most likely will succeed if his [the enemy’s] position links with a terrain that the enemy deems impassable’.[112] Mountain units should attack the enemy from several sides simultaneously in a co-ordinated fashion. Every mountain brigade must have a mountaineering company to perform reconnaissance missions and the envelopment of enemy positions across the most difficult terrain. Since it is hard to deliver ammunition to the high mountains and it is therefore usually scarce, the accuracy of infantry and artillery fire is particularly important, but distances are delusive: people tend to underestimate them when they look upward and overestimate them when they look down. Soldiers should aim at the target when shooting up and below the target when shooting down. Throwing a hand grenade uphill requires special training. Artillery fire at the slopes above enemy positions may provoke a rockfall or an avalanche intended to hit the enemy. Sound waves travel unimpeded in the mountains but are reflected by rocks; soldiers should be trained how to move noiselessly and how to identify the enemy's location by listening to echoes.[113] They need numerous exercises in the mountains to learn these peculiarities of mountain warfare.

Wagner elaborated on the qualifications of personnel of mountain formations. Since they are bound to operate in a difficult environment, these formations should consist of hand-picked soldiers. It takes time to train an alpine shooter and shape his mentality. Every officer of a mountain unit should be an experienced climber and skier. A close bond among mountain troops, who usually operate in small units, is a must: 'Every man should know everybody else's physical and moral capacity, because his life often depends on it',[114] while 'the company commander should know what every one of his men represents as a soldier and a climber and should not assign too difficult missions to privates without proper mountaineering training'.[115] In short, 'only mountain units, with special training acquired in peacetime, should be used for mountain warfare, because it would take [a long] time to adapt an improvised mountain unit raised from lowland residents to the mountain conditions. This transition involves a great effort and the overcoming of fear' that unaccustomed people often experience.[116] Not all the soldiers of a mountain brigade must be skilled climbers – in fact, only about one-third of them need to be trained to move across any terrain – but these must be motivated and physically fit enough to do their job.[117]

Wagner described in detail the climbing component of a mountain unit. A mountain brigade must have 'skilled, reliable mountaineers ... with summer and winter experience. [Officers] must seek their advice in all tactical and logistical matters, and in coping with mountain hazards. The officer who ignores the advice of mountaineers pays with blood and carries unbearable responsibility. Mountaineers should also ... supervise the climbing training and manage the climbing gear.'[118] Mountain guides should be attached to all units of a mountain brigade and should teach soldiers all aspects of mountaineering. The brigade's personnel should be rotated through mountaineering courses with a ratio of one instructor per five soldiers.[119]

Mountain guides should run two-level training courses: those targeting every soldier of the one-third selected as 'high mountain personnel' and those designed to train future climbing instructors – the best of the best. The training of high mountain personnel should enable soldiers to operate in the most difficult mountain terrain.[120] They should practise climbing, skiing, and multi-day trekking in the high mountains in all seasons, under the supervision of climbing instructors. The mountaineering course should teach the soldiers about the varieties of mountain terrain; climbing gear and its use; potential hazards and survival skills; mountaineering techniques on rocks, snow, and ice; skiing and waxing techniques for various types of snow; the transportation of weapons and injured comrades on skis and sledges; walking on one ski; shooting on skis; map reading and navigation with a compass; measurement of altitude with an aneroid; meteorology; and camp arrangement and building of igloos. Since evacuation of the wounded is difficult and slow in the mountains, every soldier must take a first-aid course, and medics should be skilled mountaineers able to help soldiers wounded in any terrain. Every company must have a rescue team consisting of three climbers, who would command the rescue work in case of a major accident, such as an avalanche. The intensive training course should last four weeks in summer and fourteen days in winter.[121]

The training of climbing instructors must be even more thorough. Only a person who, after the standard mountaineering training, has participated in six multi-week expeditions, three in summer and three in winter, can be considered an accomplished instructor. The instructor must be 'an example of courage, determination, and self-sacrifice'.[122]

The individual mountaineering gear of the high mountain personnel should include a bamboo alpenstock weighing only 0.8 kg, an ice axe, crampons, a carabiner, an avalanche cord, sunblock, a large comfortable backpack, sunglasses, and skis as well as one alcohol burner and one rope for every two persons, and a compass, an aneroid, and several ice and rock pitons for each section.[123]

Only wireless communication is viable in the mountains, which means that a mountain unit must have more portable short-range radios than a regular infantry unit of the same size would, as well as skilled radio operators able to meet the challenges of a mountainous environment. A cable car can considerably ease logistics during static action in the mountains; therefore, mountain brigades should have winches and cables.[124] According to Soviet reports, German mountain divisions had grapnel anchor launchers that allowed them to quickly cross rivers and deep ravines after shooting a rope with an anchor across them.[125]

The second German manual addressed only climbing. It instructed on various techniques and gear, mountain hazards and safety procedures.[126] While Wagner's manual was quite useful as an educational aid to Red Army mountain units, the German mountaineering manual was less important because during the interwar period Soviet civilian climbers had published several textbooks on mountaineering that were at least as good as this German manual: they described the climbing gear, proper food rations, water balance, and march tempo at various altitudes; shelter building in various types of landscapes; and a variety of mountaineering techniques, such as rope-team movement and knot tying, rappelling and belaying, the traverse of grassy and snow-encrusted slopes and screes, rock climbing with pitons, and walking across glaciers in crampons with step cutting and crevasse crossing. They also instructed on mountain hazards, the basics of meteorology, first aid and the methods of coping with acute mountain sickness, rescue operations and the gear of rescue teams, and the transportation of injured climbers. Finally, they outlined a standard training programme in an alpine camp that culminated with climbing a mountain peak.[127]

Soon after the General Staff of the Red Army acquired Wagner's manual, it produced its own draft manual. Unlike the German version, which was written by an expert on mountain warfare, the Soviet draft of 1936 was an amateurish, crude, and clumsy adaptation of the Red Army Field Manual of 1936. Most of its content was pointless demagogy irrelevant to mountain warfare. It devoted large sections to the tactics of armour and field artillery and stated, contrary to all the experience of the imperial army, that cavalry 'is a major arm in the mountains' to 'be used for daring raids across mountain passes with difficult access – that is, where the enemy expects it least'.[128]

The manual did borrow some useful points on mountain warfare from Wagner's manual, such as the importance of 'individual training and great initiative of junior officers and ... rank and file'; advice to swiftly occupy dominating heights; and emphasis on envelopments of the enemy flanks as the major assault tactic. Simultaneous frontal attacks by a fraction of the available forces were needed only to pin down the enemy.[129] In defence, 'neglecting to protect the flanks would result in a rout'; therefore, 'reconnaissance of the flanks and bypass trails deserves special attention'.[130] The manual expressed appreciation for the value of mountain artillery and stated that weapons with a steep fire trajectory, like howitzers and mortars, are particularly useful in the mountains. Finally, it stated that 'the difficulty of [earth] works in a rocky terrain demands a supply of soldiers with a large number of tools'.[131]

Although the manual's authors adopted these wise ideas from Wagner, they misinterpreted his other points, shifted emphases, omitted important sections, and inserted passages that demonstrated their ignorance about mountain warfare. The manual acknowledged that wire communications had limited use in the mountains but did not offer a viable alternative. The authors questioned the value of radio in the mountains because of the interference, the short range of portable radios, and the prohibitive weight of long-range stationary radios, suggesting that mountain troops rely instead on runners and optical communications, although these are inevitably handicapped by frequent rain, fog, and low cloud. The manual also advanced the odd idea of commanding ground troops from an airplane circling over the battlefield[132] without explaining how this could be done in the absence of landing strips in the mountains or in unstable weather. The manual presumed actions of climber units at the least accessible sections of the front,[133] but said nothing about the training procedures or their structure. It mentioned only sunglasses as the special gear needed to operate in the mountains, perhaps because its authors did not understand the meaning of the other gear described in the German manual. Except for the difficulty of ammunition supply, the draft ignored the logistics of mountain warfare. The manual expressed the misconception that mountain trails can be completely blocked by rockfalls provoked by explosions.[134] Finally, its statement that 'building strongholds in rocky soil requires much time and effort; therefore, one should always seek to find and use natural cover'[135] could convince soldiers that the landscape alone would provide enough protection and discourage them from digging in. As a whole, the draft manual turned out to be less tailored to mountain warfare, and therefore less useful, than Wagner's manual.

Marshal Egorov approved the draft, sent it to the Transcaucasian and Central Asian military districts for field tests, and requested feedback on their results.[136] In response, in September 1936, Mikhail Levandovskii, commander of the Transcaucasian Military District, launched the first large war game in the mountains ever conducted in the Soviet Union. This exercise was conspicuous for its scale rather than for a comprehensive imitation of mountain warfare. Three 'mountain' divisions and one 'mountain-cavalry' division participated in the game.[137] Its goals were to discover the limits 'of deep battle in mountain conditions', to test 'the manoeuvrability of motorised and mechanised formations in the mountains', and to identify 'the principles of combat, unit co-operation, manoeuvre, and fire in the fight for the passes'.[138] As is clear from these goals, the Transcaucasian Military District exercised in hills accessible to mechanised units rather than in the high mountains. Levandovskii chose for the game a region near Rikotskii pass and four other neighbouring passes with a maximum height of 1,000 metres and connected by a fairly good road network.[139] Such an exercise, quite useful for studying actions in the hills, did little to advance the knowledge of warfare in the high mountains, although it provided some valuable information nonetheless.

Levandovskii found that his 'mountain' divisions had no idea of mountain warfare because they interpreted earlier 'exercises in the mountains' merely as walks along ravines.[140] In fact, he wrote, 'the main and general flaw in all conducted exercises was the disregard of the peculiar mountain terrain. Units operating in the mountains often applied the methods and regulations they use on the plains.' It would be hard to expect any other outcome from divisions that have never practised war in the mountains. In terms of tactics, Levandovskii confirmed several points from the manual: 'combat in the mountains focuses on a fight for the passes'; envelopment is preferable to frontal attack; and 'the actions of small groups (section, platoon) carry the brunt of action',[141] which meant that the initiative of junior commanders and the individual training of soldiers, including in mountaineering techniques, were of utmost importance. Engineers tested artificial obstacles intended to block mountain trails: heaps of trees thrown on the paths in narrows worked well, whereas the attempts to close the trails through demolition of surrounding rocks produced somewhat disappointing results, despite the enormous amount of explosives spent.[142] The exercise exposed the serious problems of communication in the mountains. It became clear that wire and messenger communications, the main means used by the Red Army, were insufficient. Only radio was adequate in such a terrain,[143] but commanders had no experience in using radios or radio codes.[144] Since the range of radios fell considerably in the mountains, a serious effort had to be invested in selecting a proper location for radio stations and in the establishment of relay stations between headquarters and the front-line formations; consequently, the number of radios in the mountains had to be increased by at least 50 per cent in comparison with the plains.[145] The boxes with pack radio stations turned out to be unusable; nearly all horses packed with radios were injured. The stationary long-range radios were too bulky; attempts to transport them on horse-drawn carriages failed because they would not fit the mountain trails.[146] Radio batteries had to be charged every six hours, but the Red Army had no pack battery chargers, and the stationary ones, weighing 195 kilograms,[147] were too heavy for a horse, which meant, in effect, that mountain divisions could not use radios in the high mountains away from the roads; the urgency of designing portable chargers became clear.[148]

Unfortunately, this first large tactical exercise in the mountains in 1936 turned out to be the last one: Levandovskii submitted his analysis to the General Staff before the year was over, and in June 1937 he was reassigned to the Far East. His successors showed no interest in mountain warfare, especially when, in February 1938, Levandovskii was arrested and in July executed as a member of the 'fascist military conspiracy'.[149] As usually happened, those who succeeded the victims of the purge sought to disassociate themselves from everything their predecessors had done.

Nonetheless, in 1940, the Red Army published a new improved draft manual with which it entered World War II. The manual claimed to focus on warfare at altitudes of 1,000 to 2,500 metres,[150] and it advanced more and better ideas than the previous version, ideas borrowed partly from Wagner, partly from Clausewitz, partly from Korsun's work on Sarikamis, and partly from Levandovskii's field tests.

The new draft maintained that 'attack in the mountains has considerable advantage over defence' and stated prophetically: 'A broken landscape helps [the attacker] to sneak unnoticed to the enemy's flanks. Even if small forces take the heights dominating the enemy's retreat route, they can block the enemy's exit from battle … The benefits provided by terrain, if used skilfully, give an opportunity to surround [the enemy] not necessarily by superior but by equal or even inferior forces.'[151] In tune with the German manual, this draft referred to good marksmanship as a requisite of mountain warfare[152] and addressed some problems of firing in the mountains, such as the difficulty of range determination and the impact of low atmospheric pressure on ballistics, and pointed to the need for special fire-correction tables. The new draft stated that defence in the mountains should consist of tiered strongholds built with the help of explosives, thus discarding the instruction of the previous version to seek cover behind rocks. The manual repeated Wagner's points about cable cars as useful logistical means and radio as 'the main communication means in mountain warfare', notwithstanding the problems involved, and emphasised the need for portable radios.[153] The authors, however, preserved unwise references to artificial rockfalls intended to block the enemy's path, thus ignoring the results of Levandovskii's field tests;[154] they also inserted several eighteenth- and nineteenth-century ideas of the sort that 'cold steel is much more important in the mountains' than on the plains and recommended 'to proceed to bayonet charge as soon as possible'; finally, they maintained that 'stone-thrower mines [*kamnemety*] are effective weapons against attacking infantry ... All approaches to the front-line trenches ... should be covered by fused [stone-thrower] mines'[155] – counterproductive advice, as the Shipka experience had proven.

The manual devoted only two and a half of its 250 pages to actions in the high mountains, considerably fewer than to the actions of tanks or air force. This minuscule section provided few useful pieces of information. First, it specified that the envelopment of enemy positions would most likely involve climbing vertical cliffs and steep slopes, and warned, citing Wagner, that 'no mountain terrain is impassable for well-trained soldiers'.[156] Second, it identified the climbing gear necessary for such actions. Third, it emphasised that soldiers needed a ten- to twelve-day acclimatisation period before they could operate above 3,000 metres.[157] The manual's authors also added a recommendation that had dire consequences during the battle in the Caucasus: 'Military mountaineering training is conducted during the acclimatisation period: belaying, using crampons, walking across rocks and ice', as well as the study of topography, mountain hazards, and navigation.[158] This implied that the units heading to the mountains would have an acclimatisation period of ten or twelve days and that this period would provide enough time to drill soldiers from zero to a sufficient level of training for fighting in mountainous terrain. The manual did not specify who would be conducting the training during the acclimatisation period.

The manual acknowledged the need for skis and snowshoes in winter but did not explain what kind of skis and bindings were appropriate and said nothing about the training of skiers. It included a brief description of avalanche and rockfall hazards, taken from the German manual, and prompted every company to organise a rescue platoon from 'hardy, motivated, and courageous men'[159] in avalanche-prone regions; however, it did not describe any rescue techniques. Only scouts were supposed to receive camouflage coveralls:[160] all other soldiers had to fight in their green uniforms, which left them exposed against a background of snow. In short, this manual was more informative than the draft of 1936, but it was still inadequate for practical application and contained many faulty speculations unsupported by empirical evidence. Furthermore, it remained a classified draft rather than instructions to follow. Although some 'mountain' divisions received this manual, others had only the 1936 version.

Meanwhile, Brigade Commander Klement'ev summarised his own experience in a book, which provided a large amount of valuable information that supplemented the draft manual of 1940, especially with regard to marches and tactics in the high mountains, logistics, survival techniques, food rations, and equipment.[161] His book was, in fact, more useful for practising mountain warfare than the manual of 1940, but it had the lower status of a military study and was not distributed among 'mountain' divisions. Thus, by 1940, the Red Army General Staff had formulated a vague concept of mountain warfare, grasped only the basics of its tactics, and identified only some of the necessary equipment and some training requirements.

Conclusion

The effort of the Soviet state to engage civilians in sport tourism as a step towards enabling the Red Army to fight in unconventional environments – mountains, forests, or swamps – or in the challenging season of winter produced a strikingly rewarding outcome at a small cost. Born as a government-promoted enterprise and directed from a single centre in accordance with party guidelines, Soviet sport tourism, by the mid 1930s, had secured a large pool of potential recruits with desirable qualities. These were enthusiastic, patriotic, ideologically committed, physically fit, and well-educated individuals who were accustomed to strict discipline and subordination of their personal desires to the collective goal, knew how to overcome outdoor challenges with primitive gear and improvise in its absence, possessed paramilitary skills, and embraced a militarised culture. Mountaineering taught people to take the initiative while cultivating team spirit; such a mentality was a must in mountain warfare, which presumed the independent but coherent operation of small units and mutual support in action. Most mountaineers realised the challenges of Soviet multiculturalism and understood that, while travelling outside their home area, they had to make an effort to narrow the cultural gap between themselves and the local populations via consent and respect for the local customs. Unlike the typical Slavic conscript serving in the borderlands, they did not assume that their own cultural values were universal. This understanding could have helped to establish the rapport with the local population that was vital for the success of military operations across rugged terrain, where logistical assistance and local knowledge were particularly important. Unlike the average soldier, climbers knew the basics of first aid; they also knew rescue techniques in the mountains, and some were members of the professional mountaineering rescue service, which, although still embryonic, could considerably decrease the number of casualties in the numerous accidents inevitable during war in the mountains. Thousands of Soviet young men, including military officers, received basic mountaineering training, and hundreds could serve as instructors in mountain units and organise the advanced climbing training of mountain troops, rotating them through a quickly growing network of alpine camps. The reports on mountaineering expeditions, kept in the sport tourist library, provided detailed descriptions of the itineraries, sketches of the mountain passes, seasonal weather patterns, and data on population and supply opportunities; this information was priceless for planning military operations.

In short, most goals set by the Soviet government when it decided to sponsor sport tourism were attained: the state acquired excellent 'raw material' for various kinds of special forces, built an outdoor training infrastructure, identified the required gear and possible logistical solutions, and accumulated sufficient data for planning military operations in the mountains. The experiments conducted by Klement'ev and other enthusiasts of mountain warfare provided a wealth of valuable information and suggested avenues to follow to reduce the 'friction of war', exposed flaws in the equipment of Soviet 'mountain' divisions, and suggested ways to correct them. While the *Manual on Mountain Warfare* published in 1936 and refined in 1940 was far from perfect, it still offered basic tactical regulations, and the widely available textbooks on civilian mountaineering could serve as climbing aids for soldiers. It seemed that progress towards the ultimate goal – to enable the Red Army to operate efficiently in unconventional environments – had acquired a strong and steady self-sustaining impetus.

However, the Red Army failed to make the crucial step from theoretical deliberations to routine field exercises because, at the moment when it had finally secured all the necessary preconditions for such a step, the leading Soviet mountaineers and senior officers who promoted mission-oriented training and equipment were killed in the purge, while those who replaced the purge victims strived to secure their own safety by disassociating themselves from the legacy of their predecessors. The vigorous effort to secure potential personnel for mountain units, the publication of the *Manual on Mountain Warfare*, Levandovskii's field tests, and Klement'ev's experiments and studies thus had only a marginal impact on the ability of Soviet 'mountain' divisions to operate in the mountains.

3 FIRST BATTLE TESTS AND THE HANDICAPS OF SELECTIVE LEARNING

One need not drink up the entire sea to realise that its water is salty.

Bulgarian proverb

By 1939, numerous Soviet 'mountain' divisions were totally untrained for mountain warfare; their ability to operate in the mountains hardly differed from that of regular rifle formations. After the beginning of World War II, several Soviet senior officers observed that foreign mountain formations had proven their value in France, Norway, southern Poland, and Yugoslavia, while the Red Army's own combat experience in the first year of the war furnished strong arguments for the need for special forces with training and equipment adapted to peculiar battle environments. Yet Soviet generals failed to extrapolate to mountain warfare the lessons they had learned the hard way before Germans approached the Caucasus in August 1942.

The Winter War as a Wake-up Call

In the autumn of 1939, the Red Army planned a Blitzkrieg against Finland: it was to take Viipuri, the capital of Finnish Karelia, within four days and Helsinki within two weeks from the beginning of the offensive, which would end the war.[1] Its General Staff was so certain that the Blitzkrieg would bring an instant victory that, on the eve of the invasion, it rushed to issue a warning to its armies against the accidental crossing of the Swedish border more than 300 kilometres away.[2] As it happened, however, the Winter War lasted from 30 November 1939 to

13 March 1940. It took the Soviets that long to advance 100 kilometres from the Finnish border to Viipuri. A series of humiliating defeats suffered by the Red Army, despite its enormous superiority in numbers and firepower,[3] forced its General Staff to examine the problems it had encountered. A month after the Pyrrhic victory, Joseph Stalin brought together forty-six senior commanders who had participated in the Winter War to discuss the causes of the dismal performance. The conference – conducted from 14 to 17 April 1940 in the presence of Stalin and Voroshilov – was the most honest and thorough analysis of the Red Army's flaws undertaken between the beginning of the Great Purge in 1936 and the war against Germany in 1941. This analysis gave the Red Army an opportunity to shake off the ideological postulates that had governed its strategy and training procedures since the beginning of the purges and use the limited time it had left before the anticipated war against Germany to address the problems exposed by this bitter experience. Some of these problems – like the fact that after the Great Purge second lieutenants, a rank appropriate for a platoon leader, commanded battalions in the way they would command platoons[4] – could not be solved within a short timeframe. However, the Red Army still improved its winter combat capacity considerably by eliminating many flaws identified at the conference, and it passed the next major winter field test during the battle of Moscow. Many conclusions drawn at the conference were relevant to mountain warfare. The following analysis focuses on these conclusions.

The Field Manual of 1936, with which the Red Army entered the Winter War, devoted one of its thirteen chapters to actions in winter. It registered the obvious facts that deep snow 'makes an off-road march difficult without skis' and that 'the mobility of military units depends entirely on their training and the adaptation of their equipment to winter conditions and terrain. Formations untrained and unequipped for actions in winter quickly lose their combat capacity, and heavy weapons, not adapted to winter conditions, become a burden.'[5] The manual maintained that actions in winter would proceed mainly along the roads. It stated that an army should include ski units, non-existent in peacetime, but did not identify their strength, structure, equipment, or armament; it presumed merely that parts of the regular rifle divisions, the size of which was unclear, would fight on skis. The skiers were to conduct reconnaissance, protect the flanks of the main forces, envelop enemy positions outside roads, and pursue the retreating enemy. The ground forces would rely mainly on wire and messenger communication. Soldiers were supposed to receive warm uniforms and white camouflage and were to be billeted mainly in settlements. If they were to spend nights outside, they would sleep in huts made of tree branches and equipped with unidentified 'simplest warming devices'.[6] The manual presumed that soldiers' food rations would be the same in summer and in winter. Although the Red Army fought the war against Finland in accordance with this manual, a number of unexpected problems prevented it from following these vague instructions. As a conference participant put it, 'The actions of all arms suffered from basic but serious flaws ... caused by the poor skills of officers and men and their total ignorance of Finnish terrain and appropriate tactics.'[7]

Finland was covered by deep snow, and actions took place in dense forests with many swamps; the temperature was frequently −30°C, and in mid January it sometimes dropped even lower. It turned out that the Red Army was totally untrained and unequipped to operate in such conditions, because during the interwar period it had exercised only in fair weather and on easy terrain.[8] Even the divisions deployed permanently in northern regions never practised combat in winter, as if winter never happened in Russia. Red Army regulations prohibited even routine exercises near the barracks when the temperature fell below −15°C, although children were exempt from attending school only when the temperature fell below −25 °C.[9] Large-scale field exercises at subzero temperatures would inevitably result in several cases of frostbite, the common cold, and perhaps even pneumonia. However, this was the price that an army operating in a country with such climatic conditions as Russia had to pay to keep itself combat-ready. The Red Army ignored this simple axiom; the fervent search for 'wreckers' during the Great Purge ensured that commanders would keep their soldiers in barracks even when the outside temperature was well above −15 °C, because, as they frankly admitted, they worried that if their soldiers caught colds the officers could be accused of deliberately injuring them.[10] That is why the Red Army had no knowledge of winter warfare basics; when it planned the invasion of Finland, it did not take climate or the amount of daylight into account, nor did it know how to fight in winter in dense forests without roads.[11] This ignorance resulted in a number of grave problems that the Red Army had to tackle during the war.

Having undergone no field exercises in winter, the Red Army could not identify the proper uniforms or military equipment suitable for winter warfare. As it turned out, its winter uniforms were too heavy but not warm enough for strenuous marches across snowfields, and many units arrived at the front line, inexplicably, in summer uniforms. Soviet soldiers envied the Finns: 'Finnish uniforms were excellent: woollen underwear, sweaters, fur boots, sheepskin hats with ear flaps – everything was lightweight but warm and comfortable. Every soldier had a white coverall',[12] whereas Soviet soldiers found themselves exposed against the background of snow without such a simple piece of equipment.[13] Finnish Karelia was a sparsely populated region that could provide only occasional lodging; most soldiers had to spend night after night outdoors, exposed to bitter cold. Huts made with tree branches, recommended by the Field Manual, were poor shelters in subzero temperatures, especially since the army did not have the 'simplest warming devices' mentioned in the manual, nor did it have enough tents.[14] Thousands of soldiers were lost to frostbite, and many froze to death. The 44th Rifle Division alone lost 1,057 men, or about 9 per cent of its manpower, to injuries, mainly frostbite, during two days in January.[15] Most frostbitten soldiers had frozen limbs, which occurred because some divisions had no felt boots or warm foot wraps, essential footwear for prolonged stays outdoor in winter, and in other divisions many soldiers arrived at the front in disintegrating boots.[16] Some divisions had no gloves, even in late January; officers ordered their men to sew gloves from their blankets.[17] The individual infantry spades were too flimsy for digging frozen soil.[18] Nobody had thought about how soldiers would transport heavy machineguns, ammunition, and wounded men across snowfields surrounded by myriad lakes and swamps, many of which were not frozen. Since it was hard to carry wounded men across deep snow during mobile actions, many were abandoned to freeze.[19]

The conference participants believed that the Red Army had to make a radical shift from verbal instructions to practising war in the environment in which the soldiers were expected to fight.[20] The obvious extrapolation of this conclusion to mountain warfare was that soldiers of mountain divisions must exercise in various types of mountain landscape and at various altitudes in all seasons and weather conditions. Once the Red Army found that its winter uniforms were unsuitable for action in deep snow, it should have realised that soldiers operating in the mountains – often having to climb steep slopes in subzero temperatures at high elevations, even in summer – would need special uniforms that were adapted to that environment and that would provide sufficient camouflage. After the actions in winter showed that soldiers should stay overnight in tents with portable stoves rather than shiver in huts made of tree branches, it must have been clear that soldiers operating above the treeline would also need portable stoves, liquid fuel, and tents – not the large standard ones transported in trucks but small ones that could be carried in a backpack and pitched on scarce flat spots. If a Soviet infantry spade could not dig frozen soil, it must also have been useless on rocky, mountainous soil. If it was hard to transport wounded men across snowfields, it must have been at least as hard to carry them across mountainous terrain. If even Stalin realised that soldiers needed special rations containing bacon, tinned food, and vodka to survive in winter,[21] his generals must have understood that mountain divisions also needed special light but calorie-rich rations to withstand long marches through thin air. All of these problems had to be urgently addressed to turn the Soviet 'mountain' divisions into a force able to fight in the mountains.

Action in deep snow and in low temperatures required great stamina, but Soviet commanders complained that many of their men were in poor physical shape, while junior officers who had just come from cadet schools 'with fat bellies' could 'handle the horizontal bar only with a ladder'.[22] As Vasilii Chuikov, commander of the 9th Army and future hero of Stalingrad, maintained, 'We do not train soldiers and officers for tough war environments during peacetime ... If soldiers got tired after covering 5 or 10 km in gas masks, their officer was reprimanded so severely that afterwards he was afraid to train soldiers in difficult conditions.'[23] The experience of the Winter War implied that recruits who were enlisted into formations that were expected to fight in an environment demanding greater than average physical effort, such as the mountains, must be in excellent physical condition and therefore should be carefully selected among recruits.

The Winter War showed that the basic training of Soviet soldiers was 'extremely poor ... The Finnish soldier ... was definitely trained better. One Finnish soldier with a submachine-gun is worth one [Soviet] section ... Our soldiers learned how to use heavy machine-guns, hand grenades, and light machineguns [only] in combat.'[24] Since heavy weapons were often immobilised, infantry skills played a particularly important role. However, in the 50th Rifle Corps, from 20 to 30 per cent of soldiers arrived at the front line without basic military training and could not handle their weapons; the 100th and 123rd Rifle Divisions received 'absolutely untrained' reinforcements, while in the 142nd Rifle Division 47 per cent of machine-gunners did not know how their weapons operated. Such untrained soldiers, in the words of their officers, 'elevated our casualties and lowered the standards of our units'.[25] Yet untrained reinforcements were sometimes sent into action two or three hours after their arrival at the front.[26] Unlike Soviet soldiers, Finns were 'excellent marksmen'.[27] The accurate fire of Finnish snipers annoyed Soviet commanders so much that sometimes they ordered an entire artillery regiment to engage a single sniper.[28]

The basic training of Soviet junior officers was also well below the standard required for modern warfare. The commander of the 75th Rifle Division complained that officers who had recently graduated from cadet schools 'absolutely cannot handle their weapons; they are unfamiliar with topography ... and scarcely know the manuals. That is why, in combat, our lieutenants and second lieutenants quickly merged with the masses of their soldiers, thus losing the prestige of an officer.'[29] Unlike the Finns, who, according to Voroshilov, 'easily found their way in forests', only 17 per cent of the officers of the 142nd Rifle Division could navigate with a compass and a map.[30] The Winter War showed that the Red Army must urgently improve the appalling entry-level training of its soldiers and officers and then relentlessly refine their skills during intensive field exercises. Since actions in the mountains required more diverse skills than actions in forests, navigation was more difficult, and good marksmanship mattered more because of scarce heavy weapons and problematic ammunition delivery, soldiers of mountain divisions had more to learn during their basic training than did their counterparts fighting on the plains, which meant that their period of training had to be considerably longer than that of regular infantry.

The inadequate basic training ruined the Red Army's tactics when it attempted to act in conditions that it, inexplicably, had failed to anticipate.[31] Deep snow and swamps gravely impeded logistics, while limited visibility in dense forests complicated command and control. Senior commanders could set only general objectives and had no opportunity to maintain close control over their units, which meant that success depended on the initiative of junior officers acting within the framework of the general orders they had received, the individual training of their soldiers, and adequate communication means.

However, the Red Army had few dynamic commanders, because the witch-hunt during the Great Purge had taught officers at all levels that, in unforeseen circumstances, inaction in the absence of orders was a safer option for them personally than an unsanctioned action prompted by common sense.[32] If their inaction resulted in the rout of their formations, it was their superiors rather than these commanders who carried the responsibility for the defeat, whereas any minor mishap resulting from an unsanctioned action could end in a death sentence. As General Nikolai Voronov, one of the bluntest and most talented Soviet commanders, maintained, 'After 1937, such a situation emerged in the armed forces that an officer fears making a decision because each subordinate can question any of his actions at any moment by reporting to the party and Komsomol agencies or the Special Sections … and the officer may be immediately subject to investigation.'[33] Even Stalin admitted that he was stunned by the outcome of the bloodbath he had unleashed in the late 1930s, remarking: 'Modern warfare presumes well-trained, disciplined personnel with initiative. Our soldier lacks initiative. His personality is undeveloped. He is poorly trained.'[34] Finns fought in forests, deploying independent platoons that used the advantages of rough terrain.[35] Soviet junior officers could not meet the demands of warfare on broken terrain; unable to operate independently, Soviet platoons gathered around the battalion commander and, after hearing 'Follow me, forward!', attacked as a crowd and were mown down by Finnish machineguns.[36] Combat in the mountains required even more initiative from junior officers than did actions in forests, because mountain warfare was more complicated, which meant that the tactical training of mountain divisions and the individual training of their soldiers had to be urgently reformed.

Although the Field Manual presumed the wire and messenger system as the major means of communication, such a system was hard to maintain in a winter campaign: messengers struggled slowly across the snowfields; wires hanging on trees were frequently cut by accumulating ice or by combat; laid on the ground, they sank in the snow, and it was hard to find the damaged section. Radio was the optimal communication means in such conditions, but the Red Army could not use it effectively. Stalin found that 'there was not a single section of the front without complaints about communications. They [commanders] accept only wire communication but not radio.'[37] The absence of proper communications severely undermined combat performance.

The 8th Army lost track of its 20th Tank Brigade and 10th Tank Corps soon after these formations crossed the Finnish border without a single radio; they were found only after an intensive search along all the roads in the region of the offensive.[38] Numerous similar reports stated that radio was used 'on an exceptional basis' and that 'radio communication was poor, not so much because of malfunction of the hardware but because of the poor skills' of radio operators and 'radio fear'[39] – a general mistrust of radio stemming from inexperience and concern about the interception of radio conversations by the enemy. That is why radios 'were simply ignored or sometimes abandoned on the road'.[40] In the absence of contact with their units, divisional commanders had to visit the front trenches personally, at times leaving their headquarters totally empty,[41] which ensured chaos. Since the ground units did not use radio, they could not receive information from reconnaissance planes in a timely manner, while artillery spotters advancing with the infantry were in touch only as long as the cable allowed them: when they proceeded beyond it, messengers ran between spotters and the end of the cable,[42] which made artillery fire ineffective. In short, the campaign in Finland exposed the severe limitations of command and control in forested terrain covered by deep snow and suggested ways of alleviating this problem by encouraging the initiative of junior officers, investing in the individual training of soldiers, and developing a radio communication culture.

Mountains represented an even more challenging environment for command and control than forests. It was hard to reverse the lack of initiative and fear of responsibility displayed in the wake of the Great Purge at all levels of command, but the Red Army could have at least begun the tactical training of soldiers expected to operate in small units separated by mountainous terrain and invisible to their senior commanders, improved their marksmanship, and imposed wireless communication standards. A mountain environment reduced the usefulness of wire and messenger communications to a remote auxiliary of radio; consequently, mountain divisions needed a large number of portable radios, even of the available poor design, and, most importantly, skilled radio operators who would face many new challenges in mountains. The Winter War showed that the Soviet rechargeable batteries for portable radios had a short lifespan;[43] this meant that mountain divisions needed portable chargers, which Soviet industry did not produce.

The Red Army hoped to win the war against Finland before the heavy snowfalls began. That is why it deployed its regular divisions, which were structured and equipped for mechanised warfare in fair weather. When their Blitzkrieg failed and the snow began to accumulate, it turned out that Finns, who had few tanks, artillery tractors, or even trucks, easily outmanoeuvred the Soviets because Finnish logistics were well adapted to action on such terrain. General Voronov observed that 'the forest "belonged" to the Finns because of their good ski training'.[44] As war veterans recall, every Finnish soldier had skis, and 'literally all [Finnish] equipment was put on skis: machineguns, light artillery, and medical wagons. They were excellent skiers and ... they manoeuvred quickly.' In contrast, Soviet soldiers, 'having no skis, struggled through snow up to their waists thus offering targets to the Finns'.[45]

The Soviet mechanised divisions advanced slowly along the few available roads, without protective screens on the flanks, and stretched in endless columns separated by large gaps created by huge traffic jams.[46] The Finns moved into the gaps, surrounded the separated parts of Soviet columns, and sometimes cut entire divisions to pieces. In this way, Finnish lightly armed infantry won many engagements against immobilised Soviet armour and heavy artillery. This happened, Soviet commanders concluded, because 'the structure of our formations and their saturation with heavy equipment, especially artillery and supply trains, makes them unsuitable for actions on such a terrain; they are too heavy and often ... are confined to the roads. Soldiers ... are fearful of the forest and cannot ski. Finns spotted this weakness and profited from their advantage in manoeuvrability, and from local expertise.'[47] A paramedic serving in the 48th Rifle Division recalls that only thirty men of his regiment survived after it found itself immobilised in deep snow without the supplies that had been intercepted by Finnish skiers and, he adds, 'I fought [later] throughout the Great Patriotic War and marched from Leningrad to Königsberg but never experienced such a horror.'[48] The impotence of the Soviet divisions during the first half of the Winter War, even though they greatly outgunned and outnumbered the Finns, and the endless suffering from cold caused the breakdown of soldiers' morale: the 143rd Rifle Regiment had 105 incidents of self-inflicted wounds within one day, thus losing about 4 per cent of its total strength.[49] Colonel N. Raevskii pointed to the cause of the Finnish tactical superiority in his message to Voroshilov:

> Our troops suffer enormous casualties but score zero success because they cannot ski . . . Why can't the troops of the northern [military] districts ski if each of them was supposed to follow the instructions of PU-36 [Field Manual]? . . . Why did nobody think that skis had to be delivered here in advance and why did nobody start ski training at the beginning of the snowfalls? . . . Without doubt, we need light mobile ski units.[50]

Hoping for a Blitzkrieg, the Soviet armies left most or all of their skis in their depots when they began the offensive. As early as 2 December, the third day of the war, General Kirill Meretskov, commander of the Leningrad Military District, ordered the formation of ski units. This instruction was followed two weeks later by Voroshilov's directive stating that all formations departing for the front had to be 'fully supplied with skis'.[51] However, these orders did not specify the strength of the ski units, their structure, their missions, or even what 'fully supplied with skis' meant, because those who wrote them did not know the answers to these elementary questions, believing instead that all mobility problems would be solved as soon as skis were delivered to the front. Some divisions ordered skis for every infantryman, while others, like the 163rd Rifle Division, advancing across the most difficult terrain in central Finland along the only available dirt road, had no skis at all;[52] Finnish skiers surrounded that division and cut it to ribbons. Although the Soviet Union had more good skiers than Finland did, the Red Army ignored the skiing skills of recruits drafted into its divisions deployed in northern Russia, and when the front-line formations finally received skis, it turned out that few of their personnel could ski.[53] Furthermore, as commanders of the Leningrad Military District, which bordered Finland, admitted, 'None of us had any idea about combat training on skis.'[54] In the absence of experience, some commanders formed ski companies only from volunteers, while others raised ski brigades[55] that inevitably consisted mainly of men who were seeing skis for the first time in their lives. Some commanders used the ski units for the same missions as the Finns – reconnaissance and infiltration to the enemy's rear with subsequent surprise attacks – while others deployed them for frontal assaults on enemy fortifications that inevitably failed because attacks on such positions needed the support of heavy weapons that could not keep up with the skiers.

On 24 December, Voroshilov attempted to standardise the size of ski units by ordering the formation of eight ski companies in the

Belarusian and Kiev military districts, the latter being largely snowless. The skiers, recruited among 'excellent marksmen', were to operate in their standard uniforms; the only difference between them and regular infantry was that they were supplied with tents, one portable radio per company, a five-day tinned food ration to be carried in standard crude infantry sacks, and an enormous number of compasses – one per three soldiers – given without maps. These companies were to receive 'good skis', but Voroshilov did not explain what that meant.[56] In fact, Soviet military skis had only primitive bindings made of a single cross-strap that – unlike the Finnish bindings, which secured a reliable hold on the feet – were unsuitable for action through thick bush and deep snow. Even if the Red Army had attempted to replicate the Finnish bindings, the Soviet thin, tall boots, made of coarse leather, were uncomfortable for skiing and did not protect the feet from frostbite, unlike the Finnish low felt boots with gaiters designed especially for skiing. In Soviet style, Voroshilov allocated only five days for the organisation and training of ski companies. Although the training period of skiers was soon extended to fifteen days, complaints about the poor skill of skiers swamped the General Staff. The experiments with the structure and strength of ski units continued into February.[57] In the end, the Red Army raised a large ski force consisting of 259 ski companies of 150 men each.[58] After a costly trial-and-error process, the Red Army developed proper tactics for the ski units by replicating the Finnish tactics.[59] This force could never match its Finnish counterpart, nor did it attain anything similar to the spectacular successes of the Finns in the destruction of entire divisions, but it still made a belated contribution to the eventual Soviet victory by providing mobility to a part of the infantry outside the roads.

General Voronov pointed to the fact that 'it would be impossible to deploy a rifle division of the standard structure in all future military theatres; we need different ones with appropriate structures, personnel, and equipment' tailored to the anticipated battle environment.[60] When the regular rifle divisions encountered numerous problems in forests with deep snow, an environment in which a large part of the Red Army was deployed every year, it must have become clear that they would face much greater challenges in the mountains that remained terra incognita for regular infantry. Once the Red Army found that, in winter, every 'regiment must have a light ski battalion, and [every] battalion a ski company as a striking and highly mobile force',[61] it must have realised that mountain divisions must have such a mobile striking force in the mountains. The Winter War showed that, even if gear intended to enable these elite formations to operate on a certain type of terrain was available, only field tests would reveal the gear's possible flaws and suggest how to improve it, and that even excellent gear would be useless in the hands of untrained soldiers. The actions in Finland also proved that impromptu solutions required a long time to produce the desired effect, with many lives lost during trial-and-error experiments in combat. Obviously, the training of the personnel enlisted into mountain divisions would have taken much longer than the training of a skier.

Most conference participants maintained that 'the war against Finland provided rich experience for the development of our combat training'.[62] The lessons of that war can be compressed into one simple conclusion: an army expected to fight on a certain type of terrain must be trained for actions on that terrain and equipped accordingly. If elaborated, this conclusion means that this army must have uniforms, weapons and other gear, combat training, logistics, and a means of communication adapted to actions on this type of terrain in all seasons, and that its generals must take the local peculiarities into account during operational planning and choose the appropriate strategy and tactics. However, as Voroshilov frankly admitted, 'At first, neither I, the people's commissar for defence, nor the General Staff, nor the Headquarters of the Leningrad Military District had the faintest idea of the specifics and difficulties of such warfare ... Having insufficient knowledge about the enemy or the terrain, we believed that it was possible to deploy our heavy divisions and armour in any region of Finland.'[63] He also observed:

> The infantry, including not only those who arrived from southern regions but also those permanently deployed in the Leningrad Military District, as a rule, could not ski ... The troops were learning how to ski in combat but these efforts were ineffective, and in any case, they did not affect the outcomes. The enemy was superior in this matter and used his advantage skilfully and in full ... Uniforms, especially those worn by the infantry, were not suitable for winter conditions ... The food supply required serious reforms because standard rationing ... did not include a number of concentrated food items.[64]

Forests and climate in Finland and in northern Russia are similar; it was not the forests or the snow, and not the sparse forts of the Mannerheim Line,[65] but the absence of training for action in the forest and in winter that frustrated the Soviet Blitzkrieg. The Red Army's irrecoverable casualties during the Winter War equaled 126,875 men, five times the irrecoverable casualties sustained by the Finns.[66]

During the year and a half that passed from the conference of April 1940 to the battle of Moscow that began in December 1941, the Red Army undertook many important reforms that greatly improved its performance in winter. It changed the oil composition in the artillery recoil system, thus enabling the guns to operate at subzero temperatures; developed and produced warm, comfortable winter uniforms; started winter combat training; made an effort to refine the command-and-control system; and organised proper ski units. As a Soviet officer wrote, 'Had it not been for the herculean effort after the war against Finland, we would have been finished off' by the Germans in 1941.[67] Although the Red Army made little progress in the areas of tactical training of its officers and the individual training of its soldiers, its adaptation to winter conditions became an important factor in the first strategic Soviet victory during the battle of Moscow. However, the General Staff failed to extrapolate the lessons of the Winter War to mountain warfare.

Soviet Defenders of the Caucasus Versus German Mountain Troops

Germany had no mountain troops before World War I, but during the war the German Army organised several mountain battalions, although far fewer than Austria-Hungary, which maintained fourteen mountain brigades and nine independent mountain regiments.[68] The Museum of Military History in Vienna houses a display of alpine troop gear used in World War I. Even at that time, they had special uniforms suitable for climbing and a full mountaineering kit: sturdy spiked boots, eight-spike crampons, ropes, alpenstocks, ice axes, snowshoes, skis, and sunglasses. Germany ended World War I with two mountain brigades, which were disbanded in the wake of the Versailles Treaty but restored in 1935 and expanded into several divisions after 1937.[69]

The Wehrmacht had enough high-quality recruits to fill their ranks. Mountaineering, a popular form of leisure in the Alpine countries since the late nineteenth century, became a mass phenomenon in Germany during the interwar period after Arnold Fanck, a German film director, captured the audience of the Weimar Republic with his series of breathtaking films on adventures in the mountains. The romantic aura of these films – later coupled with *völkisch* and fascist ideologies extolling nationalism, physical perfection and strength, heroic struggle against deadly challenges, and self-sacrifice for the cause – gave an additional impetus to mountaineering in Germany. By 1928, the Austro-German Alpine Club had 160,000 members.[70] It was these men – enthusiastic climbers who were as comfortable in the high mountains as fish in water – whom the Wehrmacht enlisted, on a voluntary basis, into mountain divisions. German commanders studied the experience of mountain warfare during World War I, and, in tune with the axiom 'Any dilettantism will bring a lamentable outcome',[71] they trained the personnel of these divisions, using high-quality Austrian manuals on mountain warfare before they produced their own. The *Gebirgsjäger* engaged in thorough tactical exercises in the high Alps, thus adding military skills to their mountaineering experience. The Anschluss of Austria in 1938 brought to the Wehrmacht substantial manpower trained for mountain warfare. By the summer of 1941, Germany had seven mountain divisions – six Wehrmacht and one SS – that had accumulated a wealth of combat experience. They were cohesive formations that mostly corresponded to the ideal described by Wagner, with hardbitten experts in mountain warfare, well equipped for fighting in the mountains – indeed, as good as a mountain division could possibly be. How did the personnel of the Transcaucasian Front compare to their adversary?

The Red Army's Personnel Problems in the Caucasus

After the prestige of Soviet mountaineers hit rock bottom during the purges, the Red Army questioned their value as instructors or even potential personnel of mountain divisions. Could it follow the example of the Alpine countries in raising mountain divisions from residents of the mountain regions with the hope that they already possessed at least some skills needed for mountain warfare? Although the culture of sport mountaineering was alien to most ethnic groups

Figure 3.1 A German mountain trooper. Credit: Süddeutsche Zeitung Photo / Alamy Stock Photo

populating the Soviet high mountains, their local knowledge could be indispensable if they fought on native ground, as the Caucasus War of 1817–64 had demonstrated. Sent to fight to mountains elsewhere, they could rely on their general experience in such an environment. Were the Red Army to go along this path, it would have to reckon, in the case of the Caucasus, on the populations living on the northern and the southern slopes of the Main Caucasus Ridge, whose cultures differed, as did their attitudes towards the Soviet regime.

The relations between the Soviet authorities and the numerous small ethnic groups living in the high mountains of the North Caucasus varied, depending on the extent of their integration into the dominant Soviet culture and on the local impact of particular communist policies. In some regions, like Chechnya and Dagestan, traditional Islamic societies rejected the values promoted by the Soviet state; a small-scale armed resistance to Soviet policies had smouldered in these regions throughout the interwar period.[72] In the Karachai Autonomous Region and the

Kabardin-Balkar Autonomous Republic, tensions between the authorities and the local communities were less severe but still higher than in most of the Soviet Union.[73] The overall lack of allegiance of local ethnic groups to the Soviet state prompted the Red Army to abstain from their recruitment until September 1939, when a new law enforced conscription in the North Caucasus.[74]

In Transcaucasia, there were three major ethnic groups: Georgians, Armenians, and Azerbaijanis. They embraced Soviet culture to a far greater extent than did the peoples of the North Caucasus, and Soviet leaders trusted them. However, because few Azerbaijanis lived in the high mountains and because Armenia is located on a plateau surrounded by high but gentle hills rather than mountains, members of these ethnic groups were hardly better mountaineers than the Slavs. Only a small minority of recruits from Georgia – Svans, as well as some Georgians, Ossetians, and Abkhazians – lived in the high mountains and would have skills they could use to their advantage as soldiers of mountain divisions. Georgians were also the only ones who actively participated in sport mountaineering during the interwar period.

A Red Army policy pursuing, in the words of Ivan Tiulenev, commander of the Transcaucasian Military District, the integration of minorities 'into the common culture of our united multi-ethnic nation' prohibited placing recruits who came from the same region in the same small units.[75] This policy, whose long-term aim was to attain an ethnic 'melting pot', had negative repercussions in the short term. Soldiers from various ethnic groups found themselves mixed together without a shared language. Many soldiers could not speak Russian, the lingua franca of the Red Army: in 1939, that included 28.5 per cent, 33.8 per cent, and 50.5 per cent of the Georgian, Azerbaijani, and Armenian recruits, respectively. Many more spoke poor Russian that was often insufficient for smooth communication.[76] It was hard to establish close bonds with comrades from different ethnic groups; cultural differences inevitably provoked ethnic tensions, which undermined the cohesion within the divisions serving in the Caucasus. This had a particularly damaging impact on the tactics of mountain warfare presuming that small units had to operate on broken terrain independently but in concert.

The quality of the officer corps serving in Transcaucasia was lower than the Red Army average. As elsewhere, the Great Purge in the Caucasus led to a dramatic decline in aptitude among senior commanders, but the accusations of local nationalism – the fashionable and deadly demagogy of the 1930s – intensified terror in the Transcaucasian Military District and produced a particularly devastating impact. Since this district was located in the deep rear before the summer of 1942, the Red Army gradually transferred medium- and lower-level active-duty commanders to the front-line units, filling their vacated positions with drafted reservists. By December 1941, most officers and 90 per cent of sergeants in the divisions of the TCF were reservists. They were older than active-duty commanders of the same rank and far less skilled.[77] The desperate shortage of commanders from the ethnic groups of the Caucasus who, it was thought, would more easily establish rapport with soldiers of the same ethnic origin caused the Red Army to shorten the training of junior officers from these ethnic groups to only two months.[78] These were poor professionals. Sometimes local commanders of battalions and even regiments could not use a compass and had to be provided with guides familiar with this primitive navigation method.[79]

Slavic officers filled the vacant positions in divisions formed in the Caucasus. By November 1941, Slavs made up, on average, 30.6 per cent of the personnel of the TCF divisions,[80] but they constituted the majority of the officer corps in these formations. These commanders did not know the local customs or cultures and had to talk to their soldiers via interpreters.[81] Some Slavic commanders displayed ethnic prejudice and outright racism and used denigrating nicknames like 'black asses' when referring to Transcaucasian minorities.[82] Having failed to establish rapport with their subordinates, such officers maintained discipline by draconian and often extra-legal measures. It was far easier for the Soviet soldier to lose his life for a minor misdemeanour than it had been for his predecessor in the imperial army. In March 1942, Regimental Commissar Khromov, head of the Political Directorate of the Transcaucasian Military District, observed that 'some commanders still beat up, humiliate, and treat soldiers in a rude manner, ... engage in illegal repressions, ... [and] impose several consecutive penalties for the same misdemeanour'.[83] Numerous incidents of this type poisoned relations between Slavic officers and soldiers from the Caucasus. Such officers had no respect among their personnel, nor could they properly train them or maintain their morale.

Although political indoctrination was an important moulding tool of the Red Army, it was ineffective in the Caucasus. Indoctrination must be culture-specific to bear fruit, but Lev Mekhlis, the head of the Main Political Directorate of the Red Army until June 1942, followed the official internationalist dogma and dismissed the cultural peculiarities of Soviet ethnic groups. Uniform indoctrination tailored to the culture of Slavs, who were the large majority of the Red Army outside ethnic regions, had little impact on soldiers from other cultures.[84]

What was the combat worth of the personnel drafted into the Red Army from the Caucasus? The desertion rate of recruits from the North Caucasus was proportionally far higher than in central Russia, Ukraine, Belarus, or Central Asia.[85] In response to mass desertion, the People's Defence Commissariat prohibited the drafting of most ethnic groups from the North Caucasus in the spring and summer of 1942,[86] and it never regretted excluding the people of the North Caucasus from the draft.

In contrast, members of the ethnic groups populating Transcaucasia were conscripted on a regular basis. However, most divisions raised from these groups demonstrated low morale, lax discipline, and an absence of cohesion, all of which stemmed from three factors: the failure to train them properly, lower than average allegiance to the Soviet state, and ethnic tensions in their ranks. In March 1942, the General Staff of the Red Army believed that the Transcaucasian divisions did not 'meet all standards of modern combat'.[87] The soldiers' morale was poor even when they operated on the plains, before moving to high elevations with harsh weather conditions. The desertion rate was lower in these divisions than in those raised in the North Caucasus but higher than the Red Army average, even long before they arrived at the front, and any additional physical strain provoked mass desertion. When the 808th Rifle Regiment of the 394th Rifle Division, which later carried the brunt of the fighting in the high Caucasus, made a 65-kilometre march between 2 and 4 May 1942 – not a long distance to be covered in three days – forty-six of its men deserted, of whom twenty-five were Georgians and twenty-one Azerbaijanis.[88] While the 223rd Azerbaijani Division was making a several-day march in the deep Soviet rear in the summer of 1942, 168 men deserted with their weapons.[89]

When the Red Army transferred the twelve best Transcaucasian divisions to Crimea in early 1942, it found that 'these formations generally had a lower combat capacity and were less staunch than formations with predominantly Slavic personnel'.[90] After the drain of the best manpower to Crimea, the TCF found itself with third-rate personnel. By the time the Transcaucasian divisions entered actions in the Caucasus, more than half of their men had been drafted into the Red Army two or three months earlier.[91] Most of those were over 30 years old, and in some divisions, soldiers over 40 made up 40 per cent of their personnel.[92] These soldiers were cautious and unenthusiastic family heads with emerging health problems and without the stamina needed to carry heavy loads at high altitudes, and, like the older generation elsewhere in the USSR but especially in the Caucasus, they were more sceptical of the values promoted by the Soviet state and identified with their region of origin rather than the Soviet Union. All these factors lowered the morale of the TCF divisions below the Red Army average. Both Soviet and German sources assess the combat capacity of the Transcaucasian divisions as poor. The Red Army had to use these divisions primarily in the second echelon or in defence at minor parts of the front, but some could not perform even these missions. A battalion commander of the 89th Armenian Division assessed only 1 per cent of his soldiers as loyalists,[93] and Khalil Nadorshin, the head of the Political Sector of the TCF, reported that when this division experienced its first small clash with Germans 'many soldiers fled the battlefield and over 400 men defected to the enemy'.[94] Germans assessed the Transcaucasian divisions as 'quite unsteady' and 'having low combat capacity in comparison with Russian' units and noted that 'the residents of the Caucasus used every opportunity to defect. Russians were often sent into [Transcaucasian] units to prevent their disintegration.'[95]

Most top officers of the TCF – including its commander, Ivan Tiulenev – repeatedly declared their preference for Slavic recruits, thus dismissing the members of the ethnic groups from the Caucasus as poor warriors.[96] That is why more Ukrainians (10.3 per cent) than Azerbaijanis (8.9 per cent) found themselves in the units raised in Transcaucasia between September and December 1942; the percentage of Georgians and Armenians was only slightly higher: 13.1 per cent and 13.8 per cent, respectively.[97] General Ivan Maslennikov, the commander of the Northern Army Group of the TCF and a stern critic of the recruits from the Caucasus, observed that, among them, 'injuries of the left hand constitute up to 60 per cent of [overall] wounds',[98] implying that these injuries were self-inflicted, and a doctor at the field hospital in the 351st Rifle Division, which served in the North Caucasus, confirmed this allegation.[99] Such opinion was widespread, not only among Soviet senior commanders but also among rank-and-file soldiers; it is open to debate whether this opinion was based on fact or on ethnic prejudice. B. Tartakovskii, who fought in the 7th Guards Rifle Brigade, recorded his impressions about Azerbaijani reinforcements:

> Soldiers perceived them not just as poor warriors but also as individuals who used every opportunity to shirk, even temporarily, from the painful duties of a front-line infantryman. I watched occasionally how a group of five or six absolutely healthy soldiers accompanied a wounded countryman, even one lightly wounded, to the dressing station or even to a field hospital, howling loudly as do women at village funerals. Such shows irritated [other] soldiers who were freezing and soaking wet in their trenches, constantly at risk of being killed by a mine fragment or a bullet ... I have never heard similar stories about Kazakhs or Tatars.[100]

In short, the personnel of the TCF experienced many grave problems, such as the low quality of the officer corps, poor military training and discipline, lack of cohesion, and low morale.

Soviet 'Mountain' Divisions on the Eve of the Battle

How did the Soviet 'mountain' divisions look against the ideal outlined by Wagner? Germans viewed the mountain divisions as a relatively small but elite force trained especially for mountain warfare. The Red Army took the opposite approach. In the late 1930s, it expanded its armed forces to the utmost and focused on providing the new divisions with modern weapons and political indoctrination rather than combat training. This approach, common for all Soviet arms, had grave repercussions for 'mountain' divisions, especially in the late 1930s, when the Red Army assumed that future wars would be fought only in enemy territory. This dogma, reflected in the Red Army's Field Regulations of 1939, implicitly questioned the entire notion of mountain divisions because it implied that the Red Army would most likely fight in Eastern and Central Europe, in which the Carpathians – relatively low, mostly gently sloped, and fairly populated mountains – would be the worst-case mountain scenario. Soviet climbers repeatedly offered the Red Army Sport Inspectorate their expertise as instructors for training 'mountain' divisions, but the inspectorate's bureaucrats dismissed them with contempt, saying, 'We won't fight on Elbrus!',[101] a phrase these climbers bitterly recalled when they were indeed fighting on Elbrus several years later. Nobody dared to question the 'fight only on enemy territory' dogma after the Great Purge, when any doubts about official postulates were interpreted as political dissent or defeatism. Since the Red Army General Staff was uncertain whether it needed divisions specialising in mountain warfare and did not hear counter-arguments after the purge, it trained 'mountain' divisions as regular infantry. With numbers as its major criterion of strength, the Red Army raised nineteen 'mountain' divisions by 1941, three times as many as Germany.[102]

By the beginning of World War II, the Transcaucasian Military District had seven 'mountain' divisions – more than enough to protect the high Caucasus.[103] In January 1938, the top officers of the Transcaucasian Military District had a lengthy conference, during which the commanders of all 'mountain' divisions listed numerous flaws in the combat training of their formations, but no one said a word about their training for mountain warfare.[104] The Headquarters of the Transcaucasian Military District ordered its officers to pass a test on the *Manual on Mountain Warfare* of 1936 but, since the draft was classified, they could not remove it from its secured premises for field practice under threat of court martial.[105] In the 77th 'Mountain' Division, a quarter of the officers failed the test.[106] In October 1939, the commanders of 'mountain' divisions of the Transcaucasian Military District had another conference. They referred to 'the ingenious directive of Comrade Stalin, "Always be ready so that no accident and no tricks of our external enemies can catch us off-guard"',[107] and assured him in their report that they had 'made considerable progress in all aspects of combat and political training' and were 'ready to accomplish any mission assigned by the party and the government regardless of its difficulty'. However, they devoted only a few lines of the 280-page report to training for mountain warfare. Commanders of the 20th and 76th 'Mountain' Divisions wrote not a word on this type of training,[108] most likely because they did not conduct it; the training of the 9th 'Mountain' Division was confined to a single shooting exercise in the foothills;[109] the 63rd 'Mountain' Division had several shooting exercises, admitting that this was insufficient and that its officers had not yet studied the *Manual on Mountain Warfare*;[110] and the 47th and 77th 'Mountain' Divisions were the only ones that went through tactical exercises, albeit only a single round with a force of several companies that attacked and defended low hills around Kirovabad.[111] The brief conclusions of the divisions' reports stated that 'some commanders still do not know well the peculiarities of action in the mountains', that the units of 'mountain' divisions were 'poorly trained to act independently in mountain terrain', and that their rear services fell into disarray during short marches in low hills.[112] These reports implied that the training for mountain warfare was inadequate, but no senior officer expressed concern about it.

Although the draft manuals and Klement'ev emphasised that initiative at all levels of command and actions carried out by small units were basic tenets of mountain warfare, which was also implied by the experience of the Winter War, few Soviet officers could overcome the profound impact of the Great Purge on their mentality. A wave of arbitrary executions in the wake of orders No. 270 of 16 August 1941 and No. 227 of 28 July 1942 increased their fear of responsibility, and the 'mountain' divisions were no exception. These were inflexible formations unable to operate in small units, anything but a professional force. There is no evidence that any officer of the TCF examined the detailed studies of earlier campaigns in the mountains that had been conducted by the imperial General Staff. Those hundreds of officers who had engaged in mountaineering during the interwar period viewed it mostly as sport rather than applied exercise; most of them belonged to regular infantry rather than mountain units.[113] The manuals' assertions remained mostly untested declarations.

The lax attitude towards training for mountain warfare continued after the beginning of World War II. During the first six months of 1941, the Headquarters of the 63rd 'Mountain' Division failed to issue a single order related to training for mountain warfare, and this was typical of the 'mountain' divisions in the Transcaucasian Military District.[114] With the state in tight control of alpine camps during the interwar period, it was easy to register thousands of young men who passed through them as potential recruits or as instructors for 'mountain' divisions, yet, as Andrei Grechko, the commander of the 47th Army, which later fought in the North Caucasus, admitted, 'conscription offices did not register climbers for military service. That is why it was only by chance that a handful of them were drafted into mountain units at that time.'[115] With the beginning of mobilisation into the Red Army after the German attack in June 1941, the vast majority of climbers found themselves conscripted into all sorts of units that operated on the plains. Evgenii Abalakov, the most famous Soviet mountaineer, fought in the fields around Moscow in 1941; he was recalled and sent to the Caucasus only in December 1942, after the end of the battle at the MCR.[116] Leonid Gutman, the leader of the first team to have reached the summit of Pobeda, drove a tank near Leningrad. Brigade Commander Klement'ev, the pioneer of Soviet military mountaineering, spent all of World War II on the plains. And Valentina Cheredova, arguably the best female Soviet climber, who had led several successful expeditions to various peaks and was a professional who had been employed as deputy director of several alpine camps, worked as a turner at an ammunition factory.[117]

By the time the Soviet Union entered World War II, the Soviet 'mountain' divisions continued to be formations raised from recruits of average physical standards who had poor basic military training. These divisions differed from regular rifle divisions only in their structure, the types of their artillery, and the higher ratio of pack horses versus motor transport. The General Staff ignored all of Klement'ev's recommendations on special uniforms for mountain troops, except for replacing the forage cap with a brimmed hat. Soldiers wore standard infantry uniforms: long, heavy coats in which climbing was close to impossible and high boots of thin leather with flat soles that did not provide traction on slippery slopes. They quickly wore down in rocky terrain. When the 808th Rifle Regiment assigned to defend the high Caucasus made a 155-kilometre march, well over 500 soldiers, or one-sixth of its personnel, lost their boots.[118] Soldiers had no wool socks; instead, they wore cotton foot wraps that did not protect their feet from the cold and that ensured blisters during long marches.

Although the Red Army raised proper ski units after the Winter War, these units could act only on the plains because they still did not have the equipment or the skills to operate in the mountains. In 1932, OPTE had published manuals on the production of self-made modern ski bindings that replicated the designs of the Western Kandahar bindings with a string across the heel that secured a reliable hold but released the foot in case of a fall.[119] Soviet sport tourists wandering across snowy mountains used such skis. The Soviet industry had been testing these bindings for three years and began producing touring skis with steel edges and equipped with Kandahar bindings in 1940 but in meagre quantities, and few of them reached the Red Army.[120] Ivan Cherepov,

Master of Sport in mountaineering, published a good textbook on mountain skiing in 1940, and the military press promptly reprinted it as a soldiers' manual in January 1941, twenty-two months before skis could be used for combat missions in the high Caucasus.[121] The textbook explained ski techniques on various landscapes and various types of snow, ski waxing and repair, and the organisation of winter camps. However, no ski lifts existed in the Soviet Union, and mountain skiing was still perceived as exotic entertainment; it was not practised in the Red Army. Most skis in the TCF had only primitive strap bindings unusable in the mountains, and few soldiers could ski in the mountains. 'Mountain' divisions had no snowshoes, which were needed for action in thick woods.[122]

These units did have some low-quality climbing gear, but they stored it in the remotest corners of their depots as the least necessary equipment; nobody saw any item of this gear and nobody knew how to use it. The 'mountain' troops had the same old, poorly designed pack boxes that injured horses; standard heavy, long stretchers; standard low-calorie food rations; standard large tents impossible to carry in a backpack or to pitch on small flat spaces in the mountains; standard small sacks with narrow shoulder straps that did not allow soldiers to carry heavy loads; standard field kitchens that did not fit the narrow trails; and blankets instead of sleeping bags.[123] They had no portable stoves or special logistical gear, like winches and cables for cable cars. Their medical service was not adapted to mountain conditions. The Soviet radio industry produced a small number of portable radios, but no one had tested them in the mountains and 'mountain' divisions did not receive them, nor did they receive extra stationary radios, which remained bulky, with horses barely able to carry them. The Red Army still had no portable battery chargers, and the absence of this simple device in the high mountains threatened the overall command-and-control system.

In early 1941, after observing the actions in Europe, Colonel Kechiev once again attempted to press forward conclusions obvious to Red Army officers familiar with the mountains but not to its top commanders:

> Mountain warfare presumes that the personnel have special skills, are accustomed to life in the mountains, and can climb rocks and glaciers. A mountain trooper must be an excellent

> marksman because he often has only the ammunition that he carries ... Special mountain units are raised for bold actions, with orders to cross terrain deemed impassable and then launch a surprise attack on the enemy flank or rear ... It is not enough to have numerical superiority over the enemy, but it is necessary to have special mountain units raised from hand-picked climbers and skiers.[124]

Mountain troops, argued Kechiev, 'should easily navigate in the terrain, be able to spend the night on rocks and snow under severe weather conditions, preserve themselves from frostbite, and transport ammunition, machineguns, cannon, and wounded soldiers'.[125] The German mountain troops corresponded to this ideal, whereas the 'mountain' divisions of the Transcaucasian Military District had nothing in common with it.

Although the Transcaucasian Military District had six 'mountain' divisions and one 'mountain-cavalry' division when the Soviet Union entered World War II, it had lost most of them by the time the Germans approached the Caucasus. Two of these divisions, the 63rd and 77th, took part in the amphibious operation in Crimea between December 1941 and May 1942,[126] which would have been a reasonable employment of such units had they reached the mountains. As it happened, however, the Germans pinned down the Soviet offensive on the plains and destroyed most of the Soviet units that participated in it, including these divisions. With the increasing shortage of manpower, caused by the catastrophic defeats suffered by the Red Army in 1941 and the spring of 1942, its General Staff transferred two other 'mountain' divisions and the 'mountain-cavalry' division of the TCF to armies that fought on the plains.[127] In the end, the TCF retained only two 'mountain' formations in the Western Caucasus: the 9th and the 20th Divisions. Although 30 to 40 per cent of the personnel in these divisions had been drafted from residents of the Caucasus,[128] their mountaineering skill was as poor as that of their comrades of Slavic origin conscripted from the plains; in fact, the latter were probably more effective soldiers. The 9th 'Mountain' Division had only one officer who had participated in several climbing expeditions and three soldiers who had spent one stint in alpine camps; the rest had no knowledge of mountaineering.[129] Not a single soldier of this division could ski in the mountains, and few had ever engaged in cross-country skiing.[130] The 20th 'Mountain' Division had a similar lack of experience.

The TCF made a feeble attempt to train these two divisions for mountain warfare between November 1941 and May 1942: this was the mission of a single climbing instructor sent to the 9th 'Mountain' Division and four instructors sent to the 20th – a far cry from the demands of the German manual, which presumed one instructor per five trainees, or from the practice of the Soviet alpine camps, which offered one instructor per maximum of ten climbers.[131] The number of instructors given to Soviet 'mountain' divisions was sufficient only to give a crash course in the basics of mountaineering and skiing to selected officers. The course lasted several days; the trainees – three officers from each company – had then to pass on their meagre knowledge and experience to other officers and soldiers.[132] However, nobody taught the officers mountain warfare, about which these five instructors, recent draftees into the Red Army, had no knowledge.[133] The only combat-like training they undertook consisted of several shooting exercises, during which the officers were shocked to find out that they could not hit targets while shooting at high angles, and they had no manuals explaining what corrections to make.[134] Since the Headquarters of the TCF showed no interest in producing such tables, the instructor of the 9th 'Mountain' Division and his trainees developed correction tables as best they could, but the quartermasters of the TCF refused to allocate ammunition for shooting exercises using these tables, except for snipers. There are no reports that the other division had correction tables. The officers who took the mountaineering course trained without climbing gear because the quartermasters did not release it from the TCF supply depots. The 9th 'Mountain' Division received some climbing gear only after its officers had finished their training. The quartermasters refused to provide the small funds necessary to organise broader training courses,[135] and the low prestige of the formerly civilian instructors in the armed forces did not allow them to raise this matter at higher levels.

In May and June 1942, the 46th Army of the TCF, which was responsible for the defence of the MCR, ordered its 'mountain' divisions to select twelve to fifteen officers per regiment and send them to a mountaineering course given by a maximum of four instructors per division. Officers of the 9th and 20th Divisions received seventy and forty hours, respectively, of intensive climbing training.[136] Reports about this event present it as exceptional in scale and thoroughness, which shows that the earlier mountaineering exercises in November 1941 had been cursory and basic. However, officers of only some regiments participated in the training. The training took place in the foothills near Tuapse, far away from the high mountains. Nobody ever checked whether the trainees shared their knowledge with their soldiers; it is safe to assume that, given the sceptical attitude of senior commanders and the fact that most of the trainees were novices in mountaineering, they either neglected to train their soldiers or could not do it properly. The senior commanders did not understand the value of mountaineering training and did not use the few highly skilled climbers sent to 'mountain' divisions as instructors; rather, they charged them predominantly with the routine duties of regular junior infantry officers.[137]

In early June of 1942, two months before the beginning of the battle of the Caucasus, Captain O. Logofet, inspector of mountain training with the Main Directorate of the Red Army Reserves, visited the 9th and 20th 'Mountain' Divisions in order to determine whether they could operate in the high mountains. He reported that only the submachine-gunner company, two rifle companies, and the scouts and snipers of the 9th 'Mountain' Division were up to the task; all other soldiers had no knowledge of mountain warfare. The 20th 'Mountain' Division was even less skilled: four companies and scouts had 'satisfactory' training in mountain warfare – the Russian connotations of this assessment imply that they were barely fit for the job – while the rest were absolutely untrained.[138] Those units that had climbing gear could not use it. Logofet raided the supply depots of the 46th Army and was astonished when he found 15,000 metres of 'extremely scarce rope' and 40,000 'extremely useful tricouni' – spikes for mountain boots sufficient to equip 1,000 pairs of boots.[139] However, these treasures remained at the supply depots throughout most of the battle of the Caucasus. As Major Saltykov wrote *post factum*, several alpine camps, fully supplied with climbing gear, had operated in the Baksan valley before the war, and 'there were mountaineering instructors in the camps who could have given precise information about all the camps and the reserves [of food and climbing gear] and a comprehensive assessment of every pass, trail, valley, and route. Nothing of this was used.'[140]

Logofet emphasised that 'persistent training in the high mountains can greatly enhance the combat worth of these formations as mountain divisions'.[141] His call fell on deaf ears. No further mountaineering training took place in 'mountain' or any other divisions of the TCF before they went into battle. On 2 and 22 July 1942, the Headquarters of the 46th Army outlined a number of flaws in the combat training of its divisions, including 'mountain' units, that were to defend the MCR and issued a series of orders aimed to eliminate them, but they did not discuss training for mountain warfare.[142] O. Opryshko, a Soviet scholar, advanced this misleading claim: 'When war came to the Caucasus, it left no time for mountain warfare training.'[143] The 'mountain' and the other TCF divisions had stayed in the deep rear for one year after the beginning of the war and had ample time to train their personnel properly, yet they wasted this opportunity, mainly because of the ignorance, laziness, and narrow-mindedness of senior and medium-ranking commanders of the TCF.

In short, the ability of Soviet 'mountain' divisions to operate in the mountains hardly differed from that of regular rifle divisions. In the end, only one full-strength 'mountain' division, the 20th, took part in the battle at the MCR. The better-trained 9th 'Mountain' Division detached only one regiment for the battle, while the rest of it spent 1942 idling at the border with Turkey. For the defence of the MCR, the 46th Army fielded the 3rd Rifle Corps, which had – in addition to the 20th 'Mountain' Division – the 394th Rifle Division, with a large proportion of Georgians among its personnel, and the 63rd Cavalry Division raised in Tajikistan; the 155th Rifle Brigade stayed in reserve. None of these formations had any knowledge of mountain warfare.[144] For unknown reasons, the 3rd Rifle Corps assigned regular infantry and cavalry divisions to defend the highest passes of the MCR, some of which were over 3,000 metres, but deployed the 20th 'Mountain' Division in much lower terrain: two of its regiments were stationed in low hills, one near the port of Tuapse and one to the north of Sochi, a resort on the shore of the Black Sea; a third occupied Belorechenskii pass (1,782 m), and a fourth, the Pseashkha (2,014 m) and Aishkha passes (2,401 m).[145] By the summer of 1942, the Soviet armies operating in the North Caucasus had accumulated combat experience in tough battles against the Germans. In contrast, none of the divisions of the TCF that were assigned to defend the MCR had ever been in battle, and their personnel had received only cursory infantry training.[146]

These were third-rate formations that could not have matched the elite German mountain troops even if they had fought on the plains. When the 808th Rifle Regiment of the 394th Rifle Division conducted marksmanship exercises on a shooting range located on the plains in March 1942, 42 per cent of the soldiers of its first battalion failed the test; 27 per cent of the personnel in the 810th Regiment failed, as did

74 per cent of the machine-gunners.[147] Obviously, in the mountains, with the deceptive distances and with targets located at high angles, their results would have been much worse. As Aleksandr Khadeev, then commander of the 46th Army, stated, 'Poor [marksmanship] training of the personnel is due to the fact that many officers themselves cannot shoot and do not know their weapons.'[148]

Conclusion

During the Winter War, the Red Army paid a heavy toll for the lessons it had failed to learn during the interwar period and needed to learn in combat. It happened largely because the Red Army's general combat training was insufficient and because it found itself in an unfamiliar combat environment for which it had never trained but attempted to operate as it would on an ideal terrain in summer. General Voronov prophetically extended the lessons of the Winter War to another terrain on which the Red Army was unprepared to fight: 'Mountain regions are all around us but we do not study them and we are untrained to fight in the mountains. If we are now whining about the forests – after discovering forests in Finland – in the next war, we will be whining when we discover the mountains ... We must, without fail, take this aspect into account in our training procedures.'[149] Mountains were far less familiar to the Red Army than the forests and marshes covering a large part of its anticipated operational theatre, which implied that it had to urgently reform its approach to the training and equipment of 'mountain' divisions in the spirit of the reforms undertaken after the Winter War. The twenty-eight months that passed between the conference of April 1940 and the battle of the Caucasus that began in August 1942 were sufficient to extrapolate the experience of the Winter War to mountain warfare. The Red Army failed to do so.

Its preparations for war in the mountains were undermined by tendencies that emerged immediately after the Bolshevik Revolution and that received an enormous boost during the Stalinist transformation of the Soviet state in the 1930s: ideological dogma dictating strategy, the pursuit of uniformity over diversity and quantity over quality, and the reliance on improvisation instead of professionalism. All of these tendencies fed a growing uncertainty about the usefulness of special forces, including mountain formations, in the Red Army General Staff. Once the witch-hunt during the Great Purge had destroyed the prestige of Soviet mountaineering, numerous Soviet mountain climbers found themselves fighting on the plains. The native populations of the Caucasus were a poor substitute for trained climbers: not only was their allegiance to the authorities uncertain, but those of them who knew the mountains best – the people of the North Caucasus – were the least loyal citizens.

The Red Army entered World War II with no articulated concept of special forces trained for particular missions and no plans to organise them. Rather, its General Staff assumed that the outdoor skills acquired through sport tourism would help regular infantry to perform missions that in other armies were assigned to special forces. Soviet generals completely ignored the extensive knowledge of mountain warfare accumulated by their imperial predecessors; conscripted into 'mountain' divisions those who had never been in the mountains before while drafting experienced mountaineers into various arms where their expertise was irrelevant; failed to train their 'mountain' divisions for mountain warfare and squandered most of them on the plains; and entrusted the defence of the high Caucasus to a division baselessly called 'mountain', several regular infantry formations and a cavalry division, even though cavalry was useless in the high mountains, as earlier experience had unambiguously suggested. Although some small units of 'mountain' divisions had acquired basic mountaineering training, none was trained for mountain warfare. Only a dozen experienced climbers found themselves among the defenders of the MCR. The elite German mountain troops faced elderly, unenthusiastic recruits who had been drafted into the Red Army only two or three months before and were poor marksmen unable to move across rugged terrain. Many of these recruits, drafted from the local ethnic groups, were indifferent to political indoctrination incompatible with their culture and unable to understand their comrades or the commands of their substandard officers, who often despised their men and humiliated them. They were equipped with standard uniforms, field artillery and other hardware unsuitable for action in the mountains, and poor-quality climbing gear kept in depots far away from the front.

4 CONTEST OF FOLLIES: PLAN EDELWEISS AND THE GERMAN OFFENSIVE ACROSS THE HIGH CAUCASUS

It isn't anything bigger than Grunewald![1]
Adolf Hitler about the Caucasus

Operational Plans on the Eve of the Battle

The German strategic offensive towards the Caucasus began with a directive called 'Continuation of Operation "Braunschweig"'.[2] Issued by Hitler on 23 July 1942, this directive presumed an advance towards Transcaucasia by Army Group A and towards Stalingrad by Army Group B. The first offensive received the code name Edelweiss but the Germans rarely used this name. The High Command of the German Army (Oberkommando des Heeres, OKH) also planned a secondary attack within the framework of this operation: it ordered the 49th Mountain Corps to cross the MCR and to reach the Black Sea, thus severing the communications of the Soviet 18th Army, which defended the coast from the offensive of the German 17th Army. The 49th Mountain Corps, commanded by Rudolf Konrad, consisted of the 1st and 4th two-regiment Mountain Divisions,[3] nicknamed Edelweiss and Gentian after their insignias. Generals Hubert Lanz and Karl Eglseer commanded the 1st and 4th Mountain Divisions, respectively. The TCF had had ample opportunity to prepare for the defence of the Caucasus while stationed in the deep Soviet rear during the nine months between the arrival of the Germans in Rostov, the gateway to the Caucasus, in November 1941 and their approach towards the MCR in August 1942. However, the Soviet commanders had squandered this opportunity, and they paid a heavy price for this failure with the blood of their soldiers.

The attack across the Caucasus was quite an ambitious enterprise but the OKH focused mainly on the offensive towards Baku via the steppes of the Northern Caucasus rather than on the thrust across the MCR. On 12 August, three weeks after the OKH had issued the 'Continuation of Operation "Braunschweig"' directive, it ordered the 49th Mountain Corps to advance across the Caucasus towards Sukhumi, the capital of Abkhazia.[4] German generals had meagre knowledge of the prospective operational region and attempted to expand their information in the spirit of the German manual on mountain warfare, which suggested perusing tourist guidebooks in the absence of other data.[5] In July 1942, Eglseer sent Captain Max Gämmerler to the Alpine Society in Munich for two weeks to leaf through its guidebooks. This was the main source of intelligence for Germans on the conditions at the MCR; additional sketchy information was provided by several German and Austrian mountaineers who had visited the Caucasus during the interwar period. Gämmerler acquired a map with a scale of 1:200,000, too small for action in the mountains.[6] The offensive across the MCR was thus a hasty improvisation unsupported by staff work.

The best way across the Western Caucasus was via the Sukhumi Military Road, which passed from the Teberda valley at the northern foothills through the Klukhor pass to the Kodori valley, leading to the Black Sea coast (Map 4.1).

The Tyrolean booklet on the Caucasus that served as the Germans' main reference material provided contradictory information. According to that source, the Sukhumi Military Road turned into a cart trail when it entered the mountains near the Teberda resort and then, on the approach to the pass, into 'a 13-kilometer-long mule track', but the booklet also stated that 'a road through the pass began construction [*sic*] in 1936 and has since been completed'.[7] The OKH preferred to believe the latter statement. The Headquarters of the 49th Mountain Corps emphasised that the attack along the Sukhumi Military Road was the focus of the offensive because it provided the best opportunity to supply the advancing units.[8] However, since the Germans had no information on the strength of the Soviet defences at Klukhor, the two

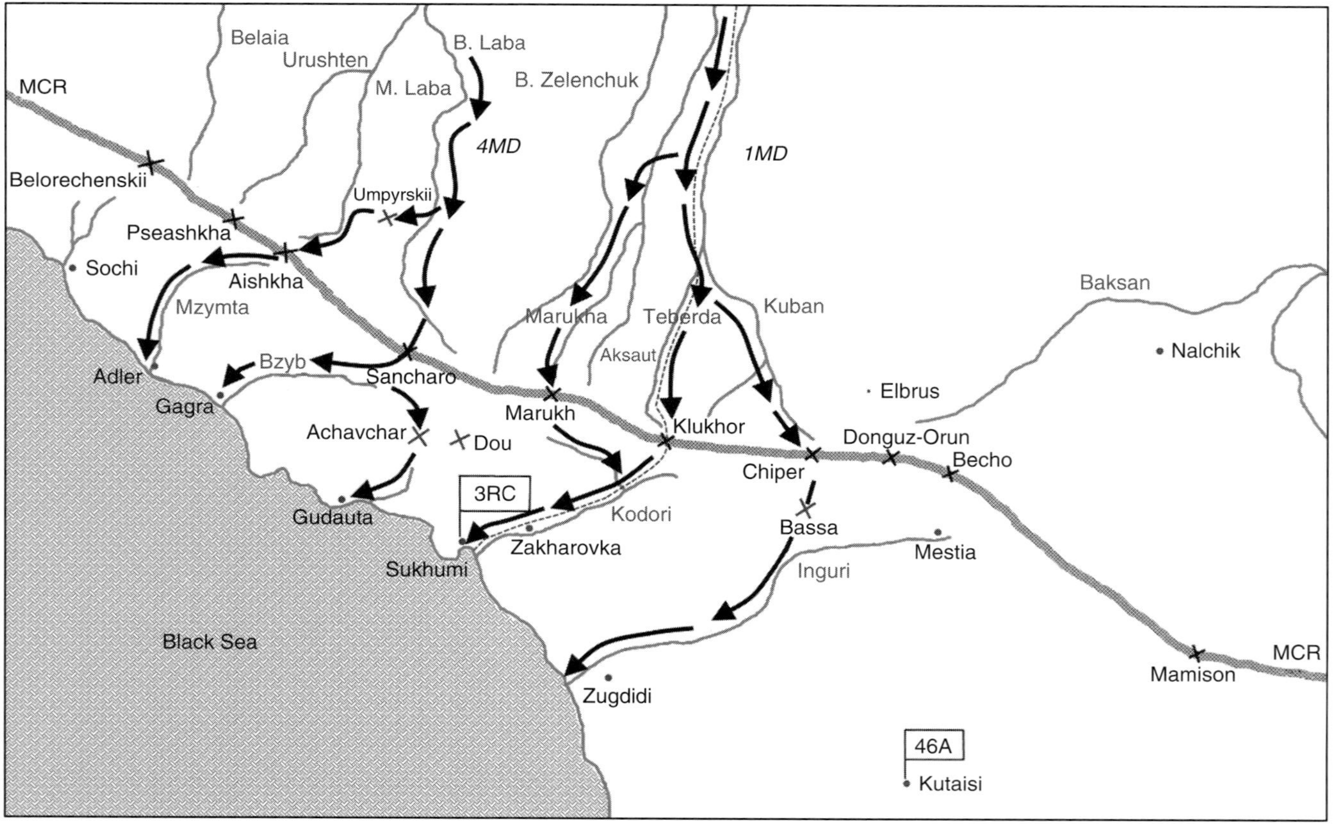

Map 4.1 Possible directions of attack across the Main Caucasus Ridge

Table 4.1 Possible routes across the Main Caucasus Ridge

Valleys in the North Caucasus from East to West	Passes	Valleys in Transcaucasia	Coastal Destination
Kuban	Elbrus group: Khotiu-Tau (3,550 m) Chiper-Azau (3,264 m) Chiper (3,285 m)[a]	Inguri	Zugdidi
Teberda	Klukhor group: Klukhor (2,781 m) Nakhar (2,885 m) Ptysh (2,995 m)[b]	Kodori	Sukhumi
Marukha	Marukh (2,748 m)	Kodori	Sukhumi
Bolshaia Laba	Sancharo group: Sancharo (2,589 m) Tsegerker (2,265 m) Allashtrakhu (2,723 m) Adzapsh (2,492 m) Chmakhara (2,486 m)	Bzyb	Gagra or Gudauta
Malaia Laba or Urushten	Aishkha (2,401 m) or Pseashkha (2,014 m)	Mzymta	Adler

[a] Soviet officers called it Chviberi pass at that time.
[b] Soviet officers called it Dombai-Ulgen pass at that time.

mountain divisions had to split their forces and advance south along several parallel valleys simultaneously to find a weak spot in the Soviet front and cross the MCR wherever possible, descending into the valleys leading towards the coast. The 49th Mountain Corps could proceed from the North Caucasus to Transcaucasia or the Black Sea coast through any one of five groups of passes as shown in Table 4.1.

In fact, although the Sukhumi Military Road was the easiest way across the MCR to the Black Sea, only the first part deserved to be called a road – the portion that led to Teberda village at the northern foothills of the Caucasus, 40 kilometres away from the Klukhor pass – after which it turned into a broad trail that crossed the pass and then led to Azhara village, 30 kilometres beyond the pass down the southern slopes of the Caucasus. From this village, a narrow cart road proceeded for 50 kilometres to Zakharovka village, 35 kilometres away from Sukhumi, where it finally turned again into a gravel road.[9] Thus, most of the distance from Teberda to the Black Sea, more than 150 kilometres, had to be covered on foot. If the Soviet defences at Klukhor were impregnable, it would be, perhaps, possible to bypass them via Marukh pass to the west of Klukhor.

The second-best route across the Western Caucasus to the Black Sea lay through the Sancharo group of passes. These passes, as well as Pseashkha and Aishkha, were located closer to the Black Sea coast and the front line than Klukhor, but it would be harder to maintain supply lines across these passes because of the long approaches via foot trails on the northern slopes of the Caucasus.

One more trail to the coast led from the Kuban valley across Chiper or Khotiu-Tau and Chiper-Azau and then over the Bassa pass into Inguri valley and along a gravel road to the town of Zugdidi near the coast, but these passes were much higher than Klukhor or Sancharo, and Zugdidi was too far away from the front line; it would be hard to sustain the 49th Mountain Corps in this remote region.

Finally, the Germans considered two other options that were beyond the operational region of the 49th Mountain Corps. At its extreme eastern flank, a gravel road from Nalchik, the capital of the Kabardin-Balkar Autonomous Republic in the Northern Caucasus, followed the Baksan valley, turning into a trail after the town of Tyrnyauz. The trail proceeded for about 100 kilometres, crossing either the Donguz-Orun (3,203 m) or the Becho (3,375 m) pass into the valley of Inguri. Although the trails across Donguz-Orun and Becho were easily passable, they were longer and of lower quality than the Sukhumi Military Road; the passes were also considerably higher than Klukhor. At the extreme western flank of the corps, a trail went from the Belaia valley in the North Caucasus via the Belorechenskii pass (1,782 m) to the Shakhe valley in Transcaucasia and then to Sochi. However, it would be impossible to surprise the enemy along this route because the 18th Army had already assembled sufficient forces in this region to terminate any German offensive.

The high mountains of the Caucasus promised severe logistical problems, which must have been clear even with the meagre information that the OKH possessed, yet the German generals ignored the potential difficulties and also the warning of Clausewitz, their military arts guru: 'Quite apart from forts that block the passes ... poor mountain roads in bad weather can be enough to drive an army to despair. More than once they have forced an army to retreat, having first utterly worn it out.'[10] As often happened to German generals during both world wars, they launched the strike across the MCR without calculating its logistical viability. When Franz Halder, chief of the OKH General Staff, expressed vague concerns, Hitler assured him and other generals that the Mountain Corps would quickly reach its objective.[11] The OKH thus put all its hopes into the element of surprise and the swift progress of the Mountain Corps to the seashore with minimal supplies; after it reached the coast, it would be supplied via the Black Sea.[12] No OKH general thought about how to maintain supply lines across the Black Sea, given the decisive superiority of the Soviet Black Sea Fleet over the minuscule Axis naval forces, whose largest ships were four Romanian destroyers,[13] nor did any senior officer ever give serious thought to how the Mountain Corps would be supplied if Soviet resistance on the way to the Black Sea delayed its advance.

There was a strong probability that the Germans would meet such resistance. Although German mountain troops were far superior to their Soviet opponents in man-for-man terms, the OKH allocated only two understaffed divisions for the offensive across the Caucasus: the 1st Mountain Division had detached one of its six battalions to the 1st Panzer Army, which was attempting to break to Ordzhonikidze,[14] and the 4th Mountain Division had been weakened by the loss of 1,600 men in earlier battles.[15] By the time these divisions were approaching the region in August 1942, the Soviet 46th Army, responsible for the defence of the Western Caucasus, had one rifle, two 'mountain', and one cavalry divisions; a rifle brigade and a frontier guard naval brigade; several cadet schools in Tbilisi, Gagra, and Sukhumi; three artillery regiments; and one trench-mortar battalion.[16] Two more rifle divisions joined the 46th Army later, after crossing the MCR from the Northern Caucasus while escaping the advancing Germans.[17] The TCF had a reserve of five rifle brigades, a tank brigade, an artillery brigade, and several artillery regiments, and it could reckon on twenty NKVD regiments, deployed in Transcaucasia.[18] Most reserve units were deployed away from the Western Caucasus but could be transferred to the MCR if necessary. Finally, the TCF included the entire 45th Army, which was guarding the border with Turkey and Iran, as a last reserve. Even the front-line force of the 46th Army, without counting the reserves, grossly outnumbered the two German mountain divisions.

The German Air Force could not assist the Mountain Corps across the Caucasus for two reasons: first, it was already overstretched in the vast operational region of Army Group A, which forced it to focus on major offensives on the steppes of the North Caucasus and along the Black Sea coast and, second, the Germans did not know whether landing strips existed in proximity to the MCR at its southern slopes, whereas unstable weather, frequent clouds in the high mountains, and powerful vertical air flows made air support of the offensive across the MCR almost impossible.[19] In contrast, the TCF had 409 combat aircraft at the beginning of the battle of the Caucasus, and 3 reserve regiments were also deployed in Transcaucasia; they had among them 125 fighter, 107 bomber, and 568 trainer aircraft, the last of which could be used for reconnaissance and supply missions.[20] In addition, the Black Sea Naval Air Force could support the TCF if necessary. The Red Air Force could operate over the southern slopes of the Caucasus from airstrips located close to the mountains. The Soviet defenders enjoyed a clear logistical advantage over the German attackers: the civilian administration of Georgia could provide far greater assistance to the 46th Army than the haphazardly organised German rear could give to the Mountain Corps. Given such a large numerical superiority of the Soviets on land and their decisive superiority in the air, the enormous problems of supplying the mountain divisions across the Caucasus, and the absence of intelligence information about the operational theatre or even proper maps, the Mountain Corps could succeed only if the Soviet defenders fled. The German plan had no provisions in case the defenders held their ground. The plan was thus a wild gamble with heavy odds against its success.

Order Writing as an Epistolary Genre

The Red Army General Staff planned to counter the German offensive across the MCR with a passive defence at its passes – a strategy against which Suvorov, Clausewitz, and even several Soviet senior officers had strongly argued. Keeping in mind the host of military and social problems in the Caucasus, the TCF began planning this defence long before the 'Continuation of Operation "Braunschweig"' directive emerged. On 12 November 1941, when the Germans were preparing their first assault on Rostov, Dmitrii Kozlov, the commander of the TCF at the time, ordered the 46th Army 'to prevent the enemy's infiltration through the passes of the MCR'. The 46th Army was 'to carry out reconnaissance of the passes through the MCR and allocate the forces needed for their defence and keep them alert ... Reconnaissance must start immediately and be completed by 20 November 1941. The fortification works must begin as soon as reconnaissance has been carried out.'[21] After the Soviet counteroffensive drove the Germans away from Rostov in late November 1941, Kozlov did not press for the implementation of his order. Aleksandr Vasilevskii, chief of the Red Army General Staff, initiated the next series of orders on 7 June 1942, when the front line was at Taganrog, 650 kilometres from the MCR. He demanded that the TCF compile a plan for the defence of the Sukhumi Military Road by 20 June; its commanders were also to conduct a 'reconnaissance of all other passes through the MCR and keep forces ready for their defence'.[22] When the deadline expired and the front line was still at Taganrog, the TCF Headquarters – and later the Stavka – started bombarding their subordinates with orders regarding the defence of the MCR (Table 4.2).

Table 4.2 The string of orders about the defence of the Main Caucasus Ridge issued between 23 June and 15 August 1942

Date	Author of the Order or Report	Summary of the Order or Report
23 June	General Ivan Tiulenev, commander of the TCF	'The adversary might attack from the North Caucasus across the MCR.' The 46th Army 'must block the enemy at the MCR'; its units must take positions at the passes by 30 June.[a]
26 June	General Vasilii Sergatskov, commander of the 46th Army	'The possibility of an enemy attack from the North Caucasus via the MCR passes cannot be excluded.' The 3rd Rifle Corps must be prepared 'to block the enemy at the MCR' and must meanwhile carry out reconnaissance of all the passes across the MCR to assess their passability, identify the locations of possible artificial obstacles, and place small garrisons in the northern foothills of the MCR. All the divisions of the 3rd Rifle Corps must allocate two-thirds of their personnel for action at the passes; these must 'be able to operate and live in the difficult conditions of high mountains'. Units assigned to defend the MCR must be fully equipped with climbing gear and plan their actions in accordance with the *Manual on Mountain Warfare*.[b]

Table 4.2 (cont.)

Date	Author of the Order or Report	Summary of the Order or Report
26 June	Headquarters of the 46th Army	Orders the destruction of the trails leading to the MCR and the building of strongholds at the passes and on the northern slopes of the Caucasus at a distance of 10 to 15 kilometres from the passes.[c]
29 June	Major Strel'tsov, chief of staff of 394th Rifle Division	Files a detailed request for mountaineering gear and spiked mountain boots sufficient to equip his division.[d]
30 June	Sergatskov	Presents a 'Plan for the Defence of the MCR': Klukhor is among 'the most probable directions of the enemy offensive'. One enemy brigade 'or a larger formation' may attack along the Sukhumi Military Road, and smaller units may advance via Sancharo and Marukh. 'The formations of the 46th Army are untrained to operate in mountains, let alone the high mountains, except for the 20th Mountain Division ... Artillery and mortar crews, and especially the supply trains of rifle divisions, are the least trained for action in the mountains.' Formations that have no pack animals, like the 394th Rifle Division, would experience the most severe logistical problems. The 46th Army must organise 6 pack companies with 150 horses each, in addition to the pack trains introduced in rifle divisions. Supply depots must be set up in the mountains and on the way to the passes. The deadline for completing reconnaissance is 15 July. Fortifications must be built between 15 July and 15 August. Training for mountain warfare must begin as soon as the mountaineering gear arrives.[e]
4 July	Sergatskov	'The probability of enemy advance from the North Caucasus via the passes of the MCR has increased.' Units allocated to defend the MCR, supplied with radios, must march to the passes immediately and build fortifications and artificial obstacles on the northern slopes. Company-strong and battalion-strong garrisons must be placed, respectively, at minor and major passes. 'Commanders must

Table 4.2 (cont.)

Date	Author of the Order or Report	Summary of the Order or Report
		immediately train their formations and supply trains for operation in the high mountains without waiting for the arrival of mountaineering gear.'[f]
11 July	Colonel Timofei Volkovich, commander of the 394th Rifle Division	Orders 'immediate training ... for action in the difficult conditions of the high mountains'. The *Manual on Mountain Warfare* must be followed during operational planning.[g]
30 July (two days after the Germans break the front at Rostov)	Vasilevskii	Repeats the order regarding the defence of the passes in the Western Caucasus.[h]
31 July (the front line is 450 km away from the MCR)	Sergatskov	'The probability of enemy advance from the Northern Caucasus via the passes of the MCR has increased.' The units assigned to defend them must immediately take positions at the passes and build strongholds by 15 August.[i]
2 August	Lieutenant-Colonel Ivan Kantaria, commander of the 394 Rifle Division	Relays Sergatskov's order of 31 July to his division and adds that its focus should be on the Klukhor and Marukh passes.[j]
3 August	Tiulenev	Units staying at the passes must complete the first series of strongholds by 10 August and then 'staunchly defend the passes'. Reliable communications must be established to maintain command and control. Commanders must 'use every minute for the improvement of defences and personnel training'.[k]
Early August	Siachin, commissar of the 394th Rifle Division	Local guides must be found; regiment commanders should 'establish friendly, Bolshevik relations with them and attend to their needs'.[l]

Table 4.2 (cont.)

Date	Author of the Order or Report	Summary of the Order or Report
5 August (the front line is 250 km away from the MCR)	General Vladimir Ivanov, deputy chief of the Red Army General Staff	'Occupy the passes not with vanguards, such as platoons or companies, as you do now but with the main forces assigned for their defence. Occupy defence positions as fast as you can.' Colonel Serafim Rozhdestvenskii, deputy chief of staff of the TCF, assures Ivanov: 'The passes are occupied by the main forces. Only the most difficult passes that exclude the actions of large enemy units are occupied by independent companies.'[m]
7 August	Sergatskov	'The probability of enemy advance via the passes in the MCR has increased.' Units staying at the passes must conduct reconnaissance at a depth of 35 to 50 kilometres to the north of the MCR.[n]
9 August	General Konstantin Leselidze, commander of the 3rd Rifle Corps	'The defence of the passes . . . should be organised in a way that excludes the sudden emergence of the enemy.'[o] Soldiers at the MCR must receive warm uniforms. The 394th Rifle Division must 'pay particular attention to the Klukhor pass'.[p]
10 August	Ivanov	The situation at the MCR causes 'great concern; it is necessary to immediately enforce garrisons at the passes and send smart, responsible commanders there and supply them with all the necessary equipment'. Aleksei Subbotin, the chief of staff of the TCF, assures Ivanov that 'all the passes are covered by garrisons of at least one battalion; they are building strongholds'. Simultaneously, he tells Sergatskov that the forces assigned to defend the passes are 'absolutely inadequate'.[q]
14 August (the first clash between the German and Soviet vanguards around Teberda,	Leselidze	The 3rd Rifle Corps must strengthen the defences of the MCR and 'by stubborn defence of the passes, destroy the enemy on the approaches to them'.[r]

Table 4.2 (cont.)

Date	Author of the Order or Report	Summary of the Order or Report
36 to 48 km away from the MCR)		
15 August (the clash at Teberda continues)	Ivanov	The Germans are heading to Transcaucasia. 'The units defending the passes are quite insignificant and cannot secure the passes. Report what measures will be taken to reinforce these units.'[s]

[a] Ivan Tiulenev to the commander of the 46th Army (23 June 1942), TsAMO, f. 401, op. 9511, d. 4, ll. 7, 8.
[b] Vasilii Sergatskov, 'Komandiram soedinenii Zakfronta' (26 June 1942), TsAMO, f. 47, op. 1063, d. 456, ll. 1–6.
[c] Headquarters of the 46th Army, 'Dnevnik boevykh deistvii soedinenii i chastei 46-i armii' (1 May–1 September 1942), TsAMO, f. 401, op. 9511, d. 58, l. 5.
[d] Major Strel'tsov (29 June 1942), TsAMO, f. 1720, op. 1, d. 23, l. 84.
[e] Sergatskov, 'Plan oborony Glavnogo Kavkazskogo Khrebta' (30 June 1942), TsAMO, f. 47, op. 1063, d. 456, ll. 9–19.
[f] Sergatskov, 'Komandiram soedinenii' (4 July 1942), TsAMO, f. 47, op. 1063, d. 456, ll. 25, 26.
[g] Colonel Timofei Volkovich (11 July 1942), TsAMO, f. 1720, op. 1, d. 23, l. 85.
[h] Aleksandr Vasilevskii, 'Direktiva General'nogo Shtaba' (30 July 1942), in U. Batyrov, S. Grebeniuk and V. Matveev, eds., *Bitva za Kavkaz* (Moscow: Triada, 2002), 312, 313.
[i] Sergatskov, 'Komandiram soedinenii' (31 July 1942), TsAMO, f. 401, op. 9511, d. 22, ll. 21–23.
[j] Lieutenant-Colonel Ivan Kantaria, 'Komandiram chastei 394-i sd' (2 August 1942), TsAMO, f. 401, op. 9511, d. 22, l. 70.
[k] Tiulenev (3 August 1942) in Batyrov, Grebeniuk and Matveev, eds., *Bitva za Kavkaz*, 319, 320.
[l] Siachin, commissar of the 394th Rifle Division (early August 1942), TsAMO, f. 1720, op. 1, d. 23, l. 107.
[m] Vladimer Ivanov to Serafim Rozhdestvenskii (5 August 1942), in V. Shapovalov, ed., *Bitva za Kavkaz v dokumentakh i materialakh* (Stavropol: SGU, 2003), 139.
[n] Sergatskov, 'Komandiram soedinenii' (7 August 1942), TsAMO, f. 47, op. 1063, d. 456, ll. 36, 37.
[o] Leselidze to the commander of the 394th Rifle Division (9 August 1942), TsAMO, f. 1720, op. 1, d. 23, l. 71.
[p] Leselidze, 'Komandiram soedinenii 3-go sk' (9 August 1942), TsAMO, f. 401, op. 9511, d. 22, l. 52.
[q] TCF Headquarters, 'Zhurnal boevykh deistvii Zakfronta' (10 August 1942), TsAMO, f. 47, op. 1063, d. 183, ll. 88, 90.
[r] Leselidze, 'Chastnyi boevoi prikaz No. 002' (14 August 1942), TsAMO, f. 1720, op. 1, d. 7, l. 126.
[s] TCF Headquarters, 'Zhurnal boevykh deistvii Zakfronta' (15 August 1942), TsAMO, f. 47, op. 1063, d. 183, ll. 119, 120.

Thus, only the High Command of the German Armed Forces can be accused of taking a wild gamble by making an impromptu decision about the strike across the MCR without preliminary staff work; in contrast, the Red Army issued numerous timely and rational orders intended to strengthen the Soviet defences in the high Caucasus long before the Germans approached. No formidable obstacles to the fulfilment of these orders existed: a large amount of manpower, fully equipped with weapons and ammunition, was at hand; most passes of the MCR were accessible to non-experts; winter uniforms and some mountaineering gear were kept at the stores of the 46th Army; and the civilian administrative infrastructure functioning among the friendly local population could greatly ease the anticipated logistical problems.

Given that the punishment for the failure to follow an order was death, the Red Army General Staff and the TCF Headquarters expected results from their numerous directives. Having begun reconnaissance of the passes in earnest in early June 1942, the 3rd Rifle Corps, assigned to defend the MCR, should have studied every inch of the areas at and around the passes and their northern approaches by mid August. Scouts should have been sent to all the valleys to the north of the MCR, ready to signal the advance of Germans the moment they saw them. From early July on, at least one battalion should have garrisoned every strategically important pass and at least one company should have covered every non-essential pass across which a large-scale attack was logistically impossible; the main forces of the defenders equalling two-thirds of the 3rd Rifle Corps, deployed close to the passes, should have headed to the top on 5 August and reached their positions the same day. The defence priority, determined on 7 June, was clear: the Klukhor pass and the Sukhumi Military Road should have been fortified particularly well, but positions at all other passes should have also been ready. Having been at the passes since early July, the Soviet garrisons should have built an elaborate system of strongholds on the northern slopes, with tiered positions to maximise firepower. Climbing gear should have begun arriving soon after 26 June, and warm uniforms soon after 9 August. The several warnings of senior commanders about the advance of the Germans towards the MCR should have prompted the 3rd Rifle Corps to address and eliminate the training flaws identified on 30 June. Having started exercises in the high mountains, in accordance with the *Manual on Mountain Warfare*, on 4 July, the regiments deployed at the MCR should have become fairly proficient by mid August. They should have established reliable communications among their units and with the Headquarters of the 3rd Rifle Corps in Sukhumi; assembled enough pack animals, harnesses, packs, and horseshoes to maintain a steady stream of supplies to the passes; and ensured the smooth operations of the supply trains after 4 July. The defenders should have set intermediate supply depots along the trails leading to the passes, thus easing logistics. The 46th Army should have maintained close links with the local communities and administrative agencies and relied on them as a source of local knowledge and logistical assistance. By the time the German vanguards were approaching the MCR on 14 August, it should have been turned into an impregnable fortress.

However, few of these logical actions were realised, and the actual Soviet hold on the MCR was quite weak. Andrei Grechko, commander of the 47th Army, fighting in the North Caucasus, attributed the failure to prepare for the defence of the MCR to the indisputable fact that the 'orders of the [Transcaucasian] Front and of the [46th] Army were fulfilled too slowly',[23] but such an argument is a gross oversimplification. The practical outcome of the frenzied order writing on the eve of the battle of the Caucasus was virtually zero: the only preparations made were the placing of small garrisons at some passes and the sending of scouts to some valleys on the MCR's northern slopes.

The mountain of orders written on the eve of the battle of the Caucasus thus produced little. This failure was due to ignorance of the potential battleground, a major strategic miscalculation of the OKW's intentions, and the lethargic state of mind of many TCF commanders at all levels, who had been corrupted by a carefree life in the deep rear for an entire year after the Soviet Union entered World War II. The effectiveness of the Soviet system of administration, whether civilian or military, depended on the extent of control maintained by superiors over their subordinates. A strategic decision produced the desired outcome only if this control was constant and close. The string of orders regarding the defence of the Caucasus came to naught because, distracted by other threats that were merely the fruit of their imagination, the commanders of the TCF, the 46th Army, and the 3rd Rifle Corps, believing that the MCR was impassable, failed to maintain close and constant control over the implementation of their orders. In the absence of control, the lower-ranking officers assigned to defend the passes merely feigned action or simply ignored the orders. A *post factum* entry in the TCF war diary stated that the local 'commanders did not fulfil the missions set by the [46th] Army superiors and, in practice, did nothing. The commanders of divisions and [smaller] units justified their inaction with poor knowledge of the terrain and the absence of descriptions of the MCR.'[24]

The 46th Army had to defend the entire western part of Transcaucasia, but Tiulenev believed, for unknown reasons, that the major threat to this region was a potential amphibious operation with a massive landing of German forces in the rear of the armies defending Novorossiisk and Tuapse. As noted in the TCF war diary, 'The commanders of the 46th Army focused on the Black Sea coast; they viewed the defence of the MCR as a secondary objective.'[25] Other contemporary observers were even blunter: 'The commanders of the 46th Army devoted all their attention ... to the coast.'[26] They spread their formations evenly all along the entire 500-kilometre stretch of the Black Sea coast between Lazarevskoe and the border with Turkey. The concerns about a potential German landing had no sound basis, given the decisive superiority of the Soviet Black Sea Fleet over the minuscule Axis naval forces, but the effort to prevent this imaginary menace consumed most of the commanders' energy.[27]

The Headquarters of the 46th Army knew that at least a dozen passes existed in the western part of the MCR and that some of them could be accessed via horse trails. However, as Lavrentii Beria, the people's commissar of the interior, found during his trip to the Caucasus in August 1942, 'As a rule, the commanders of units sent to defend the passes did not visit the passes and did not know whether proper defences had been built.'[28] He was correct: none of the senior commanders of the TCF, 46th Army, or 3rd Rifle Corps ever visited the high mountains before the Germans arrived there. Since no automobile roads to the passes existed, trekking to a pass required several days of strenuous physical effort, and senior and even medium-rank officers skipped this endeavour. Tiulenev never came any closer to the mountains than Sukhumi, a coastal town about 120 kilometres away from the MCR. His orders and memoirs advance several geographic discoveries such as the non-existent Donguz-Orun-Bashi, Dombai, and Ulgen[29] passes and the orange groves at the MCR. They also claim that mountaineers climbed vertical rocks in crampons and that 'the two primary weapons of close combat in the mountains were hand grenades and stones',[30] revealing his total ignorance of the terrain in the high Caucasus, the situation at the MCR, and the intricacies of mountain warfare. Konstantin Leselidze, commander of the 3rd Rifle Corps, made a visit to the mountains only after the first pass fell to the Germans, and even then he did not climb above 800 metres, an elevation from which he could not see the approaches to any pass, let alone the passes themselves.[31] None of his division or regiment commanders or their chiefs of staff ever visited the passes before the German assault, and most battalion commanders tasked with defending the passes had not been there either.[32] The 394th Rifle Division was supposed to carry the brunt of the action in the high Caucasus, but in early August its headquarters and the headquarters of its regiments were in Sukhumi and other coastal towns, a five-day march from the passes. The Headquarters of the 63rd Cavalry Division were in Zugdidi, a town close to the sea coast, 120 to 140 kilometres from the Gvandra, Donguz-Orun, Becho, Mestia, and Tviberi passes, all of which it was supposed to defend.[33] Although maps used by the Soviet side, produced in 1897, were obsolete, their scale of 1:42,000[34] was adequate for operations in the mountains and, unlike the German maps, they showed numerous minor trails across the Caucasus. However, despite the availability of detailed maps and the time to study the terrain, the senior commanders of the TCF and the 46th Army were almost as ignorant of the high Caucasus as were their German counterparts. Russian authors frequently explain the German successes during the first stage of the battle at the MCR with the ridiculous argument that the Germans had achieved intimate familiarity with the terrain through their pre-war visits in the area: 'before the war, many Edelweiss officers had visited this region as tourists and made an effort to remember, draw sketches, or even take photos of the mountain passes' and 'knew well every trail and every col'.[35] Nothing but their laziness and narrow-mindedness prevented the officers of the TCF, hundreds of times more numerous than the handful of German tourists, to do the same.

The TCF commanders and the Stavka maintained little control over the implementation of their numerous orders about the defence of the MCR because, as Tiulenev explained after the war, 'We did not believe that the Germans would undertake such a daring action – assault across the passes. That is why the Front Headquarters concentrated most of the 46th Army at the Black Sea coast.'[36] Soviet generals thought that passive defence at the MCR by small garrisons was a sufficient bulwark against the unlikely German attempt to cross it, exactly as the French High Command had thought about the Ardennes in 1940. The generals failed to consult the numerous Soviet climbers who knew the MCR, basing their decisions instead on the information received from regular infantrymen sent to scout the passes in mid June, when they were still covered with snow. This information was often misleading because these soldiers, novices in the mountains, inadvertently inflated the difficulty of crossing the MCR.[37] Most of the TCF senior officers believed that a reinforced company would be sufficient to garrison each pass except Klukhor, which was to be defended by two reinforced companies. They changed their opinion only well after the Germans easily took several key passes.[38] Although, under the Stavka's pressure, the reluctant commanders had to reinforce their units on Klukhor and Marukh, the actual strength of the garrisons on the eve of the German assault reflected their conviction that the MCR was 'an insurmountable obstacle' (Table 4.3).[39]

The belief that no large formations could possibly cross the MCR proved the ignorance of the Stavka and the commanders of the TCF regarding the Caucasian operational theatre. However, given that the passes were excellent defensive positions, the largest of these garrisons would have probably been sufficient if only they had arrived in advance and built strongholds, as their orders stated; consisted of soldiers who were trained and equipped for mountain warfare; possessed reliable means of communication; and had a well-established supply system. Not one of these conditions was met by the time the Germans arrived at the northern slopes of the MCR.

A *post factum* entry in the TCF war diary summarised the reasons for the failure of the Red Army to prepare positions in the high Caucasus:

> Being behind the MCR and feeling no direct enemy threat, the commander of the 46th Army, his Headquarters, and his division commanders did not particularly hurry to fulfil the orders of the TCF Military Council and failed to organise proper defences ... Troops began marching to the passes on 31 July 1942, but they advanced slowly along difficult mountain trails and, when they reached the passes, they built strongholds only at the crest but not on the northern slopes, leaving only screens there [at the passes], and kept [most] manpower on the southern slopes.

> Fortifications were built improperly [*naspekh*] because of the absence of tools ... A relaxed atmosphere reigned in the Headquarters of the 46th Army ... The negligent attitude of the 46th Army commanders ... resulted in enormous casualties and necessitated enormous efforts when the enemy broke through to the southern slopes of the Caucasus.[40]

Table 4.3 Garrisons staying at or approaching the passes of the Main Caucasus Ridge, including reconnaissance parties sent to the northern slopes between 15 and 17 August 1942

	Passes	Units Assigned for Defence	Strength
Elbrus group	Khotiu-Tau	214th Regiment of	0
	Chiper-Azau	63rd Cavalry Division	0
	Chiper		0
	Donguz-Orun		1 squadron
	Becho		1 squadron
Klukhor group	Klukhor	815th Regiment of the 394th Rifle Division	1 rifle battalion and 7 attached platoons
	Nakhar		1 rifle company
	Ptysh		0
Marukh pass		810th Regiment of the 394th Rifle Division	1 rifle battalion and 7 attached platoons
Sancharo group	Sancharo	808th Regiment of the 394th Rifle Division	2 rifle platoons and 2 attached platoons
	Tsegerker		2 rifle platoons and 1 attached platoon
	Allashtrakhu		0
	Adzapsh		0
	Chmakhara		0
	Chamashkha		1 rifle company
Aishkha		174th Regiment of the 20th 'Mountain' Division	1 'mountain' company
Pseashkha			1 'mountain' company and 3 attached platoons

Source: Major Komarov, deputy head of the Operations Section of the 46th Army, 'Svedeniia boevogo i chislennogo sostava podrazdelenii prikryvaiushchikh Kavkazskii Khrebet' (15 August 1942), TsAMO, f. 401, op. 9511, d. 22, ll. 57, 57v; Major Zhashko, chief of staff of the 394th Rifle Division, 'Svedeniia o boevom i chislennom sostave podrazdelenii, nakhodiashchikhsia na perevalakh Glavnogo Kavkazskogo Khrebta' (17 August 1942), TsAMO, f. 401, op. 9511, d. 22, l. 114; Headquarters of the 20th 'Mountain' Division, 'Zhurnal boevykh deistvii 20-i gsd' (14 and 15 August 1942), TsAMO, f. 1089, op. 1, d. 6, l. 4.

The Russian archives provide enough background information to elaborate on this summary. A week of intensive work by the entire garrison at each pass would have been sufficient to surround every pass with a system of mutually supporting strongholds. Earlier experience implied that the winner of the race for key positions in the mountains receives a sound advantage, but the 46th Army was in no hurry to get to its positions. Sergatskov believed that, after the Germans broke through at Rostov, it would take them a minimum of twenty to thirty days to reach the Caucasus. It was during this period that the units of the 46th Army were to occupy positions at the MCR.[41] As Sergatskov admitted later, 'Events, however, developed faster than we expected.'[42] Although to get to the MCR the formations of the TCF that were deployed at the coast had to cover only one-fifth of the distance that the Germans did from Rostov, the Germans arrived there only several days after these formations had reached the passes. A part of the main force assigned for the defence of the passes began marching to the MCR only around 3 August[43] but, after they reached the remote approaches to the MCR, their commanders procrastinated, delaying taking positions at the inhospitable, bare, windy passes and leaving only small vanguards there; as Beria reported, they 'failed to organise any defence but stayed in settlements between 5 and 20 kilometres away from the passes'.[44] While in these settlements, the soldiers idled and did not train for mountain warfare or mountaineering. Although these units could reach the passes within a day or two, they would arrive with zero acclimatisation and would therefore be unable to fight or even dig in effectively. Only on 14 August, the day the Germans arrived on the northern slopes of the MCR, did Sergatskov issue an urgent, categorical order to occupy the passes.[45] By this time, only one of the three battalions of the 815th Rifle Regiment, which was to defend the Klukhor pass, was at and around the pass; the second battalion was staying in Azhara village 30 kilometres away and 1,800 metres below the pass, while the third battalion was in Sukhumi, a five-day march from Klukhor.[46] The 20th 'Mountain' Division received the order to take positions at the passes only on 13 and 14 August and still had not reached them by 17 August.[47] Therefore, the manpower available for fortification works at the passes and their northern slopes was quite small.

Earlier experiences of war in the mountains suggested that the formations operating there must have additional tools to dig in on rocky terrain. The depots of the 46th Army at the Black Sea coast had enough shovels and picks but, according to a Soviet military engineer, 'many rifle units not only failed to take additional digging tools but sought to dispose of this, as they believed, useless burden' during the long and exhausting marches to the passes, often arriving at the defence line 'almost without tools'.[48] Soviet-made individual infantry spades were of such poor quality that they bent even when digging dry soil,[49] so they were virtually useless in rocky terrain. Thus, soldiers dug only a few primitive trenches at the passes' saddles rather than a tiered system of strongholds on their northern slopes, as the 1940 *Manual on Mountain Warfare* recommended. Most passes had no fortifications. A military engineer wrote that such a devil-may-care attitude to fortification works later led to 'numerous needless casualties'.[50] No one investigated the area around the passes, as the manual required. The Soviet units therefore defended only the major trails across the passes and ignored the minor ones, which they did not even know about because they had failed to undertake proper reconnaissance.[51]

The senior commanders of the 46th Army staying in cosy resorts on the shores of the Black Sea and in Kutaisi had no idea about the climate and other conditions at the MCR. They sent soldiers to the mountains in the uniforms they wore in subtropical heat and without basic food supplies, let alone climbing gear, or even sunglasses.[52] The 46th Army did literally nothing to organise a supply stream to the MCR.[53] No one made an effort to assemble supply pack trains or to prepare forage or food rations for action in the mountains. The 3rd Rifle Corps had no intermediate supply depots on the trails to the mountains, nor did the 46th Army contact the civilian administration to co-ordinate logistics or identify potential guides.[54]

By the summer of 1942, the Red Army was still inexperienced in the use of radio, and Soviet-made radios remained bulky and unreliable and had poor frequency filters. That is why, as Vasilevskii observed on 24 July, 'Unfortunately, the major type of communication remains wire communications. The command system exists as long as wire communications work, but as soon as the wire has been damaged the command is lost. Radio is used reluctantly, only under pressure ... The training of radio operators is inadequate: most of them work slowly and their knowledge of radio is poor.' He emphasised that radio communication was 'a matter of the utmost importance' and ordered division commanders to considerably broaden lower-level radio communications using simple codes.[55] This order was particularly important for actions in the Caucasus, where the great distances and the mountain landscape most often precluded the use of wire communications, but the order made little impact on the ability of the units deployed there to use radio.

Although the interwar experiments with radio in the mountains revealed a host of problems, nobody addressed these problems before 1942. The Red Army was surprised to find that radios that provided reliable communications between partisan headquarters in the Soviet mainland and partisans in the German rear refused to work in the mountains. It is unknown whether the reconnaissance parties sent to the northern slopes of the MCR had radios, but the regiment commanders who sent them received information from these parties only via messengers, and it took the messengers several days to deliver information across the MCR.[56] Having failed to establish a network of relay stations, the headquarters of the divisions sent to defend the MCR had stable contact neither with their units in the high mountains nor with the Headquarters of the 46th Army in Kutaisi or the Headquarters of the 3rd Rifle Corps in Sukhumi.[57] Thus, these headquarters did not know the location of the enemy or of their units, and most initial measures they took in response to the approach of the Germans to the MCR were belated. The headquarters had no effective control over the formations defending the passes.

Regular Soviet infantry marched to the MCR totally untrained for mountain warfare, unequipped to operate in the mountains, and ignorant of the mountain environment.[58] Some of the units had the *Manual on Mountain Warfare*, but few officers had read it. The divisions assigned to defend the MCR had only two or three maps per regiment,[59] which means that only half of the battalion commanders had maps. It must have been clear that the type of combat that was anticipated – actions by small units engaged in independent missions pursuing the same tactical objective – required having one map per platoon, but no senior officer was concerned about the shortage of maps. Soldiers arrived at positions in the high Caucasus exhausted; they were constantly short of breath without proper acclimatisation, and were unable to sleep at night because of racing hearts and bitterly cold winds. Depressed and disheartened, they shivered in their summer uniforms. The Germans came several days later.

Figure 4.1 Ivan Tiulenev, commander of the Transcaucasian Front. Credit: RGAKFD

The German Attack Across the MCR

Klukhor Group of Passes

The German assaults on the Klukhor, Elbrus, Sancharo, and Marukh groups of passes revealed the enormous gap in the tactical skills and the overall ability to operate in the mountain environment between the German mountain troops and the Soviet regular infantry and cavalry occupying the passes. The vanguards of the battalion of the 815th Rifle Regiment[60] assigned to defend the Klukhor pass, the most important of the passes, arrived there, according to various Soviet reports, between 5 and 10 August, and the rest of the battalion came on

13 August.[61] The soldiers undertook no serious effort to dig in because their commanders thought, exactly as their forefathers at Shipka and the authors of the manual of 1936 had, that the mountain landscape itself provided sufficient protection.[62] The battalion, idling at the pass for several days, eventually dug trenches sufficient only to accommodate one company.[63] Klement'ev and the Soviet manuals on mountain warfare had warned that, since the envelopment of enemy positions is a major tactic in the mountains, 'during the defence of a mountain pass, the heights adjacent to the pass's saddle are particularly important. The approaches to them should be carefully investigated and covered by strongholds ... It must be absolutely ensured that small enemy units cannot sneak [around defence positions] using the rough mountain terrain.'[64] However, unable to climb the adjacent rocks in the absence of mountaineering skills or gear, the garrison defending the Klukhor pass occupied only its saddle.

The German assault on the pass was not a surprise: the Soviets knew that the Germans were coming after several units of Soviet 242nd Rifle Division, with a total strength of 789 men, passed through Klukhor from the North Caucasus into Transcaucasia on 15 August and told the defenders that the Germans were on their heels. No one attempted to stop the retreating soldiers and use them for reinforcement of the garrison because they were reportedly 'so demoralised that they could not resist the enemy' and had abandoned most of their weapons.[65] The next piece of conclusive information about the German advance came from a scout platoon of the 815th Rifle Regiment that showed exemplary determination and discipline by repeatedly clashing with German vanguards around the villages of Verkhnii Teberdinskii (48 kilometres north of the pass) and Teberda (36 kilometres north of the pass) on 14 and 15 August, before retreating to the pass, as ordered, pursued by the Germans, who arrived at the southern slopes of the pass on 16 August (Map 4.2).[66]

A German half-battalion commanded by Captain Harald von Hirschfeld, from the 1st Mountain Division, reinforced with several platoons of heavy machineguns and mortars,[67] faced the understaffed Soviet battalion – 420 men occupying the saddle of the pass and armed with 6 heavy machineguns, 27 light machineguns, and 8 mortars, in addition to rifles.[68] For unknown reasons, the commander of the 815th Rifle Regiment placed two other companies under his command – with a total of 208 men, armed with 8 light machineguns and 3 trench

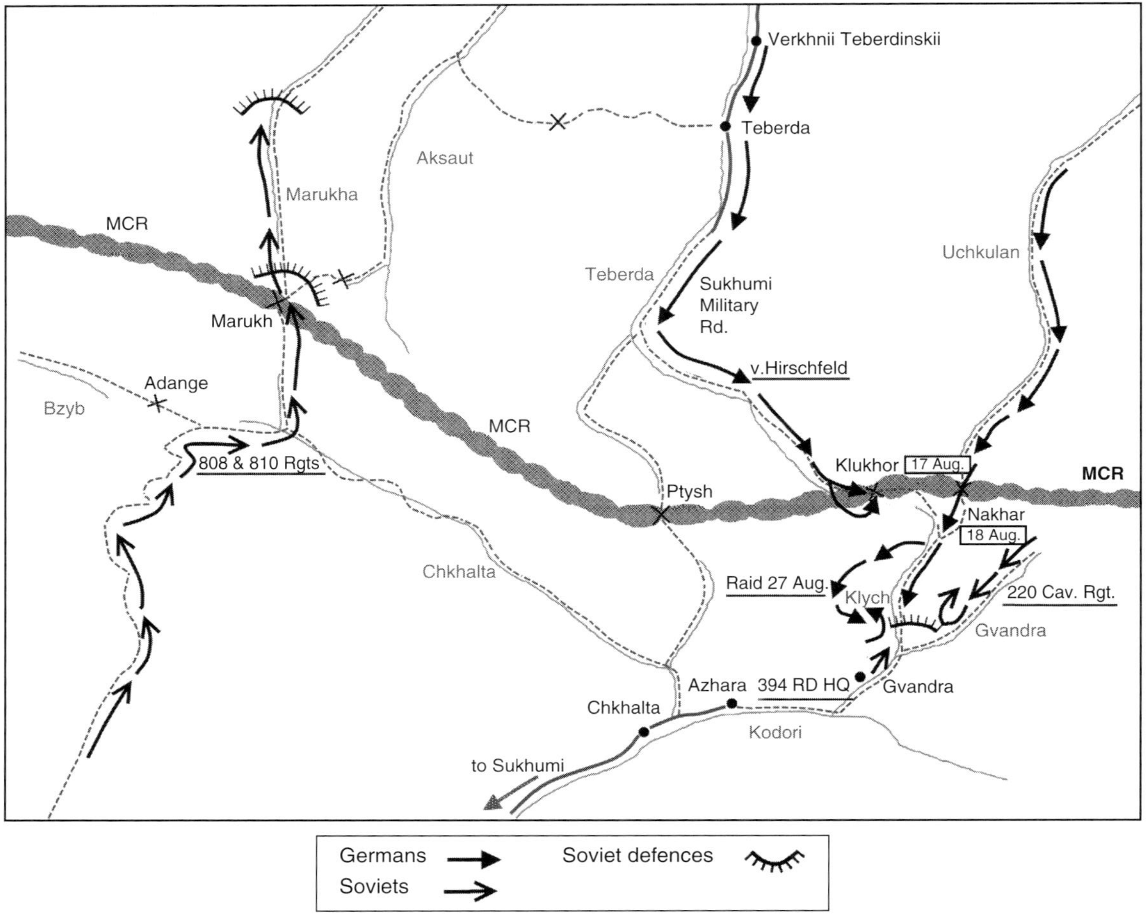

Map 4.2 The German assault on Klukhor

mortars – well below the pass on its southern foot, where they were useless for the defence of the pass.[69] With such an irrational deployment, the German vanguard roughly equalled the Soviet defenders in number and firepower, but the assault was supported by mountain and field artillery, which the Soviets did not have because regular infantry units had no mountain artillery and the trail on the southern slopes of the pass was too narrow for a horse relay pulling field guns.[70] However, the Soviet battalion at the pass was still a sufficient force to defend this excellent position.

According to the TCF war diary, the sight of the chaotic flight of the Soviet 242nd Rifle Division from the North Caucasus demoralised the defenders of Klukhor even before Hirschfeld approached the pass.[71] When the Germans began climbing Klukhor and were engaged by the Soviet garrison on 16 August, Hirschfeld acted according to the German manual on mountain warfare: he sent a company to climb the nearby rocks across the ridge and around the pass into the rear of the defenders. On the next day, a surprise attack by this company from behind aided the frontal attack by the rest of the half-battalion, and the Germans easily took the pass.[72] Everything happened according to Clausewitz's advice: in the mountains: 'the fastest way of getting results is always to give the enemy reason to fear having his line of retreat cut'.[73] According to Soviet reports, the Germans destroyed 80 per cent of the defenders during this engagement, whereas the German casualties during the action at the pass on 16 and 17 August were, according to German reports, merely 9 men dead and 32 wounded, without a single soldier missing in action, which means that the ratio of the total casualties was 1 to 8 in favour of the attackers.[74] Since the wounded German soldiers remained on the territory overrun by the Germans, whereas nearly all Soviet casualties during the engagement at the pass fell into German hands, the ratio of irrecoverable losses was probably 1 to 30 in favour of the Germans. The Germans destroyed the rest of the Soviet battalion during its retreat down the southern slopes of the pass in the following two days; only seventeen soldiers survived the ordeal unharmed. Tiulenev assessed the Soviet casualties by 21 August at and near the Klukhor pass as 'up to 500 men'[75] – it is unknown whether he counted only irrecoverable losses or included the wounded as well. The Headquarters of the 46th Army commented: 'The Klukhor pass was surrendered almost without a fight.'[76] Thus, the Germans took the most important pass across the MCR, the one through which the Sukhumi Military Road ran, at a small cost to themselves, inflicting a crushing defeat on the defenders. Unlike the Soviet regiment and division commanders who had found it too bothersome to climb Klukhor to prepare it for defence, General Lanz, commander of the German 1st Mountain Division, visited Klukhor the day after its capture to assess the available options.[77] Since no communications existed between the garrison at Klukhor and the Headquarters of the 3rd Rifle Corps, the TCF commanders learned about the emergence of Germans on the northern slopes of the MCR only two days after they had taken Klukhor.[78]

On 17 August, the 815th Rifle Regiment received an order to send a company of 105 soldiers to occupy Nakhar, the next pass to the east of Klukhor, but a German company overtook the Soviets and climbed the pass on 18 August,[79] thus acquiring without a fight another trail leading to the valley with the Sukhumi Military Road, although a steep and difficult one.

After the destruction of the Soviet garrison at Klukhor, Hirschfeld's half-battalion began descending down the southern slopes of the Caucasus along the Klych valley, which led to the Kodori River. On 20 August, it engaged the Training Battalion of the 394th Rifle Division, the only force that could slow down the German advance. This battalion of 524 men slowly retreated under German pressure, suffering heavy casualties, especially between 20 and 23 August; by 25 August, it had lost 447 men killed, wounded, and missing in action,[80] whereas Hirschfeld's force lost only 5 men dead and 47 wounded between 20 and 22 August in fights against the remnants of the battalion of the 815th Rifle Regiment and the Training Battalion; on 22 August, however, numerous Soviet reinforcements arrived, and 42 more Germans were killed and 151 wounded on 23 and 24 August while fighting against these reinforcements, which also suffered many more casualties.[81]

Elbrus Group of Passes

Meanwhile, a German High Mountain Company with seventy men, commanded by Captain Heinz Groth from the 1st Mountain Division, advanced towards the upper reaches of the Kuban River, 50 kilometres to the east of the Sukhumi Military Road, with orders to

Figure 4.2 A German mountain unit equipped with ice axes, crampons, and ropes climbs a snow slope. Credit: Süddeutsche Zeitung Photo / Alamy Stock Photo

make a reconnaissance of the Elbrus region (Map 4.3). The 3rd Rifle Corps assigned the 214th Regiment of the 63rd Cavalry Division to defend the Khotiu-Tau, Chiper, and Chiper-Azau passes. However, neither the commander of the regiment, nor his chief of staff, nor any of its battalion or company commanders had visited these passes; that is why Major Saltykov, representative of the General Staff of the Red Army in the Caucasus, wrote, 'they assessed the situation incorrectly and gave little thought to how to … defend the passes'.[82]

On 7 August, half a squadron of the 63rd Cavalry Division began marching to Chiper-Azau, but apparently only one section of eleven men with one light machinegun, commanded by an officer, climbed the pass.[83] This section soon arrived at the Priiut 11 hotel and a small weather station next door, and stayed there along with three civilian meteorologists. Built in 1939 at a height of 4,130 metres, this three-floor, forty-room hotel with an imposing architectural style was intended as a base for the mountaineers planning to climb Elbrus; it could accommodate 200 persons.[84] On 16 August, Groth led one of his platoons across the undefended Khotiu-Tau towards the foot of Elbrus; another platoon of his company took the undefended Chiper-Azau pass

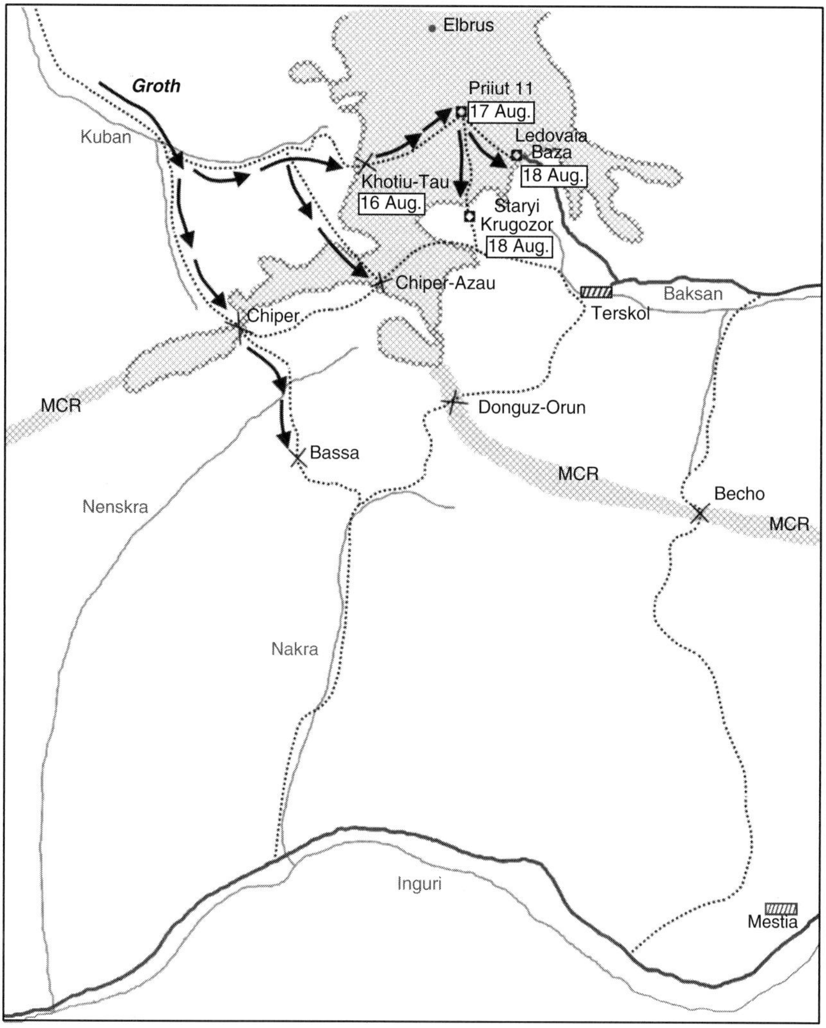

Map 4.3 The German advance to the Elbrus passes

connecting the Kuban and Baksan valleys; and yet another reconnaissance party climbed the undefended Chiper pass leading from the Kuban valley to the southern slopes of the MCR.[85] On 17 August, Groth's platoon approached the hotel occupied by the Soviet section. According to some German sources, Groth came to the Soviets with a white flag and offered them the opportunity to leave the hotel without a fight.[86] Josef Bauer, a talented writer and poet in the service of the Propaganda Ministry who was attached to this platoon, wrote that, while the Soviets

Figure 4.3 Priiut 11 hotel. Credit: Süddeutsche Zeitung Photo / Alamy Stock Photo

thought about the offer, one of them, polite 'as a hotel doorman', helped him to take his backpack to the hotel.[87] After that, the Soviet report states, the Soviet 'reconnaissance party departed [for the Baksan valley held by the Red Army] without firing a shot, leaving three men prisoner', a story confirmed by the German reports.[88] The Germans captured more than 2,000 daily food rations, including condensed milk, which they assessed as the best food for a mountaineer; a radio station; a large stock of climbing gear; excellent climbing suits; and fur jackets.[89] For a while, the High Mountain Company controlled the entire Elbrus region – and the important Khotiu-Tau, Chiper, and Chiper-Azau passes – with only one platoon of thirty-five men, while its second platoon engaged in supply operations.[90] It would have been easy for the Soviets to drive them away at that time, but nobody even considered it.

On 18 August, Groth's company arrived at the unoccupied small shelters of Staryi Krugozor and Ledovaia Baza, the latter at the end of the tractor road from the Terskol valley. Both were located well below the hotel. Several days later, the Germans marched to the undefended Bassa pass (3,057 m) nearby, which connected the two tributaries of the Inguri River. The mountain path from the Chiper pass crossed the Bassa pass and joined an excellent trail along the Inguri

Figure 4.4 A German mountain unit equipped with backpacks, alpenstocks, and snowshoes walking up a mountain path broken into the snow. Some soldiers wear Russian hats with ear flaps, which are more suitable for winter conditions than the caps worn by German mountain troops. Credit: BArch, Bild 101I-031-2417-11 / Poetsch

River, which flows to the Black Sea. The Germans set small garrisons at the Bassa, Chiper, Chiper-Azau, and Khotiu-Tau passes. In occupying Bassa, they gained the opportunity to cut the most important Soviet communication line in the Western Caucasus, between Transcaucasia and the North Caucasus via the Donguz-Orun pass, although the Soviets could still cross the MCR from the Inguri into the Baksan valley via the higher Becho pass.[91]

On 18 August, the Germans sent a reconnaissance party to the Donguz-Orun pass in an attempt to secure easy access to the Inguri valley from the Baksan valley for the anticipated offensive of the German and Romanian divisions from Nalchik in the North Caucasus into Transcaucasia.[92] However, a Soviet cavalry squadron of 182 men deployed at the pass repelled the Germans.[93] The Germans made no determined attempt to take Donguz-Orun because they had no forces to dislodge the Soviet garrison, which meanwhile was reinforced by a unit of the 8th Motorised NKVD Regiment with 271 men and, later, by a battalion of the 28th Reserve Brigade.[94] This shifted the balance of power even more towards the Soviets. The Germans did not see the capture of the pass as vital because the offensive in the North Caucasus was proceeding more slowly than expected and the route between Nalchik and the Inguri valley seemed unnecessary for the time being, given that the 1st Mountain Division had already secured the trails leading to the Inguri via the Chiper, Chiper-Azau, and Bassa passes.

Having occupied Priiut 11 and all the passes around it, the Germans held an excellent base in the high mountains that dominated the most important routes in the Elbrus region. Major Saltykov commented: 'In contrast to the inept passivity of the 63rd Cavalry Division, the enemy acted vigorously and skilfully.'[95] The Germans appreciated the strategic location of the hotel and fortified the Ledovaia Baza and Krugozor shelters, which protected the approaches to Priiut 11 from the southern and eastern valleys.

Sancharo Group of Passes

While the 1st Mountain Division took the most important passes in the Klukhor and Elbrus regions, a two-battalion German combat group of the 4th Mountain Division commanded by Colonel Walter Stettner Ritter von Grabenhofen advanced along the Bolshaia Laba River across the Sancharo group of passes to the Bzyb valley, which led to the Black Sea coast (Map 4.4). This group had a total strength of 1,100 infantrymen and 250 artillerymen serving and pulling eight mountain guns.[96] The Sancharo pass was the second most important pass, after Klukhor, across the high mountains of the Western Caucasus because a broad horse trail went across it to Bzyb.

One Soviet company of 134 men[97] stayed at Sancharo and the neighbouring Allashtrakhu pass, and 60 men occupied the Tsegerker pass; these garrisons together had three heavy machineguns, seven light machineguns, and four mortars, but no artillery pieces.[98] They arrived at the passes on 21 August, four days before the German assault, but built no strongholds there because of 'poor orders and the absence of tools'.[99] The neighbouring Adzapsh and Chmakhara passes, located to the west of Sancharo, remained undefended. One more company stayed far below at Chamashkha, a pass to the south of the MCR that separates the two tributaries of the Bzyb River; it was thus irrelevant to the actions at the Sancharo and Allashtrakhu passes.[100]

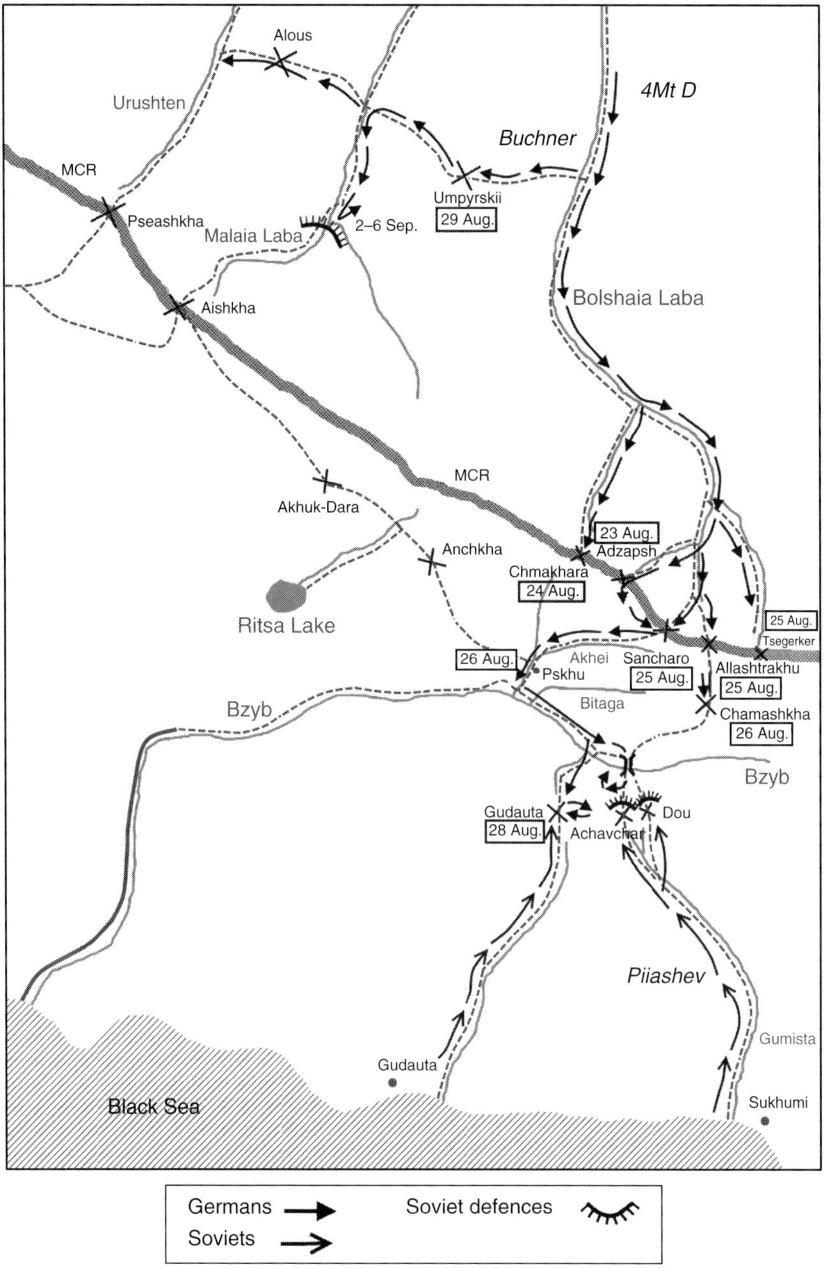

Map 4.4 The German assaults on Sancharo and Aishkha

As had been the case at Klukhor, the German attack on Sancharo was not a surprise for the defenders. A few days before the Germans arrived at its northern slopes, the 2nd battalion of the 139th Rifle Brigade and the 25th Frontier Guard Regiment had escaped the German trap in the North Caucasus by retreating south along Bolshaia Laba through Sancharo to Transcaucasia, having abandoned all their artillery and trucks with supplies. The 2nd Assembled Regiment, organised from stragglers belonging to miscellaneous units, followed them.[101] Only after the remnants of the 242nd Rifle Division, pursued by the Germans, crossed Sancharo with 2,000 men and 600 horses from the North Caucasus, thus proving that the pass was easily accessible,[102] did the Headquarters of the 46th Army decide to enforce the Sancharo garrison, but this decision came too late.

On 23 August, the Germans approached the Sancharo group of passes and climbed the Adzapsh pass. A horse trail led across Adzapsh to the Bzyb River, which flows to the Black Sea. The next day, the Germans ascended the Chmakhara pass, but the trail across it was difficult for pack animals.[103] Had the commanders of the 46th Army ordered the formations crossing the MCR from the North Caucasus to defend the Sancharo group of passes, it would have been close to impossible for the Germans to take them because this excellent defensive position would have been occupied by a force with a numerical superiority of 4 to 1 over the German attackers. However, no communications existed between the Sancharo garrison and the Headquarters of the 46th Army, and no one attempted to stop the retreating Soviet formations at the passes. As a Soviet officer explained, 'Since the [Sancharo] defence had already been organised, the commander of the 25th Frontier Guard Regiment decided to march to Sukhumi for rest.'[104] On 24 August, the astonished Germans watched from the Adzapsh pass as a large Soviet column descended the southern slopes of the MCR, leaving only one company at Sancharo.[105] That day, on the eve of the German attack on Sancharo, Sergatskov warned his subordinates: 'Most strongholds [in the mountains] can be bypassed by the enemy.'[106] This revelation came too late for the defenders of Sancharo.

The Germans used the same manual-prescribed tactics during the assault on Sancharo as they had during their attack on Klukhor, whereas the Soviets ignored every point of their own manual on mountain warfare, exactly as the Klukhor defenders had done. On 24 August, one German company[107] crossed Adzapsh, thus outflanking the Soviet garrison at Sancharo. According to the German plan, this company was to attack the Soviets from the rear on 25 August, simultaneously with the frontal assault by another company.[108] However, the next morning, when the Soviets spotted the German company traversing the southern slope of the MCR from Adzapsh into their rear, they fled without a fight. The vanguards of the German battalion that were to participate in the frontal assault climbed to the pass only three and a half hours after the outflanking unit had taken Sancharo,[109] which means that a single German company drove the Soviet company from the pass. On the same day, another German company[110] attacked the Allashtrakhu pass to the east of Sancharo. The Soviet platoon defending it resisted until two German platoons with heavy machineguns and mortars climbed the rocks towering over the pass and began firing at the defenders from above, after which the Allashtrakhu garrison retreated along the southern slopes of the MCR.[111] The trail across Allashtrakhu was more difficult than that across Sancharo, but it was still accessible to pack animals. The sixty Soviet infantrymen at Tsegerker, the last of the Sancharo group of passes, left their position without a fight, fearing being cut off by the Germans, who began descending from Sancharo and Allashtrakhu.[112] In this way, the 4th Mountain Division acquired five passes leading to the Bzyb valley, four of them passable by horse trains, having lost only two men killed and three wounded, as well as one soldier wounded the next day.[113] Leselidze attributed the 'relative ease' with which the enemy took the Sancharo system of passes to 'the confusion of commanders and the insufficient steadiness' of Soviet soldiers,[114] but since it was he who had allocated only 194 regular infantrymen, armed mainly with rifles, to defend the second most important system of passes against 1,100 German mountain troops, supported by artillery, the blame for this defeat lies primarily at his door. The commanders of the 3rd Rifle Corps alleged that the Germans began their attack 'by dropping paratroopers directly at the [Sancharo] pass and thus succeeded in advancing', but paratroopers would have had to be suicidal to engage in a mission of this sort.[115] Although several Russian authors picked up this tale,[116] German documents are silent on any air drops in the high Caucasus; they probably existed only in the imaginations of those senior Soviet officers, who had to explain the ignominious loss of the Sancharo system of passes to the furious Stavka.[117]

On 25 August, the 2nd Battalion of the 13th German Mountain Regiment began descending from Sancharo and Adzapsh down the southern slopes of the MCR into the Akhei valley leading to the Bzyb River, and on 26 or 27 August it took Pskhu village, close to the confluence of the Akhei and Bzyb rivers, easily driving away the Soviet rearguards.[118] The Germans found an airstrip at Pskhu that could be used for supply by airlift. The 3rd Battalion of the 91st Mountain Regiment descended from Allashtrakhu to the Chamashkha pass, which crossed the ridge separating Akhei from the main Bzyb valley, and one German company[119] took Chamashkha on 26 August, after a brief clash with a Soviet garrison of 125 men[120] reinforced by units that had retreated from the Sancharo, Allashtrakhu, and Tsegerker passes; the Soviet force of about 300 men hastily abandoned the pass.[121] The two German battalions descended to the Bzyb River, planning to cross the last ridge separating them from the Black Sea via the Dou and Achavchar passes and an unnamed pass that the Soviets and the Germans called, respectively, the Gudauta pass and the 1,600 pass.

On 27 August, the Germans found that a Soviet company defended the only bridge across the Bzyb River on the way to these passes; the Soviets had not destroyed the bridge, perhaps because they did not know whether all their units had retreated to the southern bank. On 28 August, the Germans built a small footbridge several kilometres downstream from the main bridge. The 3rd Battalion of the 91st Mountain Regiment crossed the Bzyb and began advancing towards the Gudauta pass but sent one company upstream to outflank the Soviet defenders of the main bridge attacked by the 2nd Battalion of the 13th Mountain Regiment from the front. The Germans took this crucial bridge intact, losing only one man killed and eight wounded in the clash.[122] On 28 August, a shepherd warned the 3rd Battalion of the 91st Mountain Regiment as it was climbing the northern slope of the Gudauta pass that a Soviet battalion was ascending the pass along its southern slope.[123] The Germans rushed to the saddle and occupied it before the Soviets could reach it. They ambushed the Soviet battalion, which was advancing carelessly without scouting screens, and threw it down. According to Soviet data, the battalion lost 189 of its 500 men; 81 of these were missing in action, most likely taken prisoner.[124] The remnants of the battalion fled in disorder, retreating 7 kilometres back. After this impressive victory, the Germans found themselves above the valley leading to the Gudauta resort on the Black Sea coast, 30 kilometres downstream. They took mountain artillery to the pass[125] and planned to take the Achavchar pass, and perhaps the Dou pass, the next day and then to march down towards either Sukhumi or Gudauta, reaching them within a couple of days.

Tiulenev and Leselidze called the loss of the Elbrus, Klukhor, and Sancharo groups of passes 'a disgrace', pointing to the fact that the enemy took them 'easily and quickly with small forces'.[126] According to Colonel Mel'nikov, chief of staff of the 3rd Rifle Corps, 'the passes were surrendered to the enemy almost without a fight'.[127] This happened largely because the Soviet regular infantry found themselves impotent against the well-trained German mountain troops, who could easily manoeuvre across rugged terrain that the Soviets regarded as inaccessible and who were far more effective in combat.

German Flags on Elbrus

In addition to inflicting disgraceful and humiliating defeats on the Soviets, the Germans gained an important propaganda victory. On 14 August, as they were approaching the foothills of the Caucasus, several officers of the 1st Mountain Division proposed to hoist a swastika banner on the summit of Elbrus.[128] The mountaineers who advanced the idea were motivated more by an irresistible passion – the desire to conquer the highest peak of Europe – than by the potential propaganda benefits, even though they probably used propaganda rhetoric to receive permission for the climb. General Konrad, commander of the 49th Mountain Corps, gave only lukewarm support to the idea because it had no military purpose. The Headquarters of Army Group A intercepted radio communications between the 1st Mountain Division and the Headquarters of the 49th Mountain Corps about the proposed adventure and initially prohibited it, reasoning that, given the shortage of forces, the mountain units should not pursue sport endeavours. Only after Konrad promised first to take all the passes in the Elbrus region did Field Marshal Wilhelm List, commander of Army Group A, permit the climb.[129]

On 19 August, a platoon of the High Mountain Company of the 1st Mountain Division began ascending the two-summit Elbrus from Priiut 11, but after a blizzard hit them at an altitude of 4,800 metres only a few men managed to climb to 5,000 metres, and the team had to turn back.[130] On 21 August, seventeen men of the same company and four men of the 4th Mountain Division made a second attempt. Captain Groth from the 1st Mountain Division and Captain Gämmerler from the 4th Mountain Division commanded the climbers, among whom were Karl von Kraus, a participant in expeditions in the Himalayas; a cameraman; and Josef Bauer, a writer employed by the Propaganda Ministry. At that time, they had already acclimatised to this altitude. They began climbing at 3:00 a.m. and were again hit by a blizzard at the same altitude of 4,800 metres, but they continued to ascend and reached the western summit, the higher one, eight hours later. They fixed the swastika banner and the flags of both mountain divisions to a tripod on the summit and made a film about the climb. Their descent was also difficult because they had to struggle through the knee-deep snow that had accumulated during the day. They returned to Priiut 11 after twelve hours of climbing, having lost one man in the blizzard, who, however, arrived at the hotel the next morning without frostbite or injury. Groth reported that the German uniforms were too thin for such extreme conditions and that they would not have been able to climb Elbrus had they not been dressed in the Soviet climbing suits captured at Priiut 11.[131]

General Richard Ruoff, commander of the German Striking Group in the Western Caucasus to which the 49th Mountain Corps belonged, wrote to Konrad: 'The climbing of Elbrus by mountaineers of the 1st and 4th Mountain Divisions led by Captain Groth is an exceptional military and sport achievement, which will be appreciated with time. The German Army and the Motherland are proud of this feat.'[132] Flattered, Lanz asked Hitler's permission to rename Elbrus as Adolf Hitler Peak 'as the highest peak of the future Europe'.[133] However, Albert Speer, the German minister of armaments and war production, described in his memoirs how Hitler exploded with blind rage when he heard the news about the climb: 'For several hours, he [Hitler] was shouting hysterically, as if this episode threatened the entire strategic plan of the Eastern Campaign. Even a week later, he could not calm down and swore at "these crazy mountaineers who deserve court-martial"' because the twenty-one 'ambitious idiots' should have advanced to Sukhumi instead of wasting three days to climb 'this damn mountain'.[134]

Nearly every Russian author attempts to dismiss this climb as unimportant, citing Speer or Kurt von Tippelskirch, who stated correctly that it 'had no tactical, let alone strategic significance'.[135] However, the outburst of the deranged dictator hardly proves that this endeavour was a waste of time. Although it was easier to climb Elbrus than many alpine peaks, the hoisting of the swastika at its top had an important symbolic significance and was an impressive propaganda coup. Lanz emphasised that 'immediate use of the photo material in the German media is in the interest of a strong propagandistic exploitation of the Caucasus operation',[136] especially given the romantic perception of mountaineering that is well rooted in German culture. The documentary about the audacious lads shown all over Germany, along with breathtaking reports published by Bauer in the major German newspapers *Das Reich* and *Frankfurter Zeitung*,[137] portrayed German soldiers as Aryan superheroes fighting not only the 'soulless animality of those narrow-eyed Asians'[138] but also the daunting challenges of nature. The pictures of the climbers in their dramatic surroundings made them national heroes[139] and persuaded the German public that the offensive in the Caucasus was proceeding as planned, when it had actually bogged down. Halder devoted only two lines to the battle on the MCR in his diary, and one of them is 'Our flag has been hoisted on Mount Elbrus',[140] which shows that he, unlike Hitler, understood the propaganda value of this act. The Soviet leaders perceived the climb as a painful humiliation[141] and, as soon as they heard about the German climb, they ordered the 46th Army to replace the German flags with the red banner, although this order could not be fulfilled as long as the Germans occupied the foot of Elbrus.

As a result of the brilliant victories at Elbrus, Klukhor, and Sancharo, the German 49th Mountain Corps occupied, at minimal cost, all the passes it had sought to take between Elbrus and Chmakhara. These easy victories, attained only two weeks after the beginning of actions in the high Caucasus, were gained by the far superior skill of the German mountain troops. Soviet soldiers were stunned by the accuracy of German infantry, mortar, and artillery fire.[142] The Germans knew how to cope with the distance delusion in the mountains and how to adjust their sights when shooting at targets above or below them. Since the Soviets had never conducted shooting exercises in the high mountains, they were usually unable to hit targets located at high angles.[143] Nor were they aware of other aspects of mountain warfare. Soviet officers acknowledged that the Germans were superior in reconnaissance because their 'personnel are mountaineers, most of whom ... belong to the best German climbing clubs. The personnel are well-trained ... They have lightweight climbing gear and uniforms.'[144] The Soviet soldiers could not move across the rugged terrain during their reconnaissance missions, having no mountaineering skills or gear, nor could they climb even gentle slopes in their regular long infantry coats and flat-soled boots. Thus, they never attempted to outflank the enemy in the high mountains, nor did they expect enemy soldiers to be able to outflank them by moving across terrain that a regular infantryman perceived as impassable. In short, the Soviets lost the passes because they were untrained and unequipped to operate in the mountains and because they arrived at the passes late and then idled. Their ignorance of proper defence tactics at such positions and the time it took them to acclimatise to the high altitude made it impossible for them to dig in and conduct a thorough reconnaissance of the area adjacent to their positions to determine potential threats to their flanks. In its conclusions on the actions in August, the TCF diary states that the German soldiers 'acted courageously and resolutely'; 'the enemy ... bypassed the [Soviet] vanguard reconnaissance units, enveloped the main defence positions, broke through them, and took the passes. This happened at Klukhor, Dombai-Ulgen, Sancharo, etc., where the defenders did not offer proper resistance and left the passes ... The actions of the 46th Army at the passes were timid; its soldiers were usually afraid of the enemy.'[145]

Conclusion

Having little knowledge of the high Caucasus, the OKW launched an extremely risky impromptu operation when it sent the 49th Mountain Corps across the MCR. It failed to prepare this operation by staff work, probably hoping that the two understaffed, two-regiment, elite divisions would easily smash the swarms of *Untermenschen* grossly outnumbering these divisions. The plan for the attack of the 49th Mountain Corps had no provisions for the possibility that these *Untermenschen* might refuse to run away. As long as the battle proceeded in the high mountains, the plan worked admirably, perhaps even exceeding the OKW's expectations. The Germans penetrated the Soviet defences as if they were butter, inflicting crushing defeats on their opponents.

Paradoxically, the Soviet defensive operation at the MCR was as impromptu an action as the German attack. As an analytical Soviet report on the battle at the MCR, written in 1943, stated, 'The great theoretician Clausewitz and the great Russian general Suvorov warned that passive defence in the mountains means rout. Our fight at the Caucasus Ridge conclusively proved it.'[146] This report, which examined the causes for the defeats in the high Caucasus, maintained:

> The Headquarters of the 46th Army ... continued to regard the defence of the coast as its priority and did not believe that the enemy could attack across the [Main Caucasus] Ridge. In fact, they started organising the defence of the passes only at the moment when they were directly threatened, and even then they did it in a haphazard and chaotic manner. This happened because of a lack of adequate reconnaissance, the belated occupation of the passes, the absence of communication and logistical plans, the total ignorance of the situation ... at the passes, ... the tactical ignorance of the commanders, and also because the garrisons at the passes had no skills for action in the mountains.[147]

Tiulenev stated in his memoirs: 'Strangely enough, we did not know the MCR and its passes well, having only meagre descriptions and outdated, quite inaccurate maps.'[148] In fact, the Soviet maps were adequate, and detailed descriptions of the passes were available in the tourist library and guidebooks, but none of the TCF or Stavka generals referred to these sources, and none of the regiment commanders and few, if any, battalion commanders made an effort to climb any pass during the summer of 1942 before the German assault. Soviet field officers, as ignorant of mountain warfare as their soldiers and short of skill to navigate and operate in an unfamiliar and frightening environment, could not competently command their men.

Clausewitz began his three chapters on defence in the mountains with the statement 'Mountainous terrain exercises a strong influence on warfare' and ended them with the brief conclusion: 'A general who allows himself to be decisively defeated in an extended mountain position deserves to be court-martialled.'[149] However, it was not only the Soviet field officers who carried responsibility for the defeats in the high Caucasus. The blame for these defeats should be attributed primarily to the General Staff of the Red Army, who ignored all the lessons of the past analysed in imperial and Soviet studies and all practical knowledge acquired in the interwar years. It failed to raise and train proper mountain divisions; sent numerous military and civilian climbers to fight on the plains; but deployed in the high Caucasus older regular infantrymen of a poor physical standard who had never been in the mountains. In turn, the TCF Headquarters spread the 46th Army evenly along the Black Sea coast in anticipation of an illusory German landing and paid no attention to the MCR, while the commanders of the 46th Army failed to develop operational and logistical plans and eschewed literally every point of the *Manual of Mountain Warfare*. Finally, the divisional commanders simply ignored the rational orders about the occupation of the passes and the building of strongholds there, thus destroying the stereotype of how a totalitarian state functions. All these generals were responsible for the disgraceful defeats in the high Caucasus and deserved, in Clausewitz's opinion, to be court-martialled.

At the end of August, the Germans descended from Klukhor down the Sukhumi Military Road and came to a good trail in the Inguri valley that led to the Black Sea. Only 30 kilometres from the coast, they enjoyed a view of the Black Sea from the Gudauta pass, and the swastika was flying over Elbrus. It seemed that the gamble taken by the OKW when it sent the 49th Mountain Corps across the Caucasus was beginning to bear fruit.

5 'NOT A STEP BACK!': THE GERMAN MOUNTAIN CORPS HITS THE WALL

Tam, gde dnem i noch'iu krutiat shkvaly,
Tonut skaly groznye v snegu,
My zakryli prochno perevaly
I ni piadi ne dali vragu.

[Battered by squalls swirling day and night
And surrounded by terrifying cliffs sinking in the snow,
We blocked the mountain passes
And did not yield an inch to the enemy.]

'Baksanskaia'

As soon as the alarmed Stavka learned about the loss of Klukhor on 18 August, it accused the TCF Headquarters of having no knowledge about the events at the MCR and demanded an urgent clarification of the situation.[1] On 20 August, the Stavka issued an order about the defence of the mountain passes, in which it pointed to the obvious fact that 'commanders who believe that the Main Caucasus Ridge is by itself an insurmountable obstacle are gravely mistaken'[2] and told Tiulenev that countering the German advance across the MCR must be the TCF's priority, rather than defending the Black Sea coast against an improbable amphibious landing. This order finally shook the commanders of the 46th Army out of their peacetime lethargy and made them react promptly to the events at the MCR.

Soviet Response to the German Victories at the MCR

Stalinist bureaucratic culture presumed that a response to any disaster had to begin with the exemplary punishment of those who were guilty in the hope that this would urge their successors to act more effectively. The commanders of the TCF understood that they were the prime candidates for such a punishment. Although Tiulenev admitted after the war that the Headquarters of the TCF 'shared responsibility' for the astounding Soviet defeats because they had 'decided unwisely that the passes were impassable', in August 1942 he sought to deflect the Stavka's anger from himself to his direct subordinates – the Headquarters of the 46th Army – who were 'asleep [*prospala*]' in the face of the German advance.[3] As the TCF war diary stated, obviously following Tiulenev's instructions, 'The commander of the 46th Army and his staff and formation commanders devoted more time to various [fantastic] plans than to the fortification of the passes. Garrisons at the passes were too weak to stop the enemy because the commander of the 46th Army and his staff failed to fulfil the orders of the front commander.'[4] Tiulenev also blamed the soldiers defending the passes who 'did not offer stubborn resistance and committed a crime by retreating without an order'.[5]

In turn, the lower-ranking commanders demonstrated vivid imaginations in their search for excuses for their failure to defend the passes, producing a series of pathetic tales intended to explain their defeats. Lieutenant-Colonel Ivan Kantaria, commander of the 394th Rifle Division, responsible for the defence of the Klukhor and Sancharo systems of passes, maintained that German commandos disguised as Soviet soldiers took the passes by surprise; he therefore ordered that 'all those arriving from the north – soldiers and civilians, men and women – whatever their identification papers, be disarmed and passed to the divisional Special Sections. Execute them if they resist.'[6] It is unknown how many people fell victim to this order, but neither Soviet nor German documents provide credible evidence of German commandos at the passes. Another tale related that, after the Germans approached Klukhor and 'all their attempts to break through failed', they drove a flock of sheep in front of them in the hope that the sheep would find an alternative trail, which they did, thus leading the Germans into the rear of the Soviet defenders. A book published in 1981 by the Soviet Academy of Science retells this tale as a fact.[7]

A more serious analysis of the defeats at the MCR pointed to the fact that 'the easy capture of such important, from a tactical point of view, passes of the MCR by the enemy became possible because some commanders had the opinion, absolutely wrong and sometimes criminal, that fortification building was unnecessary'.[8] The TCF war diary acknowledged the superiority of German tactics: 'The enemy mountain troops acted quite boldly. Independent units of well-armed soldiers moved courageously into gaps between our positions and then to our rear.'[9] To implement such tactics, which were prescribed by the Soviet manuals on mountain warfare, small units had to be able to manoeuvre across rugged terrain and operate in concert with each other while fulfilling their independent missions, pursuing a common goal identified by senior commanders. These units, led by junior officers accustomed to taking initiative, had to be well trained and well equipped for mountain warfare and had to have communication means reliable enough to secure the constant co-ordination of actions in the absence of visual contact. The Germans had such units, whereas the Soviets did not, and this was the primary reason for the Soviet fiasco at the passes.

Russian authors traditionally attribute the strengthening of the Soviet defences in the Caucasus to the Stavka's 'clear and detailed directives' issued on 20 August.[10] In fact, these directives were merely vague generalities. Among the eleven passes the Stavka identified as key passes of the Western Caucasus that needed to be defended, only five – Donguz-Orun, Klukhor, Marukh, Tsegerker, and Pseashkha – were relevant in that context, and one had already been lost to the Germans;[11] the Stavka had no knowledge of the other passes, some of which, like Sancharo, were far more important than all the passes that it did mention except for Klukhor. The Stavka did not object to the irrational decision of the TCF to send most of the 20th 'Mountain' Division to the hills and the regular infantry and cavalry to the high mountains, nor did it believe that the better-trained 9th 'Mountain' Division, idling at the Turkish border, should engage the Germans advancing across the Caucasus. By the time the TCF sent the first clear directives to its divisions on 23 August,[12] the 46th Army was facing a serious crisis: the Germans had already taken all the key passes in the Klukhor and Elbrus regions; established their major operational base at Priiut 11; occupied the Adzapsh pass, the first of the Sancharo group; and begun descending down the Sukhumi Military Road towards the

Black Sea and to the rear of the armies that opposed the major German thrust along the coast.

However, the Stavka's intervention, although belated and often incompetent, did generate a vigorous response to the German attack. The TCF reacted to the crushing defeats at the passes with a series of measures aimed to first terminate the German offensive and then throw the Germans back to the North Caucasus. Some of these measures advanced the desired objectives, while others, frustrated by poor execution, came to naught. Still others were designed merely to demonstrate zeal and thus placate furious superiors.

The first response of the 46th Army was typical of Soviet military culture at that time: its commanders sought to counter the enemy's tactical expertise with sheer numbers. As Mikhail Gioev, a junior officer who had fought at the MCR, recalled, 'Having failed in many respects, the army commander [Sergatskov] took quite desperate measures to fulfil the orders of the front commander at any cost – literally at any cost.' The commanders 'tried to correct [their] errors and save the situation at the passes by sacrificing hundreds and thousands of soldiers and ignoring the casualties'.[13] As soon as the Headquarters of the 46th Army heard about the fall of Klukhor, they sent masses of untrained soldiers to the mountains without even attempting to equip them for mountain warfare or to organise logistics.

The method the TCF chose to distribute manpower in the high mountains undermined the cohesion of Soviet defenders. In response to the surprise German attack across the Caucasus, TCF commanders first dispersed whatever divisions they could scramble in small units across great distances, and then, when it turned out that these forces were insufficient, they again dispersed the formations sent as reinforcements across a broad front. The 394th Rifle Division defended a front of 120 kilometres from Klukhor to Sancharo, mixed with the units of the 63rd Cavalry Division. When the 155th Rifle Brigade arrived to reinforce the 394th Rifle Division, it was also dispersed between the Marukh and Klukhor passes. Components of these large formations were further mixed with a host of small detachments hastily salvaged to plug numerous holes in the front: units organised from various stragglers who had retreated across the Caucasus, NKVD and frontier guard battalions, cadet and militia companies, and independent regiments and battalions detached from divisions that stayed far away from the MCR. The hotchpotch formations assembled from such a variety of units with uncertain subordination patterns, varying service cultures, and commanders who did not know each other naturally lacked cohesion, which was further reduced by the quick turnover of personnel caused by the high casualty rate.

Unsure whether the commanders of the TCF could handle the defence of the MCR even with these reinforcements, Stalin sent Lavrentii Beria, a member of the State Defence Committee and the people's commissar of the interior, to the Caucasus with orders to get the situation under control. Beria arrived on 22 August[14] with a team of top police generals: Bogdan Kobulov, his deputy; Ivan Serov, another deputy; Solomon Mil'shtein, deputy head of the Main Intelligence Directorate; Lev Vlodzimirskii, head of the Prime Cases Investigation Unit; and Lavrentii Tsanava, deputy head of the Special Sections Directorate.[15] Beria attached these generals, as well as a number of Georgian civilian party leaders, to the headquarters of the formations that were to defend the MCR, as representatives of the TCF military council. As he explained, the police officers were 'to serve as pushers [*tolkachi*]' whose objective was to facilitate the solution of identified problems leaning on their broad authority, while the Georgian party leaders were to be intermediaries between the military and civilian administrations in the organisation of logistics.[16] Along with the police generals tasked to enforce the 'victory regardless of cost' doctrine but unfamiliar with military matters, Beria added to his team General Pavel Bodin, deputy chief of the Red Army General Staff, and Colonel Sergei Shtemenko, future chief of the Operations Section of the General Staff – both of them among the ablest Soviet staff officers. Beria and most of his team stayed in the Caucasus from 22 August to mid September, although some team members continued to monitor actions until their end in late October.

The officers who wrote *post factum* about the actions at the MCR offered only polarised accounts of Beria's contribution to the defence of the Caucasus, with the date of Beria's arrest in 1953 serving as the 'great divide' in their opinions. At that time, the Soviet General Staff released a memo claiming that 'Beria, enemy of the people and of the party, sought to primarily weaken the Soviet defences at the MCR passes in order to open them for the German-fascist army' and to 'pass the Baku oil to the imperialist states'.[17] Despite the obvious absurdity of this claim, it shaped subsequent interpretations. According to the officers who testified against Beria during his trial or assessed his actions after his fall, such as Tiulenev, Grechko, and Shtemenko, Beria instilled fear and fuelled mistrust in the Headquarters of the TCF and the 46th Army and undermined the command system by creating a parallel structure dominated by police officers who were ignorant of strategy and tactics but enjoyed broad authority.[18] Tiulenev, who held the primary responsibility for the defeats at the passes, claimed that Beria 'inflicted great harm on the defence of the MCR. During his two-week stay, Beria and his faithful henchmen executed officers without a trial, disorganised the work of the TCF Headquarters, and baselessly sacked commanders'.[19] In contrast, an analytical report written a year after the battle of the Caucasus attributed the turning of the tables at the MCR mainly to structural reforms, supply arrangements, and the order-enforcement practice introduced by Beria's team.[20] Although the eulogy of Beria, one of the strongest men of the Stalinist administration, must be taken with a grain of salt, it is clear that his team identified many flaws in the functioning of the TCF and addressed them with various degrees of success.

The documents of the TCF refute the stereotypical image of Beria as a trigger-happy policeman who viewed executions as the main means of problem solving. In fact, Tiulenev and his direct subordinates showed more enthusiasm for this method of discipline enforcement than did Beria. TCF commanders routinely applied the draconian policies ordered by Stalin even before the Germans arrived in the Caucasus. On 31 July, A. Khromov, head of the TCF Political Directorate, wrote to all local commissars: 'Please ensure that every soldier be informed in his own language of the order of Comrade Stalin No. 227 of 28 July 1942 ... Resolutely unmask and destroy cowards and panic-mongers as enemy accomplices and traitors.'[21] Such orders usually resulted in numerous arbitrary executions meant simply to demonstrate zeal rather than produce tangible results. On 15, 17, and 21 August, when Beria was still in Moscow, Ivan Kantaria, commander of the 394th Rifle Division, issued several similar orders: 'Every unit [of the 394th Rifle Division] must have a blocking section ... panic-mongers and cowards must be summarily executed at the slightest attempt to ignore orders.'[22] The two other divisions defending the high Caucasus – the 20th 'Mountain' Division and the 63rd Cavalry Division – followed suit and also raised blocking units with the same purpose.[23] The public executions of 'cowards, panic-mongers, those fleeing from the battle-field', and those caught with self-inflicted wounds began in earnest on

20 August, before Beria's arrival in the Caucasus, and continued after his departure until the end of the actions at the MCR; the blocking units also operated from the beginning to the end of the battle.[24] On 21 August, Tiulenev proudly reported to the Red Army General Staff: 'After I ordered severe measures against panic-mongers, sixteen men were executed.'[25] In contrast, no researcher has found a single case of execution ordered by Beria while he was in the Caucasus.

Beria's team undertook a number of necessary steps to strengthen the defence of the Caucasus and initiated vigorous, but not always the wisest, responses to the numerous and grave problems faced by the TCF. Although at first Beria failed to announce the scope of his team's authority, a failure that increased the chaos that had reigned in the TCF Headquarters since the beginning of the German offensive across the MCR, he soon explained that the 'representatives of the Front Military Council affiliated with NKVD ... do not intervene in operational matters'; they probably continued to intervene, but less frequently.[26] Their main mission was to report the flaws they spotted in the formations to which they were attached and to offer suggestions as to how to correct these flaws. Since the powers of Beria and his team extended beyond the purely military sphere, they sometimes proposed solutions that the generals could not even imagine.

Beria's first action was reshuffling the Headquarters of the 46th Army. Between 23 and 28 August, the Stavka, on Beria's request, replaced Sergatskov with Leselidze, commander of the 3rd Rifle Corps, and gave Leselidze a new deputy with a sound combat record – the stern Colonel Ivan Piiashev, former commander of the 7th NKVD Motorised Division. The Stavka also replaced Aleksei Subbotin, chief of staff of the TCF, with General Bodin, and Beria himself demoted several commanders who had conclusively proven their ineptitude.[27] Sergatskov admitted, in conversation with his subordinates, 'We failed [*promorgali*] to occupy the passes on time.'[28] In fact, Sergatskov, Subbotin, Tiulenev, and Leselidze were all equally responsible for the loss of the passes and deserved to be demoted, yet Beria gave Tiulenev and Leselidze a second chance to prove their worth. He made no political accusations, and none of the dismissed commanders suffered harsher consequences than demotion to lower positions within the TCF.[29] The reshuffling of the 46th Army Headquarters was based not on whim, as some Soviet generals implied,[30] but on a rational attempt to improve the command. To what extent this attempt succeeded is open to

Figure 5.1 Lavrentii Beria, People's Commissar of the Interior.
Credit: RGAKFD

debate, but subsequent events showed that the TCF benefited from the replacement of Subbotin by Bodin, and Piiashev, with his bulldog grip on the assigned mission, proved adequate for the job.

Beria's team spotted several serious problems in the functioning of the TCF that had been undetected by military professionals, and they offered some viable solutions. First, they found that, since the attention of the front commanders had been focused on the protection of the sea coast against a German landing, 'everyone and nobody is responsible for [the defence of] the passes'.[31] On 23 August, the day after his arrival, Beria organised the Operations Group for the Defence of the MCR Passes (OG), a body focusing squarely on operations at the MCR and directly subordinate to Tiulenev, and appointed General Ivan Alekseevich Petrov as its commander.[32] Although the Red Army General Staff maintained during Beria's trial that Petrov, an NKVD general who had made his career as a frontier guard, had 'insufficient military experience',[33] the agency he supervised considerably improved the co-ordination among the formations defending the MCR.

Beria saw the inadequate communication system as the main flaw of Soviet command and control at the MCR and attempted to radically improve it. Because of the absence of stable radio contact between garrisons at the passes and the Headquarters of the 46th Army, and the failure to establish alternative means of communications, the commanders did not know the current situation at the MCR or even the location of their units. The OG pressed commanders to provide information as quickly as possible 'on every unit at the passes down to a platoon', but this was hardly possible with the available communication means.[34] To solve this problem, Beria requested 110 radios for the divisions defending the passes and assigned ten signals officers, as the OG's representatives, to units defending the passes; these officers were personally responsible for reliable, steady communications with the Headquarters of the 46th Army.[35]

The OG undertook a prompt effort to educate the TCF officers in the theory of mountain warfare. Since few of them had read the 1940 *Manual on Mountain Warfare* before the beginning of the battle of the Caucasus, the TCF printed, on 15 September, a surrogate *Concise Manual on Mountain Warfare*.[36] Apart from the odd instruction to end attacks with a bayonet charge, dating to Suvorov's times,[37] the manual, issued in a large number of copies, provided a considerable amount of information on the basics of mountain warfare. The TCF began distributing the manual among formations fighting at the MCR on 27 September;[38] it must have reached the front line at best in the second week of October, two weeks before the end of actions. On 6 October, General Bodin, made an urgent request for the printing of the analytical study of the nineteenth-century wars in the Caucasus written in 1940 by Nikolai Korsun. Five hundred copies were printed; the study was then distributed among the units deployed in the high Caucasus.[39]

The first reports from the passes described how the inability of soldiers to move across rugged terrain undermined Soviet tactics: 'The actions at Klukhor showed that our units, fearing difficulties, do not occupy rocks and limit their positions to plateaus. The Germans exploit this flaw; they move across rocks and strike on our flanks and from above and thus attain success.'[40] Beria was perhaps the first senior commander in the Caucasus to appreciate climbing training as a component of mountain warfare, and he attempted to accelerate it. The TCF started to search for climbers in its formations and elsewhere in order to acquire instructors who could teach soldiers. On 28 August, most likely under pressure from Beria, Tiulenev ordered the enforcement of orders issued back in June about supplying soldiers with climbing gear kept in the depots of the 46th Army.[41] Beria found that proper reconnaissance gave the Germans a solid tactical edge over the Soviet defenders, who were unable to climb steep slopes. He could not quickly improve field reconnaissance, but regular air reconnaissance flights began in late August.[42] Beria also requested ground assault missions, and Soviet aircraft engaged in frequent attacks on Germans at the MCR.[43] Beria was the first senior commander to realise that, in the high mountains, soldiers' rations should be light but calorie-dense, and he requested 90 tonnes of condensed milk and 90 tonnes of chocolate directly from Moscow.[44]

In short, under pressure from the OG, the TCF promptly undertook several important steps to strengthen Soviet defences. Along with these rational attempts to improve the Soviets' ability to fight in the mountains, the TCF made several unwise decisions, seeking to turn the tables 'at any cost'. Its commanders responded to the enemy offensive as if the actions were taking place on the plains, where the basic strategy during a retreat presumed the destruction of railways, bridges, and telegraph lines. None of those existed in the high mountains, but the Soviet commanders still sought to slow down the enemy, or even terminate the attempts to cross the Caucasus, through a series of demolitions.

The Headquarters of the 46th Army began planning these works on 26 June 1942 when it issued a directive entitled 'On Demolitions, Strongholds and Artificial Obstacles at MCR Passes', which ordered the destruction of mountain trails on the northern slopes.[45] Two days later, General Georgii Zakharov, chief of staff of the North Caucasian Front, proposed an 'innovative' approach to mountain warfare. He wrote: 'I believe it would be wise ... to close all the passes across the MCR between Elbrus and Lazarevskoe ... [Engineering] works should begin immediately.'[46] The commanders of the TCF adopted the idea. They believed that it was possible to 'close' passes through their demolition, as if these were railway bridges that could be destroyed with well-placed explosives.

On 3 August, Tiulenev gave a straightforward directive 'to block up the passes unoccupied by [Soviet] units by their demolition'.[47] On 7 August, Sergatskov ordered the 3rd Rifle Corps to 'make the passes impassable for any type of units' along both main and minor trails 'by bringing down . . . large rocks or snow and ice masses mechanically or by explosions'.[48] The TCF commanders began viewing the demolitions as a primary means of mountain warfare even though Levandovskii's experiments in 1936 had failed to provide encouraging results in this regard. The sceptical engineers reported that 'most demolitions were ineffective',[49] which made the commanders question the implementation rather than the idea of blocking the enemy advance via demolitions. Had they ever visited the mountains, they would have known that no amount of explosives could block the infantry, or even pack animals, from advancing along the mountain trails and through the passes. However, since none of them had ever seen the passes, even from a distance through binoculars, these commanders believed, or pretended to believe, that demolitions worked well. The appetite for this 'miracle weapon' rose along with the feeling of impotence in the face of the German offensive, which seemed unstoppable. The string of bizarre orders issued at all levels of the Soviet command structure gives the impression of a virus-caused collective madness. On 20 August, Stalin, Beria, Bodin, and Shtemenko also succumbed to this mass psychosis and joined the choir by approving the demolition orders.[50] The Stavka ordered Sergatskov to 'demolish and block up' with rocks nineteen mountain passes and four river valleys; in addition, they were to make the mountain trails 'unusable for dozens of kilometres'.[51] On 23 August, Tiulenev added five more passes to the demolition list; he also contributed to military thought by ordering the demolition of the Gvandra Mountain and the Tsanner Glacier.[52]

These orders, betraying a panicked reaction to the Germans' swift progress, made as little sense as Stalin's hysterical order of July 1941 calling on partisans to blow up highways and burn forests.[53] Yet, senior officers of the TCF reported that Tsegerker, Sancharo, and five other passes where no action had ever taken place 'have already been demolished'; Pseashkha, Aishkha, and two others were about to be demolished; and Belorechenskii, Donguz-Orun, and Becho were almost ready for demolition.[54]

The comforting field reports misdirected the defence strategy because they implied that the TCF could switch its attention from the 'demolished' passes to others. This self-delusion continued even after information began arriving revealing that 'after the demolitions it was still possible to bypass demolished places without much effort'.[55] Despite these revelations, on 11 September, long after the Germans had taken most of the passes they planned to take – including Sancharo and

Tsegerker, which had reportedly been 'demolished' – and the Soviet commanders had received hard proof that the strenuous demolition efforts had borne no fruit, Tiulenev and Bodin ordered the 46th Army again 'to demolish the passes that have not yet been blown up during the retreat of [the Soviet] units from the north'.[56] After Stalin's infamous 'Not a Step Back' order of 28 July 1942, which interpreted failure to follow every instruction to the letter as treason, engineers, pressed hard by Headquarters, had no option but to blindly follow the directives. They requested enormous quantities of explosives and blew up rocks, knowing that these works were futile. The Soviets carried tonnes of explosives to the passes they still held and to the southern slopes of the passes that had been lost to the Germans: 300 kilograms to Sancharo and the same amount to Tsegerker, 600 to Belorechenskii, 700 to Aishkha, 900 to Pseashkha, 1,100 to Becho, 1,200 to Klukhor and the same amount to Nakhar and Marukh, and 3,100 to Donguz-Orun.[57] These explosives were carried on horseback along steep mountain trails across distances exceeding 100 kilometres, which overstrained Soviet logistics and consumed much of the supply trains' capacity. The engineers wasted the lion's share of these explosives for 'the demolition of trails and passes' instead of using them for building tiered strongholds on the northern slopes of the MCR, as the *Manual on Mountain Warfare* instructed.

The only person who questioned this strategy was Aleksandr Kvlividze, the NKVD head in South Ossetia. On 20 August 1942, he wrote a memorandum in which he called the idea of 'destroy[ing] all trails to the passes by blowing them up' absurd – first, because the destruction of a trail, even 'for a length of just 4 or 5 kilometres, would require dozens of tonnes of ammonal', and, second, because it was 'pointless because they [the trails] would be easily repaired'. He called such a strategy 'a bungle of the [TCF] Headquarters, which has no idea of the landscape of the ridge'.[58] This local police officer hit the nail on the head; he turned out to be more insightful than the commanders of the 46th Army and the TCF, and even the General Staff of the Red Army, only because he, unlike these commanders, knew the terrain.

After the end of actions at the MCR, Colonel Olev – a representative of the General Staff of the Red Army with the 351st Rifle Division, which operated in the North Caucasus – confirmed that the orders to demolish all the trails leading to the northern slopes of the passes through the MCR could not be fulfilled in principle because 'a broad network of trails exists at the northern slopes; ... they are fairly easy to navigate and need an enormous amount of explosives for reliable demolition: 300 to 350 tonnes at the front of the 351st Rifle Division alone'.[59] Yet long after the war, Tiulenev, the most ardent advocate of 'pass demolition', proudly cited his demolition orders in his memoirs as a proper response to the German offensive, and Andrei Grechko, the general who commanded the 47th Army in the North Caucasus, regretted that 'engineers could not fulfil the entire volume of planned demolitions and had to limit themselves to the destruction of [only] some stretches of trail'.[60]

The exotic battle environment enticed those inexperienced in mountain warfare to rely on exotic weapons, grossly overestimating their efficacy. During the battle of Shipka, it was stone-throwers; during the campaign in the Beskids in 1915, Russians rolled barrels filled with explosives, iron junk, and stones downhill, hoping to horrify the Austrians.[61] During the battle of the Caucasus, the Soviet generals returned to the stone-thrower, a weapon of desperation,[62] even though those who had tried stone-throwers on Shipka assessed their effectiveness as zero. Stone-throwers had to be set 'in narrows in order to destroy enemy manpower and block the way'.[63] Colonel Grigor'evskii explained that each stone-thrower contained '43 kilograms of explosives and 2 cubic metres of stones. The fuse is set at 15 seconds ... With the approach of the enemy ... specially selected people ... will fire the stone-throwers.'[64] A series of manmade volcanos were supposed to shower the enemy with boulders at a range of 500 metres. In addition, *Instructions on the Active Defence of the Passes*, written on 25 August by Tiulenev, assured engineers that 'explosives, if placed correctly, can produce stone avalanches that hit the enemy'.[65] Soviet documents give no credible reports that stone-throwers were ever fired or that artificial avalanches ever hit the Germans. Yet, efforts to set stone-throwers, demolish trails, and provoke avalanches continued until early October.[66]

The TCF supplemented these efforts, intended simply to demonstrate vigour to angry superiors rather than block the enemy, with other futile and time-consuming engineering works. Following the Red Army Field Manual of 1939,[67] written for operations on the plains, Soviet commanders built anti-tank defences. The 46th Army laid down 10,000 anti-tank mines in the valleys leading to the MCR.[68] These mines, weighing 10 kilograms each, were totally useless because not even a two-wheeled horse-drawn light carriage, let alone a tank or a truck, could ride through any of the passes in the area of the offensive of the 49th Mountain Corps, and an anti-tank mine would not explode if a man stepped on it. In addition, the Soviets dragged sixty anti-tank rifles to the Elbrus region, forty-three to the Klukhor region, sixty-one to the Sancharo region, and seventeen to the Marukh region, along with their heavy ammunition, and fifty Molotov cocktails to the top of each pass,[69] even though no tank could possibly come even close to any of the passes.

The Germans were amused when they found Soviet anti-tank weapons at the passes.[70] They invested their time and effort in building tiered fortifications, thus making their positions nearly impregnable. If they had to retreat, they often planted hundreds of anti-personnel mines,[71] which were ten to twenty times lighter than the Soviet anti-tank mines and much more useful; they also set inventive booby traps. A Soviet report confirms that many soldiers were blown up by these mines, which made the rest cautious and considerably slowed down and constrained Soviet attacks. In contrast, the report states, Soviet 'anti-personnel minefields and booby traps were almost absent'.[72]

Thus, the Soviet attempts to demolish passes, glaciers, and mountains, block river valleys with rocks, and set anti-tank minefields and stone-throwers wasted time and explosives, misallocated engineering effort and resources, overstrained the inevitably weak logistics, and diverted the limited manpower from urgent fortification works. By 18 September, a month after the beginning of the battle at the MCR, no fortifications existed at Donguz-Orun or Becho, or on the southern slopes of the Sancharo system of passes.[73]

Termination of the German Offensive

Among all the measures taken by the Red Army in the aftermath of the defeat at the passes, the prompt sending of reinforcements, large but totally untrained for mountain warfare, played the most important role. The TCF decided to concentrate on Hirschfeld's half-battalion, which had meanwhile been reinforced to full strength and was soon joined by another battalion,[74] a hotchpotch force equalling eleven rifle battalions.[75] Soviet reinforcements rushed up the Sukhumi Military Road towards Klukhor. Among them was the 121st Regiment detached from the 9th 'Mountain' Division, deployed near Batumi.[76] This was the only component of Soviet 'mountain' force that was to operate between Elbrus and the Sancharo system of passes throughout the active stage of the battle at the MCR.

A road accessible to motor vehicles led from the sea coast to Zakharovka village, 80 kilometres from Klukhor, after which a cart road and then a broad foot trail continued to the pass. It took the first units sent from Sukhumi five days to assemble at Zakharovka and then reach the narrow Klych valley leading to Klukhor. The Training Battalion of the 394th Rifle Division suffered horrendous casualties, but its fighting retreat held Hirschfeld's force long enough to allow Soviet reinforcements to arrive before the Germans could exit the Klych valley into the broader Kodori valley, where they would have had more manoeuvrability. On 22 August, the vanguard units of these reinforcements met the Germans who had descended down the Klych valley, about 10 kilometres south of the pass at an altitude of 1,200 metres.[77] The pitched battle continued for several days. The Germans advanced two more kilometres on 25 August, meeting increasing Soviet resistance, which ultimately terminated the German attack.[78] The Headquarters of the 394th Rifle Division finally arrived at Gvandra village, near the mouth of the Klych River, and could then command the Soviet regiments blocking the Klych valley. The Germans noticed the increasing staunchness of the Soviet soldiers; it is open to debate whether this can be attributed to the draconian measures aimed to restore discipline or to the fact that these soldiers felt more comfortable in the forests at lower elevations than at the windy, bare passes surrounded by rocks permanently covered with snow.[79]

During the battle in the Klych valley, the Germans felt for the first time the impact of their failure to address potential logistical problems while planning the offensive across the Caucasus. Their heavy weapons – trench mortars and mountain guns – had a meagre ammunition supply. Soviet logistics were much easier: the Sukhumi Military Road was broad enough to allow horse relays between Zakharovka and the mouth of the Klych River. The Soviets promptly brought a light artillery battery with plenty of ammunition to the mouth of the Klych and then moved it slightly up the Klych valley, as far as the trail allowed. This battery engaged the Germans during the battle in the Klych valley on a daily basis, aided by the Red Air Force.[80]

An entry of the 46th Army war diary covering the period from 1 May to 9 September 1942 recorded the almost total absence of the German Air Force over the MCR.[81] This left the Red Air Force to operate uncontested; it frequently attacked German positions at the passes and on the southern slopes of the MCR. Even though Soviet pilots were no better trained to operate in mountains than their infantry comrades, the TCF had many obsolete I-15 and I-153 biplanes, which turned out to be the only airplanes able to attack enemy positions from a low altitude in narrow gorges inaccessible to fast but less manoeuvrable modern planes. The air force partially compensated for the absence of mountain artillery in areas inaccessible to regular artillery,[82] at times inflicting heavy losses on the Germans and even heavier damage on their supply trains.[83] The Soviet Black Sea Naval Air Force alone dropped 1,000 bombs in the Sancharo and Marukh regions.[84] Soviet field reports show that the German Air Force was incapable of doing anything similar; its actions over the MCR were limited to rare reconnaissance flights by lone aircraft that occasionally dropped one or two small bombs.[85] Perhaps even more important than the ground attacks was the logistical service performed by the Red Air Force. The large fleet of trainers that could take off from short landing strips evacuated wounded soldiers and delivered food, ammunition, and even forage to the high mountains devoid of vegetation, thus considerably extending the capacity of horse-based logistics.[86] In contrast, the Luftwaffe played no role in supplying German units across the MCR. There was a small airstrip near Pskhu village, the only one in the area of operation of the 49th Mountain Corps on the southern slopes of the ridge, but no landing of any German aircraft at this strip was ever recorded. With the number of German casualties mounting during the pitched battle in the Klych valley, the Germans finally realised how hard it was to transfer severely wounded soldiers to hospitals back across the MCR. Some could be transported on horseback, but others had to be carried on stretchers for dozens of kilometres along steep mountain trails, an agonising experience for both the wounded and the stretcher bearers.[87]

The quickly aggravating logistical situation made it clear to the Germans that they could not fight a prolonged pitched battle on the southern slopes of the MCR. In an attempt to break the stalemate, they undertook a stealthy strike on the night of 26 August by sending one battalion along the western steep slopes of the Klych valley to outflank the Soviet 815th Regiment, which was facing another

German battalion.[88] The outflanking battalion sneaked unnoticed to the Soviet rear and arrived at the confluence of the Klych and Gvandra Rivers, 3 kilometres downstream from the front line and 2 kilometres upstream from the Headquarters of the 394th Rifle Division in Gvandra village, where the Germans ran into a Soviet cavalry regiment[89] as it was descending through the Gvandra valley. The cavalrymen were so stunned to see Germans in the Soviet rear that the entire regiment fled back up the valley, making no attempt to engage them.[90] On the morning of 27 August, the Germans proceeded towards the Headquarters of the 394th Rifle Division but met the 121st 'Mountain' Regiment, which had arrived at Gvandra village the night before.[91] This regiment drove the Germans back the way they had come and surrounded one of their companies,[92] which subsequently lost many soldiers within two days.[93]

This was the first small Soviet victory at the MCR following a long series of disgraceful defeats. Even in these lower mountains in the Klych valley, the German mountain troops fought far more effectively than the Soviets, despite their great numerical inferiority. The total number of casualties of the 1st Mountain Division during the period when it attempted to break through Soviet lines in the Klych valley between 23 August and 3 September was 93 men dead, 314 wounded, and 31 missing in action,[94] including the casualties suffered at the approaches to the Marukh pass. Soviet casualties in the Klych valley alone for the same period were 1,506 men killed and wounded and an unknown number of missing in action.[95]

Although the Germans fared far better overall, the heavy casualties suffered by the company that was surrounded in the Klych valley shocked German commanders, who had been euphoric after the easy victories in the high mountains. The Germans admitted that their force in the Klych valley could not break the steadfast Soviet resistance and ordered them to go on the defensive. The commanders of the 49th Mountain Corps had informed the Headquarters of Army Group A that they needed one more mountain division to make a break to the coast in this direction but, even if this division had arrived, the available logistical resources would not have allowed its supply.[96] The decision to go on the defensive signalled the end of the German attempt to break along the Sukhumi Military Road.

Meanwhile, Stettner's soldiers, enjoying the view of the Black Sea from the top of the Gudauta pass, found their way blocked by the far superior force which the Soviets called interchangeably the Piiashev Group and the Sancharo Group.[97] Carrying only a one-day food ration but supplied by daily air drops, Colonel Ivan Piiashev quickly moved his forces north towards the Achavchar and Dou passes, which are east of the Gudauta pass, and occupied these two passes before the Germans could.[98] Piiashev turned back the Soviet 25th Frontier Guard Regiment and the Assembled Regiment rushing from the North Caucasus to the Black Sea resorts 'for rest' and deployed them at Achavchar and Dou.[99]

Stettner could not advance down to Gudauta as long as Piiashev occupied Achavchar and Dou because his units sought to descend from these passes to the Bzyb River only 4 kilometres below and cut off the German supply lines. Stettner began contemplating an assault on Achavchar. The manual-prescribed tactics presumed a combination of a frontal attack and an outflanking strike to the rear of the Achavchar defenders from the Gudauta pass. After the outflanking march failed because the German soldiers could not force their way through thick and thorny subtropical vegetation, Stettner eschewed the frontal attack.[100] He could not proceed to the coast with the available forces and asked for reinforcements.

However, the 4th Mountain Division had already deployed elsewhere the units that could have reinforced Stettner. On 26 August, Konrad made a serious mistake: instead of concentrating the available forces of the 4th Mountain Division in the Sancharo region and advancing through the passes already taken towards Gudauta and Sukhumi, he split the division, sending a large formation to take the Aishkha and Pseashkha passes leading to the Mzymta River, which flows into the Black Sea in the region of Adler. These passes were 75 kilometres away from the Sancharo system of passes.[101] The two-battalion formation,[102] commanded by Colonel Johann Buchner, was to march from the Bolshaia Laba valley via the Umpyrskii pass (2,522 m) into the Malaia Laba valley leading to the Aishkha pass (Map 4.4). Afterwards, it was to detach a part of its forces, which would cross the Alous pass (1,929 m) into the Urushten valley and then proceed up to the Pseashkha pass. By sending the Buchner Group to that region, the Headquarters of the 49th Mountain Corps extended the front of its operation to more than 200 kilometres, from Elbrus to Pseashkha.[103] This front lay across rugged terrain devoid of roads, which promised a logistical nightmare and grave co-ordination problems. This decision, prompted by 'dizziness with success' during the swift advance across the MCR, considerably weakened the striking force of the 4th Mountain Division at a crucial moment.

The 46th Army placed one reinforced company of the 174th 'Mountain' Regiment, with a total strength of 299 men, at Pseashkha and its northern approaches in the Urushten valley and three companies of the 174th 'Mountain' Regiment and a cavalry squadron, with a total strength of 651 men, at Aishkha.[104] One vanguard company of the latter force stayed at the Umpyrskii pass and another at the northern approaches to Aishkha in the Malaia Laba valley.[105] On 29 August, the Buchner Group reached Umpyrskii on its way to the Malaia Laba valley. Buchner reported that the garrison of the pass offered fierce resistance despite great inferiority in numbers and firepower, and repelled one attack, but by the end of the day the Germans had destroyed half of the Soviet defenders and driven the rest away.[106]

In the first days of September, the Buchner Group, minus one company left to protect its right flank near the Alous pass, began heading up the Malaia Laba valley towards Aishkha. However, between 2 and 6 September, one Soviet vanguard company and the remnants of Umpyrskii's defenders effectively pinned down the Buchner Group about 20 kilometres northeast of Aishkha.[107] German documents are vague on the reasons why Buchner could not overcome a handful of Soviets apart from pointing to persistent attacks by 'numerous enemy bands' on his supply trains. These attacks by Red Army regulars, belonging to formations dispersed by the Germans in the North Caucasus, inflicted serious casualties and made Buchner detach large units for the protection of his supply route, thus debilitating his formation.[108] The vigorous counterattack launched by the Soviet inferior force on 3 September against Buchner's vanguard, demonstrating the resolve of the defenders, was the last straw: on that day, Buchner reported that he could not advance further, and the Headquarters of the 49th Mountain Corps approved his decision to terminate the offensive.[109] Soviet commanders referred to the two companies that repelled Buchner as 'heroic', and rightly so.[110] The actions in this region stopped for most of September.

The Soviet Raids: The First Try Is Bound to Be a Flop

Despite this success at the northern approaches to Aishkha, the TCF was facing a severe crisis in late August of 1942. The German 49th

Mountain Corps had easily taken all the passes it planned to take, except Aishkha, and occupied positions at good trails descending to the Black Sea. The TCF Headquarters planned to terminate the German advance through stubborn defence, while simultaneously undermining the striking power of the 49th Mountain Corps by intercepting its long and vulnerable communication lines. By this time, the Stavka had already realised that the actions of partisans against enemy communications had considerably hampered the supplies of German front-line formations. The North Caucasus was good terrain for guerrilla action but the Stavka was unable to employ partisans for the interception of German communications there effectively because of their small number. No significant pro-Soviet resistance occurred in the North Caucasus for two reasons: first, local party bureaucrats – such as Mikhail Suslov, party secretary of the Stavropol region – were too inept to organise it and, second, they could not find enough volunteers. By 1 October 1942, when the Germans had overrun the Krasnodar and Stavropol regions, the Kabardin-Balkar Autonomous Republic, and most of North Ossetia, only 13 partisan bands with 816 men were reportedly operating in the entire occupied portion of the North Caucasus; their actual number was probably even lower.[111] The collaborator militia outnumbered the partisans: in the Kabardin-Balkar Autonomous Republic alone, 600 men joined its ranks. In the Karachai Autonomous Region, the militia kept the few Red partisans who operated there away from villages, thus isolating them from the local population.[112] The TCF had no option but to deploy commandos and conventional infantry for actions intended to disrupt enemy communications.

Between 19 and 26 August, Tiulenev contemplated dropping several paratroop companies to the rear of the 49th Mountain Corps: two of them would land near Teberda, and the third in the Bzyb valley near Pskhu; these paratroopers would cut the supply lines of the 1st and the 4th Mountain Divisions. A fourth company would 'close the [Bolshaia] Laba valley by explosion'; Tiulenev did not specify how the hundreds of tonnes of explosives would be delivered to that region for this mission.[113] The TCF soon abandoned these schemes. Instead, its headquarters developed a plan that presumed a three-pronged offensive converging at Teberda from the parallel eastern and western valleys (Map 5.1). The offensive from the west was to be performed by two columns. A half-battalion of conventional infantry was to cross the MCR via the Ptysh pass into the Teberda valley.[114] Ptysh, the western

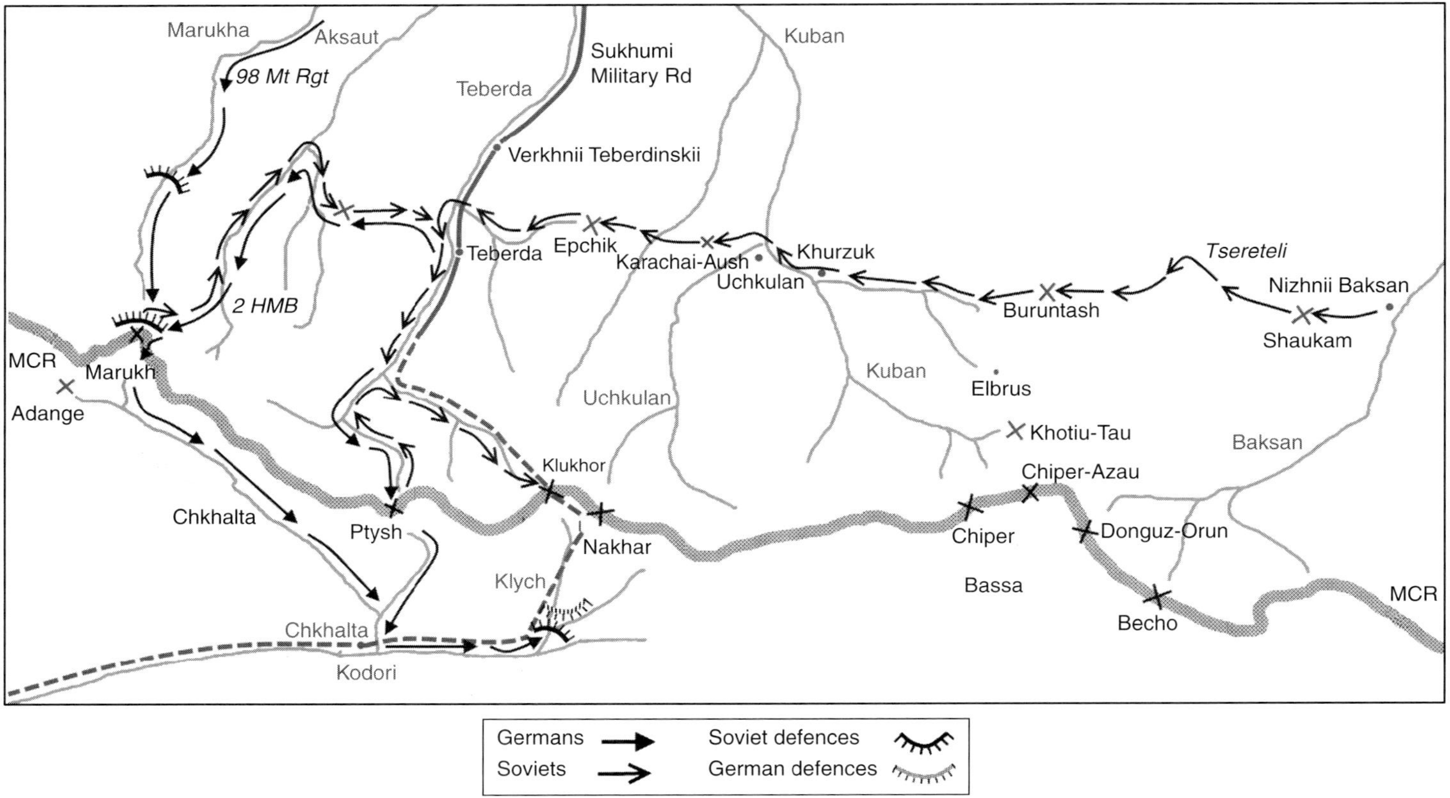

Map 5.1 Soviet and German plans for raids across the Main Caucasus Ridge

neighbour of Klukhor, was garrisoned by a Soviet section. The second column advancing from the west was to be much larger: two regiments were to cross the MCR via the Marukh pass, held by the Soviets, which was 50 kilometres and two high passes away from the Teberda valley and 90 kilometres from Klukhor. Finally, an NKVD force was to enter the Teberda valley from the east after a long trek from the Baksan valley, still held by the Red Army, in the North Caucasus.

Meanwhile, the Germans developed a similar plan. After the attack of the 1st Mountain Division along the Sukhumi Military Road bogged down, its commanders attempted to break the stalemate by sending their units via Ptysh and Marukh to the rear of the Soviet defenders in the Klych valley.[115] This meant that the two opposing forces began simultaneously converging on Ptysh and Marukh with the same goal: to clear the Sukhumi Military Road of the enemy.

The Soviet plan, born on 19 August in the Headquarters of the 46th Army in response to desperate news from Klukhor, looked impressive on paper but, in fact, it was a hasty improvisation. Although unfulfillable orders were typical of Stalinist bureaucracy, which valued vigour in response to a crisis more than the anticipated outcome, these particular orders, totally ignoring the terrain and the obvious logistical problems, hold a prominent place in the pantheon of stupidity erected by senior Soviet commanders during World War II.

The most viable of the three planned Soviet raids was that across Ptysh. However, the commanders of the 394th Rifle Division, who were in charge of operations in this region, focused primarily on keeping the Germans from moving down the Klych valley and did not reinforce the garrison of fourteen men at the pass. On 29 August, the Germans climbed Ptysh, and its defenders surrendered without firing a shot.[116] Reporting this bloodless German victory, the Soviet commanders once again demonstrated a stunning ignorance of their operational region by claiming that the Germans took the pass with tanks; they did not explain how the tanks could have climbed the impressive, steep glacier on its northern slope, accessible only to persons with at least basic mountaineering skills and gear.[117] The Germans, however, found the Ptysh route too difficult for supply trains and abandoned their plans for a strike across this pass. They kept Ptysh, but a Soviet half-battalion overtaken by the Germans on its way to the pass blocked its southern slopes.[118]

Having failed to attack the German supply lines along the most direct and logical route via Ptysh, the TCF commanders vigorously proceeded with the two far more complicated options. For the offensive from the east, obviously undertaken under pressure from Beria, the 37th Army of the TCF Northern Army Group began hastily raising several 200-man companies consisting of regular infantry, NKVD officers, and local civilians turned overnight into partisans. Their mission, explained in an order signed by Tiulenev, Beria, and Bodin on 24 August, was 'to enter the Teberda region, build a base there, and engage in combat and sabotage missions, ambushing and destroying bypassing columns, demolishing roads and bridges, and cutting [wire] communications'.[119] The companies were to depart no later than 28 August, only four days after their formation had begun. Shalva Tsereteli, deputy head of the Georgian NKVD, was to command the raid. This could have been a reasonable plan had the assigned companies been cohesive, trained for their mission, provided with a large supply train, and supported by the local people. However, none of these factors was present. Their departure was inevitably delayed; meanwhile, Tiulenev decided to greatly expand the scope of their mission. His order of 31 August stated: 'The 37th Army must organise an operation aimed at destruction of the enemy at Sancharo and interception of the enemy communications to Klukhor in the Teberda valley and to Sancharo in the Kuban valley.'[120]

Tiulenev did not even look at the map when he wrote the order: Nizhnii Baksan, the starting point of the raid, was 90 kilometres away from the Kuban valley along a trail across the Shaukam (2,945 m) and Buruntash (3,072 m) passes, and 125 kilometres away from the Teberda valley via two more passes: Karachai-Aush (2,950 m) and Epchik (2,998 m). The German communications to Sancharo went not along the Kuban valley, as Tiulenev claimed, but along the Bolshaia Laba River; in order to get there, the raiders would have had to cover an extra 100 kilometres, crossing three deep river valleys and four more high passes. This would have been an exhausting trek even for a sportsman travelling with a light backpack in midsummer in peacetime; it would have been close to impossible for soldiers who had never been in the mountains. Not only would they be heavily loaded with weapons and ammunition in September, when temperatures were below freezing at the high passes, but they would be trekking across a territory occupied by the enemy and populated by people mostly indifferent but often hostile to representatives of the Soviet regime. The German mountain units never accomplished anything even remotely similar to the trek planned by Tiulenev.

After someone enlightened him on the geography four days after he had issued this absurd order, Tiulenev again limited the mission to the Kuban and Teberda valleys, but he considerably extended the strength of the raiding party: it consisted of 5 NKVD companies of 200 men each and a regular rifle regiment.[121] The 37th Army had no time to train the huge raiding party or organise the logistics of the raid, which was a formidable task: it would have been quite challenging to feed so many people in the depopulated mountain region through which the raiders were to advance. This force was supposed to operate in concert with the regiments descending from the Marukh pass and those in the Klych valley, but since it had no radio this co-operation was impossible to accomplish. No senior commander had given it a thought.

The raid began in early September (Map 5.2). It is not clear how many men actually departed for the raid, but only about 500 dead-tired soldiers and partisans made it to the Kuban valley.[122] When, on 12 September, they approached Khurzuk village, the first settlement in the valley, collaborationist Karachai militia spotted them and alerted the Germans, who, over the next two days, easily routed the raiding party. It lost sixty-one men killed, sixty-four wounded, and ninety-five missing in action, after which its remnants fled back towards the Baksan valley, leaving the Germans to wonder at how easily the Red Army wasted its soldiers.[123]

The TCF organised the largest raid to the Teberda valley across the Marukh pass in an equally inept fashion, and it ended in a major disaster. Although on the eve of the battle of the Caucasus the commanders of the 46th Army believed that 100 men with 1 heavy machinegun would be sufficient to defend Marukh,[124] they succumbed to Tiulenev's pressure: on 14 August, they sent 2 battalions[125] of the 810th Regiment of the 394th Rifle Division to join its third battalion, which had already occupied Marukh and the area 15 kilometres to the north of it.[126] After the Germans easily threw the Soviet defenders from several key passes, Tiulenev ordered the 46th Army to reinforce the Marukh garrison further with two more battalions of the 808th Regiment of the 394th Rifle Division, deployed at the coast.[127] The distance between the trail-head at Zakharovka and Marukh was about 80 kilometres along the most logical route; the elevation gain was 2,600 metres. Two months earlier, on 30 June, Sergatskov had said that, in order to cross the MCR,

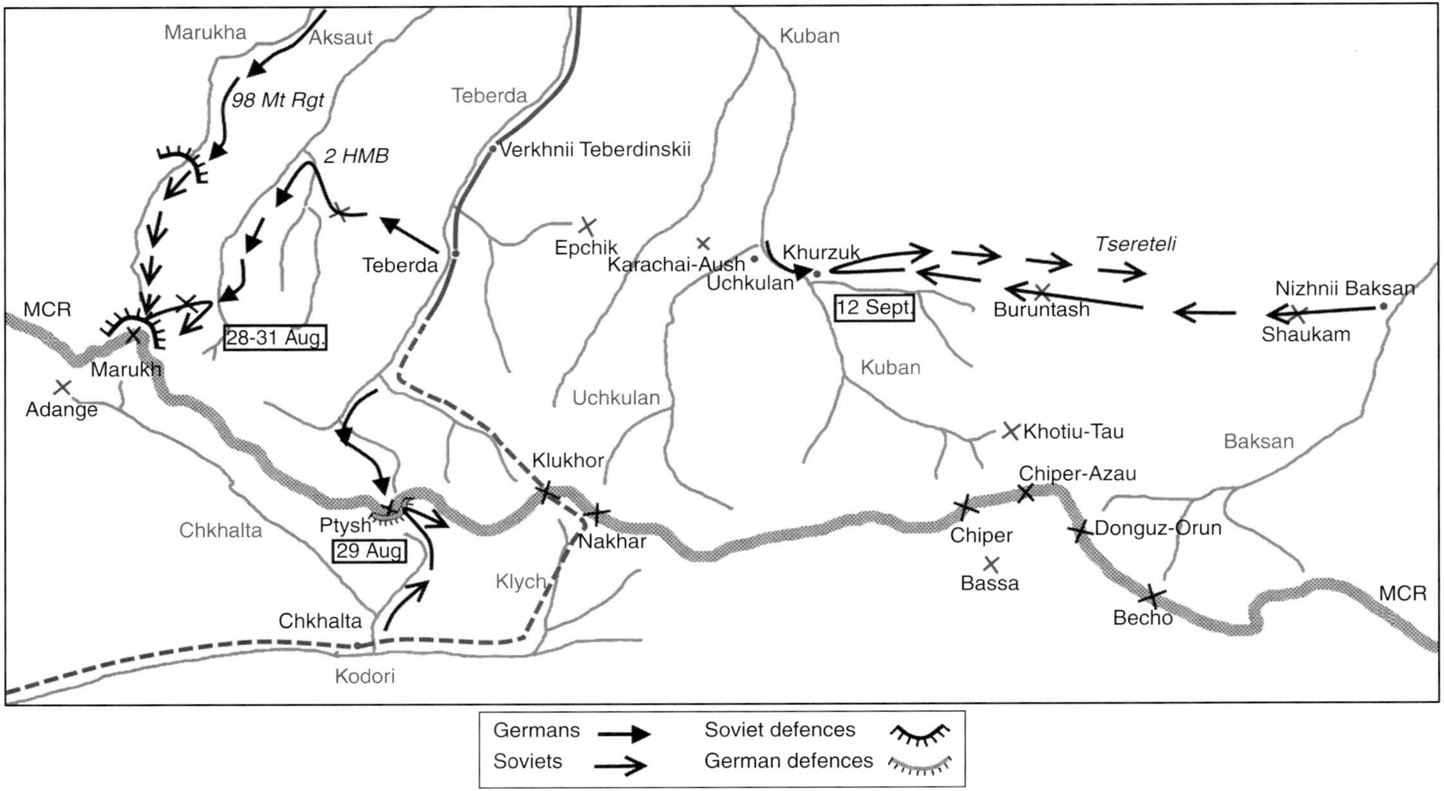

Map 5.2 Attempted Soviet raids across the Main Caucasus Ridge

'men must have climbing training, and before going to [any] pass [in the MCR], they need acclimatisation for no less than 3 or 4 days at an altitude no lower than 2,500 metres'.[128] On 20 August, however, Sergatskov passed Tiulenev's order to the 808th Regiment to leave immediately for Marukh; they were to reach it within three days and then proceed without rest for another 90 kilometres, down the northern slopes of the MCR towards Teberda, across two high ridges and a deep valley, and then take Klukhor from the north.[129] A large part of the way from Marukh to Klukhor on the northern side of the MCR was above the treeline, first across a glacier, impassable for pack animals, and then along steep trails. Colonel Vasilii Abramov, deputy commander of the 3rd Rifle Corps, who was assigned to command the raid, told Sergatskov that this mission was impossible, and Sergatskov agreed but stated that he had 'no authority to change its timeframe'.[130] On 22 August, the two-battalion 808th Rifle Regiment rushed to the pass with a three-day rusk ration and no other food.[131]

None of the commanders marching to Marukh knew the region, nor could they obtain any large-scale maps, and only after great effort did they find local civilians who gave them vague information about the route. Having no proper maps, the regiment commanders could not assess the relative difficulty of the two available routes. An excellent trail gently gained elevation, first along the Kodori and then along the Chkhalta River, through several villages, which meant that the soldiers could get at least some food on the way. However, the march to the pass from Zakharovka along this trail would have taken at least four days. Pressed to reach the pass within three days, Abramov chose a route that looked half as long on the small-scale map. However, this trail turned out to be far more difficult, leading up and down along the unpopulated ridge across several deep valleys. The regiment had enough time to collect only several pack animals to carry weapons and ammunition; the soldiers had to carry most of the load on their backs. The commanders received large-scale maps, dropped from an airplane, only on the third day of the march. On the same day, the soldiers ate their last rusks, after which they began eating their pack animals.[132] The dead-tired, famished soldiers reached Marukh only on the fifth day of the march. On the approaches to the pass, when the column was ascending the southern part of the Marukh glacier, Colonel Abramov slipped on the ice, having no crampons, and slid down to a crevasse; he managed to avoid falling into it only because it was narrow. On 26 August, the units on the northern side of the MCR requisitioned a flock of sheep, which provided the defenders with about 1 kilogram of lamb per person. They ate it raw because no firewood was available above treeline and no Soviet commander had thought about how to feed soldiers in such conditions.[133]

Colonel Abramov wrote a stunning commentary about his march to Marukh. Instead of addressing the reasons for the dismal failures of Soviet commanders to follow the orders about the defence of the passes issued during the two months before the beginning of the battle at the MCR and to prepare their units for actions in the mountains, he stated: 'I am thinking about the Soviet soldier with pride. Indeed, before the war, only a few mountaineers with special clothes and boots and not much load climbed there. We, in contrast, took an entire regiment in regular uniforms, with weapons and [military] equipment, [and it marched] the whole day without food!'[134] This bravado contrasted with the impressions of rank-and-file soldiers and junior officers who, after exhausting marches, found themselves in the mountains woefully unprepared to operate there and with their morale badly shaken even before their first engagement.[135] The regiment lacked many necessary items of military equipment, which severely handicapped its combat capacity. It had received no field telephones or digging tools, except for the soldiers' individual infantry spades; no tents; and no climbing gear.[136] Threatened by severe penalties if another pass was lost to the Germans, the commanders of the 46th Army rushed the 808th Rifle Regiment to Marukh with the order to defend it 'at any cost'; by failing to supply the soldiers even with coats, they ensured that the cost would be high indeed.[137]

By 27 August, 5 understaffed rifle battalions, 168 men of the 36th Naval Frontier Guard Battalion, and 2 mortar companies from the 155th Rifle Brigade assembled at Marukh.[138] Abramov proceeded with his orders to launch an immediate raid on Klukhor, an action planned by those who had no idea about the terrain between Marukh and Klukhor. He left two battalions at Marukh and its northern approaches[139] and sent the rest of his forces, assembled in two columns, down the northern slopes of the MCR. In the late evening of 27 August, the columns departed for their mission, led by Karachai guides. They had first to cross the northern part of the Marukh glacier and then descend into the Aksaut valley. The soldiers had no food with them but hoped to find some in the upper reaches of the Aksaut River, assuming that the valley was free of Germans. As Abramov wrote in his report, 'The success of the plan verged on the following factors: a. the columns had to consist of well-trained and properly dressed units supplied with food for three or four days; … b. surprise and stealth.'[140] He pointed to the fact that his force hardly corresponded to the first criterion of success and that stealth would be lost during the search for food on the way to Klukhor. The columns had to operate in virtual isolation: they had no working radios and communicated with Abramov, who stayed at Marukh, only through runners.[141] When the soldiers, wearing long coats unsuitable for climbing and boots with flat soles, began crossing the Marukh glacier at night, some of them slipped on the ice and fell into crevasses. Most of those died, including the commander of the 36th Naval Frontier Guard Battalion, but some, including Mikhail Okunev, deputy chief of staff of the 810th Regiment, were pulled out by their comrades, who tied together their belts or foot wraps in the absence of ropes.[142]

Meanwhile, German units, sent on 25 August to take Marukh, approached the pass. They moved along two parallel valleys: the 1st Battalion of the 98th Mountain Regiment with about 800 men went along the Marukha River, while the 2nd High Mountain Battalion of 2,000 men,[143] attached to the 1st Mountain Division, ascended the next valley to the east, containing the Aksaut River. On 26 August, a reinforced company of the 810th Rifle Regiment deployed 15 kilometres north of the pass engaged the Germans marching along the Marukha River and began a slow fighting retreat.[144]

As soon as the larger Soviet column began descending into the Aksaut valley on 28 August, it ran into the German 2nd High Mountain Battalion. This unit consisted of volunteers, mostly 21 or 22 years old, who had not yet acquired combat experience but were motivated, well trained, and well equipped with climbing gear; its commander, the Austrian Major Paul Bauer, was a famous mountaineer who had led several Himalayan expeditions, including to Kanchenjunga (8,586 m) and Nanga Parbat (8,126 m), respectively the third- and the ninth-highest mountains in the world.[145] The clashes in the Aksaut valley continued for four days; during this period, the Soviet soldiers, who had set out on the raid without food, had nothing to eat but sorrel and blackberries. They were freezing in summer uniforms while taking shelter from the snowstorm of 31 August in cavities in the ice.[146] Mountaineering textbooks published before the war warned that 'to fall asleep on a glacier without a sleeping bag or a tent means to face certain death',[147] and many soldiers met such a fate in these icy holes. On 30 August, Major Vladimir Smirnov, who was commanding the raid, reported that he could not advance because his men were debilitated by starvation and cold, rain with hail, and snow, and he received permission to return to Marukh. The decimated columns withdrew back across the Marukh glacier – as Soviet reports say, 'with enormous difficulties' – during the night of 1 September.[148] The entire Soviet rearguard covering the retreat from the Aksaut valley was lost. Several Soviet reconnaissance platoons were taken prisoner or destroyed to the last man; in one of them, seven of twenty-five men were killed and the rest froze to death.[149] During the raid, the 810th Regiment alone lost 300 men killed, 42 dead from exposure, 94 wounded, and 140 missing in action. Many Soviet survivors were suffering from hypothermia.[150] The German 1st Mountain Division reported the loss of only seven men dead and nineteen wounded between 29 August and 1 September, and some of these casualties occurred in the Marukha and Klych valleys.[151] The size of the booty of the 810th Rifle Regiment, consisting of only twelve small arms and one German prisoner,[152] confirms the great disproportion of casualties suffered by opponents in the Aksaut valley. The attempt to advance towards Teberda was a clear-cut disaster. Abramov recorded his impressions: 'The returning units of the 810th Regiment looked extremely exhausted and worn down ... they needed four or five days of rest ... Otherwise, they would be unfit to fight.'[153] He allowed the participants of the raid to descend from the pass to its southern foot, where they were irrelevant to the defence of the pass.

Meanwhile, the 2nd Battalion of the 808th Regiment and most of the 2nd Battalion of the 810th Rifle Regiment stayed at the Marukh pass without contact with the enemy. The snowstorm of 31 August covered the pass with snow. Soldiers who had never been in the mountains found themselves at an altitude of 2,748 metres in summer uniforms with disintegrating boots; they were without food, tents, sleeping bags, alcohol or kerosene burners, or sunglasses, and many had no coats.[154] The temperature plummeted below freezing at night. The Marukh pass is far above the treeline. It took the soldiers ten to twelve hours to descend down a steep path from the pass saddle to the treeline at 1,800 metres, collect firewood and take it back to the pass; one man could carry enough firewood for only one small fire, which was insufficient to cook food, so the soldier's ration consisted mainly of raw meat and rusks. Between 29 August and 5 September, the 808th Rifle Regiment lost half of its personnel to disease and starvation, and several soldiers froze to death.[155] Facing the rapid attrition of their forces, regiment commanders requested permission to leave the pass, but Abramov told them that those who 'contemplate leaving the pass will be treated as traitors';[156] after all, once he had allowed the raiding party to recuperate at the foot of the pass, he could field only two battalions, one of them with zero combat experience, to defend the pass.[157] According to Abramov, a total of 399 men with about three dozen machineguns and 17 trench mortars, and several attached small units, defended the pass. The more plausible German reports assess the Soviet force at Marukh as twice as large.[158] Indeed, a full-strength Soviet rifle battalion had almost 800 men[159] and, although the two battalions deployed at Marukh had lost many men sick, one of the two had not taken part in any action. In any case, the balance of the opposing forces at Marukh shifted dramatically between 26 August, when the 808th and 810th Rifle Regiments arrived, and 4 September, the eve of the German assault. On 26 August, the Soviets considerably outnumbered the Germans in the Marukh region. However, since the Germans suffered only light casualties between 26 August and 4 September, they retained perhaps 2,600 men, many more than the Soviets kept at the pass but still fewer than the total Soviet force, including the battered raiding party[160] staying below the pass. Although the Marukh garrison had abundant reserves of ammunition[161] – the only item regularly delivered by pack trains – its morale, badly shaken by the disastrous raid to the Aksaut valley, was further weakened by cold and hunger.

Marukh was an excellent defensive position. One Soviet company had occupied the pass at least since 5 August and was joined shortly after that by two other companies.[162] Therefore, by the time the Germans approached Marukh on 4 September, a month had passed since the first Soviet unit had arrived at the pass and nine days since the first contact with the approaching Germans on 26 August. The Soviets had ample time to turn the pass into a fortress, as the OG noted *post factum*.[163] However, the Marukh garrison failed to dig in properly, partly because of the absence of tools and partly because its commanders believed that the mountainous terrain itself provided enough cover. No trenches were dug on Marukh before the arrival on 27 August of the main forces, who needed several days to acclimatise before they could work.[164] The fortification works began soon after 27 August, but most of the strongholds were not dug-in trenches but above-ground bunkers made of rocks, which were vulnerable to artillery and even mortar fire, and which protected soldiers from fire from below but not from above. Even such bunkers were few.[165] The Soviets failed to scout the outskirts of the pass; a contemporary analysis of the battle at Marukh states bluntly: 'No reconnaissance was conducted.'[166] The defenders once again occupied only the saddle of the pass. A feeble attempt to ascend the upper part of the Marukh glacier at the extreme eastern flank of the Soviet position, and so to protect it, failed because of the absence of mountaineering skills and gear.[167]

The conduct of the Soviet and German senior field officers on the eve of the assault on Marukh revealed the dramatic difference in their ability to command their formations in the mountains. Having found Soviet forces at Marukh, 46-year-old General Lanz, commander of the 1st Mountain Division, undertook personal reconnaissance in order to investigate the available tactical options. Along with other senior divisional commanders, he climbed a peak of 3,145 metres, from which they could observe the pass well, and then proposed to act in accordance with the German manual for mountain warfare: a frontal assault on the pass saddle coupled with an outflanking attack across the rocks to the east of the saddle, which would take the Germans to the rear of the defenders and above them.[168] Lanz's Soviet counterpart, Lieutenant-Colonel Ivan Kantaria, commander of the 394th Rifle Division, which defended most of the passes, had to be relieved from command on 3 September because his heart condition did not allow him to stay even at an elevation of 800 metres.[169] Kantaria's replacement, the frontier guard Colonel Pavel Belekhov, had never climbed above 800 metres either; he admitted his inadequacy in a message to General Petrov: 'I cannot promptly and correctly assess the situation … My knowledge, my mind, and my health do not allow me to command such a huge front section in the mountains. I have never been a mountaineer.' He added that his former subordinates, lieutenants in charge of frontier guard posts, had been more competent than his current battalion commanders.[170]

Colonel Abramov, commander of the Marukh garrison, left the pass and went down to the Chkhalta valley on 4 September, one day before the German assault, when the Germans were concentrating all available forces at Marukh's northern foot. He attempted to explain this inexplicable action during the investigation conducted by the

Headquarters of the 46th Army by advancing a bizarre argument: 'Everything was quiet at the pass. Because of the absence of communications [with Headquarters], I did not know the situation at other sections of the [3rd] Corps's Front but felt responsible for them. It would be criminal to remain there – the quiet part of the front, as it seemed then – when the situation probably demanded my presence at some other pass.'[171] This argument testifies to the pitiful state of Soviet intelligence information, hampered by the inability of scouts to move across mountainous terrain, but still Abramov's decision to leave the pass on the eve of the German assault and the bewilderment of other senior officers who found themselves in the mountains for the first time, like Kantaria and Belekhov, demonstrate the enormous gaps in skill, initiative, physical conditions, and morale between the German and Soviet commanders operating in the high mountains. The dismal performance of Soviet commanders matched the performance of their men, who, in their late 30s and mid 40s, were in far worse physical shape than the young German soldiers and, unlike the Germans, were unequipped for mountain warfare or even for prolonged exposure to subzero temperatures.

On 4 September, Leselidze summarised the typical German tactics, also suggested by the Soviet *Manual on Mountain Warfare*, and the typical Soviet flaws:

> The enemy deploys small groups at the wide front in order to envelop our formations and come to their rear; [these groups] infiltrate the gaps between defences even in terrain deemed impassable … The commanders of [Soviet] formations sent to defend the passes … have not visited the passes and have not checked whether the strongholds were built correctly. These factors led to the outrageous surrender of the passes without proper resistance to the enemy: Klukhor (815th Rifle Regiment) and Sancharo (808th Rifle Regiment). Some units were unsteady and panicked when the enemy engaged them, and left their positions … Instead of taking the resolute measures presumed by Order No. 227, commanders tailed them in dismay.[172]

The next day, both the Germans and the Soviets acted at Marukh as Leselidze had described. The German assault was a masterpiece of mountain warfare. On the night of 4 September, in poor weather, two companies of the High Mountain Battalion led personally by Paul Bauer

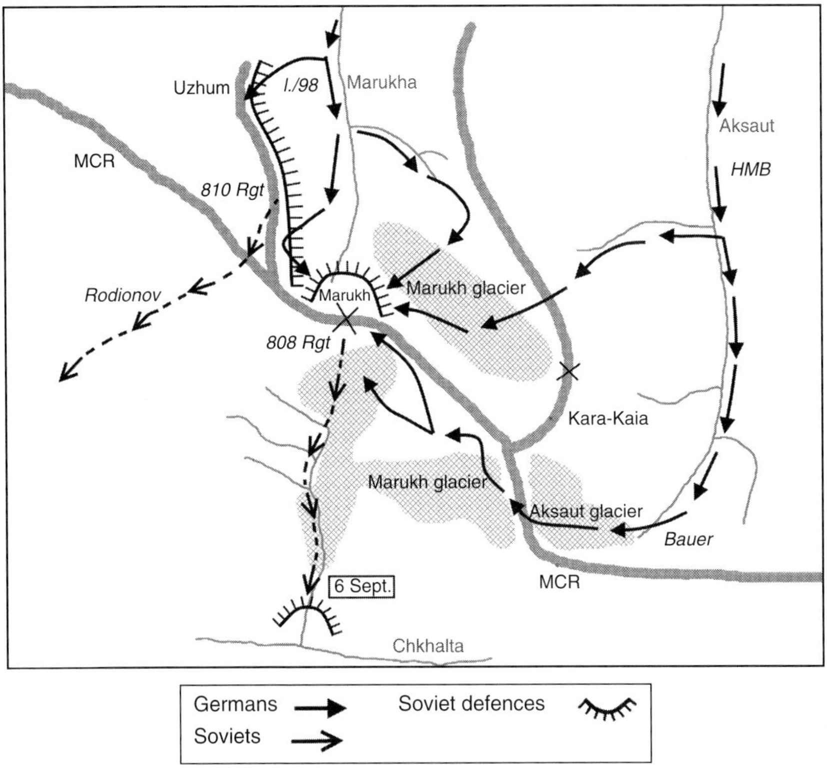

Map 5.3 The German assault on Marukh

and supplied with full mountaineering kit – crampons, ice axes, rock and ice pitons, ropes, and rope ladders – cut steps in the ice of the Aksaut glacier to the east of Marukh, belaying each other, and climbed to its upper part, invisible from Marukh, and then across the vertical rocks of the MCR. Several soldiers fell from the rocks and one died, but the others made their way to the southern side of the MCR to the rear of the defenders. One of the companies found itself on rocks towering above the pass saddle, while another rappelled down to the south of the pass saddle behind the Soviet positions.[173] It was this outflanking manoeuvre rather than the frontal assault by the remaining forces that was expected to bring success (Map 5.3).

On the morning of 5 September, the companies opened fire at the pass saddle, and this was followed by a frontal attack of the 1st Battalion of the 98th Regiment up the Marukha valley, while the two remaining companies of the High Mountain Battalion attacked across the Marukh glacier. All the assaulting units co-ordinated their actions via radio.[174] The attack from above and from the rear stunned the pass defenders. Nobody attempted to blow up the two large mines and the two 'stone-throwers' set at Marukh. The TCF war diary recorded that the Soviet soldiers 'did not offer stubborn resistance and left the pass after a brief clash'.[175] The commanders of the Marukh garrison, including Abramov and Major Smirnov, commander of the 810th Regiment, admitted that during the German surprise attack from the rocks above the saddle, a large portion of the defenders, including most of the 4th Company of the 808 Rifle Regiment, surrendered to the enemy; the regiment's 6th Company was destroyed; and many soldiers fled 'in panic down the southern slope of the pass' towards the Chkhalta valley.[176] However, retreat down this 50-degree slope was possible only along a narrow serpentine path. The Germans who had sneaked into the rear of the Soviet defenders kept this route under fire, killing the fleeing soldiers as though they were practising at a shooting range. Their fire also prevented the battalions staying at the southern foot of the pass from climbing it and, in the end, they 'retreated in disorder, offering no resistance to the enemy'.[177] Abramov explained the accuracy of the German fire from above with the allegation that the Germans 'knew our deployment and positions from some defectors';[178] the simple idea that a soldier trained to fire at high angles would do so more accurately than an untrained one did not occur to him. According to Abramov, the Germans 'destroyed the defenders of the pass almost to the last man'; the commander of the garrison and his commissar fled and thus were among the only thirteen survivors from the battalion deployed at the saddle of the pass. At least sixty-four men deserted, with their weapons, from the 810th Rifle Regiment.[179]

Although the commanders of the Marukh garrison admitted the far superior skill of the enemy,[180] nearly every Russian author explains the disaster suffered by the Soviets by making two allegations: the Germans had numerical superiority and they supported their assault with 'strong artillery and mortar fire and air force'.[181] The latter allegation comes from Abramov's order written the day after the assault, when he made a desperate attempt to explain the loss of Marukh to his superiors.[182] However, his detailed report written later states merely that one German aircraft briefly emerged over the pass and dropped several bombs on the Soviet positions – perhaps a reconnaissance plane that carried a small bomb load;[183] German archival sources and

German studies of this engagement do not mention actions of the Luftwaffe during the assault on the pass. As for German artillery, six mountain guns and three howitzers supported the assault.[184] The Soviet defenders had no artillery, except for mortars, but the OG maintained that they had 'enough manpower and firepower for the effective defence of Marukh';[185] the irrational deployment of these resources, with most units excluded from the battle, was one of the reasons why the Germans attained another easy victory.

The Germans reported having killed about 300 and taken prisoner 557 Soviet soldiers during the assault. Even if the number of enemy casualties was inflated, as was usual, the collection by the Germans of 19 heavy machineguns, 4 light machineguns, and 545 rifles on the battlefield shows the scale of the defeat suffered by the Soviets. The war diary of the 49th Mountain Corps states the total casualties of the 1st Mountain Division on 5 and 6 September as thirteen dead, thirty-four wounded, and one missing in action, including those in the Klych valley and elsewhere.[186] German authors state that the assaulting units lost only seven soldiers killed and eight wounded at Marukh.[187] This was the most impressive German victory in the battle of the Caucasus, and it showed that the Red Army had learned nothing about mountain warfare during the three weeks following the loss of Klukhor. Leselidze could not believe that the Soviet units had suffered such a crushing defeat and reprimanded his subordinates for 'the obvious understatement of his [the enemy's] casualties at Marukh', thus pressuring them to manipulate the data and downplay the scale of the disaster.[188]

Leselidze attributed the 'surrender of the Marukh pass to the enemy' to 'poor reconnaissance along ridges and bypassing trails, careless attitude, and inadequate supplies'.[189] Although this observation revealed some of the causes of the defeat, the major ones were the belated occupation of the pass, the subsequent inaction, and the absence of skills and proper equipment, including mountaineering gear. Regular infantry could not even approach the rocks across which the Germans outflanked the Soviet defenders, nor could they imagine that anyone could climb them. In the end, it was the senior TCF commanders, including Leselidze, and the General Staff of the Red Army who were primarily responsible for the disasters at the MCR because it was they who failed to raise, train, equip, and deploy proper mountain divisions in the high Caucasus. Mikhail Bonch-Bruevich, referring to the campaign of 1915 in the Carpathians, noted that Russian commanders traditionally believed that 'the Russian soldier, this primitive creature [*seraia skotinka*], can withstand anything'.[190] However, the unequipped and hungry Soviet soldiers, shivering in their tunics in subzero temperatures, could not match the well-trained, warmly dressed, and well-supplied German mountain troops.

Since the TCF commanders feared that their heads would roll in the wake of disgraceful defeats, as had happened before to failed commanders, they fervently searched for scapegoats. It did not take them long to find one: Captain V. Rodionov, commander of the 2nd Battalion of the 810th Rifle Regiment – 'a hard-working, quite competent, ... courageous, fair, and cool-headed officer',[191] according to his regiment commander. Rodionov's battalion formed the left flank of the Soviet position at Marukh; it was deployed at the Uzhum crest that joined the MCR 1 kilometre away from the Marukh saddle. According to Abramov, Rodionov's left flank was located a four-hour walk from the saddle.[192] When the Germans assaulted Marukh, they smashed through the right flank and the centre of the Soviet position, defended by the 2nd Battalion of the 808th Rifle Regiment. Rodionov's battalion also suffered heavy casualties but escaped total annihilation. After the Germans overwhelmed the defenders of the saddle and promptly began pursuing them down towards the Chkhalta valley, they cut off Rodionov's battalion from the main Soviet forces. Having no communication with the garrison commanders, who were busy fleeing from the pass, Rodionov stayed at his position, keeping in mind the penalty for unsanctioned retreat stemming from the 'Not a Step Back' order.[193] However, during the night, when his soldiers, battered by icy wind, had eaten their last rations, exhausted their ammunition, and watched several of their comrades freeze to death, Rodionov realised that with the pass lost, the continued defence of his position was pointless, and he decided to retreat. His soldiers, numbering only 100 able-bodied men by that time, descended the steep southern slopes of the MCR using tied belts and foot wraps in the absence of ropes; most likely, they left their wounded comrades behind.[194] Listening to the gunfire in the Chkhalta valley and being unsure whether the Germans pursuing the remnants of the Marukh garrison had already occupied the valley, thus barring his battalion from rejoining his regiment, Rodionov led his soldiers westward away from Chkhalta to the Bzyb valley via the Adange pass (2,299 m). The battalion undertook a hard 60-kilometre trek, during which, Rodionov reported, 'we had to eat bark, moss, and leaves, and we lost several more men who starved or froze to death'.[195] When the remaining seventy-eight frostbitten and completely exhausted soldiers finally met Soviet units in the Bzyb valley,[196] the Special Section of the 394th Rifle Division sentenced Rodionov and his commissar, Ivan Shvetsov, to death for 'abandoning their positions without an order ... and for cowardice in combat', despite the fact that Rodionov had kept his position longer than the commander of the Marukh garrison had and that he, unlike this commander, had saved at least part of his battalion from surrender or useless death from cold.[197] Both men were shot in front of the soldiers whose lives they saved. Nikolai Frolov, chief of staff of the 808th Regiment, claimed after the war that he had sent a runner to Rodionov with the order to retreat from the Uzhum crest if endangered by encirclement, but he failed to acknowledge this fact during the investigation.[198] As Konstantin Benkendorf, a member of the Dargo expedition, wrote in the nineteenth century, 'An infantry officer has two duties in combat: first ... to face enemy fire; second ... the duty of a human being and an officer makes him protect his unit and spare the lives of his soldiers as much as possible.'[199] Soviet officers were trained to focus on the first duty and ignore the second one. Leselidze, who bore the primary responsibility for the defeats at the passes, approved of the execution *post factum*. In April 1966, the Prosecutor Office of the Transcaucasian Military District revised this criminal case, dismissed all charges as baseless, and fully acquitted these officers posthumously, which prompted Soviet authors to claim, disingenuously, that 'justice was done'.[200] The lives of many other Soviet soldiers ended similarly: they were sentenced to summary execution by those who had never visited the high mountains and had no idea of the battle environment there.

The TCF Headquarters knew that the Germans had attacked Marukh but had no information about the outcome of the battle for several days.[201] At midnight on 7 September, two days after the Germans had taken Marukh, Tiulenev still assured Stalin, 'Our units offer staunch resistance to the enemy, who has been attempting to advance towards Marukh since 5 September.' Only two days later – on 9 September, after wire communication with the remnants of the Marukh garrison was established – did Tiulenev learn that the Germans had taken the pass.[202] On that day, Leselidze told Abramov, who meanwhile had rejoined the crowds retreating from Marukh: 'I am stunned by your inaction. Absolutely insignificant enemy forces threw your units, outnumbering them many times, off the Marukh pass, and continue to pursue them south. You have enough forces not just to turn the tables but also to destroy the enemy ... I repeat: not a step back!'[203] Such a warning equalled the threat of a death sentence. However, Abramov had already taken a number of vigorous steps to terminate the retreat. The same evening the Germans took the pass, he gathered the dispersed remnants of the two regiments. He counted fewer than 400 men but promptly deployed them in the narrow Marukh gorge 6 kilometres below the pass.[204] The next morning, on 6 September, Abramov, who, as Leselidze stated correctly, had 'left the front without an order at the moment when the Germans were preparing their assault',[205] regrouped the available manpower, 'resorting to the full extent of the measures presumed by Comrade Stalin's Order No. 227': he organised a blocking unit of thirty-four men, ordering it to 'pass to the tribunal [*troika*] all commanders and privates who had left their positions without order and execute them by a firing squad as traitors'.[206] Nikolai Rukhadze, chief of Special Sections of the TCF, praised Abramov's initiative, citing an incident when this blocking unit summarily shot four men for 'cowardice and panic mongering' and maintaining that the execution 'prevented potential panic among soldiers'.[207]

This draconian means, the vigorous organisation of defence positions, and the passionate appeals to protect 'the birthplace of Comrade Stalin'[208] allowed Abramov to plug the exit out of the Marukh gorge 2 kilometres before it opened into the broad Chkhalta valley. The German offensive from Marukh ended in the same way as the one in the Klukhor region had. After several Soviet units arrived between 11 and 15 September, raising the total strength of the Soviet forces in the Marukh gorge to five battalions and thus restoring Soviet numerical superiority,[209] the Germans lost the chance to break through.

Conclusion

As Beria observed, on the eve of the German assault on the MCR passes, 'TCF commanders did little to defend Transcaucasia, even though they had ample opportunity to do so.'[210] Having heard about the easy German victories in the high Caucasus and being concerned with their own safety in the face of the Stavka's fury, these commanders sought to demonstrate their vigour in response to the menace instead of focusing on the efficacy of the response and fantasised about how they would stop the Germans by blowing up mountains, mountain passes, river valleys, and glaciers. Soviet infantry arrived at the MCR without tents, climbing gear, communication means, digging tools, mountain artillery, portable radios, portable kitchens, kerosene or alcohol burners, chemical heaters, fire correction tables, sleeping bags, backpacks, special food rations, mountain boots, or warm uniforms, and sometimes even without coats, and they dragged with them useless and heavy loads of anti-tank rifles, anti-tank mines, and Molotov cocktails. The morale of Soviet raw recruits – who suffered from acute mountain sickness, spent nights in the open, were battered by strong icy winds and rains, and ate scarce rations consisting primarily of raw meat – sank even before they saw the Germans at the far approaches to their positions. The series of crushing defeats at the passes was thus the logical outcome of the thoughtless attitude to actions in the mountains that persisted in the Red Army, despite the painful experiences of the past, the detailed analysis of these experiences by military academics, interwar experiments, and the theoretical concept of mountain warfare developed on the eve of World War II.

Soviet memoirists and Russian historians attempted to explain the stunning German victories during the battle at the passes by alleging that the Germans enjoyed substantial numerical superiority. Tiulenev set an example: 'Since [only] weak forces defended the central part of the TCF, the enemy could take Klukhor, Sancharo, and Marukh.'[211] The choir of Russian authors picked up this argument, typically saying, 'The enemy drove away our small units and took several high mountain passes between Elbrus and the Umpyrskii pass.'[212] At Klukhor, however, the Soviet defenders were equal in number to the German attackers, and at Marukh they outnumbered the enemy, yet the Germans easily took these passes and also *all* – rather than 'several', as Russian authors persistently claim[213] – other passes that they attempted to take between Elbrus and Umpyrskii. Even with the irrational deployment of the available manpower at Klukhor and Marukh, the Soviet forces would have been sufficient had they been trained to operate in mountains.

In the end, however, the optimisation of the command structure undertaken by Beria's team and the resulting improved co-ordination of actions, unchallenged air superiority, and draconian discipline

Figure 5.2 A German rope-team equipped with ice axes and crampons climbing a steep snow-encrusted slope. Credit: Süddeutsche Zeitung Photo / Alamy Stock Photo

enforcement but, most importantly, the availability of large reserves helped the Red Army to terminate the German offensive across the high Caucasus. As a Russian proverb has it, 'No wrestling skills are useful against a crowbar.'[214] Superior numbers – the Soviet crowbar – defeated expertise during the battle on the southern slopes of the MCR.

6 THE SOVIET COUNTEROFFENSIVE: A STALEMATE SNATCHED FROM THE JAWS OF VICTORY

For every action, there is an equal and opposite reaction.
Newton's Third Law

The OKW planned the attack of the 49th Mountain Corps as a swift strike intended to facilitate the major offensive of Army Group A along the Black Sea coast via Tuapse. However, this attack across the Caucasus, at first quite successful, stalled as soon as the Germans began descending the southern slopes of the MCR, for two reasons: the numerical inferiority of the German forces and their neglect of logistical problems at the planning stage. Although the Germans destroyed almost all the defenders of Klukhor and Marukh, easily drove away the garrisons from the Sancharo group of passes, and captured all the passes around Elbrus without firing a shot, they still faced an enemy far superior in numbers, with much greater reserves of ammunition, and determined to drive the Germans back across the Caucasus. The 49th Mountain Corps enjoyed a decisive advantage over Soviet regular infantry at high elevations, but the lower it descended, the harder its advance became. The captured Soviet maps showed that the terrain between the MCR and the coast was more difficult than the Germans had anticipated, while deteriorating weather in early September threatened to make the trails across the MCR impassable,[1] which would cut off the supplies of the German units at the southern slopes of the MCR. In any case, the lightly armed, albeit elite, German force could not drive home an offensive against an enemy who could concentrate an enormous amount of artillery in the lower valleys and was supported by an air force that had no rival in the skies of Transcaucasia. All these factors must have been obvious before the beginning of Operation Edelweiss, but the euphoria experienced by Army Group A during its rapid advance towards the Caucasus in early August superseded the cold-headed analysis of the available options, resulting in a disastrous strategy. Meanwhile, the main offensive towards Tuapse proceeded slowly, and it became clear in late August that it could not succeed with the allocated forces, which made the attack of the 49th Mountain Corps across the MCR pointless.

On 30 August, General Konrad proposed that this attack be cancelled, and on 5 September he wrote to the Headquarters of Army Group A that the 49th Mountain Corps would be unable to hold out at the coast, even if it reached the Black Sea. He argued that given the circumstances – the failing offensive towards Tuapse, the insurmountable logistical problems experienced by the 49th Mountain Corps, and its gross inferiority in numbers – it would be wise to keep the occupied passes with minimal forces but transfer the rest of the corps to the Tuapse region and thus revitalise the major thrust along the Black Sea coast.[2] General Wilhelm List, commander of Army Group A, convinced Alfred Jodl, the OKW chief of operations, of the rationality of this plan, and on 8 September Jodl presented it to Hitler.[3] According to Keitel, 'Jodl's report . . . enraged the Führer and provoked an incredible outburst of fury . . . He dismissed the fact that the enormous logistical problems along mountain trails make this operation impossible'[4] and replaced List with Ewald von Kleist as the commander of Army Group A. However, on the next day, only four days after the brilliant victory at Marukh, Hitler reluctantly authorised the termination of the offensive across the Caucasus.[5] The 1st and the 4th Mountain Divisions transferred most of their units to the Tuapse region, leaving the entire 200-kilometre-long front along the MCR to a force equal to two regiments.[6] These regiments, dispersed in small units, were to defend all the passes that had been taken. The Headquarters of Army Group A changed the strategic objective of the operation at the MCR from a strike into the rear of the Soviet forces at the Black Sea coast to a far less ambitious but more pragmatic goal: the two mountain regiments were to pin down the forces of the TCF, as many as possible, thus keeping them away from Tuapse, while inflicting disproportional casualties on these forces with skilful defence.

The cancellation of the 49th Mountain Corps's offensive nullified all the victories it had gained at the passes. It was therefore tantamount to a strategic Soviet victory, though admittedly a quite costly one, gained mainly by decisive numerical superiority. This victory would have been complete had the Stavka been satisfied with the termination of the German offensive. However, it pressed the Headquarters of the TCF to undertake the 'urgent and heroic measures' required to retake all the passes lost to the enemy and to 'transfer the action to the northern slopes of all the passes'.[7] This goal had no strategic purpose: it became clear that severe logistical problems and deteriorating weather would frustrate a major offensive across the MCR. However, the Stavka and the TCF commanders declared the loss of the passes 'a disgrace' that needed to 'be erased [*smyt*] immediately' at any cost,[8] and the cost never concerned the Soviet leaders, military or civilian, when prestige was involved.

This objective emerged soon after the arrival of Beria, who demanded from the TCF the restoration of 'the situation that existed before 18 August 1942' and the 'full destruction of the minuscule enemy units opposing your far superior forces'.[9] Tiulenev assured his subordinates that they had 'sufficient strength and means to fulfil this mission; now everything depends on the combat skill, the determination, and the persistence of commanders'.[10] The Soviet commanders had enough persistence and determination but lacked skill in mountain warfare. The battle of the Caucasus entered a new stage marked by vigorous Soviet attacks. Already on 24 August, the Headquarters of the 3rd Rifle Corps ordered the 394th Rifle Division to take Klukhor by the evening of 26 August, and on 13 September Leselidze set 20 September as the deadline for retaking all the MCR passes.[11] After these deadlines passed without a single pass being taken, the reoccupation of all the passes remained the goal of the 46th Army until the end of the battle at the MCR in late October. By launching persistent and costly attacks against entrenched Germans, the TCF played into their hands, thus helping them to attain their new strategic objective in the high Caucasus.

The counteroffensive began on 26 August in the Klych valley and was followed by attacks in all other regions overrun by Germans, but the large numerical superiority of the TCF did not produce the expected results. The counteroffensive proceeded under conditions that were far worse than those the Germans had faced during their attack, with all the dominating heights occupied by an enemy experienced in mountain warfare and with increasingly poor weather. Russian historians maintaining that the Red Army 'relatively easily drove the

Hitlerites away from the southern slopes and retook a number of important passes, inflicting grave casualties on the enemy'[12] distort the facts. Mikhail Gioev, a junior officer of the 155th Rifle Brigade, recalled that 'each of our units paid a hefty price for every step of its advance'.[13] The Soviet offensive was slow, painful, and futile.

On 22 September, after observing the fruitless efforts to dislodge the Germans from their strongholds, Major Varlam Kakuchaia, an NKVD representative with the Military Council of the TCF and the former deputy people's commissar of the interior of Georgia,[14] a person more familiar with the local conditions than with mountain warfare, submitted an insightful memorandum to Tiulenev regarding the desirable composition, training, and equipment of Soviet forces at the MCR. He maintained that, in order to effectively confront the German mountain divisions, 'it is necessary to deploy personnel with climbing and mountain skiing skills at least at the most important sections [of the front] in the high mountains ... The major focus ... should be on quality rather than numbers, on training for action in winter, and on supply of the garrisons at the passes with gear and whatever is necessary for survival and combat.'[15] In order to have such a force, Soviet regiments at the MCR would have to run a 160-hour comprehensive training course that would last twenty days and include climbing and mountain skiing techniques, tactics of mountain warfare, transportation of wounded men, and the study of natural hazards. Mountaineering experts holding a Master of Sport title had to be immediately identified in the Red Army and summoned to the TCF; they would teach this training course with a ratio of one instructor per ten students. The commanders of the TCF must urgently find at least 2,500 skis with Kandahar bindings, ski poles, and sledges for the transportation of supplies and evacuation of the wounded. Since 'the only viable means of communication in such conditions is radio',[16] all units operating at the MCR had to be supplied with a large number of reliable portable radios. The soldiers deployed in the mountains needed special warm winter uniforms suitable for climbing, light but calorie-rich rations, anti-frostbite cream, sunglasses, and sleeping bags. They could survive and preserve their combat capacity only if they had adequate shelters – not just tents but folding huts, portable stoves, and chemical heaters; the soldiers would also have to be frequently rotated, with combat tours of about five days being followed by a ten-day rest. Hazards in the mountains multiply in winter; therefore, a permanent rescue service with special equipment such as avalanche probes, snow shovels, and portable radios had to be established.[17]

The Headquarters of the TCF followed all these recommendations but only after the events had conclusively proven Kakuchaia's insights, which happened too late to affect the actions in the high Caucasus. Meanwhile, the 46th Army sustained thousands of casualties that could have been minimised had it exercised mountain warfare in the interwar period and extrapolated the experience of the Winter War to actions in the mountains – or at least followed promptly the recommendations of the officers familiar with the local environment, such as Varlam Kakuchaia and Aleksandr Kvlividze.

Klukhor

On 25 August, the Soviets stopped the German offensive in the Klych valley 12 kilometres below the Klukhor pass. The next day, a Soviet force equal to five rifle battalions[18] began unimaginative frontal attacks towards Klukhor against two German reinforced battalions and advanced about 1 kilometre during the first three days (Map 6.1).[19] A raid by a German battalion in the rear of the attackers interrupted the Soviet offensive. However, on 3 September, the Soviet units, joined meanwhile by a force equal to a rifle regiment,[20] resumed attacks that Germans have described as determined but stereotypical.[21] The Soviets made little progress up the Klych valley: they advanced only between 400 and 800 metres from 3 to 5 September, after which the offensive bogged down.[22] During this action, the attackers suffered disproportional casualties: on 3 and 4 September, they lost 281 men killed and wounded, including Major Ivan Arshava, commander of the 121st 'Mountain' Regiment, who was killed, and Captain A. Kozhemiakin, its chief of staff, who was gravely wounded, as was A. Avtandilov, commander of the 220th Cavalry Regiment;[23] the German 1st Mountain Division, in contrast, lost only 16 soldiers killed, 50 wounded, and 2 missing in action during those two days, including the casualties sustained near Marukh.[24]

On 17 September, Soviet intelligence learned that the Germans had started to withdraw their forces to the Tuapse region, leaving one or two companies per pass. This information caused the Soviets to redouble their efforts to recapture the passes, exploiting their enormous

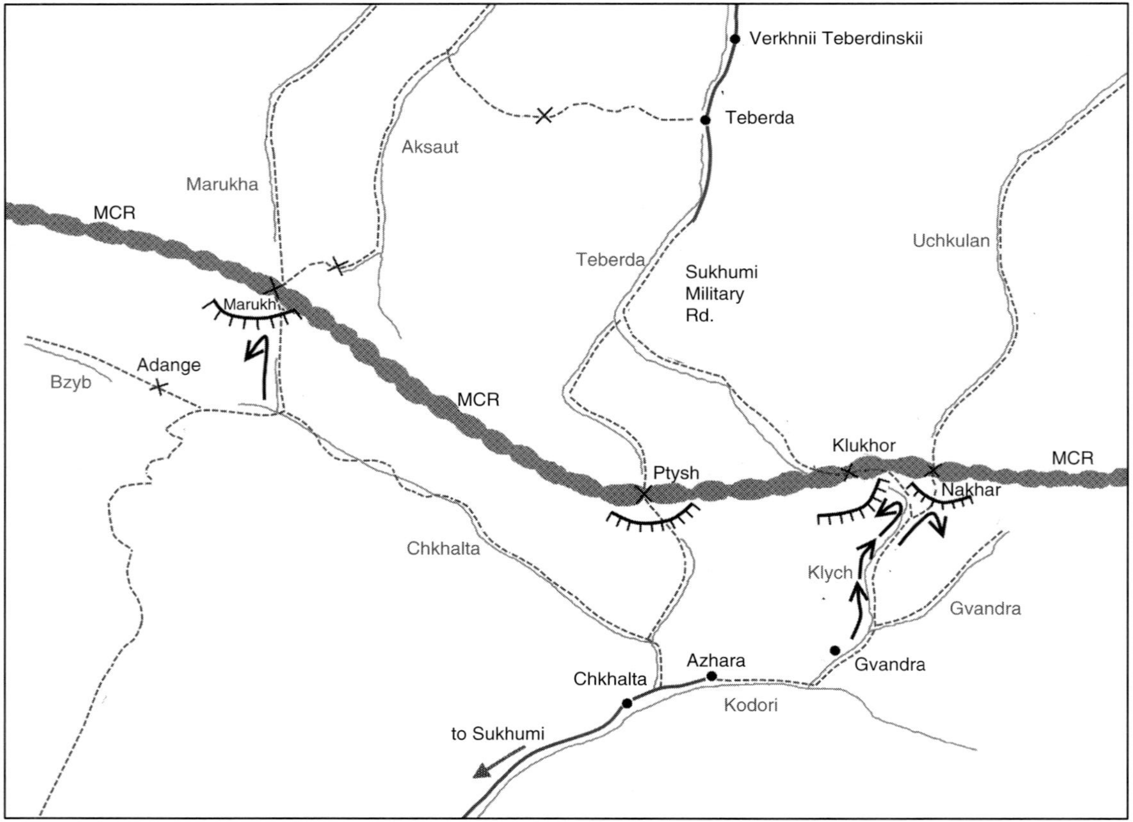

Map 6.1 Soviet assaults on Klukhor, Nakhar, and Marukh

numerical superiority. The costly Soviet attacks at Klukhor continued until 27 September; the attackers gained about 10 kilometres of ground.[25] Tiulenev claimed that the Germans 'were thrown into the abyss from Klukhor'.[26] In fact, the Germans stopped the Soviets at the southern foot of the pass.

Meanwhile, two Soviet regiments also attacked the less important Nakhar pass, next to Klukhor.[27] Although the commanders of the 394th Rifle Division claimed that on 18 September their soldiers took Nakhar[28] and, as several authors wrote later, 'threw the Hitlerites down its northern slopes',[29] in fact the Soviets were able to take only a small part of the ridge close to Nakhar rather than the pass itself. Furthermore, in the last days of September, the 121st 'Mountain' Regiment retreated from the ridge to the southern foot of Nakhar;[30] therefore, the costly capture of a small piece of the ridge had no significance. After this regiment was withdrawn from the front line on 30 September,[31] no large Soviet 'mountain' unit opposed the Germans along the longest section of the MCR front, from Elbrus to Sancharo. The Germans continued to hold the southern slopes of Klukhor and Nakhar, as well as the passes themselves, despite numerous Soviet attacks throughout October,[32] leaving them only when they chose to do so in mid January.

Between 15 August and 8 September, Soviet units lost 2,069 men killed, wounded, missing in action, and executed around Klukhor. The total casualties of the 1st Mountain Division in the Klukhor, Marukh, and Elbrus regions for these days were 141 killed, 461 wounded, and 35 missing in action.[33] Major Litvinov, the OG representative with the 394th Rifle Division, concluded that the Soviets 'suffered grave casualties but attained no success' at Klukhor.[34]

Marukh

The Soviet counteroffensive started from positions 6 kilometres away from the pass. On 9 and 10 September, the survivors of the German assault advanced 2 kilometres before they ran into strong German defences; reinforcements began arriving on 11 September, increasing the strength of the Soviets to about five battalions[35] – that is, roughly 4,000 men against an estimated 2,500 Germans. Although Russian authors alleged that 'the soldiers of the 808th and 810th Rifle

Regiments routed and drove the extolled "Edelweiss" [division] north from Marukh',[36] the documents show a different story: the Soviets could not turn the tables.

Marshal Andrei Grechko describes numerous futile attempts to take Marukh between 9 September and early October. Exactly as had happened at Klukhor, the Soviet regular infantry launched stereotypical frontal assaults that were dismissed in the Soviet *Manual on Mountain Warfare* as an incorrect tactic. It was hard to dislodge the Germans from their well-organised tiered positions behind minefields.[37] Lieutenant Shuvaev recounts the assault on a height near Marukh pass from 10 September to 13 September, when his company of 200 men finally took the height, having lost 188 men killed, wounded, and frostbitten. He concludes: 'Thus we routed the extolled mountain units of General Konrad.'[38] The total casualties of the 1st Mountain Division from 10 to 13 September were only eight men killed and twenty-five wounded, not just at this height but on all sectors of the front,[39] which makes it clear that the German mountain troops were 'extolled' for a reason.

On 14 September, the Germans retreated to the foot of the pass, about 2 kilometres from its saddle, and the Soviets were unable to take this position despite numerous attempts.[40] One of these attempts, made by the 1st Battalion of the 155th Rifle Brigade, ended with the loss of 400 of its 500 men between 25 and 29 September, with no positive results, after which the brigade was withdrawn from the front.[41] Soviet attacks in the Marukh region continued until early October.[42] On 28 October, the Germans retreated to the saddle of the pass because heavy snow made it hard to supply units at its steep southern slopes. In November, the Soviets launched one more attack on the pass, intended not to attain tangible results but merely to demonstrate the zeal of the officers after an incident that had stained their reputation. Filimonov, a Soviet cadet, described the attack: 'On the eve of the [7th] November holiday [we received] an order to assault the pass ... Officers told us that two soldiers had allegedly deserted and in order to erase this disgrace we had to take the pass ... The whole day we floundered in snow over 3 metres deep ... but could not even make our way to the glacier. Our "attack" came to naught',[43] even before the Germans could engage the Soviets. The Germans kept Marukh until 11 January 1943, after which they left it quietly and joined their comrades retreating from other passes.[44] The casualties of the 46th Army during September at Marukh alone were 424 men dead, 376 wounded, and 409 missing in

Figure 6.1 A German machinegun crew, in white camouflage capes, ready for action. Credit: Süddeutsche Zeitung Photo / Alamy Stock Photo

action, perhaps excluding the units that did not belong to this army, such as the cadets and the 36th Naval Frontier Guards Battalion. In contrast, the 1st Mountain Division lost, in total, 44 men killed, 133 wounded, and 6 missing in action in all sections of the MCR front between 1 and 26 September;[45] most of these casualties occurred in the Klych valley.

Elbrus

The Elbrus region was the highest section of the MCR front. The Germans controlled it with a force of five companies dispersed among several well-built strongholds, reinforced by mountain artillery.[46] The most important of these strongholds were the Priiut 11 hotel; the small Staryi Krugozor (2,936 m) and Ledovaia Baza (3,800 m) shelters located at the southern and the eastern approaches to Priiut 11, respectively; and the positions at the Chiper and the Chiper-Azau passes (Map 6.2).

Beginning on 23 August, a Soviet force equal to one regiment[47] made many attempts to attack the German strongholds around Elbrus.

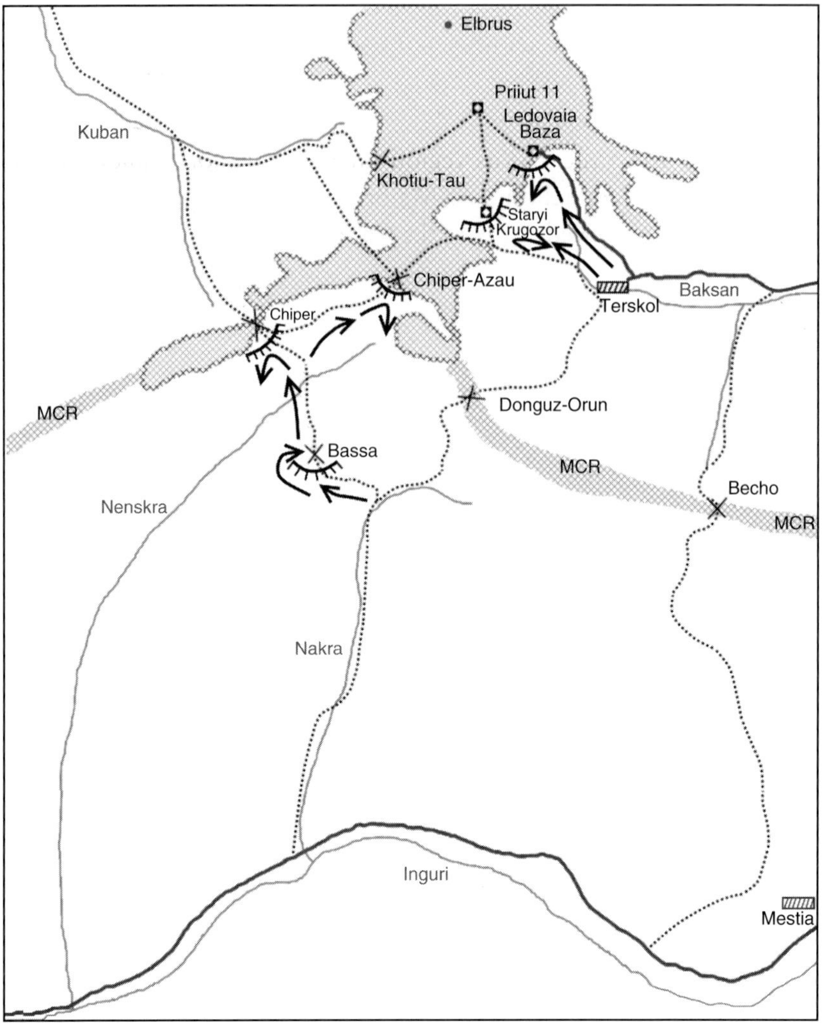

Map 6.2 Soviet attacks in the Elbrus region

These attacks were mostly raids conducted by units varying in strength between several platoons and two companies.[48] Between 1 and 7 September and 10 and 16 September, the Soviets launched such raids on Staryi Krugozor, Ledovaia Baza, and the Chiper and the Chiper-Azau passes almost daily. The Germans repelled all these raids, which sometimes ended with the total destruction of the attacking units.[49]

The commanders of the 63rd Cavalry Division, who were initially in charge of all the Soviet forces in the Elbrus area, refused to move their headquarters to the region of operation, preferring to stay in the populated Inguri valley with its mild climate and good food supply. The Mestia village that they chose for their headquarters, located at an altitude of 1,500 metres, was about 70 kilometres and several high passes away from the Elbrus region and the Gvandra valley, where their regiments were fighting. As Major Saltykov, representative of the General Staff of the Red Army in the Caucasus, wrote in his analysis of the command-and-control system, 'the shortage of communication means and their misuse deprived the Headquarters [of the 63rd Cavalry Division] of the opportunity to command. [The division commander] General [Kuz'ma] Beloshnichenko ignored all arguments about reconnaissance in person and about moving [the headquarters'] operations section closer to the pass[es].'[50] Neither Beloshnichenko nor his chief of staff, Major Romanenko, ever visited their operational region; that is why they could not grasp the scope of the daunting supply problems that their regiments experienced. Their soldiers continued to wear summer uniforms for the duration of their deployment in the high mountains.[51]

Being ignorant of the terrain and the physical demands at high altitudes, these commanders planned their actions in the same way they would for actions on the plains. A major raid on Priiut 11 that began in the early hours of 11 September was an example of such planning. The Soviets were to take the hotel with a pincer attack. A cavalry squadron,[52] reinforced by NKVD platoons, had to attack Priiut 11 from below: within two days, it had to gain 2,000 metres of altitude from Terskol village (2,100 m) in the Baksan valley, launching an assault first on Ledovaia Baza (3,800 m), occupied by a small German unit, and then on Priiut 11 (4,130 m). This assault was to be coupled with an attack by an NKVD company on Priiut 11 from the slope above it. This company had to cover, in two days, a distance of about 20 kilometres, gaining 3,100 metres of altitude from the mouth of the Irik River, at 1,700 metres, to the Elbrus slopes, at 4,800 metres. The cavalrymen and the NKVD company could not co-ordinate their actions because none of them had radios. The report on the action seems to indicate that the units had no pack animals to transport weapons and ammunition, which meant that the soldiers had to carry everything on their backs. Led by a climber, the cavalry squadron reached in one day an abandoned meteorological station below Ledovaia Baza at 3,400 metres but, when the tired soldiers attempted to move beyond it, the Germans pinned them down. The squadron was thus unable even to approach Ledovaia Baza, let alone Priiut 11. The NKVD company that was to strike Priiut 11 from above was guided by three climbers; one of them, a former director of a mountaineering camp, found some alpinist gear in the camp's depot and passed it to the soldiers. The company, wearing regular infantry uniforms and long boots with flat soles, struggled through deep snow for four days and came to Elbrus, at an altitude of 4,200 metres, only two days after the Germans had repelled the cavalrymen. The exhausted soldiers reached the glacier on the way to Priiut 11 but could not cross a wide crevasse during a severe blizzard and had to turn back without even seeing the Germans.[53]

After the TCF commanders realised that cavalry was poorly suited for actions among rocks and glaciers and requested a mountain formation to replace the cavalrymen, they received the 242nd Division. The miscellaneous units of this rifle division, with a total strength of about 2,800 men, had recently escaped the Germans by crossing the MCR via the Sancharo and Klukhor passes. Their combat record included mainly counterinsurgency operations targeting anti-Soviet guerrillas.[54] Since their total strength equalled only one regiment, while a mountain division was supposed to have four regiments, this formation received three new regiments assembled hastily from raw recruits, and was designated a 'mountain' division with the same number. The division's headquarters began organising the new formation on 29 August in Zugdidi, and already by 5 September one of its regiments[55] was marching to the highest section of the front around Elbrus, followed three days later by another.[56] These regiments replaced the 63rd Cavalry Divisions at the Donguz-Orun, Becho, and Bassa passes between 13 and 22 September.[57]

The failure of the Germans to take the Donguz-Orun pass allowed the Soviets to rescue the 392nd Georgian Rifle Division trapped in the Baksan valley to the north of the MCR. The division retreated to Donguz-Orun and crossed the pass between 4 and 19 November.[58] On 10 November, the same commanders who had repeatedly ordered raids on Priiut 11 with starting points at altitudes 2,000 metres below the target, all of which had failed, decided to use the evacuating units of the 392nd Rifle Division, along with a raw regiment of the 242nd 'Mountain' Division, to drive the Germans away from the Elbrus region. At that time, the mountains were already covered by deep snow, but these commanders argued: 'The artillery and mortars of the 392nd Rifle Division allow us to accomplish this mission quickly and without grave casualties ... If well planned, the mission, no doubt, will bring success because the enemy has only small forces ... There will be no better moment for taking [Staryi] Krugozor shelter and Priiut 11. We have the advantage in everything.'[59] These commanders once again ignored the weather conditions, the absence of training in mountain warfare, the absence of mountaineering gear, and the morale factor. Soldiers of the 392nd Rifle Division were severely demoralised by their ordeal, while the combat capacity of the 242nd 'Mountain' Division, which found itself in the high Caucasus a week after its commanders began raising it, was far less efficient than an average rifle division. Yet, on 11 November, Leselidze ordered one of its regiments[60] to gain about 1,000 metres from its positions in the Terskol valley to Priiut 11, in bitterly cold weather, and then to attack Priiut 11 across the glacier. The attack occurred on 13 November; it ended when the soldiers, struggling through deep snow, ran into a minefield, resulting in the loss of two men gravely wounded and three men with light wounds.[61] In this last action in the battle at the MCR, the commanders of the 46th Army displayed the same level of incompetence as at its beginning.

In Grechko's words, 'despite vigorous actions, it [the 242nd "Mountain" Division] could not gain success' in the many local offensives it attempted to undertake.[62] The Germans continued to defend all the strongholds near Elbrus – Krugozor, Ledovaia Baza, and Priiut 11, as well as the Chiper, Chiper-Azau, and Khotiu-Tau passes – until their general retreat from the MCR in January 1943.[63] They suffered only light casualties in this part of the front. The conclusion of the 46th Army Headquarters about the Soviet actions in the Elbrus region was brief but revealing: 'they failed to produce any positive results'.[64]

Being unable to dislodge the Germans from Priiut 11, the 46th Army ordered the destruction of the hotel. The Red Air Force and artillery repeatedly pounded the hotel and the German positions at Chiper-Azau and Khotiu-Tau from mid September to the end of the year and reported that their shells and bombs had hit their targets.[65] In light of these reports, the outrage of Soviet authors at the 'fascist barbarians' who 'soiled all the [hotel] rooms beyond recognition'[66] loses its merit.

Sancharo

While the 1st Mountain Division began its slow retreat towards the MCR on 26 August, the Stettner Group of the 4th Mountain Division was still enjoying a view of the Black Sea from the Gudauta pass. However, forces led by Colonel Piiashev blocked the southern slopes of the pass and were aiming to surround the Germans by descending to their rear from the neighbouring Achavchar and Dou passes. Piiashev's Group, consisting of regular infantry and NKVD troops, was far superior in numbers to its enemy; its inexperience in mountain warfare mattered less at lower elevations, and it possessed considerable firepower: thirty-six heavy 82-mm and 107-mm mortars, and twenty-nine cannons of 76 mm, of which, however, only three were mountain guns that could be used in the high mountains.[67]

While Stettner thought about how to attack Achavchar, Piiashev's vanguards descended from the Dou pass on 29 August and launched several attacks against the German battalion guarding the bridge across the Bzyb River; some of them ended in hand-to-hand fighting (Map 6.3).[68] These attacks threatened to sever the communication lines with the battalion positioned at the Gudauta pass.[69] Although the Germans repelled all the attacks, they were stunned by the vigour of their opponents and realised that, instead of the demoralised battalion[70] they had pursued from the Sancharo group of passes, they were now facing fresh Soviet forces that were determined and well armed, with large reserves of ammunition.[71] The Soviet heavy mortars pounded the German positions with intense and accurate fire. On 30 August, at the Gudauta pass, this fire killed twenty-five Germans and wounded many more: the German casualties were thus greater than those sustained during the assaults on Klukhor, Marukh, and Sancharo taken together, and several days later Soviet mortars inflicted serious casualties on the battalion that defended the bridge.[72] This battalion could barely keep its positions under increasing pressure. Stettner faced a potential 'Berezina', and it was clear that, if the Soviets captured the bridge, escape across the river would be problematic because the flood had swept away the temporary bridges built by the Germans and it would be hard to build new ones during the flood.

Meanwhile, the logistics of the Stettner Group began faltering. In early September, the German units south of the MCR were facing a severe shortage of ammunition, and their daily bread ration had fallen

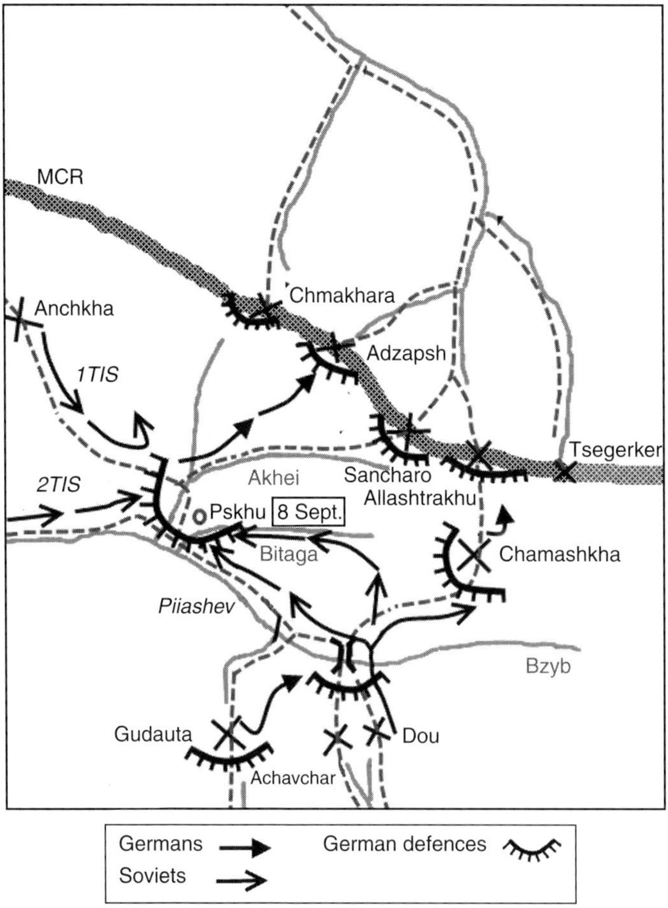

Map 6.3 Soviet attacks against the Stettner Group

from 600 grams to 150 and even 120 grams.[73] Stettner realised that, in such circumstances, he could not break through to the Black Sea; in fact, he could not even keep his positions against numerically superior forces with much greater firepower and high morale.

After the attack of the 1st Mountain Division along the Sukhumi Military Road bogged down, General Konrad decided to shift the focus of the offensive from the 1st to the 4th Mountain Division. The Stettner Group was to be reinforced by the rest of the 4th Mountain Division and also by two battalions of the 1st Mountain Division, which had to leave only screens sufficient for the defence of the passes in the Klukhor and Elbrus regions and join Stettner in his attack on Gudauta. Hitler approved of this plan,[74] which presumed that the

Stettner Group had to keep its positions for at least the two weeks needed for the arrival of reinforcements. However, it could no longer hold up against Soviet attacks. On 31 August, six days after the impressive and almost bloodless victory at Sancharo, Konrad ordered Stettner to leave the Gudauta pass, cross the Bzyb to its northern bank, and concentrate his forces around Pskhu village while waiting for reinforcements.[75] On 2 September, the German battalion holding the Gudauta pass left it, and on the same night the Germans evacuated the bridgehead on the southern bank of the Bzyb and blew up the bridge behind them.[76] The Soviets thus missed the opportunity to trap the Germans on the southern bank but, since they knew of fords across the Bzyb, they crossed the river and continued to pursue Stettner towards Pskhu. Encouraged by Piiashev's success, Leselidze ordered him, on 2 September, to destroy the Germans on the southern slopes of the MCR and retake all the passes in the Sancharo region by 7 September, thus demonstrating once again his total ignorance of the terrain and the situation on the front.[77]

On 2 September, Beria commanded the relentless bombardment of Pskhu,[78] and from 3 to 5 September Soviet bombers launched 101 sorties targeting German positions in this region.[79] The Germans could only dream of such air support. These attacks killed and wounded 61

Figure 6.2 A Soviet 120-mm mortar crew. Heavy mortars turned out to be the most effective artillery pieces in the absence of mountain guns. Credit: RGAKFD

soldiers, many of whom belonged to artillery crews and so could not be easily replaced; they also killed 106 pack horses, or more than 20 per cent of those allotted to Stettner at the beginning of his offensive and perhaps half of what he retained at this time, thus devastating the overstretched German logistics.[80] In the absence of vegetation in the high mountains, the German supply columns could move only at night to avoid air attacks, which made their progress painfully slow. Yet despite their great superiority in firepower, the Soviets continued to lose more men than the Germans. From 26 August to 3 September, the Stettner Group lost 208 men killed and wounded, many of whom fell victim to mortar fire and air force attacks, whereas Piiashev lost 342 men killed and wounded from 28 August to 3 September.[81] These data exclude those missing in action; usually, the number of missing Soviets was much greater than the number of missing Germans.

Yet Piiashev surrounded the Germans at Pskhu from three sides: his main force advanced on Pskhu from the south, one battalion attacked from the east along the Bitaga valley, and the Tbilisi Infantry School, with 400 men, approached Pskhu from the west along the Bzyb valley. The only way out of Pskhu was up the Akhei valley to the Sancharo group of passes. When another half-battalion of Tbilisi Infantry School, with 311 men, crossed the Anchkha pass from Ritsa Lake and began descending on 6 September into the Akhei valley, to the north of the Stettner Group to its rear, it threatened to close this only remaining escape route.[82] However, the Soviet forces converging on Pskhu from various directions could not act cohesively in the absence of reliable radio communications. The Soviet strikes went uncoordinated, and the Germans repelled all of them. Outraged, Leselidze described how a German platoon easily drove back to the Anchkha pass a half-battalion of the Tbilisi Infantry School, which was ten times stronger.[83] Nonetheless, when Piiashev began vigorously attacking Pskhu, it became clear that he could break through the German defences at any moment; if he had, the Germans would have found themselves in what Stettner described as a 'mousetrap'.[84] The Germans misunderstood a defector from the Tbilisi Infantry School, who told them that at least 1,000 of his comrades were to attack Pskhu; they thought that the cadet was referring to a unit that was attempting to get to their rear from Anchkha. In fact, most of these cadets were in the Bzyb valley, with only a half-battalion potentially threatening Stettner's rear.[85] This misinformation worried Stettner; it would be extremely dangerous to have

1,000 enemy soldiers between his battered force and the Sancharo passes. In the face of the Soviet preparations for a massive attack, Stettner decided to evacuate Pskhu and retreat back to the MCR without even asking permission from his superiors; they authorised the retreat only *post factum*.[86]

Although most Russian historians maintain that Piiashev 'surrounded and routed' the Stettner Group,[87] the documents of the TCF disprove these claims. Stettner's force was never fully surrounded, nor was it destroyed. Despite heavy casualties and a severe shortage of ammunition, it never fled in panic, which happened frequently to Soviet units, according to Soviet documents. On the evening of 7 September, the Germans began marching back to the Adzapsh pass, but they interrupted the retreat for two and a half hours to recover their wounded lost in the dark, something that the Soviet defenders of the Caucasus never did in similar circumstances. Stettner walked with the rearguard covering the retreat, which no senior Soviet officer assigned to the TCF had done either. The next day, the Germans reached the MCR unmolested because, as Soviets reports say, 'the pursuit was poorly organised'.[88] Stettner abandoned only a reconnaissance platoon to its fate, and that was because it had been sent on a three-day mission and could not be informed of the general retreat, but this platoon made its way to the passes six days later.[89]

Stettner attempted to hold the Chamashkha pass between the Bzyb and the MCR, but the Soviets greatly outnumbered the depleted German battalion assigned to defend the pass: two Soviet battalions attacked Chamashkha from the south,[90] and a force equal to two and a half battalions attacked it from the west along the Akhei valley in an attempt to sever the communication lines between the German defenders and the Allashtrakhu pass to the north of Chamashkha.[91] After Piiashev entered Pskhu on 8 September, airplanes carrying various supplies began landing at its airstrip, which considerably eased Soviet logistics.[92] The Germans were beating off attacks on Chamashkha for nine days, beginning on 7 September, despite an increasing shortage of food and ammunition, but on 16 September they withdrew to the Allashtrakhu and Adzapsh passes.[93] This was another failure of the numerous Soviet forces to trap and destroy the Germans. Nonetheless, Stettner's retreat to the MCR meant the end of the German plans to break to the Black Sea. The Germans left two battalions to defend the Sancharo passes.[94]

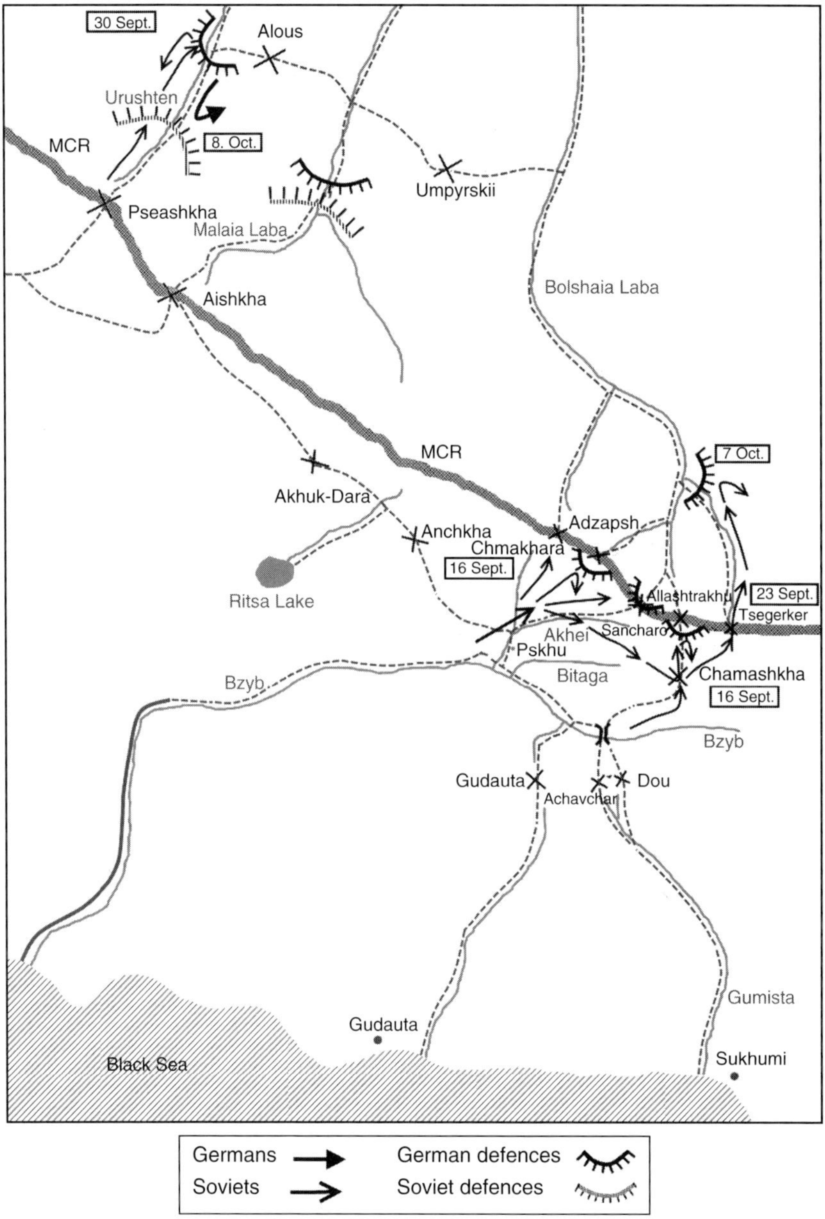

Map 6.4 Soviet attacks in the Sancharo region and actions near Aishkha and Pseashkha

Despite all the casualties suffered from late August on, by 15 September, the strength of the Piiashev Group had grown to 7,806 men, or 10 full-strength rifle battalions, against 2 German battalions weakened by heavy attrition.[95] When Leselidze's plan to take all the passes of the Sancharo group by 7 September did not materialise, he shifted the deadline, first to 15 September and then to the 20th,[96] and after the last deadline passed without any positive outcome he and Tiulenev continued to press Piiashev to meet the desired objective at any cost. Between 15 September and mid October, the Soviets engaged in an endless series of small-scale attacks by several platoons or companies at all the Sancharo passes (Map 6.4). These attacks were again stereotypical and therefore predictable; all of them failed, and again the Soviets suffered disproportional casualties.[97] A Soviet soldier recalled the desperate and fruitless assaults on Allashtrakhu and Sancharo, when he and his comrades 'had to attack along the only path upwards. At times the attackers literally ran [stepping] on the bodies of [their] comrades.'[98] Some of these attacks ended with the loss of almost an entire assault unit.[99]

As the OG concluded, 'of all the battles at the western passes [of the MCR], the toughest one occurred around Sancharo'.[100] This was probably true, although this assessment stems in part from reports filed by Piiashev, who overstated the scale of action and his progress to a greater extent than did other commanders, and the OG, headed by NKVD officers and seeking to emphasise the achievements of their NKVD colleague, duly relayed Piiashev's tales to the TCF without comment on their credibility.[101] Piiashev's reports give the impression of a slow but steady advance; his units claimed to have inflicted enormous casualties on the enemy. However, Leselidze called these claims 'inflated', giving as an example a discrepancy between the claims in daily reports of the number of Germans killed in the Sancharo region from 29 August to 1 September – a total of 405 men – and the four-day summary for the same period, where their number suddenly grew to 1,079.[102] Given that the 4th Mountain Division recorded the loss of only 34 men killed during these days, Piiashev inflated enemy casualties by 12 times in the daily reports and by 32 times in the summary. When Leselidze received Piiashev's next summary, he remarked sarcastically: 'We know that the Sancharo Group faces ... about 2,250 [German] soldiers. The combat reports of the Sancharo Group Headquarters assess the total enemy casualties from 29 August to 9 October as 3,081 men. This means that the entire enemy manpower opposing the Sancharo Group was already annihilated a long time ago.'[103] In addition to the fantastic body count, Piiashev reported falsely that his units took Adzapsh on 12 September and Allashtrakhu and Chmakhara on 16 September, the latter reportedly taken in heavy battle.[104] The reality was different: the Germans left Chmakhara on 15 September, one day before the Soviet 'assault', because it was hard to maintain the supply line to its garrison after snow and ice had covered the steep path leading from the pass to the Bolshaia Laba valley.[105] The Soviets never attempted to descend down the northern slopes of Chmakhara; therefore, the fact that they occupied its saddle had no significance. Having reported taking Adzapsh and Allashtrakhu on 16 September, Piiashev then wrote, on 10 October, that 'the enemy continues to defend Allashtrakhu ... and Adzapsh'; he repeated this information on 30 December.[106] Petrov admitted that he received 'several false reports about the taking of passes that were still kept by the enemy'.[107] Piiashev attributed these reports to the insufficient navigation skills of Soviet commanders – a poor excuse for bombastic and false victory claims.[108] Frustrated, Leselidze compared the effectiveness of Soviet and German actions: 'The enemy easily and quickly occupied the Klukhor and Marukh regions with small forces ... The 394th Rifle Division and Piiashev Group were launching numerous attacks for a month and suffered grave casualties but could not take the passes.'[109] The Germans kept Adzapsh and Allashtrakhu until early January, well after the end of the battle at the MCR.[110]

In addition to Chmakhara, the Soviets also occupied the Tsegerker pass: on 23 September, a unit of the 25th Frontier Guard Regiment climbed to its top.[111] The circumstances of this event are unclear because neither the Soviets nor the Germans reported action at Tsegerker. Perhaps the Germans abandoned it because of logistical considerations, as they had abandoned Chmakhara. On 25 September, 300 frontier guards descended from Tsegerker down the Bolshaia Laba valley to its confluence with the Sancharo River, seeking 'to cut the trail that goes along Bolshaia Laba to the [Sancharo] pass and ... to strike the rear of the enemy Sancharo garrison from the north'.[112] This was a rational plan within the mountain warfare canon, but nothing came out of it, for unknown reasons, despite the fact that, according to Soviet reports, the frontier guards remained on the northern side of the MCR and the weather still allowed actions at the MCR. Only on 7 October did a small reconnaissance party of frontier guards repeat this raid, but it was repelled by a German platoon before it could reach the German supply route at the confluence with the Sancharo River, after which the scouts returned to the northern slopes of Tsegerker.[113] There were no further attempts to intercept the German communications with the Sancharo, Allashtrakhu, and Adzapsh passes from Tsegerker. Perhaps this inexplicable inaction during the three weeks of fair weather occurred because field commanders at Tsegerker had adopted a 'live and let live' philosophy and did not want to risk losing Tsegerker again, which could have happened had they begun threatening German communications.

The OG perceived Piiashev as the ablest field commander at the MCR and believed that, if pressed hard, he could take all the Sancharo passes. However, Piiashev, frustrated with the lack of progress despite heavy casualties, rebelled. On 20 September, he wrote to the Headquarters of the 46th Army that he saw no opportunity to take the well-defended Sancharo with regular infantry dressed in summer uniforms, nor did he see any tactical or strategic reason for continuing the attacks. He explained that subzero temperatures turned the steep slopes, soaked with water after daily heavy rains, into icy slides that were impossible to climb without mountaineering gear. It addition to the gear, Piiashev requested the urgent delivery of 7,880 sets of winter uniforms and alcohol burners, adding that 'it would be wise to abstain from crossing the passes but to build strong and impregnable positions at their [southern] slopes' because, according to local people, snowfalls would close all trails in the high Caucasus within one or two weeks; even if his force crossed the passes, it would be impossible to supply them on the northern side of the MCR.[114] After General Petrov called these strong arguments 'spurious [*nadumannye*]',[115] the Military Council of the 46th Army summoned Piiashev to its Headquarters for explanations. The content of this meeting is unknown, but upon his return Piiashev continued the offensive on Sancharo, which, from his point of view, was pointless.

Two Soviet companies began the final assault on Sancharo on 14 October; it continued for the next two days.[116] Piiashev reported that his forces had taken the saddle of Sancharo on 16 October and had repelled a German counterattack during the following night. The commanders of the 46th Army perceived this report as a major victory won during the battle of the MCR. However, Piiashev still admitted that 'small enemy groups' remained at the pass and that the Germans still occupied its northern slopes. According to Piiashev, the Soviet casualties between 15 and 17 October were 24 killed and 267 wounded.[117]

The abnormally small proportion of killed versus wounded suggests that his soldiers suffered severe casualties from frostbite. Piiashev failed to mention any soldiers missing in action; the Germans claimed to have taken thirty-five prisoners.[118] The 4th Mountain Division reported its total casualties from 15 to 17 October in all parts of the front – including the Tuapse region, where more severe fights occurred – as three men killed, eighteen wounded, and one missing in action.[119] The Soviets thus lost at least fifteen soldiers for every German they killed or wounded during this assault. Furthermore, the credibility of Piiashev's claim about taking Sancharo is uncertain because the Germans maintained that they repelled the attacks on Sancharo on 16 and 17 October in hand-to-hand fighting.[120]

Thus, contrary to the claims of numerous Russian authors that the Soviets took 'the entire group of Sancharo passes', and that 'the well-armed and well-trained Hitlerist Jägers suffered a crushing defeat',[121] the Red Army secured only Chmakhara, which had been abandoned by the Germans; Tsegerker, probably also abandoned; and perhaps a part of Sancharo's saddle. The great disproportion of casualties during the assault on Sancharo shows that this alleged victory was, in any case, a Pyrrhic one. Furthermore, the reoccupation of these passes had no tactical, let alone strategic, significance because after the snowstorm of 18 to 21 October covered the slopes of the MCR with 2 metres of snow and the temperatures at the passes began fluctuating between −10 and −20 °C, with windchill temperatures much lower, large-scale actions became impossible.[122] On 21 October, five days after the alleged victory at Sancharo, Leselidze ordered the 46th Army to stop the offensive for the duration of winter and to descend to the southern feet of the MCR passes, where the Soviet formations could survive.[123] In the Sancharo region, the Soviets took positions about 800 metres below Tsegerker, 1,200 metres below Allashtrakhu, and 1,900 metres below Chmakhara.[124] The Germans continued to hold the Sancharo passes until their general retreat from this region.[125]

The Piiashev Group did attain limited success, but it enjoyed a greater numerical superiority over the enemy than the Soviets had elsewhere, and it also paid a hefty price for its small victories. The Soviet casualties in the Sancharo region during September were 258 men killed, 902 wounded, and an unknown number of missing in action. The total casualties of the 4th German Mountain Division in all parts of the front, including the approaches to the Aishkha Pass, between 1 and

26 September and before its units engaged in the Tuapse region on 27 September, were 108 men killed, 333 wounded, and 10 missing in action.[126] This disparity in casualties shows that in the Sancharo region, the Germans also attained their strategic goal pursued during the second phase of the battle in the high Caucasus: they tied up much larger Soviet forces than they deployed themselves and inflicted much greater casualties on the Soviets than they suffered themselves.

Aishkha, Pseashkha, and Belorechenskii

When the Headquarters of the 46th Army saw that Piiashev's offensive had lost its steam at the approaches to the Sancharo passes, they decided to ease his mission with another raid to the enemy rear. Encouraged by the fact that a mere two companies[127] of the 20th 'Mountain' Division had pinned down the Buchner Group at the far approaches to Aishkha, Leselidze reinforced the Soviet units in this region and sent some of them to cut the German communication lines to the Sancharo passes in the Bolshaia Laba valley. The Buchner Group had occupied the same positions since early September: its main forces stayed in the Malaia Laba valley, while one company, guarding the right flank of the Buchner Group, crossed the undefended Alous pass to the Urushten valley.[128]

The first step of the Soviet raid was to be an offensive towards the Umpyrskii pass, which separates the Malaia Laba and Bolshaia Laba valleys. The same two companies that had opposed the Buchner Group since late August were reinforced by one regiment,[129] which gave the Soviets numerical superiority with a ratio of 2:1. They attacked on 20 September down the Malaia Laba, but the Germans held their ground.[130] On 30 September, two other Soviet companies[131] converged on the German company in the Urushten valley, almost surrounding it and inflicting grave casualties.[132] These Soviet companies planned to cross the Alous pass and get to the rear of the Buchner Group in the Malaia Laba valley, thus trapping it between two Soviet forces, destroying it, and then proceeding to the Umpyrskii pass.[133] In response, the Headquarters of the 49th Mountain Corps sent a formation of 1,277 men from Sancharo to the Urushten valley; in this way, the Germans gained a large numerical superiority there. This formation relieved the remnants of the surrounded German company and pushed the Soviets back along the Urushten valley on 5 October.[134]

Inspired by this small success, the Headquarters of the 49th Mountain Corps, on 7 October, ordered an attempt to take the Pseashkha pass.[135] Marching through steady rain, Buchner's Group pursued the two Soviet companies until it ran into a series of huge heaps of downed trees 7 kilometres away and 600 metres below Pseashkha. This obstacle, of the sort used by Chechens during the Caucasus War in the nineteenth century, turned out to be the most effective of all the artificial obstacles erected by the Red Army at the MCR. Soviet engineers built six such barricades, each between 1,000 and 4,000 square metres in size, across the approaches to Aishkha and another ten across the approaches to Pseashkha.[136] It required strenuous physical effort for soldiers to force their way even through unmanned barricades several dozen metres deep; engineers had to work for many hours to clear the trail for pack animals. Having made their way through one or two such obstacles on 8 October, the Germans came to a barricade built in a narrow gorge that precluded envelopment. The two Soviet companies that Buchner had pursued from Alous defended the barricade protected by anti-personnel mines and well-camouflaged positions. The Germans could attack only with small forces along a narrow front, while the rest of their units had to idle at the trail below. Such attacks were ineffective in the absence of artillery support, which was impossible to provide because of the limited visibility in the dense forest. An outflanking strike across the cliffs, squeezing the gorge, would have required an enormous physical effort, which the German soldiers, soaking wet from the steady rain, could not undertake, being too exhausted first from the long and swift march from Sancharo to Urushten and then from carrying up loads of weapons and ammunition weighing 40 to 45 kilograms via a muddy and slippery trail along Urushten. The chaotic combat at close quarters, the only action possible in thick forest, nullified their tactical superiority. The Soviet defenders inflicted serious casualties on the Germans during their futile attacks.[137] The tormenting march from Sancharo and the inability to overcome the barricades undermined the morale of the Buchner Group.[138]

After Buchner personally came to the front line from Malaia Laba via the Alous pass to inspect the situation, he cancelled the offensive. The actions in the Malaia Laba and Urushten valleys thus ended in a stalemate: the Germans could not advance to Aishkha and Pseahkha, and the Soviets could not drive the Germans down the valleys.[139] Although the war diary of the TCF reported on 16 and 20 October that the 174th 'Mountain' Regiment took the Umpyrskii pass, this was merely wishful thinking; a later Soviet report admitted that the Germans kept Umpyrskii until the end of the battle at the MCR.[140] As usual, the Soviets paid a heavy price for their limited success: by 9 October, when major actions in this region stopped, the 20th 'Mountain' Division had lost, in total, 553 men: 152 killed, 266 wounded, 126 missing in action, and 9 taken prisoner.[141] Most of these casualties occurred in the Malaia Laba and Urushten valleys. Nonetheless, the stalemate away from the passes was a Soviet tactical victory, attained despite the substantial numerical superiority of the Germans. The Soviet engineers who built the tree barricades and the lower-level commanders who chose their locations were the heroes of this victory.

The Soviets gained a second and perhaps even more important victory at the relatively low Belorechenskii pass (1,782 m) at the extreme west of the MCR, outside the operational area of the 49th Mountain Corps but within that of the Soviet 20th 'Mountain' Division. Two of its companies[142] were at the pass when a German Jäger regiment[143] began advancing towards it. The actions at the far approaches to the Belorechenskii pass took place between 21 August and mid October.[144] The Jäger units were trained and equipped for action on exactly such a terrain: woody mountains up to 1,000 metres high. Had the Germans taken the pass, they would have found themselves close to a road leading to Sochi, the Black Sea coastal resort. The TCF urgently dispatched the 23rd NKVD Frontier Guard Regiment and 33rd NKVD Motorised Regiment to Belorechenskii. By the time the frontier guards arrived on 23 August, the Germans were already close to the pass.[145] The Soviets had a slight numerical superiority, and they also had mountain guns, in addition to mortars. For unknown reasons, the Soviets placed their 'mountain' companies in the second echelon, leaving only NKVD regiments to face the Germans. Yet in the lower mountains, what mattered was the ability of small units to act independently rather than mountaineering skills, and the frontier guards, accustomed to operating in small units, displayed more initiative than regular infantry. The Soviet reports emphasised the exceptionally staunch resistance of the frontier guards who, by 3 September, had stopped the German offensive in a pitched battle.[146] Both NKVD regiments suffered such grave casualties that they almost ceased to exist as combat units, but by 11 September they had driven the Germans away from Belorechenskii and were continuing their slow advance, pushing the Germans north.[147] The 'mountain' troops staying in the second echelon missed their chance to acquire martial glory, leaving this victory to NKVD soldiers.[148]

Conclusion

The Germans enjoyed a solid tactical edge over the Soviets throughout the battle of the Caucasus. To be able to sneak around enemy positions along several routes and then launch a co-ordinated joint assault on these positions from flanks and rear, the attackers should know the exact location of the enemy, find ways to bypass their positions, and have small units trained to operate independently but in concert. The Germans could use such tactics, unlike the Soviets. The major tactical handicaps of the Red Army during the battle at the MCR stemmed from its ignorance of mountain warfare, the lack of mobility across rugged terrain, the poor standard of infantry training, and the absence of proper means of communication or inexperience in their use. A report written after the end of the battle at the MCR states: 'Commanders were untrained for leading [their] units in the mountains and could not navigate quickly or read a map'[149] or use a compass, which most Soviet reconnaissance parties did not have.[150] Soviet small units were unable to operate independently, and junior commanders lacked the initiative necessary for such actions. The Germans had much better intelligence about the location of enemy positions, the strength of the enemy in a certain part of the front, and possible outflanking routes because their reconnaissance parties could move across terrain that Soviet regular infantry believed to be impassable. Major Bozhenko, the smart chief of staff of the 242nd 'Mountain' Division, compared the ability of the Germans and the Soviets to manoeuvre across the mountainous landscape:

> Deploying reconnaissance parties on a broad front, the enemy searches for envelopment routes with one clear objective: to reach the southern slopes of the passes and strike us from the rear ... Our units conduct reconnaissance on a narrow front; they do not try [to find ways that allow us] to envelop the enemy

> by crossing ridges and to infiltrate the enemy's rear. Because of insufficient reconnaissance, commanders and headquarters do not know who opposes them, how strong the enemy is, and what his intentions and actions are, and, since the enemy moves from one height to another thus creating the impression of a large force, they [the commanders] inflate his strength.[151]

Having no climbing gear or mountaineering skills, these scouts chose predictable routes protected by German screens; several Soviet reconnaissance parties vanished without a trace, ambushed by Germans expecting them to come from obvious directions, which made the following parties reluctant to take risks and approach the German positions.[152] The Soviet scouts could not take a single prisoner in the Klukhor and Elbrus regions for the entire period of action at the MCR, whereas the Germans made four attempts to take Soviet prisoners around Elbrus and succeeded in three.[153] When a Soviet reconnaissance platoon of eighteen men received an order to take a German prisoner on 3 December and ran into four Germans, the entire platoon fled, led by its commander.[154] The absence of detailed and timely intelligence resulted in tactical errors.

Bozhenko also made an unflattering comparison of the German and Soviet defence and attack practice. In defence, 'Germans always build tiered positions at heights', whereas the Soviets 'stay, as a rule, in defiles and ignore dominating heights ... In fact, [the Soviet soldiers] take positions only at passes' saddles, leaving neighbouring heights unoccupied. This gives the enemy the opportunity to climb these heights unopposed and then fire at the flanks of our units deployed at the passes.' During offensives, the Soviet infantry 'launch mainly frontal attacks, pushing the enemy away instead of surrounding and destroying him. They attack on a narrow front and their units are deployed in depth. As a result, only the vanguard unit engages the enemy, whereas all others sit behind rocks and watch, sustaining sometimes unnecessary casualties.'[155] General Petrov advanced a trivial but sound explanation of the flawed Soviet tactics: 'Most officers do not know the peculiarities of mountain warfare ... [That is why they] lack imagination and resourcefulness.'[156]

In addition to numerous tactical handicaps stemming from inexperience in mountain warfare, the Soviet forces at the MCR suffered from poor general infantry training. The 307th Regiment of the

61st Rifle Division was the largest formation of the Piiashev Group. Inspectors who assessed the combat capacity of this division believed that its training

> is inadequate and does not correspond to the demands of modern warfare ... Most officers cannot handle their weapons ... The individual training of soldiers and the cohesion of sections and platoons are poor, especially when they operate on mountainous and forested terrain. [Tactical] exercises at the level of the company and above have never been conducted. The [tactical] training of officers ... is inadequate.[157]

Five of the eight platoons that were examined failed their marksmanship test.

The 242nd Division provides a grotesque example of the Soviet approach to mountain warfare. Raw recruits who found themselves in the high Caucasus a week after their commanders had started organising this formation and who therefore lacked even basic military training made up the large majority of their personnel; Bozhenko referred to the 900th Regiment as 'absolutely untrained'.[158] While the division was still replacing the cavalry at the MCR beginning in mid September, it received an order to throw the Germans down from Khotiu-Tau, Chiper-Azau, and Chiper and take Priiut 11 by 20 September 1942 – a mission that would have been impossible to accomplish within the given timeframe even with well-trained mountain troops, let alone with raw recruits who had just arrived at the front line and were totally unfamiliar with the terrain.[159] Naturally, these recruits could not fulfil the order, and they were the last to blame for this failure, which had to be attributed primarily to the Headquarters of the 46th Army, who believed that a formation raised from scratch three weeks earlier could perform complicated missions in the mountains.

The 242nd 'Mountain' Division remained in the high Caucasus until late 1942, but its skills remained inadequate until the very end of its deployment in the high Caucasus. Bozhenko wrote on 30 November, long after actions at the MCR had stopped: 'The division's manpower came from the plains of Georgia, the Ordzhonikidze region, and Ukraine. These personnel found themselves in the mountains for the first time, and at present they are still insufficiently trained for actions in the mountains. The vast majority cannot ski on the plains, and nobody can ski in the mountains.'[160] Although during the battle at the MCR, the

Soviet officers came to the conclusion that snipers were 'extraordinarily important in the mountains',[161] a report on marksmanship exercises conducted in late December 1942 in the 903rd 'Mountain' Regiment of this division stated that, of the 275 soldiers picked randomly from various units, 7 men, or 2.5 per cent, received an 'excellent' mark; 23 men, or 8.4 per cent, showed 'good' results; 65 men, or 23.6 per cent, scored a 'satisfactory' mark; and 180 men, or 65.5 per cent, failed to hit the target.[162] Having spent three and a half months at the front line, the regiment attained these pitiful results at a shooting range located in a flat area without any impact from the enemy. Obviously, they could hit almost no target during their front-line tour, when they had to adjust their sights while firing at enemy positions located at high angles and while being sprayed by enemy bullets. Colonel Georgii Kurashvili, the division's commander, wrote that 'soldiers and even some officers cannot load and unload their weapons, let alone take aim and fire' accurately; they 'continue to remain as raw as they were three months ago'.[163] That is why all their attempts to take Priiut 11 and other nearby heights failed. The German mountain troops demonstrated far greater tactical skills, even at lower elevations, than their Soviet counterparts, including those belonging to 'mountain' divisions, and their general infantry training was also superior.

7 MOSAICS OF MOUNTAIN WARFARE: COMPARATIVE MILITARY EFFECTIVENESS IN THE HIGH CAUCASUS

Otstavit' razgovory!
Vpered i vverkh! A tam . . .
Ved' eto nashi gory,
Oni pomogut nam!

[Shut up and climb!
After all,
These are our mountains;
They will help us!]

Vladimir Vysotskii, 'Edelweiss Troops'

Apart from individual and tactical training, many other factors affected Soviet and German actions in the high Caucasus. This chapter compares these factors in terms of their impacts on the performance of the opposing sides during the battle at the MCR. Some of these factors favoured the Soviets, but most benefited the Germans, because the latter had exercised mountain warfare before World War II, while the former had not.

Firepower

Only 'mountain' Soviet divisions had mountain artillery comparable to that of the Germans;[1] the rifle and cavalry divisions, which constituted the large majority of those who fought in the high Caucasus, had only standard field artillery, which could not be moved along narrow mountain trails. By mid September, one month after the beginning of the battle at the MCR, the Soviet artillery along the 200-kilometre front was limited to only two three-gun mountain batteries, one each at Donguz-Orun and Bassa; one three-gun 76-mm field artillery battery in Klukhor; and twenty-nine guns of 76 mm in Sancharo of which only one three-gun battery had mountain guns that could be carried into the high mountains. In addition, several mountain guns defended the Belorechenskii pass. Five mountain batteries and an anti-tank battery at Aishkha and Pseashkha never saw action. The Marukh defenders had no artillery at all.[2] The German reports confirm that where Soviet artillery existed it performed adequately,[3] but the Soviets had too few guns at high altitudes to attain substantial results. The two German two-regiment mountain divisions had between them seventy-two mountain guns and forty-eight efficient 105-mm mountain howitzers.[4] Unlike the Soviets, the Germans were able to bring all these guns to the MCR; furthermore, they had been trained to operate at high elevations and knew how low atmospheric pressure affected ballistics. Thus, in terms of artillery, the German superiority at high altitudes was overwhelming.

In the absence of mountain artillery, only mortars could support the Soviet infantry in the high Caucasus; in fact, they constituted the bulk of Soviet heavy weapons. The Soviet mortars were similar to those used by the German mountain divisions, and the two sides had roughly the same number of such weapons per regiment. Soviet commanders were surprised to discover that heavy long-range 82-mm and 107-mm mortars proved to be effective, unlike 50-mm ones – the major mortar type used at the beginning of the battle at the MCR.[5] By mid September, the Soviets had 102 heavy mortars in the Klukhor, Marukh, and Sancharo regions, along with an unknown number in the Elbrus region and around Aishkha and Pseashkha, compared to 72 heavy mortars possessed by the two German mountain divisions.[6] Soviet commanders, however, came to appreciate mortars as the major means of infantry support in the mountains only during the second stage of the battle at the MCR and, even then, their use of these weapons was flawed: they concentrated them in their own hands, as they were trained to do with field artillery, instead of distributing them among small units fulfilling independent missions.[7]

The Soviets and the Germans had roughly equal numbers of machineguns and small arms per regiment. However, the only type of heavy machinegun that the Soviet defenders of the Caucasus had was the one that had been designed by Hiram Maxim and produced in Russia since 1910. Its technical parameters, such as a weight of 62 kilograms and a rate of fire of 600 shots per minute, were far inferior to the German MG-34, which weighed only 12 kilograms and had a rate of fire of 800 shots per minute.[8] It was quite an effort to take the heavy Maxim, along with the water needed for cooling its muzzle, to the positions at the MCR; it was hard to manoeuvre across rugged terrain with the Maxim, and it was impossible to climb rocks with it. The light DP machinegun, the main Soviet long-range automatic weapon, weighed as little as the German MG-34; however, its magazine held only 47 cartridges compared to the 250 in the MG-34's belt, it took longer to load the magazine, and the rate of fire was only 600 shots per minute when the muzzle was cold and much lower when the weapon overheated.[9] Soviet regiment commanders complained about 'the insufficient training of infantry, machinegun and mortar crews who could not determine distance in the mountains; their fire produced poor results, and the enemy suffered insignificant casualties'.[10]

However, the Soviets had absolute superiority in air power to the south of the MCR. Although not trained to co-operate with the ground forces and frequently unable to fly because of low clouds or poor weather, the air force gave the Soviets substantial additional firepower. At times, air strikes inflicted heavy casualties on the Germans and devastated their supply columns.[11] Despite the control of the air exercised by the Soviets, the Germans would still have had superiority in firepower had they had enough ammunition. However, since what mattered was not the ratio of guns but the ratio of shells that could be fired daily, and the Soviets had far greater reserves of ammunition on the southern slopes of the Caucasus, the firepower of the opponents was more or less on a par.

Command and Control

During manoeuvres across rugged terrain, units seeking to outflank the enemy are often separated by ridges, gorges, forest, and clouds and are therefore invisible to each other and to their superiors. Mountain warfare thus presents a great challenge to command and control. Rugged terrain and strong winds preclude wire communication, and runners are

Figure 7.1 A Soviet artillery crew transporting a disassembled 76.2-mm mountain gun. Credit: RGAKFD / Maksim Alpert

too slow to be effective. Only radio can secure adequate command of action in the mountains.

The Soviet problems with radio communications in the Caucasus revolved around the poor designs and low manufacturing quality of available radios, their small number and prohibitive weight, the insufficient skills of radio operators, and the conservatism of field commanders. Because the Soviet radio industry was well behind Western industries, the technical parameters of German long-range stationary radios and short-range portable radios were far better and their reliability much greater than those of the Soviet radios. Countless Red Army reports stemming from all arms say that Soviet-made radios were obsolete, bulky, and unreliable and had poor filters that could not hold the desired frequency or eliminate interference.[12] Not only did the Red Army have fewer radios per unit than the Wehrmacht, but at any one time many or even most Soviet radios were broken down or were perceived as such by untrained operators who could not make them work. These deficiencies and the overblown concern about interception of radio communications by the enemy made Soviet commanders suspicious of radio. After the Winter War exposed the flaws of the Red Army communication system, its General Staff issued numerous orders seeking to change the attitudes of officers, but they continued to rely

Figure 7.2 A German 75-mm mountain gun. Credit: BArch, Bild 183-B23252 / Fred Rieder

mainly on telephones rather than radios. Such problems with communication culture and radio design had particularly grave repercussions not only on the actions of mobile arms, such as armour and air force, but also on action in the mountains.

Although the Germans also complained about the frequent interruption of radio contact in the high Caucasus,[13] on most days, the Headquarters of the 49th Mountain Corps received daily reports

Figure 7.3 A Soviet section dragging a 62-kg Maxim machinegun up to the rocks. It was difficult to change a position on the rugged terrain under enemy fire with such a heavy machinegun. Credit: RGAKFD / P. Troshkin

Figure 7.4 A German 20-mm Flak 38 anti-aircraft gun in action. Credit: BArch, Bild 146-1970-033-04

from every regiment and were able, from a distance of about 80 kilometres as the crow flies, to effectively direct the actions of the two mountain divisions advancing along several valleys, even after these regiments crossed the MCR.[14] The reliable short-range portable radios allowed the Germans to co-ordinate the actions of small units manoeuvring around Soviet positions.

In contrast, the Soviets could not establish reliable radio contact between units deployed in the high mountains and their divisional headquarters in the foothills, or between divisional headquarters and army headquarters in the far rear. The absence of information about the situation at the MCR produced tremendous confusion and long delays in response to enemy actions and led to a string of irrelevant orders and fantastic plans prompted mainly by a panicked reaction to surprise rather than by strategic considerations.

The Headquarters of the 46th Army usually received the reports of the units deployed near the MCR with a three-day delay: that much time was needed for messengers to get to the closest telephone wire. Its orders issued in response to an event that had happened three days earlier travelled back with the same speed, arriving six days after the event.[15] The commanders of the 46th Army learned about the advance of the Germans towards the MCR only on the fourth day after the scouts of the 394th Rifle Division had clashed with German vanguards on 14 August near Verkhnii Teberdinskii village, 48 kilometres north of Klukhor; consequently, the orders to defend this village and 'prepare the main road between Teberda village and Klukhor for destruction and destroy it with the advance of the enemy' were sent only in the late evening of 17 August, when the Germans had already taken Klukhor.[16] On 20 August, the Headquarters of the 46th Army began planning an outflanking march to Klukhor via the Nakhar pass, which had already been taken by the Germans on 18 August.[17] The main Soviet forces allocated for the defence of the MCR began marching to the passes only after the Germans had already taken Klukhor, Nakhar, and most passes in the Elbrus region, but even then the Headquarters of the 46th Army could not monitor their advance. When the 220th Regiment of the 63rd Cavalry Division left Khaishi village for the MCR on 21 August, the divisional headquarters lost all contact with the regiment for seven days, although the distance it covered during that time was only about 50 kilometres.[18] In early September, all contact with the Piiashev Group was lost for four days. In mid September, the 20th 'Mountain' Division requested at least three radios; it is unclear whether it had any working radios at that time. The Red Air Force communicated with infantry marching in the mountains by dropping messages that were hard to find or to fetch; if infantrymen had to pass a message to the air force, they hung a rope with a message between two trees, and the pilot caught the rope with a hook attached to a rope he held in his hands.[19] Colonel Pavel Belekhov, commander of the 394th Rifle Division, explained that the absence of portable radios in reconnaissance parties often devalued the intelligence they had acquired with great effort because it was delivered with a delay of several days.[20]

The structure of the Soviet formations aggravated the communication problems. The German mountain divisions arrived in the high Caucasus with all their integral components, including signals units. In contrast, a large part of the Soviet forces operating at the MCR were either hotchpotch formations assembled from battalions or from regiments detached from their original divisions without signals units, or independent NKVD units that never had a proper signals service. Such practice considerably reduced the saturation of Soviet formations at the MCR with signalling equipment and signals personnel, in comparison with regular rifle formations of equal size.[21] The large hotchpotch formation raised by the 37th Army for a deep raid to Klukhor along the northern slopes of the MCR was supposed to co-operate with Soviet formations across the Caucasus, but it had no signals units and, accordingly, no contact with either the Headquarters of the 37th Army or the formations south of the MCR. After the raid failed, the 37th Army could not rescue the demoralised soldiers retreating without food across two high passes because it did not know what had happened to them. Only after a Soviet airplane spotted the raiding party by chance several days after its defeat did the air force deliver food; without it, these soldiers would probably all have perished.[22]

The German assault on Marukh was one of many examples demonstrating that adequate radio communications gave the German mountain units as solid a tactical edge over the Soviet defenders as they enjoyed in mountaineering. The Germans sent eighteen radios of different ranges to their two battalions converging on Marukh. After partisans ambushed and destroyed the supply column carrying the radios, the Germans sent more radios, and they had enough of them to co-ordinate the assault on the pass from three sides and to maintain permanent radio contact with the Headquarters of the 1st Mountain

Division in Teberda village, beyond two high ridges.[23] In contrast, the two Soviet regiments deployed at Marukh had only one stationary radio with a meagre reserve of batteries, after a horse carrying half of the batteries fell into an abyss. From late August to mid September, the Headquarters of the 3rd Rifle Corps in Sukhumi recorded the absence of radio contact with Marukh garrison, 55 kilometres away as the crow flies, almost daily.[24] In the absence of radio contact, the Marukh garrison and the Headquarters of the 3rd Rifle Corps in Sukhumi continued to rely on messengers, whose return trip, a distance of 130 kilometres, took eight to ten days.[25] Messages sent by Suvorov in the late eighteenth century travelled faster than did those between the Marukh garrison and headquarters. The defenders of Marukh had no portable short-range radios; units deployed there communicated with each other by phone, which worked only during static defence and only as long as the wires, frequently cut by strong winds, remained undamaged.[26] One day before the German assault on the pass, the Headquarters of the 46th Army, aware of the forthcoming attack, suddenly recalled the cipher officer, who left along with his cipher book, leaving the commanders of the Marukh garrison with no opportunity to communicate with headquarters via radio, even in those rare moments when the radio worked. The Headquarters of the TCF learned that the Germans had taken the pass only four days after it had happened, meanwhile issuing a string of irrelevant orders about its defence.[27]

Soviet divisions entered the battle in the high Caucasus with bulky RKR stationary radios weighing 47 kilograms, with a range of 20 kilometres in telegraphic mode, and 'portable' 12-RP radios weighing over 25 kilograms, with a range of 8 kilometres in telephone mode and 16 kilometres in telegraphic mode. Since their rechargeable batteries lasted for only six hours in transmission mode and eighteen to twenty hours in receiving mode, both types required a charger that could not be delivered to the high mountains because of its prohibitive weight.[28] Beria's order about the urgent delivery of new radio designs to the MCR was promptly fulfilled, and on 4 September 100 radios, along with 92 operators, arrived in the southern foothills of the MCR, followed by further deliveries: in total, the 46th Army sent 174 radios to the mountains.[29] These were new stationary Prima radios transported in three packs weighing, in total, 36 kilograms, with a range of 300 kilometres in telegraphic mode and supplied with batteries that could be charged by a generator working from muscle power, as well as 13-RA portable radios weighing 20 kilograms, with a range of 12 kilometres and powered by fairly light non-rechargeable batteries.[30]

The arrival of the new designs and radio operators eased the communication problems but did not eliminate them. The capacity of non-rechargeable batteries plummeted to 60 per cent at a temperature of −10 °C,[31] which meant that batteries had to be delivered to the mountains at almost twice the rate of those brought to units serving at that time on the plains; the standard battery supply schedule for that season led to a severe shortage of batteries. The range of the radios also fell dramatically in the mountains; furthermore, the 13-RA design had poor frequency filters, while the Prima radio turned out to be too flimsy for mountain warfare, and its manufacturing quality was low. Some of these new radios were damaged during transport, and it took five days to fix them after their arrival in the mountains.[32] As it turned out, only eighteen of the ninety-two new radio operators were able to use and service the radios without supervision, and fifty-seven operators, mainly women who had graduated from crash radio courses, were poorly trained and unfamiliar with the available designs. They received another five-day crash training course and departed for the mountains on 9 September. The remaining signals personnel, formally called 'radio operators', were totally untrained and had to remain in reserve while taking additional courses.[33] The 23rd Frontier Guard Regiment had fairly good operators, according to Soviet standards, but, as Major Pavel Kazak, its commander, explained, 'The regiment was fighting in the mountains for the first time ... Neither privates nor officers had experience in organising and maintaining signals service in the mountains.'[34] The radio operators typically did not know that they had to invest serious effort in experimenting with location, antennae position, and radio frequency in the mountains to establish an adequate connection. The outcome of this inexperience was the frequent absence of radio contact.[35] This frustrated the cohesion of infantry units and the co-operation of infantry, artillery, and air force, which, in General Petrov's words, resulted in 'the waste of thousands of rounds of mines and bullets that were very hard to deliver to the mountains'.[36]

Soviet commanders continued to complain that the 'radio almost never worked'.[37] Because of these daunting problems, Soviet units continued to communicate with each other mainly via telephone, if such an opportunity existed, or via messengers, who struggled across rugged terrain, some vanishing without a trace – presumably killed or captured by the Germans or buried by avalanches.[38] The understaffed signals personnel gradually extended telephone cables from the coast to the mountains. This improved the command and control at a strategic level but not at a tactical one, because Soviet units still could not coordinate their actions once they had left their positions. Furthermore, soon after the telephone wires finally reached the front line, accumulating ice and avalanches began cutting them, and heavy snowfalls concealed the damaged cables, making repairs difficult.[39]

Only by the end of October, when actions on the MCR had already stopped, did the Soviets solve most problems with radio communications: the 394th Rifle Division reported that it had twenty-four radios and the 20th 'Mountain' Division had forty-six.[40] However, even in late December 1942, the 33rd NKVD Regiment, fighting at the Belorechenskii pass, had only one working radio instead of the ten that a rifle unit of this size was supposed to have; the 23rd Frontier Guard Regiment, deployed at the same pass, had only three working radios, and the Assembled Regiment, fighting at the Sancharo pass, had seven but only one worked, and it had no battery charger.[41] In sum, the small number of radios, their poor quality and heavy weight, the absence of portable battery chargers and the inadequate supply of non-rechargeable batteries, the inexperience of radio operators, and the absence of a radio communication culture in the Red Army greatly hampered Soviet actions in the mountains, which gave the Germans a sound advantage in the area of command and control.

Logistics

The experience of the imperial army showed that logistics in the mountains faced numerous challenges. Obviously, modern warfare required far larger volumes of supplies than had the wars of the nineteenth century or even World War I, but since no automobile roads reached the MCR, supply was possible only with thousands of pack animals, which had to be collected and distributed among baggage trains and provided with packs, harnesses, and horseshoes. However, neither side had thought about logistics on the eve of the battle of the Caucasus, and both committed numerous blunders that aggravated the inevitable logistical problems.

For the Germans, faltering logistics was as serious a challenge as their numerical inferiority. The dismal failure to foresee this challenge should be attributed not to the 49th Mountain Corps but to the OKW, which pressed a sceptical OKH to launch the offensive across the Caucasus without calculating its logistical viability. German supply trucks had to cover about 200 kilometres from the railway to the trail-heads along poor dirt roads. A round trip took two or three days and required many trucks and much fuel, which the Army Group A could hardly spare.[42] The OKH counted on the Sukhumi Military Road as the major supply artery but found that the road turned into a mule trail on the approaches to Klukhor. Once the supplies reached the trailheads, they had to be loaded, first onto carts and then, as the trails deteriorated, onto horses. On 19 August, when the triumphant 1st Mountain Division secured the Elbrus region with all its passes and began descending from Klukhor, the Headquarters of the 49th Mountain Corps recorded, for the first time, its concern about the logistical viability of the operation, and on the same day the OKW expressed its first doubts about whether the corps could reach the Black Sea coast.[43] On 21 August, immediately following a series of stunning victories at the passes, Hitler went into a fury over the slow rate of the offensive, which was, in fact, the outcome of his initial perception of the high Caucasus as hardly 'anything bigger than Grunewald',[44] an opinion probably shared by the OKW generals who sanctioned the operation. The first snowfall at the passes on 21 August, the day the Germans hoisted their banner on Elbrus, gave a sobering warning of imminent supply problems. The Stettner Group began experiencing supply shortages on 23 August, when it was still on the northern slopes of the MCR; these shortages multiplied as soon as the group crossed the MCR. The Germans considered taking the carts apart, dragging them across the Caucasus, and reassembling them on the southern slopes, but since they could not reach any cart road in Transcaucasia they dropped the idea.[45] It turned out that the loads carried by pack animals had to be much smaller along steep trails at high altitudes than on the plains: a horse was able to carry a load of only about 50 kilograms for long distances, and a donkey's maximum load was about 30 kilograms.[46] Therefore, an army needed many more animals to maintain supplies in the high mountains. The number of pack animals that the 49th Mountain Corps managed to mobilise was inadequate from the start; the animals had to work day and night, and their progressive exhaustion resulted in rapid attrition, which was exacerbated by attacks of the Red Air Force and led to a dramatic reduction in supplies.

A mountain division needed, ideally, 30 tonnes of supplies daily.[47] The 4th Mountain Division operated farther from the automobile roads than did the 1st Mountain Division. Had the entire 4th Mountain Division crossed the Caucasus, it would have needed at least 3,000 horses for an uninterrupted flow of supplies across the MCR;[48] it began its offensive with half of this number, and because of the improvised nature of the operation the Germans did not have enough harnesses even for the horses they were able to acquire.[49] When the Soviets retreated across the MCR, they destroyed most bridges behind them. Heavy autumn rains turned trails into mud pools and swelling rivers made the numerous fords dangerous at best and impassable at worst, thus straining German logistics to breaking point. The Germans engaged eleven pioneer platoons in the maintenance of communication lines, yet it took the horses four days to take supplies along the steep trails across the MCR to Bzyb.[50] The hopes for an airlift came to naught when the Soviets recaptured the airstrip at Pskhu, the only one in the Transcaucasian area occupied by the Germans.[51]

Once the snowfalls began, only porters could access the highest positions, which meant that German units had to allocate much of their manpower to porter duty, thus draining their combat strength. Soviet POWs were an important component of German logistics. The Germans forced them to carry supplies and to evacuate wounded men, both Germans and, sometimes, captured Soviets, on trail sections inaccessible to pack animals.[52] With communication lines extending across the MCR, the 4th Mountain Division requested 6,000 porters, but it did not have that many POWs; even after the Germans mobilised an additional 900 civilians as porters, it was still not enough.[53] The porters had to be fed; they thus consumed some of the food that was delivered with much effort across the MCR. The Germans reduced the volume of cargo by cutting below survival level the rations of porters mobilised from POWs, which caused their high death rate. As in other German elite formations raised on a voluntary basis, many soldiers in the mountain divisions were committed Nazis; they treated POWs like animals and killed those who were too exhausted to carry heavy loads. Both Soviet and German sources recorded these murders, sometimes committed en masse against the orders of senior officers concerned with the supply situation. After the Germans retreated up the Klych valley, the advancing Soviets found more than 100 bodies of Soviet POWs allegedly killed by the Germans; Soviet reports also acknowledge that other porters recruited among Soviet POWs were killed by Soviet artillery.[54]

Although the number of partisans operating in the North Caucasus was small,[55] the numerous Red Army regulars, cut off by the Germans during the chaotic retreat of their divisions and dispersed across mountain valleys in the rear of the 49th Mountain Corps, organised themselves into combat units and engaged in guerrilla warfare. These bands, several hundred men strong and some of them led, according to Germans, by 'quite talented' commanders, operated without a clear strategic plan or contact with the Red Army, but they nonetheless attacked the extended communication lines of the 49th Mountain Corps almost daily and at times intercepted and destroyed entire supply columns.[56] This forced the 49th Mountain Corps to erect a network of strongholds along the supply routes: on the way to Bzyb, the Germans built twenty-seven blockhouses and twenty ammunition bunkers; they had to provide manpower to garrison these strongholds and detach units to protect supply columns between strongholds, which drained their combat strength.[57] The Germans deployed a mountain battalion, a collaborationist Azerbaijani battalion,[58] and a company of Georgian collaborators to protect their supply routes. They destroyed several Soviet bands but could not eradicate the guerrillas, who skilfully manoeuvred across foothills and had an efficient intelligence network among civilians, especially among the refugees who had evacuated from urban centres and settled in the villages of the North Caucasus. The commanders of the 49th Mountain Corps believed that these attacks on already overstrained logistics could frustrate the entire operation.[59] Many logistical problems experienced by the 49th Mountain Corps must have been easy to foresee, given the nature of the terrain. However, the OKW demonstrated, once again, a typical flaw of German strategic thought: the neglect of logistics during operational planning.

The Soviets were exposed to the same weather conditions as the Germans were; both the lengths and quality of foot trails to the MCR were about the same as those covered by the Germans; and since, as Beria and Tiulenev observed, the commanders of the 46th Army had made no logistical arrangements for potential action in the mountains, the Soviet supply operations were as improvised as the German ones.[60] The logistics of the German mountain divisions were based on pack animals from the start, and their supply units had experience in at least short-distance hauling operations in the mountains, whereas the logistics of Soviet regular infantry and NKVD soldiers, the large majority of those deployed at the MCR, were based on trucks or horse-driven wagons, neither of which could travel along the mountain trails. However, the Soviets had far broader opportunities to organise their logistics than the Germans did – first, because they operated among friendly Georgian people and, second, because they relied on regional administrative agencies that could mobilise local resources far more effectively than the Germans, who had no such infrastructure. The civilian administration confiscated pack animals from the locals, whom they then mobilised as muleteers; the TCF also requisitioned the combat horses of the 63rd Cavalry Division for hauling supplies.[61] By 13 September, five horse companies of 886 heads, two donkey companies of 150 heads, and one mixed donkey/horse company of 213 heads were hauling loads in the Marukh and Klukhor regions, and four horse companies of 759 heads and one donkey company of 256 heads were working in the Sancharo region.[62] The Soviets had fewer pack animals per unit than the Germans had, but the Soviet supply trains did not have to cross the MCR, which simplified their operation considerably.

Yet Soviet logistics faced numerous problems stemming from inexperience in large-scale hauling operations in the mountains. Both sides found that a donkey was 'the best [pack animal] in the mountains. This animal can pass along a path accessible only to a soldier with spiked boots, and it does not require [much] fodder', which was scarce in the high mountains; it was also easier to help donkeys move along these paths than horses.[63] People in Transcaucasia kept more donkeys than did residents in the North Caucasus; accordingly, the Soviets had the opportunity to mobilise more donkeys than the Germans. However, since donkeys were not listed in the inventory of the Red Army, the divisions deployed at the MCR had no horseshoes, packs, or harnesses for them. The Georgian administration conscripted hundreds of smiths and harness-makers to produce these items, but it took time to make them.[64] Furthermore, Soviet regular infantry had no pack boxes. Instead of proper packs, muleteers used improvised boxes of various sizes that were uncomfortable and quickly mutilated the animals.[65] These injuries may have caused a rate of attrition of Soviet supply trains as high as that inflicted on German ones by the Red Air Force.

The German logistical problems in the high Caucasus eased considerably when their mountain divisions used their standard equipment to build several cable-car lines along the northern slopes of the MCR. Cable cars quickly delivered food supplies, firewood, and ammunition to the passes and evacuated wounded men, who were thus spared the torment of transportation on stretchers along steep trails. The Soviet divisions had no cable-car equipment, but airlifts partially compensated for the flaws of Soviet ground logistics. A large fleet of small biplanes able to land at short airstrips delivered up to 60 tonnes of supplies daily, weather permitting – an amount equal to the daily needs of the two German mountain divisions.[66] In total, during the actions on the MCR, the Red Air Force brought 4,088 tonnes of cargo to divisions fighting on the ridge and evacuated about 5,600 wounded soldiers.[67]

With the airlift, the Soviets delivered larger cargo volumes to the MCR than the Germans did, but their soldiers still endured much greater privations, because the Headquarters of the 46th Army, ignorant of the environment in the high mountains, misjudged the supply priorities. They focused mainly on ammunition: Soviet field commanders rarely complained about ammunition shortages, and Germans frequently envied the inexhaustible Soviet stockpiles.[68] However, the 46th Army supplied its divisions in the high Caucasus in the same way it would on the plains, overloading logistics with useless heavy items, such as anti-tank weapons, but assigning a low priority to articles necessary for soldiers' survival in conditions the senior Soviet commanders could not even imagine. Ignorance of mountain warfare and the environment in the high Caucasus, along with the inflexibility and inertia of military bureaucracy, ensured that Soviet soldiers, unlike the Germans, were starving and freezing in the mountains.

Food Supplies

A person performing hard work at high altitudes requires a special food ration to preserve physical fitness, especially given that, at high elevation, appetite diminishes and food tastes change. By the late 1930s, Soviet mountaineers had identified food rations that were light but calorie-dense, relatively tasty, and easy to consume at high altitude. Such rations included protein- and fat-rich foods that required no cooking or were easy to cook, such as smoked sausages, ham and

Figure 7.5 A German supply train. Credit: Süddeutsche Zeitung Photo / Alamy Stock Photo

Figure 7.6 A German cable car. The cable-car system considerably eased German logistics in the Caucasus. Credit: BArch, Bild 183-B22462 / Kintscher

Figure 7.7 A Soviet airlift. The large fleet of Po-2 biplanes able to land on short airstrips was a vital asset of Soviet logistics. Credit: RGAKFD / O. Knorring

tongue, cheese, tinned meat and fish, nuts, quick-cooking concentrates, bouillon cubes, and egg powder; sweets that the body could quickly assimilate, thus receiving a fast boost, such as chocolate, sugar, candies, cookies, and condensed milk; and spicy or sour items that provided vitamins and whetted the appetite, like garlic, onions, dried fruit, and cranberry or currant syrup.[69] Some senior Soviet officers argued that soldiers fighting in the high Caucasus needed such rations – as much as the depleted food industry could provide them.[70] However, pressed by the Stavka after the belated discovery of Germans at the MCR and fearing stiff penalties for the failure to protect the passes across the Caucasus, the TCF Headquarters rushed its formations, scattered all along the Black Sea, to the mountains without any reserves of food, let alone special rations. The supply departments did not receive orders in time and refused to allocate food to the regiments departing for the MCR despite its availability in army deports.[71] To send unfed soldiers on long marches was not unusual in Red Army practice.[72] This habit generally had no grave consequences on the populated plains, where soldiers could live off the land, but few people inhabited the high Caucasus. Having failed to take this fact into account, the senior commanders doomed their soldiers to debilitation and sometimes death from starvation.

A vanguard company heading to Sancharo left without food and had nothing to eat, except its pack horses, for four days after it arrived at the pass. Only on the day the Germans attacked Sancharo did the supply train reach the pass; hunger may have been responsible for the failure to resist the Germans.[73] Such an ordeal was the rule rather than an aberration during the first several weeks of the battle at the MCR. When the 46th Army rushed the 808th and 810th Regiments of the 394th Rifle Division to Marukh, it expected that their mission would last at least ten days under the most favourable circumstances. However, the 810th Regiment received only several kilograms of rusks, 800 grams of herring, and 300 grams of sugar per person and nothing else. As a soldier recalled, 'after several days, we had exhausted our rations and afterwards ate whatever we could find in the forest'.[74] These soldiers were, however, luckier than their comrades from the 808th Regiment, who received nothing more than a three-day rusk ration.[75] The 220th Cavalry Regiment also marched to the MCR with only three-day rations, and when it reached its positions, slightly below 3,300 metres, its men received only several rusks a day for the next two weeks.[76] When the soldiers of the first-wave formations slaughtered their pack animals, they could not cook the meat because the standard field kitchens ordered by Tiulenev to be delivered to the mountains only on 23 August, nine days after the beginning of battle at MCR,[77] could not pass along the narrow, steep trails, as the experience of the imperial army and Klement'ev's experiments in the interwar period had suggested. The effort to find pack kitchens failed: by late December, long after the end of actions at the MCR, the 33rd NKVD Regiment, occupying the lower Belorechenskii pass, had acquired only one pack kitchen instead of the ten it was supposed to have, while units deployed at high passes usually had none. As long as soldiers were marching through forests, they could roast horse meat on fires or boil it in their helmets in the absence of buckets, but above the treeline, they had to consume it raw because no fuel was available.[78] Soviet soldiers relayed numerous stories of being fed with raw horse meat or lamb even in the second week of September, a month after the beginning of the battle at the MCR.[79] If they had anything to eat at all, it was the standard heavy, low-calorie rations.

It is safe to assume that the Soviet troops at the MCR were less picky than Suvorov's soldiers, who often rejected blue cheese because they suspected it was rotten.[80] The campaign in the Caucasus was almost as static as the campaign in the Balkans in 1877, but the food of Soviet soldiers was far worse than that of their forefathers in Bulgaria, who, even during the worst weather, had hot tea three times a day and picked only the meat out of food buckets, scorning the rest of their rich but cold meals. During the campaign in the Carpathians in 1915, Russian soldiers received tinned food equal to one and a half regular rations when the melting snow made supply with hot meals difficult.[81] The Soviet soldiers deployed on the TCF would have envied Suvorov's men, the defenders of the Shipka pass, or those who had fought in the Carpathians. By the end of September, the soldier's ration at Marukh consisted only of rusks, meat, and sugar; occasionally, they consumed uncooked porridge concentrate, but they had no butter, vegetables, or vodka, all of which every front-line soldier was supposed to receive. Although the depots of the 63rd Cavalry Division were stuffed with food, its soldiers deployed in the Elbrus region had only flour and raw grain, which they could not cook in the absence of firewood.[82] Since units in the high mountains received no fresh vegetables or vitamins, the medics noticed signs of scurvy in positions located less than 100 kilometres away from abundant mandarin gardens. The defenders of the high Caucasus lost dozens of men to starvation.[83] When a battalion, fighting at Sancharo, was relieved in early October, it was necessary to send a rescue party of 100 men to bring it down because many of its soldiers were so weakened that they could not descend without assistance.[84]

Unlike their forefathers in the imperial army, the soldiers deployed in the high Caucasus were desperately short of tinned food until the very end of the action. Being a rarity, tins were reserved mainly for reconnaissance parties, but even scouts frequently received raw meat as their rations. Although on 3 September, three weeks after the beginning of action at the MCR, Beria, one of the most powerful members of the Politburo, requested 90 tonnes of chocolate and 90 tonnes of condensed milk for the soldiers in the high Caucasus,[85] these items arrived long after action at the MCR had ended, and several officers were court-martialled for their misappropriation. Only on 26 November did the 242nd 'Mountain' Division acquire enough tins of meat, condensed milk, chocolate, and sausages to supply its scouts – but only them.[86]

The heavy snowfalls that began in late October interrupted the food supplies, since only porters could ascend the icy paths; the amount that they brought was inevitably less than what had earlier been delivered by pack animals. On 13 November, General Petrov reported that 'rations are monotonous and insufficient and lack vitamins';[87] however, it was not the monotony but the shortage of food that tormented the soldiers. The calorie value of the soldiers' rations at that time was half or one-third of the Red Army standard. Some days, they received no food at all; and they often scavenged for rotten horse carrion.[88]

Beginning in October 1942, when it became difficult to carry firewood along the paths covered with snow and ice, soldiers often had to consume their meagre rations frozen. The inspectors examining the living conditions in the mountains filed their first requests for kerosene stoves or alcohol burners on 5 September; these requests were repeated by Major Varlam Kakuchaia, an NKVD representative of the TCF Military Council, on 22 September.[89] However, it turned out that Soviet industry, which produced thousands of excellent tanks and aircraft every month, was unable to supply the TCF with kerosene stoves. General Petrov issued an urgent request that 300 kerosene stoves be bought in Iran, and by mid November, a month after the end of action at the MCR, the first portable kerosene and firewood stoves arrived at the front line, but the Rear Directorate had forgotten that the kerosene stoves needed kerosene.[90] On 17 November, Colonel Dreev, the OG chief of staff, wrote: 'Soldiers on the passes do not receive hot meals because of the absence of fuel, the delivery of which has not been organised yet. The personnel are poorly fed; they receive only dry food: herring, dry bread, and [porridge] concentrate.'[91] Such a regimen provoked severe thirst, but the only source of water was snow, which soldiers could not melt in the absence of fuel. Instead, they had to suck on the snow, which caused hypothermia; many soldiers became sick and had to be evacuated to hospitals.[92]

In contrast, German mountain troops received steady special food rations that were richer and tastier than those allotted to regular infantry, and they had portable stoves and alcohol burners to cook or warm up meals above treeline, as well as thermoses to keep their drinks warm.[93] It is easy to imagine what Soviet soldiers were thinking about their own commanders when they listened to a German prisoner from the 2nd High Mountain Battalion complaining that he, at times, had received no hot meals and was reduced to eating dry rations like tinned goulash, potatoes, beans, and veal, as well as ham, sausages, cheese, bacon, butter, jam, chocolate, and candies; he had also regularly received vitamin pills.[94] German commanders followed the Napoleonic maxim, 'An army marches on its stomach', whereas their Soviet counterparts ignored it in the belief that this aspect of supply was secondary to weapons and ammunition. However, an adequate food supply was vital at high altitudes, where no opportunity to supplement rations with requisitions existed; every action required a greater physical effort than it would on the plains, and the ability to resist atrocious weather made the difference between life and death. Severe debilitation undermined the combat capacity of Soviet soldiers, ruined their morale, and resulted in a high proportion of non-combat casualties.

Clothes and Gear

Uniforms and other gear items of the German mountain troops, identified during a long trial-and-error process, were adapted to the anticipated battle environment: every soldier had a warm woollen balaclava and a cap with ear flaps and a neck cover; two pairs of warm underwear; three shirts, a woollen sweater, and a tunic large enough to wear over a sweater; a water-resistant hooded jacket comfortable for climbing, with double-cloth shoulders to withstand months of carrying a backpack and with a white lining so it could be turned inside out and serve as camouflage against the snow; loose-fitting trousers with laces at the ankles to protect from snow and ticks; gaiters, three pairs of socks, and sturdy spiked mountain boots that could fit over two or three pairs of socks; waterproof wax; and sunglasses and sunblock.[95] The Germans slept in warm sleeping bags and had small tents that were easy to pitch on rough mountain terrain and able to withstand strong winds.[96] How did the Soviet approach to the supply of items believed to be essential for survival in the high mountains compare with that of their opponents?

Every previous campaign fought by Russians in the mountains, including the recent experience of the Winter War, had shown that uniforms and other gear had to be adapted to the conditions in which the army was planning to operate; those relying on standard equipment in an unanticipated battle environment suffered enormous combat and non-combat casualties. Since the Red Army had no proper mountain divisions and little equipment suitable for operating in the mountains, the TCF could have at least supplied its soldiers sent to the mountains with standard winter kits. It failed to do so. When the Germans began advancing towards the Caucasus, the divisions of the 3rd Rifle Corps, scattered along the Black Sea coast, were wearing summer uniforms. When its headquarters rushed these divisions to the MCR, their soldiers did not receive winter uniforms because Soviet bureaucracy, both military and civilian, followed rigid regulations ruling out quick reactions to surprises. These regulations stated that, in Transcaucasia, soldiers would change uniforms in the late autumn. Many senior commanders at different levels had to sign every unanticipated request coming from the field. None of these signatories imagined weather conditions in the high mountains. Although in late August, the night temperature could drop to 0 °C even at the relatively low Sancharo pass and below freezing at the Marukh pass,[97] this was incomprehensible to senior officers who were sweating in humid tropical heat in Kutaisi or at the resorts on the Black Sea coast. Being accustomed to a relaxed work pace in this remote rear region and too inert to respond promptly to the sudden avalanche of orders during the crisis at the MCR, they considered the delivery of winter clothes a matter of secondary priority, given that many soldiers lacked even essential items of the summer uniforms. When Beria arrived at the TCF in late August, he found that the supply of soldiers with uniforms was 'organised with criminal negligence: in some units from 50 per cent to 70 per cent of soldiers have no coats or boots'.[98] He counted 300 barefoot men among those sent to the mountains.[99] These revelations addressed only the tip of the iceberg.

After the embarrassment of the Winter War, the Red Army General Staff knew exactly what a standard winter uniform kit had to be. However, it took a long time to supply the soldiers deployed in the mountains with these kits. The pile of directives intended to provide winter uniforms to the front-line formations was only one chapter in the lengthy and sterile order-writing saga that began on the eve of the German assault on the MCR and continued throughout the conflict: despite numerous instructions issued by top officers of the TCF, most soldiers were not properly dressed until the very end of the battle of the Caucasus. On 30 June, one and a half months before the beginning of action, Sergatskov ordered the organisation of intermediate supply depots that would store all the items needed to equip the first wave of MCR defenders. Leselidze filed the first explicit request for winter uniforms on 9 August, a week before the first clash of Soviet reconnaissance parties with the vanguards of the 49th Mountain Corps. On 20 August, General Khadeev, deputy commander of the TCF, set 5 September as the

Figure 7.8 Soviet regular infantry in winter uniforms but unequipped for mountain warfare struggle across a snowfield in the high Caucasus. Credit: RGAKFD / Maksim Alpert

deadline for the delivery of winter uniforms for the units that were occupying the highest passes, Becho and Donguz-Orun.[100] On 24 August, Sergatskov again wrote that 'the soldiers defending the passes must be supplied with winter uniforms and warm boots'.[101] The next day, Tiulenev submitted a list of equipment to be sent urgently to the mountains, including hats with ear flaps, warm underwear, wadded jackets, winter gloves, felt boots, mountain boots, and portable stoves. On 26 and 28 August and 4 September, Tiulenev repeated his order of 25 August about winter uniforms, and General Khadeev did the same on 31 August.[102]

The failure of the 46th Army to organise intermediate supply depots on the way to the MCR was primarily responsible for the lack of winter uniforms at the front line. Once the battle began, it was much harder to deliver equipment to the mountains. The Rear Directorate of the TCF sent most of the requested items from stores of the 46th Army to divisional depots located far away from the front line, but only on 6 September,[103] a month after the first explicit request for winter uniforms had been filed. It took a long time to transport these items to divisional depots, and even longer to deliver them to the front line. The total weight of the uniforms for such a force was about 380 tonnes, given a maximum strength of the Soviet forces in the Klukhor, Marukh, and Sancharo regions of about 20,500 men;[104] a combat attrition of about 5,000 men in these regions; and the weight of the full winter uniform kit, including sheepskin coat and the felt boots, of about 15 kilograms. The force deployed in these regions, equal to two divisions, needed, in theory, 60 tonnes of supplies daily,[105] but the air force could deliver, at best, only about 50 tonnes on days with good weather;[106] the rest had to be transported first in carts, which was relatively easy, and then on horseback. The capacity of the Soviet supply trains operating beyond the cart roads in these regions was about 100 tonnes for a single trip,[107] and the round trip from the end of the cart roads to the front-line positions took, depending on the region, from two to four days; this meant that supply trains could deliver 20 to 40 tonnes daily, given that some of these pack animals were engaged in hauling cargo from airstrips to the front line. This amount was probably adequate for keeping the formations at the MCR functioning, but additional strains, such as the delivery of winter uniforms, were often beyond its capacity, and the supply officers continued to perceive this cargo as a secondary priority.

The great contrast between the optimistic claims of the Rear Directorate of the 46th Army on supply matters and the grim field reports persisted until the very end of the battle at the MCR.[108] On 12 September, General Petrov maintained that 'winter uniforms were sent to the 20th Mountain Division, the 394th Rifle Division, and the 63rd Cavalry Division, but nobody knows whether they arrived at the passes'.[109] They did not. Even in late September, six weeks after the beginning of action at the MCR, reinforcements were arriving in the high mountains in summer uniforms, and often without essential items of these uniforms. General Petrov recorded his impressions of the 242nd 'Mountain' Division as it came to positions located at an altitude of 3,300 metres in mid September, when night temperatures at these positions dropped at times to −10 °C: all soldiers arrived in incomplete summer uniforms; nobody had a cape, the primary means of protection from wind and rain; of 8,300 men, 1,012 had no coats; and 'some soldiers walked barefoot and were ragged [*obodrannye*]'.[110] Many other reports register similar shortages of most essential items. By mid September, soldiers deployed in the Klukhor region had received winter underwear but only about 10–15 per cent of the other winter uniform items; many of those stationed near Elbrus and Marukh had no winter uniforms even in late September.[111]

During his field tests in the interwar years, Colonel Klement'ev came to the conclusion that a soldier deployed in the mountains needed a lightweight, warm uniform comfortable for climbing; sunglasses and a woollen mask for protection from icy wind; a backpack instead of the standard shapeless infantry sack; a water-resistant sleeping bag instead of the standard thin blanket; mountain boots; climbing gear; and small tents accommodating three persons instead of the large standard tents for twenty men, which were hard to carry and pitch in the mountains and were easily swept away by strong winds. Few Soviet soldiers sent to the high Caucasus had any of these items. They wore long infantry coats unsuitable for climbing. Reconnaissance parties sent for multi-day missions carried ammunition and other supplies in standard clumsy sacks. The defenders of the MCR had received only 300 sleeping bags by the end of action.[112] By mid November, the 20th 'Mountain' Division had only 58 mountain tents, which, in total, could accommodate at most 232 soldiers and only if they slept on their sides, while the 242nd 'Mountain' Division had none.[113] Consequently, most Soviet soldiers who fought at the MCR survived frequent heavy rains and snowfalls in holes dug in the ground, huddling under the few available capes and shivering under thin standard blankets.[114] In the absence of firewood, kerosene stoves, or alcohol burners, they burned the boots of their fallen comrades, filling these holes with pungent smoke.[115] The divisions of the TCF consisted largely of soldiers drafted from the Transcaucasian populations, most of whom had lived in a mild climate; they had not experienced severe cold and did not know how to preserve their bodies from frostbite. Having no woollen masks for face protection, Leselidze ordered lamb fat as an anti-frostbite means on 13 September, but only on 17 November, a month after the end of actions at the MCR, did Colonel Dreev report that the fat had finally arrived at the stores of the 242nd 'Mountain' Division, and a week later Tiulenev wrote that most front-line units still had no fat.[116] Soldiers sent to the high mountains suffered not only from cold but also from severe ultraviolet radiation reflected by snow.[117] Most soldiers had no sunglasses; their eyes were painfully raw and some were temporarily blinded by the blazing glare. None of the senior TCF commanders thought about sunblock until casualties with sunburns began arriving at hospitals. Only in mid November did sunblock arrive, and then only at the divisional stores rather than the front line.[118]

Table 7.1 Winter uniforms delivered to divisional depots as a percentage of those requested, 29 September 1942

	Belorechenskii	Sancharo	Marukh	Klukhor
Hats with ear flaps	72.9	89.1	96.8	78.1
Wadded jackets	65.4	108.5	35.6	87.1
Wadded trousers	46.5	149.7	61.3	67.3
Sets of two warm shirts	55.0	59.6	39.9	64.6
Sets of two winter underwear	55.2	35.0	42.4	63.4
Gloves	65.4	56.2	86.0	88.0
Camouflage coveralls	0	0	0	0
Capes	123.5	47.5	0	53.1
Sets of two pairs of winter foot wraps	100	51.8	96.4	78.3

Source: Lieutenant-Colonel Leshukov, 'Spravka o potrebnosti i obespechennosti voisk' (29 September 1942), TsAMO, f. 47, op. 1063, d. 643, ll. 129–133.

A small number of mountain boots were available in TCF depots, but soldiers departing for the front were inexperienced in mountaineering and did not appreciate their advantages. Given a choice between them and regular boots, they preferred the latter because they weighed much less. Although adequate on the plains, the regular boots did not protect the feet from severe cold or the ankles from twisting, nor did they provide traction on slippery mountain paths. It was also hard to ski in such boots or to fix crampons to them.[119] The lifespan of regular boots was about three weeks on mountainous terrain. Already by 13 September, 40–45 per cent of the soldiers sent to the mountains needed boot replacement, and in some regiments, only 20 per cent of the personnel had boots assessed as wearable. Despite the periodic delivery of new boots, the proportion of those needing replacement grew to 50 per cent in mid November and to 60 per cent in mid December.[120] Many soldiers injured their feet wearing disintegrating footwear in snow, and some fell to their deaths having slipped on glaciers or icy steep trails in their flat-soled regular boots.

On 29 September, the commanders of the TCF finally received an inventory of the winter uniforms, delivered to divisional depots located at the ends of cart roads (Table 7.1). These data show that even had all the items been delivered from the divisional depots to the front line, which never happened, many soldiers would have lacked essential uniform items: one-third of them would have had no wadded jackets or trousers; most would have been without capes, spare underwear, and shirts; many would have had no gloves or spare foot wraps; and nobody would have had a white camouflage coverall. It was hard to survive in subzero temperatures without wadded jackets and trousers in the absence of tents or capes; a soldier could not fight without gloves; and in the absence of spare sets, there was no opportunity to dry underwear, shirts, and foot wraps soaked by heavy rain and snow.

The Soviet administrative system worked only if superiors constantly monitored their subordinates, but TCF commanders could only trace the path of the equipment to divisional depots. Knowing the quantities that arrived at and left from these depots, they pressed the divisional supply officers to pass the winter uniforms on to soldiers as soon as possible. Experiencing this pressure to empty the depots and being aware that transportation to the high mountains was difficult, the supply officers chose an easy way to demonstrate their zeal: they provided winter uniforms first to nearby units. These units, stationed in valleys with a pleasant warm climate, received them much faster than those shivering at high altitudes. In late September, only soldiers deployed at Belorechenskii, the lowest pass defended by the TCF, with the warmest climate, received felt boots and sheepskin coats.[121] By mid November, a month after the end of action at the MCR, units located in low valleys had received full sets of winter uniforms, whereas only a quarter of the personnel serving in the high mountains had received sheepskin coats, despite their availability in divisional depots.[122]

The TCF had no white coveralls; admittedly, its commanders carried less responsibility for their failure to provide them than did their colleagues in northern Soviet regions, because winters in Transcaucasia are usually free of snow except in the mountains, where the TCF Headquarters did not plan to operate. The white coveralls, simple items that were easy to produce, could have saved thousands of lives, yet images of Soviet soldiers running in dark coats across snowfields under enemy fire are a constant feature of documentaries and memoirs on World War II. Most Soviet soldiers in the Caucasus and elsewhere, even reconnaissance parties, had no coveralls, thus becoming easy targets for Germans.[123]

In the total absence of washing facilities in the mountains or even soap,[124] the lack of spare underwear and shirts led to the proliferation of lice.[125] Before the war, if medics found lice on even one soldier in the Transcaucasian Military District, this was an extraordinary event entailing prompt disinfection.[126] In November and December, the 46th Army found that nine of every ten men in front-line units of the 808th Regiment of the 394th Rifle Division were infected, as were nearly all soldiers of the 897th Regiment of the 242nd 'Mountain' Division.[127] Lice tormented the soldiers day and night, creating conditions for a typhus outbreak.

Although the warm-clothing supply improved in November and December, it happened not because of a change in the supply practice but because of a reduction of Soviet manpower at the MCR: soon after severe snowstorms stalled all action at the MCR, the 46th Army transferred most men to other sections of the front, which allowed it, to a degree, to saturate the units remaining in the high mountains with winter uniforms.[128] However, even then, the 242nd 'Mountain' Division, deployed at the highest and coldest part of the front near Elbrus, had no gloves; soldiers of the 394th Rifle Division still had only one warm shirt and one set of underwear, one in three men in this division had no gloves, and only one in four had a sheepskin coat.[129]

The criminal neglect of their men by the TCF commanders set a record of misery on the Eastern Front. The horrific suffering from hunger and cold experienced by Soviet soldiers in the high Caucasus exceeded the privations from these factors nearly anywhere else, including the trenches around starving Leningrad and frozen Stalingrad. Filimonov, a 17-year-old cadet, recalled that his cadet school was suddenly shut down and all the cadets rushed to Marukh. His position was a hole in a rock 1.5 metres square, which he had to share with three other men. In late October, these future officers were

> always wet up to the knees, hungry and covered with lice. Our rations, delivered not even every day, consisted of a piece of rusk, a tiny rotten herring, a piece of raw meat, a spoonful of sugar, a handful of raw rice or beans, 100 millilitres of vodka, and a pinch of tobacco. We ate [the whole ration] at once: the rice mixed with sugar, the herring together with its giblets and scales, and the raw meat. In contrast, the Germans defending the passes received hot food delivered to them by a cable car. Our faces and hands were black from sun radiation and mud; the skin peeled off; our eyes festered from the wind and sun

> glare, whereas the Germans had sunglasses ... Half-blind, frost-bitten, and swollen from starvation, we sometimes succumbed to a feeling of doom.[130]

Filimonov later fought at Novorossiisk, as well as in Crimea, Belarus, and Poland, but, he writes, 'even now I remember the actions in the high mountains of the Caucasus as a time of subhuman misery ... I have never experienced anything similar since then. It was not as if we were facing death all the time, nor were there stunning displays of courage. However, the tenacity, fortitude, and determination [we showed] in the mountains were truly heroic.'[131] Mikhail Gioev, a junior officer of the 155th Rifle Brigade sent to Marukh, seconds Filimonov's impressions:

> Soaking wet, in coats covered with ice, deprived even of the opportunity to make a fire to warm themselves up and have a drink of hot water ... many soldiers were frostbitten and even died from hypothermia ... Those who fought at the [mountain] passes believe unanimously that all the nightmares of war they ever experienced no doubt pale in comparison with the misery and privations they endured in the high Caucasus.[132]

Hypothermia and Frostbite as Casualty Factors

The savage conditions suffered by Soviet soldiers in the mountains became unbearable as the weather deteriorated in the autumn. By 7 September, when the temperature at the Black Sea coast, where senior commanders were staying, was still in the mid twenties Celsius, twenty-one men from the Marukh garrison froze to death, and several more froze during attempts to attack the Chiper and Chiper-Azau passes.[133] Bitter cold often frustrated Soviet actions. When, in early September, a company of the 121st 'Mountain' Regiment, dressed in summer uniforms, was ascending the Nakhar pass at night in order to retake it the next morning, the attack had to be abandoned before it had started after the temperature fell to −10 °C and many soldiers were lost to frostbite.[134] In September, the garrison of Donguz-Oruns[135] lost thirty-five men wounded by enemy fire, thirty-six men sick, five men frostbitten, and thirteen injured – that is, almost half of its non-lethal casualties were due to hypothermia.[136] In mid October, the night temperature plummeted to −10 °C, even at the feet of the passes,[137] and at the top of Donguz-Orun and Becho it was below −20 °C; with the strong winds above the treeline, windchill temperatures were much lower. When the Soviets received inaccurate intelligence data alleging that the Germans had left Marukh, a reconnaissance party of fifteen men sent to verify this information on 30 November could not climb the pass because every man was frostbitten during this attempt.[138]

The massive snowstorm that raged from 18 to 21 October terminated action in the high Caucasus, but the Soviets repeated the experience of their forefathers at Shipka: their forces quickly dwindled because of frostbite and diseases caused by hypothermia. During this snowstorm, frostbite incapacitated 450 men in the 394th Rifle Division; the Piiashev Group lost 359 men frostbitten and 3 frozen to death;[139] and the two companies garrisoning the Donguz-Orun and Bassa passes lost 23 men frozen to death and 163 frostbitten – about half of their personnel.[140] It took a rescue party of 150 men, sent to evacuate the victims, two days to make their way through waist-deep snow to Bassa and four days to Donguz-Orun.[141] During this time, many frostbite victims sustained grave injuries in the absence of medical assistance. In the month of October, 1,052 soldiers of the 46th Army were frostbitten, and many more had to be evacuated as sick.[142]

Paradoxically, the Germans, staying at altitudes between 2,000 and 4,100 metres – far above the Soviet positions, most of which were at about 1,800 metres – felt more at ease in the Caucasus than the Soviets did. Their field reports and memoirs leave the impression that the German soldiers experienced nothing even remotely resembling the privations of their enemies, except on days with particularly severe weather. According to Gioev, 'While our soldiers and officers shivered in ice-covered uniforms in bitter cold, the Germans had everything, including footballs to work out after spending the night in warm sleeping bags.'[143] The Germans also suffered casualties from the snowstorm in late October, but they were lighter than those sustained by the Soviets: the 1st Battalion of the 91st Regiment, one of the two battalions guarding the entire group of Sancharo passes, lost 1 man frozen to death and 79 frostbitten, compared to 3 Soviet soldiers frozen to death and 359 frostbitten in the same region.[144] Referring to the prolonged snowfall in late October, Colonel Bulyga, the OG chief of staff, blamed the high number of Soviet casualties not so much on the severe weather but on the fact that 'the formations of the 46th Army defending the passes were not ready for winter conditions and because of this suffered extremely heavy casualties from frostbite'. Among the main reasons for the disaster, he named the absence of instructions on frostbite prevention and the failure to supply soldiers with sheepskin coats, felt boots, and spare uniform items that would have allowed them to change into dry clothes.[145]

As long as the Soviets kept their positions in the high mountains, they continued to sustain massive frostbite casualties. By 1 November, the 394th Rifle Division alone had lost, in the Klukhor and Marukh region, 3,725 men wounded, injured, and sick, of which 72 men (2 per cent), were evacuated with concussions and other non-combat traumas, 586 (16 per cent) were frostbitten, and 704 (19 per cent) were evacuated as sick; 60 per cent of the latter suffered from fever and the rest from the flu and dysentery.[146] Therefore, non-combat injuries and disease were responsible for 37 per cent of the non-lethal casualties. In total, according to official data, the TCF divisions that fought at the MCR lost 1,416 men frostbitten; of these, 716 had second-degree frostbite, which meant that they were excluded from action at the MCR for several weeks, and 149 were permanently disabled from third-degree frostbite.[147] It is safe to assume that many more first- and second-degree frostbite cases went unreported and many more sick soldiers were not evacuated beyond the front-line dressing stations.

When the Stavka received data on such an enormous number of non-combat casualties at the MCR, it sought to punish those responsible. Commanders at all levels hurried to shift the responsibility to their subordinates. Tiulenev, the primary culprit, argued, 'So many cases of frostbite occurred only because [field] commanders do not take care of their men.'[148] The field commanders rushed to relay the responsibility down the line. Major Aleksandr Korobov, commander of the 815th Rifle Regiment, who had never visited any mountain pass in the MCR, primarily blamed the victims. He wrote: 'We have many frostbitten soldiers. This has happened because officers do not monitor their men and allow negligent persons [*razgil'diai*] to get their feet frozen, and some wavering [soldiers] do it on purpose . . . I'll regard any frostbite as a self-inflicted wound, and the guilty will suffer penalties up to execution by a firing squad, and [their] commanders will be demoted to private.'[149] It is unknown how many frostbite victims died as a result of this and other similar orders. Such a primitive explanation for the huge number of non-combat casualties veiled the genuine roots of the disaster: the failure of the General Staff to raise proper mountain divisions and equip and train them for action in winter conditions; the ignorance of TCF commanders, at all levels, of their operational terrain; and the inertia of military administrators of the 46th Army, who failed to fulfil orders about the establishment of intermediate supply depots, first issued in late June, misallocated the supply priorities, and could not deliver items essential for survival at high altitudes.

The TCF did learn some peculiarities of logistics and supply in the high mountains from bitter experience, but not quickly enough to counteract the deteriorating weather. After sustaining grave non-combat casualties during and after the massive snowstorm in late October, Tiulenev finally ordered survival training for all soldiers at the MCR and explicitly demanded that those deployed at high altitudes be given preference in food and equipment over those in the foothills; he distributed the eleven-page *Instructions for Frostbite Prevention* and also pressed for the production of special uniform items absent in the Red Army, like woollen face masks and woollen codpieces.[150] However, all these wise steps began having an impact only long after the action at the MCR had ended.

Figure 7.9 German mountain troops resting in a snow cave. Credit: BArch, Bild 183-L27357 / Leander Gofferjé

The Plight of the Wounded

Neither the Germans nor the Soviets had thought about the challenges of medical service when they planned action in the high Caucasus. German field hospitals remained stationed to the north of the MCR, and German commanders were, inexplicably, surprised by the difficulty of transporting the wounded across the ridge along steep, narrow mountain trails. At least eight men had to be allotted for carrying each stretcher for long distances, which greatly depleted the force available for combat. Many wounded Germans did not survive the tormenting ordeal.[151] The difficulty of evacuation across the MCR was among the key arguments the commanders of the 49th Mountain Corps used when they requested termination of the offensive.

The Soviets were as indifferent as the Germans to this thorny problem, although the experience of the imperial army and Klement'ev's experiments in the interwar period had shown that there were no easy solutions. The *Manual on Mountain Warfare* of 1940 stated, 'In order to avoid frostbite, wounded and sick men should be evacuated as quickly as possible ... Stretcher bearers should have sleeping bags, fur socks, gloves, and hats for the wounded.'[152] However, not a single order issued on the eve of the battle of the Caucasus by the TCF, the 46th Army, or the 3rd Rifle Corps or any of its divisions addressed medical service in the mountains; explained how to evacuate the wounded; or requested extra stretchers, not to mention equipment presumed by the manual or suggested by Klement'ev.[153] Medical service was to be 'business as usual', conducted in the same way as on the plains.

Such an attitude ensured that the horrific privations experienced by Soviet soldiers in the high mountains paled in comparison with the sufferings of the wounded. Front-line dressing stations often had no dugouts because it was hard to dig them in the rocky soil; the standard large medical tents could not be pitched above the treeline. Consequently, the wounded lay in the open, with, at best, a cape as a roof. They were able to receive only first aid at the dressing station and had to be taken to field hospitals for surgery.[154] Although airplanes evacuated most wounded men, those had first to reach airstrips or field hospitals along mountain trails. Because many of them could not sit on horseback during the ride across the steep slopes, they had to be carried all the way in stretchers. The Marukh field hospital was located 30 to 40 kilometres away from the front-line positions. It generally took three to five days to carry the wounded there from the front-line dressing stations; those wounded in the remotest regions reached field hospitals only after eight or nine days.[155] Since evacuation took so long that field medical sections found themselves short of stretchers, many of the wounded had to be carried in capes or blankets for dozens of kilometres, which increased their suffering.[156]

Heavy rain and snowfall often stalled the transportation of the wounded. As Mikhail Gioev recalled, 'It was impossible to reach the positions of some platoons and companies for several days after each downpour turned the rocks into ice walls ... Gravely wounded men died in pain and suffering ... because it was impossible to evacuate them.'[157] Given the large loss of combat strength to the evacuation of those gravely injured, officers could not allocate men to accompany the lightly wounded and sick soldiers to the field hospitals. They had to walk there themselves down steep paths. With the approach of winter, such treks sometimes had lethal outcomes. An OG representative reported, 'The evacuation of the wounded is organised quite poorly ... On 25 October 1942, twelve wounded and frostbitten soldiers [of the 242nd "Mountain" Division] were sent down from the Donguz-Orun pass without any assistance or monitoring ... eight of them died on the way.'[158] Only in late October, after the end of action at the MCR, did the 46th Army send 2,900 sleeping bags for the evacuation of wounded men; they probably did not reach the front line until mid November.[159] Meanwhile, dozens, perhaps hundreds, of wounded succumbed to freezing temperatures during the lengthy evacuation process. On 13 November, three weeks after the end of the battle, General Petrov found medical service 'unacceptable in most units'; Tiulenev shared this opinion.[160]

The ordeal of the wounded did not end when they reached stationary hospitals in small towns in the foothills, because these facilities were overwhelmed. Yet, typical of the Soviet system, Aleksei Sadzhaia, the first deputy premier of Georgia, forbade the use of the abundant resources of the numerous Georgian resorts, reserved for the communist elite, to relieve the desperate shortage of hospital equipment. Outraged, Major Sedykh wrote on 17 September: 'I believe it is a crime to keep wounded soldiers on bare floors in Shovi hospitals, while the Shovi resorts are packed with mattresses and bedding.'[161] It is unknown whether his report had any impact on the plight of the wounded.

Lieutenant-Colonel Zav'ialov, who studied the experience of the battle at the MCR a year after its end, concluded that 'in mountain warfare, the evacuation of the wounded and medical assistance should be given special attention'. He went on to recommend pack stretchers mounted on donkeys and horses and the establishment of several 'warming stations' along the evacuation routes.[162] The Russian imperial General Staff and Colonel Klement'ev had come to these conclusions long before the battle of the Caucasus.[163]

Morale

The austere, frightening, but beautiful environment of the MCR produced a large body of romantic war mythology in the Soviet Union – tales about heroes who, cornered by Germans, refused to surrender, jumping instead into an abyss and blowing themselves up with hand grenades while plunging to their death, or those who, during a stealthy approach to enemy positions at night across precarious cliffs, slipped and 'fell into the abyss in complete silence, so they would not expose their comrades'. Narratives like these still dominate Russian writing.[164] However, the archival files of the TCF and the uncensored memoirs of those who fought in the Caucasus refute such epic stories, intended to veil the blunders of Soviet senior officers and their criminal neglect of the men under their command.

Soviet soldiers demonstrated remarkable resilience in savage conditions, but their morale was ruined by the feeling of inferiority to their skilled enemy, the utmost misery they experienced, and the awareness of their likely fate if wounded. Many of them were twice as old as their opponents;[165] they lacked the youthful enthusiasm and optimism typical of the German mountain troops, and they were less fit physically. Major Saltykov, a representative of the General Staff of the Red Army in the TCF, examined the causes for plummeting morale among the Soviet defenders and found that 'commanders, and especially political officers, ignore the fact that the mountains depress untrained soldiers, which undermines their capacity and endurance. The poor food supply, with frequent interruptions, and the total absence of medical monitoring and assistance aggravate the situation even more.'[166]

In addition, the Soviet soldiers lacked the strong bonds and team spirit necessary for survival in such a severe environment. Most of those sent to the high Caucasus belonged to local ethnic groups with dissimilar cultures and pervasive ethnic prejudices. These soldiers often did not share a language and had no tradition of military service for the state. Furthermore, since Soviet culture and communist ideology had penetrated the Caucasus to a lesser extent than the Slavic regions of the USSR, recruits from the Caucasus, immune to patriotic propaganda spread in Russian, were less inclined to risk their lives in defence of the Soviet state. The Red Army neglected the political training of non-Slavic soldiers until 17 September 1942, when Aleksandr Shcherbakov, the new head of the Red Army's Main Political Directorate, issued a directive entitled 'On the Education of Red Army Privates and Junior Commanders of Non-Russian Backgrounds', which reprimanded commissars who 'forgot that each of them [ethnic minorities] has their native language, customs, and well-rooted traditions, and treated them all alike, ignoring their ethnic cultures'.[167] This directive, ordering ethnic-tailored propaganda in the local languages and other measures aimed at bridging the gaps among the ethnic groups in the Red Army, emerged too late to affect the battle of the Caucasus. As Khalil Nadorshin, head of the Political Section of the Northern Army Group of the TCF, concluded on 18 October, the day when action at the MCR stopped, 'the combat capacity of most ethnic divisions is still poor because of neglect of the political work targeting their personnel, the insufficient communication with men, and absence of the slightest effort to improve the cohesion of the units and their combat training'.[168]

Another factor contributing to 'the unhealthy morale'[169] was the unanticipated consequence of Stalin's 'Not a Step Back' order. The order gave officers of all ranks sweeping powers over their subordinates, including the right of summary execution, in case of unauthorised retreat. It presumed that officers would use these powers responsibly and only to prevent flight from the battlefield. Although the draconian measures often helped to terminate such flight, the aura of officer impunity created by the order provoked many commanders to abuse their broad powers and impose disproportional punishment on soldiers for misdemeanours that did not fit the framework of the order or to tyrannise those who had committed no offences but whom the officers personally disliked. As General Leselidze observed,

> some officers perpetrate outrageous acts: they summarily execute innocent soldiers or those who have committed minor offences and humiliate [others]. Such officers think that they tighten discipline by such acts. In fact ... they undermine it. For

> example, Captain Navodchikov, commander of the 4th Rifle Battalion of the 51st Independent Rifle Brigade, summarily executed ... Private Chumburidze for coming to the battalion commander without a rifle. Lieutenant Shevtsov, from the 174th Regiment of the 20th Mountain Division, intended to summarily execute Private Dzagunaridze for sleeping on sentry duty. During the execution, Private Dzagunaridze fell into a ravine unharmed and played dead, after which he got out of the ravine, came back to his company, and reported the incident. Captain Antonenko, commander of the 51st Independent Auto Battalion, ordered the summary execution of Private Karimov only because the latter, being frightened by aerial bombardment, had stopped his truck and hidden in the bushes ... Similar incidents of summary execution and beatings have occurred in other units and formations of the [46th] Army.[170]

The TCF documents describe scores of similar incidents. Lieutenant Pupenko, from the 155th Independent Rifle Brigade, committed 'an absolutely disgraceful and totally outrageous crime' when he 'baselessly shot dead Shavla Sisoevich Baramiia, a soldier of his company'.[171] A court-martial protocol states that Lieutenant Ivan Voloshin, company commander from the 9th 'Mountain' Division,

> routinely beat up soldiers and humiliated them ... On 30 September 1942, the defendant Voloshin called Private Khvadashvili into his dugout and started to beat him up with sticks, feet, and fists for sleeping on sentry duty ... and then tied his feet to his hands and left him in that position for four hours ... When Voloshin saw that Private Garibashvili had dropped a jar containing food and broken it, he hit his [Garibashvili's] neck with a stick and then arrested him and left him unfed for three days.[172]

All the criminals with officer ranks mentioned in these reports were Slavs and all their victims belonged to the local ethnic groups, which fuelled ethnic tensions in the formations of the TCF. The clash of cultures between predominantly Slavic commanders and recruits from the Caucasus, and the particular sensitivity of the latter to affronts on male dignity, created an atmosphere of mistrust between soldiers and officers. The executions within the framework of the 'Not a Step Back' order and the arbitrary murders outside its framework reached such a scale that the Military Council of the 46th Army felt obliged to restrict the rate of repression by demanding that its divisions 'suspend the execution of pronounced sentences for various offences until the end of the war and send the sentenced to the front line, giving them the opportunity to atone for their guilt. If they show themselves staunch defenders of the Motherland, their punishment may be void or reduced upon the request of their officers.'[173] Most soldiers with suspended sentences found themselves in penal companies.

Sentence to a penal unit was another type of punishment for unsanctioned retreat suggested by the 'Not a Step Back' order. However, as with summary executions, many soldiers were sent to penal service outside the framework of the order. As General Vladimir Kurdiumov, deputy commander of the TCF, observed, 'Soldiers and sergeants were frequently sentenced to penal companies not for cowardice or lack of moral fibre or grave crimes but for minor offences liable to punishment in accordance with the Disciplinary Manual of the Red Army.' He gave a list of the soldiers who found themselves in penal units for the following 'crimes': for one private, 'everything was a joke; he always laughed', while another missed a morning exercise; a sergeant displayed an 'untidy appearance and undue familiarity', while two female soldiers were 'sexually promiscuous', and several men were sent to penal companies for being sick.[174] A sentence to a penal company, which typically engaged in the most dangerous missions, was a severe punishment most often entailing death or injury.[175]

Misuse of the broad powers given to officers by the 'Not a Step Back' order damaged both the prestige of these officers and the morale of their units. A commissar described the psychological climate in a reconnaissance platoon of the 815th Regiment deployed near Klukhor. In this unit, engaged in stealthy action in no-man's land for which an internal bond was particularly important, half of the soldiers 'hate the platoon commander for his rude manners: he allegedly threatens them with execution for every trifle, and when [I] talked to soldiers, Private Ermakovskii stated that, if the platoon commander shoots a soldier, "he himself will be riddled with bullets"'.[176] Such relations between commanders and soldiers would have been unthinkable in German mountain units, which cultivated comradeship as a precondition for success in the difficult missions they performed.

Many soldiers who did not feel allegiance to the Soviet state viewed surrender to the enemy, defection, or desertion as a way to escape the misery they suffered in the high mountains. The difference in the number of prisoners taken by the two opposing forces during the battle at the MCR and the circumstances of their capture are indicative of morale. The 394th Rifle Division, the largest formation operating at the MCR, failed to take a single German prisoner during October and the first three weeks of November, despite many attempts. Neither the 63rd Cavalry Division nor the 242nd 'Mountain' Division were able to capture a single prisoner in the Elbrus region.[177] When Soviet soldiers managed to take one or two prisoners, this was an extraordinary event worth reporting to the TCF Headquarters.[178] Most German prisoners taken by the Soviets were either wounded or otherwise incapacitated, as happened in an incident described by Aleksandr Gusev, a Soviet mountaineer who fought in the Caucasus: two German soldiers from a company surrounded in the Klych valley, having no food, attempted in vain to sneak back across the front for twenty days, until one of them starved to death and the other was found unconscious next to the body of his comrade.[179] Since most German prisoners were taken in similar circumstances, their number was meagre. For the entire period of action at the MCR, the Red Army took prisoner only thirty-three German privates and three sergeants; they were unable to capture a single officer.[180] In contrast, Soviet soldiers surrendered and deserted in droves. The Germans reported having taken 557 prisoners during one day in the battle over the Marukh pass;[181] they also took hundreds of prisoners at and near Klukhor,[182] and Soviet documents mention many incidents when entire platoons vanished without trace,[183] which never happened to Germans except in one incident, during the battle in the Klych valley, when most of the surrounded Germans died in battle rather than surrendered.

The ratio of missing in action to other casualties shows a similar pattern. In September and October, the 20th 'Mountain' Division, which performed slightly better than the other formations deployed in the high Caucasus, lost 724 men killed, wounded, sick, and missing in action, with the last category numbering 177 men, or 24 per cent of those lost.[184] In contrast, the 1st and the 4th German Mountain Divisions lost, respectively, 36 and 13 of their soldiers missing in action, or 5 per cent and 2 per cent of their total casualties, from 14 August to 26 September.[185] The 46th Army counted, in total, 1,102 soldiers missing in action at the MCR from 19 August to 13 October, whereas the German 49th Mountain Corps claimed to have taken 2,495 prisoners between 16 August and 17 September to the north and south of the MCR.[186] Such a great disparity in the number of prisoners taken by Germans and Soviets and in those missing in action versus other casualties reflects the difference in their morale.

Not a single German soldier defected to the Red Army during the battle at the MCR, whereas both Soviet and German documents provide numerous examples of Soviet defections. One instance occurred on 31 August 1942, when the Germans attacked the Soviet positions on Umpyrskii pass and a Soviet blocking platoon – a unit organised from 'the best, staunchest and most motivated soldiers'[187] ordered to prevent unauthorised retreat – defected to the Germans, unlike the rest of the garrison, which stubbornly resisted the enemy.[188] Several reconnaissance parties, and even some officers, also defected.[189] Most defectors were from the Caucasus.[190] Soviet commanders complained that the Germans received detailed intelligence information from defectors; at times, the Germans ambushed and destroyed Soviet raiding parties because defectors had allegedly divulged the plans of their commanders.[191]

Although desertion from the formations of the TCF was never as rife as it was among the units raised in the North Caucasus, it continued in fairly large numbers until the end of battle of the Caucasus, despite public executions of captured deserters and the warnings of commissars about the repression that awaited the families of deserters and defectors.[192] Reports about desertions, including those committed by communists and Komsomol members, arrived from most large formations engaged in the high Caucasus.[193] In addition, some soldiers were caught with self-inflicted wounds.[194] Even in December, long after action in the high mountains had stopped, Major Bozhenko, the chief of staff of the 242nd 'Mountain' Division, wrote that 'disgraceful incidents of desertion and defection … still continue in our division'.[195] In an attempt to prevent such incidents, he established a free-fire zone of 200 metres in front of the Soviet positions and ordered men to fire at any Soviet soldier spotted in this zone; to this he added the summary execution of captured deserters. Only reconnaissance parties were allowed to cross the free-fire zone, but members of these parties had to be selected 'exclusively among true patriots preapproved by the Special Section'.[196] The 46th Army preserved blocking units at the

MCR, even after the battle had ended, to prevent potential defections.[197]

Most soldiers who deserted, surrendered, or defected to the Germans were not anti-communist; they did it partly because they felt impotent when facing the superior tactics and skill of German mountain troops and partly because their tyrannical officers and the privations they suffered in harsh environments, even in the absence of combat, made their lives unbearable. When fourteen men defected to the Germans near Marukh on 31 August, and five more the next day, these soldiers were so debilitated that they could barely stand on their feet; two of them slipped while fording a river and drowned.[198] Having been driven to such a state, many soldiers believed, wrongly, that German captivity would give them a better chance of survival.

Relations with the Local Populations

Instead of identifying the absence of training for mountain warfare as the most obvious reason for the defeats at the MCR, some commanders, in the spirit of Stalinism, offered treason as an explanation. The Headquarters of the 46th Army explained its failure to defend the passes with the allegation that 'the enemy had a great advantage in intelligence acquisition, gaining information from numerous traitors'.[199] Those traitors allegedly belonged to the local ethnic groups. Karachais populated the northern slopes of the Caucasus in the operational area of the German 49th Mountain Corps. On 19 August, a day after Tiulenev and his chief of staff, Aleksei Subbotin, learned about the loss of Klukhor and still had only vague information about the actions at the pass, they attributed the successful German attack to treason. They informed Stalin that 'by employing Karachai guides, the enemy gained access relatively easily and quickly' to Klukhor.[200] According to the war diary of the TCF, 'guides played quite an important role in this tactic: the local population knew all the trails to the passes, and guides brought the Germans to our defence positions. ... The enemy emerged from directions that our soldiers did not anticipate.'[201] Tiulenev added a ludicrous story about a local person who allegedly guided the Germans climbing the

Elbrus via radio from Tyrnyauz, a town located 40 kilometres away and 3,000 metres below Priiut 11.[202] With the increasing tendency of the Soviet state to identify traitors in ethnic terms, the commanders of the TCF and the top police officers in the Caucasus began categorising the complex Caucasian society into loyal and disloyal ethnic groups, with Christians belonging mainly to the former and Muslims constituting the overwhelming majority of the latter.

To what extent did the allegations about treason in the North Caucasus reflect the facts? After the beginning of the war, civilians experienced various forms of pressure all across the Soviet Union: heavy taxes, requisitions of livestock and horses, the labour draft, and even hostage taking in families that failed to report for the labour draft.[203] Those who had adopted Soviet values perceived these extraordinary wartime measures as the price for eventual victory, whereas most residents of the North Caucasus, both native and Russian, did not share the main Soviet wartime goal of victory at all costs, and a minority were even ready to collaborate with the Germans. When the authorities, distracted by numerous war-related problems, weakened their grip on the North Caucasus, a resistance to Soviet policies, both armed and passive, emerged. Those who had escaped the military and labour drafts gathered in the mountains and occasionally attacked Soviet administrators. These attacks happened mostly in Chechnya and Dagestan, where the conflict between Soviet authority and the local people was smouldering throughout the interwar period, finally bursting into widespread insurgency after the government attempted to enforce first the Collective Farm Charter in 1940 and then conscription in 1941.[204] Soviet security forces counted more than 2,000 insurgents in the Itum-Kale and Galain-Chozh districts of mountainous Chechnya alone, as well as many bands of several dozen men that were scattered throughout Chechnya and Dagestan and actively supported by the local population, who often fled to the mountains, to the last person.[205] In the North Caucasus, counterinsurgency operations at times resulted in large-scale engagements with hundreds of casualties. When Chechen insurgents in the Shatili district of Georgia, which borders Chechnya, ambushed and destroyed a platoon of the 28th Reserve Rifle Brigade, killing 16 and capturing 8 soldiers on 19 September 1942, and then moved on to Chechnya, the Soviet security forces launched a massive counterinsurgency operation in early October, killing 152 alleged insurgents and capturing 231.[206] However, these clashes happened outside the Karachai Autonomous Region, where the battle of the MCR occurred.[207] In this region, fugitives merely sought to escape conscription rather than to resist, but, when the Germans arrived, some enlisted in collaboratorationist militia. Most local people, however, kept their neutrality in the war between the Red Army and the Wehrmacht.

The Germans reported that the Karachais were 'very friendly'; they often greeted the Germans with the Nazi salute, provided intelligence, repaired bridges destroyed by the retreating Red Army, and organised militias that clashed occasionally with Soviet stragglers. However, the Germans also often referred to those Karachais who collaborated as bandits motivated by self-interest rather than by hatred for the Soviet regime or love for the Germans.[208] Balkars also resided in the high mountains, but most lived outside the area of the MCR where action occurred. Nonetheless, Beria also accused them of joining the 'collaboratorationist guide' club. Neither reports of the 49th Mountain Corps nor memoirs of German soldiers mention Karachais or other minorities of the North Caucasus serving the Germans as mountain guides, although they do mention fifteen Georgian guides who arrived on 8 September, by which date the Germans had already taken all the passes they planned to take between Elbrus and Chmakhara.[209]

The 'Father and Teacher' of the Soviet nation promptly reacted to the accusations of collaboration. The decrees of the Presidium of the Supreme Soviet of the USSR issued after the Red Army reoccupied the regions where Karachais and Balkars lived ordered the wholesale deportations of these ethnic groups, stating that they 'assisted the fascist invaders by guiding them to the passes of the Caucasus'.[210] Soviet collective war memory embraced these baseless allegations, despite their obvious absurdity and despite the partial tacit acquittal of the unfortunate ethnic groups in 1956 and the official full acquittal in 1989. In fact, all the ethnic groups of the North Caucasus taken together provided fewer collaborators than did Slavic Cossacks living in the nearby lowlands, but the latter were not deported for mass treason.

The social situation in Transcaucasia was different. Some strain between the local populations and the Red Army emerged when hungry soldiers stole 'unowned [*beznadzornye*] flocks of sheep',[211] as Soviet authors put it, from those living in the foothills of the MCR. Since population density was low in these regions, the constant theft of livestock hit people hard, which aggravated the inevitable clash of cultures with Slavic soldiers and those belonging to other non-local ethnic groups.

The Headquarters of the 46th Army appreciated the logistical assistance provided by local civilians but, being busy with other matters, turned a blind eye to what it called 'petty plunder, rudeness, and hooliganism'[212] until Major Saltykov, a representative of the Red Army in the TCF, submitted a report on the potential danger of such an attitude. His memo stated:

> Relations with the local civilians are of utmost importance for the success of our actions in the mountains. Commanders and soldiers must know the customs of the ethnic groups living in the combat area, respect their traditions, and abstain from alienating the local population. As long as local civilians have been respected, they have helped us and they will continue to help. Their assistance is absolutely vital during actions in the mountains ... This aspect has been ignored so far, and there have been several incidents when soldiers embittered the people. All soldiers must receive comprehensive instructions [on attitudes towards locals]. Otherwise, the enemy will turn them against us.[213]

Given the precedent of anti-Soviet insurgency in the North Caucasus, the Headquarters of the 46th Army reacted promptly to this memo and co-operated with local party agencies to defuse the brewing tensions between the army and civilians. It was easier to do this in Transcaucasia than in the North Caucasus because the Georgians, Svans, Ossetians, and Abkhazians living in the areas near the front had accepted Soviet authority, and the strain between them and the Red Army did not have deep roots. No popular armed resistance ever occurred in Transcaucasia, where the internal strife was limited to grumbling and several skirmishes with bands of armed deserters numbering no more than a dozen men; not having local support, they were quickly destroyed.[214] Unlike the rear of the 37th Army in the North Caucasus, the rear of the TCF was safe, and the civilians of Georgia made a substantial contribution to the termination of the German offensive across the Caucasus by providing logistical assistance and food supplies.

Conclusion

The interpretation of a battle as a success or a failure stems primarily from the correlation among the goals set during its planning, the results attained, and the cost of those results. The OKW's initial goal was to sever the communications of the 18th Army and thus open the way for a major offensive along the Black Sea coast. As long as action took place in the high Caucasus, German mountain troops were far superior in man-for-man terms to Soviet 'mountain' personnel, regular infantry, cavalry, and frontier guards, all of whom found themselves in the mountains for the first time in their lives and had no proper equipment. Skill in mountain warfare brought glorious victories to the 49th Mountain Corps. However, when the Germans descended to lower altitudes in late August and early September, those particular skills mattered less, and their superiority in general infantry training turned out to be insufficient to break through the lines defended by the enemy, who massively outnumbered the Germans, had more ammunition, and enjoyed full control of the air. As a result, all of the astounding victories won by the Germans at the passes turned out to be hollow. The German offensive across the Caucasus was a thoughtless and sloppy improvisation that ignored both the huge imbalance in resources available to Soviets and Germans at this part of the front and the potential logistical problems. Had the Germans been able to reach a dirt road, they would have been exposed to Soviet heavy artillery and tanks and most likely would have been completely destroyed. This wild gamble was doomed to failure from the start.

The Red Army's goal from the beginning of the battle at the MCR to its end was not just to prevent the invasion of Transcaucasia but also to keep the Germans on the northern slopes of the MCR, preferably at its remote approaches, which it failed to do. Tiulenev, nonetheless, finished his description of the battle in the high Caucasus as follows: 'The 1st Mountain Division left the Khotiu-Tau and Chiper-Azau passes under the strikes of our units and fled to the northern slopes of the [Main Caucasus] Ridge ... Our counterattacks at the Klukhor and Marukh passes routed the German fascist troops.'[215] This happened only in his dreams, but most Russian authors describe the end of the battle at the MCR along the lines set by Tiulenev: the Red Army 'held firmly the key passes to Transcaucasia', 'stubbornly defended every metre of mountain trails', 'reconquered the passes that Hitlerites had taken in summer', and threw the Germans down from the ridge; 'a large part' of the 49th Mountain Corps 'was buried on the passes of the MCR'.[216] Some authors even claim that the Soviets pursued the fleeing Germans along the northern slopes of the Caucasus, thus creating the impression of a hard-won but clear-cut victory.[217] Few Russian studies avoid the cliché that the Red Army 'routed [*razgromila nagolovu*]' the 'extolled [*khvalenye*]' German mountain divisions. This cliché is engraved on numerous monuments that were erected at the passes of the MCR after the war, thus bolstering the victory claim. In fact, after the OKW changed the ultimate goal of the operation and sought to pin down as many Soviet forces in the mountains as possible in order to ease the progress of the main offensive along the coast, the battle shifted back to higher ground, and Germans again enjoyed the advantage of their mountaineering skills. They did attain this new goal, which, however, did not result in victory at the coast. The battle in the high Caucasus thus ended in a stalemate.

In the absence of an obvious winner, the ratio of casualties suffered by the two opposing sides adds a dimension to the interpretation of the outcome. In mid September, the 49th Mountain Corps withdrew most of its manpower from the high passes and transferred it to the Tuapse region, leaving a mixture of units from both mountain divisions at the MCR. The daily casualty statistics of the 49th Mountain Corps can be traced with considerable accuracy from the beginning of action at the MCR until 27 September, the day it engaged in the battle of Tuapse, which was much costlier than the actions in the high Caucasus; after that day its reports on the total daily casualties reflected mainly its losses near Tuapse. The daily reports slightly understated the number of casualties because sometimes the situation at remote positions was still uncertain by the evening, but they included the casualties inflicted by partisans in the North Caucasus.[218] It is clear from German war diaries that the casualties of the 1st Mountain Division at the MCR decreased greatly after mid September,[219] whereas the casualties of the 4th Mountain Division continued at a constant rate until the first week of October, after which they decreased. The Soviet 46th Army presented only data on the total casualties it sustained for the period from 19 August to 13 October: that is, these data exclude the hundreds of soldiers lost at Klukhor, the hundreds lost during the raid launched by the 37th Army into the rear of the 1st Mountain Division, the casualties of partisans and militia, and probably the casualties of cadets and NKVD units that were not integral parts of the 46th Army. These two sets of data are presented in Table 7.2. Although these data are imperfect, they still show who 'routed' whom in the high Caucasus and why the German mountain troops were 'extolled'.

The total casualties of either German mountain division roughly equalled the Soviet casualties sustained during one day of fighting on Marukh on 5 September. The Germans lost, in total, 37 officers killed, wounded, and missing in action, while the 46th Army lost 589 officers.[220] The ratio of total irrecoverable casualties – including the various attached formations, partisans, and NKVD units – was no less than 1:10 in favour of the Germans, despite the substantial numerical superiority of the Soviets; their better ammunition supply; and the uncontested domination of the Red Air Force, which killed and wounded many German soldiers, greatly eased Soviet logistics, and seriously hampered those of the Germans. The Germans easily took Khotiu-Tau, Chiper, Chiper-Azau, Bassa, Nakhar, Klukhor, Ptysh, Marukh, Umpyrskii, Tsegerker, Sancharo, Adzapsh, Allashtrakhu, Chmakhara, Chamashkha, and Gudauta – that is, nearly all the passes they attempted to take, except for Aishkha, Pseashkha, and Belorechenskii, the latter being outside the operational area of the 49th Mountain Corps. They held nearly all of the passes they took, except for three across minor ridges – Bassa, Chamashkha, and Gudauta – and two across the MCR – Chmakhara and Tsegerker. They abandoned the latter two passes because of logistical difficulties; soon after their reoccupation, the Soviets had to evacuate them for the same reason. The Germans defended the passes with far inferior forces at a low cost against numerous futile Soviet attacks, and they left them in January 1943, without any pressure from the TCF, when the Wehrmacht began its general strategic retreat from the Caucasus.[221] Lieutenant-Colonel Mezentsev summarised the outcome of the battle in the high Caucasus thus: 'we suffered grave casualties but could not attain our objectives'.[222]

What were the primary reasons for such an outcome? As the TCF Headquarters found, even in late November, few officers had the *Manual on Mountain Warfare* and 'almost nobody ever used it'.[223] Indeed, the Soviet forces fought in the high Caucasus in a way that contradicted nearly every point of the manual and nearly every conclusion of the field experiments run by Klement'ev and Levandovskii in the

Table 7.2 Soviet and German casualties in the battle at the Main Caucasus Ridge

Casualties of the German Mountain Divisions, from 14 August to 26 September, Killed (K), Wounded (W), and Missing in Action (M)						Total German Casualties	Casualties of the Soviet 46th Army, from 19 August to 13 October, Killed (K), Wounded (W), Missing in Action (M), Taken Prisoner (POW), and Sick					Total Soviet Casualties
1st Mountain Div.			4th Mountain Div.									
K	W	M	K	W	M		K	W	M	POW	Sick	
149	504	36	159	493	13	1,354, of which 357 irrecoverable	1,890	4,168	1,102	47	745	7,952, of which 3,039 irrecoverable

Source: 49th Mountain Corps, 'Zahlenmässige Übersicht def Uffz. und Mannsch.-Verluste vom 4.6.42 mit 17.12.1942', BA-MA, RH 24-49/232, Anlage 3; Beliavskii, 'Svedeniia o poteriakh v voiskakh 46-i armii s 19 avgusta po 13 oktiabria 1942' (no date), TsAMO, f. 47, op. 1063, d. 655, l. 165.

interwar years. The instructions on tactics suggested by the manual dismissed frontal assaults in favour of daring envelopments across rugged terrain; they prescribed the swift occupation of dominating heights, tiered defensive positions with protected flanks, and the support of infantry with mountain artillery.[224] Action in the mountains, preceded by a thorough collection of intelligence by reconnaissance teams 'recruited from commanders and soldiers most skilled in mountaineering', was to be 'conducted by small well-trained mountain units' that had climbing gear and knew how to use it;[225] were able to manoeuvre across any terrain; were acclimatised to the altitudes at which they were operating; and were led by junior officers who had great initiative, could easily navigate in the mountains with a map and a compass, and co-ordinated their actions via portable radios. The manual emphasised the need for cable-car equipment, special mountain food rations, pack kitchens, warm tents, individual light stoves, alcohol burners, and chemical heaters.[226] The field experiments revealed the need for special medical and logistical arrangements to be made before the start of a campaign in the mountains, which were necessary to secure the proper care for the wounded and an uninterrupted flow of supplies.[227] In fact, the Soviet tactics, gear, artillery, food rations, supply and medical practices, standards of the officers, and skills of the soldiers deployed at the MCR did not correspond to any of these requirements determined by the manual as conditions for success in mountain warfare. This happened because Soviet generals had never trained for mountain warfare and completely ignored the experience of earlier wars that had revealed most of the factors that were to surprise these generals during the battle at the MCR.

A year after the end of the battle at the MCR, Lieutenant-Colonel Zav'ialov wrote a detailed and fairly honest analysis of the Soviet problems in the mountains. Among the major tactical flaws, he mentioned

> the absence of reliable reconnaissance, frontal attacks instead of envelopment, which had particularly grave consequences in mountain warfare, and thoughtless deployment in defence ... our units occupied valleys and passes, leaving the neighbouring heights unprotected, which allowed the enemy to easily climb these heights and then force our units to evacuate their positions by firing from the flanks.[228]

These flaws stemmed from tactical ignorance and the limited mobility of Soviet regular infantry on mountainous terrain, as well as the poor skills of field commanders who lacked initiative and who either ignored radios, even after they received better designs, or had no radio batteries or operators trained to work in the mountains. These factors precluded sophisticated tactics and forced the Soviets to engage in unimaginative, predictable, and costly frontal attacks that defied the *Manual on Mountain Warfare* and all the earlier experiences of the Russian imperial army. Paradoxically, Zav'ialov ended his devastating criticism of the TCF with a stunning conclusion, an idea picked up later by numerous postwar Soviet authors: the experience of the battle at the MCR allegedly 'showed that not just special mountain troops but all types of units can fight in the mountains'; after all, 'with the acquisition of experience that cost a lot of blood, the tactics of our units changed dramatically'.[229] The casualty statistics revealed by the TCF documents put the phrase 'a lot of blood' in context: the Soviet regular infantrymen managed to terminate the German offensive only because of their overwhelming numbers and the flawed German strategy, and they paid such an enormous price for the modest results they attained exactly because they did not know how to fight in the mountains. Contrary to Zav'ialov's final statement, the TCF documents show no tangible improvement in the combat performance of the Soviets until the very end of the battle at the MCR.

After the snowfalls began, it became difficult to climb the steep southern slopes of the MCR, even without enemy impact, and it was extremely difficult to dislodge the Germans from their impressive system of strongholds in the absence of mountain artillery. During the counteroffensive launched in September and October, the Soviet formations continued to suffer attrition much faster than the German forces, not only because of their primitive tactics but also because the Germans suffered lighter non-combat casualties. The German mountain units had identified all the items necessary for survival in the mountains through a long trial-and-error process during exercises throughout the interwar period. They secured sufficient comfort for their soldiers to help them maintain high morale, even when they were battered by atrocious weather and faced a numerically superior enemy.

The Soviet divisions defending the Caucasus had no proper equipment because their senior commanders, staying at the Black Sea coast, did not know what their soldiers needed to act effectively in the high mountains. The TCF had no uniforms suitable for climbing, and it failed to deliver the available winter uniforms from the stores to the MCR because it took the generals time to realise what soldiers needed for weather conditions at high altitude and because they failed to establish intermediate supply depots during the ample time they had after receiving orders in late June prompting them to do so. Once the action began, it was hard to deliver these uniforms to the mountains because the Soviet logistics, hastily organised only after the Germans had taken the first passes, were overburdened with other items believed to be of higher priority, including useless anti-tank weapons. Having failed to secure portable kitchens, kerosene stoves, tinned food, or special high-altitude food rations, Soviet commanders fed their soldiers with raw frozen meat and raw grain. These soldiers were exposed to icy rains and whipped by fierce winds; many were frostbitten; their lips festered and their throats became raw from sucking snow in the absence of water; lacking sunglasses, they suffered from sharp pain in their eyes; and they were tormented by lice. Aware of their dire prospects if wounded, feeling impotent against younger and more skilled German mountain troops, and threatened with execution for minor misdemeanours, they could not be an effective combat force, and some chose to desert or defect to the enemy. Nonetheless, the pompous Russian claims that 'the defenders of the passes showed mass heroism' and 'barred the enemy's way to the icy positions in the high Caucasus with their bodies [*grud'iu pregradili*]'[230] are in fact correct: as it had during the Winter War, the Red Army countered the enemy's skill with greater numbers of untrained, unequipped, and underfed soldiers who paid with their lives and health for the failure of the Red Army General Staff to raise proper mountain divisions, whereas the Germans were as comfortable in the Soviet mountains as the Finns had been in their forests.

Colonel Dreev described the outcome of the Soviet counteroffensive: 'After occupying the passes, fortifying them, and placing small but well-trained mountain units there, the enemy tied down large forces of the TCF who were obliged to secure the southern slopes of the passes. Our attempts to take the passes were, as a whole, futile and resulted in grave casualties despite ... our overwhelming numerical superiority.' As a result, the enemy 'was able to secure the passes with a relatively weak force and transfer most units from these regions to other parts of the front'.[231] The success of the Germans in strategic defence at the MCR was as clear-cut as their failure to break through to the Black Sea: they tied down far superior Soviet forces,[232] thus preventing their relocation to the Tuapse region; they killed and wounded many more Soviet soldiers than they lost themselves and left the MCR when they chose to. General Konstantin Skorobogatkin, head of the Military Studies Directorate with the General Staff of the Soviet Army, wrote later that the Soviet 'actions on the passes of the Main Caucasus Ridge from August to October 1942 cannot serve as an instructive example for lecturing on tactics and operational art'.[233]

Nevertheless, by the end of the battle at the MCR, the TCF had taken a number of important and rational steps intended to improve Soviet combat capacity in the mountains in the long run. First, it made an effort to systematise knowledge about the operational theatre and the tactics of mountain warfare earned at the MCR. On 8 October, General Petrov requested from the commanders of all formations involved in the battle at the MCR a detailed analysis of the problems encountered in every particular region and the possible solutions to these problems. He wrote: 'Your report should focus on tactics and be based solely on your combat experience rather than on theoretical speculations ... with concrete examples, conclusions, and proposals.'[234] He inquired about the specifics of offensive and defensive tactics in the mountains, including the independent actions of small units and snipers; mortar and artillery fire; the effectiveness of artificial obstacles in mountainous terrain; the possibilities of air support; the desirable structure of mountain formations; suggested changes in weapons, uniforms, and food rations; the logistical arrangements, including estimates of the number of porters and pack animals needed to supply units of various strengths at various altitudes; the designs of packs and the proper ratio of horses to donkeys in supply trains; the problems of medical service; the co-ordination of military effort with local civilian agencies; and the recruitment of local guides.[235] Petrov also demanded that a detailed description of every mountain pass be entered into a standardised form. The description for each pass was to include topography and detailed sketch-maps, weather data, information on trails and their seasonal passability, water sources and vegetation usable for fortifications and firewood, possible fortification solutions and the potential location of artificial obstacles and their types, fords across rivers streaming from the pass, possible communication means between the pass and the valley leading to it, and suggested transportation means across the pass. Also required was an estimate of the garrison strength needed to defend the pass; a tactical defence plan, including co-operation with guerrilla units; and proposals on the evacuation of wounded men.[236] Abundant information began streaming to the TCF Headquarters in early November. The commanders determined appropriate tactics for summer and winter; discussed the impact of the high mountain environment on the morale and physical conditions of soldiers; emphasised the special value of marksmanship, initiative, individual training, and adequate signals service; and highlighted the need for camouflage coveralls, portable kitchens, and individual alcohol burners.[237]

The TCF should have addressed all these issues long before the German attack across the Caucasus. It failed to do so, and all these valuable analyses of mountain warfare were conducted too late to help fight Germans at the MCR. However, the strenuous effort to collect comprehensive information on the operational terrain, systematise the scattered bits of experience-based knowledge on the peculiarities of mountain warfare, analyse the identified problems, and suggest possible solutions created a blueprint of the actions needed to establish formations able to fight effectively in the mountains. As Colonel Dreev maintained, 'One of the reasons for the failure of our assaults [on the MCR] was either the absence of special mountain units or their poor training.'[238] According to him,

> The experience of mountain warfare showed that special mountain units are necessary for successful actions in the mountains. This is confirmed by (a) the successful defence of German mountain units against our [numerically] superior forces; (b) the heavy casualties of our regular and poorly trained mountain units in offensives on the passes of the MCR and the futility of many offensives.[239]

The next chapter describes the Soviet effort to raise genuine rather than nominal mountain units able to fight their German counterparts on equal terms.

8 LEARNING MOUNTAIN WARFARE THE HARD WAY

Victory must be gained by skill rather than numbers!

Alexander Suvorov[1]

After the Germans easily took nearly all the passes they had planned to take, inflicting crushing defeats on the Soviet garrisons, the TCF commanders began thinking about how to improve the combat performance of their formations in the mountains. At first, they raised ad hoc units from the fittest soldiers selected among regular infantry and sent them on risky raids, organised, in General Petrov's words, with 'criminal negligence'.[2] The most determined attempt to drive the Germans away from Priiut 11 serves as an example. A company commanded by Lieutenant Guren Grigoriants and consisting mainly of hand-picked soldiers of the 897th 'Mountain' Regiment, with an attached platoon of the best and most experienced soldiers of the 214th Cavalry Regiment, received the order to advance, on the evening of 27 September, from an elevation of 3,268 metres in Terskol valley and attack Priiut 11 that same night. In order to reach the hotel, the company had to gain 1,000 vertical metres and cross a 3-kilometre-wide glacier.[3] It was virtually impossible to climb so quickly at such altitudes and then navigate across the glacier, broken by crevasses, in the dark, especially given that subzero temperatures forced the soldiers to carry sheepskin coats in addition to weapons and ammunition. It took the company nine hours to climb to the glacier, and the soldiers had crossed most of it by the time daylight broke. The Germans discovered the dead-tired soldiers when they were 1 kilometre away from Priiut 11, at which point a German platoon feigned flight, luring the Soviets onto an open snowfield, where the Germans surrounded and completely destroyed the company: of its 102 men, only 4, including the commissar, escaped, all of them wounded.[4] The Germans claimed to have taken 57 prisoners, including the wounded commander – more than the total number of German prisoners taken by the Soviets throughout the battle in the high Caucasus.[5]

After a series of similar spectacular failures, some commanders began arguing that Suvorov's maxim was valid for the battle of the Caucasus and that not only motivation and fitness but also special training, gear, and uniforms were necessary to fight effectively in the mountains.[6] These officers pinpointed three general flaws in Soviet actions. First, Soviet commanders did not know their operational terrain because they had failed to study it on the eve of the battle. The Germans did not know it either, but their general mountaineering experience allowed them to outmanoeuvre the Soviets. Second, the Germans had a solid edge in the tactics of mountain warfare. Third, even after the Soviets learned about these tactics from the Germans, they could not replicate them because their soldiers had no mountaineering skills or gear, appropriate combat training and uniforms, or reliable communication means. The Soviet analysts offered extensive observations on each of these handicaps by making unflattering comparisons between Soviet clumsiness and German tactical sophistication.[7] Having reached a consensus about the poor efficiency of the Soviet forces in the mountains, identified most of their flaws, and grasped at least some tenets of mountain warfare, the TCF commanders thought about how to correct these shortcomings. They had to learn the tactics of mountain warfare from scratch, but before that they had to train their soldiers to manoeuvre across mountainous terrain and supply them with climbing gear. The adaptation to mountain warfare evolved painfully along several avenues, some of which led to dead ends while others promised encouraging results.

Supply of Climbing Gear

Since 'mountain' divisions never used the climbing gear allocated to them during the interwar period, this gear lay in the remotest corners of TCF depots as the least valuable equipment. Few officers understood the difference between the primitive four-spike crampons that worked only on flat icy surfaces and the ten-spike crampons that allowed the climbing of steep icy slopes, or the differences between an alpenstock and an ice axe, mountain tents and regular army tents, alpine skis and cross-country skis, or climbing rope and the rope used for everyday army needs. Nobody knew what gear the TCF had or in which depots it was kept. The Headquarters of the 46th Army assumed that a quarter of the personnel deployed in the high mountains had to be supplied with climbing gear,[8] which was a reasonable estimate but, having no experience in mountain warfare, they did not know which of the various gear items, and in what quantities, a unit fighting in the mountains should have.

On 26 June, General Sergatskov issued the first order for the delivery of gear to the regiments that he planned to send to the high mountains. Four days later, he wrote that 'success in this matter [the defence of the Caucasus] cannot be attained ... in the absence of climbing gear'.[9] The 46th Army planned to deploy a force equal to one division of 12,000 men at the MCR; they were to receive, by 10 July, 1,200 ice axes, 2,400 sets of crampons, 4,200 pairs of spiked mountain boots, and 4,800 alpenstocks. In addition, every 100 men were to receive one rope of 25 metres along with three pitons and three carabiners.[10] Although the number of carabiners and the amount of allotted rope were woefully inadequate, this gear would have been sufficient for climbing training. The Rear Directorate of the TCF had sufficient time to pass the gear from its stores to the formations assigned to defend MCR, but the commanders of the 46th Army failed to monitor the fulfilment of their orders. Furthermore, the Rear Directorate ignored the orders because neither the military bureaucrats nor the field commanders understood that such items were essential for a soldier fighting in the mountains, and they viewed them as fanciful, exotic contraptions. When the regiments of the 46th Army rushed to the MCR in mid August, they had none of this gear. On 23 August, after the Germans had demonstrated the tactical advantage of military mountaineering, Tiulenev again ordered that the soldiers in the passes be supplied with the climbing gear kept in the depots of the 46th Army. Sergatskov duplicated this order on 24 August; Petrov, and then Tiulenev, did the same on 25 August, as did Major Litvinov, an OG representative with the 394th Rifle Division, on 19 September.[11] However, since the strength of the Soviet forces at the MCR turned out to be much larger than the TCF had initially planned and the vast majority of those were rifle units with no climbing gear, the Rear Directorate had only a fraction of the gear necessary to supply these forces. Some gear began arriving at the front line bit by bit, but its quantity, let alone quality, was never adequate. When this became obvious, the TCF Headquarters requested that the Georgian administration urgently produce 10,000 pairs of crampons, 15,000 pitons, 5,000 ice axes, 10,000 sleeping bags, 80,000 metres of climbing rope, 5,000 mountaineering suits, and 5,000 backpacks. However, the administration rejected the request, referring to the absence of production capacities and the necessary metals, and the 46th Army continued to suffer from a desperate shortage of gear.[12] As the snow began to fall, the requests for climbing gear mounted, but its supply always lagged far behind the demand.

The inspectors who visited the 20th 'Mountain' Division in late September reported that the available gear was 'absolutely insufficient' and attributed the poor climbing skills of its soldiers partly to this fact.[13] By 20 November, when action at the MCR had already stopped, this division still lacked most of the gear it was supposed to have. Only on 6 December did the OG send most of the required gear to the division's depots, which means that the front-line units would have received it, at best, in late December, when the Germans holding positions at the MCR had already begun their overall retreat from the Caucasus (Table 8.1).

Still, the 20th 'Mountain' Division was in a privileged position in terms of gear supply as compared to the 394th Rifle Division or the 242nd 'Mountain' Division, the latter of which was sent to the MCR a week after it had received its 'mountain' designation; those two formations had no climbing gear in their depots and pleaded with the TCF Headquarters to deliver urgently whatever gear could be scrambled together (Table 8.2).

Such an uneven distribution of gear among the formations at the MCR occurred because, at the outset of the battle, the Rear Directorate of the 46th Army had no plan for supplying gear to formations deployed at the MCR. Field commanders often attributed the disasters experienced by their units to the absence of climbing gear, thus implicating the Rear Directorate as the culprit.[14] In response, supply bureaucrats, to avert the anger of the TCF Headquarters, hurried to send to the front line, in a haphazard fashion, whatever gear they found. It was only in the second half of November, a month after action at the MCR had

Table 8.1 Climbing gear delivered as a percentage of that requested by the 20th 'Mountain' Division

	Requested Items in Absolute Numbers	Percentage Delivered by 20 November to the Division's Depots	Percentage Available on 20 November to Front-Line Units	Percentage Delivered by Late December to the Division's Depots
Crampons	1,500 pairs	100	84	100
Ice axes	500	86	44	100
Carabiners	1,500	?	9	?
Rock pitons	3,000	57	19	84
Ice pitons	1,500	5	5	57
Sunglasses	6,000 pairs	71	40	100
Backpacks[a]	2,000	13	13	13
Mountain uniforms	1,500	0	0	100
Mountain boots	1,500 pairs	33	20	100
Rope	9,000 m	18	8	18
Climbing cord	9,000 m	0	0	22
Cross-country skis	1,500 pairs	100	64	100
Snowshoes	600 pairs	50	33	100

Source: Lieutenant Purtseladze, TCF inspector of mountaineering training, 'Gornaia i gorno-lyzhnaia podgotovka' (26 November 1942), TsAMO, f. 47, op. 1063, d. 692, l. 144; Colonel Spotkai, 'Svedeniia obespechennosti 20 gsd spetsial'nym al'pinistskim snariazheniem' (3 December 1942), TsAMO, f. 47, op. 1063, d. 692, l. 149; A. Gusev, head of Operations Section of Headquarters of the 46th Army, 'Svedeniia o nalichii al'pinistskogo imushchestva' (20 November 1942), TsAMO, f. 47, op. 1063, d. 695, l. 517.
Note: [a] The available data show only the actual number of backpacks rather than the supposed number. The supposed number of backpacks is taken from the inventory of the 242nd 'Mountain' Division.

ended, that the 46th Army began to record the gear received by its formations deployed in the mountains and stored in various depots and attempted to compensate shortages in an orderly fashion. Soldiers fighting in the high mountains were desperately short of rope, crampons, ice axes, mountain boots, and woollen socks. The severe shortage of climbing rope stemmed mainly from its criminal squandering. Although the 20th 'Mountain' Division initially had enough high-quality climbing rope, its officers wasted it for everyday needs, leaving

Table 8.2 Climbing gear delivered as a percentage of that requested by the 242nd 'Mountain' and 394th Rifle Divisions

	242nd 'Mountain' Division			394th Rifle Division[a]	
	Requested Items in Absolute Numbers	Percentage Delivered to the Division's Depots by 15 November	Percentage Available on 15 November to Front-Line Units	Percentage Available on 20 November to the 815th Regiment in the Klukhor Region	Percentage Available on 20 November to the 808th and 810th Regiments in the Marukh Region
Mountain boots	10,000 pairs	25	0	34	0
Crampons	1,000 pairs	81	20	46	20
Rope	20,000 m	0	0	7	?
Ice axes	1,500	18	18	97	66
Climbing cord	4,000 m	66	65	0	5
Rock pitons	5,000	2	1	0	3
Mountain tents	500	0	0	0	?
Mountain uniforms	2,000	50	0	0	0
Backpacks	2,000	0	0	0	0
Alcohol burners	100	0	0	0	0
Sunglasses	3,000 pairs	70	55	0	32
Woollen gloves	3,000 pairs	0	0	?	?
Woollen socks	6,000 pairs	19	19	0	0
Ski bindings	500 pairs	0	0	0	?
Kerosene stoves	2,200	0	0	?	?
Skis with bindings	1,500 pairs	57	17	84	4
Snowshoes	2,000 pairs	0	0	0	24

Source: Major Bozhenko, chief of staff of the 242 'Mountain' Division, 'Donesenie po potrebnosti i obespechennosti 242-i gsd gornym i gorno-lyzhnym snariazheniem' (15 November 1942), TsAMO, f. 47, op. 1063, d. 695, l. 515; A. Gusev, head of Operations Section of Headquarters of the 46th Army, 'Svedeniia o nalichii al'pinistskogo imushchestva' (20 November 1942), TsAMO, f. 47, op. 1063, d. 695, l. 517; Gusev, 'Svedeniia o nalichii al'pinistskogo imushchestva' (28 November 1942), TsAMO, f. 47, op. 1063, d. 695, l. 519.
Note: [a] The available data show only the numbers of the gear items available to the 394th Rifle Division rather than the numbers requested by its headquarters. The regimental request inventory submitted by the 20th 'Mountain' Division is used as a benchmark to calculate the percentage of gear available to the regiments of the 394th Rifle Division.

the soldiers in the mountains without this vital mountaineering tool. In addition to lack and misuse of gear, much of the Soviet gear was of poor quality. Nearly all crampons in the 20th 'Mountain' Division were primitive four-spike ones, and the spikes of Soviet-made crampons and the tips of ice axes easily bent and broke.[15] Without gear, Soviet soldiers could not climb rocks, cross glaciers, traverse steep slopes, or even walk along icy paths, which gave the Germans a broad tactical edge.

With the approach of the winter season in October, the mobility of the Soviet defenders, compared to that of their enemies, became even more constrained. The Soviets envied the easy manoeuvres of the Germans across snowfields on alpine skis, which allowed them to patrol the front line in the high mountains with moderate physical effort.[16] Soviet 'mountain' divisions were also supposed to be able to move across snowy mountains. On paper, the TCF had many more skis than it needed for actions at the MCR: 7,000 pairs in the depots of the 46th Army and 25,000 more in the depots of the TCF. However, Lieutenant Purtseladze, the TCF inspector of climbing training, found that the ski stock of the 20th 'Mountain' Division consisted mainly of cross-country skis of 'quite poor quality – worn out; the toes are flat and about 60 per cent have strap bindings unusable in the mountains'.[17] On 4 September, the TCF Headquarters ordered the Rear Directorate to equip 50 per cent of front-line personnel with touring skis carrying Kandahar bindings by 1 October, wildly inflating their needs.[18] Since the Red Army had few such skis, the OG organised their production, but it took time to make them. By 6 October, the first 1,500 pairs were sent to the mountains, and by the time action at the MCR stopped in late October, their number had increased to 5,000.[19] Yet even in late November, as Purtseladze wrote, 'nobody [in the 20th "Mountain" Division] has yet checked the conditions of the skis or used them, although winter has already arrived'.[20] This happened, in part, because few Soviet soldiers had the skills to ski in the mountains, even on touring skis with steel edges and proper bindings. As a result, the skis never became a prominent factor in the Red Army's mobility in the high Caucasus; only reconnaissance parties used them, and then only occasionally. The Red Army initially had no snowshoes, needed for action in dense vegetation; only after the battle of Caucasus had begun did the TCF order the production of 2,000 pairs of snowshoes at the Tbilisi furniture factory. The factory delivered 500 pairs by 5 November, but, having no experience manufacturing them, it had made the snowshoes flimsy and too small to keep a soldier on the snow's surface.[21] Aleksandr Gusev, one of the few climbing instructors who found themselves in the Caucasus, observed that 'having no [alpine] skis and proper training, reconnaissance parties could not approach the MCR' between late October, when the heavy snowfalls began, until January, when the Germans left.[22] The TCF continued to experience a shortage of mountain uniforms, mountain tents, all items of climbing gear, touring skis, and snowshoes until the Germans retreated from the Caucasus.[23]

During World War I, Russian imperial generals acquired ill fame by sending a second wave of soldiers into attack unarmed and telling them to pick up the rifles of their fallen comrades from the first wave. TCF commanders deserve an equally poor reputation for sending their soldiers to the high mountains without climbing gear. However, the shortage of gear was only one among several major problems impeding the ability of the Soviet divisions to manoeuvre across mountains. The German mountain units not only had the appropriate climbing gear, identified by trial and error in peacetime, but also knew how to use it. That is why they moved across rugged terrain with much greater ease than did the Soviet regular infantry, even if the latter had climbing gear. As several Soviet officers remarked, training for mountain warfare was 'possible even with the [meagre] available climbing gear', but 'most of it is kept in depots, and the personnel underestimate the gear and use it rarely because they are untrained to do so'.[24] Climbing training was a prerequisite to exploring the opportunities provided by the gear.

Soviet 'Mountain' Divisions in the Battle at the MCR

While the 242nd Division received a 'mountain' designation a week before it marched to its positions in the high Caucasus and therefore was no more effective in the mountains than a regular rifle division, the 9th and 20th Divisions of the 46th Army had been so designated since 1931. How did they perform during the battle at the MCR?

After some officers of the 9th 'Mountain' Division took crash mountaineering courses in the autumn of 1941 and the spring of 1942, this formation had more men with basic climbing skills than any other

Figure 8.1 German patrol on mountain skis. Skis considerably enhanced the mobility of German mountain troops in the late autumn. Credit: BArch, Bild 101I-031-2417-34 / Poetsch

TCF unit. However, during the battle of the Caucasus, the division idled in the lowlands near the sea coast, protecting the border with Turkey. The 46th Army detached only the 121st Regiment of this division and sent it to Klukhor. The regiment entered action on 27 August against a German battalion that was outflanking the Soviet position in the Klych valley; the fight continued for two days. On 3 September, the regiment spearheaded the Soviet offensive in the Klych valley, but it engaged only in straightforward frontal attacks, making no attempt to outmanoeuvre the enemy. It advanced only 500 metres on that day and 150 metres the next, losing, in those two days, 140 men killed and wounded, or 11 per cent of its personnel of 1,235 men.[25] The regiment resumed the attack on 10 September, and by 15 September it was reduced to merely two companies with a total strength of 220 men – that is, it lost more than 1,000 men, or 82 per cent of its manpower, during the actions of 27–28 August and 3–4 and 10–15 September.[26] Other Soviet units in the Klych valley suffered similar casualties,[27] whereas the German 1st Mountain Division reported having lost – during the same days and in all parts of the front, including Marukh – only 55 men killed, 132 wounded, and 30 missing in action.[28] The remnants of the 121st Regiment engaged in a fight near Nakhar and briefly occupied a part of the MCR near the pass. However, as the ratio of casualties suffered by the 121st 'Mountain' Regiment and the German 1st Mountain Division shows, the soldiers of this regiment were no match for their adversary.

The 20th 'Mountain' Division was another formation assessed by Captain O. Logofet, inspector of mountaineering training with the Main Directorate of the Red Army Reserves, as familiar with some elements of mountain warfare but with worse training than the 9th 'Mountain' Division. The 20th 'Mountain' Division participated in the battle of the MCR mainly with one of its four regiments, and the 174th Regiment, unlike the 121st Regiment of the 9th 'Mountain' Division, scored several impressive successes: one of its companies resisted the attack of the much larger Buchner Group on the Umpyrskii pass for the entire day of 29 August, and this was followed by two companies pinning down the Germans on the far approaches to the Aishkha pass. Later, two other companies of the division prevented Buchner from approaching the Pseashkha pass. However, judging from the fact that on 15 November, long after these events, General Petrov assessed the training of this division in mountain warfare as 'particularly poor',[29] its successes near Aishkha and Pseashkha should probably be attributed to a lucky engineering solution – Chechen-style barricades – rather than to its special skills. In short, 'mountain' divisions provided no convincing empirical proof that they were more effective in the mountains than regular infantry.

Soviet Climbers in Combat

Having observed the dismal performance of their forces in the mountains, the TCF Headquarters realised that they needed experts who would enhance the combat capacity of the units deployed at the MCR by familiarising soldiers with the operational region, guiding them across the mountains, and running some training in climbing. Before the battle at the MCR, Soviet commanders believed that local guides would enable regular infantry to defend the high Caucasus effectively.[30] They sent two local militia platoons to Klukhor and Marukh and one militia company to Sancharo, planning to use them as mountain guides.[31] However, those who had enlisted in the militia were mostly urban dwellers or, at best, villagers living in the foothills of the MCR; they knew their regions of residence well, but they had never been in the high mountains. Most TCF commanders soon realised that climbers would be able to provide more detailed information on the operational theatre; they could also personally participate in actions by guiding the Soviet formations and training them.

In Russian collective war memory, the climbers are perceived as a crucial component of the Soviet forces defending the Caucasus.[32] According to NKVD general Pavel Sudoplatov, Beria was the first among members of the TCF Military Council to come up with the trivial idea that a soldier trained and equipped for mountain warfare would fight in the mountains more effectively than a man in a standard uniform without climbing gear who had never been in the mountains. In August, Sudoplatov alleges, Beria ordered that a company of 150 mountaineers, fully equipped with climbing gear, be raised within 24 hours in Moscow and delivered to the Caucasus by airplane. Sudoplatov describes their actions vaguely, saying only that they 'blew up oil reservoirs and destroyed motorised German infantry' but suffered heavy casualties because they had no military training.[33] However, this is mere legend: TCF documents say nothing about this unit, nor were there any 'motorised German infantry' at the MCR.

These documents show that Russian war memory grossly inflates the contribution of Soviet climbers to the combat in the high Caucasus. The authors who mention them as a component of the Soviet forces are frequently referring to regular infantrymen with climbing gear or even regular units without climbing gear guided by one or two mountaineers.[34] In fact, there is no evidence that any of the numerous

Soviet mountaineers took part in the defence of the MCR before the Germans occupied all the passes they had planned to take. Only on 31 August did General Petrov request that the TCF transfer forty-five climbers, sixty-one men 'who knew the passes' across the MCR, and eighty-nine experienced skiers from the North Caucasus to Transcaucasia.[35] Since Petrov was an NKVD general, it is plausible that it was indeed Beria who initiated this request. However, since nobody knew where the thousands of Soviet climbers were serving, it took time to identify some of them in divisions dispersed all over the plains of the Eastern Front and then to summon them to the Caucasus. The TCF was able to find only about a dozen such experts, several of whom were top-class climbers holding Master of Sport titles.[36]

When the TCF began summoning climbers to the Caucasus, it had no clear idea how to employ them. Having acquired only a handful, the TCF Headquarters first attempted to use them as mountain guides leading regular infantry to the enemy's rear across rugged terrain. Several such raids scored minor successes, such as the retaking of the Bassa pass. In late August, after the Germans captured Bassa, which connects two confluent streams in the upper reaches of the Inguri River close to the MCR, they had the opportunity to fire from Bassa at Soviet supply trains moving between the Inguri and Baksan valleys.[37] Although this was the main regional transportation artery, connecting the North Caucasus and Transcaucasia via the Donguz-Orun pass, the Germans underestimated the value of Bassa and placed only one platoon there. The commanders of the 46th Army worried about the possibility of losing such an important route and sought to retake Bassa as soon as possible. On 28 August, after several fruitless frontal attacks, the dismounted 214th Regiment of the 63rd Cavalry Division concentrated forces at the foot of the pass that were at least five times as large as the German platoon at its saddle. In the night of 29 August, Leonid Kels, an experienced climber, led a Soviet platoon, equipped with climbing gear, around the German position across a neighbouring height and launched a surprise attack from the rear simultaneously with a frontal attack by the main forces, thus driving the Germans away from the pass.[38] The Soviets retained Bassa until the end of action at the MCR.

Another well-documented action in which climbing guides participated was an attack on an unnamed pass, about 2,500 metres high, connecting the Klych and Gvandra valleys leading to the MCR (Map 8.1). A dismounted cavalry unit of about 300 men,[39] guided by

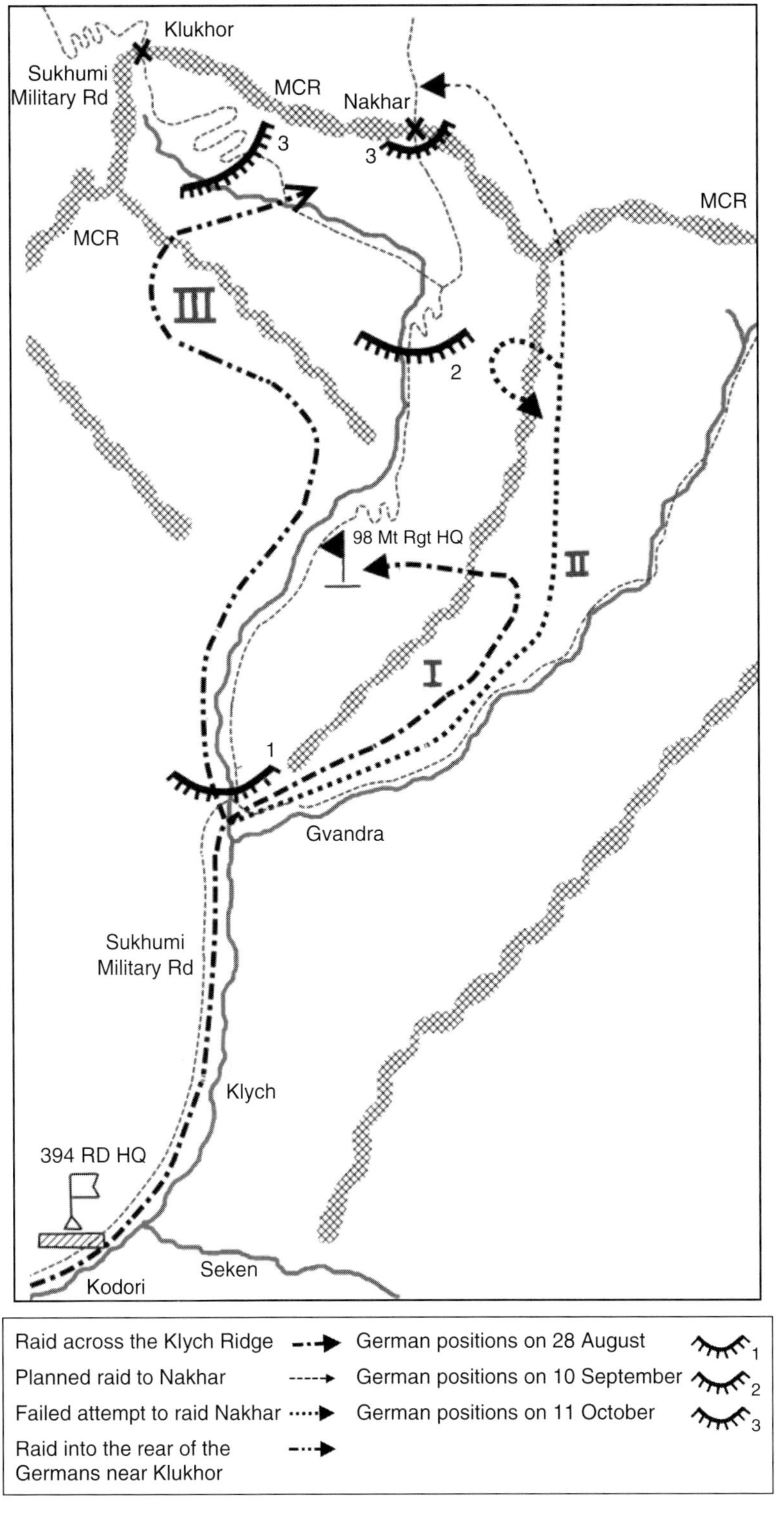

Map 8.1 Actions of units led by Soviet climbers

several climbers, received its battle order on 28 August. It had to outflank the two German battalions defending the Klych valley by crossing the Klych Ridge, perpendicular to the MCR, and then attacking the German headquarters in the Klych valley simultaneously with a frontal assault by two Soviet regiments[40] up the Klych valley on 3 September. The entire distance the cavalrymen were to cover was about 14 kilometres. However, it turned out that one or two German platoons occupied the pass, thus blocking the way. The cavalrymen advanced in four groups separated by broken terrain, and none of them had radios; they communicated only via messengers, which frustrated co-ordinated actions. While they climbed the ridge, the Germans ambushed them twice: the cavalrymen lost an entire platoon of twenty-four soldiers in one instance and then nearly a whole squadron of ninety men, as well as dozens of men in other episodes.[41] Only on 9 September, six days after the frontal attack in the Klych valley had begun, did the depleted cavalrymen drive the Germans away from the ridge. The frontal attack up the Klych River failed, but the outflanking strike across the Klych Ridge threatening the German rear in the Klych valley forced the Germans to abandon their positions and withdraw about 8 kilometres upstream to the feet of the Klukhor and Nakhar passes.[42] The Soviets again paid a disproportionate price for a victory that had minor tactical significance but was the greatest attained in the Klukhor region during the entire period of the Soviet counteroffensive there. It looked particularly impressive against the background of futile frontal attacks by the main Soviet forces in the Klych valley on 3 and 4 September, which resulted in grave casualties.

Climbers guided soldiers in several other minor actions, such as the failed raid intended to outflank Nakhar. Colonel Pavel Belekhov, acting commander of the 394th Rifle Division, who admitted that he understood nothing about mountain warfare,[43] gave only two days to a platoon of twenty men, consisting of conventional infantry without climbing gear, to accomplish an impressive trek of 25 kilometres. The platoon had to gain about 2,000 metres, cross the MCR, and then traverse its northern slope before striking the German rear; this suicidal mission ended well before the platoon reached the MCR because most of its soldiers were frostbitten and had to return without even seeing the Germans.[44] Sometimes, climbers guided reconnaissance teams, and the reports stated that they saved several such teams that were, 'no doubt, doomed to death', being battered by severe weather.[45] However, few reconnaissance teams had climbing guides, and even the teams that did could not match their German counterparts because none of their members, except the attached climber, knew the basics of mountaineering and neither the climbers nor the other soldiers were trained for mountain warfare.

None of the experienced Soviet climbers attached to the TCF was killed or wounded during the battle in the high Caucasus, which shows that their participation in combat was marginal. They contributed to the Soviet effort mainly with their expertise rather than by fighting and, in this respect, their contribution was far greater than their numbers suggested. The most impressive actions in which Soviet climbers participated were the evacuations of civilians and military units from the Baksan valley across the MCR. Between 11 August and 2 September, three experienced climbers – Aleksandr Sidorenko, Aleksei Maleinov, and Georgii Odnobliudov – guided 1,500 civilian refugees, including many women, elderly people, and 230 children, across the Becho pass into Transcaucasia without the loss of a single life.[46] A second similar episode happened between 11 and 16 November, when the 392nd Rifle Division, trapped by the enemy without supplies in the Baksan valley, escaped across the MCR via Donguz-Orun to Transcaucasia.[47] Before the Axis forces overran the Tyrnyauz Wolfram-Molybdenum Concentrating Factory, its administration evacuated and delivered to the MCR several truckloads of precious wolfram and molybdenum concentrate needed for the production of armour plates. The 392nd Rifle Division abandoned most of its heavy weapons, but every soldier carried on his back several kilograms of concentrate. In total, 7,636 able-bodied soldiers crossed the pass, bringing with them 15 tonnes of concentrate, 297 of their 450 wounded men, 6 light artillery pieces, 19,172 head of cattle and sheep, and 512 horses. The climbers provided consultation to two independent 'mountain' companies, and three engineering companies on how to organise safe evacuations.[48] Their competent leadership secured success in these two episodes.

First Steps Towards Proficiency in Mountain Warfare

Even before the battle of the Caucasus, several senior TCF officers understood that special skills were necessary for effective actions in the mountains but did not know what these skills were. The string of generic, and therefore meaningless, directives on training for mountain warfare began with the order issued by General Sergatskov on 26 June. He demanded that the formations assigned to defend the MCR begin such training 'in the regions of their action after receiving climbing gear'.[49] On 4 July, Sergatskov corrected his first directive by ordering the immediate beginning of training 'for actions in the high mountains without waiting for the arrival of climbing gear'.[50] This order would have been sufficient to initiate the basic training of the formations assigned to defend the MCR, had their commanders known how to approach the training process. Since they did not, they quietly ignored the order, as they did all the subsequent generic directives on training for mountain warfare issued by the TCF Headquarters on 25 August and 11 and 30 November.[51] None of these orders affected the ability of the 46th Army to fight in the mountains.

Most TCF commanders acknowledged the tactical superiority of German mountain troops and pointed to the numerous handicaps of their own formations.[52] However, some of them, like Tiulenev, believed that the Red Army would radically improve its performance in the mountains as soon as the divisions deployed at the MCR received climbing gear, warm uniforms, and the *Concise Manual on Mountain Warfare*. Other senior officers understood that the soldiers would be unable to replicate German tactics even with the gear and the manual because they lacked mountaineering skills and had never practised mountain warfare, thus having had no opportunity to learn its peculiarities. Such officers emphasised the necessity of immediate and intensive exercises 'on mountainous terrain in any weather, in the daytime and at night',[53] which was a radical departure from pre-war training practices; they also argued that the training process should be shaped in a way that would develop the initiative of soldiers and teach them flexible small-unit tactics.[54] On 12 October, Major Saltykov, a representative of the Red Army General Staff, wrote a sketch of the training reform needed to attain the desired goal in the long run:

> A soldier must be prepared for operating in the mountains in summer and winter through a well-designed combat and political training programme and through routine exercises of marches along mountain trails, [and across] passes, ridges, and valleys, and on skis in winter. Soldiers should not idle at one location as

> they do now. Officers and soldiers must know their operational terrain perfectly ... Climbing and ski training supervised by climbing and alpine ski instructors deserve particular attention. Soldiers holding positions [in the mountains] should have at least ten days of rest every month, during which ... they must train. Such a system of training and combat exercises not only precludes fear of the mountains but inspires love for them and for mountaineering. Officers should ... study the experience of past campaigns in the mountains. A major goal of officer training [for actions] in the mountains should be a detailed study of the terrain and the learning of proper timing and tempo of manoeuvres; these are vital issues during operational planning.[55]

Most of these prescriptions were self-evident but the Red Army did not arrive at these ideas during the interwar period; rather, they were drawn from the costly mistakes committed when its generals sent untrained soldiers to fight in the high Caucasus.

After the TCF commanders realised that special skills were necessary for effective actions in the mountains, they had to answer two basic questions: who would run this training and who should be trained? The actions in which a handful of climbers participated – such as the reconquering of Bassa, the attack across the Klych Ridge to the rear of the Germans that prompted their retreat, and the successful reconnaissance missions and evacuations across the Becho and Donguz-Orun passes – demonstrated for the first time, in practice as opposed to theory, the potential value of mountaineering skills. The failed raid on Nakhar showed that this potential could be realised only with a fairly large force and only if the senior officers planning operations in the mountains understood the basic tactics and logistics of mountain warfare. These discoveries prompted several senior TCF commanders to initiate long-term training programmes for mountain warfare.

The first step would be to recall the handful of skilled mountaineers who served as guides for regular infantry and employ them as climbing instructors. In early October, the OG organised a Mountaineering Section from a dozen such climbers, headed by Aleksandr Gusev, a man with a solid mountaineering record.[56] The section was to supervise climbing training and propose the gear needed for actions at the MCR. The second step would be to identify the potential trainees. While most senior officers eventually agreed that the absence of training for mountain warfare was at the root of the Soviet mishaps in the high mountains, no consensus existed as to exactly whom the instructors were to train: should they train all the formations deployed in the mountains, the 'mountain' divisions, or only a small elite force raised solely for mountain warfare? The TCF decided to proceed along all three avenues simultaneously, but the intensity of the training programmes was to be different. Regular front-line infantry had to learn the very basics of mountain warfare; the training of 'mountain' divisions would be more thorough but would inevitably be limited by the available resources. Only the small elite units were expected to be trained to the level of the German mountain troops.

Moving along the first of those avenues, TCF commanders ordered all the second-echelon and reserve units deployed at the MCR to complete a thirty-hour climbing and alpine skiing course, taught during two-hour daily exercises beginning on 1 October.[57] However, regular officers could not teach their soldiers mountain warfare because they were as ignorant as their men and did not know the nuts and bolts of the training process. That is why, wrote Battalion Commissar Khoshtariia, 'the divisional headquarters ignored the orders of the 46th Army about the [thirty-hour] mountaineering course'.[58] Lieutenant Purtseladze described how the 20th 'Mountain' Division reacted to the directives demanding the enforcement of the thirty-hour course: 'Despite the fact that the division had fought in the mountains from 20 August to 1 November 1942, which must have exposed all the flaws in special training',[59] and despite all the orders issued in this regard by the Headquarters of the 46th Army, only one company of its 265th Regiment allocated six hours to climbing exercises during November, and in those six hours, soldiers studied only the simplest elements of mountaineering – slope and scree traversing and knots – rather than mountain warfare.[60] This was merely eyewash under the pressure of superiors rather than a sincere desire to learn appropriate techniques.

It became clear that in order to be effective, exercises needed to be constantly monitored by professionals, but the TCF had only a dozen such experts. Consequently, before proceeding to a serious training programme, the TCF had to acquire enough instructors. The climbers suggested to the OG that the most rational approach would be to re-create the training system that had existed in pre-war mountaineering: the climbers would run several crash training cycles intended to create a large pool of instructors able to teach basic mountaineering to all units deployed in the mountains.

The training programme went ahead and quickly gained momentum. The instructor training course took place first in the 351st Rifle Division of the TCF's Northern Army Group. General Sergatskov, commander of the division, ordered every regiment to select ten junior officers – 'healthy, strong men, preferably familiar with mountaineering and alpine skiing'. They trained ten hours a day between 10 and 20 October in the Tsei alpine camp located in Ossetia. The training programme allocated two hours to the study of climbing gear, eight hours to safety measures, ten hours to marching techniques, twenty-six hours to rock climbing and marksmanship exercises, twenty hours to the climbing of icy and snow-encrusted slopes, ten hours to the transportation of wounded men and river crossing, and twenty hours to peak climbing.[61] During peacetime, a mountain guide course generally lasted twice as long,[62] but such fast-track training, roughly equal to what was needed to be qualified as Alpinist of the USSR 1st Class before the war, was probably justified in the circumstances. This course was immediately followed by a similar course in the Georgian mountain resort of Bakuriani between 20 October and 5 November, although this later course embraced many more officers. By 6 November, 8 climbing experts, most of them well-educated persons holding the Master of Sport title, had trained 188 officers who graduated as instructors of mountaineering and were then required to pass their knowledge on to their soldiers during two-hour daily exercises.[63] The next instructor training cycle began on 12 December.[64]

While the future instructors studied mountaineering, Aleksei Maleinov, senior climbing inspector with the 242nd 'Mountain' Division, a man with a sound record that included the traverse of Ushba, developed a comprehensive programme of basic training for the personnel of 'mountain' divisions. The 49-hour course, more thorough than that offered to regular infantry, balanced mountaineering theory and practice and included the study of a wide variety of elements: particular passes across the Caucasus; climbing gear; hazards in the mountains and ways to evade them; navigation techniques and the choice of routes; belaying and knots; marching tempo, breathing, and water consumption; traversing of grassy slopes, scree, and glaciers; rock and ice climbing; rescue techniques, first aid, and transportation of injured men; and, finally, combat in the mountains. Maleinov emphasised the practical aspects of training: every 'class should start with the demonstration of certain techniques and then proceed to exercising them. Daily exercises [must be conducted] along sample routes (rocks, snow, ice).'[65] This was the most comprehensive programme of rank-and -file climbing training produced in the Red Army to this point. After Maleinov submitted his draft to the division commander on 15 November, the latter ordered the rotation of all companies through a six-day intensive course.[66]

However, while securing a good starting point for the training of units operating in the mountains, this programme provided only the first step towards raising a force competent in mountain warfare. The few expert climbers whom the TCF initially gathered did everything they could to improve the combat capacity of Soviet divisions, but they were former civilians recently drafted into the army with a rank of lieutenant; they had no previous military experience. As such, they could teach soldiers mountaineering but not the tactics of mountain warfare, about which they knew little: as Aleksandr Gusev later admitted, 'I was a hydrologist rather than a military officer.'[67] Consequently, the courses these instructors taught tilted heavily to mountaineering rather than combat in the mountains. Maleinov allocated only 10 of the 49 hours to mountain warfare, and those only to aspects he knew about from experience: actions in defence and reconnaissance.[68] Such instructors could not match the professional officers of German mountain troops, even if they were better climbers, and the TCF continued to experience a desperate shortage of expert instructors affiliated with its divisions on a permanent basis: by 20 November, the 242nd 'Mountain' Division had only one;[69] the 394th Rifle Division had six, all of them near Marukh and none around Klukhor; and the 20th 'Mountain' Division had twenty-six instructors.[70] After the new instructors who had taken crash climbing courses began arriving in late November to the divisions deployed at the MCR, they often could not start training the soldiers immediately because of the absence of climbing gear. While these officers had enough enthusiasm to teach their men, most other officers, who still had the mentality of regular infantry, perceived the actions at the MCR as a brief aberration from regular practice and were reluctant to study mountaineering, despite their painful experience that plainly demonstrated the need for special training. As E. Smirnov, an OG liaison officer, wrote on 1 December, 'Given the current situation with gear and personnel, the combat capacity of the units [belonging to the 20th "Mountain" Division] and their ability to perform special missions remain limited ... I found no overpowering urge towards the pursuit of daily progress or the enforcement of the basic steps leading to the adaptation to modern [mountain] warfare.'[71]

All these obstacles would have been overcome with time. Most importantly, the climbers quickly established the infrastructure needed for turning the nominal 'mountain' divisions into genuine ones. In November and December, the OG Mountaineering Section registered all the climbers who had, by chance, found themselves in Transcaucasia,[72] and the OG recalled them to fill the positions of instructors permanently affiliated with the formations serving at the MCR. The TCF assembled enough instructors to organise a School of Military Mountaineering and Alpine Skiing in Bakuriani. The school eventually employed two dozen top-class climbers as instructors, including Evgenii Abalakov, arguably the best Soviet climber, and Ivan Cherepov, author of several textbooks on mountaineering.[73] The plan was to rotate the entire personnel of the formations serving in the high mountains through fifteen-day crash mountaineering courses, with one instructor teaching fifteen soldiers; this would accomplish a vital transition from ad hoc to routine, methodical training.[74] Dozens of instructors, attached permanently to the units fighting at the MCR, were to monitor continuous exercises within these units. All the preparations for the massive training of soldiers deployed at the MCR were to be completed by 1 January 1943.

An Effort to Raise Mountain Units

Along with the basic training of regular rifle and 'mountain' divisions, the TCF decided to organise elite mountain units (*gornostrelkovye otriady*): well trained, well equipped, and engaged exclusively in mountain warfare. The circumstances in which the TCF found itself made it clear that this new force would inevitably be small and would consist of volunteers willing to perform difficult missions that were beyond the capacity of regular infantry. The TCF hoped that superior skills, full climbing gear, and pride of belonging to the military elite would enable this force to fight the 'extolled' enemy on equal terms and to cope with severe weather, natural hazards, and the narrow margin of error typical of war in the mountains. The new force was structured as independent mountain companies to be used in reconnaissance, envelopments of enemy positions across rugged terrain, and raids into the enemy rear.[75]

Vague talk about such a force emerged in the TCF Headquarters on 14 August, when the German and Soviet vanguards clashed for the first time near Teberda. On that day, Tiulenev ordered the raising of 10 independent companies with 1,050 men in total. This first attempt to organise units that were baselessly called 'mountain' was merely a sham in the tradition of Stalinist culture that valued vigour over effectiveness in responding to a crisis. Only four days later, on 18 August, Aleksei Subbotin, the TCF chief of staff, reported that these companies had departed for their assigned destinations; they had to perform 'reconnaissance missions and set ambushes on the approaches to the passes'.[76] Having poor knowledge of MCR geography and no information on the location of the Germans, Sergatskov sent five of these companies, numbered from 1 to 5, to the east of the Becho pass, an area that the Germans never attempted to reach; three others (the 6th, 7th, and 8th) were to cross the Caucasus, and the 9th and 10th were to take positions to the west of Sancharo and Pseashkha, where no German soldier ever went.[77] Of all these units, only the 7th Company could have theoretically fulfilled the order; the 6th and 8th Companies could not reach their destinations because their way lay through passes already occupied by the Germans. It is unknown how many of these ten companies actually existed and how many of them departed for the MCR, although it is clear that four were eventually rerouted to Klukhor.[78] The records of the 46th Army give little information about the actions of these companies, although they mention briefly two raids that were probably undertaken by these companies. One of them, led by Officer Gokhonidze, attempted, in late August, to replicate the German raid in the Klych valley and to envelop the enemy positions via the steep valley slopes. The report on this action states that the company 'was formed from handpicked soldiers of the TCF … The mission failed because of lack of food and special climbing gear. Of the total 190 soldiers, 26 men deserted; 23 became sick or were malingerers; 17 lost contact with the unit; and 23 vanished after being assigned independent missions.'[79] Thus, this company lost almost half of its personnel without having any contact with the enemy because it was ill equipped, underfed, and untrained for fighting in the mountains. Another such company, led by Lieutenant Khomenko, attempted to outflank the German positions near Nakhar but was destroyed by the Germans.[80] None of the four companies sent to Klukhor scored any success.

On 28 August, six days after his arrival in the Caucasus, Beria undertook a more serious effort to raise proper mountain units. He instructed the Military Council of the 46th Army: 'Study enemy tactics and begin urgently organising mountain units ... for which pick the fittest and best-trained fighters and commanders and also instructors among the members of the Georgian Mountaineering Association. NKVD agencies must help you to assemble and train mountain units.'[81] This order initiated the formation of the genuine mountain units. The TCF decided to raise twelve mountain companies attached to rifle and 'mountain' divisions.[82] On 11 September, General Bodin reported that all the companies had been organised. Their strength fluctuated between 234 and 305 men, and climbing instructors were included in their personnel.[83] The 'mountaineers', as soldiers of these companies were speciously called, were to receive impressive sets of equipment: warm uniforms comfortable for climbing, including American ski jackets; backpacks instead of the sacks used by regular soldiers; skis with Kandahar bindings; snowshoes; sunglasses; sleeping bags and mountain tents; portable kitchens and alcohol burners for warming up food in woodless areas; five portable radios per company; and climbing gear – crampons, ice axes, ice and rock pitons, mountain boots, ropes, and avalanche cords.[84]

Nearly all Russian authors claim that these mountain companies helped the Red Army to turn the tables at the MCR, typically arguing along the following lines: 'The 49th Mountain Corps [initially] had an advantage that determined the outcome of the actions at the high passes, but it [the advantage] vanished after the arrival of well-trained and well-armed Soviet mountain units equipped with climbing gear.' These units allegedly 'took most positions in the high mountains', and, 'from that moment on, professionals fought the enemy'.[85] However, the combat reports of the 46th Army show that these authors grossly overstate the proficiency of the new mountain companies, the quality of their equipment, and, most importantly, their contribution to the battle of the Caucasus.

By mid September, these companies were still 'mountain' units only in designation: they consisted of untrained recruits without climbing gear, radios, or compasses; only one in five soldiers had mountain boots.[86] The TCF made a vigorous effort to supply them with gear, but it took time to find and deliver it. Bodin believed that the companies 'must begin special exercises as soon as they arrive at the regions of action', after which they could be sent to the front line.[87] Gusev claimed in his memoirs that the companies 'were raised from mountaineers sent by the People's Defence Commissariat, climbing instructors, and Transcaucasian mountaineers',[88] but the TCF documents show that their personnel were drafted mainly from the 28th Reserve Rifle Brigade and NKVD troops – rear formations with combat experience limited to counterinsurgency.[89] The soldiers of these companies may have been motivated and fitter than average, but their knowledge of mountain warfare was limited, at most, to a two-week crash mountaineering course taught by one or two civilian instructors in military uniform attached to these companies. Although they knew more about mountaineering than regular infantry and were eventually much better equipped than 'mountain' divisions, their overall combat capacity was modest because many of their soldiers did not have even basic military training.[90] Colonel Zinov'ev, the OG deputy chief of staff, examined the 11th and 12th Mountain Companies that arrived at Marukh on 5 and 6 October 1942. He referred to their training as pathetic: 'There are only two mountaineers ... in the 12th Company, while the rest of the personnel have no special [climbing] training except for a thirteen-day special course in conditions *similar*[91] to the mountains. Half of the personnel had received weapons for the first time and had never practised shooting rifles, let alone automatic weapons.'[92] Having inspected these mountain companies, the commanders in the Marukh region sent them to another fifteen-day training course, during which they had to spend six hours a day studying tactics, reconnaissance, and the peculiarities of marksmanship in the mountains and another six hours practising engineering works and camouflage.[93]

Several Soviet authors describe the Soviet mountain companies as well armed[94] but, in fact, most of their small arms did not fulfil the requirements of mountain warfare. The Germans knew from experience that in the mountains, where intensity of combat was inevitably low, the approach to enemy positions was slow, and ammunition had to be carried on soldiers' backs, the volume of fire delivered by small arms was of secondary importance to their range and accuracy. The German mountain troops were armed mainly with long-range machineguns and non-automatic Mauser rifles, accurate at 800 metres. In contrast, the TCF commanders, not having yet received feedback on mountain warfare from the front-line units, equipped their new mountain companies with weapons more suitable for commando actions than for combat in the mountains: mainly submachine-guns consuming much ammunition but accurate only at a maximum distance of 150 metres.[95]

The proportion of short-range submachine-guns to long-range rifles was 4 to 1 in Soviet mountain companies, and each of them carried two heavy anti-tank rifles, which were totally useless in the mountains.[96] Every Soviet company had only one heavy and three light long-range machineguns, two and four times fewer, respectively, than those carried by a German mountain company.[97] Since German machineguns had a higher rate of fire and carried five times as many cartridges in their belts as did the magazines of Soviet light machineguns, the machine-gunners of a German mountain company had an even greater advantage over their Soviet counterparts. The Soviet mountain units thus enjoyed greater firepower only in combat at close quarters, but the Germans could greatly reduce the number of Soviet soldiers before the latter could engage the enemy.

Soviet regular infantry envied equipment received by the new mountain companies.[98] Indeed, the TCF supplied these companies with climbing gear much better than that of other units, but it still overestimated its resources when it decided to raise twelve mountain companies. Half of them were fully equipped, but the TCF cut corners with the supplies provided to the companies it raised last. The 12th Mountain Company arrived at the front in ordinary rather than mountain boots and lacked much of the mountaineering gear; it had few snowshoes and only several pairs of skis, and, since only a handful of men could ski in the mountains anyway, the company surrendered its skis to a rescue team. The 11th Mountain Company arrived in summer uniforms and had no working radios. By 30 December, seventy soldiers of this company, or one-quarter of its personnel, were sick and injured; fifty of them had to be evacuated with severe frostbite.[99] The mountain companies were supposed to receive high-calorie food rations but, after snowfalls cut the supply lines in late October, the 11th Mountain Company deployed at the Naur pass received only one rusk per meal. After an airplane dropped several sacks of food, their rations increased to two or three rusks per meal and 70 to 100 grams of sugar per day.[100] Such privations ruined discipline and morale. The report by Captain Igol'nikov, an OG senior liaison officer, shows that this company was anything but a crack unit. Five soldiers deserted and three more defected to the enemy, which is not surprising considering the deplorable conditions:

> Commissar Kostomakha, deputy commander of the mountain company, being drunk, launched a mock execution of the

> following officers: Lieutenant Sitnikov, ... Commissar Tselishchev, ... and Lieutenant Makarov ... Intimidation and physical abuse [*rukoprikladstvo*] are common ... The company's surgeon amputates frostbitten limbs in unsanitary conditions, which causes sepsis and death. There were six such cases. Self-inflicted injuries are common among the personnel.[101]

German mountain units never displayed such poor morale and discipline in the Caucasus. The first six of the Soviet companies were probably in a better shape than the other six, but it is hard to assess their worth from their meagre combat record.

Russian authors typically praise the uniforms and gear of the new mountain companies but give little information about their actions. In fact, few of these companies ever engaged the enemy. One or two of them took part in action in late September and early October,[102] but on 25 September half of the companies, the 7th to the 12th, were still in Gori, Telavi, and eastern Georgia, far away from the front, undertaking mountaineering and military training, the intensity of which varied from unit to unit because of the shortage of climbing instructors and the total absence of experts on mountain warfare. In early October, the last four of the twelve companies departed for the mountains.[103] The companies were deployed in pairs at the most important sections of the front: the 5th and 6th Companies went to Elbrus, the 1st and 9th took positions around Klukhor, the 11th and 12th departed for Marukh, the 2nd and 10th headed for Sancharo, the 7th and 8th were sent to the 20th 'Mountain' Division, and the 3rd and 4th were assigned to the Mamison pass and thus were excluded from action, since the Germans never reached Mamison.[104]

It is not known how many of these units saw combat before the snowstorm that began on 18 October and terminated actions at the MCR. The 9th Mountain Company undertook its first mission – the protection of the southern slopes of the Ptysh pass – only on 22 October. Its commander reported that during the following eleven weeks, until 11 January, the company 'did not participate directly in combat, except for machinegun and mortar skirmishes', in which it lost three men killed and five wounded.[105] The combat history of other mountain units was similar: the 11th Mountain Company went to the front line only in November;[106] the 242nd 'Mountain' Division had only one attached mountain platoon by 5 November 1942 and two platoons by

24 November.[107] In the North Caucasus, the Soviets also raised eight well-equipped companies from cadets of the Telavi, Buinaksk, Ordzhonikidze, and Grozny infantry schools, but by 15 October none of them had been in combat, and it is unknown whether they ever fought at the MCR.[108]

Only one action of a mountain company is well documented. The 1st Mountain Company came to Klukhor on 30 September without combat experience and then engaged in intensive training.[109] On the night of 10 October, the soldiers rappelled from the cliff of a ridge perpendicular to the MCR, thus sneaking to the rear of a German company blocking the Klych valley, thereby cutting it off from the Klukhor pass. They launched a surprise attack at dawn, along with a simultaneous frontal attack by the 815th Regiment of the 394th Rifle Division. Aleksandr Gusev, the climber who guided the mountain company, stated that only 'a handful of Jägers' escaped to the Klukhor pass, and they lost 'about a hundred soldiers and officers killed and twelve men taken prisoner'.[110] It is impossible to verify the extent to which Gusev inflated the enemy casualties from the records of the 1st Mountain Division, which reported a loss of 39 men killed, 103 wounded, and 2 missing in action on 11 October but, at this time, it was suffering greater casualties at Tuapse than in the Klych valley.[111] However, the German report confirms a surprise Soviet attack from above that forced the Germans to retreat by about 800 metres up the Klych valley.[112] This small victory was still exceptional among the Soviet actions at the MCR, because this time the Soviets dislodged a well-entrenched German company at a cost of only light casualties, which demonstrated the potential that the Red Army wasted by failing to raise proper mountain units before the war.

There are no more documents on Soviet mountain companies in combat, although several reports describe reconnaissance missions conducted by their soldiers, and Soviet authors tell several fantastic tales about their daring actions.[113] Most mountain companies arrived at the front too late to participate in the battle for the MCR; their combat proficiency remained untested and the numerous claims of Russian historians that Soviet mountain companies 'were the first superb mountain units in the Red Army that matched the mountain units of other states, including those of the German Army'[114] have no empirical proof. Most of these units engaged only in reconnaissance. Some senior commanders, including Leselidze, played with the idea of deep raids into enemy territory across the MCR to attack the supply bases and headquarters of the Germans defending the passes and to intercept their communications.[115] However, since the Germans controlled all the passes except Belorechenskii, Aishkha, and Pseashkha, these would have been suicidal missions, so nothing came of these ideas. The only attempt to cross the MCR, via the Gvandra pass, failed when a Soviet platoon, ambushed by a German ski platoon, retreated, losing six men dead and three wounded.[116]

After the massive snowstorm of 18 to 21 October forced the Soviets to terminate their offensive and descend to the southern feet of the MCR passes, Soviet regular infantry, reinforced by mountain companies, garrisoned the approaches to the passes, conducted reconnaissance, and patrolled their slopes.[117] The mountain platoons occasionally probed the German defences, but the Germans easily kept them at bay. The *Instructions on Garrisoning and Defence of the MCR Passes in Winter* ordered the rotation of Soviet garrisons every five or ten days, depending on weather conditions. According to the instructions, the garrisons were to be fully supplied with gear: every soldier was to receive a backpack instead of a regular infantry sack, a sleeping bag, skis with Kandahar bindings, sunglasses, and a carabiner, while every section was to be supplied with three ice axes, three pairs of crampons, a 30-metre piece of climbing rope, 40 metres of thin cord, ski wax, an avalanche cord, one kerosene stove, two alcohol burners, one candle per day, and tinned food along with the regular rations.[118]

Although the contribution of the mountain companies to the battle of the Caucasus was meagre, it became clear that the TCF had finally found the correct path towards raising effective mountain units, and its senior officers continued to analyse the experience of mountain warfare gained in the Caucasus. The TCF Mountaineering Section was vigorously building a training infrastructure. It served as an advisory body during operational planning; supervised the drill of mountain companies; suggested proper rations and uniforms for soldiers operating in the mountains; developed manuals for action and survival in the mountains, including instructions on how to avoid and cure frostbite and how to dig shelters in the snow; and prepared a reference book on the passes across the MCR.[119] The officers of the Mountaineering Section knew the terrain well and participated in air reconnaissance and interpretation of photos taken by airplanes, thus improving the quality of intelligence data; they also corrected old maps.[120]

The Mountaineering Section compiled an inventory of the gear available in various depots and alpine camps, designed new gear such as touring skis and snowshoes, and monitored their urgent production.[121] When it became clear how hard it was to preserve combat capacity at high altitudes in winter, the Mountaineering Section promptly designed folding plywood huts – an item that, at this point, had existed neither in the Red Army nor in the Wehrmacht. By 25 November, the Tbilisi furniture factory had produced 100 huts and was planning to produce 100 more.[122] Aleksandr Gusev argued that these huts 'allow us to advance garrisons close to the passes, which was impossible earlier because of the absence of shelter. Kerosene stoves provide adequate room temperature in the huts even during severe frosts and winds, which enables the personnel to have proper rest and take care of weapons and uniforms'.[123] In consultation with climbers, Colonel Eliseev, head of the Basic Combat Training of the 46th Army, developed a programme of four-month winter exercises, conducted between 15 November and 15 March on difficult mountain terrain, 'as in actual battle instead of simulations'. They included river fording, shooting practice in the mountains, skiing across snowfields and up and down hills, navigation at night, rock climbing, and topography. The soldiers had to 'patiently correct their flaws' and 'refine their skills to automatism'.[124]

In a summary analysis of the actions of the 46th Army written on 30 December, Lieutenant-Colonel Mezentsev, senior assistant to the OG Chief of Staff, planned to summon 'all climber reserves' and enrol them into a total of twenty mountain companies that were to be supplied with all the equipment, the inventory of which had already been compiled, including portable radios to be manned by operators trained to work in the mountains.[125] In January 1943, General Petrov wrote to Tiulenev:

> The actions at the MCR confirmed once again that special training is essential for the formations operating in the mountains ... [The effort to raise] mountain units was fully justified. It is necessary to preserve the well-trained military mountaineering personnel in view of their future deployment in mountainous operational regions. I believe it would be expedient ... to complete their special training, supply them with gear, and reorganise them ... into one [large] formation.[126]

Tiulenev supported the initiative and wrote a draft order proposing that all mountain companies be incorporated into a mountain brigade.[127] Therefore, in striking contrast with grandiose plans made in the inter-war period, which presumed that the TCF would have seven mountain divisions, its commanders now believed that they had resources for only one well-trained mountain brigade. The brigade, dispersed in companies, was to bear the brunt of the fighting in the mountains. Its headquarters would have three senior positions reserved for top-rate climbers holding Master of Sport titles: deputy commander responsible for climbing training, head of the mountaineering section, and head of the mountain rescue service. The Brigade Mountaineering Section would include two dozen climbing instructors responsible for training and the supply of climbing gear.[128]

The appreciation of special skills as a precondition for effective action in the mountains, the vigorous effort to develop a training infrastructure, the intent to replace most regular infantry with well-equipped mountain units, and the detailed instructions on gear and the rotation of soldiers serving in the high mountains showed that the TCF had finally learned at least some basic tenets of mountain warfare. All these rational steps would have borne fruit in the long run, but they were taken too late to affect the battle of the Caucasus: by the time the first wave of new instructors had arrived in the TCF divisions and the soldiers of mountain companies – and only they – had acquired basic mountaineering skills and most necessary gear, action at the MCR had already stalled.

Struggle Against the White Death

Although the *Manual on the Active Defence of the MCR Passes* and the *Concise Manual on Mountain Warfare* warned soldiers about avalanches, they provided no detailed instructions as to how to identify this hazard or evade it, because their authors were ignorant on this subject.[129] Because of this, wrote Battalion Commissar Khoshtariia, 'divisional headquarters . . . plan the trails incorrectly, mostly across avalanche-exposed slopes'.[130] As a result, from November until the retreat of the Germans from the Caucasus in January, avalanches inflicted heavier casualties than enemy fire. During December 1942, the 46th Army lost eight men killed in action, but more than forty died in avalanches and many of those rescued were gravely injured and frostbitten.[131]

Figure 8.2 Climbing training of Soviet mountain troops. Credit: RGAKFD / Maksim Alpert

The Soviets sustained their first casualties from avalanches during the snowstorm of 18–21 October, and in December and January such incidents became routine. Since the 46th Army failed to accumulate

Figure 8.3 Soviet mountain troops equipped for mountain warfare but armed with short-range submachine-guns. Credit: RGAKFD / Maksim Alpert

food, firewood, and ammunition reserves close to the positions at the MCR before the snowfalls, when supply by pack animals had still been possible, porter teams bringing supplies were now struggling through

Figure 8.4 A Georgian soldier, a member of a Soviet mountain company. Few Soviet soldiers had white camouflage coveralls. Credit: ITAR-TASS Photo Agency / Alamy Stock Photo

deep snow and being exposed to avalanche danger.[132] When a company of 205 men[133] was delivering firewood to Donguz-Orun on 1 December, an avalanche swept away 70 soldiers, 21 of whom were killed and 6 gravely injured.[134] The survivors did little to help those buried by the avalanche because they did not know how. When a rescue team led by climbers arrived, they dug out seventeen bodies of soldiers who, a climber maintained, could have been saved had their comrades been familiar with basic rescue procedures.[135] Georgii Kurashvili, commander of the 242nd 'Mountain' Division, held that a disaster of such a scale 'could happen only because of the absence of elementary safety precautions, such as distance [between soldiers], [the presence of quick-response] rescue teams, and the identification of avalanche hazard'.[136]

The Soviet files on the defence of the MCR are full of similar stories. On 4 December, an avalanche killed seventeen men descending from the Adange pass. On 8 December, ten soldiers died in an avalanche on their way to the Chmakhara pass. On 5 January, an avalanche hit eighteen men from the 11th Mountain Company, of whom twelve died, including its commander, and on 6 January, an avalanche buried an entire supply platoon of twenty-five men from the 33rd NKVD Regiment near Aishkha pass; when another platoon of twenty-one men rushed to their rescue, a second avalanche hit. Only six of those forty-six men were dug out alive.[137] The 394th Rifle Division alone lost fifty-eight men to avalanches or to slipping on icy trails and falling into abysses.[138] These horrific accidents provoked rumours that wildly inflated the casualties from avalanches. Feeling defenceless against the fury of nature, soldiers believed these rumours, which further undermined their morale, already shaken by the shortage of food, severe cold, and delays in their rotation caused by severe weather.

German sources mention, rather rarely, casualties from frostbite, but they report no calamities similar to those inflicted by avalanches on the Soviets, perhaps because the Germans, unlike the Soviets, could identify avalanche hazards and set positions in safe places. They picked supply routes with minimal exposure; moved across dangerous slopes only at night, when avalanche probability was low; and had well-equipped and well-trained rescue teams that minimised the casualties.[139]

No mountain rescue service existed in the Red Army,[140] and the embryonic civilian rescue service that had begun operating in the interwar period disintegrated during the war. On 22 September, well before heavy snowfalls began, Major Varlam Kakuchaia, an NKVD representative at the TCF Military Council, argued that it was essential to establish a permanent rescue service that would co-ordinate actions of quick-response teams consisting of climbers and paramedics and equipped with special gear, such as avalanche probes, snow shovels, and reliable portable radios.[141] However, Kakuchaia's superiors ignored his memo, as well as the warnings of local people about the imminent danger. An avalanche cord, a 25-metre piece of coloured thin cord tied to one's body on exposed slopes, greatly eases the rescue of those hit by an avalanche. Few Soviet soldiers had this simple safety tool; the 11th Mountain Company had none, and it is safe to assume that regular infantry had none either.[142]

As usual, the Headquarters of the 46th Army addressed the problem only after it had proven to be acute, and as usual, it first attempted ad hoc solutions. Improvised rescue teams began operating after the snowstorm of 18–21 October had completely cut communications with the formations still attempting to dislodge the Germans from the MCR. These formations began suffering such enormous casualties from frostbite that they could have perished altogether. Colonel Kurashvili organised three large rescue teams within the 242nd 'Mountain' Division, two of which were led by four skilled climbers and the third assembled from local civilians and militia, and sent them to the Bassa, Donguz-Orun, and Becho passes. These teams – equipped with snowshoes, snow shovels, and mountaineering gear – saved most of the soldiers at these passes by securing their evacuation along safe routes.[143] The 20th 'Mountain' Division also organised similar rescue teams that evacuated soldiers incapacitated by frostbite.[144]

When grave avalanche danger emerged in addition to bitter cold, Soviet commanders realised that two steps were necessary to reduce the casualties. First, soldiers deployed at the MCR had to learn how to identify avalanche hazards; second, a professional rescue service had to be established, with well-equipped teams trained and led by climbers. On 15 November, three weeks after the first avalanches began roaring down the slopes of the MCR, Aleksei Maleinov submitted a plan proposing the organisation of a mountain rescue platoon within the division. The platoon was to teach soldiers basic precautionary measures and rescue techniques, monitor avalanche hazards in all sections of the division's front, mark safe routes, lay ski trails, fix ropes along steep slopes, assist with the transportation of wounded men, deliver messages in poor weather, and organise rescue works. Commanded by a senior climbing instructor, the platoon would include two additional climbing instructors, a medic, a radio operator with a portable radio, and other personnel selected from 'among fit, well-trained, and motivated men, … experts in mountaineering and alpine skiing, having medical and special mountain rescue skills'.[145] Maleinov compiled a training programme for rescue platoons that included climbing, alpine skiing and rescue techniques, and paramedical basics; the latter would be learned during a 21-hour course, combining theory and practice and taught by a doctor.[146] Maleinov emphasised that the rescue platoon had to act immediately upon receiving a distress signal, and he prepared a detailed inventory of its equipment. On the day he submitted his plan, Colonel Georgii Kurashvili endorsed it and set 1 December as the deadline for the completion of rescue training.[147] The establishment of a permanent rescue service was another step towards professionalism in mountain warfare.

Russian memoirs on the battle of the Caucasus and other writings contain many stories about the destruction of German units by snow and stone avalanches triggered intentionally by the Soviets. Allegedly, 'Our soldiers several times used explosives and grenades to provoke avalanches hitting the Hitlerites: tonnes of snow fell, gaining speed and burying outposts, strongholds, and entire enemy units.'[148] Gusev claimed to have witnessed a Soviet air attack near Klukhor on 9 September, when pilots 'dropped bombs on the slopes over the road where the Jägers were. The explosions tore off many huge rocks. The terrifying rock fall gained speed and ... swept away nearly all the Jägers. The horses and mules that remained alive stampeded madly along the slope, crushing the soldiers who had survived, by some miracle, this rocky hell.'[149] The fact that the 1st Mountain Division recorded no casualties on this day taints the vivid picture painted by Gusev.[150] German sources do not mention avalanches triggered by the Soviets, let alone casualties inflicted by such alleged incidents. Given the far superior skills of the Germans in the mountains and the fact that, having taken the passes across the MCR, they were, for the most part, holding higher positions, it would be logical to assume that they must have used this exotic weapon more frequently and effectively, and a Soviet field report and several Soviet memoir authors mention some such incidents.[151] Unfortunately, the field report does not assess the inflicted damage, and memoir authors grossly exaggerate the impact of the avalanches triggered by German shelling, maintaining that they buried entire companies or even battalions,[152] which never happened, according to Soviet field reports. In any case, the fury of nature proved to be far deadlier than the attempts to bury the enemy with artificial avalanches. In total, ninety-six Soviet soldiers were listed as missing after being swept away by avalanches during the battle at the MCR; this number excludes those whose bodies were recovered.[153] The TCF Headquarters eventually developed a set of appropriate measures to minimise avalanche impact, but not before they had lost well over a hundred soldiers.

Tearing Down the German Banner from Elbrus

After two main offensives of Army Group A along the northern slopes of the Caucasus and along the Black Sea coast failed, the OKH saw no more reason to hold the passes across the MCR. When, on

1 January 1943, the TCF Northern Army Group launched a major counteroffensive along the northern foothills of the Caucasus, it threatened to cut off the German formations at the MCR. Army Group A ordered its units to leave the passes. The Germans evacuated their positions unmolested and with all their weapons. Not a single engagement between the units of the 46th Army and the Germans occurred during the retreat. On 11 January, a Soviet reconnaissance party climbed Marukh and found no enemy at the pass. The 46th Army sent scouts to climb Sancharo, Chiper-Azau, Klukhor, Nakhar, and Adzapsh on 11, 13, 14, 18, and 20 January, respectively, and they reported that the Germans had evacuated all the passes, leaving behind only their warm shelters.[154]

The final episode of the battle in the high Caucasus was the winter climb of Elbrus, which was intended to erase the humiliation inflicted by the German climbers who had hoisted their banner at its summit. Tiulenev claims in his memoirs that the swastika 'flew for only a short time' until a team of Soviet climbers 'broke to the summit in battle' and 'tore down the fascist banner'.[155] In fact, the banner flew from 21 August to mid February, long after the last German soldier had left Elbrus. The Soviet generals who emphatically denied the significance of this fact gave their first order to tear the banner down on 11 September. An NKVD company that was to launch a raid on Priiut 11 planned to send a team to climb Elbrus immediately after the destruction of the German garrison at the hotel. The raid failed but the TCF Political Directorate was determined to repeat the attempt at the first opportunity.[156]

No such opportunity presented itself as long as the Germans held Priiut 11. On 5 January 1943, Nikolai Gusak, an instructor in the TCF Mountaineering Section, initiated the flag removal campaign. He wrote to General Petrov: 'I strongly suggest that you consider the political importance of my proposal and allow me, in the next several days, to organise a team of four or five mountaineering instructors … and climb both Elbrus summits in order to tear away the German fascist flags and hoist the banners of the USSR.'[157] On 30 January 1943, two weeks after the Germans had left the Elbrus region, Petrov assigned this mission to a team of twenty skilled climbers.[158] The winter climb of Elbrus was a far more challenging enterprise than the climb undertaken by the Germans in August, when the temperature at the summit was only slightly below freezing.

According to Gusev, in February, the temperature was almost −40 °C at Priiut 11. If this is true, it had to be close to −50 °C at the summit. On 13 February, six climbers, led by Gusak, left for the western summit at 2:30 a.m. during a pitch-black night and returned, after fifteen hours of fighting with the blizzard, with the scraps of the German banner, which had been torn apart by the winds. On 17 February, fourteen climbers, led by Gusev, began the climb to the eastern summit, once again struggling against strong winds.[159] They claimed to have reached the summit, and Liubov' Korotaeva, the only woman on the team, later wrote: 'I remember our fury when we tore the enemy flag down.'[160] Gusev also describes this episode in his memoirs, even though the Germans never visited the eastern summit.[161] Gusev's team included a cameraman, who was supposed to make a film eclipsing the German one, a mission impossible at such temperatures. While the German film turned the mountaineering endeavour into a great propaganda coup, the few seconds of the Soviet film, allegedly shot during the triumphal climb, went unnoticed by the Soviet public. Both the film depicting climbers saluting the red banner supposedly hoisted at the summit and the picture of a climber holding the banner against a background of mountain peaks, presented in Russian military histories and memoirs with the caption, 'A Soviet banner at the Elbrus summit',[162] are obvious fakes: the background mountains are considerably higher than the point where the film has been shot and the picture taken; furthermore, neither the film nor the photo shows the tripods fixed at the summits, and the team shown in the film, supposedly ascending the eastern summit, consists of sixteen persons instead of fourteen.[163] Notwithstanding these fakes, the team that climbed the western summit definitely reached it and brought the remnants of the German flag to Tiulenev as proof.[164]

The reactions of German and Soviet top commanders to the idea of hoisting a flag on Elbrus were quite different: the Headquarters of Army Group A reluctantly approved the climbers' initiative, and this provoked Hitler's hysterical outburst. Captain Groth, who led the German mountaineers, tried to downplay the climb in his report, emphasising the purely military missions as his company's priority. No German received a decoration for the climb.[165] In contrast, the TCF commanders explicitly ordered two teams to risk their lives in the midst of winter to replace one piece of cloth with another of the same colour; these teams had no military missions to perform in this region, and upon the completion of the climbs, all participants were decorated.[166] The Stavka thus viewed the hoisting of flags on Elbrus as a much more important enterprise than the OKW did.

Conclusion

The failure to raise genuine mountain formations in the interwar years, despite the large available pool of potential manpower, led to graver consequences than the failure to occupy the MCR passes on the eve of the German assault. Thousands of Soviet climbers were fighting on the plains, while the TCF could field only regular infantry, cavalry, and NKVD soldiers, untrained and unequipped for mountain warfare, against the 49th Mountain Corps. After senior commanders acknowledged the platitude that soldiers operating in the mountains had to 'undertake climbing training and be fully equipped with climbing gear',[167] their belated effort to prepare regular infantry and the personnel of 'mountain' divisions for mountain warfare brought limited results. Having no resources to turn the nominal 'mountain' divisions into genuine ones, these commanders decided to raise a small but well-equipped and well-trained force, which was a rational choice in the circumstances. Only a tiny fraction of these personnel, selected according to criteria of fitness and motivation, were climbers, but most still perceived themselves as military elite, had higher morale, eagerly studied mountaineering taught by top-class climbers, and quickly acquired entry-level climbing proficiency. Their military training was mediocre, but they could have improved it with time. Some senior officers realised that this force, potentially able to perform difficult missions that were beyond the capacity of regular infantrymen, should be used only for such missions. As Colonel Dreev, the OG chief of staff, argued in January 1943, 'It would obviously be inexpedient to use mountain units as regular infantry', but their deployment in the high Caucasus could 'allow us to refine the training of mountain units necessary for future operations . . . in other regions, e.g. in Crimea'.[168]

The TCF Mountaineering Section quickly compiled a viable, comprehensive, and standardised training programme with clear guidelines; built a solid training infrastructure; and gave impetus to the sustainable expansion of climbing training to all mountain units in the

Caucasus. Climbing gear began arriving, and the School of Military Mountaineering could have rotated the entire personnel serving in the mountains through crash training courses within a short period of time, while climbing instructors incorporated into large formations could have refined the entry-level training acquired in the school. Gusev claimed to have trained 5,000 soldiers, mainly after the end of the battle at the MCR.[169] The Mountaineering Section monitored the training, identified and requested missing gear, introduced advanced designs developed by Soviet mountaineers in the interwar period, and suggested new equipment such as folding huts. It advised on safety in the mountains; organised a professional rescue service, thus reducing the number of non-combat casualties; and published new manuals on climbing and alpine skiing. The Mountaineering Section lacked the knowledge to teach soldiers the military aspect of mountain warfare, but its effective management of the climbing aspect contrasted with the vague and incompetent orders that the TCF Headquarters had issued when it attempted to address the challenges of war in this unfamiliar environment, such as those demanding the demolition of mountain passes and glaciers; the insistence on using 'stone-throwers'; the dispatch of soldiers to the passes without food, coats, or tents; the launching of deep raids across the MCR without any logistical arrangements; the instructions on bayonet charges in the mountains; and the attempts to maintain command and control with a wire-and-messenger network. This contrast demonstrated the potential wasted by the Red Army when it failed to enrol the thousands of climbers and other sport tourists into mountain divisions while instead enlisting personnel who had never been in the mountains.

The collection of comprehensive data on the operational terrain, the systematisation of the scattered bits of empirical knowledge on the peculiarities of mountain warfare, and the effective training programme in the anticipated battle environment under the supervision of mountaineering experts would probably have borne fruit. It is open to speculation whether these efforts, if consistent, would have allowed the Soviets to match the German mountain troops, but they would have greatly improved the ability of the Red Army to operate in the mountains. However, all these wise steps were taken too late to affect the outcomes of the battle at the MCR. The embryonic mountain companies emerged only at the end of the battle, and their contribution to the defence of the Caucasus was negligible. The popular Russian perception of the battle in the high Caucasus as a confrontation between Soviet and German climbers turned out to be simply a part of the vast Soviet wartime mythology. The next chapter shows how the Red Army applied the knowledge and experience gained on the MCR to its subsequent operations in the mountains.

9 LESSONS IGNORED: DÉJÀ VU AT TUAPSE (1942) AND IN THE CARPATHIANS (1944)

Esli nado, vnov' voz'mem granaty,
Finku, pistolet i avtomat.
Esli nado, to poidet v Karpaty,
Al'pinistov boevoi otriad.

[If ordered, we'll again take hand grenades,
Knives, pistols, and submachine-guns.
If ordered, the unit of military mountaineers
Will head to the Carpathians.]

Later addition to 'Baksanskaia'

During the actions in the high Caucasus, the TCF accumulated rich experience of combat in the mountains, analysed the winning tactics, identified the necessary equipment, produced a series of helpful manuals, established training procedures and infrastructure, and raised mountain companies that could potentially attain proficiency in mountain warfare. The Red Army became involved in two more battles in the mountains during World War II: the defence of Tuapse, in the autumn of 1942, and the offensive from Poland to Slovakia across the Beskids, in the autumn of 1944. This chapter surveys these two episodes and shows that, despite the costly experience gained in the high Caucasus and the clear path towards the creation of a worthy mountain force, the Red Army failed to switch from an ad hoc to a systematic approach to mountain warfare. Its performance in the mountains only marginally improved, and even this improvement was primarily due to the easier terrain rather than to sharpened skills.

Actions in the Mountains During the Defence of Tuapse

One of the two major German offensives presumed by Operation Edelweiss was to proceed along the Black Sea coast to Transcaucasia. The OKH believed that this offensive would decide the entire campaign in the Caucasus.[1] The Black Sea Army Group, organised within the TCF on 1 September 1942, defended the 220-kilometre -long stretch of coastline from Novorossiisk to Lazarevskoe.[2] The group consisted of the 47th, 56th, and 18th Armies. The German 17th Army intended to strike across the foothills of the Caucasus and reach the coast at Tuapse, thus severing from the rest of the TCF the 47th and 56th Armies that defended the northern part of the coast (Map 9.1). After that, the Germans planned to advance against the 18th Army towards Sukhumi. Combat in the mountains was an important component of the battle at the approaches to Tuapse.

After the Soviet 18th Army pinned down the first German offensive 80 kilometres from Tuapse in early September, the 17th Army attempted to turn the tables by deploying half of the 49th Mountain Corps, recently transferred from the MCR, at the left flank of their forces advancing towards the coast. The new German offensive, codenamed Attika, was to combine a strike by the Bavarian 97th and the Baden-Württemberger 101st Jäger Divisions along the major road leading from Maikop to Tuapse via the low Goitkh pass (336 m) and across the adjacent hills with an outflanking attack by the so-called Lanz Division of the 49th Mountain Corps across mountains that were 800 to 1,100 metres high and covered with thick vegetation.[3] Named after its commander, the Lanz Division was assembled from the 98th Regiment of the 1st Mountain Division, the 13th Regiment of the 4th Mountain Division, and the attached artillery units. The attack across the mountains was to bring the Lanz Division into the rear of the Soviet formations that defended the road to Tuapse, thus facilitating the offensive of the main forces along the road. In total, the German 17th Army allocated six divisions – three infantry, one motorised, two Jäger, and one mountain – to the new offensive, whereas the Soviet 18th Army initially had seven rifle and two cavalry divisions, four brigades, and an independent regiment (Table 9.1).[4] Although Soviet rifle divisions were smaller than German infantry divisions, their numerical strength roughly equalled the German Jäger and mountain divisions assigned for this mission. Therefore, even at the start of the German attack, the Soviets had a slight numerical superiority.

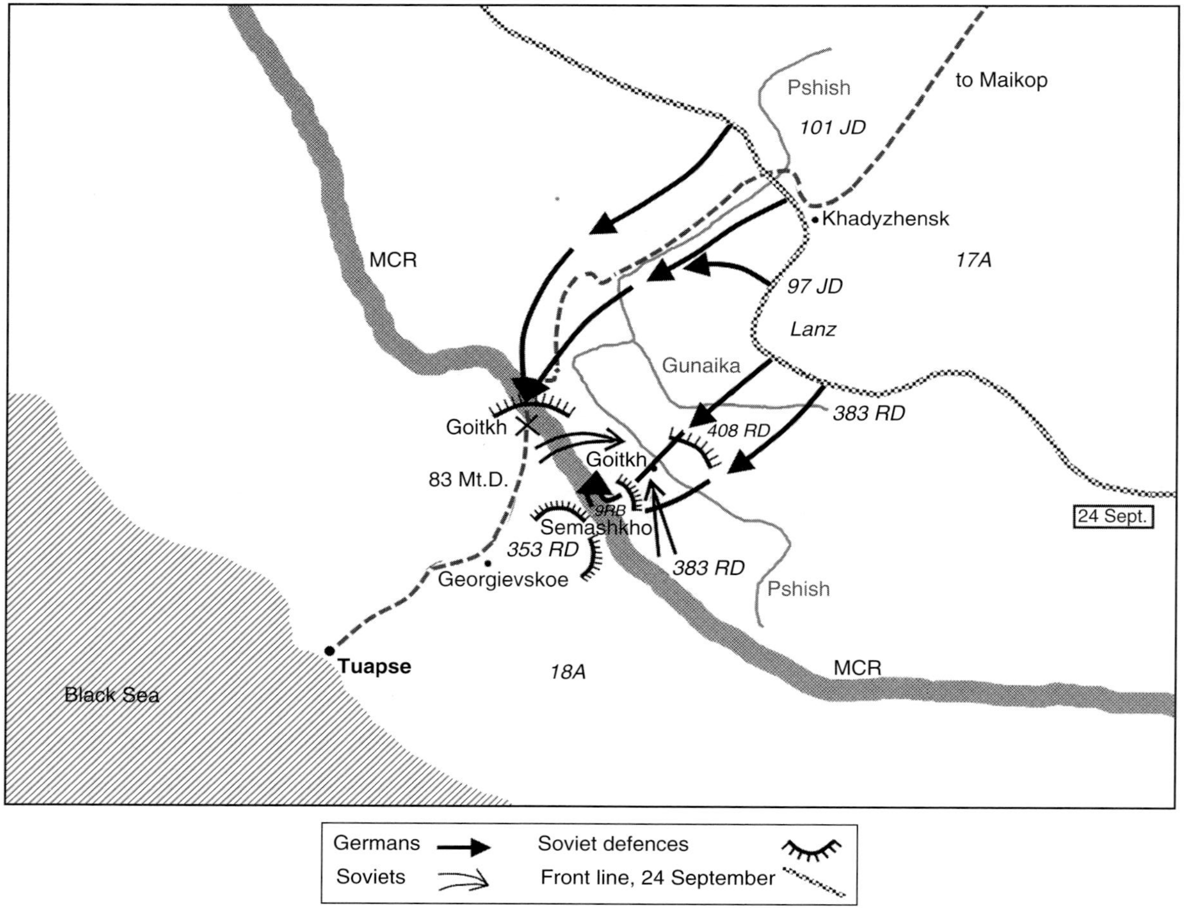

Map 9.1 The German assault on Tuapse, September–December 1942

Table 9.1 Ratio of forces on the eve of the battle of Tuapse

Wehrmacht	Red Army
• 46th, 125th, and 198th Infantry Divisions • 1st Slovak Motorised Division • 101st and 97th Jäger Divisions • Lanz Mountain Division	• 236th, 328th, 383rd, 395th, and 408th Rifle Divisions and 31st and 32nd Guards Rifle Divisions • 11th and 12th Guards Cavalry Divisions • 40th Motorised Brigade • 119th Rifle Brigade • 68th and 76th Marine Brigades • 145th Marine Regiment

Source: Wilhelm Tieke, *The Caucasus and the Oil* (Winnipeg: J. J. Fedorowicz, 1995), 197; Andrei Grechko, *Bitva za Kavkaz* (Moscow: MO SSSR, 1971), 152, 153.

In the battle that followed, both sides displayed the same assets and flaws as they had during the battle at the MCR. The German mountain troops again demonstrated impressive flexibility, enviable skills, and high motivation, but their tactical excellence could not offset the OKH's thoughtless strategy. The 17th Army launched Operation Attika with no reserves[5] against a numerically superior enemy on terrain that was easier to defend than to attack; thick vegetation confined the Lanz Division to only a few narrow, muddy trails. Although infantry could move, with great difficulty, outside these trails, supply columns could not, and navigation was extremely difficult given inadequate maps and the total absence of visibility, which limited tactical options. The Soviets again deployed only conventional forces against the German mountain and Jäger formations. However, the Black Sea Army Group had accumulated large reserves and possessed the remarkable ability to shift these reserves swiftly to crucial sections of the front along the coastal railway.

The Headquarters of the 18th Army anticipated a new German attack along the road to Tuapse and made thorough preparations to meet this challenge. When the Germans resumed their offensive on 25 September, the 101st Jäger Division made little progress against stubborn Soviet resistance. However, having concentrated most of its forces along the road, the 18th Army did not expect an attack across the wooded mountains at its right flank and so had deployed in that area only the 383rd Rifle Division, spread thinly across 25 kilometres of front. The Lanz Division hit it on 27 September, attaining complete surprise. As the Stavka observed, 'despite the presence of sufficient forces ... that had spent a long time at their defensive positions, it took the enemy [only] several days to get to the flank and the rear of the 18th Army's formations defending the road ... Despite the overall numerical superiority, the units of the 18th Army were weaker in every direction of the enemy's strikes.'[6]

The Lanz Division was making impressive gains despite difficult terrain.[7] On 21 October, it came to the positions of the 408th Rifle Division. This formation, raised in Armenia, was well equipped but had limited combat experience. The Soviet report states that, when the division was hit by an airstrike and an artillery barrage, it 'retreated in disorder, and this retreat turned later into a panicked flight'.[8] Building on its success, the Lanz Division crossed the Pshish River on the same day and two days later, on 23 October, reached the northeastern slopes of Semashkho Mountain (1,035 m), one of the highest in the region, thus covering more than half the distance between its initial position and the Black Sea. The German mountain troops enveloped the flank of the main Soviet forces near the road, forcing them to retreat up the northern slopes of the Goitkh pass, the last obstacle before Tuapse.[9] Only 25 kilometres separated Lanz's position at Semashkho from the Black Sea; the Germans were again watching the sea from the summit.[10] However, by 31 October, a fierce but costly Soviet counter-attack drove most of the Germans 8 kilometres back to the Pshish River; only two German mountain battalions continued to hold Semashkho, being connected to the main forces of the Lanz Division by a narrow corridor.

On 15 November, the Lanz Division resumed its offensive. Its attack sent the Soviet 9th Guards Rifle Brigade, in a panicked flight, away from Semashkho; the flight ended at Georgievskoe village, about 8 kilometres from the point of maximum penetration of the Germans in this direction.[11] This offensive relieved the two German battalions cornered at Semashkho; however, the Germans were unable to advance beyond it. The battle of Tuapse was far more intense than anything the German mountain divisions had ever experienced in the high Caucasus; they often faced stubborn resistance and suffered far greater casualties than they had sustained at the MCR. The Soviet local counteroffensives frequently drove the Germans back, recovering the ground that the Germans had acquired at a high cost.[12] Such pitched battles drained the strength of the German units, whereas the Soviets constantly received reinforcements. The daily field reports of the 1st Mountain

Division state its total casualties during the 44 days of fighting at the MCR, from its first clash with Soviets screens on 14 August to the beginning of the battle of Tuapse on 27 September, as 689 men, of whom 149 were killed, 504 wounded, and 36 missing in action, whereas the Lanz Division lost ten times as many soldiers during the 96 days from 27 September to 31 December: 6,884 men in total, of whom 1,267 were killed, 4,009 wounded, 182 missing in action, and 1,426 sick. Its companies were reduced to 40 soldiers.[13] Having no reserves, the 17th Army had no time to properly train the new recruits who were arriving to compensate for battle attrition; many of these were unenthusiastic *Volksdeutsche*, Soviet citizens of German descent mobilised against their will.[14] Meanwhile, the Soviet 18th Army reinforced the defenders of Tuapse with three divisions – one rifle, one 'mountain', and one cavalry; six brigades; an NKVD regiment; and an independent marine battalion.[15] The rapidly increasing gap in numbers decided the outcome of the battle. On 25 November, the 18th Army, having attained a decisive numerical superiority, terminated the German offensive. Relentless rain turned the supply routes into mud pools, which led to a great attrition of horses: in late November and early December, the Lanz Division was losing sixty horses daily.[16] The swelling waters of the Pshish River destroyed the only bridge across it and made fording extremely difficult. This crucially undermined the supplies of the nine depleted German battalions positioned around Semashkho; they found themselves under severe Soviet pressure without food and ammunition but with a multiplying number of wounded soldiers, whom they could not evacuate.[17] The Germans eventually restored the bridge, and on 17 December they retreated back to the northern bank of the Pshish River, after which the actions stopped. This termination of the major German offensive amounted to a Soviet strategic victory; in mid January, Army Group A began its general retreat from the Caucasus to avoid encirclement by the Soviet armies rolling quickly westward along the northern foothills of the Caucasus.

Since the Black Sea Army Group belonged to the TCF, it was easy to extrapolate the lessons of the actions in the high Caucasus to operations in the Tuapse region. The battle of Tuapse began on 25 September, six weeks after the beginning of action at the MCR. During these six weeks, the TCF had identified many aspects of mountain warfare that needed to be addressed before its divisions could perform adequately in the mountains and took a set of belated but wise steps to adapt its forces in the high Caucasus to the requirements imposed by this environment. It undertook similar measures during the battle of Tuapse, but the six weeks between the beginnings of the two battles was not enough time for the lessons learned at the MCR to produce a tangible improvement in Soviet combat capacity at the approaches to Tuapse.

The analysis of the battle made by Lieutenant-Colonel Konstantin Belokonov, head of the TCF Operative Section, shows that the TCF suffered from the same flaws during this episode as those it had experienced at the MCR. As in the high Caucasus, the Black Sea Army Group fielded regular infantry untrained for action in the mountains and having ill-suited logistical, signals, and medical services. As in the high Caucasus, the Soviet report states, 'the inability of staff officers to command their units in the mountains had extremely negative consequences'.[18] Soviet senior commanders did not know their operational terrain or the situation at the front line.[19] Field officers had only small-scale maps that were useless in the mountains, so they frequently lost their way when manoeuvring across rugged terrain. The 18th Army had numerous artillery units, but their mobility was limited to the low foothills and their fire was often ineffective because the crews were not trained to operate in the mountains, which led to costly attacks without artillery support. The TCF issued and distributed the *Concise Manual on Actions in Wooded Mountains* only in late December, after the end of action in this part of the front. As in the high Caucasus, the Soviets could not climb the dominating heights; the Germans occupied them and easily drove away the defenders with fire at their flanks from above.[20] Senior commanders sent their men to the mountains without shovels and other tools needed for fortification works on rocky ground, and again the Stavka observed, 'most units have [only] unfinished trenches or do not have them at all ... Many commanders still adhere to the completely wrong view ... that, in the Caucasus, boulders and trees substitute for fortifications.' That is why, as Andrei Grechko, commander of the 18th Army, wrote, 'although the terrain provided the opportunity to make the defence positions impregnable and there was ample time to do so, they [the positions] remained weak'.[21] Soviet analysts again referred with high respect to the tactical skills of the German mountain troops and with disdain to Soviet tactics. German strikes 'typically had no clichés', except that the Germans feigned frontal assaults with only a fraction of their forces while the rest tried to outflank the Soviets.[22] They were able to do this because their mountain units could move across broken terrain inaccessible to Soviet regular infantry, had good tactical intelligence acquired via reconnaissance teams raised from mountaineers, and co-ordinated their actions effectively via portable radios. In contrast, the report stated, 'our reconnaissance teams did not have the skills needed for operation in the mountains'; Soviet forces, 'having insufficient intelligence data, often launched frontal attacks and suffered grave casualties but could not attain their objectives'.[23] Furthermore, all the formations suffered from severe communications problems: they had only about 20 per cent of the telephone cable and telephones that they needed, while 'radio communications never worked properly because of the absence of portable radios and code tables, and the poor radio training of commanders at all levels ... Often runners were the only means of communication.'[24] Without radio or visual contact, the Soviet units, separated by hills and thick vegetation, could not act in concert, nor could reconnaissance teams deliver tactical intelligence in a timely fashion.

The German mountain troops again displayed high morale and discipline. The Germans claimed to have taken 1,800 POWs during the first three weeks of Operation Attika, whereas the Soviets took few German prisoners and proudly reported the capture of every single one.[25] The German mountain troops never fled in panic in entire formations, as did the 408th Rifle Division and the 9th Guards Rifle Brigade.[26] Two German mountain battalions that found themselves almost completely surrounded near Semashkho on 24 October continued to resist for three weeks, until they were relieved on 15 November by a new German offensive.[27] The absence of timely intelligence did not allow the Soviets, greatly superior in numbers, to trap the Germans at Semashkho; the latter withdrew at night unnoticed, along with most of their artillery,[28] a stealthy manoeuvre similar to that undertaken by Stettner during his retreat from the Bzyb River.

As in the high Caucasus, the Soviets had no special means to evacuate their wounded. When the Germans hit an NKVD company with heavy mortar fire, wounding 20 soldiers, the company's combat strength declined from 150 to 50 men because 4 men were needed to carry every wounded soldier on a standard heavy stretcher for a long distance across the wooded hills, and, as the Soviet report states, 'similar incidents occurred in the 383rd Rifle Division and the 9th Guards Rifle Brigade'.[29] Since commanders could not afford such a diversion of manpower, heavily wounded men were often evacuated on improvised sledges made of two trees laid side by side with their crowns tied together, the wounded soldier lying on the crowns and the trunks harnessed to a horse as shafts. Aleksandr Luchinskii, commander of the 83rd 'Mountain' Division, remarked: 'One can imagine how the wounded must have felt' during such an evacuation.[30] This division set its hospital 4 kilometres away from the front line; it took lightly wounded soldiers up to six hours to cover this distance on foot along steep trails. Once again, the mortality rate of the wounded men and the number of non-combat casualties were abnormal, and 'there were frequent incidents when even lightly wounded [men] did not reach the dressing stations but froze to death'.[31] The conclusion of the Black Sea Army Group on the battle at the approaches to Tuapse is remarkably self-evident: 'It is necessary to know the mountains, and the advantages and disadvantages of [mountainous] terrain ... The Tuapse operation revealed the insufficient training of our soldiers for action in wooded mountains.'[32]

Some measures taken by the TCF Headquarters during the defence of Tuapse can be traced back to the experience gained in the high Caucasus. Ivan Efimovich Petrov, commander of the Black Sea Army Group (not to be confused with OG commander Ivan Alekseevich Petrov), was a general with an impressive record who had acquired a cursory experience in mountain warfare while commanding the 44th Army in the North Caucasus. He ordered the logistics of the rifle units deployed at the approaches to Tuapse to be restructured along the lines adopted in mountain divisions with mules, donkeys, and horses instead of trucks and demanded the urgent transfer of officers with combat experience in the mountains to the Black Sea Army Group. He also requested some equipment proven essential for actions in the mountains, such as portable radios, mountain artillery, detailed maps with a scale of 1:42,000, portable kitchens, and light but calorie-rich mountain rations.[33] These wise measures, ordered a month after the beginning of the battle of Tuapse, addressed only a few of the many problems that the Red Army had to solve before it could fight effectively in the mountains.

Granted, the environment in the Tuapse region was far less challenging and more forgiving than that at the MCR: even the highest mountains were only one-third the elevation of the highest passes of the MCR. Tactical ignorance on such terrain and the absence of mountaineering skills and special gear had less severe consequences because the low wooded mountains offered more opportunities for manoeuvre to regular infantry, inexperienced in mountain warfare, and allowed for greater margins of error than the vertical and bald rocks of the high Caucasus. In addition, the climate was considerably warmer than at the MCR,[34] and there were no strong winds in the wooded mountains, which provided unlimited firewood; all of this allowed soldiers, dressed in summer uniforms,[35] to maintain tolerable living conditions and, accordingly, the men, even though unaccustomed to the mountains, were less depressed. German reports from the Tuapse region, unlike those from the high Caucasus, repeatedly refer to 'the fanatical ferocity' of Soviet resistance and the persistent Soviet counterattacks that sometimes ended in hand-to-hand fighting.[36] At times, especially at the lower elevations to the north of the Tuapse road, where Soviet divisions could get away with conventional tactics, their capacity matched that of the German Jäger divisions.

The only Soviet 'mountain' formation that participated in the battle – the understaffed 83rd 'Mountain' Division – arrived at the front line, from Iran, on 22 November, two months after the beginning of Operation Attika.[37] Its tactical skills were only marginally better than those of regular infantry, and it had no climbing instructors. However, despite the justified complaints of Soviet senior officers about 'the poor training and inappropriate gear and uniforms of Soviet mountain units' at Tuapse,[38] this division, with mountain guns and logistics based on pack animals, could manoeuvre more easily than rifle divisions across broken terrain and was able to deliver firepower to areas inaccessible to field artillery. The actions of the 83rd 'Mountain' Division against German mountain regiments, which had been bled white in previous engagements, were unspectacular but adequate; the series of attacks that it launched around Semashkho, supported by artillery and heavy mortars, helped the 18th Army repulse the Germans beyond the Pshish River. However, as a whole, the performance of Soviet units in the mountains to the southeast of the road leading from Maikop to Tuapse was still far inferior to that of the German mountain troops. The Red Army scored a strategic victory by terminating the German offensive not because its skills in the mountains had radically improved but because it was able to quickly transfer its divisions from other parts of the front and pit them against German forces, which rapidly shrank in the absence of reinforcements.

The approach of the Red Army to mountain warfare demonstrated the validity of a proverb used by Russians to describe their national character: 'A man does not think of salvation until he hears thunder.'[39] This proverb also implies that a man forgets about salvation as soon as the thunderstorm is over. The Red Army acted in accordance with this proverb. Having suffered crushing defeats in the high Caucasus, it undertook a number of vigorous but belated reforms that created all the conditions for acquiring proper mountain units. However, as soon as the war shifted from the mountains to the plains in the spring of 1943, the Red Army curtailed the training of its 'mountain' divisions; in the summer and early autumn of that year, it disbanded the mountain companies and sent their soldiers to 'mountain' divisions or even to regular infantry, and it closed the School of Military Mountaineering.[40] The Red Army preserved several divisions with the 'mountain' designation, but their training for mountain warfare was limited to what they had received in the wake of the battle of the Caucasus in the winter and spring of 1943, and the subsequent attrition reduced the number of trained soldiers. New divisions that received the 'mountain' designation were untrained for mountain warfare. Since the Red Army reached many correct conclusions on mountain warfare only near the end and after the battle of the Caucasus, and these conclusions had few practical consequences, the extensive search for proper tactics, drill, equipment, and logistics enabling it to fight the enemy on equal terms ended up being primarily an academic exercise, and the potential created during a painful trial-and-error process was not realised.

The Carpathian–Dukla Operation

The third and last operation conducted by the Red Army in the mountains in the European military theatre was an attempt to cross the Beskids, the lowest part of the Carpathians, in September and October 1944. This was a much larger operation than the battles in the high Caucasus and at Tuapse. In August 1944, the 1st Ukrainian Front – commanded by Ivan Konev, a marshal with a glorious military record – advanced westwards in southern Poland until it paused near Krosno, a town at a major road connecting Poland and Slovakia via the low and broad Dukla pass (502 m), 40 kilometres south of Krosno.[41]

Konev planned to continue the strategic offensive in the same westward direction along the northern foothills of the Carpathians towards Krakow, Breslau, and Berlin.[42] However, events in Slovakia abruptly intervened. In the summer of 1944, when the Red Army approached the Slovak frontier, the Slovak National Council, a major anti-Nazi resistance group, decided to launch an uprising. The council stated that at the beginning of the uprising, two Slovak divisions protecting the northern border of Slovakia would occupy the Dukla pass and the approaches to it and hold their positions until the arrival of the Red Army.[43] The Stavka decided to exploit the uprising, which could potentially destabilise the German rear, and break south across the Beskids and then across Slovakia towards the Hungarian plains and Miskolc into the rear of Army Group South, deployed in Transylvania, thus cutting off a part of the German 1st Tank Army and the entire 1st Hungarian Army.[44] The offensive took place in the same general area where the Russian Army had fought the Austrians in the winter of 1915; it was also as improvised as the campaign of 1915, ending in a similar bloody stalemate (Map 9.2).

On 5 August, the Stavka designated a part of the 1st Ukrainian Front as a separate 4th Ukrainian Front. On 15 August, the General Staff of the Red Army gave a directive to the 4th Ukrainian Front to prepare for actions in wooded mountains, and on 27 August the front's commanders received a clear operational order to plan an offensive across the Carpathians.[45] On 29 August, while the Stavka was thinking about how to deploy the 4th Ukrainian Front, the uprising erupted. Two days later, Konev suggested that his front, rather than the 4th Ukrainian Front, deliver the main strike across Dukla. Since the Germans were moving promptly to suppress the uprising, Konev asked for only seven days to prepare the operation. The Stavka approved his idea on 2 September and ordered him to begin what it called the Carpathian–Dukla Operation on 8 September. Konev's plan presumed that the reinforced 38th Army of the 1st Ukrainian Front would advance across Dukla; the occupation of the pass by Slovaks was 'an important aspect of the plan'.[46] Simultaneously, the reinforced 1st Guards Army of the 4th Ukrainian Front would launch a strike across the Beskids to the east of Dukla, first facilitating the offensive of the 38th Army and later assuming a primary role in the offensive towards Hungary. Both Konev and Kirill Moskalenko, commander of the 38th Army, maintained that 'the offensive across the

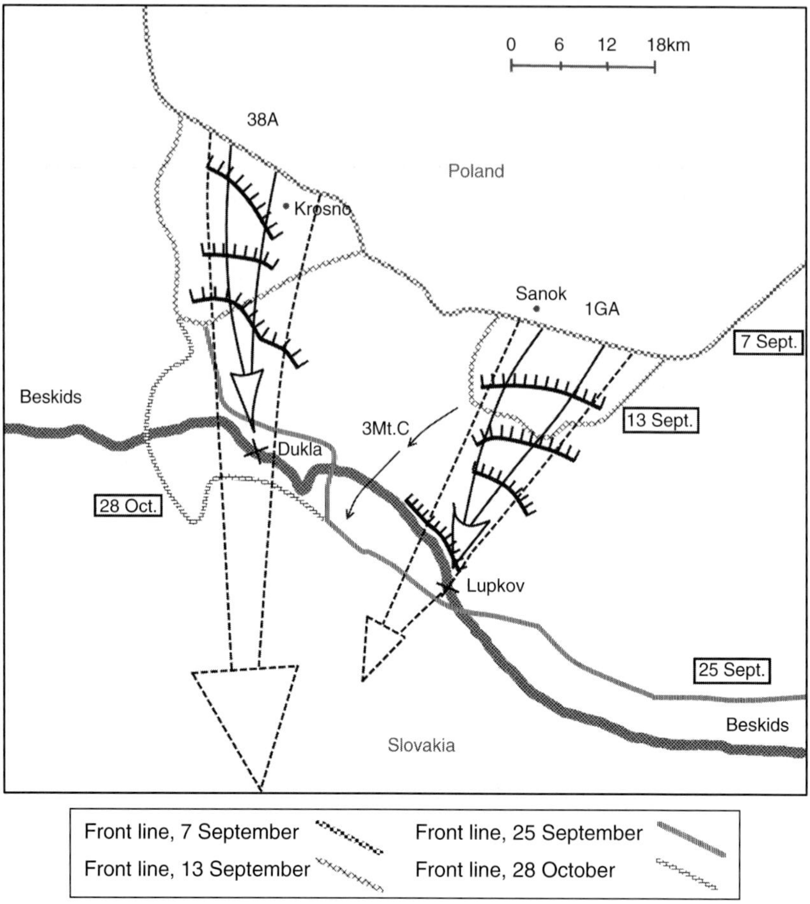

Map 9.2 The Red Army's attempt to break through the Beskids to Slovakia, September–October 1944

Carpathians had no strategic or operational imperatives but only a political goal: to help the rising Slovak people'.[47] Russian historiography promotes this thesis. However, the Soviet leaders, like the leaders of any other state, would not help foreigners if it entailed thousands of casualties, which their soldiers would inevitably suffer while fighting their way across difficult terrain; indeed, it would have been criminal to do so. The Stavka must have sanctioned the operation in the hope that the offensive across the Beskids would quickly bring the Soviet armies to the rear of Army Group South. In fact, Konev was sure that the two armies of the 1st and 4th Ukrainian Fronts would easily break through the Beskids and then drive their tanks across first the Slovak and then the Hungarian plain. He planned to reach the Slovak plain on the fifth day of the offensive.[48]

The Beskids can hardly be called mountains; they are high wooded hills with a maximum altitude of about 800 metres and an elevation above the surrounding plains of only 300 metres.[49] The northern slopes of the Beskids are gently sloped, which must have eased the attack planned by the Stavka. It takes only about fifteen hours to walk across the Beskids from the Polish to the Slovak plains, even without a road. Infantry could cross the Beskids anywhere along numerous paths. It required no mountaineering training, special uniforms, or gear, except for ropes to pull the artillery. However, in order to break to the Slovak plain, the Red Army had to overcome several low parallel ridges perpendicular to the direction of its advance.[50] These ridges, thickly forested and impassable for tanks or heavy artillery, were good defensive positions.

The Axis kept the Army Group Heinrici, consisting of the 1st Tank Army and the 1st Hungarian Army, spread all the way along the 300-kilometre front in the northern Carpathians. Konev assessed the enemy forces in front of the 38th Army as 'rather weak'[51] and believed that the enormous Soviet superiority in numbers and firepower in this part of the front would grant him success (Table 9.2).

Both Soviet and German formations in this region were at half of their full strength. About 16,000 Soviet and Slovak partisans operated in the rear of the Germans and could, potentially, facilitate the Soviet offensive by attacking the German supply lines.[52] Two Soviet air armies were to provide air support.[53] Moskalenko shared Konev's optimism but also believed that 'the success of the mission depended on a quick rout of the enemy at the foothills of the Carpathians and a swift strike by mobile formations – cavalry and tank corps'. Furthermore, as he wrote, 'we put our special hopes on the "god of war". Soviet artillery demonstrated that it well deserved this title by its splendid actions in all operations of the Great Patriotic War.'[54] However, as Moskalenko admitted, 'all three and a half years of war, we [he and his commanders] had fought on the plains ... Now we would have to gain experience of mountain warfare, and not in training grounds, because we had no time for it, but in combat', exactly as the TCF had done in 1942.[55] The 38th Army had no mountain units. Even though the force allocated for an attack needed no mountaineering training, it still had to know the tactics of mountain warfare and rely

Table 9.2 Ratio of forces on the eve of the Carpathian–Dukla operation, 8 September 1944

38th Army	German forces opposing the 38th Army	1st Guards Army	German forces opposing the 1st Guards Army[a]
• 121st, 140th, 183rd, 211th, 241st, 304th, 305th, 340th Rifle Divisions and 70th Guards Rifle Division • 1st Guards Cavalry Corps • 25th Tank Corps • Czechoslovak Corps • Artillery division • Two mortar brigades and two independent mortar regiments • Anti-aircraft division	• 68th, 208th, and 545th Infantry Divisions	• 30th, 141th, 155th, 161st, 167th, 237th, 276th Rifle Divisions and 129th Guards Rifle Division • Tank brigade • Tank regiment • Regiment of self-propelled guns • Artillery brigade • Howitzer regiment • Four artillery anti-tank regiments • Four mountain mortar regiments • Anti-aircraft artillery division • Anti-aircraft artillery regiment	• 96th, 168th, and 254th Infantry Divisions • Units of the 101st Jäger Division

Source: Ivan Konev, *Zapiski komanduiushchego frontom* (Moscow: Nauka, 1972), 307, 308; Kirill Moskalenko, *Na iugo-zapadnom napravlenii, 1943–1945* (Moscow: Nauka, 1973), II:438; General V. Korovikov, head of Operations Section of the 4th Ukrainian Front, and Colonel Levshuk, head of Section for Utilising War Experience, 'Karpatskaia operatsiia 4-go Ukrainskogo Fronta' (no date), TsAMO, f. 244, op. 3000, d. 723, ll. 80, 101, 103, 111.
Note: [a] Only the 96th and 168th Divisions were in the first echelon. Grechko also mentions the 6th Hungarian Division as allegedly opposing the 1st Guards Army, but it stayed in the region of Strilky, well to the east of the area where the 1st Guards Army operated and did not take part in the action: A. Grechko, *Cherez Karpaty* (Moscow: MO SSSR, 1972), 82, 111–14, Map 5.

on weapons and logistics effective on such terrain. The commanders of the 1st Ukrainian Front had no time to adapt their formations to the mountainous environment and planned the operation as if it would proceed on a plain.

In contrast, the 4th Ukrainian Front had three weeks to prepare for actions in the mountains. Its commander, Ivan Efimovich Petrov, knew from experience that mountain warfare rarely brings swift victory and did not share the optimism prevailing in the Headquarters of the 1st Ukrainian Front. Believing that 'the skill of the entire personnel, from private to general, is a necessary precondition for successful actions in the mountains',[56] he understood that many arrangements had to be made before his rifle divisions could perform adequately in the Beskids. On 11 August, Petrov issued 'Directives on the Preparations for Actions in the Mountains', followed by a *Manual on Actions in Wooded Mountains*, *Instructions on Artillery Actions in the Mountains*, and *Instructions on Engineering Support in Wooded Mountains*.[57] These directives outlined the basic aspects of combat in the mountains; emphasised flexibility and initiative, at all levels of command, as imperatives in mountain warfare; and confirmed that 'envelopment is the major form of action in the mountains: small forces should pin down the enemy with fire and frontal attack, whereas the main forces should make their way to the heights dominating enemy flanks'.[58] Petrov arranged a series of lectures for corps and division commanders with topics such as 'Training and Tactics in the Mountains' and 'Actions of a Rifle Division in Wooded Mountains'. These commanders then had to deliver similar lectures to regiment commanders, who in turn had to organise lectures for battalion and company commanders, adjusting the topics to the corresponding levels of command. The lectures targeting junior officers examined the tactics of mountain warfare, such as attack on a mountain summit by a rifle company at night or in conditions of poor visibility, navigation in wooded mountains with and without a compass, and a march across mountains without roads. Division commanders organised a war game on maps. The Soviets had good maps of the Beskids, with a scale of 1:50,000. Every officer received a compass. Petrov reminded the commanders that radio is the most reliable and flexible means of communication in the mountains.[59]

Although the Beskids are a series of low, narrow mountain ridges, Petrov expected to face a serious logistical challenge. He maintained that 'the number of guns is secondary to the number of shells these guns can fire',[60] thus emphasising the importance of proper logistics. Since the interwar period, the Red Army had striven to mechanise its artillery and supply services as much as possible, but now the 4th Ukrainian Front switched its logistics back to horses for crossing the Beskids. The 1st Guards Army managed to raise only three horse companies, which would be inadequate to secure the steady flow of supplies if the operation took longer than planned. In order to alleviate the shortage of horses, Petrov wrote a devious instruction suggesting that 'company commanders be granted broad powers in acquiring horses but not by confiscating them from civilians', thus giving carte blanche for requisitions while paying lip service to political constraints.[61] Every rifle division had to make packs for the horses, and muleteers had to be trained how to load horses without injuring them. Petrov ordered his officers to leave their personal belongings in divisional depots to free the supply trains of inessential loads. Every field gun was to be fitted with straps so that infantry could drag the guns to places where horses could not pass. The 1st Guards Army was to receive pack kitchens as well as dry mountain rations for every man.[62] To inspire his soldiers, Petrov referred to Suvorov's Swiss campaign, when 'the Russian Army won brilliant victories over the enemy, and gained eternal glory'.[63]

Unlike Tiulenev in the Caucasus, Petrov monitored the implementation of his orders, and most of them were fulfilled. His subordinates trained for ten to twelve hours a day, practising navigation, night marches, and combat in forests, including envelopments and the co-operation of infantry, artillery, and engineers. Remembering the lessons of the Caucasus, the 1st Guards Army acquired winches to pull guns across the mountains, made enough horse-driven sledges for the evacuation of wounded men, and even produced primitive crampons, although they were unnecessary in the Beskids. In short, Petrov did whatever he could to enlighten his soldiers on mountain warfare and prepare the offensive, but his officers admitted that their units received only 'minimal training in wooded mountains'[64] because of time constraints and also because the scope of training was inevitably limited since the 1st Guards Army was deployed on the plains at that time, where it could study the theoretical aspects of tactics in the mountains but was unable to practise them.

On 7 August, the Stavka began relocating the 3rd Mountain Corps, the only mountain formation the Red Army had at that time on the Eastern Front, from Crimea to the Beskids.[65] Two of the corps's three divisions had experience in mountain warfare: its 242nd Mountain Division had defended the Elbrus region during the battle in the high Caucasus, while the 128th Guards Mountain Division, formerly the 83rd 'Mountain' Division, had participated in the battle of Tuapse. The 318th Division had received its 'mountain' designation only that summer and had no training in mountain warfare. The corps had mountain artillery, portable radios, and horse-based logistics suitable for action in the mountains.[66]

The Stavka's plans went wrong even before the operation began. On 1 and 2 September, the Germans disarmed the two Slovak divisions that were to occupy Dukla.[67] The Stavka was unsure about the course of events in Slovakia and decided to proceed with the operation, although it soon became clear that the easy drive along the highway across the Beskids was no longer an option. Furthermore, Konev grossly underestimated the strength of the German defences to the north of the Beskids, dozens of kilometres away from the mountains. Andrei Grechko, commander of the 1st Guards Army, attributed the slow tempo of advance from the outset in part to poor weather, but field reports show that September was a good season for an offensive: the weather was warm, with an average low and high of 13 and 22 °Celsius; there were only nine rainy days during that month and the rains were light, so the forest roads were in good condition.[68] However, fierce German resistance reduced the speed of the Soviet offensive to a snail's pace. By 13 September, the day on which Konev had planned to reach the Slovak plain, his vanguards had gained only 25 kilometres from their initial positions and were still on the Polish plain with the Beskids ahead of them. Meanwhile, from 9 to 11 September, the Germans reinforced their formations facing the 38th Army with three infantry divisions[69] and most of the units of the 8th Tank Division and, later, with a tank regiment of the 1st Tank Division.[70]

The problems encountered by the attackers multiplied when they finally reached the foothills of the Beskids in the second half of September. As Moskalenko recalled,

> the closer [Soviet] units came to the [Dukla] pass, the tougher became the terrain and the clearer were the errors made during planning, especially those regarding the tempo of the advance ... The absence of tactical skills in wooded mountains was making an ever graver impact ... The personnel had never endured such strenuous physical efforts ... as they did during the Carpathian–Dukla Operation.[71]

During the battle of the Beskids, Soviet divisions faced some of the same problems their comrades had encountered in the Caucasus, and again they had to learn how to solve them. Officers complained about the delusive distances in the mountains, which seemed shorter than they actually were if one looked uphill and longer if one looked downhill, and once again they discovered the need for sight adjustments when a target was located at an angle higher than 30 degrees. In one instance, soldiers set their rifle sights at a distance between 100 and 230 metres when in reality the distance they needed to cover was 530 metres; their commanders concluded that 'only persistent training in distance calculation ... gives a positive outcome'.[72] The Soviets were again impressed with the ability of the Germans to operate in small units on broken terrain, observing that 'the enemy groups of uneven strength literally stuck to our spearheads from all sides, thus surrounding them'.[73] By 1944, the Red Army had received many reliable portable radios via Lend-Lease, which considerably improved its command and control in operations on broken terrain, but the logistics on such terrain remained a great challenge.

The few paved roads in this region followed valley bottoms and were blocked by numerous German strongholds, so the Red Army had to advance across wooded hills, along dirt roads, at best, and often with no roads at all. Tanks and heavy artillery – the main arms the commanders of the 38th Army had hoped for when they were planning the operation – were immobilised and had to be left behind. Field artillery was sometimes able to advance, with great effort, across the mountainous terrain: every gun was drawn by seven pairs of horses and scores of infantrymen pulling ropes but, as was to be expected, the artillery's progress lagged 7 to 12 kilometres behind the infantry.[74] In the absence of heavy artillery, 82-mm and 107-mm mortars became the primary means to support the infantry; however, the pack animal trains turned out to be insufficient to deliver ammunition fast enough, so the firepower of Soviet field artillery and mortars was much weaker than their number suggests. The inadequate artillery support was a major reason for the slow advance.[75] The Germans retreated step by step from one ridge to another, inflicting heavy casualties on the attackers. Assault on every subsequent ridge required substantial preparations. The Soviets made a consistent effort to bypass the German strongholds and envelop their flanks along mountain paths, and, unlike in the Caucasus, they could do this in the low Beskids.[76] They gained many small tactical victories, but often, when the infantry finally breached the front, it had to wait a long time for the artillery to arrive; meanwhile, the Germans sealed the breach. The average daily rate of Soviet advance was 1 to 2 kilometres.[77] Although every rifle corps was reinforced with two or three engineering battalions, in addition to the integrated engineering units, such support turned out to be inadequate to secure a way around

German strongholds.[78] When Moskalenko attempted to break the stalemate and sent his cavalry corps into a breach in the front, hoping that its raid would create havoc in the enemy rear, the corps could only drag less than half of its field artillery. Though it suffered only light casualties in manpower, within several days the corps lost 37 per cent of its horses, mostly those pulling artillery and hauling packs, and had to break back across the front, having failed to fulfil its mission.[79]

Only the mountain guns of the 3rd Mountain Corps could move at the infantry's pace. It took time to relocate the corps from Crimea; it entered the battle on 19 September. By this time, the 1st Guards Army had already made its way through the first ridge of the Beskids. As soon as the corps reached the front line, it made significant progress and, on 20 September, it became the first Soviet formation to cross the main ridge of the Beskids into Czechoslovakia, having taken twelve Slovak villages.[80] However, once out of the mountains, its light artillery could not provide sufficient support against the German heavy tanks that arrived along the better road network in Slovakia, and the corps had to stop its offensive. Between 2 and 12 October, the corps was relocated 40 kilometres to the east and again spearheaded the Soviet offensive in the higher mountains. Although the offensive failed, the corps performed better than other formations.[81]

It became clear that the Carpathian–Dukla Operation had lost its steam. On 27 September, Konev suggested that it be terminated because the 38th Army 'turned out to be structurally unprepared for an offensive in wooded mountains'; that is why 'the mountains helped the enemy'.[82] However, the Stavka ordered him to press on. Only on 6 October, having crossed three ridges, did the 38th Army and the Czechoslovak Corps take Dukla, but the Germans continued to hold the southern slopes of the pass. The 38th Army advanced 50 kilometres during the first month of the offensive; most of this distance lay along the plain at the northern approaches to the Beskids.[83] The 38th and 1st Guards Armies crossed the main ridge of the Beskids in several places and gained several kilometres of Slovak territory along its southern slopes, but they could advance no farther.

The weather became much worse in October. Rain poured nonstop from 1 to 5 October, making the dirt roads impassable, even for light field artillery. Half of the last twenty days of October were also rainy. The heavy, sticky black clay turned into knee-deep mud, stalling

Soviet logistics. Even infantrymen found it difficult to move across the mud fields.[84] When the weather was good, the numerous bombers supporting the Soviet offensive could launch more than 800 sorties within several hours, but thick fog prevented them from operating during most days in October.[85]

The Soviet forces continued to attack, losing many of their soldiers, until the last days of October. Russian sources do not give the numbers of casualties sustained by the 1st Guards Army but the total casualties of the 4th Ukrainian Front, including those suffered during a secondary offensive in the eastern Carpathians, equalled 66,837 men, or a quarter of its initial strength of 264,000 men; of these, 10,060 were killed, 41,387 wounded, 1,806 missing in action, and 13,584 sick. The 1st Ukrainian Front lost 62,014 men during this operation, with 13,264 of these being irrecoverable casualties, which means that it lost two-thirds of its initial strength of 99,100 men. The Czechoslovak Corps lost 5,699 of its 14,900 men, of which 1,630 were irrecoverable casualties.[86] According to Soviet estimates, surely inflated, the total German casualties in the Carpathian–Dukla Operation equalled 70,000 men.[87] It is likely that the Red Army lost two or three times as many soldiers as the Germans.

Konev and Moskalenko claimed that the Stavka insisted on the continuation of the offensive long after it became clear that it had failed because the General Staff had decided to tie down the German formations sent to the Beskids, thus keeping them away from the eastern Hungarian plains, while the 2nd Ukrainian Front broke through the German lines on 6 October and quickly advanced across Transylvania.[88] However, the Soviet forces deployed in the Beskids were much more numerous than the German forces there. While the Germans received considerable reinforcements during the battle of the Beskids, so did the Soviets.[89] In the end, the 38th Army had the equivalent of ten rifle, five tank, and five artillery divisions, while the opposing Germans had only six depleted infantry divisions and two tank divisions, excluding the attached artillery.[90] As for the 1st Guards Army, by 19 September, it had twelve rifle and mountain divisions, a tank brigade, and the equivalent of four artillery and three mortar divisions[91] against six German infantry and Jäger divisions, units of a tank division, and some auxiliary formations.[92]

It is clear, therefore, that the Red Army kept two or three times as large a force in the Beskids as the Germans did, a force it had diverted from its offensive towards Germany. If the Stavka indeed planned to tie down the enemy forces in the Beskids, the rationality of this decision is uncertain. Its outcome appears far less impressive than the outcome of the German defence in the high Caucasus, when the Germans tied down an equivalent of four Soviet divisions with the forces of two regiments, thus preventing the transfer of those divisions in the direction of the main German strike at Tuapse, and inflicted far heavier casualties on the Soviets than they suffered themselves. In the Beskids, the Stavka allegedly sought to tie down inferior German forces and, again, the Soviets suffered greater casualties than the Germans. However, the Red Army had more manpower on the Eastern Front than the Germans did and perhaps could afford such strategic decisions if their cost was ignored, which it was. After all, despite the impressive success of the Germans' defence in the high Caucasus, their major offensive at Tuapse failed, whereas the offensive of the 2nd Ukrainian Front, facilitated perhaps by the diversion of some German forces to the Beskids, brought a strategic victory. In the end, as had happened during the second stage of the battle in the high Caucasus, the Germans, who had frustrated the Soviet attempts to break through the Beskids in September and October, had to retreat in November, when the 2nd Ukrainian Front advanced towards Debrecen into the rear of the Heinrici Army Group.

Granted, as Konev admitted, 'tying up large forces of the Hitlerite army in the Carpathians was not the main mission of the left flank of the 1st Ukrainian Front. Our main mission was the swift advance towards the insurgents. However, the difficult mountain terrain and the fierce resistance of the enemy greatly reduced the pace of our advance' until it stalled.[93] Therefore, apart from the controversial decision to tie down an inferior German force in the Beskids, the overall outcome of the Soviet offensive there is clear. If the battle in the high Caucasus was a draw and the battle at Tuapse was a clear-cut albeit costly victory for the Red Army, the attempt to break across the Beskids was a strategic failure. It did not attain any of its military or political objectives: the Red Army did not manage to break through to the Slovak and Hungarian plains, nor did it save the Slovak uprising suppressed by the Germans in late October. The roots of the failure lay in strategy rather than tactics: the Stavka and Konev gravely underestimated the difficulty of an offensive across the mountains, and, as Soviet historians have admitted, 'the Red Army and the Czechoslovak Corps were not trained for an offensive in wooded mountains and had no proper equipment'.[94] A Russian saying stemming from a satirical song written by Leo Tolstoy about the disastrous attack of the Russian Army at Chernaia River in 1854 asserts: 'Since their map sheets were flat, they ignored the ravines on their way.'[95] This saying applies to the operation in the Beskids as well.

Konev's main conclusion about the attempt of the 38th Army to cross the Beskids is striking in its naivety: 'The experience of mountain warfare showed clearly that formations must be familiar with the peculiarities of the mountainous terrain and be supplied with climbing gear and suitable equipment, and lighter weapons.'[96] The Red Army General Staff should have learned that much during the battle in the high Caucasus two years earlier. It had established Sections for Utilising War Experience within the staffs of armies and fronts, and several senior officers wrote detailed studies of the battle at the MCR right after it ended.[97] However, only those generals who had fought in the Caucasus were to learn these lessons, rather than the Stavka or other commanders. To be fair, the 38th Army had to launch an offensive on short notice with no time for thorough training. The commanders of the 4th Ukrainian Front had more time and utilised it with moderate efficiency. Having gained limited experience of mountain warfare, General Petrov vigorously addressed the anticipated problems, whereas Konev was unaware of the potential challenges. It was Konev who initiated the operation and the Stavka, captivated by his extravagant promise to prepare the offensive within a mere seven days and then to cross the Beskids within five days, chose to ignore the lessons of the Caucasus and once again squandered the lives of Soviet soldiers. The 1st Guards Army, which had undertaken cursory training for mountain warfare, advanced faster than the 38th Army, and across more rugged terrain, but was not fast enough to tip the balance, and its offensive was planned as an auxiliary strike, meant to facilitate the main attack across Dukla. The Stavka launched the operation hoping that strategic surprise would allow the 38th Army to quickly break through the mountains. When stubborn German resistance at the approaches to the Beskids frustrated this hope, the improvised attempt to cross the fortified mountains with formations that were well armed but unskilled in mountain warfare had a predictable outcome.

The Red Army did not earn martial glory in the mountains: it suffered much heavier casualties than the enemy in every battle it fought, despite the considerable numerical superiority it usually enjoyed. Naturally, the greatest disparity of casualties occurred in an environment that provided the narrowest margin of error, thus giving a sound advantage to the army that had appropriate skills and gear over those that ventured into the mountains untrained and unequipped. In the lower mountains, the substantial superiority of the Red Army in firepower coupled with lesser demands for mission-tailored training could, to a degree, offset its inexperience in mountain warfare and reduce the ratio of casualties; nonetheless, the latter still remained in the enemy's favour. Yet, even in the low Beskids, the 3rd Mountain Corps fought more effectively than regular rifle divisions because its weapons and logistics were better suited to actions in the mountains and some of its soldiers had gained experience in mountain warfare in the Caucasus, while the 4th Ukrainian Front, which made an effort to adjust to an anticipated battle environment, attained better results than the 1st Ukrainian Front, which undertook no such effort. The actions in the mountains during World War II thus provided empirical proof of a simple thesis: an army planning to operate in a certain environment must be trained and equipped for actions in such an environment.

10 DISDAIN FOR MILITARY PROFESSIONALISM AS A COMPONENT OF THE UNIVERSAL STALINIST PARADIGM

Train hard – fight easy!

Alexander Suvorov[1]

Conventional wisdom suggests that the dismal performance of Soviet formations in the mountains may be attributed primarily to their dilettantism in mountain warfare. After all, in the interwar period, the Red Army had mostly planned for campaigns on the plains. It was well equipped for such combat: it had many more weapons, often of a better quality, than the Germans did; Soviet summer uniforms were as suited to these battle conditions as were the German ones, while Soviet winter uniforms and logistics were superior. It would be logical to assume, then, that the basic training acquired by Red Army soldiers before they were sent to their first battle enabled them to operate on the plains markedly better than in the mountains. A plethora of candid war memoirs and uncensored studies published in the post-communist period provides enough information for testing this hypothesis. These new sources reveal the attitude of top Soviet commanders towards military specialisation and also describe the training procedures followed by various Red Army branches intended for actions on the plains, the nature of their drills, and the range of skills they believed sufficient to perform adequately in combat. The skills of the Soviet 'mountain' troops can be measured against these parameters used as a benchmark.

By World War II, most top Red Army commanders had adopted the Bolshevik 'it's not rocket science'[2] stance that had emerged with the foundation of the Soviet state in 1917 but became prevalent during the Stalinist modernisation in the 1930s. This approach presumed that any person supplied with proper tools and fortified by communist ideology could do any job. As Oleg Suvenirov observes,

> [Viacheslav] Molotov, a college dropout, was perceived as an eminent scholar; the paramedic [Sergo] Ordzhonikidze supervised the entire heavy industry of the state; [Kliment] Voroshilov, who had attended school for only 'two winters', commanded the armed forces for fifteen years and also supervised military studies; [Nikolai] Ezhov with his 'unfinished primary education' was the terrifying NKVD chief and secretary of the Central Committee of the Communist Party . . . ; and nobody knows whether [Lazar'] Kaganovich, a key Politburo member, had any formal education.[3]

In Hannah Arendt's words, 'Totalitarianism in power invariably replaces all first-rate talents, regardless of their sympathies, with those crackpots and fools whose lack of intelligence and creativity is still the best guarantee of their loyalty.'[4] Stalinist leaders – following the captivating populist slogan 'anyone can become a hero'[5] coupled with proud assertions of their own ignorance, 'We have not graduated from academies!'[6] – implied that enthusiasm, improvisation, hard work, and the total mobilisation of resources were more important than expertise, painstaking calculation, and skill. Applied to the Red Army, this stance meant that high numbers, modern hardware, and ideological zeal were of higher value than professionalism. The government sought to raise the largest army in Europe and to supply it with high-quality weapons, while commanders had to follow simplified training procedures that would allow them to process the enormous number of recruits within a short timeframe. Many senior Soviet commanders, having been swiftly promoted through several ranks during the civil war, found themselves in positions for which they had no training or education, yet they believed that they could handle their jobs. A commission that investigated Voroshilov's actions during the civil war came to the conclusion that a battalion was the largest unit he could possibly command,[7] but he received the rank of marshal in 1935, supervised the Red Army during his term as people's commissar of defence from 1925 to 1940, and served briefly as its commander-in-chief during the Winter War.[8] The legacy of the civil war coupled with

Bolshevik ideology formed the mentality of most officers holding the highest positions in the Red Army: the total victory of the semi-amateurish Red Army over its numerous professional foes during the civil war was a hard fact; the Red Army won the civil war because it was always several times larger than the armies of all its enemies taken together. The strong motivation to join the ranks secured numerical superiority and was therefore more important than professionalism. Only victory mattered, and its cost was irrelevant.

The elimination of the brightest minds in the Red Army during the Great Purge and the massive influx of junior commanders and political commissars into senior positions in its wake further undermined professionalism. Many top Soviet commanders had no military education, including Marshal Voroshilov; the head of the Red Army's Political Directorate, Lev Mekhlis, who held the rank of a four-star general; and half of the commanders of the armies in the Kiev Special Military District.[9] This top component of the Soviet officer corps – consisting, in David Glantz's words, 'largely of political hacks, sycophants and cronies of Stalin'[10] – expressed contempt for expertise, having no understanding that modern warfare required a qualitatively higher level of professionalism than that with which they had won the civil war. The numerous overnight promotions of junior officers and commissars to senior positions vacated by the purges – when battalion and platoon commanders were appointed to command corps and regiments, respectively[11] – implied that professional training, especially the time-consuming kind that involved mission-tailored diversified skills, was a bourgeois luxury. The beneficiaries of the purge perceived basic military drill merely as a means to infuse recruits with loyalty and discipline.

This lack of professionalism became the Red Army's Achilles heel. The combat skills of Soviet officers were far inferior to those of their German counterparts, even after the Wehrmacht expanded greatly after 1935 and before the Red Army started an expansion in 1939. The training gap increased dramatically after the beginning of World War II. As the Abwehr reported ten days before the attack on the Soviet Union, 'Inflexible and stereotypical tactics, the absence of determination, and fear of responsibility are typical features of the Russians … Commanders of all ranks still have no skill sets to handle large modern formations.'[12] The events of the following months proved the validity of this assessment. With time, Soviet senior commanders gained sufficient expertise to match the Wehrmacht in tactics and to outperform it in operational art and strategy; however, they were able to learn the business of war only because they had a much greater opportunity to survive the long and tormenting learning process than did front-line junior officers and rank-and-file soldiers, most of whom lost their lives or health before they could acquire sound skills.

How, then, did the individual entry-level training of junior officers and men who fought on the plains compare to the training of those who found themselves in the mountains? A two-stage analysis can answer this question. It starts with identifying the general Red Army training features and then provides a survey of drill procedures in its various arms. This analysis yields data for the assessment of the skills that the Red Army General Staff believed to be sufficient for a soldier sent into battle.

What were the key characteristics of Soviet military training? First, such training became extremely brief and superficial during the Red Army expansion in 1939–41, while the Soviet Union was still neutral, and it shortened and weakened even further after the German invasion. Soviet officer schools recruited cadets among both civilians and those who had already passed through universal military service. In the interwar period, it took the cadets two to three years to attain the rank of officer. After 1939, the Red Army General Staff decided to sacrifice the quality of the junior officer corps for quantity by severely cutting the training time: cadets, even those recruited among civilians, received their officer commission after a mere six months. Of all Soviet officers serving in 1940, only 4.3 per cent had graduated from the military academy, 13 per cent had taken additional training courses after graduation from military schools, 36.5 per cent had graduated from regular military schools, 3.3 per cent had received their commission after one year of studies and 27.2 per cent after only six months of studies, and 15.9 per cent had no military education.[13] Thus, almost half of the Soviet officers had either a superficial military education or no education at all. Most of the platoon and company commanders – that is, those who trained rank-and-file soldiers – were officers who had received their commission after a six-month training period and were themselves poor professionals. The youngest Wehrmacht privates who found themselves in combat on the Eastern Front in the summer of 1941 were those drafted in the early autumn of 1940. Therefore, an average German private knew the war business better than the Soviet lieutenants who had graduated from a six-month programme in the summer of 1941. The report of the Kiev Special Military District written in early 1941 stated: 'The commanders of platoons, companies, and battalions have no skills to organise and run combat training in their units; subsequently, the drill methodology in most units of the district is poor.'[14] The thirteen months that passed between the entrance of the Soviet Union in the war and the arrival of the Germans in the Caucasus was sufficient time to attain the level of professionalism required for mountain warfare, had the officers read the manuals developed in the interwar years, known the peculiarities of training procedures, and been keen to acquire the necessary skills. However, the TCF Headquarters approached training like the headquarters of other fronts and thus failed to prepare their soldiers and officers for the upcoming battle in the mountains.

Another flaw in the Red Army drill was the unwarranted shift of training priorities from combat exercises to remote secondary aspects of the military profession. As Clausewitz wrote, although exercises are 'a feeble substitute for the real thing', they can considerably reduce the 'friction' in a future war if they are conducted in conditions closely simulating the battle environment. Such exercises not only sharpen combat skills but also help to maintain morale when the real test comes, because 'when exceptional efforts are required of him in war, the recruit is apt to think that they result from mistakes, miscalculations and confusion at the top. In consequence, his morale is doubly depressed. If maneuvers prepare him for exertions, this will not occur.'[15] Few survivors of the purges read Clausewitz, and the Red Army ignored his recommendations. Rather than field exercises, the most salient features of the training procedures were indoctrination and parade drill. During the interwar years, Soviet soldiers spent more time at political lectures than practising combat,[16] and in the Caucasus indoctrination was even more time-consuming than elsewhere because of the anticipated lower-than-average loyalty of local ethnic groups. The love for parade drill was inherited from Russian imperial generals, who adopted this minor aspect of Prussian military training but ignored the main one – professionalism. The former sergeants, who had now become senior Red Army commanders, continued the old tradition. Parade drill, arduous but useless, took a large share of the brief training period, whereas combat practice fell well below the bare minimum a soldier needed to perform his duties. Soviet veterans have a unanimous opinion of parade drill: 'every soldier in his right mind hated it'.[17] The mountain terrain provided few opportunities for parades, and indoctrination did little to prepare soldiers for fighting in conditions where frightening abysses, severe fatigue, high altitude, and harsh weather undermined the morale of novices much more than their scepticism of official values did.

The gross misallocation of resources in defence policy was another factor undermining the Red Army's professionalism. The Soviet government invested the lion's share of these resources into ever-expanding hardware production but left the Directorate for Combat Training to scrape the bottom of the barrel. Funds allocated to training, woefully insufficient from the start, dried up almost completely after the beginning of general mobilisation and the loss of the enormous military stockpiles in the western regions. The desperate shortages of equipment, fuel, and ammunition ruined the already handicapped training procedures and led to purely theoretical instructions in the absence of practice. Having no weapons or ammunition, infantrymen studied tactics with wooden rifle replicas and imitated machinegun fire with rattles.[18] A Soviet veteran summarised his activities during his infantry training: 'We undertook parade drill and studied bayonet fighting. We had [only] one rifle with a bayonet and we lined up to stab an effigy. We were told how to shoot but had no shooting practice.'[19] After such 'training', he was sent to the front. The extremely brief time allotted to training forced training departments to produce 'narrow specialists' unable to handle other weapons that they were bound to see on the battlefield. Every infantry section had rifles and one light machinegun, and it might also have submachine-guns. Even those Soviet riflemen who were taught how to handle a rifle studied submachine-guns and light machineguns only in theory, with no firing practice. Such infantrymen were thus unable to replace their comrades even within their section, and they were completely unfamiliar with other infantry weapons, such as mortars, anti-tank rifles, or heavy machineguns.[20] The shortage of proper gear and funds allocated for exercises in the mountains – a trend common for all arms – was, in part, responsible for the poor performance of Soviet soldiers in the Caucasus.

The widespread perception that training was optional caused two interrelated tendencies in the Red Army: assigning soldiers to jobs that had nothing to do with what they had been taught during their basic training and meeting immediate personnel shortages by forcing specialists who had undergone prolonged training to perform jobs that required only basic skills. War memoirs provide scores of examples demonstrating these two tendencies. When soldiers arrived at the front, they often received weapons that they were seeing for the first time or were given jobs for which they were totally untrained. A private trained as a mortar gun layer was assigned to a reconnaissance unit that had no mortars. Conversely, an infantry cadet was appointed as a mortar gun layer; before he found himself with the mortar on the battlefield, he had seen it only once, from a distance.[21] Artillery officers taught to operate large howitzers found themselves in charge of small anti-tank guns, for which they had had no training.[22]

The habit of assigning specialists who had, according to lax Soviet standards, sound skills to simple jobs for which they were untrained caused a rapid attrition of valuable manpower. One member of a mortar crew, recalling that his battery commander was a pilot, commented, 'Such incidents were frequent: young pilots for whom no aircraft were available fought in the infantry, the artillery, and God knows where else.'[23] After the 137th Tank Brigade lost most of its tanks but was ordered, on 19 September 1942, to attack Mamaev Hill, dominating Stalingrad, it sent its tank crews, who were waiting for the arrival of repaired tanks, to fight as infantry. Having no knowledge of infantry tactics, these personnel suffered grave casualties.[24] Only in December 1942 did Stalin finally prohibit the use of tank and air force crews and other specialists as infantry.[25] The battle of the Caucasus took place before this simple idea had occurred to him. Thus, the Stavka's usual way to address immediate problems was to send thousands of climbers to fight on the plains; employ 'mountain' divisions, with their primitive logistics and weak firepower, on the steppes; defend the Caucasus primarily with rifle and cavalry divisions untrained and unequipped for fighting in the mountains; and mobilise the cadets as privates.

The uncensored memoirs of Soviet soldiers published recently reveal a sentiment absent in sources dated to the communist period: their profound respect for the enemy's skill. An infantry veteran recalled one episode, reflecting on the Germans' expertise:

> We attacked a village and fired a lot. When we took it, we … found 30 or 40 killed Germans, but we had lost about 700 men. Our officers and privates asked themselves: 'What is going on?

> We suffer casualties but the Germans seem not to.' ... They were very skilled warriors. Their army was well-trained, hardened by combat experience ... A section of theirs with a machinegun could pin down an [entire] company of ours.[26]

It was not only soldiers fighting in the Caucasus who were stunned by the enemy's professionalism; most authors of memoirs published in the post-Soviet period admit their professional inferiority to the Germans or even the Finns.[27] Deficiencies of the Red Army's entry-level training – such as its brevity, shortened even further by lengthy indoctrination and parade drill; the prevalence of theoretical instruction over exercises; and narrow specialisation, coupled with arbitrary assignments to positions for which no training was provided – were typical of all Soviet arms, as was the thoughtless waste of skilled personnel.

Regular riflemen drafted into the Red Army at the beginning of the war received the shortest and most cursory training, lasting only a month; an infantry sergeant received his rank after only two months of training. Many infantry veterans say that their shooting practice was limited to one or two exercises, during which they were allowed only three rifle shots at a firing range.[28] But they were lucky compared to some recruits who were sent to the front after spending several days in conscription offices without a single shooting exercise, having learned, in the words of war veterans, only two commands: 'Attention!' and 'At ease!'[29] The recruits were not taught how to throw hand grenades and, when they found themselves on the front, they were afraid to use them, fearing that the grenades would blow up in their hands.[30]

Mountain troops also belonged to the infantry, but they were supposed to have special mission-tailored skills; the acquisition of such skills required longer and more diverse drills. How did the training of other infantry specialists, expected to possess mission-tailored skills, compare to that of regular riflemen? The training of a Soviet sniper lasted four months, during which a raw recruit learned mainly how to crawl and take aim but fired only twelve to fifteen shots, and only some of those from a sniper rifle.[31] The training period of a raw recruit assigned to anti-aircraft machine-gunners was to be five months, but in practice it lasted one to two-and-a-half months; even those who studied for the maximum term had a total of four shooting exercises during their training period, and only one of them involved a vertical target – the tops of 20-metre poplars that were to imitate enemy aircraft.[32] Long raids on skis around the flanks of an enemy immobilised by deep snow required the knowledge of special tactics, good skiing technique, and excellent physical health, but skiers were trained for only one month, and only as regular infantrymen; some recruits drafted into ski units were 40 years old, and many skied poorly.[33] A mortar was often the only means of artillery support on broken terrain, but the Red Army conducted no training of mortar crews before the Winter War, during which the crews were hastily assembled from infantrymen who had never fired a mortar before coming to the front; these crews suffered so many accidents that some infantry officers explicitly prohibited the firing of mortars because they allegedly were 'dangerous to handle'.[34]

Every rifle regiment had two platoons of scouts, another type of infantry specialist. A major mission of scouts was to snatch prisoners from enemy trenches and bring them back alive across no-man's land. This was an extremely dangerous job: Soviet veterans recall that sometimes many scout teams perished in futile attempts to capture a single prisoner.[35] Such a job required exceptional courage, motivation, initiative, stamina, patience, ruthlessness, team spirit, and sound skills in hand-to-hand combat, especially given that the Germans were, on average, physically stronger than the Soviets. The soldiers of reconnaissance units were supposed to be a hand-picked elite who had volunteered for this tough job. They were to be provided with special training, as well as special privileges as compensation for the greater risk they had accepted. Finally, since it was not easy to replace such soldiers, they were supposed to be used solely for reconnaissance missions. However, at the beginning of the war, Red Army reconnaissance units did not differ from regular infantry in their training, skills, composition, or status. The Red Army had no special field reconnaissance schools, exactly as it had no special mountaineering schools before the end of 1942.[36] It was only during the second half of the war that commanders realised the need for a special force to perform this duty but, even then, the training period of an infantry junior officer requalified as a commander of a reconnaissance unit lasted at most three weeks.[37] The rank and file of this force were mostly volunteers but, since few regular soldiers volunteered for this dangerous job, a large part of the reconnaissance personnel were criminals drafted from labour camps or penal soldiers, who could easily receive a full pardon once they volunteered.[38] As a reconnaissance platoon commander recalled, half of his subordinates were 'bandits who were serving their terms. Ordinary people would not enlist as scouts.'[39] Although scouts did acquire a tacit elite status with time and enjoyed certain privileges like better food rations, separate quarters, and lax off-duty discipline, few of them received special training from professional instructors in hand-to-hand fighting, camouflage technique, night actions, and crossing rivers; they had to learn this job the hard way during their missions.[40] No codified regulations about the employment of reconnaissance units existed, and the scope of their missions depended on the personal attitude of commanders: some accepted the concept of an elite force and assigned to scouts only the duties they were supposed to perform[41] whereas others rejected this concept and frequently used scouts as regular infantry.[42] Like Soviet 'mountain' troops, scouts often expressed admiration for the skill of their German counterparts: the Germans 'snatched many of our soldiers. Smart fellows! As scouts we learned ruses, camouflage, and combat techniques from them. [They were] cool-headed men – every bullet on target!'[43]

The airborne forces were also infantry with special skills. The Soviet approach to raising such a force resembled its approach to raising mountain divisions. The Red Army General Staff again relied on numbers while paying little attention to quality and ignoring vital details that would have made this new arm effective. The Germans realised that both mountain and airborne divisions should be few but elite, and by 1941 they had raised seven mountain divisions and one airborne division, all of which had proven their professionalism after the beginning of World War II. By the same time, the Red Army had raised nineteen 'mountain' divisions and four 'cavalry-mountain' divisions, all untrained for mountain warfare, and five 'airborne' corps with 100,000 soldiers, most of whom had never jumped with a parachute, and without airplanes able to transport large airborne units.[44] The Soviet airborne force did receive better training than regular infantry: paratroopers had more practice on a firing range with various weapons and were taught navigation with a map and a compass, basic demolition, and, for some, even hand-to-hand fighting. But even in 1943 many paratroopers had to jump behind enemy lines after only one training jump, and some had never jumped before.[45] The Soviet airborne divisions could not perform a basic airborne procedure: landing their soldiers, ready for action, at a certain point behind enemy lines. The jumps sometimes ended in horrific accidents because inexperienced pilots dropped paratroopers at night into a forest or a lake; many paratroopers were killed, injured, or drowned. When the Soviets launched their last large airborne operation on 24 September 1943, seeking to attack the Germans defending the western bank of the Dnepr River, untrained pilots dropped various paratrooper units not in the 10- by 14-kilometre area as planned but spread across a 30- by 90-kilometre region; some were dropped into the Dnepr and drowned, while others landed at the Soviet positions.[46] As the Germans reported, 'The whole action carries the stamp of dilettantism.'[47] The soldiers jumped at night without flashlights, or flares, and without being given a reserve meeting place; radio operators and those who carried radio batteries flew on different planes and could not find each other.[48] Having no appropriate training, Soviet paratroopers did not distinguish themselves in spectacular missions of the sort conducted by paratroopers during the German assault on the Danish Masnedø and Belgian Eben-Emael forts and Storstrøm Bridge in 1940, the British assault on Pegasus Bridge, or the American landing in Normandy in June 1944.

These examples of Soviet infantry specialists show that, although all they did indeed train for a longer time and, unlike mountain troops, on the terrain on which the Red Army had always expected to fight, the skills they acquired were still inadequate for the missions they were expected to accomplish. The Red Army's General Staff grossly underestimated the necessity, scope, and diversity of mission-tailored training for infantry specialists. The ability of Soviet 'mountain' units to fulfil their duties after basic training was as poor as the ability of other infantry specialists – snipers, skiers, mortar crews, scouts, or paratroopers. In the case of 'mountain' divisions, this universal underappreciation of special training, coupled with the lack of funds allotted for training and the shift of priorities from field exercises to parade drills and indoctrination, resulted in numerous flaws: the absence of climbing skills, gear, and proper uniforms; the recruitment of elderly residents of the plains; officers' tactical ignorance; poor marksmanship; the impotence of scouts and radio operators in the mountains; and the overall professional inferiority of Soviet 'mountain' personnel compared to their German counterparts.

How did the ability of infantry specialists to perform their duties and oppose their enemy after their basic training compare to that of soldiers operating heavy weapons requiring technical sophistication, such as artillery, tanks, and combat aircraft? After Stalin called artillery 'the god of modern war', Soviet propaganda turned his phrase into a cliché. The quality of Soviet artillery weapons was at least equal and sometimes superior to that of German ones.[49] However, the Germans manned their weapons with much greater skill. Even during the Winter War, when the Red Army experienced no shortage of men or ammunition, the training of artillery crews was at times limited to loading a gun with wooden dummy shells and taking aim; they frequently went to the front without having fired a single shot.[50] The painful experience of the Winter War made little impact on artillery drill and, with the entrance of the Soviet Union into the war against the Axis, the training time of artillery cadets was reduced to six to nine months.[51] One of them recalled that his time in artillery school was filled mainly with 'dull everyday parade drills ... We rarely had shooting exercises. At the final exam, only several men from each battery were tested. I shot only once, and once I performed as artillery spotter. [During the entire period of study] we shot at dummy tanks pulled by winches only twice.'[52] In 1941 and 1942, the Soviet 45-mm anti-tank gun was an adequate piece with an excellent sight, superior to the 37-mm Pak 36, the Wehrmacht's basic anti-tank gun of that time.[53] However, it could destroy German tanks only from a distance of several hundred metres; survival of its crew depended on their ability to deliver fast and accurate fire within seconds before tanks discovered their position and returned fire, which was deadly at such a distance.[54] It would have been logical to enforce particularly rigorous training of anti-tank crews to secure coherent action and good marksmanship but that was not the case. The training for this extremely dangerous job lasted only four months and was conducted in a manner that an anti-tank gun layer, the most important man in the crew, described thus: 'The training was brief ... On a training ground, we were allowed for the first time to shoot an armour-piercing shell at a dug-in tank. I hit it and after many pleas was allowed a second shot. Soon we were on a train heading for the Voronezh Front.'[55]

An artillery officer expressed his opinion about the enemy, which coincided with that of infantrymen: 'It was hard to fight the Germans. They were excellent, natural-born soldiers.'[56] Most Soviet senior officers ignored the fact that it was thorough training that turned German recruits into excellent soldiers. By 9 July 1941, the Red Army had lost 19,000 of the 32,900 artillery pieces that its front-line formations had on 22 June,[57] which made General Nikolai Vatutin, chief of staff of the North-Western Front, issue desperate directives in

Instructions on Anti-Tank Actions, prompting soldiers 'to collect mud and throw it into tanks' periscopes'.[58] The poor training of those who served the 'god of modern war' was largely responsible for the situation in which mud became the Red Army's anti-tank weapon a mere two weeks into the campaign.

The Red Army built an enormous armoured force to implement the Deep Operation doctrine, the main doctrine it followed before, during, and after the war. Given the perception of armour as the primary weapon of modern war, the General Staff should have paid particular attention to the efficacy of this force. In theory, a tank commander should have known tank design and armour tactics and been able to substitute for any crew member if needed, and every crew member should have been trained to substitute for any of his comrades.[59] How did the skills of Soviet tank crews correspond to this standard?

The Red Army attempted to attain this standard before the war but, when it expanded the number of its mechanised corps from eight to twenty-nine after February 1941, the new tank divisions, grossly underequipped and absolutely untrained, made up two-thirds of Soviet armour. In order to provide enough tank officers during this enormous expansion, the Red Army cut the training period of tank cadets to only six months, the same time as infantry cadets.[60] As one tank commander commented on his firing and driving practice in tank school, 'I shot three shells and emptied one machinegun magazine. What kind of training was that? There was some driving practice on a BT-5 [an obsolete model]. We were taught the very basics: how to make a move and drive straight forward.'[61] This tank commander was lucky compared to others who did not participate in even one session of firing practice before departing to the front.[62] The commander of the 8th Mechanised Corps admitted in June 1941 that, 'throughout the entire period of its existence, the corps's equipment and personnel had taken part in practically no tactical exercises'.[63] Most such exercises were theoretical: cadets practised tactics without tanks; they walked 'the way a tank rides' across the training ground, as the Reichswehr had done in the 1920s,[64] but the Reichswehr had no tanks at that time, whereas in June 1941 the Red Army had three times as many tanks as the Wehrmacht and all its European allies.[65] A cadet described the scope of tactical drill he received before going to battle thus: 'After our platoon and company were formed, we exercised once as a platoon and then once as a company, then we held a 50-kilometre march, and that was it.'[66] The Stavka and senior tank commanders issued numerous orders addressing the poor tactical skills of armour: the incoherent actions of tanks, infantry, and artillery; the piecemeal deployment of dispersed large formations, which sapped their strength; the stereotypical frontal attacks against strong anti-tank defences that led to enormous casualties; and the frequent loss of command and control because of poor radio skills.[67] These flaws were the outcome of woefully inadequate tactical training of tank commanders.

Other crew members were also undertrained: the 15th and 21st Mechanised Corps entered action in June 1941 with 60 per cent and 70 per cent, respectively, of their manpower conscripted only a month or two earlier.[68] After the beginning of the war, the training period of a tank driver was cut from one year to three months.[69] Many drivers arrived at the front with only two hours of practice. In most tank crews, nobody had enough training to replace the driver,[70] which meant that the entire crew became incapacitated if the driver was killed or injured. A tank gunner's practice was limited to ten or twelve shots in tank school, and tank commanders admitted that 'our tank crews shot quite inaccurately';[71] that may be why they occasionally rammed German tanks instead of seeking to destroy them from a distance with their powerful guns.[72] Although the survival of a tank crew depended on the coherent actions of all its members, they generally met for the first time only a few days before they left for the front and typically had only one brief training-ground practice together.[73] A tank commander described the crew assigned to him just before their departure for the front: the driver 'could basically not drive a tank after the brief training. The gun layer was ... a fat elderly man who could barely get into the tank. The gun loader ... was somewhat mentally impaired ... and feared the recoil.'[74] Such crews had little chance of survival on the battlefield.

Like the tank forces of other countries, Soviet tank divisions experienced their greatest attrition from breakdowns rather than combat. Colonel Dedov, chief of the armoured forces of the 6th Army, observed during the first days of the war: 'Most crews of KV and T-34 tanks ... are unable to fix even minor breakdowns', while Soviet mechanics were trained to operate only in shops.[75] Since Red Army armour conducted no long-range marching exercises, its General Staff did not understand that the tank force would dwindle quickly if ordered to undertake such marches. Stricken by panic in the first days after the German attack, the Red Army moved large armour formations back and forth across huge distances, losing most of its tanks during these marches without even having contact with the enemy.[76] The 19th Regiment of the 10th Tank Division, armed with brand new KV tanks, lost 86 per cent of them during a march on 22 and 23 June. The 12th Tank Division engaged in a 415-kilometre march, arriving at its destination four days later with only 75 of the 300 tanks that had begun the march; the rest were left broken down on the road.[77] Sometimes, SMERSh executed crews whose tanks broke down, suspecting foul play, but commanders attributed these grave losses without contact with the enemy primarily to the inexperience of the personnel, who either drove tanks in the wrong gear or could not fix minor breakdowns.[78]

The Red Army believed that it did not matter which designs were used in tank schools, most of which had only obsolete light BT tanks[79] that weighed 11.5 to 14 tonnes. New graduates were assigned to whatever tanks were available, including heavy KV tanks that weighed 47.5 tonnes and were to perform missions different from those of light tanks. Tank crews who found themselves in a tank of unfamiliar design usually had no time to retrain for their tank model. A tank commander describes his 'retraining' from a BT to a KV tank: when all the graduates arrived at the city square, where there were three KVs, 'we were allowed to get into the heavy tank to drive it to Lenin's monument, switch into reverse, and return'.[80] From this 'training course', he went directly to the battlefield, armed only with the knowledge of the KV tank that he had acquired in the city square. Such crews had to gain the necessary skills in combat, paying a hefty price for the lessons.

Although all reported advantages of the German armoured force 'were to be nullified by the courage and audacity of the Soviet crews',[81] the primitive training of Soviet armour guaranteed its enormous attrition and the gross imbalance of casualties in encounters with the well-trained Wehrmacht: within two weeks after the beginning of Operation Barbarossa, the Red Army had lost 11,700 of its 22,600 tanks,[82] and the Southwestern Front had lost 50 tanks for every German tank its soldiers had destroyed.[83] Such stunning casualties made little impact on the Red Army's approach to the training of tank crews in 1941–2. In the summer of 1942, most tank drivers sent to the 13th and 23rd Tank Corps of the Stalingrad Front had three to five hours of driving practice.[84] Only in the autumn of 1943, after the Stavka had calculated the price it had paid for the victory at Kursk, did it extend the training period of tank commanders to eight, twelve, or even eighteen months. From that point on, they were to spend several weeks on the training ground practising tactics, tank driving, and shooting; other crew members were to go through six months of training.[85] This improved the performance of Soviet armour to a degree, but the reinforcements arriving fresh from tank schools still had insufficient practice for the jobs they were supposed to perform; they still found themselves in unfamiliar tank types, and they had little opportunity to refine their training before going to battle. As a tank commander recalled, 'upon arrival, new reinforcements received only superficial instructions. They heard mainly two phrases: "You will learn in combat" and, directly before the engagement, "Do as I do!"'[86] Some of these crews did learn in combat and became experienced soldiers matching the Germans, but many, perhaps most, were killed or wounded during their first action.

The life expectancy of the Soviet tank crews was low compared to that of German crews. In October 1942, the Stavka prohibited the use of tanks against enemy tanks 'unless an overwhelming [numerical] superiority over the enemy has been secured'.[87] This happened long before the Germans deployed on the Eastern Front new-generation heavy tanks with greater firepower than the Soviet medium ones. In this way, the Stavka tacitly admitted that Soviet tank units armed with T-34, the best medium tank in the world, had little chance of winning an engagement against German tank crews driving obsolete models. Vasilii Briukhov, one of the most famous Soviet tank commanders, stated: 'I have to pay credit to German soldiers and officers: they were good warriors and in one-to-one combat they always caused a lot of trouble and casualties.'[88] If the training of Red Army armour, believed to be the primary weapon of modern war, was poor in comparison with their enemy's, it should have caused no surprise that the Soviet 'mountain' force, raised mainly as a concession to foreign trends rather than as a strategic imperative, could not match its German counterpart.

Surrounded by a romantic aura, 'Stalin's Falcons', as Soviet propaganda called the Red Air Force, enjoyed more public attention and admiration in the interwar years than all other arms taken together. By 1 October 1939, the Red Army had more combat aircraft than the air force of any of the other participants in World War II.[89] Pilots were the favourites of party leaders and perceived themselves as the cream of the Soviet officer corps. To what extent did their proficiency correspond to this perception?

During the interwar period, pilot cadets studied for two-and -a-half or three years before receiving their commissions as air force officers, and during the first year they received only theoretical instruction.[90] By the time a fighter pilot graduated from the air force school, he had acquired about forty-five hours of flight on combat aircraft, fifteen firing exercises at air targets, and ten individual exercises in air combat, but no practice in team air combat or in flying in clouds or poor weather. The air force rarely conducted winter exercises.[91] Such training was inadequate for the modern air force, especially if compared to the Luftwaffe, where pilots had to accumulate 250 hours of independent flight, during which they learned aerobatics, flying in difficult meteorological conditions, and individual and team air combat. After graduation, they joined reserve Luftwaffe units, and only after refining their skills there were they allowed to fly combat missions.[92]

The expansion of the Red Army after the beginning of World War II undermined the quality of air force pilot training as much as it did the training of tank crews, but it had an even worse impact on the ability of the Red Air Force to face the Luftwaffe than on the ability of Soviet armour to fight its German counterpart; Soviet armour could compensate, to a degree, for deficiencies in training with its considerable superiority in tank designs, whereas most new Soviet aircraft designs were slightly inferior to the German ones. However, the gap in the efficiency of the Luftwaffe versus the Red Air Force was much wider than the narrow margin in design quality would suggest. With the beginning of the air force expansion, the average training period of a Soviet combat pilot starting from zero dropped to twelve months and, of those who had graduated from civilian flying school, to eight or sometimes even four months.[93]

The Winter War demonstrated the poor proficiency of the Red Air Force even in the virtual absence of air combat. It was untrained to co-operate with infantry, so, when land forces requested close air support, the air command demanded that these forces be withdrawn from their vanguard positions to a distance of 2 kilometres before the aircraft bombed the enemy front trenches, to preclude hitting their own. Bomber navigators were trained only to conduct carpet bombing, releasing bombs upon the signal of their squadron leader rather than dropping them on a target independently; accurate bombing was thus beyond their capacity.[94] When Stalin ordered the destruction of a bridge over the Kuman River, the air force sent eighty bombers, which lined up one after another and dropped their bombs in turn from 1,200 metres. Only one bomb hit the bridge; it remains unclear from the report whether the bridge survived.[95]

Obviously, the air war against Germany would be a far tougher challenge than the actions against the Finns, but the Red Air Force failed to improve its training procedures. A severe fuel shortage forced commanders to replace flying exercises with a great range of activities unrelated to combat training. As Mark Solonin writes, by 1941, the Red Air Force had 'a gigantic network of flying schools but their cadets were busy perfecting their parade drill and unloading freight cars'.[96] During the first three months of 1941, the 9th Mixed Air Division had 1.3 shooting exercises per pilot and no bombing exercises. The pilots of the Kiev Special Military District gained only four hours of flight time during the same period and participated, on average, in less than one bombing, shooting, or air combat exercise per crew. Pilot schools had no trainers equipped with radio; therefore, the radio training of graduates was zero.[97] A young pilot who joined the air force in the summer of 1940 and was assigned to fly an I-16 fighter admitted that he learned little during his first year of service: 'Neither I nor my schoolmates could master this aircraft. What would you expect? We undertook only several dozen flights in circles and flew a bit over the airfield. We had no shooting exercises, nor did we practise dog fights. We would constantly lose our way, being unable to follow the [assigned] route.'[98]

About half of the aircraft designs that the Red Air Force had by 1941 – not only the obsolete I-16 fighter but also the new types, such as the LAGG-3, MIG-1, Pe-2, and Il-4 – were difficult to fly,[99] and most Soviet pilots had insufficient training to fly them safely. In Solonin's words, 'the "relaxed" attitude to combat drill ... resulted in a brutally high rate of lost aircraft and lives',[100] especially when, after the beginning of the war against Germany, pilots often had to fly in difficult weather conditions, which they had not encountered earlier. From 22 June to 3 July, the 161st and 163rd Fighter Regiments lost sixteen aircraft in combat and nineteen on the ground, and seventy-six aircraft crashed. The first actions against the Luftwaffe revealed that even most of the pilots who had entered service before the war 'had poor knowledge of the air combat tactics adopted by their own air force and by the enemy and could not effectively use aircraft weapons, either guns or bombs'.[101]

One veteran recalled that, after the Soviet Union entered the war, 'all training programmes went to hell: either we had no fuel, or something else. We basically stopped flying.' Another commented that pilots 'were trained [only] to be cadaver candidates'.[102] Air school graduates generally accumulated a mere five or six hours of independent flight on combat aircraft, and some had only one hour.[103] An instructor told a fresh lieutenant assigned to a fighter regiment: 'They will shoot you down on the second or the third day and that'll be it. What can you do? Hold the stick, take off, and land.'[104] Bomber pilots graduated from flying schools after only two or three bombing exercises and one long flight to a target.[105] Instructors trained them exclusively in 'safe' mode to avoid accidents, for which they were severely punished. As a result, a pilot recalled, 'the pilotage we had been taught in school was useless in combat ... Sharp turns were not just discouraged – they were banned. God forbid a hedge-hopping flight! ... The punishment was most severe, up to a court-martial ... However, as we found after arrival at the front, the sharper a manoeuvre the better.'[106] Lucky fighter cadets had two or three exercises in firing at air targets; the unlucky ones had none. When one of them asked his instructor, 'How can I go to the front without a single shooting exercise?', the latter replied, 'You'll learn how to shoot at once if you want to live!'[107] Many pilots did not know how to use aircraft sights, so fighter pilots were trained to open fire at enemy aircraft only from the extremely short distance of about 50 metres or less, whereas German fighters usually hit their targets from a distance four times as great.[108] The original Il-2 ground assault model had an accurate collimator gun sight, but it turned out to be too complicated for poorly trained pilots, and in 1942 it was replaced with a primitive mechanical sight that such pilots could handle.[109] When a new bomber crew was assembled, it was allowed to make three to five training flights to a 'target' to attain at least some cohesion among crew members. The pilot and navigator needed considerably more training together in order to successfully find a target located several hundred kilometres in the enemy rear, approach it with a series of evasive manoeuvres, and hit it, but they received no such training opportunity.[110] The Soviet Pe-2 dive bomber was far superior to the German Ju 87 model: much faster, more robust, better armed, and able to carry a heavier bomb load. Yet the Germans attained greater results with the obsolete Ju 87 than the

Soviets did with the Pe-2 because few Soviet pilots and navigators were taught dive bombing before the summer of 1943, so the vast majority bombed from a flat trajectory, thus forfeiting accuracy, the main asset of dive bombers. Until the very end of the war, Pe-2 crews bombed predominantly from a flat trajectory because of inadequate pilot training.[111]

Casualties caused by poor training were as devastating to the air force as they were to armour. As one veteran pilot admitted, 'We did not exercise dog fights ... We practised during action; that is why we suffered [heavy] losses.' At the beginning of the war, said another, 'a squadron lasted three or four days – and these were our best pilots'.[112] The reinforcements who arrived after graduating from a shortened flying programme sustained even heavier casualties. Within five weeks of the German attack in June 1941, the Red Air Force had lost half of its 20,000 aircraft.[113] Soviet war memoirs narrate devastating losses: how a Soviet air assault regiment lost all but two of its thirty-plus aircraft in one mission, while a bomber regiment sustained steady casualties of 20 to 25 per cent per mission; how fifteen aircraft crashed when they were flying through a thunderstorm because their pilots were unaware of the risk; and how fifty-six bombers were lost in one raid on a well-protected port.[114] The Luftwaffe never suffered similar disasters.

Many fighter pilots and perhaps most ground assault and bomber crews had never jumped with a parachute before they went into action. Such pilots kept their parachutes in bags without repacking them; the parachutes became compressed and often failed to open when they had to jump.[115] For this reason, many preferred to crash-land if they were hit instead of bailing out, even if the chances of a successful crash-landing were minuscule; thus, many paid with their lives for the absence of parachute training.

As with armour, pilot schools used obsolete aircraft types for exercises, and the time allotted to graduates to familiarise themselves with the modern aircraft they were to fly in combat was extremely brief. A pilot who had previously flown only an obsolete I-153 biplane was allowed to make only two flights in a modern Iak-7 fighter and one flight in a modern La-5 fighter, after which he went into combat in a La-5.[116] When a Soviet bomber regiment received American A-20 Boston bombers via Lend-Lease, its commander told the pilots: 'Today we'll study them; tomorrow we'll have training flights; and the day after tomorrow we'll fly combat missions.'[117] He stuck to his word and they went into battle two days later. Since all the inscriptions on the aircraft gadgets and switches were in English, which nobody could read, the pilots did not learn some of their functions until the end of the war.

After the disasters suffered by the Red Air Force in the first years of the war, its commanders concluded that 'the main reason for the high casualties among young pilots was the sheer stupidity and tactical ignorance of regiment and squadron commanders. They threw a large number of young pilots into battle without properly checking their pilotage skills and without additional combat training.'[118] After commanders acknowledged this fact, they began sending the fresh graduates of pilot schools to reserve air regiments, where they spent between ten days and three months refining their skills and practising air combat on the type of aircraft they were to fly. Only after such additional training were they transferred to front-line units and attached one-on-one to experienced pilots who coached them in combat.[119] However, this practice became the rule only in 1943, and even then a Soviet pilot lasted, on average, merely two months after his arrival at the front. War veterans state that only after mid 1944 did new pilots begin receiving adequate training in reserve regiments,[120] but this opinion may reflect primarily the overwhelming numerical superiority over the Luftwaffe attained by that time rather than the qualitative improvement of training.

Thus, throughout most of the war, Soviet novices could not match the proficiency of Luftwaffe beginners, and the Red Air Force continued to bet on numbers rather than skill. When asked to name at least one flaw of German fighter pilots in 1942, a veteran fighter pilot of the Red Air Force answered: 'None that I can think of.'[121] Other pilots agreed that most Luftwaffe personnel 'were excellent pilots; their fire accuracy was superb, their tactics were almost always impeccable, and they co-ordinated their actions in combat very well ... At the beginning of the war ... German pilots had almost perfect training ... By 1943, when we had killed many German pilots with pre-war training, the proficiency of their new arrivals became considerably lower.'[122] Yet even in 1943, when German flying schools cut their programme to 100 hours of independent flight, the Luftwaffe training was still much more thorough than the training Soviet beginners ever received before or during the war. As one Soviet veteran observed, 'German pilots fought admirably to the last day'; another noted, 'We always suffered higher casualties.'[123]

It is a well-known fact that the quality of the Red Army's training was lower than that of the Wehrmacht. However, the view from below, offered by soldiers' memoirs, exposes the stunning enormity of this gap. Most Soviet veterans assessed the entry-level skills of Red Army manpower as inferior, and actions in 1941 and 1942 proved that Soviet soldiers fighting in more habitual terrain displayed no more professionalism than their comrades in the mountains. Skill deficiencies were largely responsible for the loss of half of the Red Army's heavy weapons during the first weeks of Operation Barbarossa and for the 1:28 ratio of German and Soviet non-recoverable personnel casualties on the Eastern Front in 1941.[124]

Granted, the superior training of the Wehrmacht did not necessarily reflect a difference in the overall combat capacities of the respective armed forces, because professionalism was only one of many factors affecting combat capacity. Soviet generals learned, with time, how to fight a modern war with the force they had at hand – poorly trained but larger than that of the enemy and supported by overwhelming numbers of high-quality weapons. The Red Army had more time to adapt to modern warfare on the plains than in the mountains, and its effort eventually bore fruit: in 1943, it began attaining its operational and strategic goals more effectively than the Wehrmacht. It seems, therefore, that the Red Army's effectiveness against the enemy depended less on the battle environment than on the length of the learning process. In the high Caucasus, the trial-and-error process was too short to produce tangible results: although the new mountain companies were trained and equipped much better than the units that had fought during the active phase of the battle, their combat capacity against the German mountain troops remained untested.

Even on the plains the half-hearted efforts to improve the Red Army's drill procedures brought only modest results: the gap in training between German and Soviet soldiers narrowed with time but continued to exist until 1945. The Red Army won the war with soldiers whose skill remained inferior to that of their German counterparts, generously paying for the victory with the lives of their men. An artillery officer remarked, 'It would be possible to win by other methods, but we focused squarely on victory … regardless of cost.' Another officer observed: 'Germans sought to spare their men and equipment; this is an indisputable fact. We, in contrast, shed our blood like water.'[125] When the Red Army launched Operation Bagration in the summer of

1944, arguably its most spectacular World War II operation, it enjoyed a superiority of 4.6:1 in manpower, 8:1 in tanks, and 11.5:1 in aircraft at that section of the front, but it lost two men for every German casualty. During Operation Barbarossa in the same region in the summer of 1941, when the German Army Group Centre and the opposing Soviet forces were roughly equal in numbers, the Germans attained an even more spectacular success while losing thirty times fewer men than the Red Army did during Operation Bagration.[126] The imbalance in professionalism was primarily responsible for these outcomes.

Since the Red Army could not properly train its manpower even for actions in the terrain in which it had always expected to operate, its failure to train mountain formations – a low-priority force intended for an exotic battle environment – is hardly surprising. Soviet generals raised three times as many divisions designated as 'mountain' as the Germans did and believed that this force, even if untrained, would be adequate to handle a potential low-probability challenge. The ratio of casualties in every battle the Red Army fought in the mountains proved them wrong. However, since mountain warfare was a minor aspect of the war on the Eastern Front, the untrained 'mountain' divisions constituted a less severe handicap for the Red Army than the untrained regular infantry, radio operators, artillerists, armour, and air force.

That is why, perhaps, the overall negative World War II experience of the Red Army in the mountains made no impact on the Soviet approach to mountain warfare: the Soviet Army disbanded the few mountain divisions that existed by the end of the war and it stepped on the same rake again during its next serious mountain challenge, in Afghanistan in 1979–89, when, having no mountain troops, it had to deploy conventional infantry and airborne divisions, and also Spetsnaz, in the Hindu Kush. Although much better trained than regular infantry, the Spetsnaz units were few and small, and neither they nor the paratroopers received training in mountaineering or the tactics of mountain warfare, nor did they have climbing gear. The absence of a mountain force was one of the reasons why the Soviets could neither seal the border with Pakistan to cut the endless flow of supplies, weapons, and manpower to insurgents nor protect their own supply lines from frequent attacks. The First Chechen War, in 1994–6, again demonstrated the advantages enjoyed by those who knew the mountains over those who did not. Only the Second Chechen War, in 1999–2009, prompted Russia to restore several mountain brigades, beginning in December 2007; by 2014, 7,000 soldiers had passed through mountaineering training.[127] Islamic radicalism, with guerrilla warfare as its strategy of choice, will be Russia's major military challenge in the foreseeable future. The new mountain brigades will soon have a chance to prove their worth.

ACKNOWLEDGEMENTS

This project was supported by a generous grant awarded by the Social Sciences and Humanities Research Council of Canada, which allowed me to develop it in depth. This funding also enabled me to participate in an excellent conference at the Royal Military Academy Sandhurst, organised by Simon Trew and Robert von Maier, at which I received valuable input from top military historians. The University of Calgary Centre for Military, Security, and Strategic Studies invited me to present a guest lecture on the battle of the Caucasus, thus giving me an opportunity to share my findings with affiliates of this most respected military history agency in Canada. I am indebted to Michael Watson who guided the revisions of my manuscript with inexhaustible patience; to Karen Anderson, a copy-editor of great competence; to Darina Mladenova and Ioana Mikhailova, who produced maps for this book; to Igor Matveev, whom I consulted on radio communications in the mountains; to Alexandr Nepomniashchii, who joined me in retracing Alexander Suvorov's march across the Swiss Alps; to Marina Zakharova, who helped me to acquire photographs for this book; and to the many sport tourists who shared their views on Soviet wartime military mountaineering: Vladimir Chukov, polar explorer; Grigorii Don, Vladimir Korenev, Aleksandr Erkovich, Pavel Kibardin, and Vladimir Tolpegin from the Moscow Globus Tourist Club; Nikolai Riazanskii, Anatolii Serebrennikov, Ramil Deianov, Vladislav Popchikovskii, Aleksandr Lifanov, Leonid Levitin, Evgenii Lapshin, Leonid Direktor, Andrei Lebedev, Mikhail Studitskii, Mikhail

Vasil'ev, Ravil Aibatulin, Sergei Klimin, David Lekhtman, Evgenii Nizhnikovskii, Alexandr Stupakov, and Svetlana Tsvetkova from the Moscow City Tourist Club; Boris Gusev and Dmitrii Shagaev from the Riazan Tourist Club; and members of the Odessa Romantik Tourist Club.

NOTES

Introduction: The Path Towards the Top Summits of World War II

1. N. Kurchev, *Gory v nashikh serdsakh* (St Petersburg: Professiia, 2001), 18, 19.
2. Such as 'Barbarisovyi kust' written by Nikolai Morenets in 1942 and 'U kostra', ibid., 19, 20, 82, 86, 87.
3. Vladimir Vysotskii, 'Edelweiss Troops' (1966). See also Vladimir Vysotskii, 'K vershine' (1969), in Kurchev, *Gory v nashikh serdsakh*, 489, 490.
4. Numerous interviews carried out with present-day Russian and Ukrainian sport tourists on this subject demonstrate this. For some unknown reason, Russians refer to all German mountain troops who fought in the Caucasus as 'Edelweiss', the nickname of the 1st German Mountain Division, thus ignoring the 4th Mountain Division, nicknamed 'Gentian'.
5. 'Priiem v Kremle v chest' uchastnikov parada Pobedy', *Pravda* 152 (27 June 1945), 2.
6. Hubert Lanz, *Gebirgsjäger* (Bad Nauheim: Hans-Hennig Podzun, 1954); Rudolf Konrad and E. Wolf Rümmler, *Kampf um dem Kaukasus* (Munich: Copress, 1954); Josef Martin Bauer, *Unternehmen 'Elbrus'* (Munich: Herbig, 1976); Helmut Blume, *Zum Kaukasus 1941–1942. Aus dem Tagebuch und Briefen eines jungen Artilleristen* (Tübingen: Narr Francke Attempto, 1993).
7. Joachim Hoffmann, *Kaukasien 1942/1943. Das deutsche Heer und die Orientvölker der Sowjetunion* (Freiburg: Rombach Verlag KG, 1991).
8. Alex Buchner, *Kampf im Gebirge* (Munich: Schild, 1957); Alex Buchner, *Gebirgsjäger an allen Fronten* (Berg am See: Kurt Vowinckel, 1984); Ronald Kaltenegger, *Gebirgsjäger im Kaukasus* (Graz: Leopold Stocker Verlag, 1995); Wilhelm Tieke, *The Caucasus and the Oil* (Winnipeg: J. J. Fedorowicz, 1995).
9. I. V. Tiulenev, *Cherez tri voiny* (Moscow: MO SSSR, 1960); I. V. Tiulenev, *Krakh operatsii 'Edelveis'* (Ordzhonikidze: Ir, 1975); Pavel Sudoplatov, *Spetsoperatsii* (Moscow: Olma-Press, 1999).
10. Khadzhi Murat Ibragimbeili, *Krakh 'Edel'veisa' i blizhnii vostok* (Moscow: Nauka, 1977).

11. O. Opryshko, *Zaoblachnyi front Priel'brus'ia* (Moscow: MO SSSR, 1976); V. Gneushev and A. Poput'ko, *Taina Marukhskogo lednika* (Moscow: Sovetskaia Rossiia, 1966); V. I. Lota, *Sorvat' 'Edelveis'* (Moscow: Kuchkovo pole, 2010); Il'ia Moshchanskii, *Stoiat' nasmert'!* (Moscow: Veche, 2010); Il'ia Moshchanskii, *Oborona Kavkaza* (Moscow: Veche, 2009).
12. M. M. Bobrov, *Front nad oblakami* (St Petersburg: Sankt-Peterburgskii gumanitarnyi universitet profsoiuzov, 2005); N. I. Medvenskii, *Boevye operatsii na perevalakh Abkhazii v khode bitvy za Kavkaz 1942–1943 gg.* (Sukhum, 2012).
13. A. Gusev, *El'brus v ogne* (Moscow: MO SSSR, 1980); A. Grechko, *Bitva za Kavkaz* (Moscow, MO SSSR, 1969); V. Abramov, *Na ratnykh dorogakh* (Moscow: MO SSSR, 1962).
14. V. Bekishvili, 'Oborona kavkazskikh perevalov' (PhD dissertation, Tbilisi, 1977).
15. V. Zolotarev and G. Sevost'ianov, eds., *Velikaia Otechestvennaia voina, 1941–1945* (Moscow: Nauka, 1998), vol. I, 380.
16. S. Linets and S. Ianush, *Oborona Severnogo Kavkaza v gody Velikoi Otechestvennoi voiny* (Moscow: Ileksa, 2010).
17. V. Shapovalov, ed., *Bitva za Kavkaz v dokumentakh i materialakh* (Stavropol: SGU, 2003); U. Batyrov, S. Grebeniuk and V. Matveev, eds., *Bitva za Kavkaz* (Moscow: Triada, 2002).
18. Carl von Clausewitz, *On War* (Princeton: Princeton University Press, 1984), 170, 171.

1 Russia's Historical Experience in Mountain Warfare

1. Clausewitz, *On War*, 170.
2. Ibid., 170, 171.
3. Dmitrii Miliutin, *Istoriia voiny 1799 goda mezhdu Rossiei i Frantsiei* (St Petersburg: Imperatorskaia Akademiia Nauk, 1857), III:476.
4. Clausewitz, *On War*, 101, 119.
5. Suvorov to Rastopchin (13 October 1799) in Egor Fuks, *Istoriia rossiisko-avstriiskoi kampanii 1799 g.* (St Petersburg: Voennaia tipografiia General'nogo Shtaba, 1825–6), III:387; Nikolai Griazev, 'Pokhod Suvorova v 1799 g.', in S. Semanov, ed., *Aleksandr Vasil'evich Suvorov* (Moscow: Russkii mir, 2000), 205.
6. Griazev, 'Pokhod Suvorova', 219–21.
7. Miliutin, *Istoriia voiny 1799 goda*, II:298; III:520.
8. Suvorov himself wrote on 13 and 14 October that he had only 10,000 able-bodied men, 'barefoot and naked', which did not include Cossacks: Suvorov to Rastopchin in Fuks, *Istoriia*, III:387; Miliutin, *Istoriia voiny 1799 goda*, II:323.
9. The French assessed their casualties during the fifteen days of the Swiss campaign – including the actions against another Russian corps and the Austrians allied with the Russians – as 6,000 men killed, wounded, or taken prisoner: Miliutin, *Istoriia voiny 1799 goda*, III:526.
10. Carl von Clausewitz, *Shveitsarskii pokhod Suvorova* (Moscow: Voennoe izdatel'stvo, 1939), 133.
11. Konstantin Benkendorf, 'Vospominaniia', in Ia. Gordin, ed., *Darginskaia tragediia* (St Petersburg: Zvezda, 2001), 228; Nikolai Del'vig, 'Vospominanie ob ekspeditsii v Dargo', ibid., 425; Aleksandr Dondukov-Korsakov, 'Moi vospominaniia', in Iakov Gordin, ed., *Osada Kavkaza* (St Petersburg: Zvezda, 2000), 434, 435.

12. V.N.N., 'Kavkazskaia ekspeditsiia v 1845 godu', in Gordin, ed., *Darginskaia tragediia*, 131, 132, 216, 217. The author of the latter memoir wrote under the pen name V.N.N. His identity is unknown.
13. Benkendorf, 'Vospominaniia', 231; Del'vig, 'Vospominanie', 409.
14. Benkendorf, 'Vospominaniia', 268–70; V.N.N., 'Kavkazskaia ekspeditsiia', 101; Del'vig, 'Vospominanie', 413; V. Geiman, '1845 god', in Gordin, ed., *Darginskaia tragediia*, 346, 347; Erast Andreevskii, 'Darginskii pokhod', ibid., 501; Dondukov-Korsakov, 'Moi vospominaniia', 200.
15. August-Wilhelm von Merklin, 'Vospominaniia', in Gordin, ed., *Darginskaia tragediia*, 520.
16. G. Filipson, 'Vospominaniia', in Gordin, ed., *Osada Kavkaza*, 104–7, 175, 176; V.N.N., 'Kavkazskaia ekspeditsiia', 152–4; Del'vig, 'Vospominanie', 426, 427; M. Ol'shevskii, 'Zapiski', in Gordin, ed., *Osada Kavkaza*, 306; Aleksandr Nikolai, 'Iz vospominanii o moei zhizni', in Gordin, ed., *Darginskaia tragediia*, 473.
17. Nikolai Gorchakov, 'Ekspeditsiia v Dargo', in Gordin, ed., *Darginskaia tragediia*, 453.
18. Dondukov-Korsakov, 'Moi vospominaniia', 500; Del'vig, 'Vospominanie', 409.
19. V. Achkasov et al., *Russko-turetskaia voina 1877–1878* (Moscow: Voenizdat, 1977), 24, 57.
20. Nikolai Vyrypaev, *Shest' mesiatsev na Shipke* (St Petersburg: Chtenie dlia soldat, 1884), 8.
21. Achkasov et al., *Russko-turetskaia voina*, 115, 116.
22. I. Gerua, ed., *Opisanie russko-turetskoi voiny 1877–1878 gg.* (St Petersburg: Voennaia tipografiia, 1912), VIII/2:219.
23. Ibid., IV/1:32; Vyrypaev, *Shest' mesiatsev*, 21, 24, 40.
24. Gerua, *Opisanie*, IV/1:96, 97, 104.
25. I. Prochko, *Istoriia razvitiia artillerii* (Moscow: Poligon, 1994), 415, 421; Vyrypaev, *Shest' mesiatsev*, 74, 75.
26. 'Materialy dlia istorii Shipki', *Voennyi sbornik* 135(1) (1880):35; 'Materialy dlia istorii Shipki', *Voennyi sbornik* 135(2) (1880):266.
27. Gerua, *Opisanie*, VIII/1:78.
28. V. Nemirovich-Danchenko, *God voiny: dnevnik russkago korrespondenta* (St Petersburg: Novoe vremia, 1878), II:106; 'Materialy dlia istorii Shipki', *Voennyi sbornik* 135(2) (1880):252.
29. 'Zhurnal voennykh deistvii 24-i pekhotnoi divizii', in *Sbornik materialov po russko-turetskoi voine 1877–1878 gg. na Balkanskom poluostrove* (St Petersburg: Izdanie Voenno-Istoricheskoi Komissii Glavnago Shtaba, 1898), VI:93–111; Gerua, *Opisanie*, VIII/1:82, 83, 86, 87.
30. Gerua, *Opisanie*, VIII/1:155–8; 'Materialy dlia istorii Shipki', *Voennyi sbornik* 135 (2) (1880):273.
31. Edward Erickson, *Ordered to Die* (Westport, CT: Greenwood Press, 2001), 53–5.
32. Nikolai Korsun, *Sarykamyshskaia operatsiia* (Moscow: Voenizdat, 1937), 10, 14, 20, 82.
33. Ibid., 30, 66, 69.
34. Ibid., 61, 62, 65, 82, 145.
35. Although Erickson maintains that the temperature dropped to −40 °C, such temperatures are hardly possible in this region: Erickson, *Ordered to Die*, 59. The Russian sources mention −20 °C as the lowest temperature: A. Kersnovskii, *Istoriia russkoi armii* (Moscow: Golos, 1993), IV:132.
36. Korsun, *Sarykamyshskaia operatsiia*, 54, 64.
37. Ibid., 129, 130.

38. Kersnovskii, *Istoriia russkoi armii*, IV:134.
39. Ibid., IV:134.
40. Korsun, *Sarykamyshskaia operatsiia*, 103, 111; Erickson, *Ordered to Die*, 59.
41. M. Bonch-Bruevich, *Poteria nami Galitsii v 1915 g.* (Moscow: 20-ia gosudarstvennaia tipografiia, 1920), I:27, 28.
42. Graydon Tunstall, *Blood on the Snow* (Lawrence: University Press of Kansas, 2010), 1.
43. Aleksei Brusilov, *Moi vospominaniia* (Moscow: Rosspen, 2001), 120, 121.
44. Tunstall, *Blood on the Snow*, 38, 40, 52, 69, 76, 159.
45. Headquarters of the 8th Army to General Pustovoitenko (1 February 1915), Rossiiskii gosudarstvennyi voenno-istoricheskii arkhiv (hereafter cited as RGVIA), f. 2067, op. 1, d. 303, l. 109; General Zarin to Headquarters of the Southwestern Front (23 January 1915), RGVIA, f. 2067, op. 1, d. 303, l. 270; Kersnovskii, *Istoriia russkoi armii*, III:266.
46. Brusilov, *Moi vospominaniia*, 131.
47. Tunstall, *Blood on the Snow*, 61, 66, 116, 211.
48. Ibid., 37, 49, 67, 83, 92, 155; 'Spravka' (no date), RGVIA, f. 2067, op. 1, d. 307, ll. 81, 82.
49. Bonch-Bruevich, *Poteria nami Galitsii*, 91.
50. Tunstall, *Blood on the Snow*, 12.
51. Bonch-Bruevich, *Poteria nami Galitsii*, 113.
52. Miliutin, *Istoriia voiny 1799 goda*; Fuks, ed., *Istoriia rossiisko-avstriiskoi kampanii 1799 g.*; Clausewitz, *Shveitsarskii pokhod Suvorova*; M. Bogdanovich, *Pokhody Suvorova v Italii i Shveitsarii* (St Petersburg: Voennaia tipografiia, 1846); Rudolf von Reding-Biberegg, *Pokhod Suvorova cherez Shveitsariiu* (St Petersburg: T-vo khudozhestvennoi pechati, 1902); *Obzor voennykh deistvii na Kavkaze v 1845 godu* (Tbilisi: Shtab otdel'nago kavkazskago korpusa, 1846); V.N.N., 'Kavkazskaia ekspeditsiia'; R. Fadeev, *60 let Kavkazskoi voiny* (Moscow: Gosudarstvennaia publichnaia istoricheskaia biblioteka Rossii, 2007); Gerua, *Opisanie russko-turetskoi voiny*; 'Materialy dlia istorii Shipki', *Voennyi sbornik* 135(2) (1880); Franz von Kuhn, 'Gornaia voina', *Voennyi sbornik* 133 (1880); *Sbornik materialov po russko-turetskoi voine 1877–1878 gg. na Balkanskom poluostrove*. See also interwar studies by former imperial senior officers: Korsun, *Sarykamyshskaia operatsiia*; N.R., 'Sarykamysh', *Voina i revoliutsiia* 3 (1927); Bonch-Bruevich, *Poteria nami Galitsii*.
53. Kuhn, 'Gornaia voina', 20.
54. Clausewitz, *Shveitsarskii pokhod Suvorova*, 243.
55. Korsun, *Sarykamyshskaia operatsiia*, 100, 154, 157.
56. Ibid., 155–8.
57. Ibid., 151–3, 156–8.
58. A. Kavtaradze, 'A. V. Suvorov v otechestvennoi istoriografii', in A. Beskrovnyi and A. Preobrazhenskii, eds., *Aleksandr Vasil'evich Suvorov* (Moscow: Nauka, 1980), 45.
59. Ibid., 52.
60. S. Lukirskii, ed., *Taktika v trudakh voennykh klassikov* (Moscow: Gosudarstvennoe voennoe izdatel'stvo, 1926), vol. II; D. Skorodumov, 'Plan Shveitsarskogo pokhoda Suvorova', *Voenno-istoricheskii zhurnal* 2 (1941), 65.
61. Vladimir Lenin, 'IV Konferentsiia professional'nykh soiuzov i fabrichno-zavodskikh komitetov Moskvy', in Lenin, *Polnoe sobranie sochinenii* (Moscow: Izdatel'stvo politicheskoi literatury, 1967), XXXVI:438.

62. Kirill Moskalenko, *Na iugo-zapadnom napravlenii, 1943–1945* (Moscow: Nauka, 1973), II:435. Nikolai Korsun never calls Yudenich by name in the study of the Sarikamis operation, referring to him only by his title.
63. General Pavel Bodin, chief of staff of the TCF (6 October 1942), Tsentral'nyi arkhiv Ministerstva oborony Rossiiskoi Federatsii (hereafter cited as TsAMO), f. 47, op. 1063, d. 161, l. 19.
64. Vladimir Lenin, 'Sotsializm i voina', in Lenin, *Polnoe sobranie sochinenii*, XXVI:316.
65. Korsun, *Sarykamyshskaia operatsiia*, 152.
66. Clausewitz, *On War*, 418.
67. Ibid., 420.
68. Ibid., 422.
69. Ibid., 423, 424.
70. M. Al'tgovzen, 'Polkovodcheskoe iskusstvo Suvorova v Shveitsarskom pokhode', in A. Sukhomlin, ed., *Suvorovskii sbornik* (Moscow: AN SSSR, 1951), 148.

2 Soviet Preparations for War in the Mountains

1. V. Antonov-Saratovskii, 'Turizm, partiia i gosudarstvo', *Na sushe i na more* (hereafter *NSINM*) 1 (1930), 1.
2. I. Kuznetsov, 'Iz istorii turizma', *NSINM* 5 (1941), 20.
3. V. Antonov-Saratovskii, 'Na vysshuiu stupen'', *NSINM* 11 (1930), 2.
4. G. Dolzhenko, *Istoriia turizma v dorevoliutsionnoi Rossii i SSSR* (Rostov-on-Don: Izdatel'stvo Rostovskogo Universiteta, 1988), 77; Grigorii Usyskin, *Ocherki istorii rossiiskogo turizma* (St Petersburg: Gerda, 2000), 103.
5. 'Sotsialisticheskoe stroitel'stvo i turizm', *NSINM* 2(1930), 1.
6. Ibid., 1, 2.
7. 'Ot redaktsii', *NSINM* 1 (1930), 1.
8. Usyskin, *Ocherki istorii*, 107; Igor' Orlov and Elena Iurchikova, *Massovyi turizm v stalinskoi povsednevnosti* (Moscow: Rosspen, 2010), 76, 77.
9. Orlov and Iurchikova, *Massovyi turizm*, 8.
10. A. Livshin and I. Orlov, 'Sovetskaia vlast' plius voenizatsiia vsei strany', in A. V. Surin et al., *Istoriki razmyshliaiut* (Moscow: Universitetskii gumanitarnyi litsei, 1999), 217.
11. M. Pogrebetskii, *Tri goda bor'by za Khan-Tengri* (Kharkov: Ukrains'kyi robitnyk, 1935), 116.
12. Nikolai Aretov, 'Emotsii, identichnost, literatura i natsionalna mitologiia: mnogoposochnost na vruzkite', in Nikolai Aretov, ed., *Purva radost e za mene. Emotsionalnoto sudurzhanie na bulgarskata natsionalna identichnost: istoricheski koreni i suvremenni izmereniia* (Sofia: Kralitsa Mab, 2012), 11; V. Dobkovich, *Turizm v SSSR* (Leningrad: Vsesoiuznoe obshchestvo po rasprostraneniiu politicheskikh i nauchnykh znanii, 1954), 3.
13. 'Sotsialisticheskoe stroitel'stvo i turizm', 2.
14. Antonov-Saratovskii, 'Turizm, partiia i gosudarstvo', 2.
15. A. De-Lazari, 'Kul'turnaia revoliutsiia i turizm', *NSINM* 3 (1930), 14; A. Gashchuk and V. Vukolov, *Turizm v vooruzhennykh silakh SSSR* (Moscow: Voenizdat, 1983), 16.
16. L. Gurvich, 'Turizm i oborona', *NSINM* 13 (1932), 10.
17. N. Pokrovskii, 'Turizm i oborona', *NSINM* 1 (1941), 4.

18. L. Barkhash, 'Distsiplina sredi turistov', *NSINM* 11 (1930), 15, 16.
19. V.P., 'Kak vesti dnevnik', *NSINM* 11 (1930), 15; L. Mashuk, 'Uchet i obmen opytom leta', *NSINM* 21 (1931), 2; 'Poriadok utverzhdeniia marshrutov', *NSINM* 6 (1933), 14.
20. Vasilii Semenovskii, *Al'pinizm* (Moscow: FiS, 1936); V. Abalakov, A. Get'e and D. Gushchin, *Vysokogornye uchebnye pokhody i ekspeditsii* (Moscow: Fizkul'tura i turizm, 1937); M. Pogrebetskii, 'Tekhnika gorovoskhozhdeniia', *NSINM* 17 (1932), 14, 15; B. Dzerdzeevskii, 'Prognoz pogody zimoi', *NSINM* 2 (1941), 12.
21. L. Gurvich, 'Izvlechem bol'shevistskii urok', *NSINM* 31–2 (1932), 15; L. Barkhash, 'Vnimanie, samodeiatelnye turisty', *NSINM* 1 (1935), 4.
22. I. Cherepov, 'Kak sokhranit' turistskoe snariazhenie', *NSINM* 15 (1933), 15.
23. Industry in the post-communist space followed the lead of amateur designers and began producing high-quality gear on the basis of these designs.
24. Antonov-Saratovskii, 'Na vysshuiu stupen'', 2.
25. F. Traskovich, 'Za rost obshchestva i razvitie samodeiatel'nogo turizma', *NSINM* 6 (1935), 2.
26. N. Krylenko, 'Al'pinizm na novom etape', *NSINM* 4 (1936), 4; G. Arem'ev, 'OPT v Kabardino-Balkarii', *NSINM* 12 (1929), 15.
27. Pogrebetskii, *Tri goda bor'by*, 52–4; Mashuk, 'Uchet i obmen opytom leta', 1; A. Zhemchuzhnikov, 'Turist – na gornye lyzhi', *NSINM* 2–3 (1933), 7; O. Aristov and Iu. Korobkov, 'Po tropam iuzhnoi Kirgizii', *NSINM* 17 (1933), 8–10.
28. M. Pogrebetskii, 'Kak byl vziat Khan-Tengri', *NSINM* 7 (1932), 4, 5; M. Pogrebetskii, 'Kak byl vziat Khan-Tengri', *NSINM* 9 (1932), 8, 9; D. Gushchin, 'Kak byl vziat pik Stalina', *NSINM* 18 (1933), 5–7; Dolzhenko, *Istoriia turizma*, 89.
29. Gusev, *El'brus v ogne*, 148.
30. 'Polozhenie o znachke Al'pinist SSSR I stupeni', in L. Gutman, S. Khodakevich and I. Antonovich, *Uchebnoe posobie dlia nachinaiushchikh al'pinistov* (Moscow: Fizkul'tura i sport, 1939); S. Ianin, 'Kursy v gorakh', *NSINM* 1 (1935), 7; S. Nikolaev, 'Gornye massovki i uchebnye pokhody', *NSINM* 10 (1933), 14.
31. Zinaida Rikhter, *Shturm El'brusa: vtoraia al'piniada RKKA* (Moscow: Molodaia gvardiia, 1935), 9.
32. Orlov and Iurchikova, *Massovyi turizm*, 72; 'Instruktory po turizmu', *NSINM* 5 (1941), 2; L. Gutman, S. Khodakevich and I. Antonovich, *Tekhnika al'pinizma* (Moscow: Fizkul'tura i sport, 1939), 14.
33. D. Gushchin, 'Shkola al'pinizma', *NSINM* 8 (1935), 13.
34. Krylenko, 'Al'pinizm na novom etape', 6; Gutman, Khodakevich and Antonovich, *Tekhnika al'pinizma*, 14.
35. Tsentral'nyi Sovet OPTE, *Spasatel'naia rabota v gorakh* (Moscow: Put' Oktiabria, 1936).
36. O. Kotovich, 'Pobezhdat' gory bez avarii', *NSINM* 5 (1941), 8; German Andreev, 'Istoriia spasatel'noi sluzhby SSSR – Rossii', http://alpklubspb.ru/ass/46.htm (accessed on 8 May 2017).
37. Livshin and Orlov, 'Sovetskaia vlast'', 218.
38. K. Furst, 'Turizm za granitsei', *NSINM* 9 (1930), 20.
39. 'Ustav Obshchestva proletarskogo turizma RSFSR', in Orlov and Iurchikova, *Massovyi turizm*, 169.
40. 'Krepi oboronu SSSR', *NSINM* 22 (1930), 1.
41. Gashchuk and Vukolov, *Turizm v vooruzhennykh silakh*, 17.
42. De-Lazari, 'Kul'turnaia revoliutsiia i turizm', 14.
43. 'Vsem otdeleniiam OPTE', *NSINM* 15 (1930), 1.
44. V. Perlin, 'Shkola al'pinista i boitsa', *NSINM* 18 (1931), 3.

45. 'Krepi oboronu SSSR', 2.
46. Furst, 'Turizm za granitsei', 20; K. Grigor'ev, 'Turizm za granitsei', *NSINM* 3 (1930), 19; K. Grigor'ev, 'Voennyi turizm na zapade', *NSINM* 4 (1931), 18–20.
47. Pokrovskii, 'Turizm i oborona', 4, 5; V. Vorob'ev, 'Kavkaz pod bokom', *NSINM* 1 (1932), 15; P. Noskov, 'Boevye zadachi lodochnogo turizma', *NSINM* 5 (1930), 3; V. Koval'chuk et al., eds., *Dobrovol'nye obshchestva v Petrograde-Leningrade v 1917–1937 gg.* (Leningrad: Nauka, 1989), 137; Dolzhenko, *Istoriia turizma*, 92.
48. Obshchestvo sodeistviia oborone, aviatsionnomu i khimicheskomu stroitel'stvu (Association for Assistance to Defence, Aviation, and Chemistry).
49. 'Novaia popytka podniat'sia na Belukhu', *NSINM* 25 (1931), 9.
50. N. Koritskii, 'Voenizatsiia turizma', *NSINM* 3 (1930), 2.
51. Pavel Sudoplatov, *Spetsoperatsii* (Moscow: Olma-Press, 1999), 235. The NKVD (Narodnyi komissariat vnutrennikh del SSSR (USSR People's Commissariat of Internal Affairs)) was the overarching term for the Soviet police, including the secret police.
52. 'Gornomu turizmu – boevye tempy', *NSINM* 16 (1932), 2.
53. V. Vorob'ev, 'Tekhnika gornogo turizma dybom', *NSINM* 15 (1932), 13.
54. 'Gornomu turizmu – boevye tempy', 2.
55. Perlin, 'Shkola al'pinista i boitsa', 2, 3; V. Vorob'ev, 'Na kruton pod'eme', *NSINM* 20 (1931), 5.
56. Nikolaev, 'Gornye massovki i uchebnye pokhody', 14.
57. Vorob'ev, 'Na kruton pod'eme', 4.
58. De-Lazari. 'Kul'turnaia revoliutstiia i turizm', 14.
59. '*Shutkam ne uchat v nashikh lageriakh.*
Esli pridetsia voevat' v gorakh,
Vmeste s ledorubom voz'mesh ty avtomat
I, kak na strakhovke, sozhmesh eto priklad': 'Baksanskaia', in Kurchev, *Gory v nashikh serdsakh*, 19.
60. M. Demin, 'Molodye turisty-bezbozhniki', *NSINM* 3 (1930), 21.
61. Gurvich, 'Turizm i oborona', 10.
62. Pokrovskii, 'Turizm i oborona', 4.
63. S. Kamenev, 'Turizm i oborona', *NSINM* 11 (1929), 9.
64. 'Proletarskii turizm – na sluzhbu oborone strany', *NSINM* 4 (1933), 8–10.
65. A. Sediakin, 'Turizm i al'pinizm v Krasnoi armii', *NSINM* 4 (1935), 5. See also V. Perlin, 'Turizm i Krasnaia armiia', *NSINM* 4 (1931), 1, 2; A. Nesterov, 'Turizm na sluzhbe oborone SSSR', *NSINM* 4 (1933), 3, 4; 'Turistskii den'', *NSINM* 4 (1933), 2.
66. Koritskii, 'Voenizatsiia turizma', 2.
67. 'Proletarskii turizm – na sluzhbu oborone strany', 8–10.
68. 'Za massovyi turizm v Krasnoi armii', *NSINM* 12 (1930), 8; Grigor'ev, 'Voennyi turizm na zapade', 18–20.
69. 'Za massovyi turizm v Krasnoi armii', 5.
70. M. Sitnikov, 'Dva goda raboty', in V. Perlin, *Turizm v Krasnoi armii* (Moscow: Fizkul'tura i turizm, 1930), 39.
71. S. Pankratov, 'Pod znakom rosta', ibid., 39.
72. Orlov and Iurchikova, *Massovyi turizm*, 130.
73. N. Krylenko, ed., *V lednikakh: vysokogornye pokhody komandirov RKKA v 1934 g.* (Moscow: Gosudarstvennoe voennoe izdatel'stvo, 1935), 9.
74. V. Perlin, 'Turizm v Krasnoi armii', *NSINM* 10 (1931), cover.
75. Perlin, ed.,*Turizm v Krasnoi armii*, 3–4; Blagomyslov, '2,000 kilometrov na shliupkakh', ibid., 76, 77.

76. S. Pankratov, 'Turizm i oborona', *NSINM* 5 (1932), 2, 3; Dolzhenko, *Istoriia turizma*, 88.
77. B. Kal'pus, 'Turizm v RKKA', *NSINM* 2 (1936), 13.
78. N. Ialukhin, I. Dolgikh and G. Mukhoedov, eds., *Shturm Belukhi* (Novosibirsk: Zapadno-Sibirskoe Kraevoe Izdatel'stvo, 1936), 156–8.
79. 'Pokhod zakavkazskoi pekhotnoi shkoly', *NSINM* 22 (1930), 10; Pankratov, 'Turizm i oborona', 2.
80. V. Perlin, 'Na loshadiakh cherez Shari-Vtsek', *NSINM* 21 (1930), 6, 7.
81. Gashchuk and Vukolov, *Turizm v vooruzhennykh silakh*, 10.
82. Dolzhenko, *Istoriia turizma*, 87; V. Klement'ev, *Cherez lednikovye perevaly Kavkaza: voenno-turistskii pokhod* (Moscow: Fizkul'tura i turizm, 1931), 22; V. Klement'ev, 'Voskhozhdenie na Kazbek', in Perlin, ed., *Turizm v Krasnoi armii*, 60; V. Klement'ev, 'Na vershinu El'brusa', ibid., 108.
83. Dolzhenko, *Istoriia turizma*, 89; V. Perlin, 'Krasnaia zvezda na El'bruse', *NSINM* 17 (1933), 5, 6; Gashchuk and Vukolov, *Turizm v vooruzhennykh silakh*, 20, 24.
84. Krylenko, 'Al'pinizm na novom etape', 4.
85. 'Turizm v Krasnoznamennoi Kavkazskoi', *NSINM* 19 (1930), cover.
86. Vasilii Klement'ev, *Boevye deistviia gornykh voisk* (Moscow: Voenizdat, 1940), 40.
87. Ibid., 76, 85, 193.
88. Ibid., 176, 178, 185; Klement'ev, *Cherez lednikovye perevaly*, 123, 124.
89. Klement'ev, *Boevye deistviia*, 178, 189, 190; Klement'ev, *Cherez lednikovye perevaly*, 8, 14, 33, 34, 111–24, 147, 152.
90. Klement'ev, *Boevye deistviia*, 181–5.
91. Ibid., 194, 198; Klement'ev, *Cherez lednikovye perevaly*, 152.
92. Klement'ev, *Boevye deistviia*, 93, 197.
93. Budylin, 'Ratsiia na Elbruse', *NSINM* 22–4 (1932), 26. See also B. Kudinov, 'Radiostantsiia v gorakh', *NSINM* 8 (1935), 14; Ialukhin, Dolgikh and Mukhoedov, eds., *Shturm Belukhi*, 201–5; Evgenii Abalakov, *Na vysochaishikh vershinakh Sovetskogo Soiuza* (Moscow: AN SSSR, 1962), 43, 51.
94. Gashchuk and Vukolov, *Turizm v vooruzhennykh silakh*, 22, 26; Kal'pus, 'Turizm v RKKA', 13.
95. Kal'pus, 'Turizm v RKKA', 13.
96. N. Krylenko, *Po neissledovannomy Pamiru* (Moscow: Gosudarstvennoe izdatel'stvo geograficheskoi literatury, 1980), 325; K. Voroshilov, 'Prikaz Narkoma Soiuza SSR', *NSINM* 1 (1935), 2.
97. Voroshilov, 'Prikaz Narodnogo Komissara Oborony' (21 December 1934), in Krylenko, ed., *V lednikakh*, 3. The correct height is 5,642 metres but they did not know it at that time.
98. Gusev, *El'brus v ogne*, 145. The badge was introduced in February 1934, and in 1934 and 1935 about 5,000 men and women earned it annually: *NSINM* 2 (1936), 2; Krylenko, 'Al'pinizm na novom etape', 5.
99. V. Zhigulin, 'Nositeli znachkov', *NSINM* 5 (1941), 18.
100. The full-strength Soviet mountain division was to have 8,829 soldiers: Moshchanskii, *Stoiat' nasmert'!*, 17. However, one-third of its personnel did not require mountaineering training – artillery crews, engineers, and members of the signals and transportation units.
101. I. Il'ina, *Obshchestvennye organizatsii Rossii v 1920-e gody* (Moscow: IRI RAN, 2000), 71.
102. Usyskin, *Ocherki istorii*, 123.

103. Orlov and Iurchikova, *Massovyi turizm*, 101, 105; V. Savel'ev, 'Gotovim gornykh strelkov', *NSINM* 5 (1941), 2.
104. L. Golovkova, 'Shpionazh na vershinakh', in V. Shantsev et al., eds., *Butovskii poligon, 1937–1938 gg.* (Moscow: Al'zo, 2002), VI:46.
105. Ibid., VI:48–53; Vladimir Kizel', *Gory zovut* (Moscow: Lokis, 2005), 46, 47.
106. Oleg Suvenirov, *Tragediia RKKA, 1937–1938* (Moscow: Terra, 1998), 373, 375, 382.
107. Grigor'ev, 'Turizm za granitsei', 19. The Scottish Highlanders never fought in the mountains during World War I, but these Soviet officers had heard that they fought well and mistook them for mountain troops.
108. De-Lazari, 'Kul'turnaia revoliutsiia i turizm', 15. This is a reference to the Soviet punitive expedition of 700 soldiers, most of them residents of the plains, outmanoeuvred and exterminated by poorly armed Dagestani rebels in the Arakan Gorge in October 1920: Donogo Khadzhi-Murad, 'Arakanskii sindrom', http://muhajir.netai.net/yaseen/arkans.htm (accessed on 8 May 2017).
109. Levandovskii, commander of the Transcaucasian Military District, 'Tsirkuliarnoe pismo' (1935), Rossiiskii gosudarstvennyi voennyi arkhiv (hereafter cited as RGVA), f. 25873, op. 1, d. 102, ll. 257–320; Levandovskii, 'Tsirkuliarnoe pismo' (July 1935), RGVA, f. 25873, op. 1, d. 102, ll. 354–362; Zhukov, deputy head of the RKKA Cavalry Inspectorate, 'Zamechaniia i ukazaniia po khodu boevoi podgotovki chatei 2-i gorno-kavaleriiskoi kavkazskoi divizii' (29 September 1935), RGVA, f. 25873, op. 1, d. 103, ll. 17–25.
110. 'Doklad kapitana Vagnera: "Gornaia voina. Ee osobennosti, osnovnye polozheniia i organizatsiia"' (before October 1937) (hereafter cited as 'Doklad kapitana Vagnera'), RGVA, f. 25873, op. 1, d. 102, l. 126.
111. Ibid., ll. 116–118.
112. Ibid., ll. 141, 200.
113. Ibid., ll. 125, 134, 135, 137, 147.
114. Ibid., ll. 135, 136.
115. Ibid., ll. 140.
116. Ibid., l. 122.
117. Ibid., ll. 130, 131.
118. Ibid., ll. 124, 125.
119. Ibid., ll. 242, 243.
120. Ibid., ll. 247, 248.
121. Ibid., ll. 140, 240, 245–252.
122. Ibid., ll. 133, 246.
123. Ibid., ll. 232–235, 254, 255.
124. Ibid., ll. 120, 230, 241.
125. Aleksei Tereshkin, *Istoriia otechestvennogo voennogo al'pinizma* (documentary film, 2012), part 2.
126. I. Cherepov, ed., *Nastavlenie dlia gorno-strelkovykh chastei germanskoi armii* (Moscow: Voenizdat, 1941).
127. V. Abalakov, Get'e and Gushchin, *Vysokogornye uchebnye pokhody i ekspeditsii*; Semenovskii, *Al'pinizm*; Vitalii Abalakov, *Osnovy al'pinizma* (Moscow: FiS, 1941); Gutman, Khodakevich and Antonovich, *Tekhnika al'pinizma*; I. Cherepov, *Al'pinizm* (Moscow: Fizkul'tura i sport, 1940); I. Cherepov, *Gornolyzhnyi sport* (Moscow: Fizkul'tura i sport, 1940).
128. General'nyi shtab Krasnoi Armii [General Staff of the Red Army], *Nastavlenie dlia deistvii voisk RKKA v gorakh* (Moscow: NKO SSSR, 1936), 24.
129. Ibid., 9, 10, 47, 77.

130. Ibid., 10, 47.
131. Ibid., 11, 27.
132. Ibid., 15, 31–4.
133. Ibid., 9.
134. Ibid., 62, 100.
135. Ibid., 14.
136. Ibid., 3.
137. These were the 9th Caucasus, the 47th Georgian, and the 63rd Georgian 'Mountain' Divisions and the 17th Caucasian 'Mountain-Cavalry' Division: Mikhail Levandovskii to Aleksandr Egorov, 'Doklad nachal'niku shtaba RKKA o krupnom uchenii 1936 g.' (20 June 1936), RGVA, f. 25873, op. 1, d. 116, l. 7.
138. Levandovskii, 'Krupnoe uchenie voisk Zakavkazskogo voennogo okruga' (1936) (hereafter cited as 'Krupnoe uchenie'), RGVA, f. 25873, op. 1, d. 111, l. 3.
139. Levandovskii to Egorov, 'Doklad nachal'niku shtaba RKKA', RGVA, f. 25873, op. 1, d. 116, l. 8.
140. 'Stenogramma plenuma Revvoensoveta Kavkazskoi Krasnoznamennoi Armii' (December 1933), RGVA, f. 25873, op. 1, d. 95, l. 65.
141. Levandovskii, 'Krupnoe uchenie', ll. 105, 106.
142. Ibid., l. 180.
143. Colonel Ivanov, head of the Communications Department of the Transcaucasian Military District, 'Obshchie vyvody: voprosy upravleniia i sviazi na krupnom uchenii v 1936 g.' (1936) (hereafter cited as 'Obshchie vyvody'), RGVA, f. 25873, op. 1, d. 116, l. 660.
144. Ibid., l. 657.
145. Levandovskii, 'Krupnoe uchenie', l. 157.
146. Ivanov, 'Obshchie vyvody', ll. 661, 662.
147. Glavnoe upravlenie sviazi [Main Signals Directorate], *Spravochnik po voiskovym i tankovym radiostantsiiam* (Moscow: Voennoe izdatel'stvo NKO, 1943), III:157.
148. Ivanov, 'Obshchie vyvody', l. 663.
149. Suvenirov, *Tragediia RKKA*, 375.
150. D. Shebalin, ed., *Nastavlenie dlia deistvii voisk v gorakh* (Moscow: NKO SSSR, 1940), 3.
151. Ibid., 149.
152. Ibid., 16.
153. Ibid., 12, 20, 45, 126, 139.
154. Ibid., 25, 138, 158.
155. General'nyi shtab Krasnoi Armii, *Nastavlenie*, 92, 102; Shebalin, *Nastavlenie*, 5, 224, 234.
156. Shebalin, *Nastavlenie*, 9, 78, 124; 'Doklad kapitana Vagnera', l. 200.
157. 'Doklad kapitana Vagnera', 223.
158. Ibid.
159. Ibid., 6, 56, 217, 218.
160. Ibid., 72, 217.
161. Klement'ev, *Boevye deistviia gornykh voisk*.

3 First Battle Tests and the Handicaps of Selective Learning

1. O. Manninen, 'Pervyi period boev', in E. Kul'kov and O. Rzheshevskii, eds., *Zimniaia voina, 1939–1940* (Moscow: Nauka, 1998), I:148.

2. Mark Solonin, *'Uprezhdaiushchii udar' Stalina* (Moscow: Iauza-Katalog, 2014), 79.
3. The peacetime Finnish Army had 60 times fewer men, 100 times fewer combat aircraft, and 350 times fewer tanks than the peacetime Red Army: Solonin, ibid., 15.
4. Major Mukhin and General Iurii Novosel'skii in Kul'kov and Rzheshevskii, eds., *Zimniaia voina,* II:50, 57.
5. Narodnyi Komissariat Oborony [People's Commissariat of Defence], *Vremennyi Polevoi Ustav RKKA PU-36* (Moscow: Gosudarstvennoe Voennoe Izdatel'stvo NKO SSSR, 1937), 165.
6. Ibid., 166–9.
7. General Nikolai Voronov (April 1940) in V. A. Zolotarev, ed., *Tainy i uroki zimnei voiny, 1939–1940* (St Petersburg: Poligon, 2002), 394.
8. General Mikhail Kirponos and Marshal Boris Shaposhnikov in Kul'kov and Rzheshevskii, eds., *Zimniaia voina,* II:31, 190.
9. Kirponos, General Vladimir Kurdiumov and Joseph Stalin, ibid., II:31, 127, 190.
10. General Stepan Oborin, ibid., II:38.
11. Voronov, in Zolotarev, ed., *Tainy i uroki*, 396, 417.
12. Kirponos and Kurdiumov in Kul'kov and Rzheshevskii, eds., *Zimniaia voina,* II:32, 125; N. Kaliazintsev in V. Sebin, ed., *Pamiat' i skorb'* (Petrozavodsk: Administration of Pitkiaranty, 1999), 77.
13. Zolotarev, ed., *Tainy i uroki*, 128–9, 192–3.
14. Lev Mekhlis, head of the Main Political Directorate of the Red Army, in Kul'kov and Rzheshevskii, eds., *Zimniaia voina,* II:169.
15. Mekhlis (10 January 1940) in Zolotarev, ed., *Tainy i uroki*, 270.
16. General Stepan Cherniak, General Vasilii Chuikov and Kurdiumov in Kul'kov and Rzheshevskii, eds., *Zimniaia voina,* II:59, 102, 127.
17. Battalion Commissar Mikhail Butkovskii (28 December 1939) and General Andrei Zelentsov (20 January 1940) in Zolotarev, ed.,*Tainy i uroki*, 224, 297.
18. Kurdiumov in Kul'kov and Rzheshevskii, eds., *Zimniaia voina,* II:126.
19. Mekhlis in Zolotarev, ed., *Tainy i uroki*, 271.
20. Kirponos, Oborin, General Semen Nedvigin and Kurdiumov in Kul'kov and Rzheshevskii, eds., *Zimniaia voina,* II:31, 38, 70, 129; Voronov in Zolotarev, ed., *Tainy i uroki*, 407.
21. Stalin in Kul'kov and Rzheshevskii, eds., *Zimniaia voina,* II:243.
22. Colonel Ivan Roslyi, Oborin and Nedvigin, ibid., II:26, 39, 70.
23. Chuikov, ibid., II:110.
24. General Vladimir Grendal', ibid., II:236. See a similar claim by Army Commissar Aleksandr Zaporozhets, ibid., II:240.
25. Semenov, Roslyi, General Arkadii Ermakov, and Zaporozhets, ibid., II:22, 27, 224, 240.
26. Nedvigin, ibid., II:70.
27. General Nikolai Iakovlev (11 February 1940) in Zolotarev, ed., *Tainy i uroki*, 333, 334; Zaporozhets in Kul'kov and Rzheshevskii, eds., *Zimniaia voina,* II:240.
28. Mukhin in Kul'kov and Rzheshevskii, eds., *Zimniaia voina,* II:50.
29. Nedvigin, ibid., II:69. See similar comments in Oborin, ibid., II:36; and in Voronov in Zolotarev, ed., *Tainy i uroki*, 410.
30. Kliment Voroshilov (no date) in Zolotarev, ed., *Tainy i uroki*, 429; General Petr Pshennikov in Kul'kov and Rzheshevskii, eds., *Zimniaia voina,* II:27. See similar comments in General Filipp Alabushev and Kurdiumov, ibid., II:48, 125; Voronov in Zolotarev, ed., *Tainy i uroki*, 411.
31. Pshennikov and Kurdiumov in Kul'kov and Rzheshevskii, eds., *Zimniaia voina,* II:29, 125.

32. Suvenirov, *Tragediia RKKA*, 330.
33. Voronov in Zolotarev, ed., *Tainy i uroki*, 410.
34. Stalin in Kul'kov and Rzheshevskii, eds., *Zimniaia voina*, II:280.
35. Novosel'skii, Colonel Vladimir Kriukov, Nedvigin, General Valerian Frolov and Grendal', ibid., II:56, 68, 70, 100, 236.
36. Pshennikov and Novosel'skii, ibid., II:29, 56, 57.
37. Stalin, ibid., II:84. See also Kirill Meretskov (6 December 1939) in Zolotarev, ed., *Tainy i uroki*, 152.
38. Murav'ev in Kul'kov and Rzheshevskii, eds., *Zimniaia voina*, II:84.
39. Brigade Commissar Konstantin Murav'ev, ibid., II:83.
40. Oborin, Kurdiumov and Zaporozhets, ibid., II:37, 125, 241.
41. Kurdiumov, ibid., II:125.
42. General Semen Zhavoronkov (14 December 1939) and Voronov in Zolotarev, ed., *Tainy i uroki*, 192, 388.
43. Ermakov in Kul'kov and Rzheshevskii, eds., *Zimniaia voina*, II:224.
44. Voronov in Zolotarev, ed., *Tainy i uroki*, 392.
45. G. Paramoshkov and N. Koliazintsev in Sebin, ed., *Pamiat' i skorb'*, 58, 77.
46. Frolov and Colonel Petr Shevchenko in Kul'kov and Rzheshevskii, eds., *Zimniaia voina*, II:98, 118; Nikishev in Zolotarev, ed., *Tainy i uroki*, 264.
47. Nikishev in Zolotarev, ed., *Tainy i uroki*, 254. See also Voronov, ibid., 392, 402, 414.
48. I. Giatsintov in Sebin, ed., *Pamiat' i skorb'*, 49.
49. Zaporozhets in Kul'kov and Rzheshevskii, eds., *Zimniaia voina*, II:242.
50. Colonel N. Raevskii (31 December 1940) in Zolotarev, ed., *Tainy i uroki*, 232–4.
51. Meretskov (2 December 1939) and Voroshilov (18 December 1939), ibid., 131, 200.
52. Chuikov in Kul'kov and Rzheshevskii, eds., *Zimniaia voina*, II:104; General Sokolov (28 November 1939) in Zolotarev, ed., *Tainy i uroki*, 237.
53. Novosel'skii, Shevchenko and Kurdiumov in Kul'kov and Rzheshevskii, eds., *Zimniaia voina*, II:58, 118, 125.
54. Nedvigin, ibid., II:71.
55. Stavka (7 February 1940) in Zolotarev, ed., *Tainy i uroki*, 240, 241.
56. Voroshilov (6 February 1940) and Vladimir Grendal' (24 February), ibid., 238, 245.
57. Voroshilov (6 February 1940), Stavka (7 February 1940), and General Semen Timoshenko (14 January 1940), ibid., 238, 240, 268.
58. General Pavel Egorov (8 February 1940) and Stavka (9 February 1940), ibid., 243, 244.
59. Stavka (7 February 1940), ibid., 240, 241.
60. Voronov, ibid., 403.
61. Nikishev, ibid., 256.
62. Shaposhnikov in Kul'kov and Rzheshevskii, eds., *Zimniaia voina*, II:187.
63. Voroshilov (no date) in Zolotarev, ed., *Tainy i uroki*, 426.
64. Voroshilov (no date), ibid., 433.
65. The author walked along the Mannerheim Line from the Baltic coast to Leipiasuo Station – the region where the major actions took place – and was surprised to see how inflated, for different political reasons, the strength of the defences was by both sides of the conflict.
66. Grigorii Krivosheev, ed., *Rossiia i SSSR v voinakh XX veka* (Moscow: OLMA Press, 2001), 211.
67. Rostislav Zhidkov in Artem Drabkin, ed., *Vstavai, strana ogromnaia* (Moscow: Iauza-Eksmo, 2010), 184.
68. Lanz, *Gebirgsjäger*, 10.

69. Ibid., 10, 13–17.
70. V. Abalakov, Get'e and Gushchin, *Vysokogornye uchebnye pokhody i ekspeditsii*, 6.
71. 'Doklad kapitana Vagnera', l. 113.
72. Leont'ev, head of the NKVD Struggle Against Banditry Department, 'Doklad o rezul'tatakh bor'by s banditizmom' (30 August 1944), Gosudarstvennyi arkhiv Rossiiskoi Federatsii (hereafter cited as GARF), f. 9478, op. 1, d. 63, ll. 8, 9, 12.
73. Alexander Statiev, 'The Nature of Anti-Soviet Armed Resistance, 1942–1944: The North Caucasus, the Kalmyk Autonomous Republic, and Crimea', *Kritika: Explorations in Russian and Eurasian History* 6/2 (2005), 295.
74. A. Bezugol'nyi, *Narody Kavkaza i Krasnaia armiia* (Moscow: Veche, 2007), 139–41.
75. Ibid., 140, 141; Colonel Volkovich, commander of the 394th Rifle Division, 'Doklad Voennogo Soveta 46-i armii' (14 May 1942), TsAMO, f. 1720, op. 1, d. 8, l. 64.
76. Bezugol'nyi, *Narody Kavkaza,* 146, 196, 199.
77. Ibid., 196, 200, 201.
78. General Ishchenko, 'Doklad nachal'nika shtaba Zakavkazskogo voennogo okruga' (13 March 1942), ibid., 345.
79. Conversation between General Ivan Maslennikov, commander of the Northern Army Group, and General Vasilii Khomenko, commander of the 44th Army (25 December 1942), ibid., 369.
80. Ibid., 144, 199.
81. Mikhail Gioev, *Bitva za Kavkaz: razdum'ia frontovogo ofitsera* (Vladikavkaz: Ir, 2007), 78, 79; Abramov, *Na ratnykh dorogakh*, 152.
82. Bezugol'nyi, *Narody Kavkaza*, 243, 275, 276, 287.
83. Commissar Khromov, 'Vsem voenkomam chastei 9-i gsd' (2 March 1942), TsAMO, f. 1064, op. 1, d. 40, l. 25.
84. Bezugol'nyi, *Narody Kavkaza*, 196, 197, 285, 302.
85. Statiev, 'The Nature of Anti-Soviet Armed Resistance', 289.
86. On 13 October 1943, the State Defence Committee ordered the TCF to draft recruits of 'only Russian, Ukrainian, Belorussian, and other non-Caucasus ethnic groups', thus excluding not only the ethnic groups of North Caucasus but also those of Transcaucasia: Bezugol'nyi, *Narody Kavkaza,* 159, 184.
87. Ibid., 200, 201, 219.
88. Volkovich, 'Doklad Voennogo Soveta 46-i armii' (14 May 1942), TsAMO, f. 1720, op. 1, d. 8, ll. 64, 67.
89. Kh. Nadorshin, head of the Political Section of the Northern Army Group (18 October 1942), in V. Iampol'skii et al., eds., *Organy gosudarstvennoi bezopasnosti SSSR v Velikoi Otechestvennoi voine* (Moscow: Rus', 2003), III/2:400.
90. Bezugol'nyi, *Narody Kavkaza*, 307.
91. Nadorshin in Iampol'skii et al., eds., *Organy*, III/2:399.
92. Colonel Dreev, 'Spetssoobshchie o sostoianii 394-i sd' (17 November 1942), TsAMO, f. 47, op. 1063, d. 692, l. 212; Major Litvinov, senior signals officer of the Operations Group for the Defence of TCR with the 394th Rifle Division, to Lieutenant-Colonel Popov, deputy head of the Operations Group (12 November 1942), TsAMO, f. 47, op. 1063, d. 691, l. 40v; Bezugol'nyi, *Narody Kavkaza*, 198.
93. Bezugol'nyi, *Narody Kavkaza*, 223, 226; Nadorshin in Iampol'skii et al., eds., *Organy,* III/2:400.
94. Nadorshin in Iampol'skii et al., eds., *Organy*, III/2:400, 401.
95. Bezugol'nyi, *Narody Kavkaza*, 227.

96. 'Zhurnal boevykh deistvii Zakfronta' (15 August 1942), TsAMO, f. 47, op. 1063, d. 183, ll. 118, 119; Bezugol'nyi, *Narody Kavkaza*, 240. During Beria's trial in July 1953, Tiulenev blamed him for banning ethnic divisions, especially Azerbaijani ones, from the front line because of their alleged cowardice: Bezugol'nyi, *Narody Kavkaza*, 224.
97. Bezugol'nyi, *Narody Kavkaza*, 357.
98. Ibid., 240.
99. Grigorii Lesin in Artem Drabkin, ed., *Vytashchit' s togo sveta* (Moscow: Eksmo, 2012), 323.
100. Bezugol'nyi, *Narody Kavkaza*, 233.
101. Gusev, *El'brus v ogne*, 11.
102. David Glantz, *Stumbling Colossus: The Red Army on the Eve of World War* (Lawrence: University of Kansas Press, 1998), 152.
103. The 9th, 20th, 47th, 63rd, 76th and 77th 'Mountain' Divisions and the 17th 'Mountain-Cavalry' Division: Colonel Levushkin, 'Spravka' (15 December 1939), RGVA, f. 25873, op. 1, d. 145, l. 487.
104. 'Stenogramma soveshchaniia ob itogakh boevoi i politicheskoi podgotovki' (3 January 1938), RGVA, f. 25873, op. 1, d. 132, ll. 7, 8, 13, 33, 37, 38.
105. Colonel Konstantin Leselidze, acting commander of the 63rd 'Mountain' Division (2 April 1938), RGVA, f. 34446, op. 1, d. 29, ll. 62, 63.
106. 'Stenogramma soveshchaniia ob itogakh boevoi i politicheskoi podgotovki' (3 January 1938), RGVA, f. 25873, op. 1, d. 132, l. 63.
107. Colonel Grishchenko, 'Doklad Voennomu Sovetu Zak.VO po boevoi i politicheskoi podgotovke' (11–12 October 1939), RGVA, f. 25873, op. 1, d. 144, l. 126.
108. Colonel Neskubo, 'Tezisy doklada na rasshirennom zasedanii Voennogo Soveta Zak.VO po 20-i gsd' (11–12 October 1939), RGVA, f. 25873, op. 1, d. 144, ll. 208–217; Colonel Makshanov, 'Tezisy doklada na rasshirennom zasedanii Voennogo Soveta Zak. VO po 76-i gsd' (11–12 October 1939), RGVA, f. 25873, op. 1, d. 144, ll. 245–259.
109. Colonel Maslov, 'Tezisy doklada na rasshirennom zasedanii Voennogo Soveta Zak.VO po 9-i gsd' (11–12 October 1939), RGVA, f. 25873, op. 1, d. 144, l. 232.
110. Colonel Andreev, 'Tezisy doklada komandira 63-i gsd' (11–12 October 1939), RGVA, f. 25873, op. 1, d. 144, ll. 199, 205.
111. Grishchenko, 'Doklad Voennomu Sovetu Zak.VO po boevoi i politicheskoi podgotovke' (11–12 October 1939), RGVA, f. 25873, op. 1, d. 144, l. 133; Battalion Commissar Romanov, 'Tezisy doklada na rasshirennom zasedanii Voennogo Soveta Zak.VO po 77-i gsd' (11–12 October 1939), RGVA, f. 25873, op. 1, d. 144, l. 276; Colonel Sakharov, 'Otchet o dvustoronnem takticheskom uchenii, provedennom chastiami 77-i gsd' (June 1939), RGVA, f. 25873, op. 1, d. 145, ll. 528–551.
112. Grishchenko, 'Doklad Voennomu Sovetu Zak.VO po boevoi i politicheskoi podgotovke' (11–12 October 1939), RGVA, f. 25873, op. 1, d. 144, ll. 134, 143; Colonel Seredkin, 'Tezisy doklada na rasshirennom zasedanii Voennogo Soveta Zak. VO po itogam boevoi i politicheskoi podgotovke voisk okruga' (11–12 October 1939), RGVA, f. 25873, op. 1, d. 144, ll. 13, 14.
113. Gusev, *El'brus v ogne*, 11.
114. RGVA, f. 34446, op. 1, d. 37.
115. Grechko, *Bitva za Kavkaz* (1969), 168.
116. E. Abalakov, *Na vysochaishikh vershinakh*, 10, 261.

117. Sankt-Peterburg Alpine Club, 'Al'pinisty severnoi stolitsy', http://alpklubspb.ru/ass/a155-3.htm (accessed on 8 May 2016).
118. Volkovich, 'Doklad Voennogo Soveta 46-i armii' (14 May 1942), TsAMO, f. 1720, op. 1, d. 8, l. 65.
119. I. Cherepov, 'Kreplenie lyzhnika-turista', *NSINM* 31–2 (1932), 14.
120. Gusev, *El'brus v ogne*, 17; Cherepov, *Gorno-lyzhnyi sport*, 35, 49, 50.
121. Cherepov, *Gorno-lyzhnyi sport*; I. Cherepov, *Gornolyzhnaia podgotovka* (Moscow: Voenizdat, 1941).
122. Gusev, *El'brus v ogne*, 17, 19.
123. Grishchenko, 'Doklad Voennomu Sovetu Zak.VO po boevoi i politicheskoi podgotovke' (11–12 October 1939), RGVA, f. 25873, op. 1, d. 144, l. 143.
124. Colonel Kechiev, 'V gorakh Albanii', *NSINM* 2 (1941), 14.
125. Colonel Kechiev, 'Boevye deistviia v Al'pakh', *NSINM* 4 (1941), 13, 14.
126. Bezugol'nyi, *Narody Kavkaza*, 194, 203.
127. Lieutenant-Colonel Zav'ialov, 'Oborona Glavnogo Kavkazskogo Khrebta' (22 September 1943) (hereafter cited as 'Oborona Glavnogo Kavkazskogo Khrebta'), TsAMO, f. 47, op. 1063, d. 504, l. 16v.
128. Nagovitsyn, 'Svedeniia o natsional'nom sostave' (no date), TsAMO, f. 401, op. 9511, d. 111, l. 81; Bezugol'nyi, *Narody Kavkaza*, 221.
129. Gusev, *El'brus v ogne*, 14.
130. Ibid., 17.
131. 'Doklad kapitana Vagnera', ll. 242, 243; 'Gornye lageri', *NSINM* 4 (1936), 2; Purtseladze, TCF inspector of mountaineering training, 'Gornaia i gorno-lyzhnaia podgotovka' (26 November 1942), TsAMO, f. 47, op. 1063, d. 692, l. 143; Gusev, *El'brus v ogne*, 12.
132. Gusev, *El'brus v ogne*, 12.
133. Captain O. Logofet, inspector of mountaineering training with the Main Directorate of the Red Army Reserves, 'O prodelannoi rabote v gornostrelkovykh chastiakh' (13 June 1942) (hereafter cited as 'O prodelannoi rabote'), TsAMO, f. 401, op. 9511, d. 30, l. 74.
134. Gusev, *El'brus v ogne*, 18; Logofet, 'O prodelannoi rabote', l. 74.
135. Gusev, *El'brus v ogne*, 26, 35, 36; Logofet, 'O prodelannoi rabote', ll. 74, 75.
136. Logofet, 'O prodelannoi rabote', ll. 74, 76.
137. Purtseladze, 'Gornaia i gorno-lyzhnaia podgotovka', l. 143.
138. Logofet, 'O prodelannoi rabote', ll. 76, 77. Moshchanskii writes that the inspectors found the '9th Mountain Division the best', but he does not mention that it was the best of only two divisions inspected: Moshchanskii, *Stoiat' nasmert!*, 41.
139. Logofet, 'O prodelannoi rabote', l. 75.
140. Major Saltykov, 'Doklad' (12 October 1942), TsAMO, f. 47, op. 1063, d. 691, l. 3.
141. Logofet, 'O prodelannoi rabote', l. 77.
142. Vasilii Sergatskov, 'Voiskam 46-i armii Zakfronta' (2 July 1942), TsAMO, f. 401, op. 9511, d. 16, ll. 220–221v; Sergatskov, 'O boevoi gotovnosti podvizhnykh otriadov' (22 July 1942), TsAMO, f. 401, op. 9511, d. 16, ll. 222–226.
143. Opryshko, *Zaoblachnyi front Priel'brus'ia*, 26.
144. Tiulenev (3 August 1942) in Batyrov, Grebeniuk and Matveev, eds., *Bitva za Kavkaz*, 319; 'Kopiia protokola doprosa L. P. Beriia', in O. Mozokhin, ed., *Politbiuro i delo Beriia* (Moscow: Kuchkovo pole, 2012), 213.
145. The 67th, 265th, 379th, and 174th Regiments respectively: Major Komarov, 'Dislokatsiia chastei i podrazdelenii prikryvaiushchikh Glavnyi Kavkazskii Khrebet' (14 August 1942), TsAMO, f. 401, op. 9511, d. 22, l. 56.

146. Batyrov, Grebeniuk and Matveev, eds., *Bitva za Kavkaz*, 63.
147. Khadeev, 'Komandiru i voennomu komissaru 394-i sd' (13 March 1942), TsAMO, f. 1720, op. 1, d. 8, l. 9.
148. Khadeev, 'Komandiru i voennomu komissaru 9-i gsd' (14 March 1942), TsAMO, f. 1720, op. 1, d. 8, l. 29.
149. Voronov in Kul'kov and Rzheshevskii, eds., *Zimniaia voina*, II:262.

4 Contest of Follies: Plan Edelweiss and the German Offensive Across the High Caucasus

1. Franz Halder, *The Halder Diaries: The Private War Journals of Colonel General Franz Halder* (Boulder: Westview Press, 1976), 1583.
2. Adolf Hitler, 'Weisung Nr 45 für die Fortsetzung der Operation "Braunschweig"', in Walter Hubatsch, ed., *Hitlers Weisungen für die Kriegsfürung, 1939–1945* (Munich: Deutscher Taschenbuch Verlag, 1965), 228, 229.
3. 49th Mountain Corps, Kriegstagebuch (hereafter cited as KTB) (15 August 1942), Bundesarchiv-Militärarchiv, Freiburg, Germany (hereafter cited as BA-MA), RH 24-49/72, S. 67v.
4. 49th Mountain Corps, KTB (12 August 1942), BA-MA, RH 24-49/72, S. 42v.
5. 'Doklad kapitana Vagnera', l. 184.
6. Kaltenegger, *Gebirgsjäger im Kaukasus*, 91, 120. Mikhail Gioev alleges that the Germans had 'the newest maps compiled by their agents, who had flooded the Caucasus on the eve of the war': Gioev, *Bitva za Kavkaz*, 9. These claims are baseless.
7. Tieke, *The Caucasus and the Oil*, 99, 100.
8. 49th Mountain Corps, KTB (12 August 1942), BA-MA, RH 24-49/72, S. 50v; Document No. 297, 'Korpsbefehl' (14 August 1942), BA-MA, RH 24-49/79.
9. 'Pereval Marukh' (no date), TsAMO, f. 47, op. 1063, d. 666, l. 3.
10. Clausewitz, *On War*, 426.
11. Halder, *The Halder Diaries*, 1583.
12. Andreas Hillgruber, ed., *Kriegstagebuch des Oberkommandos der Wehrmacht* (Munich: Bernard & Graefe, 1982), II/1:597, 622.
13. Alexander Statiev, 'Romanian Naval Doctrine and Its Tests in the Second World War', *War in History* 15(2) (2008), 198.
14. The detached battalion was the 1st Battalion of the 99th Mountain Regiment: Lanz, *Gebirgsjäger*, 160.
15. 49th Mountain Corps, KTB (15 August 1942), BA-MA, RH 24-49/72, S. 67v.
16. The 394th Rifle Division, the 63rd Cavalry Division, the 155th Rifle Brigade, the 9th and 20th 'Mountain' Divisions, and the Tbilisi cadet schools: Ivan Tiulenev, commander of TCF (3 August 1942), in Batyrov, Grebeniuk and Matveev, eds., *Bitva za Kavkaz*, 319. During the battle of the Caucasus, both sides split their forces into a great variety of small units. In the interest of readability, the precise lengthy identifications of these units are placed in endnotes.
17. These were the 242nd and the 392nd Rifle Divisions: TCF Headquarters, 'Zhurnal boevykh deistvii Zakfronta' (14 August 1942), TsAMO, f. 47, op. 1063, d. 183, l. 139; Zav'ialov, 'Oborona Glavnogo Kavkazskogo Khrebta', l. 2.
18. 'Kopiia protokola doprosa L. P. Beriia', 216; Tiulenev (3 August 1942) in Batyrov, Grebeniuk and Matveev, eds., *Bitva za Kavkaz*, 319.
19. Georgii Pshenianik, *Krakh plana 'Edel'veis'* (Moscow: Tsentrpoligraf, 2013), 183.

20. Ibid., 169.
21. Dmitrii Kozlov, commander of TCF, to the Commander of the 46th Army (12 November 1941), TsAMO, f. 47, op. 1063, d. 10, ll. 16, 17.
22. Aleksandr Vasilevskii, 'Direktiva General'nogo Shtaba' (7 June 1942), in Batyrov, Grebeniuk and Matveev, eds., *Bitva za Kavkaz*, 317.
23. Grechko, *Bitva za Kavkaz* (1969), 156.
24. TCF Headquarters, 'Zhurnal boevykh deistvii Zakfronta' (13 August 1942), TsAMO, f. 47, op. 1063, d. 183, l. 112.
25. Ibid.
26. Zav'ialov, 'Oborona Glavnogo Kavkazskogo Khrebta', l. 4.
27. Grechko, *Bitva za Kavkaz* (1969), 154. The Germans conducted no amphibious operations in the Black Sea, whereas the Soviets launched several such operations.
28. Lavrentii Beria to the Military Council of the 46th Army (28 August 1942), TsAMO, f. 401, op. 9511, d. 30, l. 121.
29. Tiulenev, 'Plan oborony perevalov Glavnogo Kavkazskogo Khrebta' (23 August 1942), TsAMO, f. 47, op. 1063, d. 644, ll. 17, 18.
30. Tiulenev, *Cherez tri voiny*, 226, 227; Tiulenev, *Krakh operatsii 'Edel'veis'*, 79. Donguz-Orun-Bashi is a peak rather than a pass, and Dombai-Ulgen was the old name for the Ptysh pass rather than for two separate passes. No oranges grow in the Caucasus. Crampons are used for climbing icy slopes rather than vertical rocks.
31. Zav'ialov, 'Oborona Glavnogo Kavkazskogo Khrebta', l. 5. The highest point Leselidze ever reached during the battle at the MCR was Gentsvish village, at about 800 metres.
32. Beria to the Military Council of the 46th Army (28 August 1942), TsAMO, f. 401, op. 9511, d. 30, l. 121.
33. Lieutenant-Colonel Kantariia, 'Prikrytie perevalov cherez Kavkazskii Khrebet' (no date), TsAMO, f. 401, op. 9511, d. 22, l. 31; TsAMO, f. 401, op. 9511, d. 23.
34. TsAMO, f. 1720, op. 1, d. 23, l. 62; Aleksei Maleinov, senior inspector of mountaineering in the 242nd 'Mountain' Division, 'Programma gorno-fizicheskoi podgotovki' (15 November 1942), TsAMO, f. 1524, op. 1, d. 9, l. 158.
35. Gneushev and Poput'ko, *Taina Marukhskogo lednika* (1966), 133; Gioev, *Bitva za Kavkaz*, 94; Opryshko, *Zaoblachnyi front*, 9; Gusev, *El'brus v ogne*, 97; V. Evnevich, 'Bitva za Kavkaz v istorii vtoroi mirovoi voiny', in U. Batyrov, ed., *Materialy mezhdunarodnoi nauchnoi konferentsii posviashchennoi 60-letiiu bitvy za Kavkaz* (Vladikavkaz: Iriston, 2003), 12.
36. Gneushev and Poput'ko, *Taina Marukhskogo lednika* (1966), 354, 355.
37. The author could cross Marukh in early May, when the snow cover was much greater than in mid June.
38. Leselidze, 'Chastnyi boevoi prikaz No. 002' (14 August 1942), TsAMO, f. 1720, op. 1, d. 7, ll. 126, 126v; Headquarters of the 46th Army, 'Plan oborony perevalov ot reki Bol'shaia Laba do reka Malaia Laba' (22 August 1942), TsAMO, f. 401, op. 9511, d. 18, ll. 37, 38; Headquarters of the of 46th Army, 'Plan oborony perevalov ot Marukhskogo do Sancharskogo perevalov' (22 August 1942), TsAMO, f. 401, op. 9511, d. 18, l. 41.
39. Tiulenev, 'Operativnaia direktiva No. 530' (23 August 1942), TsAMO, f. 401, op. 9511, d. 4, l. 11.
40. TCF Headquarters, 'Zhurnal boevykh deistvii Zakfronta' (13 August 1942), TsAMO, f. 47, op. 1063, d. 183, l. 113.
41. Sergatskov, 'Plan oborony Glavnogo Kavkazskogo Khrebta' (30 June 1943), TsAMO, f. 47, op. 1063, d. 456, l. 17.

42. Headquarters of the 46th Army, 'Dnevnik boevykh deistvii' (1 May–1 September 1942), TsAMO, f. 401, op. 9511, d. 58, l. 6.
43. TCF Headquarters, 'Zhurnal boevykh deistvii Zakfronta' (4–5 August 1942), TsAMO, f. 47, op. 1063, d. 183, l. 48.
44. Zav'ialov, 'Oborona Glavnogo Kavkazskogo Khrebta', l. 5v.
45. 'Pis'mo polkovnika Mel'nikova', in Mozokhin, ed., *Politbiuro i delo Beriia*, 945.
46. Grechko, *Bitva za Kavkaz* (1969), 162.
47. Headquarters of the 20th 'Mountain' Division, 'Zhurnal boevykh deistvii 20-i gsd' (14 August 1942), TsAMO, f. 1089, op. 1, d. 6, l. 3.
48. B. Badanin, *Na boevykh rubezhakh Kavkaza* (Moscow: MO SSSR, 1962), 55.
49. Iurii Apel', *Dokhodiaga* (Moscow: Rosspen, 2009), 34.
50. Badanin, *Na boevykh rubezhakh Kavkaza*, 55.
51. Grechko, *Bitva za Kavkaz* (1969), 156.
52. Beria to the Military Council of the 46th Army (28 August 1942), TsAMO, f. 401, op. 9511, d. 30, l. 121; Gioev, *Bitva za Kavkaz*, 90.
53. A. Zav'ialov and T. Kaliadin, *Bitva za Kavkaz* (Moscow: MO SSSR, 1957), 77.
54. Abramov, *Na ratnykh dorogakh*, 153; Tiulenev, *Cherez tri voiny*, 225.
55. Aleksandr Vasilevskii, 'Direktiva nachal'nika General'nogo Shtaba' (24 July 1942), TsAMO, f. 47, op. 1063, d. 31, ll. 1, 2.
56. Tiulenev, *Cherez tri voiny*, 225.
57. Ivanov to Subbotin (18 August 1942) in Shapovalov, ed., *Bitva za Kavkaz*, 152; Batyrov, Grebeniuk and Matveev, eds., *Bitva za Kavkaz*, 94.
58. General Konstantin Skorobogatkin to Marshal Matvei Zakharov (22 January 1963), TsAMO, f. 1720, op. 1, d. 10, l. 5.
59. Dreev to Petrov (9 September 1942), TsAMO, f. 47, op. 1063, d. 667, l. 19v.
60. The 1st Battalion of the 815th Rifle Regiment of the 394th Rifle Division: Major Zhashko, 'Svedeniia o boevom i chislennom sostave podrazdelenii, nakhodiashchikhsia na perevalakh Glavnogo Kavkazskogo Khrebta' (17 August 1942) (hereafter cited as 'Svedaniia o boevom i chislennom sostave'), TsAMO, f. 401, op. 9511, d. 22, l. 114.
61. Colonel Belekhov, acting commander of the 394th Rifle Division, 'Opisanie Klukhorskogo i Nakharskogo perevala' (18 October 1942), TsAMO, f. 401, op. 9511, d. 73, l. 15; TCF Headquarters, 'Zhurnal boevykh deistvii Zakfronta' (5 August 1942), TsAMO, f. 47, op. 1063, d. 183, l. 54.
62. Badanin, *Na boevykh rubezhakh Kavkaza*, 48.
63. Tiulenev, 'Prikrytie perevalov i prokhodov cherez Glavnyi Kavkazskii Khrebet' (17 August 1942), TsAMO, f. 47, op. 1063, d. 689, l. 3.
64. Klement'ev, *Boevye deistviia gornykh voisk*, 151, 153; General'nyi shtab Krasnoi Armii, *Nastavlenie*, 77; Shebalin, ed., *Nastavlenie*, 149.
65. TCF Headquarters, 'Zhurnal boevykh deistvii Zakfronta' (18 August 1942), TsAMO, f. 47, op. 1063, d. 183, l. 139; TCF Headquarters, 'Zhurnal boevykh deistvii Zakfronta' (August 1942), TsAMO, f. 47, op. 1063, d. 183, l. 221.
66. TCF Headquarters, 'Zhurnal boevykh deistvii Zakfronta' (18 August 1942), TsAMO, f. 47, op. 1063, d.1 83, l. 139; 'Operativno-razvedyvatel'naia svodka No. 2' (22 August 1942), TsAMO, f. 47, op. 1063, d. 671, ll. 19, 20.
67. The 2nd Battalion of the 98th Mountain Regiment: Tieke, *The Caucasus and the Oil*, 102, 109.
68. The 1st Battalion of the 815th Regiment: Zhashko, 'Svedeniia o boevom i chislennom sostave', l. 114.

69. The 5th Company of the 2nd Battalion of the 815th Regiment and the 1st Company of the 1st Battalion of the 810 Regiment. Both regiments belonged to the 394th Rifle Division: ibid.
70. The German mountain battalion had ten heavy machineguns, thirty-six light machineguns, fifteen mortars, and two mountain guns. Hirschfeld had a half-battalion, but it was reinforced with an attached artillery unit that had mountain guns and howitzers: Lanz, *Gebirgsjäger*, 315.
71. TCF Headquarters, 'Zhurnal boevykh deistvii Zakfronta' (21 August 1942), TsAMO, f. 47, op. 1063, d. 183, l. 159.
72. 49th Mountain Corps, KTB (17 August 1942), BA-MA, RH 24-49/72, SS. 68v, 72v; Tieke, *The Caucasus and the Oil*, 103.
73. Clausewitz, *On War*, 539.
74. 49th Mountain Corps, 'Zahlenmässige Übersicht def Uffz. und Mannsch.-Verluste vom 4.6.42 mit 17.12.1942' (hereafter cited as 'Zahlenmässige Übersicht'), BA-MA, RH 24-49/232, Anlage 3. These casualty numbers come from the daily field reports filed by the 49th Mountain Corps; they exclude officer casualties, which were light. Although, as elsewhere, both sides inflated the casualties they inflicted on the opponents, and the Soviets inflated them more than the Germans, Soviet and German reports on their own casualties were fairly accurate. The Soviets maintained daily statistics on casualties only at the small-unit level and, given the poor communications, reports at higher levels included mainly summaries of the casualties suffered in certain actions or during a certain period. The Germans maintained daily casualty data at the corps level. These reports sometimes arrived after a small delay because of intermittent radio communications; they also slightly understated the number of casualties because of the uncertainty of what had happened to some temporarily missing soldiers. The Germans probably added, if they could, omitted casualty data for the previous evening to the casualties suffered during the current day. In order to reduce the impact of the possible delay in the communication of daily statistics, I sometimes give the numbers of German casualties not just for the day of action but also for the next day, when all the reports for the previous day must have arrived.
75. Belekhov, 'Opisanie Klukhorskogo i Nakharskogo perevala' (18 October 1942), TsAMO, f. 401, op. 9511, d. 73, ll. 13v, 14; TCF Headquarters, 'Zhurnal boevykh deistvii Zakfronta' (21 August 1942), TsAMO, f. 47, op. 1063, d. 183, l. 155.
76. Headquarters of the 46th Army, 'Dnevnik boevykh deistvii' (1 May–1 September 1942), TsAMO, f. 401, op. 9511, d. 58, l. 6.
77. Serov, deputy people's commissar of the interior, to Kobulov (3 September 1942), TsAMO, f. 47, op. 1063, d. 671, l. 22.
78. TCF Headquarters, 'Zhurnal boevykh deistvii Zakfronta' (September 1942), TsAMO, f. 47, op. 1063, d. 194, l. 246.
79. The 7th Company of the 3rd Battalion of the 815th Rifle Regiment: Zhashko, 'Svedeniia o boevom i chislennom sostave', l. 114; 49th Mountain Corps, KTB, Anlagen (19 August 1942), BA-MA, RH 24-49/79.
80. Captain Agaev, commander of the Training Battalion, 'Svedeniia o nalichii i poteriakh' (25 August 1942), TsAMO, f. 815sp, op. 39410, d. 1, ll. 171, 171v.
81. 49th Mountain Corps, 'Zahlenmässige Übersicht'.
82. Major Zarelua, head of the NKVD Special Section of the 46th Army, 'Vypiska iz doneseniia' (no date), TsAMO, f. 47, op. 1063, d. 664, l. 5; Saltykov, 'Doklad' (12 October 1942), TsAMO, f. 47, op. 1063, d. 691, l. 3.
83. TCF Headquarters, 'Zhurnal boevykh deistvii Zakfronta' (7 August 1942), TsAMO, f. 47, op. 1063, d. 183, l. 68; Captain Heinz Groth, 'Bericht über die Ersteilung des Elbrus' (28 August 1942), BA-MA, RH 24-1/171, S. 215.

84. A. Rakovskii, 'Kak my stroili priiut OPT', *NSINM* 11 (1929), 16; G. Dolzhenko and Iu. Putrik, *Istoriia turizma v Rossiiskoi imperii, Sovetskom Soiuze i Rossiiskoi Federatsii* (Moscow and Rostov-on-Don: MarT, 2010), 118.
85. Groth, 'Bericht über die Ersteilung des Elbrus', SS. 214, 215; 49th Mountain Corps, KTB (16 August 1942), BA-MA, RH 24-49/72, SS. 60v, 64v.
86. Tieke, *The Caucasus and the Oil*, 106; Lanz, *Gebirgsjäger*, 158.
87. Bauer, *Unternehmen 'Elbrus'*, 160.
88. Saltykov, 'Doklad' (12 October 1942), TsAMO, f. 47, op. 1063, d. 691, l. 3; Groth, 'Bericht über die Ersteilung des Elbrus', S. 215; Bauer, *Unternehmen 'Elbrus'*, 163; 49th Mountain Corps, KTB (16 August 1942), BA-MA, RH 24-49/72, S. 76v.
89. Groth, 'Bericht über die Ersteilung des Elbrus', S. 218; Saltykov, 'Doklad' (12 October 1942), TsAMO, f. 47, op. 1063, d. 691, l. 3; Saltykov, 'Doklad o metodakh i taktike deistvii protivnika v raione g. Elbrus' (24 October 1942), TsAMO, f. 47, op. 1063, d. 691, l. 26.
90. Groth, 'Bericht über die Ersteilung des Elbrus', S. 216.
91. Saltykov, 'Doklad' (12 October 1942), TsAMO, f. 47, op. 1063, d. 691, l. 3; Saltykov, 'Doklad o metodakh i taktike deistvii protivnika v raione g. Elbrus' (24 October 1942), TsAMO, f. 47, op. 1063, d. 691, l. 26.
92. Lanz, *Gebirgsjäger*, 160.
93. The 3rd Squadron of the 214th Cavalry Regiment of the 63rd Cavalry Division: Major Komarov, deputy head of the Operations Section of the 46th Army, 'Svedeniia boevogo i chislennogo sostava podrazdelenii prikryvaiushchikh Kavkazskii Khrebet' (15 August 1942), TsAMO, f. 401, op. 9511, d. 22, l. 57v. Opryshko grossly inflates the scale of this clash, stating that the victorious Soviets 'counted more than sixty enemy corpses at the battlefield near Elbrus', having lost only nine men killed: Opryshko, *Zaoblachnyi front Priel'brus'ia*, 32. In fact, the total losses of the 1st Mountain Division, including the casualties in the Klych valley, were stated as only one man killed and four wounded on 18 August and three men killed and five wounded on 19 August: 49th Mountain Corps, 'Zahlenmässige Übersicht'.
94. General Ivan Petrov, OG commander, 'Operativnaia svodka No. 4' (27 August 1942), TsAMO, f. 47, op. 1063, d. 65g, l. 19; Bogdan Kobulov, deputy head of NKVD, to Beria (16 September 1942), TsAMO, f. 47, op. 1063, d. 655, l. 10.
95. Saltykov, 'Doklad o metodakh i taktike deistvii protivnika v raione g. Elbrus' (24 October 1942), TsAMO, f. 47, op. 1063, d. 691, l. 26.
96. The combat group consisted of the 3rd Battalion of the 91st Mountain Regiment, the 2nd Battalion of 13th Mountain Regiment, and an artillery company: Buchner, *Kampf im Gebirge*, 47.
97. The 5th Company of the 2nd Battalion of the 808th Rifle Regiment: Zhashko, 'Svedeniia o boevom i chislennom sostave', l. 114.
98. Ibid.
99. Major Zarelua (1 September 1942), TsAMO, f. 47, op. 1063, d. 668, l. 27.
100. The 2nd Company of the 1st Battalion of the 808th Rifle Regiment: Zhashko, 'Svedeniia o boevom i chislennom sostave', l. 114.
101. Gneushev and Poput'ko, *Taina Marukhskogo lednika* (1971), 302.
102. Colonel Rasskazov, chief of staff of the 46th Army (22 August 1942), TsAMO, f. 47, op. 1063, d. 456, l. 44.
103. 49th Mountain Corps, KTB (23 and 25 August 1942), BA-MA, RH 24-49/72, SS. 109v, 127v; Buchner, *Kampf im Gebirge*, 31; 'Tagesmeldungen' (25 August 1942), BA-MA, RH 24-49/75.

104. General Petrov, 'Operativnaia svodka No. 1' (24 August 1942), TsAMO, f. 47, op. 1063, d. 658, l. 6; V. Gneushev and A. Poput'ko, *Taina Marukhskogo lednika* (Moscow: Sovetskaia Rossiia, 1971), 302.
105. 49th Mountain Corps, KTB (24 August 1942), BA-MA, RH 24-49/72, S. 125v.
106. Sergatskov, 'Operativnaia direktiva No. 0011' (24 August 1942), TsAMO, f. 47, op. 1063, d. 692, l. 6.
107. The 13th Company of the 91st Mountain Regiment.
108. The 11th Company of the 91st Mountain Regiment: 49th Mountain Corps, KTB (24 August 1942), BA-MA, RH 24-49/72, S. 125v.
109. Buchner, *Kampf im Gebirge*, 32, 33.
110. The 12th Company of the 91st Mountain Regiment.
111. Buchner, *Kampf im Gebirge*, 33.
112. Komarov, 'Svedeniia boevogo i chislennogo sostava podrazdelenii prikryvaiushchikh Kavkazskii Khrebet' (15 August 1942), TsAMO, f. 401, op. 9511, d. 22, l. 57; Colonel Mikhail Mikeladze, chief of staff of the 46th Army, 'Itogovaia operativnaia svodka No. 2' (6 November 1942), TsAMO, f. 401, op. 9511, d. 112, l. 4.
113. 49th Mountain Corps, 'Zahlenmässige Übersicht'.
114. Leselidze (2 September 1942), TsAMO, f. 401, op. 9511, d. 51, l. 55.
115. General Petrov, 'Operativnaia svodka No. 3' (26 August 1942), TsAMO, f. 47, op. 1063, d. 658, l. 12; Illarion Gagua, people's commissar of the interior of Abkhazia, to Bogdan Kobulov (3 September 1942), TsAMO, f. 47, op. 1063, d. 668, l. 16.
116. Linets and Ianush, *Oborona Severnogo Kavkaza*, 282, Batyrov, Grebeniuk and Matveev, eds., *Bitva za Kavkaz*, 99; Grechko, *Bitva za Kavkaz* (1969), 166; Bekishvili, 'Oborona kavkazskikh perevalov', 63; Ibragimbeili, *Krakh 'Edel'veisa'*, 109; Tiulenev, *Krakh operatsii 'Edel'veis'*, 83; Moshchanskii, *Stoiat' nasmert!*, 103; Pshenianik, *Krakh plana 'Edel'veis'*, 117. As in the summer of 1941, when the bewildered Soviet commanders attributed the tremendous confusion caused by the German attack to omnipresent enemy paratroopers, TCF commanders were obsessed with alleged German airborne drops that in reality had never occurred: Mark Solonin, *Iiun' 41-go: okonchatel'nyi diagnoz* (Moscow: Iauza-Eksmo, 2014), 240, 314.
117. Later, the Soviet narrative changed to the equally unsubstantiated allegation that Germans dropped forty paratroopers near the Dou pass and that this paratrooper unit was 'completely destroyed': Zav'ialov, 'Oborona Glavnogo Kavkazskogo Khrebta', l. 14v. Germans would certainly have reported such an incident, but their documents do not mention it.
118. Buchner, *Kampf im Gebirge*, 34; Hillgruber, ed., *Kriegstagebuch des Oberkommandos der Wehrmacht*, 651.
119. The 12th Company of the 3rd Battalion of the 91th Mountain Regiment.
120. Zhashko, 'Svedeniia o boevom i chislennom sostave', l. 114.
121. 49th Mountain Corps, KTB (24 August 1942), BA-MA, RH 24-49/72, S. 142; Buchner, *Kampf im Gebirge*, 34.
122. Buchner, *Kampf im Gebirge*, 36, 39.
123. Ibid., 38; General Petrov, 'Konspekt' (2 September 1942), TsAMO, f. 47, op. 1063, d. 689, l. 28.
124. The 4th Battalion of the 155 Rifle Brigade: Petrov, 'Konspekt' (2 September 1942), TsAMO, f. 47, op. 1063, d. 689, l. 28.
125. Buchner, *Kampf im Gebirge*, 38, 39, 162.
126. Leselidze, 'Komandiram soedinenii i chastei 46-i armii' (16 October 1942), TsAMO, f. 1720, op. 1, d. 7, l. 11; 'Zhurnal boevykh deistvii Zakfronta'

(22 August 1942), TsAMO, f. 47, op. 1063, d. 183, l. 163; Tiulenev, 'Operativnaia direktiva No. 530' (23 August 1942), TsAMO, f. 401, op. 9511, d. 4, l. 11.
127. 'Kopiia protokola doprosa L. P. Beriia', 213.
128. Lanz, *Gebirgsjäger*, 158.
129. 49th Mountain Corps, KTB (16 August 1942), BA-MA, RH 24-49/72, SS. 63v–64v; Konrad to List (16 August 1942), BA-MA, RH 24-49/79, Document No. 310.
130. Groth, 'Bericht über die Ersteilung des Elbrus', S. 216.
131. Ibid., SS. 217, 218.
132. General Richard Ruoff (23 August 1942), BA-MA, RH 24-49/79, Document No. 356.
133. Lanz to Konrad (21 August 1942), BA-MA, RH 24-49/79, Document No. 344.
134. Al'bert Shpeer, *Vospominaniia* (Smolensk: Rusich, 1997), 331.
135. Grechko, *Bitva za Kavkaz* (1969), 163; Andrei Grechko et al., *Istoriia vtoroi mirovoi voiny 1939–1945* (Moscow: MO SSSR, 1975), V:218; Ibragimbeili, *Krakh 'Edel'veisa'*, 107; Opryshko, *Zaoblachnyi front*, 12, 13; Moshchanskii, *Stoiat' nasmert!*, 65; A. Kardanova, 'Zashchita perevalov Kavkaza', in Batyrov, ed., *Materialy mezhdunarodnoi nauchnoi konferentsii*, 55.
136. Daniel Uziel, *The Propaganda Warriors* (Oxford: Peter Lang, 2008), 294.
137. Ibid., 292, 293.
138. Ingo Stoehr, *German Literature of the Twentieth Century* (Rochester: Camden House, 2001), 186, 187.
139. Gusev, *El'brus v ogne*, 168.
140. Halder, *The Halder Diaries*, 1513.
141. Many years after the war, this action continued to offend the Soviet public, and the person who commanded it fuelled particular hatred. Bekishvili even states that Captain Groth was buried by an avalanche provoked by bombs intentionally dropped by Soviet bombers at the slope of Elbrus above the German positions: Bekishvili, 'Oborona kavkazskikh perevalov', 99. In fact, Groth ended the war as the commander of the 99th Regiment of the 1st Mountain Division: Lanz, *Gebirgsjäger*, 311. He became a judge and lived until 1994.
142. Saltykov, 'Doklad o metodakh i taktike deistvii protivnika v raione g. Elbrus' (24 October 1942), TsAMO, f. 47, op. 1063, d. 691, l. 26v; Colonel Belekhov, 'Doklad o prakticheskikh vyvodakh' (19 October 1942), TsAMO, f. 401, op. 9511, d. 73, l. 43.
143. Gusev, *El'brus v ogne*, 18.
144. Belekhov, 'Doklad o prakticheskikh vyvodakh' (19 October 1942), TsAMO, f. 401, op. 9511, d. 73, l. 43.
145. 'Zhurnal boevykh deistvii Zakfronta' (29 August 1942), TsAMO, f. 47, op. 1063, d. 183, ll. 222, 231.
146. Zav'ialov, 'Oborona Glavnogo Kavkazskogo Khrebta', l. 16.
147. Ibid., ll. 15v, 16v.
148. Ibid., l. 15v; Tiulenev, *Krakh operatsii 'Edelveis'*, 83.
149. Clausewitz, *On War*, 417, 432.

5 'Not a Step Back!': The German Mountain Corps Hits the Wall

1. Ivanov to Subbotin (18 August 1942) in Shapovalov, ed., *Bitva za Kavkaz*, 152, 153.
2. Grechko, *Bitva za Kavkaz* (1969), 157.

3. Tiulenev, *Krakh operatsii 'Edel'veis'*, 56, 57.
4. 'Zhurnal boevykh deistvii Zakfronta' (21 August 1942), TsAMO, f. 47, op. 1063, d. 183, l. 159.
5. Tiulenev, 'Operativnaia direktiva No. 530' (23 August 1942), TsAMO, f. 401, op. 9511, d. 4, l. 11.
6. Lieutenant-Colonel Kantariia, 'Komandiram chastei 394-i sd' (17 August 1942), TsAMO, f. 401, op. 9511, d. 22, l. 113.
7. Bekishvili, 'Oborona kavkazskikh perevalov', 60; A. Kharitonov, 'Na gornykh perevalakh Kavkaza', in A. Basov et al., *Narodnyi podvig v bitve za Kavkaz* (Moscow: Institut Istorii AN SSSR, 1981), 122.
8. Leselidze, 'Komandiram soedinenii i chastei 46-i armii' (16 October 1942), TsAMO, f. 1720, op. 1, d. 7, l. 11.
9. 'Zhurnal boevykh deistvii Zakfronta' (September 1942), TsAMO, f. 47, op. 1063, d. 194, l. 245.
10. Linets and Ianush, *Oborona Severnogo Kavkaza*, 290; Batyrov, Grebeniuk and Matveev, eds., *Bitva za Kavkaz*, 103; Zav'ialov and Kaliadin, *Bitva za Kavkaz*, 78.
11. Grechko, *Bitva za Kavkaz* (1969), 158.
12. Linets and Ianush, *Oborona Severnogo Kavkaza*, 259.
13. Gioev, *Bitva za Kavkaz*, 89, 90.
14. 'Zhurnal boevykh deistvii Zakfronta' (no date), TsAMO, f. 47, op. 1063, d. 183, l. 160.
15. Shapovalov, ed., *Bitva za Kavkaz*, 467.
16. 'Kopiia protokola doprosa L. P. Beriia', 213, 214.
17. Ibid., 216; Linets and Ianush, *Oborona Severnogo Kavkaza*, 128.
18. Shapovalov, ed., *Bitva za Kavkaz*, 467; Abramov, *Na ratnykh dorogakh*, 155; A. Bezugol'nyi, 'Uchastie vysshikh gosudarstvennykh deiatelei SSSR v rukovodstve oboronoi Kavkaza', in Batyrov, ed., *Materialy mezhdunarodnoi nauchnoi konferentsii*, 65. Researchers should be sceptical about these testimonies, which were produced to political order.
19. Gneushev and Poput'ko, *Taina Marukhskogo lednika* (1966), 354, 355.
20. Zav'ialov, 'Oborona Glavnogo Kavkazskogo Khrebta', l. 16.
21. Khromov, head of the Political Directorate of the TCF (31 July 1942), TsAMO, f. 1089, op. 1, d. 32, l. 50.
22. Lieutenant-Colonel Kantariia, 'Komandiram chastei 394-i sd' (17 August 1942), TsAMO, f. 401, op. 9511, d. 22, l. 113.
23. Nikolai Rukhadze, chief of TCF Special Sections, to Tiulenev, 'Spetsial'noe soobshchenie o nedochetakh v ispol'zovanii zagradotriadov 46-i armii' (15 November 1942), TsAMO, f. 47, op. 1063, d. 28, l. 101.
24. TsAMO, f. 815sp, op. 39410, d. 1, ll. 109, 111, 196.
25. 'Zhurnal boevykh deistvii Zakfronta' (21 August 1942), TsAMO, f. 47, op. 1063, d. 183, l. 155.
26. Petrov to Beria (1 September 1942), TsAMO, f. 47, op. 1063, d. 689, l. 8; Colonel A. Rasskazov, chief of staff of the 46th Army (no date), TsAMO, f. 47, op. 1063, d. 689, l. 9.
27. Beria to the Military Council of the 46th Army (28 August 1942), TsAMO, f. 401, op. 9511, d. 30, ll. 121, 121a; Shapovalov, ed., *Bitva za Kavkaz*, 468; 'Zhurnal boevykh deistvii Zakfronta' (22 August 1942), TsAMO, f. 47, op. 1063, d. 183, ll. 168, 169.
28. Abramov, *Na ratnykh dorogakh*, 152.
29. Bezugol'nyi, 'Uchastie vysshikh gosudarstvennykh deiatelei SSSR', 65. Sergatskov was appointed commander of the 351st Rifle Division, whereas Subbotin became

a representative of the Red Army General Staff with the TCF: Beria, 'Prikaz predstavitelia GKO' (28 August 1942), in Shapovalov, ed., *Bitva za Kavkaz*, 179.

30. Grechko, *Bitva za Kavkaz* (1969), 161. Colonel Vasilii Abramov, one of those who accused Beria *post factum* of 'arbitrary dismissals' and explained them with the assumption that Beria was 'a master [*materyi*] spy and enemy of the Soviet people', had left the Marukh pass entrusted to him one day before the German assault: Abramov, *Na ratnykh dorogakh*, 155. Bogdan Kobulov, Beria's deputy, argued with good reason that Abramov had 'bungled [*provalil*] the defence of Marukh': Kobulov to Beria (17 August 1942), TsAMO, f. 47, op. 1063, d. 689, l. 54. Yet, despite this dismal failure, Abramov retained his position as deputy commander of the 3rd Rifle Corps after a brief temporary demotion.
31. Colonel M. Romanov, OG deputy chief of staff, to Komarov (27 August 1942) in Shapovalov, ed., *Bitva za Kavkaz*, 176.
32. Beria, 'Donesenie predstavitelia GKO' (23 August 1942), ibid., 161.
33. 'Kopiia protokola doprosa L. P. Beriia', 213. This frontier guard general should not be confused with Ivan Efimovich Petrov, commander of the 44th Army of the North Caucasus Front, who did not participate in the battle in the high Caucasus.
34. Romanov to Komarov (27 August 1942) in Shapovalov, ed., *Bitva za Kavkaz*, 177.
35. Bezugol'nyi, 'Uchastie vysshikh gosudarstvennykh deiatelei', 62, 63; General Petrov, 'Operativnaia svodka No. 2' (25 August 1942), TsAMO, f. 47, op. 1063, d. 658, l. 10.
36. Tiulenev, 'Instruktsiia po aktivnoi oborone perevalov GKKh' (25 August 1942), TsAMO, f. 47, op. 1063, d. 655, ll. 96–125; Colonel Andrei Bulyga, OG chief of staff (15 September 1942), TsAMO, f. 1720, op. 1, d. 7, ll. 282–289.
37. Tiulenev, 'Instruktsiia po aktivnoi oborone perevalov GKKh' (25 August 1942), TsAMO, f. 47, op. 1063, d. 655, l. 98.
38. General Petrov, 'Doklad o sostoianii oborony perevalov GKKh' (13 November 2013) (hereafter 'Doklad o sostoianii oborony perevalov'), TsAMO, f. 47, op. 1063, d. 655, l. 132.
39. General Bodin (6 October 1942), TsAMO, f. 47, op. 1063, d. 161, l. 19.
40. Bazarnyi, chief of staff of the 20th 'Mountain' Division, 'Boevoe rasporiazhenie No. 4' (24 August 1942), TsAMO, f. 1089, op. 1, d. 4, l. 23.
41. Tiulenev, 'Operativnaia direktiva No. 00530' (28 August 1942), TsAMO, f. 47, op. 1063, d. 31, l. 44.
42. Grechko, *Bitva za Kavkaz* (1969), 159.
43. Komarov to the commander of TCF air force (after 22 August 1942), TsAMO, f. 401, op. 9511, d. 30, l. 110.
44. Beria to Anastas Mikoian, deputy chair of the Council of People's Commissars, 'Khodataistvo predstavitelia GKO' (3 September 1942), in Shapovalov, ed., *Bitva za Kavkaz*, 200.
45. Headquarters of the 46th Army, 'Dnevnik boevykh deistvii' (1 May–1 September 1942), TsAMO, f. 401, op. 9511, d. 58, l. 5.
46. TCF Headquarters, 'Zhurnal boevykh deistvii Zakfronta' (28 July 1942), TsAMO, f. 47, op. 1063, d. 183, l. 14.
47. TCF Headquarters, 'Zhurnal boevykh deistvii Zakfronta' (3 August 1942), TsAMO, f. 47, op. 1063, d. 183, l. 33.
48. Sergatskov, 'Komandiram soedinenii' (7 August 1942), TsAMO, f. 47, op. 1063, d. 456, ll. 36, 37.
49. Headquarters of the 46th Army, 'Dnevnik boevykh deistvii' (1 May–1 September 1942), TsAMO, f. 401, op. 9511, d. 58, l. 5.

50. Beria, 'Donesenie predstavitelia GKO' (23 August 1942), 161; 'Zhurnal boevykh deistvii Zakfronta' (no date), TsAMO, f. 47, op. 1063, d. 183, l. 168.
51. Stalin and Bodin, 'Direktiva Stavki' (20 August 1942), in Batyrov, Grebeniuk and Matveev, eds., *Bitva za Kavkaz*, 322–4.
52. Tiulenev, 'Plan oborony perevalov Glavnogo Kavkazskogo Khrebta' (23 August 1942), TsAMO, f. 47, op. 1063, d. 644, ll. 17, 18.
53. Alexander Statiev, 'The Soviet Union', in Philip Cooke and Ben Shepherd, eds., *European Resistance in the Second World War* (Barnsley: Pen & Sword, 2013), 192.
54. Colonel Zhibkov to Romanov (no date), TsAMO, f. 47, op. 1063, d. 664, l. 43; General Petrov, 'Operativnaia svodka No. 3' (26 August 1942), TsAMO, f. 47, op. 1063, d. 658, l. 14.
55. Petrov, 'Doklad o sostoianii oborony perevalov', l. 145.
56. Tiulenev and Bodin, 'Operativnaia direktiva No. 015' (11 September 1942), in Shapovalov, ed., *Bitva za Kavkaz*, 221.
57. Zaitsev, chief of staff of the TCF Engineers, 'Opersvodka po zagrazhdeniiam No. 5' (4 September 1942), TsAMO, f. 47, op. 1063, d. 662, l. 6; Vodop'anov, chief of staff of the TCF Engineers, 'Opersvodka po zagrazhdeniiam No. 16' (4 October 1942), TsAMO, f. 47, op. 1063, d. 662, l. 20; Vodop'anov, 'Opersvodka po zagrazhdeniiam No. 17' (4 October 1942), TsAMO, f. 47, op. 1063, d. 662, l. 21.
58. Aleksandr Kvlividze, NKVD head in South Ossetia (20 August 1942), in Shapovalov, ed., *Bitva za Kavkaz*, 157, 158.
59. Colonel Olev, 'Vypiska iz doklada ofitsera Genshtaba' (24 October 1942), TsAMO, f. 47, op. 1063, d. 31, l. 115.
60. Tiulenev, *Krakh operatsii 'Edel'veis'*, 77; Grechko, *Bitva za Kavkaz* (1969), 153.
61. Headquarters of the 8th Army to the Headquarters of the Southwestern Front (7 February 1915), RGVIA, f. 2067, op. 1, d. 305, l. 11.
62. Badanin, *Na boevykh rubezhakh Kavkaza*, 50.
63. Sergatskov, 'Komandiram soedinenii' (7 August 1942), TsAMO, f. 401, op. 9511, d. 22, l. 48.
64. Colonel Grigor'evskii, chief of staff of the 61st Rifle Division, 'Voenno-topograficheskoe opisanie perevala Akhuk-Dara' (17 October 1942), TsAMO, f. 401, op. 9511, d. 73, l. 5.
65. Tiulenev, 'Instruktsiia po aktivnoi oborone perevalov' (25 August 1942), TsAMO, f. 47, op. 1063, d. 655, l. 99.
66. Vodop'anov, 'Inzhenernaia svodka po zagrazhdeniiam No. 17' (4 October 1942), TsAMO, f. 47, op. 1063, d. 10, l. 92.
67. Narodnyi Komissariat Oborony [People's Commissariat of Defence], *Polevoi ustav RKKA PU-39* (Moscow: Gosudarstvennoe Voennoe Izdatel'stvo NKO SSSR, 1941).
68. Badanin, *Na boevykh rubezhakh Kavkaza*, 50.
69. Lieutenant-Colonel Mezentsev, 'Itogovyi doklad o deistviiakh voisk 46-i armii' (30 December 1942) (hereafter cited as 'Itogovyi doklad'), TsAMO, f. 47, op. 1063, d. 692, ll. 188v–190; Colonel Zhashko (10 August 1942), TsAMO, f. 1720, op. 1, d. 23, l. 115.
70. Buchner, *Kampf im Gebirge*, 49.
71. Litvinov (12 November 1942), TsAMO, f. 47, op. 1063, d. 691, l. 38v.
72. Petrov, 'Doklad o sostoianii oborony perevalov', ll. 145, 146.
73. Major Bozhenko, chief of staff of the 242nd 'Mountain' Division, 'Kharakteristika 242-i gsd' (30 November 1942), TsAMO, f. 1524, op. 1, d. 12, l. 97; Leselidze, 'Komandiram soedinenii i chastei 46-i armii' (16 October 1942), TsAMO, f. 1720, op. 1, d. 7, l. 11.

74. The 3rd Battalion of the 99th Regiment of the 1st Mountain Division: Tieke, *The Caucasus and the Oil*, 110.
75. The Soviet forces in the Klych valley consisted of the Training Battalion of the 394th Rifle Division, the 2nd and 3rd Battalions of the 815th Regiment, the 1st Company of the 810th Regiment of the 394th Rifle Division, the 121st Regiment of the 9th 'Mountain' Division with 1,235 men, the 220th Regiment of the 63rd Cavalry Division and the 2nd and 3rd Battalions of 155th Rifle Brigade, the 36th Naval Frontier Guard Unit of 300 men, two companies of the Sukhumi Infantry School with 270 men, the 5th and 6th Special Companies with about 300 men, and an NKVD unit of about 300 men: 'Khod boevykh deistvii na Klukhorskom i Marukhskom napravleniiakh', TsAMO, f. 47, op. 1063, d. 504, korobka 5785; Zav'ialov, 'Oborona Glavnogo Kavkazskogo Khrebta', l. 5; 'Zhurnal boevykh deistvii Zakfronta' (20 August 1942), TsAMO, f. 47, op. 1063, d. 183, l. 146; Sergatskov, 'Plan chastichnoi peregruppirovki i usileniia chastei 46-i armii' (27 August 1942), TsAMO, f. 401, op. 9511, d. 18, l. 99; Gioev, *Bitva za Kavkaz*, 108; 'Skhema polozheniia chastei klukhorskoi gruppirovki' (27 August 1942), TsAMO, f. 47, op. 1063, d. 691, l. 28; Tiulenev, 'Plan oborony perevalov Glavnogo Kavkazskogo Khrebta' (23 August 1942), TsAMO, f. 47, op. 1063, d. 644, l. 18.
76. Sergatskov, 'Plan chastichnoi peregruppirovki i usileniia chastei 46-i armii'(27 August 1942), TsAMO, f. 401, op. 9511, d. 18, l. 99.
77. General Konstantin Skorobogatkin to Marshal Matvei Zakharov (22 January 1963), TsAMO, f. 1720, op. 1, d. 10, l. 5.
78. 49th Mountain Corps, KTB (25 August 1942), BA-MA, RH 24-49/72, S. 128v.
79. 49th Mountain Corps, KTB (20, 21 and 25 August 1942), BA-MA, RH 24-49/72, SS. 96, 97v, 127v.
80. 49th Mountain Corps, KTB (19 August 1942), BA-MA, RH 24-49/72, S. 84v; Bauer, *Unternehmen 'Elbrus'*, 226.
81. Headquarters of the 46th Army, 'Dnevnik boevykh deistvii' (1 May–1 September 1942), TsAMO, f. 401, op. 9511, d. 58, l. 7.
82. Pshenianik, *Krakh plana 'Edel'veis'*, 116, 175, 183.
83. 49th Mountain Corps, KTB (6 September 1942), BA-MA, RH 24-49/72, S. 219v.
84. Pshenianik, *Krakh plana 'Edel'veis'*, 115.
85. Tiulenev, *Cherez tri voiny*, 230; Abramov, *Na ratnykh dorogakh*, 160.
86. Pshenianik, *Krakh plana 'Edel'veis'*, 118, 119; Colonel Tetiukhin, head of the TCF Rear, to Romanov (13 September 1942), TsAMO, f. 47, op. 1063, d. 692, l. 9.
87. Lanz, *Gebirgsjäger*, 160.
88. The 2nd Battalion of the 98th Mountain Regiment: Lanz, *Gebirgsjäger*, 160.
89. The 220th Regiment of the 63rd Cavalry Division.
90. 'Skhema polozheniia chastei klukhorskoi gruppirovki' (27 August 1942), TsAMO, f. 47, op. 1063, d. 691, l. 28.
91. 'Karta polozheniia voisk armii na Klukhorskom napravlenii' (no date), TsAMO, f. 401, op. 9511, d. 116.
92. The 8th Company of the 98th Mountain Regiment: BA-MA, RH 24-49/72, l. 148v.
93. The first Soviet reports on this action, filed on 27 and 28 August, stated that a group of 'up to 100 German submachine-gunners' came to the confluence of the Gvandra and Klych Rivers, but all except ten or twelve men were killed and four were taken prisoner: Tiulenev to Stalin, 'Boevoe donesenie No. 015' (27 August 1942), TsAMO, f. 47, op. 1063, d. 166, l. 44; 'Zhurnal boevykh deistvii Zakfronta' (28 August 1942), TsAMO, f. 47, op. 1063, d. 183, l. 191. Subsequent reports

quickly inflated the scale of this engagement and the success scored by the Soviets: the number of German casualties in various Soviet sources fluctuated between 200 and 300: Zav'ialov, 'Oborona Glavnogo Kavkazskogo Khrebta', l. 10; 'Karta polozheniia voisk armii na Klukhorskom napravlenii' (January 1943), TsAMO, f. 401, op. 9511, d. 116. The 1st Mountain Division reported thirty-one men killed, fifty-seven wounded, and twenty-eight missing in action in total, including the casualties suffered in the Marukh region, on 27 and 28 August: 49th Mountain Corps, 'Zahlenmässige Übersicht'.

94. 49th Mountain Corps, 'Zahlenmässige Übersicht'.
95. Beria, 'Donesenie predstavitelia GKO' (9 September 1942), in Shapovalov, ed., *Bitva za Kavkaz*, 217.
96. 49th Mountain Corps, KTB (26 and 28 August 1942), BA-MA, RH 24-49/72, SS. 130v, 134v, 153v, 158v.
97. The Piiashev Group grew and eventually included the 307th Regiment with 2,005 men of the 61st Rifle Division transferred from the 45th Army, the 1st Battalion of the 66th Regiment of the 61st Rifle Division, the 25th NKVD Frontier Guard Regiment with 1,123 men, the 4th Battalion and a part of the 1st Battalion of the 155th Rifle Brigade, the 1st Battalion of the 808th Regiment of the 394th Rifle Division, the 4th Battalion of the 51st Rifle Brigade with 956 men, a half-battalion from the 1st Tbilisi Infantry School with 311 men advancing from Lake Ritsa via the Anchkha pass and another half-battalion from the 1st Tbilisi Infantry School with 400 men advancing along the Bzyb, the Sukhumi Infantry School with 395 men, an NKVD Destruction Battalion of 150 men, and a company of submachine-gunners and the attached artillery. Several of these battalions were fused into the Assembled (*svodnyi*) NKVD Regiment: Leselidze, 'Operativnaia direktiva No. 00896' (4 September 1942), TsAMO, f. 47, op. 1063, d. 456, l. 49; 'Kratkoe opisanie perevala Sancharo' (no date) (hereafter cited as 'Kratkoe opisanie perevala Sancharo'), TsAMO, f. 47, op. 1063, d. 668, l. 4; 'Zhurnal boevykh deistvii Zakfronta' (September 1942), TsAMO, f. 47, op. 1063, d. 194, l. 5; Bulyga, 'Svedeniia o chastiakh i podrazdeleniiakh oboroniaiushchikh i prikryvaiushchikh GKKh' (15 September 1942) (hereafter 'Svedeniia o chastiakh'), TsAMO, f. 47, op. 1063, d. 655, l. 73; General Petrov, 'Operativnaia svodka No. 3' (26 August 1942), TsAMO, f. 47, op. 1063, d. 658, l. 13.
98. 'Kratkoe opisanie perevala Sancharo', l. 4; Gneushev and Poput'ko, *Taina Marukhskogo lednika* (1971), 310.
99. Gneushev and Poput'ko, *Taina Marukhskogo lednika* (1971), 308.
100. Buchner, *Kampf im Gebirge*, 43.
101. 49th Mountain Corps, KTB (26 August 1942), BA-MA, RH 24-49/72, S. 135v.
102. The Buchner Group included one regular battalion – the 3rd Battalion of the 91st Mountain Regiment; another of its battalions was a hotchpotch unit made up of the Training Battalion of the 94th Mountain Regiment and a reconnaissance company of the 13th Mountain Regiment. It also had two mountain guns: Buchner, *Kampf im Gebirge*, 158.
103. 49th Mountain Corps, KTB (28 August 1942), BA-MA, RH 24-49/72, S. 155v.
104. Bulyga, 'Svedeniia o chastiakh', l. 73. Alex Buchner grossly inflates the strength of the Soviet forces in the Aishkha and Pseashkha regions in the main text of his book, claiming that the Buchner Group was facing four regiments of the 20th 'Mountain' Division: the 174th and the 67th Regiments in the Urushten valley, the 265th Regiment in the Malaia Laba valley, and the 379th Regiment at the southern approaches to the Pseashkha pass. However, in the attachments, he assesses the total strength of the enemy forces opposing the Buchner Group as four companies:

Buchner, *Kampf im Gebirge*, 138, 159. Indeed, only four Soviet companies of the 174th Regiment and a cavalry squadron with a total strength of 950 men were deployed in the Malaia Laba and Urushten valleys throughout September: Bulyga, 'Svedeniia o chastiakh', l. 73. Units of the 265th Regiment entered the battle only on 5 October, when most actions had already stopped: Zav'ialov, 'Oborona Glavnogo Kavkazskogo Khrebta', l. 12v.

105. These were the 2nd and the 4th Companies of the 174th 'Mountain' Regiment: Headquarters of the 20th 'Mountain' Division, 'Zhurnal boevykh deistvii 20-i gsd' (14 and 15 August 1942), TsAMO, f. 1089, op. 1, d. 6, l. 11; Zav'ialov, 'Oborona Glavnogo Kavkazskogo Khrebta', l. 12v.
106. 49th Mountain Corps, KTB (29 August 1942), BA-MA, RH 24-49/72, SS. 161v, 164v. Soviet sources state that the defenders repelled the German attack on 28 August and resisted until the night of 30 August, having killed or wounded 500 German soldiers: Zav'ialov, 'Oborona Glavnogo Kavkazskogo Khrebta', l. 12v. However, German reports state that the Buchner Group took the pass in 'a heavy battle' on 29 August, killing twenty Soviet soldiers: 49th Mountain Corps, KTB (29 August 1942), BA-MA, RH 24-49/72, S. 164v. The 4th Mountain Division stated its total losses on 29 August as eleven men killed, twenty-two wounded, and one missing in action, and on 30 August as nine men killed and twenty-eight wounded, including the casualties of the Stettner Group: 49th Mountain Corps, 'Zahlenmässige Übersicht'.
107. Headquarters of the 20th 'Mountain' Division, 'Zhurnal boevykh deistvii 20-i gsd' (11 September 1942), TsAMO, f. 1089, op. 1, d. 6, l. 17; Zav'ialov, 'Oborona Glavnogo Kavkazskogo Khrebta', l. 12v.
108. 49th Mountain Corps, KTB (31 August and 1 September 1942), BA-MA, RH 24-49/72, SS. 178v, 182v.
109. 49th Mountain Corps, KTB (3 September 1942), BA-MA, RH 24-49/72, SS. 192v, 193v.
110. Zav'ialov, 'Oborona Glavnogo Kavkazskogo Khrebta', l. 12v.
111. 'Partizanskie otriady v polose sovetskikh voisk Zakavkazskogo fronta', in Shapovalov, ed., *Bitva za Kavkaz*, 244, 245.
112. Nikolai Bugai and Askarbi Gonov, *Kavkaz: narody v eshelonakh* (Moscow: INSAN, 1998), 123, 164.
113. Tiulenev to Stalin, 'Boevoe donesenie No. 05' (19 August 1942), TsAMO, f. 47, op. 1063, d. 166, l. 13; Tiulenev to Stalin, 'Boevoe donesenie No. 013' (26 August 1942), TsAMO, f. 47, op. 1063, d. 166, l. 36; 'Zhurnal boevykh deistvii Zakfronta' (20 August 1942), TsAMO, f. 47, op. 1063, d. 183, ll. 147, 151.
114. 'Zhurnal boevykh deistvii Zakfronta' (19 August 1942), TsAMO, f. 47, op. 1063, d. 183, l. 143.
115. 49th Mountain Corps, KTB (25 August 1942), BA-MA, RH 24-49/72, S. 128v.
116. Captain Bobovskii, 'Opisanie perevala Dombai-Ul'gen' (October 1942), TsAMO, f. 401, op. 9511, d. 73, l. 35; General Petrov, 'Operativnaia svodka No. 7' (30 August 1942), TsAMO, f. 47, op. 1063, d. 658, l. 36.
117. Major Panin, 'Kratkoe opisanie perevala Klukhor' (no date), TsAMO, f. 47, op. 1063, d. 671, l. 10.
118. The half-battalion comprised a company of the 155th Rifle Brigade with 153 men and an NKVD company of 147 men: Major Zhashko, chief of staff of the 394th Rifle Division, 'Skhema obstanovki chastei Klukhorskogo napravleniia' (1 October 1942), TsAMO, f. 47, op. 1063, d. 671, l. 24.

119. Tiulenev, Beria and Bodin (24 August 1942), TsAMO, f. 47, op. 1063, d. 644, ll. 39–40.
120. Ibragimbeili, *Krakh 'Edel'veisa'*, 109.
121. Tiulenev to the commander of the Northern Army Group (3 September 1942), TsAMO, f. 47, op. 1063, d. 31, l. 68.
122. Zav'ialov, 'Oborona Glavnogo Kavkazskogo Khrebta', l. 9v.
123. Headquarters of the 37th Army to Beria (28 September 1942), TsAMO, f. 47, op. 1063, d. 31, l. 73; 49th Mountain Corps, KTB (12 and 13 August 1942), BA-MA, RH 24-49/72, SS. 255v, 262v; Hillgruber, ed., *Kriegstagebuch des Oberkommandos der Wehrmacht* (14 and 16 September 1942), 723, 730; Bauer, *Unternehmen 'Elbrus'*, 236, 237. Several Russian authors mention this episode, which demonstrated the utter incompetence of TCF Headquarters, but nobody comments on it: Linets and Ianush, *Oborona Severnogo Kavkaza*, 261, 265, Batyrov, Grebeniuk and Matveev, eds., *Bitva za Kavkaz*, 96; Moshchanskii, *Stoiat' nasmert!*, 103; Grechko, *Bitva za Kavkaz* (1969), 164; Ibragimbeili, *Krakh 'Edel'veisa'*, 109.
124. Headquarters of the 46th Army, 'Plan oborony perevalov ot Marukhskogo do Sancharskogo' (22 August 1942), TsAMO, f. 401, op. 9511, d. 18, l. 41.
125. Without the 1st and the 9th Companies deployed in the Klych valley and at the Adange pass.
126. General Petrov, 'Operativnaia svodka No. 4' (27 August 1942), TsAMO, f. 47, op. 1063, d. 658, l. 19; 'Pereval Marukh' (after September 1942), TsAMO, f. 47, op. 1063, d. 666, l. 7; Gneushev and Poput'ko, *Taina Marukhskogo lednika* (1971), 113.
127. The 2nd and the 3rd Battalions of the 808th Rifle Regiment: Abramov, *Na ratnykh dorogakh*, 153.
128. Sergatskov, 'Plan oborony Glavnogo Kavkazskogo Khrebta' (30 June 1942), TsAMO, f. 47, op. 1063, d. 456, l. 15.
129. Colonel Abramov, 'Doklad o voennykh deistviiakh na Marukhskom napravlenii' (20 September 1942) (hereafter cited as 'Doklad o voennykh deistviiakh'), TsAMO, f. 47, op. 1063, d. 692, l. 35.
130. Abramov, *Na ratnykh dorogakh*, 155.
131. The 1st Battalion of the 808th Regiment was deployed in the Sancharo region.
132. Abramov, 'Doklad o voennykh deistviiakh', 34, 35, 155, 156.
133. Abramov, *Na ratnykh dorogakh*, 161; Abramov, 'Doklad o voennykh deistviiakh', l. 36; Gneushev and Poput'ko, *Taina Marukhskogo lednika* (1966), 17.
134. Abramov, *Na ratnykh dorogakh*, 162.
135. Gioev, *Bitva za Kavkaz*, 89–92.
136. Abramov, 'Doklad o voennykh deistviiakh', l. 50. Only one or two companies had short ropes and several ice axes: 'Vospominaniia starshego leitenanta Shuvaeva', in Shapovalov, ed., *Bitva za Kavkaz*, 240; Gneushev and Poput'ko, *Taina Marukhskogo lednika* (1966), 71, 74.
137. Abramov, *Na ratnykh dorogakh*, 153; General Konstantin Skorobogatkin to Marshal Matvei Zakharov (22 January 1963), TsAMO, f. 1720, op. 1, d. 10, l. 8.
138. The 2nd and 3rd Battalions of the 808th Rifle Regiment, and all three battalions of the 810th Rifle Regiment: Gneushev and Poput'ko, *Taina Marukhskogo lednika* (1966), 34, 281, 282.
139. The 2nd Battalion of the 808th Rifle Regiment and the 2nd Battalion of the 810th Rifle Regiment.
140. Abramov, 'Doklad o voennykh deistviiakh', ll. 36, 37.
141. Abramov, *Na ratnykh dorogakh*, 166; Gneushev and Poput'ko, *Taina Marukhskogo lednika* (1966), 35.

142. Gneushev and Poput'ko, *Taina Marukhskogo lednika* (1966), 34, 41, 106, 109, 282.
143. Buchner, *Kampf im Gebirge*, 56, 65.
144. The 5th Rifle Company: General Petrov, 'Operativnaia svodka No. 4' (27 August 1942), TsAMO, f. 47, op. 1063, d. 658, l. 19; 49th Mountain Corps, KTB (27August 1942), BA-MA, RH 24-49/72, S. 142.
145. Buchner, *Kampf im Gebirge*, 49.
146. Gneushev and Poput'ko, *Taina Marukhskogo lednika* (1966), 18, 75, 76.
147. Semenovskii, *Al'pinizm*, 190.
148. 'Vospominaniia starshego leitenanta Shuvaeva', 243; Abramov, 'Doklad o voennykh deistviiakh', l. 38.
149. Colonel Rasskazov, 'Opersvodka No. 395' (3 September 1942), TsAMO, f. 1089, op. 1, d. 3, l. 18; Gneushev and Poput'ko, *Taina Marukhskogo lednika* (1966), 28, 78, 86, 109; Bekishvili, 'Oborona kavkazskikh perevalov', 73.
150. Abramov, 'Doklad o voennykh deistviiakh', l. 39; Gneushev and Poput'ko, *Taina Marukhskogo lednika* (1966), 110, 125.
151. 49th Mountain Corps, 'Zahlenmässige Übersicht'.
152. Abramov, 'Doklad o voennykh deistviiakh', l. 39.
153. Ibid., ll. 39, 43.
154. Ibid., l. 37; Gneushev and Poput'ko, *Taina Marukhskogo lednika* (1966), 17; 'Vospominaniia starshego leitenanta Shuvaeva', 240, 243.
155. Abramov, 'Doklad o voennykh deistviiakh', ll. 41, 42; General Konstantin Skorobogatkin to Marshal Matvei Zakharov (22 January 1963), TsAMO, f. 1720, op. 1, d. 10, l. 8.
156. Abramov, 'Doklad o voennykh deistviiakh', l. 43.
157. The 2nd Battalion of the 808th Rifle Regiment and the 2nd Battalion of the 810th Rifle Regiment.
158. Abramov, 'Doklad o voennykh deistviiakh', ll. 41, 42; Buchner, *Kampf im Gebirge*, 64.
159. Kul'kov and Rzheshevskii, eds., *Zimniaia voina*, II:105.
160. It consisted of the remnants of the 3rd Battalion of the 808th Rifle Regiment and the 1st and 3rd Battalions of the 810th Rifle Regiment.
161. Buchner, *Kampf im Gebirge*, 49.
162. The 5th Company of the 810th Regiment arrived first and, by 17 August, was joined by its 4th and 6th Companies: 'Zhurnal boevykh deistvii Zakfronta' (5 August 1942), TsAMO, f. 47, op. 1063, d. 183, l. 54; Zhashko, 'Svedeniia o boevom i chislennom sostave', l. 114. Alex Buchner and Wilhelm Tieke, who takes most of his information from Buchner's writings, claim that, on 25 August, the Soviets threw a platoon of the 13th Mountain Regiment down from Marukh: Buchner, *Kampf im Gebirge*, 51; Tieke, *The Caucasus* and *the Oil*, 110. However, they do not provide sources. According to Major Zhashko, chief of staff of the 394th Rifle Division, on 17 August, the 2nd Battalion of the 810th Rifle Regiment had already taken position at Marukh, and its vanguards were 15 kilometres down the northern slopes: Zhashko, 'Svedeniia o boevom i chislennom sostave', l. 114. The Germans would have had to undertake a serious effort to drive this battalion from the pass, but neither the war diary of the 49th Mountain Corps nor any Soviet document mentions any engagements near Marukh between 20 August, the first day when any unit of the 13th Mountain Regiment could have theoretically reached the pass, and 26 August, when the Soviets and the Germans recorded the first clash 15 kilometres north of the pass. The 1st Mountain Division received an order to take Marukh only on 25 August: 49th Mountain Corps, KTB

(25 August 1942), BA-MA, RH 24-49/72, S. 128v. Most likely, the allegation about the clash at Marukh on 25 August is false.

163. Buchner, *Kampf im Gebirge*, 52; Colonel Zinov'ev, OG deputy chief of staff, 'Dokladnaia zapiska o sostoianii oborony perevalov Marukhskogo napravleniia' (8 August 1942) (hereafter cited as 'Dokladnaia zapiska'), TsAMO, f. 47, op. 1063, d. 692, l. 66.
164. Zinov'ev, 'Dokladnaia zapiska', ll. 66, 67; Petrov, 'Doklad o sostoianii oborony perevalov', l. 147; Kumchiev, commissar of the 394th Rifle Division, to the Chief of Staff of the 3rd Rifle Corps (23 August 1942), TsAMO, f. 1720, op. 1, d. 23, l. 195.
165. Abramov, 'Doklad o voennykh deistviiakh', l. 46; Colonel Abramov, 'Voennomu sovetu 46-i armii' (29 September 1942) (hereafter cited as 'Voennomu sovetu 46-i armii'), TsAMO, f. 47, op. 1063, d. 692, l. 56; General Petrov, 'Operativnaia svodka No. 8' (31 August 1942), TsAMO, f. 47, op. 1063, d. 658, l. 42.
166. Zinov'ev, 'Dokladnaia zapiska', l. 67.
167. Abramov, 'Doklad o voennykh deistviiakh', l. 40.
168. Buchner, *Kampf im Gebirge*, 56, 57.
169. Gneushev and Poput'ko, *Taina Marukhskogo lednika* (1966), 247; General Petrov, 'Operativnaia svodka No. 11' (3 September 1942), TsAMO, f. 47, op. 1063, d. 658, l. 58.
170. Colonel Pavel Belekhov to General Petrov (21 November 1942), TsAMO, f. 47, op. 1063, d. 692, ll. 216, 216v.
171. Abramov, 'Voennomu sovetu 46-i armii', l. 58.
172. Leselidze, 'Operativnaia direktiva No. 00896' (4 September 1942), TsAMO, f. 47, op. 1063, d. 456, l. 46.
173. Buchner, *Kampf im Gebirge*, 59, 61; Kaltenegger, *Gebirgsjäger im Kaukasus*, 121.
174. Buchner, *Kampf im Gebirge*, 62–4.
175. Zaitsev, chief of staff of the TCF Engineers, 'Opersvodka po zagrazhdeniiam No. 5' (4 September 1942), TsAMO, f. 47, op. 1063, d. 662, l. 6; 'Zhurnal boevykh deistvii Zakfronta' (September 1942), TsAMO, f. 47, op. 1063, d. 194, l. 246.
176. Abramov, 'Voennomu sovetu 46-i armii', l. 56; Abramov, 'Doklad o voennykh deistviiakh', l. 45; Zav'ialov, 'Oborona Glavnogo Kavkazskogo Khrebta', l. 5v.
177. 'Pereval Marukh' (no date), TsAMO, f. 47, op. 1063, d. 194, l. 6v; Abramov, 'Doklad o voennykh deistviiakh', l. 45; Zinov'ev, 'Dokladnaia zapiska', l. 67. Russian authors misinform their readers that 'the 808th and the 810th Regiments of the 394th Georgian Division fought the fascists to the last bullet', 'the units of the 810th Rifle Regiment … being surrounded … fought their way out despite suffering heavy casualties', and 'the whole 4th Company fell in unequal battle but nobody panicked and nobody took a step back': Linets and Ianush, *Oborona Severnogo Kavkaza*, 127, 128; Gneushev and Poput'ko, *Taina Marukhskogo lednika* (1971), 105.
178. Abramov, 'Doklad o voennykh deistviiakh', l. 45.
179. Ibid., l. 44; Abramov, 'Voennomu sovetu 46-i armii', ll. 56, 57; Major Vladimir Smirnov, commander of the 810th Rifle Regiment, to Colonel Tronin (no date), TsAMO, f. 47, op. 1063, d. 692, l. 75.
180. Smirnov to Zinov'ev (12 November 1942), TsAMO, f. 47, op. 1063, d. 691, l. 43v.
181. 'Zhurnal boevykh deistvii Zakfronta' (September 1942), TsAMO, f. 47, op. 1063, d. 194, ll. 4, 89; General Petrov, 'Operativnaia svodka No. 14' (6 September 1942), TsAMO, f. 47, op. 1063, d. 658, l. 72; Zav'ialov, 'Oborona Glavnogo Kavkazskogo Khrebta', l. 5v; Batyrov, Grebeniuk and Matveev, eds., *Bitva za Kavkaz*, 98; Linets and Ianush, *Oborona Severnogo Kavkaza*, 280; Gneushev and Poput'ko, *Taina Marukhskogo lednika* (1966), 110.

182. Colonel Abramov, 'Boevoi prikaz No. 04' (6 September 1942), TsAMO, f. 47, op. 1063, d. 692, l. 51.
183. Abramov, 'Doklad o voennykh deistviiakh', l. 44; Abramov, 'Voennomu sovetu 46-i armii', l. 56.
184. Buchner, *Kampf im Gebirge*, 65.
185. Zinov'ev, 'Dokladnaia zapiska', l. 66.
186. 49th Mountain Corps, KTB (8 September 1942), BA-MA, RH 24-49/72, S. 231v; 49th Mountain Corps, 'Zahlenmässige Übersicht'.
187. Buchner, *Kampf im Gebirge*, 64.
188. Leselidze, 'Postanovlenie Voennogo soveta 46-i armii' (1 November 1942), TsAMO, f. 1524, op. 1, d. 9, l. 110.
189. Ibid.
190. Bonch-Bruevich, *Poteria nami Galitsii*, I:115.
191. Gneushev and Poput'ko, *Taina Marukhskogo lednika* (1971), 145, 146.
192. Abramov, 'Voennomu sovetu 46-i armii', l. 57.
193. Ibid., l. 57.
194. Gneushev and Poput'ko, *Taina Marukhskogo lednika* (1971), 154, 155.
195. Bekishvili, 'Oborona kavkazskikh perevalov', 76.
196. Gneushev and Poput'ko, *Taina Marukhskogo lednika* (1971), 156.
197. Leselidze, 'Postanovlenie Voennogo soveta 46-i armii' (1 November 1942), TsAMO, f. 1524, op. 1, d. 9, l. 109.
198. Gneushev and Poput'ko, *Taina Marukhskogo lednika* (1971), 158.
199. Benkendorf, 'Vospominaniia', 235.
200. Leselidze, 'Postanovlenie Voennogo soveta 46-i armii' (1 November 1942), TsAMO, f. 1524, op. 1, d. 9, l. 109; Gneushev and Poput'ko, *Taina Marukhskogo lednika* (1971), 158.
201. General Petrov, 'Operativnaia svodka No. 14' (6 September 1942), TsAMO, f. 47, op. 1063, d. 658, l. 72.
202. Tiulenev to Stalin, 'Boevoe donesenie No. 026' (7 September 1942), TsAMO, f. 47, op. 1063, d. 166, l. 100v; Tiulenev to Stalin (9 September 1942), TsAMO, f. 47, op. 1063, d. 166, l. 126.
203. Leselidze to Abramov (9 September 1942), TsAMO, f. 401, op. 9511, d. 18, l. 96.
204. Abramov, 'Doklad o voennykh deistviiakh', l. 46.
205. Leselidze, 'Postanovlenie Voennogo soveta 46-i armii' (1 November 1942), TsAMO, f. 1524, op. 1, d. 9, l. 214v.
206. Abramov, 'Doklad o voennykh deistviiakh', ll. 46, 49; Abramov, 'Boevoi prikaz No. 04', TsAMO, f. 47, op. 1063, d. 692, l. 51.
207. Nikolai Rukhadze, chief of TCF Special Sections, to Tiulenev, 'Spetsial'noe soobshchenie o nedochetakh v ispol'zovanii zagradotriadov 46-i armii' (15 November 1942), TsAMO, f. 47, op. 1063, d. 28, l. 101.
208. Abramov, 'Doklad o voennykh deistviiakh', l. 47.
209. Abramov, 'Voennomu sovetu 46-i armii', l. 58. The reinforcements included the 1st Battalion of the 107th Rifle Brigade, a battalion from the 2nd Tbilisi Infantry School, a part of the 1st Battalion of the 155th Rifle Brigade, and a company of 110 men from the 36th Naval Frontier Guard Unit that joined the remnants of sailors who had survived the raid across the MCR: 'Pereval Marukh' (no date), TsAMO, f. 47, op. 1063, d. 666, l. 8; Abramov, 'Doklad o voennykh deistviiakh', l. 48; General Petrov, 'Operativnaia svodka No. 15' (7 September 1942), TsAMO, f. 47, op. 1063, d. 658, l. 80; Gneushev and Poput'ko, *Taina Marukhskogo lednika* (1966), 282.
210. Beria, 'Donesenie predstavitelia GKO' (23 August 1942), 160.

211. Tiulenev, *Krakh operatsii 'Edelveis'*, 56.
212. Ibragimbeili, *Krakh 'Edel'veisa'*, 105.
213. Iampol'skii et al., eds., *Organy gosudarstvennoi bezopasnosti*, III/2:169; Ibragimbeili, *Krakh 'Edel'veisa'*, 102, 104; I. Basik, 'Voennoe iskusstvo soverstkikh voisk v oboronitel'nukh operatsiiakh bitvy za Kavkaz', in Batyrov, ed., *Materialy mezhdunarodnoi nauchnoi konferentsii*, 30; Bezugol'nyi, 'Uchastie vysshikh gosudarstvennykh deiatelei', 62; Zav'ialov and Kaliadin, *Bitva za Kavkaz*, 76.
214. *'Protiv loma net priema.'*

6 The Soviet Counteroffensive: A Stalemate Snatched from the Jaws of Victory

1. Hillgruber, ed., *Kriegstagebuch*, II/1:691; 49th Mountain Corps, KTB (5 September 1942), BA-MA, RH 24-49/72, S. 207v.
2. 49th Mountain Corps, KTB (5 September 1942), BA-MA, RH 24-49/72, SS. 208–215v.
3. Hillgruber, ed., *Kriegstagebuch*, 691, 695.
4. Document No. 21, 'Iz pokazanii V. Keitelia' (30 September 1946), in Shapovalov, ed., *Bitva za Kavkaz*, 89.
5. Hillgruber, ed., *Kriegstagebuch*, 691, 697.
6. Tieke, *The Caucasus and the Oil*, 192–6.
7. Beria to the Military Council of the 46th Army (28 August 1942), TsAMO, f. 401, op. 9511, d. 30, l. 123; Abramov, *Na ratnykh dorogakh*, 153.
8. 'Zhurnal boevykh deistvii Zakfronta' (August 1942), TsAMO, f. 47, op. 1063, d. 183, l. 163.
9. 'Zhurnal boevykh deistvii Zakfronta' (2 September 1942), TsAMO, f. 47, op. 1063, d. 194, l. 27; 'Zhurnal boevykh deistvii voisk 46-i armii' (1 September 1942), TsAMO, f. 401, op. 9511, d. 9, l. 25v.
10. General Tiulenev, 'Operativnaia direktiva No. 015' (11 September 1942), in Shapovalov, ed., *Bitva za Kavkaz*, 221.
11. Major Aleksandr Korobov, commander of 815th Rifle Regiment, 'Boevoi prikaz' (24 August 1942), TsAMO, f. 815sp, op. 39410, d. 1, l. 1; Leselidze, 'Operativnaia direktiva No. 916' (13 September 1942), TsAMO, f. 401, op. 9511, d. 18, l. 46.
12. Badanin, *Na boevykh rubezhakh Kavkaza*, 49.
13. Gioev, *Bitva za Kavkaz*, 108.
14. The NKVD rank of major corresponded to the rank of brigade commander in the Red Army.
15. Varlam Kakuchaia to Tiulenev (22 September 1942), TsAMO, f. 47, op. 1063, d. 664, ll. 312, 314.
16. Ibid., ll. 312–314.
17. Ibid., ll. 313, 316.
18. This force included two battalions of the 815th Rifle Regiment, the 220th Cavalry Regiment, the remnants of the training battalion of the 394th Rifle Division, the 36th Naval Frontier Guard Battalion with 280 men, the 1st Company of the 810th Rifle Regiment, a unit from the Sukhumi Infantry School with 277 men, the 5th and 6th Independent 'Mountain' Companies with a total strength of 350 men, and two militia platoons: Petrov to Beria (29 August 1942), TsAMO, f. 47, op. 1063, d. 689, l. 12; Tiulenev to Stalin (29 August 1942), TsAMO, f. 47, op. 1063, d. 689, l. 19;

Leselidze, 'Operativnaia direktiva No. 00896' (4 September 1942), TsAMO, f. 47, op. 1063, d. 456, l. 48; Gneushev and Poput'ko, *Taina Marukhskogo lednika* (1966), 281.

19. 'Zhurnal boevykh deistvii voisk 46-i armii' (1 September 1942), TsAMO, f. 401, op. 9511, d. 9, l. 26.
20. The reinforcements included the 121st 'Mountain' Regiment and the 3rd Battalion of the 155th Rifle Brigade: General Petrov, 'Operativnaia svodka No. 4' (27 August 1942), TsAMO, f. 47, op. 1063, d. 658, l. 18; 'Perechen' soedineniii i chastei oboroniaiushchikh perevaly' (20 September 1942), TsAMO, f. 47, op. 1063, d. 655, l. 60v. In addition, a company of the 1st Battalion of the 155th Rifle Brigade with 153 men and an NKVD company with 147 men were deployed at the foot of the neighbouring Ptysh pass: Major Zhashko, chief of staff of the 394th Rifle Division, 'Skhema obstanovki chastei Klukhorskogo napravleniia' (1 October 1942), TsAMO, f. 47, op. 1063, d. 671, l. 24.
21. Buchner, *Kampf im Gebirge*, 182.
22. Litvinov to Popov (12 November 1942), TsAMO, f. 47, op. 1063, d. 691, l. 38v.
23. 'Zhurnal boevykh deistvii voisk 46-i armii' (2 September 1942), TsAMO, f. 401, op. 9511, d. 9, l. 34; Tiulenev to Stalin, 'Boevoe donesenie No. 024' (5 September 1942), TsAMO, f. 47, op. 1063, d. 166, l. 90v; Colonel Rasskazov, 'Opersvodka No. 395' (3 September 1942), TsAMO, f. 1089, op. 1, d. 3, l. 18.
24. 49th Mountain Corps, 'Zahlenmässige Übersicht'.
25. Document No. 90, Bogdan Kobulov, 'Donesenie zamestitelia Narkoma vnutrennikh del' (17 September 1942), in Shapovalov, ed., *Bitva za Kavkaz*, 228; Kakuchaia to Tiulenev (22 September 1942), TsAMO, f. 47, op. 1063, d. 664, l. 315; Mikeladze, chief of staff of the 46th Army 'Itogovaia operativnaia svodka No. 2' (6 November 1942), TsAMO, f. 401, op. 9511, d. 112, l. 3.
26. Tiulenev, *Krakh operatsii 'Edel'veis'*, 77. No abysses exist near Klukhor.
27. These were the 815th Rifle Regiment of the 394th Divisions and 121st Regiment of the 9th 'Mountain' Division.
28. General Petrov, 'Operativnaia svodka No. 27' (19 September 1942), TsAMO, f. 47, op. 1063, d. 658, l. 159; Zav'ialov, 'Oborona Glavnogo Kavkazskogo Khrebta', l. 10; Major Panin, 'Kratkoe opisanie perevala Klukhor' (no date), TsAMO, f. 47, op. 1063, d. 671, ll. 11, 11v; Grechko, *Bitva za Kavkaz* (1969), 163.
29. Opryshko, *Zaoblachnyi front*, 67.
30. Gusev, *El'brus v ogne*, 112; Hillgruber, ed., *Kriegstagebuch*, 755; Major Agaev, commander of the 121st 'Mountain' Regiment, 'Skhema zanimaemoi pozitsii 121-go gsp' (no date), TsAMO, f. 815sp, op. 39410, d. 1, l. 323.
31. Litvinov to Popov (12 November 1942), TsAMO, f. 47, op. 1063, d. 691, l. 38v.
32. Colonel Belekhov to Korobov, 'Boevoe rasporiazhenie No. 6' (14 October 1942), TsAMO, f. 815sp, op. 39410, d. 1, l. 273; Korobov, 'Boevoi prikaz No. 6' (8 October 1942), TsAMO, f. 815sp, op. 39410, d. 1, l. 270; 'Raspolozhenie ognevykh tochek protivnika i nasha oborona' (21 November 1942), TsAMO, f. 815sp, op. 39410, d. 1, l. 448; Belekhov to Korobov, 'Boevoe rasporiazhenie No. 19' (28 November 1942), TsAMO, f. 815sp, op. 39410, d. 1, l. 456; Rybin to Petrov, 'Opersvodka No. 20' (9 January 1943), TsAMO, f. 47, op. 1063, d. 692, l. 203; Lieutenant-Colonel Mezentsev, senior assistant to the OG Chief of Staff, 'Pis'mennyi doklad' (16 December 1942), TsAMO, f. 47, op. 1063, d. 691, l. 68; Gusev, *El'brus v ogne*, 126.
33. Litvinov, OG representative with the 394th Rifle Division, to Romanov (19 September 1942), TsAMO, f. 47, op. 1063, d. 692, l. 27; 49th Mountain Corps, 'Zahlenmässige Übersicht'.

34. Litvinov to Popov (12 November 1942), TsAMO, f. 47, op. 1063, d. 691, l. 40v.
35. The reinforcements included the 1st Battalion of the 155th Rifle Brigade, minus one company, which was engaged near the Ptysh pass; the 2nd Battalion of the 155th Rifle Brigade; the 1st Battalion of the 107th Rifle Brigade, minus one company; a battalion from the Tbilisi Infantry School; and a company from the Sukhumi Infantry School: 'Opersvodka No. 410' (18 September 1942), TsAMO, f. 47, op. 1063, d. 655, l. 22; Abramov, 'Doklad o voennykh deistviiakh' l. 48; Document No. 98, K. Shuvaev, 'Vospominaniia byvshego komandira otriada razvedchikov' (August–September 1942), in Shapovalov, ed., *Bitva za Kavkaz*, 244. The battalion of the 107th Rifle Brigade arrived without shovels: Gneushev and Poput'ko, *Taina Marukhskogo lednika* (1971), 171, 178, 200. By this time, the 808th and the 810th Rifle Regiments in the Marukh region equalled at most a battalion each.
36. Ibragimbeili, *Krakh 'Edel'veisa'*, 111.
37. Grechko, *Bitva za Kavkaz* (1969), 165; Zav'ialov, 'Oborona Glavnogo Kavkazskogo Khrebta', l. 14v.
38. Shuvaev, 'Vospominaniia byvshego komandira otriada razvedchikov', 244. See also Gioev, *Bitva za Kavkaz*, 105.
39. 49th Mountain Corps, 'Zahlenmässige Übersicht'.
40. 'Karta polozheniia voisk armii na Klukhorskom napravlenii' (January 1943), TsAMO, f. 401, op. 9511, d. 116.
41. Gioev, *Bitva za Kavkaz*, 102; Gneushev and Poput'ko, *Taina Marukhskogo lednika* (1966), 140, 143.
42. 49th Mountain Corps, KTB (5 September 1942), BA-MA, RH 24-49/73, S. 168v.
43. Document No. 130, V. Filimonov, 'Iz vospominanii uchastnika Velikoi Otechestvennoi voiny' (hereafter cited as 'Iz vospominanii uchastnika'), in Shapovalov, ed., *Bitva za Kavkaz*, 309.
44. Rybin, chief of staff of the 13th Rifle Corps, to Petrov, 'Opersvodka No. 23' (12 January 1943), TsAMO, f. 47, op. 1063, d. 692, l. 206; 'Karta polozheniia voisk armii na Klukhorskom napravlenii' (January 1943), TsAMO, f. 401, op. 9511, d. 116.
45. Colonel Mikeladze, 'Itogovaia operativnaia svodka No. 2' (6 November 1942), TsAMO, f. 401, op. 9511, d. 112, l. 4; 49th Mountain Corps, 'Zahlenmässige Übersicht'. Most of the 1st Mountain Division was transferred to the Tuapse region and entered into much more intensive actions on 27 September.
46. Tieke, *The Caucasus and the Oil*, 192.
47. Two squadrons of the 214th Regiment of the 63rd Cavalry Division and a half-battalion of the 8th Motorised NKVD Regiment with 271 men, reinforced later by a battalion of the 28th Training Rifle Brigade and a battalion of the 51st Rifle Brigade: General Petrov, 'Operativnaia svodka No. 4' (27 August 1942), TsAMO, f. 47, op. 1063, d. 658, l. 19.
48. Mezentsev, 'Itogovyi doklad', l. 188v; 49th Mountain Corps, KTB (2 and 12 September 1942), BA-MA, RH 24-49/72, SS. 188v, 261v.
49. General Petrov, 'Operativnaia svodka Nos. 11, 17–23' (3, 10–15 September 1942), TsAMO, f. 47, op. 1063, d. 658, ll. 57, 96, 100, 104, 114, 123, 128; Rasskazov, 'Opersvodka Nos. 401–408' (9–15 September 1942), TsAMO, f. 1089, op. 1, d. 3, ll. 22, 25, 28, 34, 37, 41, 44; 49th Mountain Corps, KTB (2, 3, 9, 12 September 1942), BA-MA, RH 24-49/72, SS. 188v, 191v, 252v, 254v.
50. Saltykov, 'Doklad' (12 October 1942), TsAMO, f. 47, op. 1063, d. 691, l. 4v.

51. Captain Ivanchenko, OG representative with the 63rd Cavalry Division, to Romanov (18 September 1942), TsAMO, f. 47, op. 1063, d. 692, ll. 28–30; Bulyga, 'O nedostatkakh v snabzhenii voisk oboroniaiushchikh perevaly' (23 September 1942), TsAMO, f. 47, op. 1063, d. 643, l. 16.
52. From the 214th Regiment of the 63rd Cavalry Division.
53. Opryshko, *Zaoblachnyi front*, 47–55.
54. TCF Headquarters, 'Zhurnal boevykh deistvii Zakfronta' (18 August 1942), TsAMO, f. 47, op. 1063, d. 183, l. 139; Colonel Rasskazov, chief of staff of the 46th Army (22 August 1942), TsAMO, f. 47, op. 1063, d. 456, l. 44; Batyrov, Grebeniuk and Matveev, eds., *Bitva za Kavkaz*, 180.
55. The 897th 'Mountain' Regiment.
56. The 900th 'Mountain' Regiment.
57. Romanov, 'Operativnaia svodka No. 30' (22 September 1942), TsAMO, f. 47, op. 1063, d. 658, l. 171; Bozhenko, 'Kharakteristika 242-i gsd' (30 November 1942), TsAMO, f. 1524, op. 1, d. 12, l. 95.
58. Zav'ialov, 'Oborona Glavnogo Kavkazskogo Khrebta', l. 2.
59. Major Zarelua, head of the NKVD Special Section of the 46th Army (10 November 1942), TsAMO, f. 47, op. 1063, d. 456, ll. 116, 117.
60. 897th 'Mountain' Regiment.
61. Bozhenko, 'Opersvodka No. 64' (13 November 1942), TsAMO, f. 1524, op. 1, d. 12, l. 78; Opryshko, *Zaoblachnyi front*, 114.
62. Grechko, *Bitva za Kavkaz* (1969), 164.
63. Ivanchenko, 'Doklad' (3 November 1942), TsAMO, f. 47, op. 1063, d. 692, l. 117; Aleksandr Gusev, Military Engineer of the 3rd Rank, to Petrov (17 January 1943), TsAMO, f. 47, op. 1063, d. 692, l. 273.
64. Zav'ialov, 'Oborona Glavnogo Kavkazskogo Khrebta', l. 9v.
65. 49th Mountain Corps, KTB (5 September 1942), BA-MA, RH 24-49/72, S. 261v; Major Zhibkov, 'Operativnaia informatsiia k 14:00' (6 November 1942), TsAMO, f. 401, op. 9511, d. 52, l. 17; Colonel Mikeladze, 'Boevoe donesenie No. 42' (13 November 1942), TsAMO, f. 401, op. 9511, d. 52, l. 41; Opryshko, *Zaoblachnyi front*, 56, 89, 103, 105, 129.
66. Gusev, *El'brus v ogne*, 198, 200; Evgenii Simonov, 'Geroi El'brusa',*Turist* 3 (1967), 3.
67. 'Kratkoe opisanie perevala Sancharo', l. 4; Bulyga, 'Svedeniia o chastiakh', l. 73; Mezentsev, 'Itogovyi doklad', l. 190. According to Beria's report filed on 9 September 1942, the Germans took the Dou and the Achavchar passes on 31 August: Beria, 'Donesenie predstavitelia GKO' (9 September 1942), 218. The war diary of the 49th Mountain Corps states that, on 30 August, Stettner received an order to take Dou and Achavchar, but the next day he received a new order to retreat to the north of the Bzyb: 49th Mountain Corps, KTB (30 and 31 August), BA-MA, RH 24-49/72, SS. 171, 175v. Neither Soviet nor German sources give information on actions at these passes. Most likely, the Germans did not attempt to take either Dou or Achavchar.
68. 49th Mountain Corps, KTB, Document No. 395 (29 August 1942), BA-MA, RH 24-49/79; Gneushev and Poput'ko, *Taina Marukhskogo lednika* (1971), 303; Bekishvili, 'Oborona kavkazskikh perevalov', 81. The 2nd Battalion of the 13th Mountain Regiment defended the bridge.
69. The 3rd Battalion of the 91st Mountain Regiment defended the pass.
70. This was the 1st Battalion of the 808th Rifle Regiment.
71. Buchner, *Kampf im Gebirge*, 182.
72. Ibid., 45, 169.

73. Kaltenegger, *Gebirgsjäger im Kaukasus*, 75; Buchner, *Kampf im Gebirge*, 161.
74. 49th Mountain Corps, KTB (5 September 1942), BA-MA, RH 24-49/72, SS. 193v, 194v; Hillgruber, ed., *Kriegstagebuch*, 677.
75. 49th Mountain Corps, KTB (31 August 1942), BA-MA, RH 24-49/72, S. 175v.
76. Buchner, *Kampf im Gebirge*, 165–70; 'Zhurnal boevykh deistvii voisk 46-i armii' (2 September 1942), TsAMO, f. 401, op. 9511, d. 9, ll. 29–31; Colonel Rasskazov, 'Opersvodka No. 395' (3 September 1942), TsAMO, f. 1089, op. 1, d. 3, l. 18.
77. Rasskazov, 'Opersvodka No. 395' (3 September 1942), TsAMO, f. 1089, op. 1, d. 3, l. 18; 'Kratkoe opisanie perevala Sancharo', l. 4v.
78. Rasskazov to Petrov (2 September 1942), TsAMO, f. 47, op. 1063, d. 644, l. 63.
79. General Petrov, 'Operativnaia svodka Nos. 11, 12 and 13 (3–5 September)', TsAMO, f. 47, op. 1063, d. 658, ll. 59, 63, 68; Rasskazov, 'Opersvodka No. 395' (3 September 1942), TsAMO, f. 1089, op. 1, d. 3, l. 19.
80. Buchner, *Kampf im Gebirge*, 47, 171; 49th Mountain Corps, KTB (4 September 1942), BA-MA, RH 24-49/72, S. 199v.
81. 49th Mountain Corps, KTB (4 September 1942), BA-MA, RH 24-49/72, S. 199v; Piiashev to Kobulov (11 September 1942), TsAMO, f. 47, op. 1063, d. 668, l. 15.
82. Buchner, *Kampf im Gebirge*, 173; TCF Headquarters, 'Zhurnal boevykh deistvii Zakfronta' (25 August 1942), TsAMO, f. 47, op. 1063, d. 183, l. 180.
83. Leselidze, 'Komandiram soedinenii i chastei Zakfronta' (11 September 1942), TsAMO, f. 47, op. 1063, d. 456, l. 118.
84. 49th Mountain Corps, KTB (7 September 1942), BA-MA, RH 24-49/72, S. 225v.
85. Buchner, *Kampf im Gebirge*, 173; General Petrov, 'Konspekt' (2 September 1942), TsAMO, f. 47, op. 1063, d. 689, ll. 28, 29.
86. 49th Mountain Corps, KTB (7 September 1942), BA-MA, RH 24-49/72, SS. 224v, 225v.
87. Ibragimbeili, *Krakh 'Edel'veisa'*, 108; Gneushev and Poput'ko, *Taina Marukhskogo lednika* (1966), 272; Moshchanskii, *Stoiat' nasmert!*, 78.
88. Zav'ialov, 'Oborona Glavnogo Kavkazskogo Khrebta', l. 11v.
89. Buchner, *Kampf im Gebirge*, 177, 178.
90. These were the 1st and 3rd Battalions of 25th Frontier Guards Regiment: Piiashev to Kobulov (11 September 1942), TsAMO, f. 47, op. 1063, d. 668, l. 14.
91. This force included the 2nd Battalion of the 25th Frontier Guards Regiment, an Assembled NKVD 'Regiment' of 700 men, and 305 men from the Tbilisi Infantry School: 'Kratkoe opisanie perevala Sancharo', l. 5; Piiashev to Kobulov (11 September 1942), TsAMO, f. 47, op. 1063, d. 668, ll. 5v, 14; Petrov, 'Operativnaia svodka No. 18' (11 September 1942), TsAMO, f. 47, op. 1063, d. 658, l. 101.
92. Gneushev and Poput'ko, *Taina Marukhskogo lednika* (1971), 287.
93. 49th Mountain Corps, KTB (21 September 1942), BA-MA, RH 24-49/73, S. 19v; 'Kratkoe opisanie perevala Sancharo', ll. 5v–7v.
94. These were the 1st and 2nd Battalions of the 91st Mountain Regiment: Buchner, *Kampf im Gebirge*, 184.
95. Bulyga, 'Svedeniia o chastiakh', l. 73.
96. Leselidze to Piiashev (2 September 1942), TsAMO, f. 401, op. 9511, d. 40, l. 21; Leselidze to Piiashev (13 September 1942), TsAMO, f. 401, op. 9511, d. 18, l. 107; Leselidze, 'Chastnyi boevoi prikaz No. 009' (15 September 1942), TsAMO, f. 1089, op. 1, d. 3, ll. 51, 52; Ibragimbeili, *Krakh 'Edel'veisa'*, 112.
97. Hillgruber, ed., *Kriegstagebuch*, 730; Buchner, *Kampf im Gebirge*, 190.
98. Gneushev and Poput'ko, *Taina Marukhskogo lednika* (1966), 273.

99. Buchner, *Kampf im Gebirge*, 187–90.
100. Mezentsev, 'Itogovyi doklad', l. 189v.
101. 'Kratkoe opisanie perevala Sancharo', ll. 4v–10v.
102. Leselidze, 'Prikaz voiskam 46-i armii' (17 November 1942), TsAMO, f. 1524, op. 1, d. 9, l. 110.
103. Ibid. Leselidze had a surprisingly accurate estimate of the initial strength of the Stettner Group: Buchner, *Kampf im Gebirge*, 47. He called the Soviet field reports on the casualties inflicted on the enemy 'eyewash', but in the end his headquarters still stated that the 46th Army killed and wounded 7,313 German soldiers in September alone, whereas the actual casualties of the two German mountain divisions between 1 and 26 September equalled 160 men killed, 478 men wounded, and 17 missing in action, or a total of 655 men: Lieutenant-Colonel Komarov, deputy chief of operations of the 46th Army, TsAMO, f. 401, op. 9511, d. 51, l. 174; 49th Mountain Corps, 'Zahlenmässige Übersicht'. Therefore, the 46th Army inflated the casualties it inflicted on the enemy by eleven times.
104. General Petrov, 'Operativnaia svodka No. 21' (13 September 1942), TsAMO, f. 47, op. 1063, d. 658, l. 115; Petrov, 'Operativnaia svodka No. 24' (16 September 1942), TsAMO, f. 47, op. 1063, d. 658, l. 137; Kobulov to Beria (16 September 1942), TsAMO, f. 47, op. 1063, d. 655, l. 12; Kobulov to Beria (17 September 1942), TsAMO, f. 47, op. 1063, d. 658, l. 54; 'Kratkoe opisanie perevala Sancharo', ll. 6v, 7v; Colonel Mikeladze, 'Opersvodka No. 408' (16 September 1942), TsAMO, f. 1089, op. 1, d. 3, l. 44.
105. 49th Mountain Corps, KTB (15 September), BA-MA, RH 24-49/72, S. 272v.
106. 'Kratkoe opisanie perevala Sancharo', l. 11; 'Zhurnal boevykh deistvii Zakfronta' (11 October 1942), TsAMO, f. 47, op. 1063, d. 196, l. 87.
107. General Petrov, 'Doklad o sostoianii oborony perevalov GKKh' (13 November 2013), TsAMO, f. 47, op. 1063, d. 655, l. 135.
108. Mezentsev, 'Itogovyi doklad', l. 191v.
109. Bekishvili, 'Oborona kavkazskikh perevalov', 84.
110. 49th Mountain Corps, KTB (5, 10 and 14 October), BA-MA, RH 24-49/73, SS. 132v, 168v, 214v; Zav'ialov, 'Oborona Glavnogo Kavkazskogo Khrebta', l. 12; Mezentsev, 'Itogovyi doklad', l. 188; Colonel Mikeladze, 'Opersvodka No. 469' (29 October 1942), TsAMO, f. 1089, op. 1, d. 3, l. 70.
111. Piiashev, 'Boevoe donesenie' (23 September 1942), TsAMO, f. 47, op. 1063, d. 692, ll. 15, 16; Leselidze (22 October 1942), TsAMO, f. 401, op. 9511, d. 40, l. 59.
112. 'Kratkoe opisanie perevala Sancharo', l. 8v; Romanov, 'Operativnaia svodka No. 33' (25 September 1942), TsAMO, f. 47, op. 1063, d. 658, l. 183.
113. Romanov, 'Operativnaia svodka No. 36' (28 September 1942), TsAMO, f. 47, op. 1063, d. 658, l. 193v; 'Kratkoe opisanie perevala Sancharo', l. 10; Buchner, *Kampf im Gebirge*, 191.
114. Piiashev to the Military Council of the 46th Army (20 September 1942), TsAMO, f. 47, op. 1063, d. 692, ll. 59, 60.
115. Petrov to Kobulov (21 September 1942), TsAMO, f. 47, op. 1063, d. 689, l. 59.
116. 49th Mountain Corps, KTB (14 and 16 October 1942), BA-MA, RH 24-49/73, SS. 210v, 231v, 236v.
117. 'Kratkoe opisanie perevala Sancharo', l. 11.
118. Buchner, *Kampf im Gebirge*, 190, 191.
119. 49th Mountain Corps, 'Zahlenmässige Übersicht'.
120. Buchner, *Kampf im Gebirge*, 191.

121. Grechko, *Bitva za Kavkaz* (1969), 166; Grechko et al., eds., *Istoriia Vtoroi mirovoi voiny*, V:218; Iampol'skii et al., eds., *Organy gosudarstvennoi bezopasnosti*, III/2: 437; Batyrov, Grebeniuk and Matveev, eds., *Bitva za Kavkaz*, 100; Bekishvili, 'Oborona kavkazskikh perevalov', 85, 86; Moshchanskii, *Stoiat' nasmert!*, 104; Ibragimbeili, *Krakh 'Edel'veisa'*, 112.
122. 49th Mountain Corps, KTB (19 October 1942), BA-MA, RH 24-49/73, S. 257; Buchner, *Kampf im Gebirge*, 184.
123. Leselidze, 'Boevoe donesenie No. 18' (20 October 1942), TsAMO, f. 401, op. 9511, d. 51, l. 223; Mezentsev, 'Itogovyi doklad', l. 190v.
124. Captain Igol'nikov to Dreev (30 October 1942), TsAMO, f. 47, op. 1063, d. 692, l. 111.
125. Rybin, chief of staff of the 13th Rifle Corps, to Petrov, 'Opersvodka No. 20', 'Opersvodka No. 23' (9 and 12 January 1943), TsAMO, f. 47, op. 1063, d. 692, ll. 203, 206; Igol'nikov to Litvinov, 'Donesenie' (12 January 1943), TsAMO, f. 47, op. 1063, d. 692, l. 233.
126. Colonel Mikhail Mikeladze, 'Itogovaia operativnaia svodka No. 2' (6 November 1942), TsAMO, f. 401, op. 9511, d. 112, l. 4; 49th Mountain Corps, 'Zahlenmässige Übersicht'.
127. These were the 2nd and 5th Companies of the 174th 'Mountain' Regiment.
128. The 1st Company of the 13th Mountain Regiment.
129. The 265th 'Mountain' Regiment.
130. Leselidze, 'Chastnyi boevoi prikaz No. 009' (15 September 1942), TsAMO, f. 1089, op. 1, d. 3, ll. 51, 52; Headquarters of the 20th 'Mountain' Division, 'Zhurnal boevykh deistvii 20-i gsd' (1 October 1942), TsAMO, f. 1089, op. 1, d. 6, l. 25; 'Kratkoe opisanie perevala Pseashkho' (no date), TsAMO, f. 47, op. 1063, d. 664, l. 25v.
131. These were the 1st Company of the 174 'Mountain' Regiment and the 2nd Company of the 67th 'Mountain' Regiment, 'Boevoe donesenie No. 76' (1 October 1942), TsAMO, f. 1089, op. 1, d. 5, l. 123.
132. 'Opersvodka No. 45' and 'Opersvodka No. 53' (23 September and 1 October 1942), TsAMO, f. 1089, op. 1, d. 5, ll. 106, 124; Headquarters of the 20th 'Mountain' Division, 'Zhurnal boevykh deistvii 20-i gsd' (2 October 1942), TsAMO, f. 1089, op. 1, d. 6, l. 27; Buchner, *Kampf im Gebirge*, 140, 141.
133. 'Opersvodka No. 53' (26 September), TsAMO, f. 1089, op. 1, d. 5, l. 113.
134. A reinforced company of the Training Battalion of the 94th Regiment, the 1st Reconnaissance Company of the 94th Regiment, field and mountain artillery units, and the entire 3rd Battalion of the 91st Mountain Regiment were dispatched urgently from the Sancharo region and the lower Laba valleys after the failure to break to Gudauta: Buchner, *Kampf im Gebirge*, 144–9, 158.
135. Ibid., 152.
136. Vodop'anov, 'Inzhenernaia svodka po zagrazhdeniiam No. 17' (4 October 1942), TsAMO, f. 47, op. 1063, d. 10, l. 91.
137. Headquarters of the 20th 'Mountain' Division, 'Zhurnal boevykh deistvii 20-i gsd' (2 October 1942), TsAMO, f. 1089, op. 1, d. 6, l. 30; Buchner, *Kampf im Gebirge*, 150, 154–8.
138. Kaltenegger, *Gebirgsjäger im Kaukasus*, 85; Buchner, *Kampf im Gebirge*, 158.
139. Bekishvili, 'Oborona kavkazskikh perevalov', 56.
140. TCF Headquarters, 'Zhurnal boevykh deistvii Zakfronta' (16 and 20 October 1942), TsAMO, f. 47, op. 1063, d. 196, ll. 110, 127; Mezentsev,

'Itogovyi doklad', l. 190; Mezentsev, 'Pis'mennyi doklad' (16 December 1942), TsAMO, f. 47, op. 1063, d. 691, l. 68.

141. Captain Glazunov, OG representative with the 20th 'Mountain' Division, 'Dokladnaia zapiska' (9 October 1942), TsAMO, f. 47, op. 1063, d. 692, l. 90.

142. These were the 3rd and 4th Companies of the 379th Regiment of the 20th 'Mountain' Division.

143. The 207th Regiment of the German 97th Jäger Division, belonging to the 44th Army Corps.

144. Headquarters of the 20th 'Mountain' Division, 'Zhurnal boevykh deistvii 20-i gsd' (2 October 1942), TsAMO, f. 1089, op. 1, d. 6, l. 7.

145. Ibid., l. 15; General Petrov, 'Operativnaia svodka No. 6' (29 August 1942), TsAMO, f. 47, op. 1063, d. 658, l. 32.

146. General Petrov, 'Operativnaia svodka No. 6' (4 and 6 September 1942), TsAMO, f. 47, op. 1063, d. 658, ll. 62, 73; Headquarters of the 20th 'Mountain' Division, 'Zhurnal boevykh deistvii 20-i gsd' (2 October 1942), TsAMO, f. 1089, op. 1, d. 6, l. 15.

147. Iakubov, OG representative with the Headquarters of the 46th Army, 'Doklad' (after 11 September 1942), TsAMO, f. 47, op. 1063, d. 692, l. 20; Zav'ialov, 'Oborona Glavnogo Kavkazskogo Khrebta', l. 13.

148. Zav'ialov, 'Oborona Glavnogo Kavkazskogo Khrebta', l. 2v.

149. Mezentsev, 'Itogovyi doklad', l. 191v.

150. Litvinov to Popov (12 November 1942), TsAMO, f. 47, op. 1063, d. 691, l. 40v; Gneushev and Poput'ko, *Taina Marukhskogo lednika* (1966), 307–11.

151. Bozhenko, 'Iz opyta boev na perevalakh GKKh' (25 November 1942), TsAMO, f. 1524, op. 1, d. 9, l. 162.

152. Gneushev and Poput'ko, *Taina Marukhskogo lednika* (1971), 218.

153. Leselidze, 'Komandiram chastei i soedinenii Zakfronta' (11 November 1942), TsAMO, f. 47, op. 1063, d. 456, l. 118v; Litvinov to Popov (12 November 1942), TsAMO, f. 47, op. 1063, d. 691, l. 39; Saltykov, 'Doklad' (12 October 1942), TsAMO, f. 47, op. 1063, d. 691, l. 6.

154. Colonel Georgii Kurashvili, 'Prikaz chastiam 242-i gsd' (3 December 1942), TsAMO, f. 1524, op. 1, d. 9, l. 208.

155. Bozhenko, 'Iz opyta boev na perevalakh GKKh' (25 November 1942), TsAMO, f. 1524, op. 1, d. 9, ll. 162, 163.

156. Petrov, 'Doklad o sostoianii oborony perevalov', l. 132.

157. Leselidze, 'Prikaz voiskam 46-i armii' (28 October 1942), TsAMO, f. 1524, op. 1, d. 9, l. 148.

158. Bozhenko, 'Kharakteristika 242-i gsd' (30 November 1942), TsAMO, f. 1524, op. 1, d. 12, l. 95.

159. Colonel Georgii Kurashvili, commander of the 242nd 'Mountain' Division, 'Boevoi prikaz No. 005' (18 September 1942), TsAMO, f. 47, op. 1063, d. 456, l. 33; Bozhenko, 'Kharakteristika 242-i gsd' (30 November 1942), TsAMO, f. 1524, op. 1, d. 12, l. 95.

160. Saltykov, 'Doklad' (12 October 1942), TsAMO, f. 47, op. 1063, d. 691, l. 4v; Bozhenko, 'Kharakteristika 242-i gsd' (30 November 1942), TsAMO, f. 1524, op. 1, d. 12, l. 98.

161. Bozhenko, 'Itogi voennykh deistvii v gorakh chastei 242-i gsd' (30 October 1942), TsAMO, f. 47, op. 1063, d. 691, l. 35.

162. Colonel Georgii Kurashvili, 'Prikaz chastiam 242-i gsd' (31 December 1942), TsAMO, f. 1524, op. 1, d. 9, l. 272v.

163. Ibid.

7 Mosaics of Mountain Warfare: Comparative Military Effectiveness in the High Caucasus

1. V. Shunkov, *Oruzhie Krasnoi armii* (Minsk: Kharvest, 1999), 185–8; V. Shunkov, *Oruzhie Vermakhta* (Minsk: Kharvest, 1999), 186, 187.
2. Bozhenko, 'Kharakteristika 242-i gsd' (30 November 1942), TsAMO, f. 1524, op. 1, d. 12, l. 98; Tiulenev, 'Plan oborony perevalov Glavnogo Kavkazskogo Khrebta' (23 August 1942), TsAMO, f. 47, op. 1063, d. 644, l. 283; Bulyga, 'Svedeniia o chastiakh', l. 74; Mezentsev, 'Itogovyi doklad', l. 190; Komarov, 'Svedeniia boevogo i chislennogo sostava podrazdelenii prikryvaiushchikh Kavkazskii Khrebet' (15 August 1942), TsAMO, f. 401, op. 9511, d. 22, ll. 57, 57v.
3. Bauer, *Unternehmen 'Elbrus'*, 226.
4. Lanz, *Gebirgsjäger*, 315; Shunkov, *Oruzhie Vermakhta*, 201, 202.
5. Smirnov to Zinov'ev (12 November 1942), TsAMO, f. 47, op. 1063, d. 691, ll. 42v, 43; Zav'ialov, 'Oborona Glavnogo Kavkazskogo Khrebta', l. 17; Tiulenev, *Cherez tri voiny*, 231.
6. Bulyga, 'Svedeniia o chastiakh', ll. 73, 74; Lanz, *Gebirgsjäger*, 315.
7. Bozhenko, 'Iz opyta boev na perevalakh GKKh' (25 November 1942), TsAMO, f. 1524, op. 1, d. 9, ll. 162, 164.
8. Shunkov, *Oruzhie Krasnoi armii*, 79; Shunkov, *Oruzhie Vermakhta*, 93–8.
9. Shunkov, *Oruzhie Krasnoi armii*, 68, 69; Shunkov, *Oruzhie Vermakhta*, 93–8.
10. Major Titov, commander of the 810th Rifle Regiment, 'O zadachakh boevoi i politicheskoi podgotovki na dekabr' 1942' (Novemver 1942), TsAMO, f. 1720, op. 1, d. 7, l. 189.
11. Leselidze, 'Komandiram soedinenii 46-i armii' (17 September 1942), TsAMO, f. 47, op. 1063, d. 79, l. 16; Bauer, *Unternehmen 'Elbrus'*, 200, 204.
12. Vitalii Klimenko, Nikolai Dudnik, Nikolai Golodnikov, Sergei Gorelov, Grigorii Krivosheev, and Ivan Kozhemiako in Artem Drabkin, ed., *My dralis' na istrebiteliakh* (Moscow: Iauza-Eksmo, 2014), 44, 55, 173, 314, 357, 408.
13. Bauer, *Unternehmen 'Elbrus'*, 217.
14. Buchner, *Kampf im Gebirge*, 34–6, 142, 172.
15. Iakubov, OG representative at the Headquarters of the 46th Army, 'Doklad' (after 11 September 1942), TsAMO, f. 47, op. 1063, d. 692, ll. 19, 20.
16. Lieutenant-Colonel Kantariia, 'Komandiram chastei 394-i sd' (17 August 1942), TsAMO, f. 401, op. 9511, d. 22, l. 111.
17. 'Zhurnal boevykh deistvii Zakfronta' (19 and 20 August 1942), TsAMO, f. 47, op. 1063, d. 183, ll. 144, 146.
18. Beria to the Military Council of the 46th Army (28 August 1942), TsAMO, f. 401, op. 9511, d. 30, l. 121.
19. Gneushev and Poput'ko, *Taina Marukhskogo lednika* (1971), 303.
20. Belekhov to Petrov (16 October 1942), TsAMO, f. 47, op. 1063, d. 691, ll. 19, 19v.
21. Major Bakhtadze, deputy head of the TCF Signals Directorate, 'Otchet o prodelannoi rabote' (8 October 1942), TsAMO, f. 47, op. 1063, d. 688, l. 63; Petrov, 'Doklad o sostoianii oborony perevalov', l. 149; Iakubov, 'Doklad' (after 11 September 1942), TsAMO, f. 47, op. 1063, d. 692, l. 21.
22. Pshenianik, *Krakh plana 'Edel'veis'*, 95.
23. Buchner, *Kampf im Gebirge*, 49, 58.
24. Abramov, *Na ratnykh dorogakh*, 161, 158, 163; TsAMO, f. 1089, op. 1, d. 3.

25. Abramov, 'Doklad o voennykh deistviiakh', l. 49; Glazunov, 'Dokladnaia zapiska' (9 October 1942), TsAMO, f. 47, op. 1063, d. 692, l. 92.
26. Smirnov to Zinov'ev (12 November 1942), TsAMO, f. 47, op. 1063, d. 691, l. 43v.
27. Tiulenev to Stalin, 'Boevoe donesenie No. 022' (3 September 1942), TsAMO, f. 47, op. 1063, d. 166, l. 81v; Abramov, 'Doklad o voennykh deistviiakh', l. 49; Tiulenev to Stalin, (9 September 1942), TsAMO, f. 47, op. 1063, d. 166, l. 126.
28. Petrov, 'Doklad o sostoianii oborony perevalov', l. 150; Glavnoe upravlenie sviazi, *Spravochnik*, I:14, 22, 26.
29. Major Bakhtadze, 'Doklad' (4 September 1942), TsAMO, f. 47, op. 1063, d. 688, l. 9; Petrov, 'Doklad o sostoianii oborony perevalov', l. 149.
30. Petrov, 'Doklad o sostoianii oborony perevalov', l. 150; Glavnoe upravlenie sviazi, *Spravochnik*, I:19; 2:83, 84.
31. Glavnoe upravlenie sviazi, *Spravochnik*, III:169.
32. Bakhtadze, 'Doklad o sostoianii sviazi' (no date), TsAMO, f. 47, op. 1063, d. 688, l. 123; General Petrov, 'Operativnaia svodka No. 15' (7 September 1942), TsAMO, f. 47, op. 1063, d. 658, l. 83.
33. Bakhtadze, 'Doklad' (4 September 1942), l. 10; General Petrov, 'Operativnaia svodka No. 15' (7 September 1942), TsAMO, f. 47, op. 1063, d. 658, l. 83.
34. Major Pavel Kazak, commander of the 23rd Frontier Guard Regiment, 'Doklad ob organizatsii sviazi' (28 December 1942), TsAMO, f. 47, op. 1063, d. 688, l. 113.
35. Colonel Kutasin, commander of Defence District No. 2, to Petrov (14 October 1942), TsAMO, f. 47, op. 1063, d. 691, l. 8; Bakhtadze, 'Doklad o sostoianii sviazi' (no date), TsAMO, f. 47, op. 1063, d. 688, l. 123.
36. Petrov, 'Doklad o sostoianii oborony perevalov', l. 136.
37. Belekhov, 'Opisanie Klukhorskogo i Nakharskogo perevalov' (18 October 1942), TsAMO, f. 401, op. 9511, d. 73, l. 15v.
38. Litvinov to Romanov (19 September 1942), l. 26; Moshchanskii, *Stoiat' nasmert!*, 91, 95, 119, 124, 125, 164.
39. Lieutenant Borzenko to Dreev (19 December 1942), TsAMO, f. 47, op. 1063, d. 692, l. 166; Belekhov to Petrov (21 November 1942), TsAMO, f. 47, op. 1063, d. 692, l. 216v.
40. Colonel Mikeladze, 'Donesenie o chislennom i boevom sostave soedinenii i otdel'nykh chastei 46-i armii' (1 November 1942), TsAMO, f. 401, op. 9511, d. 54, ll. 1, 2.
41. Glazunov, 'Dokladnaia zapiska' (23 December 1942), TsAMO, f. 47, op. 1063, d. 692, ll. 257v, 258; Kazak, 'Doklad ob organizatsii sviazi' (28 December 1942), TsAMO, f. 47, op. 1063, d. 688, l. 113; Mezentsev, 'Itogovyi doklad', l. 173v.
42. 49th Mountain Corps, KTB (28 August 1942), BA-MA, RH 24-49/72, S. 155v.
43. Hillgruber, ed., *Kriegstagebuch*, 609.
44. Halder, *The Halder Diaries*, 1512, 1583.
45. Hillgruber, ed., *Kriegstagebuch*, 619; Buchner, *Kampf im Gebirge*, 31; 49th Mountain Corps, KTB (23 August 1942), BA-MA, RH 24-49/72, S. 117v.
46. Petrov, 'Doklad o sostoianii oborony perevalov', l. 157.
47. Buchner, *Kampf im Gebirge*, 211.
48. 49th Mountain Corps, KTB (23 August 1942), BA-MA, RH 24-49/72, S. 117v.
49. The Stettner Group, consisting of two battalions and an attached artillery group, had 510 horses when it began crossing the MCR: Buchner, *Kampf im Gebirge*, 47. If horses were distributed equally among the units of the mountain division at the

MCR, an extrapolation of this number to the entire mountain division, with its six battalions, equals about 1,500 horses per division.

50. 49th Mountain Corps, KTB (1 September 1942), BA-MA, RH 24-49/72, S. 182v; Buchner, *Kampf im Gebirge*, 210.
51. 49th Mountain Corps, KTB (23 August 1942), BA-MA, RH 24-49/72, S. 118v.
52. Buchner, *Kampf im Gebirge*, 208; Gneushev and Poput'ko, *Taina Marukhskogo lednika* (1966), 28.
53. 49th Mountain Corps, KTB (5 September 1942), BA-MA, RH 24-49/72, S. 205v; Buchner, *Kampf im Gebirge*, 212.
54. General Petrov, 'Operativnaia svodka No. 16' (9 September 1942), TsAMO, f. 47, op. 1063, d. 658, l. 91; Kaltenegger, *Gebirgsjäger im Kaukasus*, 118, 126; Gioev, *Bitva za Kavkaz*, 110; Bezugol'nyi, *Narody Kavkaza*, 383. Another allegation of the atrocities committed by the 49th Mountain Corps refers to the massacre in Teberda village, which hosted sanatoria for children sick with tuberculosis. It also accommodated many Jewish refugees – children, their parents, and other Jewish adults. During the occupation of the village by the 49th Mountain Corps, many of them were killed, which the Soviets discovered as soon as they reconquered Teberda. The Soviet and German versions of the cause of their death are different. Josef Bauer claims to have witnessed a raid of the Red Air Force on Teberda and describes several thousand children screaming in horror while the Soviet planes bombarded the sanatoria, inflicting casualties among them: Bauer, *Unternehmen 'Elbrus'*, 194. Bauer, however, worked for the Nazi Propaganda Ministry; this fact casts doubt on the credibility of his version. A Soviet field report states that, during their retreat, the Germans executed 300 adult Jews and 47 children: Arutiunov, 'Opersvodka No. 38' (22 January 1943), TsAMO, f. 401, op. 9511, d. 111, l. 303. This alleged murder would be consistent with the deeds of the 1st Mountain Division in other parts of the world, such as the deadly pogrom in Lviv in June 1941, while the 1st Mountain Division was in charge of the area; the destruction of Borovë village in Albania on 6 July 1943, with the execution of 107 civilians aged between 4 months and 80 years; the execution of between 4,905 and 9,640 Italian POWs in Cephalonia between 13 and 24 September 1943; and the murder of 1,204 civilians in Greece during Operation Panther against ELAS on 22 October 1943: Hermann Frank Meyer, *Blutiges Edelweiss: Die 1. Gebirgs-Division im Zweiten Weltkrieg* (Berlin: Ch. Links, 2008), 64, 163, 422, 529. However, the Soviet propaganda machine also tended to attribute the war crimes committed by the Soviet forces in the Caucasus and elsewhere to the Germans, as they did in the case of the Verkhniaia Balkaria massacre and the Katyn affair: Statiev, 'The Nature of Anti-Soviet Armed Resistance', 290, 291.
55. The fantastic tales about the feats of partisans, who defended the passes of the Caucasus and supposedly destroyed '1,700 fascists, 11 light tanks and armoured cars, and 22 motor vehicles and blew up 17 bridges', are not credible: Kardanova, 'Zashchita perevalov Kavkaza', in Batyrov, ed., *Materialy mezhdunarodnoi nauchnoi konferentsii*, 57.
56. 49th Mountain Corps, KTB (29 and 31 August, 1, 3, 8, 12 and 13 September 1942), BA-MA, RH 24-49/72, SS. 165v, 178v, 184v, 191v, 232v, 256v, 262v, 263.
57. Buchner, *Kampf im Gebirge*, 210, 211.
58. This was the 804th Hilfswillige Battalion, 49th Mountain Corps, KTB (3 and 6 September 1942), BA-MA, RH 24-49/72, SS. 192v, 219v.
59. 49th Mountain Corps, KTB (3, 8, 9 and 13 September 1942), BA-MA, RH 24-49/72, SS. 192v, 234v, 238v, 263, 265v; 49th Mountain Corps, KTB (19 September 1942), BA-MA, RH 24-49/73, S. 5v.

60. Beria, 'Prikaz predstavitelia GKO', 178; Tiulenev, *Krakh operatsii 'Edel'veis'*, 76.
61. Bekishvili, 'Oborona kavkazskikh perevalov', 64, 113.
62. Tetiukhin to Romanov (13 September 1942), TsAMO, f. 47, op. 1063, d. 643, l. 60.
63. Bozhenko, 'Itogi voennykh deistvii v gorakh chastei 242-i gsd' (30 October 1942), TsAMO, f. 47, op. 1063, d. 691, l. 35; Abramov, *Na ratnykh dorogakh*, 158; Mezentsev, 'Itogovyi doklad', l. 191v; Captain Groth, 'Bericht über die Ersteilung des Elbrus' (28 August 1942), BA-MA, RH 24-1/171, S. 215.
64. Major Zhukov (5 October 1942), TsAMO, f. 47, op. 1063, d. 643, l. 62; Gneushev and Poput'ko, *Taina Marukhskogo lednika* (1966), 213.
65. Gioev, *Bitva za Kavkaz*, 96; Dreev to Petrov (9 September 1942), TsAMO, f. 47, op. 1063, d. 667, l. 18v.
66. Zav'ialov, 'Oborona Glavnogo Kavkazskogo Khrebta', l. 17v.
67. Pshenianik, *Krakh plana 'Edel'veis'*, 120.
68. Buchner, *Kampf im Gebirge*, 138, 182, 190.
69. V. Abalakov, Get'e and Gushchin, *Vysokogornye uchebnye pokhody*, 59, 60; Ialukhin, Dolgikh and Mukhoedov, eds., *Shturm Belukhi*, 162–70; V. Iatsenko, *V gorakh Pamira* (Moscow: Izdatel'stvo geograficheskoi literatury, 1950), 122, 136, 149; Rikhter, *Shturm El'brusa*, 90.
70. Belekhov to Petrov (16 October 1942), TsAMO, f. 47, op. 1063, d. 691, l. 21; Khadeev, deputy commander of the TCF (31 August 1942), TsAMO, f. 47, op. 1063, d. 644, ll. 46, 46v.
71. Abramov, *Na ratnykh dorogakh*, 154, 158.
72. See, for instance, Solonin, *Iiun' 41-go*, 533.
73. This was the 5th Company of the 808th Rifle Regiment: Major Zarelua, head of the NKVD Special Section of the 46th Army (1 September 1942), TsAMO, f. 47, op. 1063, d. 668, l. 27.
74. Gneushev and Poput'ko, *Taina Marukhskogo lednika* (1966), 16.
75. Abramov, 'Doklad o voennykh deistviiakh', l. 34.
76. Beria, 'Prikaz predstavitelia GKO', 178; Lieutenant Rozhkov, 'Kopiia materialov proverki obespechennosti chastei na per. Donguz-Orun' (5 September 1942), TsAMO, f. 47, op. 1063, d. 692, l. 11.
77. Tiulenev, 'Operativnaia direktiva' (23 August 1942), in Batyrov, Grebeniuk and Matveev, eds., *Bitva za Kavkaz*, 327.
78. Glazunov, 'Dokladnaia zapiska' (23 December 1942), TsAMO, f. 47, op. 1063, d. 692, ll. 257v, 258; Gneushev and Poput'ko, *Taina Marukhskogo lednika* (1966), 269.
79. Gneushev and Poput'ko, *Taina Marukhskogo lednika* (1966), 17, 140, 163.
80. Nikolai Griazev, 'Pokhod Suvorova v 1799 g.', in Semanov, ed., *Aleksandr Vasil'evich Suvorov*, 205.
81. Vyrypaev, *Shest' mesiatsev na Shipke*, 116; 'Materialy dlia istorii Shipki', *Voennyi sbornik* 135(2) (1880):266; General Brusilov (21 March 1915), RGVIA, f. 2067, op. 1, d. 307, l. 189.
82. Romanov, 'Operativnaia svodka No. 36' (28 September 1942), TsAMO, f. 47, op. 1063, d. 658, l. 195v; Ivanchenko to Romanov (18 September 1942), TsAMO, f. 47, op. 1063, d. 692, ll. 28–30.
83. Dreev to Petrov (9 September 1942), TsAMO, f. 47, op. 1063, d. 667, l. 19; Mezentsev, 'Itogovyi doklad', l. 191v.
84. The 4th Battalion of the 155th Rifle Brigade: Gneushev and Poput'ko, *Taina Marukhskogo lednika* (1966), 265.
85. Colonel Kutasin to Petrov (14 October 1942), TsAMO, f. 47, op. 1063, d. 691, l. 8v; Beria to Anastas Mikoian, deputy chair of the Council of People's Commissars,

'Khodataistvo predstavitelia GKO' (3 September 1942), in Shapovalov, ed., *Bitva za Kavkaz*, 200.

86. Litvinov (12 November 1942), TsAMO, f. 47, op. 1063, d. 691, l. 41v; Bozhenko (26 November 1942), TsAMO, f. 1524, op. 1, d. 9, l. 167.
87. Petrov, 'Doklad o sostoianii oborony perevalov', l. 159.
88. Senior Lieutenant Teliatnikov, 'Doklad o sostoianii oborony' (no date), TsAMO, f. 47, op. 1063, d. 692, l. 93v; Bulyga, 'Spetssoobshchenie' (21 November 1942), TsAMO, f. 47, op. 1063, d. 643, l. 218; Gneushev and Poput'ko, *Taina Marukhskogo lednika* (1971), 138.
89. Lieutenant Rozhkov, 'Kopiia materialov proverki obespechennosti chastei na per. Donguz-Orun' (5 September 1942), TsAMO, f. 47, op. 1063, d. 692, l. 11; Kakuchaia to Tiulenev (22 September 1942), TsAMO, f. 47, op. 1063, d. 664, l. 313.
90. Dreev, 'O sostoianii podrazdelenii 242-i gsd oboroniaiushchikh perevaly' (17 November 1942), TsAMO, f. 401, op. 9511, d. 30; Petrov (11 November 1942), TsAMO, f. 47, op. 1063, d. 643, l. 243.
91. Ivanchenko, 'Doklad po tabeliu srochnykh donesenii' (16 November 1942), TsAMO, f. 47, op. 1063, d. 695, l. 448.
92. Ivanchenko, 'Doklad' (3 November 1942), TsAMO, f. 47, op. 1063, d. 692, l. 117; Lieutenant Borzenko to Dreev (19 December 1942), TsAMO, f. 47, op. 1063, d. 692, l. 166. Frozen food consumed in subzero temperatures quickly cools the body down from inside; intensive and prolonged movement is required to restore body temperature and prevent hypothermia.
93. Bekishvili, 'Oborona kavkazskikh perevalov', 41; Moshchanskii, *Stoiat' nasmert!*, 9.
94. Interrogation of a German prisoner (no date), TsAMO, f. 47, op. 1063, d. 655, l. 89v.
95. 'Doklad kapitana Vagnera', ll. 232–235, 254, 255; Interrogation of a German prisoner (no date), TsAMO, f. 47, op. 1063, d. 655, l. 90; Captain Groth, 'Bericht über die Ersteilung des Elbrus' (28 August 1942), BA-MA, RH 24-1/171, SS. 218, 219.
96. Bekishvili, 'Oborona kavkazskikh perevalov', 41.
97. Buchner, *Kampf im Gebirge*, 28, 50.
98. Beria, 'Prikaz predstavitelia GKO', 178.
99. TCF Headquarters, 'Zhurnal boevykh deistvii Zakfronta' (26 August 1942), TsAMO, f. 47, op. 1063, d. 183, l. 185.
100. Sergatskov, 'Plan oborony Glavnogo Kavkazskogo Khrebta' (30 June 1943), TsAMO, f. 47, op. 1063, d. 456, ll. 9–19; Leselidze to the commander of the 394th Rifle Division (9 August 1942), TsAMO, f. 1720, op. 1, d. 23, l. 71; General Khadeev (20 August 1942), TsAMO, f. 47, op. 1063, d. 642, l. 7.
101. Sergatskov, 'Operativnaia direktiva No. 0011' (24 August 1942), TsAMO, f. 1720, op. 1, d. 7, l. 130v.
102. Tiulenev, 'Direktiva po tylu No. 06' (25 August 1942), TsAMO, f. 47, op. 1063, d. 643, l. 109; Tiulenev, 'Plan material'nogo obespecheniia voisk oboroniaiushchikh GKKh' (26 August 1942), TsAMO, f. 47, op. 1063, d. 643, ll. 112–113; Tiulenev, 'Operativnaia direktiva No. 00530' (28 August 1942), TsAMO, f. 47, op. 1063, d. 31, l. 44; Tiulenev and Bodin, 'Operativnaia direktiva No. 015' (4 September 1942), TsAMO, f. 47, op. 1063, d. 645, l. 10; General Khadeev (31 August 1942), TsAMO, f. 47, op. 1063, d. 644, ll. 46, 46v.

103. Petrov, 'Operativnaia svodka No. 14' (6 September 1942), TsAMO, f. 47, op. 1063, d. 658, l. 76.
104. Slightly more than 8,000 men were deployed around Klukhor, slightly less than 8,000 in the Sancharo region, and about 4,500 men at Marukh at that time.
105. Buchner, *Kampf im Gebirge*, 211.
106. The total cargo delivered to all the passes, including those in the Elbrus region, was about 60 tonnes daily: Zav'ialov, 'Oborona Glavnogo Kavkazskogo Khrebta', l. 17v.
107. The Soviets had about 1,750 horses and about 500 donkeys in the Klukhor, Sancharo, and Marukh regions. In the high mountains, the horses and donkeys could carry 50 and 30 kilograms each respectively: Petrov, 'Doklad o sostoianii oborony perevalov', l. 157; Tetiukhin to Romanov (13 September 1942), TsAMO, f. 47, op. 1063, d. 643, l. 60.
108. Colonel Nikolai Spotkai, OG deputy commander, 'Nachal'niku upravleniia tyla' (22 November 1942), TsAMO, f. 47, op. 1063, d. 643, l. 284.
109. Petrov, 'Dokladnaia zapiska' (12 September 1942), TsAMO, f. 47, op. 1063, d. 642, l. 40.
110. Bulyga, 'O nedostatkakh v snabzhenii 63 kd and 242 sd' (after 19 September 1942), TsAMO, f. 47, op. 1063, d. 643, l. 17; Khadeev (20 August 1942), TsAMO, f. 47, op. 1063, d. 642, l. 7; Petrov, 'Dokladnaia zapiska' (12 September 1942), TsAMO, f. 47, op. 1063, d. 642, l. 41.
111. Dreev to Petrov (9 September 1942), TsAMO, f. 47, op. 1063, d. 667, l. 18v; Petrov, 'Operativnaia svodka No. 24' (16 September 1942), TsAMO, f. 47, op. 1063, d. 658, l. 139; Gioev, *Bitva za Kavkaz*, 101; Bulyga, 'O nedostatkakh v snabzhenii voisk oboroniaiushchikh perevaly' (23 September 1942), TsAMO, f. 47, op. 1063, d. 643, l. 16.
112. Lieutenant-Colonel Leshukov, 'Spravka o kolichestve al'piiskogo imushchestva' (23 October 1942), TsAMO, f. 47, op. 1063, d. 695, l. 433.
113. Purtseladze, TCF inspector of mountaineering training, 'Gornaia i gorno-lyzhnaia podgotovka' (26 November 1942), TsAMO, f. 47, op. 1063, d. 692, l. 144; Bozhenko, 'Donesenie po potrebnosti i obespechennosti 242 gsd gornym i gorno-lyzhnym snariazheniem' (15 November 1942), TsAMO, f. 47, op. 1063, d. 695, l. 515.
114. Lieutenant-Colonel Ostrovskii, 'Otchet o poezdke na per. Becho' (5 September 1942), TsAMO, f. 47, op. 1063, d. 692, l. 13.
115. Gneushev and Poput'ko, *Taina Marukhskogo lednika* (1966), 174.
116. Leselidze, 'Operativnaia direktiva No. 916' (13 Septenber 1942), TsAMO, f. 401, op. 9511, d. 18, l. 48; Dreev, 'O sostoianii podrazdelenii 242-i gsd oboroniaiush-chikh perevaly' (17 November 1942), TsAMO, f. 401, op. 9511, d. 30; Tiulenev, 'Prikaz voiskam Zakavkazskogo fronta' (25 November 1942), TsAMO, f. 401, op. 9511, d. 10, l. 133.
117. The author crossed Marukh one sunny day without using sunblock. By the end of the day, every member of his team was suffering from severe sunburn, with extensive blisters on exposed areas.
118. Petrov, 'Doklad o sostoianii oborony perevalov', l. 159.
119. Gusev, *El'brus v ogne*, 22.
120. Tetiukhin to Romanov (13 September 1942), TsAMO, f. 47, op. 1063, d. 692, l. 9; Romanov, 'Operativnaia svodka No. 36' (28 September 1942), TsAMO, f. 47, op. 1063, d. 658, l. 195v; Teliatnikov to Litvinov (21 November 1942), TsAMO, f. 47, op. 1063, d. 692, l. 154; Teplichnyi, deputy commander of the 33rd NKVD

Regiment, 'Spravka o sostoianii snabzheniia polka' (28 November 1942), TsAMO, f. 47, op. 1063, d. 695, l. 461; Glazunov, 'Dokladnaia zapiska' (23 December 1942), TsAMO, f. 47, op. 1063, d. 692, ll. 257v, 258.

121. Ivanchenko, 'Doklad' (3 November 1942), TsAMO, f. 47, op. 1063, d. 692, l. 117; Leshukov, 'Spravka o potrebnosti i obespechennosti voisk' (23 October 1942), TsAMO, f. 47, op. 1063, d. 695, ll. 129–133.
122. Dreev (10 November 1942), TsAMO, f. 47, op. 1063, d. 689, l. 116; Dreev, 'O sostoianii podrazdelenii 242-i gsd oboroniaiushchikh perevaly' (17 November 1942), TsAMO, f. 401, op. 9511, d. 30.
123. Ivan Kobets, Shalom Skopas and Aleksandr Solov'ev in Artem Drabkin, ed., *My khodili za liniiu fronta* (Moscow: Iauza-Eksmo, 2011), 46, 73, 260; Vladimir Zimakov in Artem Drabkin, ed., *Glavnoe – vybit' u nikh tanki* (Moscow: Iauza-Eksmo, 2011), 204; P. Solov'ev and V. Shevchenko in Vladimir Pershanin, ed., *Stalingradskaia miasorubka* (Moscow: Iauza-Eksmo, 2012), 175, 246.
124. In some units, not a single soldier received a piece of soap: Major Zarelua, head of the NKVD Special Section of the 46th Army (1 September 1942), TsAMO, f. 47, op. 1063, d. 668, l. 27.
125. Dreev, 'Spetssoobshchebie o sostoianii 394-i sd' (17 November 1942), TsAMO, f. 47, op. 1063, d. 692, l. 212; Ivanchenko, 'Doklad' (3 November 1942), TsAMO, f. 47, op. 1063, d. 692, l. 120.
126. Regiment Commissar Abaulin, 'Prikaz' (January 1941), RGVA, f. 34446, op. 1, d. 37, l. 31; Senior Lieutenant Beldii, 'Komandiru 63-go str. polka' (12 February 1941), RGVA, f. 34446, op. 1, d. 37, l. 39.
127. Kabakadze, acting head of 46th Army's Rear Directorate (17 November 1942), TsAMO, f. 47, op. 1063, d. 691, l. 59; Colonel Georgii Kurashvili, 'Prikaz chastiam 242 gsd' (10 December 1942), TsAMO, f. 1524, op. 1, d. 9, l. 287; Dreev, 'Spetssoobshchebie o sostoianii 394-i sd' (17 November 1942), TsAMO, f. 47, op. 1063, d. 692, l. 212.
128. Senior Lieutenant Vorob'ev, 'Obespechennost' zimnim obmundirovaniem 242-i gsd' (16 November 1942), TsAMO, f. 47, op. 1063, d. 695, l. 452.
129. Ivanchenko, 'Doklad' (3 November 1942), TsAMO, f. 47, op. 1063, d. 692, l. 118; Litvinov, 'Svedeniia o potrebnosti i obespechennosti zimnim obmundirovaniem' (1 December 1942), TsAMO, f. 47, op. 1063, d. 692, l. 159.
130. Filimonov, 'Iz vospominanii uchastnika', 308, 309.
131. Ibid., 310.
132. Gioev, *Bitva za Kavkaz*, 94, 95.
133. Leselidze to Subbotin (7 September 1942), TsAMO, f. 401, op. 9511, d. 51, l. 62; Opryshko, *Zaoblachnyi front*, 66.
134. Moshchanskii, *Stoiat' nasmert!*, 100.
135. The 214th Regiment of the 63rd Cavalry Division.
136. Lieutenant-Colonel Danilenko, chief of staff of the 63rd Cavalry Division, 'Donesenie o poteriakh lichnogo sostava' (October 1942), TsAMO, f. 3587, op. 1, d. 83, l. 1.
137. Teliatnikov, 'Doklad o sostoianii oborony' (no date), TsAMO, f. 47, op. 1063, d. 692, l. 93.
138. Glazunov, 'Dokladnaia zapiska' (23 December 1942), TsAMO, f. 47, op. 1063, d. 692, l. 189v.
139. Bulyga (28 October 1942), TsAMO, f. 47, op. 1063, d. 689, l. 110.
140. They belonged to the 897th Regiment of the 242nd 'Mountain' Division: Belekhov to Petrov (21 November 1942), TsAMO, f. 47, op. 1063, d. 692, l. 216; Colonel

Mikeladze, 'Opersvodka No. 465' (27 October 1942), TsAMO, f. 1089, op. 1, d. 3, l. 68; Bozhenko, 'Opersvodka No. 46' (26 October 1942), TsAMO, f. 1524, op. 1, d. 12, l. 56.

141. Opryshko, *Zaoblachnyi front*, 124, 125.
142. Tiulenev, 'Prikaz voiskam Zakavkazskogo Fronta' (25 November 1942), TsAMO, f. 401, op. 9511, d. 10, l. 133.
143. Gioev, *Bitva za Kavkaz*, 95.
144. Buchner, *Kampf im Gebirge*, 192; Bulyga (28 October 1942), TsAMO, f. 47, op. 1063, d. 689, l. 110.
145. Bulyga (28 October 1942), TsAMO, f. 47, op. 1063, d. 689, l. 110.
146. Litvinov to Popov (12 November 1942), TsAMO, f. 47, op. 1063, d. 691, l. 40.
147. Mezentsev, 'Itogovyi doklad', l. 191.
148. Tiulenev, 'Prikaz voiskam Zakavkazskogo Fronta' (25 November 1942), TsAMO, f. 401, op. 9511, d. 10, l. 133.
149. Major Korobov, commander of the 815th Rifle Regiment, 'Prikaz No. 276' (30 October 1942), TsAMO, f. 815sp, op. 39411, d. 2, ll. 160, 160v.
150. Tiulenev, 'Prikaz voiskam Zakavkazskogo Fronta' (25 November 1942), TsAMO, f. 401, op. 9511, d. 10, l. 133.
151. 49th Mountain Corps, KTB (5 September 1942), BA-MA, RH 24-49/72, S. 205v; Bauer, *Unternehmen 'Elbrus'*, 208, 226, 227; 49th Mountain Corps, KTB (16 August 1942), BA-MA, RH 24-49/72, S. 76v.
152. Shebalin, *Nastavlenie*, 220.
153. Litvinov to Popov (12 November 1942), TsAMO, f. 47, op. 1063, d. 691, l. 40.
154. Teliatnikov, 'Doklad o sostoianii oborony' (no date), TsAMO, f. 47, op. 1063, d. 692, l. 93v; Romanov, 'Operativnaia svodka No. 36' (28 September 1942), TsAMO, f. 47, op. 1063, d. 658, l. 195v.
155. Dreev to Petrov (9 September 1942), TsAMO, f. 47, op. 1063, d. 658, l. 18v; Petrov, 'Doklad o sostoianii oborony perevalov', l. 158; Litvinov to Popov (12 November 1942), TsAMO, f. 47, op. 1063, d. 691, l. 40.
156. Smirnov to Zinov'ev (12 November 1942), TsAMO, f. 47, op. 1063, d. 691, l. 43v.
157. Gioev, *Bitva za Kavkaz*, 92, 95.
158. Ivanchenko, 'Doklad' (3 November 1942), TsAMO, f. 47, op. 1063, d. 692, l. 119v.
159. Dreev (10 November 1942), TsAMO, f. 47, op. 1063, d. 689, l. 116v.
160. Petrov, 'Doklad o sostoianii oborony perevalov', l. 159; Tiulenev, *Cherez tri voiny*, 232.
161. Major Sedykh (17 September 1942), TsAMO, f. 47, op. 1063, d. 643, l. 69.
162. Zav'ialov, 'Oborona Glavnogo Kavkazskogo Khrebta', l. 17v.
163. Klement'ev, *Boevye deistviia*, 93, 197, 198; Klement'ev, *Cherez lednikovye perevaly*, 152.
164. Gneushev and Poput'ko, *Taina Marukhskogo lednika* (1966), 84, 356; Opryshko, *Zaoblachnyi front*, 34, 68; A. Kharitonov, 'Na gornykh perevalakh Kavkaza', in Basov et al., *Narodnyi podvig v bitve za Kavkaz*, 124.
165. Most men of the Soviet 394th Rifle Division were 30 to 38 years old, whereas most soldiers of the German 2nd High Mountain Battalion were 18 or 19 years old: Dreev, 'Spetssoobshchebie o sostoianii 394-i sd' (17 November 1942), TsAMO, f. 47, op. 1063, d. 692, l. 212; Litvinov to Popov (12 November 1942), TsAMO, f. 47, op. 1063, d. 691, l. 40v; Bezugol'nyi, *Narody Kavkaza*, 198.
166. Saltykov, 'Doklad' (12 October 1942), TsAMO, f. 47, op. 1063, d. 691, l. 5.

167. Main Political Directorate of the Red Army, 'O vospitatel'noi rabote s kranoarmeitsami i mladshimi komandirami nerusskoi natsional'nosti' (17 September 1942), TsAMO, f. 1089, op. 1, d. 32, l. 143.
168. Khalil Nadorshin (18 October 1942) in Iampol'skii et al., eds., *Organy gosudarstvennoi bezopasnosti*, III/2:399.
169. TCF Headquarters, 'Zhurnal boevykh deistvii Zakfronta' (10 October 1942), TsAMO, f. 47, op. 1063, d. 196, l. 79.
170. Leselidze, 'O sluchaiakh samoupravstva i izdevatel'stva nad krasnoarmeitsami' (7 October 1942), TsAMO, f. 1089, op. 1, d. 32, l. 145.
171. Markov, head of the Political Section of the 46th Army to Matus, head of the Political Section of the 155th Independent Rifle Brigade (5 October 1942), TsAMO, f. 1983, op. 1, d. 1, l. 53.
172. 'Prigovor' (27 October 1942), TsAMO, f. 1064, op. 1, d. 40, l. 181. The Military Tribunal sentenced Voloshin to ten years in labour camps.
173. Emel'ianov, member of the Military Council of the 46th Army (18 September 1942), TsAMO, f. 1983, op. 1, d. 1, l. 44.
174. General Vladimir Kurdiumov, deputy commander of the TCF, 'Prikaz voiskam Zakfronta' (2 November 1942), TsAMO, f. 401, op. 9511, d. 10, ll. 104v, 105.
175. No comprehensive data on the turnover of penal personnel exist, but the statistics on the 1st Independent Penal Company of the 57th Army show that, of the 3,348 penal soldiers who passed through it between August 1942 and September 1945, 796 (23.8 per cent) were killed; 1,939 (57.9 per cent) were wounded; 457 (13.6 per cent) were pardoned for outstanding conduct; 117 (3.5 per cent) were released after they had served their term; and 39 (1.2 per cent) were missing in action or had deserted. See Alexander Statiev, 'Penal Units in the Red Army', *Europe-Asia Studies* 62(5), July 2010, 738.
176. Commissar of the Reconnaissance Platoon, 'Boevoe donesenie' (18 November 1942), TsAMO, f. 815sp, op. 39410, d. 1, l. 427.
177. Belekhov to Petrov (21 November 1942), TsAMO, f. 47, op. 1063, d. 692, l. 216; Bozhenko, 'Itogi voennykh deistvii v gorakh chastei 242-i gsd' (30 October 1942), TsAMO, f. 47, op. 1063, d. 691, l. 33; Saltykov, 'Doklad' (12 October 1942), TsAMO, f. 47, op. 1063, d. 691, l. 6.
178. General Petrov, 'Operativnaia svodka No. 5', 'Operativnaia svodka No. 6', 'Operativnaia svodka No. 11' (28 and 29 August and 3 September 1942), TsAMO, f. 47, op. 1063, d. 658, ll. 26, 32, 58.
179. Gusev, *El'brus v ogne*, 113.
180. Mezentsev, 'Itogovyi doklad', l. 191.
181. 49th Mountain Corps, KTB (8 September 1942), BA-MA, RH 24-49/72, S. 231v.
182. TCF Headquarters, 'Zhurnal boevykh deistvii Zakfronta' (21 August 1942), TsAMO, f. 47, op. 1063, d. 183, l. 155.
183. Glazunov, 'Dokladnaia zapiska' (9 October 1942), TsAMO, f. 47, op. 1063, d. 692, l. 91; Petrov, 'Operativnaia svodka No. 4' (27 August 1942), TsAMO, f. 47, op. 1063, d. 658, l. 21; Gneushev and Poput'ko, *Taina Marukhskogo lednika* (1971), 313, 331.
184. Nagovitsyn to Semenovskii (2 November 1942), TsAMO, f. 1089, op. 1, d. 5, l. 189.
185. 49th Mountain Corps, 'Zahlenmässige Übersicht'.
186. Beliavskii, 'Svedeniia o poteriakh v voiskakh 46-i armii s 19 avgusta po 13 oktiabria 1942' (no date), TsAMO, f. 47, op. 1063, d. 655, l. 165; 49th Mountain Corps, BA-MA, RH 24-49/268.
187. Tiulenev, 'Prikaz voiskam Zakfronta' (5 June 1942), TsAMO, f. 401, op. 9511, d. 10, l. 45.

188. Colonel Rasskazov, 'Opersvodka No. 392' (31 August 1942), TsAMO, f. 1089, op. 1, d. 3, l. 17.
189. Rateriaev, commander of the Reconnaissance Section of the 46th Army, 'Organizatsiia i vedenie razvedki' (17 October 1942), TsAMO, f. 47, op. 1063, d. 691, l. 10; Litvinov to Popov (12 November 1942), TsAMO, f. 47, op. 1063, d. 691, l. 41v; Serov to Beria (30 August 1942), TsAMO, f. 47, op. 1063, d. 671, l. 17.
190. Vechtomov (9 September 1942), TsAMO, f. 1089, op. 1, d. 32, l. 112; Serov to Beria (30 August 1942), TsAMO, f. 47, op. 1063, d. 671, l. 16.
191. 'Zhurnal boevykh deistvii 20-i gsd' (24 October 1942), TsAMO, f. 1089, op. 1, d. 6, l. 42; Zhibkov, 'Informatsiia k 14:00' (21 October 1942), TsAMO, f. 401, op. 9511, d. 51, l. 227v; 'Dnevnik boevykh deistvii soedinenii i chastei 46-i armii' (September 1942), TsAMO, f. 401, op. 9511, d. 58, l. 9.
192. General Petrov, 'Operativnaia svodka No. 12' (4 September 1941), TsAMO, f. 1089, op. 1, d. 658, l. 65; Aleksandr Shcherbakov, head of the Red Army's Main Political Directorate (28 August 1942), TsAMO, f. 1089, op. 1, d. 32, l. 96.
193. Markov, head of the Political Section of the 46th Army (12 October 1942), TsAMO, f. 1089, op. 1, d. 32, l. 158; Major Rudenko, head of the Political Section of the 20th 'Mountain' Division (27 November 1942), TsAMO, f. 1089, op. 1, d. 32, l. 249; Zhibkov, 'Informatsiia k 14:00' (21 October 1942), TsAMO, f. 401, op. 9511, d. 51, l. 227v.
194. Major Medzmariashvili, 'Imennoi spisok ranenykh', TsAMO, f. 3587, op. 2, d. 3, l. 23v.
195. Bozhenko, 'Vsem komandiram chastei' (11 December 1942), TsAMO, f. 1524, op. 1, d. 9, l. 232.
196. Ibid.
197. Colonel Tronin (10 December 1942), TsAMO, f. 1720, op. 1, d. 7, l. 228.
198. Kaltenegger, *Gebirgsjäger im Kaukasus*, 118.
199. Headquarters of the 46th Army, 'Dnevnik boevykh deistvii' (1 May–1 September 1942), TsAMO, f. 401, op. 9511, d. 58, l. 9.
200. 'Zhurnal boevykh deistvii Zakfronta' (21 August 1942), TsAMO, f. 47, op. 1063, d. 183, l. 160; Tiulenev to Stalin, 'Boevoe donesenie No. 05' (19 August 1942), TsAMO, f. 47, op. 1063, d. 166, l. 13.
201. 'Zhurnal boevykh deistvii Zakfronta' (September 1942), TsAMO, f. 47, op. 1063, d. 194, l. 245.
202. Tiulenev, *Krakh operatsii 'Edel'veis'*, 27, 28.
203. Bezugol'nyi, *Narody Kavkaza i Krasnaia armiia*, 164, 165.
204. Statiev, 'The Nature of Anti-Soviet Armed Resistance', 286–91.
205. Dreev, 'Materialy po prikrytiiu i oborone GKKh' (no date; probably January 1943), TsAMO, f. 47, op. 1063, d. 689, ll. 170, 171v; Romanov, 'Operativnaia svodka No. 33' (25 September 1942), TsAMO, f. 47, op. 1063, d. 658, ll. 184, 185; Romanov, 'Operativnaia svodka No. 36' (28 September 1942), TsAMO, f. 47, op. 1063, d. 658, l. 194; Romanov, 'Operativnaia svodka No. 39' (1 October 1942), TsAMO, f. 47, op. 1063, d. 658, l. 204v.
206. Romanov, 'Operativnaia svodka No. 31' (23 September 1942), TsAMO, f. 47, op. 1063, d. 658, l. 176; Dreev, 'Materialy po prikrytiiu i oborone' (no date; probably January 1943), TsAMO, f. 47, op. 1063, d. 689, l. 171v.
207. Zaboev, deputy head of the Struggle Against Banditry Department, 'Spravka o kolichestve likvidirovannykh bandgrupp' (20 October 1944), GARF, f. 9478, op. 1, d. 137, ll. 1, 2, 5.

208. 49th Mountain Corps, KTB (23 August 1942), BA-MA, RH 24-49/72, S. 120v; Lanz, *Gebirgsjäger*, 157; Bauer, *Unternehmen 'Elbrus'*, 115, 116, 123, 128.
209. 49th Mountain Corps, KTB (8 September 1942), BA-MA, RH 24-49/72, S. 234v.
210. N. Pobol' and P. Polian, *Stalinskie deportatsii* (Moscow: Demokratiia, 2005), 489. During Beria's trial in 1953, Roman Rudenko, the chief prosecutor of the USSR, accused the defendant of being soft on the Karachais and Balkars, 'who served as guides and provided considerable help to the Germans in taking the passes', even though these two ethnic groups had suffered genocidal attrition as a result of their deportation: 'Kopiia protokola doprosa L. P. Beriia', 214.
211. Gneushev and Poput'ko, *Taina Marukhskogo lednika* (1971), 161.
212. Senior Lieutenant Makarov, head of NKVD Operations Section, to Belekhov (no date), TsAMO, f. 1720, op. 1, d. 7, l. 16.
213. Saltykov, 'Doklad' (12 October 1942), TsAMO, f. 47, op. 1063, d. 691, l. 7.
214. General Petrov, 'Operativnaia svodka No. 26' (18 September 1942), TsAMO, f. 47, op. 1063, d. 658, l. 155.
215. Tiulenev, *Krakh operatsii 'Edel'veis'*, 81; Tiulenev, *Cherez tri voiny*, 228.
216. Kardanova, 'Zashchita perevalov', 55, 56; Gusev, *El'brus v ogne*, 164; Ibragimbeili, *Krakh 'Edel'veisa'*, 103, 111, 112, 122; Gioev, *Bitva za Kavkaz*, 94, 105; Opryshko, *Zaoblachnyi front*, 137; Lota, *Sorvat' 'Edel'veis'*, 408.
217. Gneushev and Poput'ko, *Taina Marukhskogo lednika* (1966), 253, 254.
218. The summary of the war diary of the 49th Mountain Corps on the casualties of the 1st Mountain Division between 10 and 31 August lists 104 killed, 426 wounded, and 30 missing, whereas the totals of the daily reports for these dates are 99 killed, 361 wounded, and 28 missing in action: 49th Mountain Corps, KTB (5 September 1942), BA-MA, RH 24-49/72, S. 201v; 49th Mountain Corps, 'Zahlenmässige Übersicht'.
219. The 1st Mountain Division lost only seventeen men wounded and no one killed or missing in action between 13 and 26 September: 49th Mountain Corps, 'Zahlenmässige Übersicht'.
220. BA-MA, RH 24-49/232; Beliavskii, 'Svedeniia o poteriakh v voiskakh 46-i armii s 19 avgusta po 13 oktiabria 1942', TsAMO, f. 47, op. 1063, d. 655, l. 165.
221. A. Gusev, deputy chief of staff of the 46th Army, 'Itogovaia operativnaia svodka' (3 February 1943), TsAMO, f. 401, op. 9511, d. 112, l. 40.
222. Mezentsev, 'Itogovyi doklad', l. 191v.
223. Purtseladze, 'Gornaia i gorno-lyzhnaia podgotovka' (26 November 1942), TsAMO, f. 47, op. 1063, d. 692, ll. 144v–145v; Petrov, 'Doklad o sostoianii oborony perevalov', l. 132; Colonel Olev, 'Vypiska iz doklada ofitsera Genshtaba polkovnika Pisareva "O sostoinii oborony MCR na uchastke 351 sd"' (24 October 1942), TsAMO, f. 47, op. 1063, d. 31, l. 118.
224. General'nyi shtab Krasnoi Armii, *Nastavlenie*, 11, 77; Shebalin, *Nastavlenie*, 126, 139; Tiulenev, 'Instruktsiia po aktivnoi oborone perevalov GKKh' (25 August 1942), TsAMO, f. 47, op. 1063, d. 655, ll. 101, 123.
225. Tiulenev, 'Instruktsiia po aktivnoi oborone perevalov GKKh' (25 August 1942), TsAMO, f. 47, op. 1063, d. 655, l. 115; Shebalin, *Nastavlenie*, 78, 124, 149, 221; General'nyi shtab Krasnoi Armii, *Nastavlenie*, 47, 75; Klement'ev, *Boevye deistviia*, 178, 189, 190; Klement'ev, *Cherez lednikovye perevaly*, 8, 14, 33, 34, 111–24, 147, 152.
226. Bulyga, 'Kratkaia instruktsiia po deistviiam voisk v gorakh' (15 September 1942), TsAMO, f. 1720, op. 1, d. 7, l. 283v; Shebalin, *Nastavlenie*, 73, 223; Klement'ev, *Boevye deistviia*, 176, 178, 181–5; Tiulenev,

'Instruktsiia po aktivnoi oborone perevalov GKKh' (25 August 1942), TsAMO, f. 47, op. 1063, d. 655, ll. 117, 118.

227. Levandovskii, 'Krupnoe uchenie', ll. 168, 173; Klement'ev, *Boevye deistviia gornykh voisk*; Tiulenev, 'Instruktsiia po aktivnoi oborone perevalov GKKh' (25 August 1942), TsAMO, f. 47, op. 1063, d. 655, l. 125.
228. Zav'ialov, 'Oborona Glavnogo Kavkazskogo Khrebta', l. 16v.
229. Zav'ialov and Kaliadin, *Bitva za Kavkaz*, 98; Zav'ialov, 'Oborona Glavnogo Kavkazskogo Khrebta', l. 16v.
230. Batyrov, Grebeniuk and Matveev, eds., *Bitva za Kavkaz*, 103; Ibragimbeili, *Krakh 'Edel'veisa'*, 104, 112.
231. Dreev, 'Materialy po prikrytiiu i oborone GKKh' (no date; probably January 1943), TsAMO, f. 47, op. 1063, d. 689, l. 173v. See similar conclusion in Petrov, 'Doklad o sostoianii oborony perevalov', l. 132.
232. In December, the Germans held the entire front in the high Caucasus between Pseashkha and Elbrus with a force of five battalions: the 2nd and 3rd Battalions of the 99th Regiment of the 1st Mountain Division, the Training Battalion and the Reconnaissance Battalion of the 94th Regiment of the 4th Mountain Division, and the 2nd High Mountain Battalion: Tieke, *The Caucasus and the Oil*, 195, 196. The Soviets deployed more than six full-strength battalions in the Klukhor region alone: Litvinov, 'O khode stroitel'stva inzhenernykh sooruzhenii na perevalakh Klukhorskom i Marukhskom' (5 December 1942), TsAMO, f. 47, op. 1063, d. 692, l. 157.
233. General Konstantin Skorobogatkin to Marshal Matvei Zakharov (22 January 1963), TsAMO, f. 1720, op. 1, d. 10, l. 8.
234. General Petrov (8 October 1942), TsAMO, f. 401, op. 9511, d. 30, ll. 143, 144.
235. General Petrov to commanders of the 46th Army (8 October 1942), TsAMO, f. 47, op. 1063, d. 644, ll. 102, 103.
236. General Petrov (8 October 1942), TsAMO, f. 401, op. 9511, d. 30, ll. 143, 144.
237. Smirnov to Zinov'ev (12 November 1942), TsAMO, f. 47, op. 1063, d. 691, ll. 42v, 43; Bozhenko, 'Itogi voennykh deistvii', TsAMO, f. 47, op. 1063, d. 691, ll. 33–36; Bozhenko, 'Perechen' takticheskikh voprosov po organizatsii obshchevoiskovoi oborony v vysokogornoi mestnosti' (no date), TsAMO, f. 1524, op. 1, d. 9, l. 235.
238. Dreev, 'Materialy po prikrytiiu i oborone GKKh' (no date; probably January 1943), TsAMO, f. 47, op. 1063, d. 689, l. 173v. See a similar conclusion in the TCF war diary, TCF Headquarters, 'Zhurnal boevykh deistvii Zakfronta' (August 1942), TsAMO, f. 47, op. 1063, d. 183, l. 117.
239. Dreev, 'Materialy po prikrytiiu i oborone GKKh' (no date; probably January 1943), TsAMO, f. 47, op. 1063, d. 689, l. 177.

8 Learning Mountain Warfare the Hard Way

1. Semanov, ed., *Aleksandr Vasil'evich Suvorov*, 385.
2. Petrov, 'Doklad o sostoianii oborony perevalov', ll. 135, 136.
3. Bozhenko, 'Prikazanie' (no date), TsAMO, f. 1524, op. 1, d. 9, l. 10; Opryshko, *Zaoblachnyi front*, 98–100.
4. Bozhenko, 'Opersvodka No. 23' (3 October 1942), TsAMO, f. 1524, op. 1, d. 12, l. 32.

5. Bozhenko, 'Kharakteristika 242-i gsd' (30 November 1942), TsAMO, f. 1524, op. 1, d. 12, l. 96; Saltykov, 'Doklad o metodakh i taktike deistvii protivnika v raione g. Elbrus' (24 October 1942), TsAMO, f. 47, op. 1063, d. 691, l. 26; Tieke, *The Caucasus and the Oil*, 193, 194. Post-war Soviet sources allege that the commander committed suicide: Opryshko, *Zaoblachnyi front*, 100. However, the action report states that 'Lieutenant [Guren] Grigoriants, wounded in both legs, was left at the battlefield': Bozhenko, 'Opersvodka No. 23' (3 October 1942), TsAMO, f. 1524, op. 1, d. 12, l. 32. Some post-communist authors present this disaster as a sound victory: Lota, *Sorvat' 'Edel'veis'*, 314–19.
6. Grechko, *Bitva za Kavkaz* (1969), 168.
7. Colonel Olev, 'Vypiska iz doklada ofitsera Genshtaba polkovnika Pisareva "O sostoinii oborony GKKh na uchastke 351 sd"' (24 October 1942), TsAMO, f. 47, op. 1063, d. 31, l. 118; Leselidze, 'Komandiram chastei i soedinenii Zakfronta' (11 November 1942), TsAMO, f. 47, op. 1063, d. 456, ll. 118v, 119.
8. 'Svedeniia na potrebnoe al'pinistskoe imushchestvo' (22 October 1942), TsAMO, f. 47, op. 1063, d. 643, l. 190.
9. General Vasilii Sergatskov, 'Komandiram soedinenii Zakfronta' (26 June 1942), TsAMO, f. 47, op. 1063, d. 456, l. 6; Sergatskov, 'Plan oborony Glavnogo Kavkazskogo Khrebta' (30 June 1943), TsAMO, f. 47, op. 1063, d. 456, l. 11.
10. Major Strel'tsov, chief of staff of the 394th Rifle Division (29 June 1942), TsAMO, f. 1720, op. 1, d. 23, l. 84.
11. General Ivan Tiulenev, 'Operativnaia direktiva' (23 August 1942), in Batyrov, Grebeniuk and Matveev, eds., *Bitva za Kavkaz*, 327; Sergatskov, 'Operativnaia direktiva No. 0011' (24 August 1942), TsAMO, f. 47, op. 1063, d. 692, l. 7; Petrov, 'Operativnaia svodka No. 2' (25 August 1942); TsAMO, f. 47, op. 1063, d. 658, l. 9; Tiulenev, 'Direktiva po tylu No. 06' (25 August 1942), TsAMO, f. 47, op. 1063, d. 643, l. 109; Litvinov to Romanov (19 September 1942), TsAMO, f. 47, op. 1063, d. 692, l. 27.
12. Simon Khoshtariia, deputy premier of Georgia, to Tiulenev (4 January 1943), TsAMO, f. 47, op. 1063, d. 695, l. 522.
13. Colonel Piiashev (30 November 1942), TsAMO, f. 47, op. 1063, d. 692, l. 147.
14. Teliatnikov, 'Doklad o sostoianii oborony' (no date), TsAMO, f. 47, op. 1063, d. 692, l. 93; Colonel Piiashev (30 November 1942), TsAMO, f. 47, op. 1063, d. 692, l. 147.
15. Purtseladze, 'Gornaia i gorno-lyzhnaia podgotovka', ll. 144, 144v. Even those who climbed Elbrus to dispose of the German flags after the battle of the Caucasus and who received the best available gear complained that the spikes of their crampons were easily bent: Opryshko, *Zaoblachnyi front*, 142.
16. Gusev to Petrov (17 January 1943), TsAMO, f. 47, op. 1063, d. 692, ll. 273–274v; 'Opersvodka No. 72' (20 October 1942), TsAMO, f. 1089, op. 1, d. 5, l. 168; Saltykov, 'Doklad o metodakh i taktike deistvii protivnika v raione g. Elbrus' (24 October 1942), TsAMO, f. 47, op. 1063, d. 691, l. 26; Gusev, *El'brus v ogne*, 185; Opryshko, *Zaoblachnyi front*, 93, 107, 132.
17. Purtseladze, 'Gornaia i gorno-lyzhnaia podgotovka', l. 144
18. Tiulenev and Bodin, 'Operativnaia direktiva No. 015' (4 September 1942), TsAMO, f. 47, op. 1063, d. 645, l. 10.
19. Kobulov to Beria (17 September 1942), TsAMO, f. 47, op. 1063, d. 658, l. 54; Petrov, 'Doklad o sostoianii oborony perevalov', l. 155; Leshukov, 'Spravka o kolichestve al'piiskogo imushchestva' (23 October 1942), TsAMO, f. 47, op. 1063, d. 695, l. 433.

20. Purtseladze, 'Gornaia i gorno-lyzhnaia podgotovka', l. 144v.
21. Ibid., l. 144v; Spotkai, 'Intendantu Zakfronta Kudrinskomu' (6 November 1942), TsAMO, f. 47, op. 1063, d. 643, l. 254.
22. Gusev to Petrov (17 January 1943), TsAMO, f. 47, op. 1063, d. 692, ll. 273–274.
23. Spotkai to Kudrinskii (1 December 1942), TsAMO, f. 47, op. 1063, d. 643, l. 310; E. Smirnov, OG liaison officer, to Petrov, 'Raport' (1 December 1942), TsAMO, f. 47, op. 1063, d. 692, l. 278.
24. Petrov to Piiashev (3 December 1942), TsAMO, f. 47, op. 1063, d. 692, l. 148; Purtseladze, 'Gornaia i gorno-lyzhnaia podgotovka', l. 144v.
25. Zav'ialov, 'Oborona Glavnogo Kavkazskogo Khrebta', l. 10; Major Panin, 'Kratkoe opisanie perevala Klukhor' (no date), TsAMO, f. 47, op. 1063, d. 671, l. 10v; Sergatskov, 'Plan chastichnoi peregruppirovki i usileniia chastei 46 armii' (27 August 1942), TsAMO, f. 401, op. 9511, d. 18, l. 99; Bekishvili, 'Oborona kavkazskikh perevalov', 66.
26. Bulyga, 'Svedeniia o chastiakh', l. 73.
27. By mid September, the 815th Rifle Regiment, which was twice as large as the 121st 'Mountain' Regiment, had been reduced to 581 men, and its 1st Battalion had lost 80 per cent of its men: Bulyga, 'Svedeniia o chastiakh', l. 73; Belekhov, 'Opisanie Klukhorskogo i Nakharskogo perevalov' (18 October 1942), TsAMO, f. 401, op. 9511, d. 73, l. 13v.
28. 49th Mountain Corps, 'Zahlenmässige Übersicht'.
29. Petrov to Brigade Commissar Efimov (15 November 1942), TsAMO, f. 47, op. 1063, d. 692, l. 127.
30. Siachin, commissar of the 394th Rifle Division (early August 1942), TsAMO, f. 1720, op. 1, d. 23, l. 107.
31. Colonel Rasskazov, chief of staff of the 46th Army, 'Komandiru 3-go sk' (25 August 1942), TsAMO, f. 47, op. 1063, d. 692, l. 1.
32. Grechko, *Bitva za Kavkaz* (1969), 168, 169; Lota, *Sorvat' 'Edel'veis'*, 216–18.
33. Sudoplatov, *Spetsoperatsii*, 234, 235.
34. Gusev, *El'brus v ogne*, 105; Moshchanskii, *Stoiat' nasmert!*, 69, 85, 90.
35. Petrov to the TCF Military Council (31 August 1942), TsAMO, f. 47, op. 1063, d. 689, l. 50.
36. NKVD major Varlam Kakuchaia to Tiulenev (22 September 1942), TsAMO, f. 47, op. 1063, d. 664, l. 312; Gusev, *El'brus v ogne*, 169, 170; Opryshko, *Zaoblachnyi front*, 121.
37. Opryshko, *Zaoblachnyi front*, 57.
38. General Petrov, 'Konspekt' (2 September 1942), TsAMO, f. 47, op. 1063, d. 689, l. 26; Gusev, *El'brus v ogne*, 170, 171; Opryshko, *Zaoblachnyi front*, 58, 59.
39. From the 220th Regiment of the 63rd Cavalry Division.
40. These were the 121st Regiment of the 9th 'Mountain' Division and 815th Regiment of the 394th Rifle Division.
41. Gusev, *El'brus v ogne*, 70, 79, 88–92.
42. Litvinov to Romanov (19 September 1942), TsAMO, f. 47, op. 1063, d. 692, l. 25; Petrov, 'Operativnaia svodka No. 17' (10 September 1942), TsAMO, f. 47, op. 1063, d. 658, l. 96; Gusev, *El'brus v ogne*, 97.
43. Belekhov to Petrov (21 November 1942), TsAMO, f. 47, op. 1063, d. 692, ll. 216, 216v.
44. A map in Gusev's memoir shows that his unit crossed the MCR; his text is ambiguous in its description of how far they reached, and he blames poor weather for the failure of his mission: Gusev, *El'brus v ogne*, 69, 107–12. However, several combat reports state that the raid failed long before his unit reached the MCR: Major Panin,

'Kratkoe opisanie perevala Klukhor' (no date), TsAMO, f. 47, op. 1063, d. 671, l. 11; Major Zhashko, chief of staff of the 394th Rifle Division, 'Skhema obstanovki Klukhorskogo napravleniia' (8 September–1 October 1942), TsAMO, f. 47, op. 1063, d. 671, l. 24; 'Opersvodka No. 410' (18 September 1942), TsAMO, f. 47, op. 1063, d. 655, l. 22.

45. Opryshko, *Zaoblachnyi front*, 121.
46. Ibid., 18, 22.
47. Document No. 118, Kuparadze, commander of the 392nd Rifle Division (November 1942), in Shapovalov, ed., *Bitva za Kavkaz*, 275; Opryshko, *Zaoblachnyi front*, 107.
48. Bozhenko, 'Kharakteristika 242-i gsd' (30 November 1942), TsAMO, f. 1524, op. 1, d. 12, l. 97; Opryshko, *Zaoblachnyi front*, 110, 113. Aleksandr Gusev and, after him, Il'ia Moshchanskii, who plagiarised two pages of Gusev's memoirs, wrongly present as one event two different evacuations from the Baksan valley – an evacuation of civilians via the Becho Pass and an evacuation of the 392nd Rifle Division via the Donguz-Orun Pass: Gusev, *El'brus v ogne*, 176, 177; Moshchanskii, *Stoiat' nasmert!*, 152, 153. In fact, the first evacuation occurred in mid August, whereas the second took place between 11 and 16 November.
49. Sergatskov, 'Komandiram soedinenii Zakfronta' (26 June 1942), TsAMO, f. 47, op. 1063, d. 456, l. 6; Sergatskov, 'Plan oborony Glavnogo Kavkazskogo Khrebta' (30 June 1943), TsAMO, f. 47, op. 1063, d. 456, l. 19.
50. Sergatskov, 'Komandiram soedinenii' (4 July 1942), TsAMO, f. 47, op. 1063, d. 456, l. 26.
51. Petrov, 'Operativnaia svodka No. 2' (25 August 1942), TsAMO, f. 47, op. 1063, d. 658, l. 9; Leselidze, 'Komandiram soedinenii i chastei Zakfronta' (11 November 1942), TsAMO, f. 47, op. 1063, d. 456, l. 119v; Colonel Piiashev (30 November 1942), TsAMO, f. 47, op. 1063, d. 692, l. 147.
52. Belekhov to Petrov (16 October 1942), TsAMO, f. 47, op. 1063, d. 691, l. 23.
53. Colonel Eliseev, head of basic combat training of the 46th Army (4 November 1942), TsAMO, f. 401, op. 9511, d. 16, l. 273.
54. Rateriaev, 'Organizatsiia i vedenie razvedki' (17 October 1942), TsAMO, f. 47, op. 1063, d. 691, l. 11.
55. Saltykov, 'Doklad' (12 October 1942), TsAMO, f. 47, op. 1063, d. 691, l. 5.
56. Petrov to Leselidze (21 November 1942), TsAMO, f. 47, op. 1063, d. 692, l. 135.
57. Tiulenev, 'Ob al'pinistskoi i gorno-lyzhnoi podgotovke' (19 September 1942), TsAMO, f. 47, op. 1063, d. 672, l. 46; Colonel Mikeladze, chief of staff of the 46th Army, 'Komandiram divizii i brigad' (19 September 1942), TsAMO, f. 1720, op. 1, d. 7, l. 4.
58. Battalion Commissar Khoshtariia to Petrov (31 October 1942), TsAMO, f. 47, op. 1063, d. 692, l. 126.
59. Purtseladze, 'Gornaia i gorno-lyzhnaia podgotovka', l. 144v.
60. Ibid., l. 145.
61. Sergatskov, 'Prikaz chastiam 351 sd' (6 October 1942), TsAMO, f. 47, op. 1063, d. 456, ll. 97, 98.
62. In 1965, the mountain guide training programme consisted of 240 hours of intensive training: 'Stenogramma IV Plenuma sektsii massovykh vidov turizma i 1-go organizatsionnogo Plenuma TsMKK' (24 December 1964), GARF, f. 9520, op. 2, d. 8, l. 95.
63. E. Abalakov, G. Klimushkin, P. Zakharov, A. Komissarov, A. Bogrov, I. Cherepov, A. Arutiunov, and V. Kudinov: 'O rezultatakh podgotovki instruktorov al'pinizma' (10 November 1942), TsAMO, f. 47, op. 1063, d. 672, l. 45; Tiulenev, 'Ob

al'pinistskoi i gorno-lyzhnoi podgotovke' (19 September 1942), TsAMO, f. 47, op. 1063, d. 672, l. 46.
64. Bozhenko, 'Vsem komandiram chastei' (9 December 1942), TsAMO, f. 1524, op. 1, d. 9, l. 227.
65. Aleksei Maleinov, senior climbing inspector with 242nd 'Mountain' Division, 'Programma gorno-fizicheskoi podgotovki' (15 November 1942), TsAMO, f. 1524, op. 1, d. 9, ll. 156–159.
66. Bozhenko, 'Vsem komandiram polkov' (3 December 1942), TsAMO, f. 1524, op. 1, d. 9, l. 211.
67. Gusev, *El'brus v ogne*, 71.
68. Maleinov, 'Programma gorno-fizicheskoi podgotovki' (15 November 1942), TsAMO, f. 1524, op. 1, d. 9, ll. 156–158.
69. Later, their number grew to twenty-eight: Opryshko, *Zaoblachnyi front*, 121.
70. Bozhenko, 'Donesenie po potrebnosti i obespechennosti 242-i gsd gornym i gorno-lyzhnym snariazheniem' (15 November 1942), TsAMO, f. 47, op. 1063, d. 695, l. 515; Gusev, 'Svedeniia o nalichii al'pinistskogo imushchestva' (20 and 28 November 1942), TsAMO, f. 47, op. 1063, d. 695, ll. 517, 519.
71. Smirnov to Petrov, 'Raport' (1 December 1942), TsAMO, f. 47, op. 1063, d. 692, l. 278.
72. Junior Lieutenant Kudinov, deputy head of the OG Mountaineering Section, 'Otchet o rabote al'pinistskogo otdeleniia Opergruppy Zakfronta' (19 December 1942), TsAMO, f. 47, op. 1063, d. 691, l. 71; Dreev (20 December 1942), TsAMO, f. 401, op. 9511, d. 30, l. 180.
73. Grechko, *Bitva za Kavkaz* (1969), 168. Evgenii Abalakov arrived from Moscow as a permanent instructor only in December, although he did occasionally take part in training in October and early November: Smirnov to Petrov, 'Raport' (1 December 1942), TsAMO, f. 47, op. 1063, d. 692, l. 279.
74. Tiulenev, 'O podvizhnykh shkolakh al'pinizma' (10 November 1942), TsAMO, f. 47, op. 1063, d. 672, l. 44.
75. Litvinov (12 November 1942), TsAMO, f. 47, op. 1063, d. 691, l. 38v.
76. 'Zhurnal boevykh deistvii Zakfronta' (August 1942), TsAMO, f. 47, op. 1063, d. 183, l. 138.
77. 'Zhurnal boevykh deistvii Zakfronta' (August 1942), TsAMO, f. 47, op. 1063, d. 183, l. 117.
78. Leselidze, 'Operativnaia direktiva No. 00896' (4 September 1942), TsAMO, f. 47, op. 1063, d. 456, l. 48.
79. Serov to Beria (30 August 1942), TsAMO, f. 47, op. 1063, d. 671, l. 17.
80. Petrov, 'Doklad o sostoianii oborony perevalov GKKh', l. 136.
81. Lavrentii Beria, 'Voennomu sovetu 46 armii' (28 August 1942), TsAMO, f. 47, op. 1063, d. 28, l. 64. See similar instructions issued on 4 September and then on 13 September: Tiulenev and Bodin, 'Operativnaia direktiva No. 015' (4 September 1942), TsAMO, f. 47, op. 1063, d. 645, l. 9; Leselidze, 'Operativnaia direktiva No. 916' (13 September 1942), TsAMO, f. 401, op. 9511, d. 18, l. 47.
82. Petrov, 'Operativnaia svodka No. 13' (5 September 1942), TsAMO, f. 47, op. 1063, d. 658, l. 68; Petrov to Beria (8 September 1942), TsAMO, f. 47, op. 1063, d. 691, l. 159.
83. General Pavel Bodin to Leselidze (11 September 1942), TsAMO, f. 47, op. 1063, d. 31, l. 33; Bulyga to Shtemenko (21 October 1942), TsAMO, f. 47, op. 1063, d. 655, l. 176.

84. Spotkai to Glinkin (20 November 1942), TsAMO, f. 47, op. 1063, d. 643, l. 303; Romanov, 'Operativnaia svodka No. 34' (26 September 1942), TsAMO, f. 47, op. 1063, d. 658, l. 190; Gusev, *El'brus v ogne*, 144.
85. Ibragimbeili, *Krakh 'Edel'veisa'*, 106; Gioev, *Bitva za Kavkaz*, 88; Linets and Ianush, *Oborona Severnogo Kavkaza*, 282; Moshchanskii, *Stoiat' nasmert!*, 172.
86. Petrov to Beria (8 September 1942), TsAMO, f. 47, op. 1063, d. 691, ll. 159, 160.
87. Bodin to Leselidze (11 September 1942), TsAMO, f. 47, op. 1063, d. 31, l. 33.
88. Gusev, *El'brus v ogne*, 144.
89. Petrov, 'Operativnaia svodka No. 13' (5 September 1942), TsAMO, f. 47, op. 1063, d. 658, l. 68.
90. Belekhov to Petrov (16 October 1942), TsAMO, f. 47, op. 1063, d. 691, l. 21.
91. Emphasis is mine. The original text gives the dates of their arrival as '5 and 6 September', but this is an obvious typo, as is clear from another document stating that the last four companies left for the MCR on 2 October: Bulyga to Shtemenko (21 October 1942), TsAMO, f. 47, op. 1063, d. 655, l. 176.
92. Zinov'ev, OG deputy chief of staff, 'Dokladnaia zapiska o sostoianii oborony perevalov' (8 October 1942), TsAMO, f. 47, op. 1063, d. 692, l. 73.
93. Ibid., ll. 73, 74.
94. Gneushev and Poput'ko, *Taina Marukhskogo lednika* (1966), 96.
95. Shunkov, *Oruzhie Vermakhta*, 51; Shunkov, *Oruzhie Krasnoi armii*, 39.
96. Gusev, *El'brus v ogne*, 148.
97. Bulyga to Shtemenko (21 October 1942), TsAMO, f. 47, op. 1063, d. 655, l. 176; Lanz, *Gebirgsjäger*, 315.
98. Gusev, *El'brus v ogne*, 144; Gneushev and Poput'ko, *Taina Marukhskogo lednika* (1966), 96.
99. Zinov'ev, 'Dokladnaia zapiska o sostoianii oborony perevalov' (8 October 1942), TsAMO, f. 47, op. 1063, d. 692, l. 74; Gneushev and Poput'ko, *Taina Marukhskogo lednika* (1966), 305; Igol'nikov, OG senior liaison officer, 'Raport' (30 December 1942), TsAMO, f. 47, op. 1063, d. 692, l. 220.
100. Gneushev and Poput'ko, *Taina Marukhskogo lednika* (1971), 214. In January 1943, the daily ration of the 9th Mountain Company was limited to only 150 or 200 grams of rusks: General Petrov (18 January 1943), TsAMO, f. 47, op. 1063, d. 695, l. 506.
101. Igol'nikov, 'Raport' (30 December 1942), TsAMO, f. 47, op. 1063, d. 692, l. 220.
102. Belekhov, 'Boevoi prikaz No. 6' (11 September 1942), TsAMO, f. 815sp, op. 39410, d. 1, l. 214.
103. Bodin to Leselidze (11 September 1942), TsAMO, f. 47, op. 1063, d. 31, l. 33; Bodin to General F. Kurdiumov, TCF deputy commander (25 September 1942), TsAMO, f. 47, op. 1063, d. 31, l. 47. Commanders of the 174th Regiment of the 20th 'Mountain' Division mentioned briefly a unit of seventy-five men they called 'climbers' during a failed attack towards Umpyrskii pass on 21 September, but since the 7th and 8th Mountain Companies arrived at this division only in the second half of October, the unit mentioned in their reports most likely belonged to the first-generation 'mountain' companies – an unequipped regular infantry led by a climber: 'Opersvodka No. 44 and 47' (21 and 23 September 1942), TsAMO, f. 1089, op. 1, d. 5, ll. 103, 111; Turchinskii, commander of the 20th 'Mountain' Division, 'Boevoe rasporiazhenie No. 6' (24 October 1942), TsAMO, f. 1089, op. 1, d. 4, l. 83.
104. Bulyga to Shtemenko (21 October 1942), f. 47, op. 1063, d. 655, l. 176.
105. Lieutenant Sergienko, chief of staff of the 9th Mountain Company, 'Spravka' (January 1943), TsAMO, f. 47, op. 1063, d. 692, l. 250.

106. Gneushev and Poput'ko, *Taina Marukhskogo lednika* (1971), 214.
107. Mikeladze, 'Svedeniia o chislennom i boevom sostave garnizonov 242 gsd' (5 and 24 November 1942), TsAMO, f. 401, op. 9511, d. 54, ll. 3, 12.
108. 'Obespechennost' veshchevym i obozno-khoziaistvennym imushchestvom gornostrelkovykh rot sformirovannykh iz sostava Telavskogo i Buinakskogo pekhotnykh uchilishch' (15 October 1942), TsAMO, f. 47, op. 1063, d. 695, ll. 329–330; 'Obespechennost' veshchevym i obozno-khoziaistvennym imushchestvom gornostrelkovykh rot sformirovannykh iz sostava OVPU i groznenskogo VPU' (15 October 1942), TsAMO, f. 47, op. 1063, d. 695, ll. 331–332; Colonel Kutasin, commander of Defence District No. 2, to Petrov (14 October 1942), TsAMO, f. 47, op. 1063, d. 691, l. 8.
109. Gusev, *El'brus v ogne*, 148; Zhashko, 'Skhema obstanovki chastei Klukhorskogo napravleniia' (1 October 1942), TsAMO, f. 47, op. 1063, d. 671, l. 24.
110. Gusev, *El'brus v ogne*, 159.
111. 49th Mountain Corps, 'Zahlenmässige Übersicht'.
112. 49th Mountain Corps, KTB (13 October 1942), BA-MA, RH 24-49/73, S. 206v.
113. Some authors maintain that Soviet 'special mountain units' pursued Germans along the northern slopes of the Caucasus: Moshchanskii, *Stoiat' nasmert!*, 174. Ivan Golota, commissar of the 1st Independent Mountain Company, claims that when his unit received an order to 'to throw Germans down from Klukhor Pass and liberate Teberda within two days', 'our skiers rushed [uphill] on German positions, shooting from the submachine-guns while they skied. The fascists did not expect the attack and left their strongholds, shooting chaotically, and rushed to the descent from the pass', but the Soviets pursued them, burdened with ammunition boxes and food, until they came to Teberda and liberated it in battle by midnight of the same day: Gneushev and Poput'ko, *Taina Marukhskogo lednika* (1966), 253–8. It is impossible to reach Teberda from the southern slopes of Klukhor pass within one day, even without fighting and without the heavy loads that the Soviets reportedly carried. In any case, Soviet field reports state that the Germans left the Klukhor pass unnoticed and without any pressure from the Red Army.
114. Gusev, *El'brus v ogne*, 144. See also Lota, *Sorvat' 'Edel'veis'*, 218; Ibragimbeili, *Krakh 'Edel'veisa'*, 106; Linets and Ianush, *Oborona Severnogo Kavkaza*, 282.
115. Turchinskii, 'Boevoe rasporiazhenie No. 6' (25 October 1942), TsAMO, f. 1089, op. 1, d. 4, l. 85; Turchinskii, 'Komandiru 265 gsp' (12 October 1942), TsAMO, f. 1089, op. 1, d. 4, l. 39; Mikeladze to Turchinskii (29 October 1942), TsAMO, f. 1089, op. 1, d. 4, l. 87; Leselidze, 'Komandiram soedinenii i chastei Zakfronta' (11 November 1942), TsAMO, f. 47, op. 1063, d. 456, l. 119; Petrov to Leselidze (21 November 1942), TsAMO, f. 47, op. 1063, d. 692, l. 135; Bozhenko, 'Komandiram 105 i 106 gso' (15 November 1942), TsAMO, f. 1524, op. 1, d. 9, l. 133; Bozhenko, 'Komandiram 900, 903 and 897 gsp' (10 December 1942), TsAMO, f. 1524, op. 1, d. 9, l. 228.
116. Gusev to Petrov (17 January 1943), TsAMO, f. 47, op. 1063, d. 692, l. 273v.
117. General Petrov, 'Instruktsiia o sluzhbe garnizonov po oborone perevalov Glavnogo Kavkazskogo Khrebta v zimnii period' (no date), TsAMO, f. 1524, op. 1, d. 9, ll. 171a, 171b; 'Plan oborony perevalov' (3 November 1942), TsAMO, f. 401, op. 9511, d. 59, ll. 46–48.
118. Petrov, 'Instruktsiia o sluzhbe garnizonov po oborone perevalov Glavnogo Kavkazskogo Khrebta v zimnii period' (no date), TsAMO, f. 1524, op. 1, d. 9, ll. 171b, 171g, 171d; Opryshko, *Zaoblachnyi front*, 125.

119. Gusev, *El'brus v ogne*, 174, 175; Kudinov, 'Otchet o rabote al'pinistskogo otdeleniia' (19 December 1942), TsAMO, f. 47, op. 1063, d. 691, l. 71; I. Cherepov, ed., *Pamiatka boitsa lyzhnika-al'pinista* (Uchebnaia gornolyzhnaia baza Upraforma Zakavkazskogo Fronta, December 1942).
120. Gusev to Petrov (17 January 1943), TsAMO, f. 47, op. 1063, d. 692, l. 273; Petrov to Leselidze (21 November 1942), TsAMO, f. 47, op. 1063, d. 692, l. 135; General Kuz'ma Beloshnichenko, commander of the 63rd Cavalry Division, 'Dokladnaia zapiska' (1 October 1942), TsAMO, f. 47, op. 1063, d. 456, l. 59.
121. Kudinov, 'Otchet o rabote al'pinistskogo otdeleniia' (19 December 1942), TsAMO, f. 47, op. 1063, d. 691, l. 71; Smirnov to Petrov, 'Raport' (1 December 1942), TsAMO, f. 47, op. 1063, d. 692, l. 279.
122. Kudinov, 'Akt' (25 November 1942), TsAMO, f. 47, op. 1063, d. 695, l. 495; Simon Khoshtariia, 'Postanovlenie SNK Gruzinskoi SSR' (1 November 1942), TsAMO, f. 47, op. 1063, d. 695, l. 504.
123. Gusev to Petrov (17 January 1943), TsAMO, f. 47, op. 1063, d. 692, l. 273.
124. Colonel Eliseev, 'Ukazaniia po boevoi podgotovke gorno-lyzhnykh otriadov na zimnii period' (no date), TsAMO, f. 1720, op. 1, d. 7, l. 307.
125. Mezentsev, 'Itogovyi doklad', ll. 192v, 193.
126. Petrov to Tiulenev (23 January 1943), TsAMO, f. 47, op. 1063, d. 689, l. 150.
127. Tiulenev, 'Postanovlenie Voennogo soveta Zakfronta' (January 1943), TsAMO, f. 47, op. 1063, d. 689, l. 151.
128. Ibid., ll. 151–154v.
129. Tiulenev, 'Instruktsiia po aktivnoi oborone perevalov GKKh' (25 August 1942), TsAMO, f. 47, op. 1063, d. 655, ll. 113, 114.
130. Battalion Commissar Khoshtariia to Petrov (31 October 1942), TsAMO, f. 47, op. 1063, d. 692, l. 126.
131. Mikeladze, 'Svedeniia o poteriakh i trofeiiakh chastei 46-i armii' (31 December 1942), TsAMO, f. 401, op. 9511, d. 112, l. 22.
132. Mikeladze, 'Opersvodka No. 455' (22 October 1942), TsAMO, f. 1089, op. 1, d. 3, l. 62; Captain Mashin, chief of staff of the 33rd NKVD Regiment, 'Boevoe donesenie' (11 January 1943), TsAMO, f. 47, op. 1063, d. 692, ll. 240–242.
133. From the 897th Regiment of the 242nd 'Mountain' Division.
134. Colonel Georgii Kurashvili, commander of the 242nd 'Mountain' Division, 'Prikaz chastiam 242-i gsd' (10 December 1942), TsAMO, f. 1524, op. 1, d. 9, l. 287.
135. Gusev, *El'brus v ogne*, 162, 163; Opryshko, *Zaoblachnyi front*, 126, 127.
136. Kurashvili, 'Prikaz chastiam 242-i gsd' (10 December 1942), TsAMO, f. 1524, op. 1, d. 9, l. 287.
137. Komarov, 'Opersvodka No. 544' (4 December 1942), TsAMO, f. 1089, op. 1, d. 3, l. 106; Piiashev to Leselidze, 'Boevoe donesenie No. 020' (15 January 1943), TsAMO, f. 47, op. 1063, d. 692, l. 225; Gneushev and Poput'ko, *Taina Marukhskogo lednika* (1971), 216; General Petrov (18 January 1943), TsAMO, f. 47, op. 1063, d. 695, l. 506; Captain Mashin, 'Boevoe donesenie' (11 January 1943), TsAMO, f. 47, op. 1063, d. 692, ll. 240–242.
138. Leselidze, 'O preduprezhdenii snezhnykh obvalov' (December 1942), TsAMO, f. 401, op. 9511, d. 16, l. 287.
139. Buchner, *Kampf im Gebirge*, 186.
140. Tiulenev, 'Prikaz voiskam Zakavkazskogo Fronta' (25 November 1942), TsAMO, f. 401, op. 9511, d. 10, l. 133.
141. Kakuchaia to Tiulenev (22 September 1942), TsAMO, f. 47, op. 1063, d. 664, l. 314.

142. Gneushev and Poput'ko, *Taina Marukhskogo lednika* (1966), 219.
143. Colonel Kurashvili, 'Meropriiatiia po organizatsii pomoshchi garnizonu, nakhodiashchemusia na per. Becho' (22 October 1942), TsAMO, f. 1524, op. 1, d. 9, l. 84; Kurashvili, 'Ukazanie instruktoram al'pinizma' (22 October 1942), TsAMO, f. 1524, op. 1, d. 9, ll. 85, 86.
144. Turchinskii, 'Boevoe rasporiazhenie' (24 October 1942), TsAMO, f. 1089, op. 1, d. 4, l. 84.
145. Maleinov, 'Polozhenie o spasatel'noi gruppe gs polka' (15 November 1942), TsAMO, f. 1524, op. 1, d. 9, l. 161; Bozhenko, 'Komandiram 900, 903 and 897 gsp' (25 December 1942), TsAMO, f. 1524, op. 1, d. 9, l. 263.
146. Gurov, doctor of the 242nd 'Mountain' Division, 'Programma po sanitarnoi podgotovke dlia polkovykh spasatel'nykh otraidov' (15 November 1942), TsAMO, f. 1524, op. 1, d. 9, l. 160.
147. Kurashvili, 'Prikaz chastiam 242-i gsd' (15 November 1942), TsAMO, f. 1524, op. 1, d. 9, l. 155.
148. Opryshko, *Zaoblachnyi front*, 127. See similar stories in Gusev, *El'brus v ogne*, 155, 156; Gneushev and Poput'ko, *Taina Marukhskogo lednika* (1966), 242; Bekishvili, 'Oborona kavkazskikh perevalov', 99; Abramov, *Na ratnykh dorogakh*, 167, 174; Tiulenev, *Cherez tri voiny* (1960), 227; Gashchuk and Vukolov, *Turizm v vooruzhennykh silakh*, 32. Soviet film producers picked up these tales: a movie depicts a section of Soviet climbers blowing up a large charge on a slope dominating German defences and thus burying Germans under a snow avalanche: Stanislav Govorukhin, *Belyi vzryv* (film, 1969).
149. Gusev, *El'brus v ogne*, 98.
150. The next day, the 1st Mountain Division reported three men killed and two wounded on all sections of the front: 49th Mountain Corps, 'Zahlenmässige Übersicht'. Therefore, even if the report on casualties was delayed until the next day, the casualties from the alleged artificial avalanche could not have been higher than one or two men.
151. Rateriaev, 'Organizatsiia i vedenie razvedki' (17 October 1942), TsAMO, f. 47, op. 1063, d. 691, l. 12; Gioev, *Bitva za Kavkaz*, 95.
152. Filimonov, 'Iz vospominanii uchastnika', 309; Gneushev and Poput'ko, *Taina Marukhskogo lednika* (1966), 96, 97, 135, 136, 229, 230, 282.
153. Mezentsev, 'Itogovyi doklad', l. 191.
154. Arutiunov, deputy chief of staff of the 13th Rifle Corps, to Petrov, 'Opersvodka Nos. 24 and 26' (13 and 15 January 1943), TsAMO, f. 47, op. 1063, d. 692, ll. 207, 227; Arutiunov, 'Opersvodka No. 30' (18 January 1943), TsAMO, f. 401, op. 9511, d. 111, l. 276; Colonel Rybin, chief of staff of the 13th Rifle Corps, to Petrov, 'Opersvodka No. 23' (12 January 1943), TsAMO, f. 47, op. 1063, d. 692, l. 206; Colonel Piiashev, 'Vneocherednoe boevoe donesenie 13-go sk No. 66' (11 January 1943), TsAMO, f. 401, op. 9511, d. 111, l. 232; Gusev, 'Itogovaia operativnaia svodka' (3 February 1943), TsAMO, f. 401, op. 9511, d. 112, l. 40; Igol'nikov to Litvinov, 'Donesenie' (12 January 1943), TsAMO, f. 47, op. 1063, d. 692, l. 233.
155. Tiulenev, *Krakh operatsii 'Edel'veis'*, 57; Gioev, *Bitva za Kavkaz*, 86.
156. Opryshko, *Zaoblachnyi front*, 51–5; Gusev, *El'brus v ogne*, 194.
157. Nikolai Gusak, instructor of TCF Mountaineering Section, to Petrov (5 January 1943), TsAMO, f. 47, op. 1063, d. 691, l. 66.
158. Petrov, 'Prikaz voiskam Zakfronta' (30 January 1943), TsAMO, f. 47, op. 1063, d. 672, l. 70; Gusev, *El'brus v ogne*, 197.
159. Gusev, *El'brus v ogne*, 200–2.

160. V. Al'binin, 'Pomnish granatu i zapisku v nei . . .', *Turist* 8 (1976), 31.
161. Gusev, *El'brus v ogne*, 203. Several Soviet authors wrongly state that the Germans climbed both Elbrus summits: Ibragimbeili, *Krakh 'Edel'veisa'*, 107; Moshchanskii, *Stoiat' nasmert!*, 194; Gashchuk and Vukolov, *Turizm v vooruzhennykh silakh*, 33.
162. Gusev, *El'brus v ogne*, 128, 129; Grechko, *Bitva za Kavkaz* (1969), 160, 161.
163. See www.youtube.com/watch?v=eiZXCsCnFHQ.
164. Opryshko, *Zaoblachnyi front*, 144.
165. Captain Groth, 'Bericht über die Ersteilung des Elbrus' (28 August 1942), BA-MA, RH 24-1/171, SS. 214–216; Kaltenegger, *Gebirgsjäger im Kaukasus*, 103.
166. Opryshko, *Zaoblachnyi front*, 144.
167. Belekhov (19 October 1942), TsAMO, f. 401, op. 9511, d. 73, l. 41.
168. Dreev, 'Materialy po prikrytiiu i oborone GKKh' (no date; probably January 1943), TsAMO, f. 47, op. 1063, d. 689, l. 177v.
169. Aleksandr Gusev, 'Slovo znamenostsam', *Turist* 3 (1967), 3.

9 Lessons Ignored: Déjà Vu at Tuapse (1942) and in the Carpathians (1944)

1. 49th Mountain Corps, KTB (22 September 1942), BA-MA, RH 24-49/73, S. 25v.
2. Lieutenant-Colonel Konstantin Belokonov, 'Proval nastupleniia nemtsev na Tuapsinskom napravlenii' (no date) (hereafter cited as 'Proval nastupleniia nemtsev'), TsAMO, f. 47, op. 1063, d. 144, l. 11.
3. Konrad and Rümmler, *Kampf um dem Kaukasus*, 35, 36; Tieke, *The Caucasus and the Oil*, 198, 199.
4. Tieke, *The Caucasus and the Oil*, 197; Andrei Grechko, *Bitva za Kavkaz* (Moscow: MO SSSR, 1971), 152, 153.
5. Konrad and Rümmler, *Kampf um dem Kaukasus*, 37.
6. Grechko, *Bitva za Kavkaz* (1971), 157. Russian authors list units participating in the battle of Tuapse but claim disingenuously that Germans enjoyed numerical superiority, contrary to the contemporary assessment of the General Staff of the Red Army: Linets and Ianush, *Oborona Severnogo Kavkaza*, 316; Grechko, *Bitva za Kavkaz* (1971), 153.
7. Linets and Ianush, *Oborona Severnogo Kavkaza*, 326.
8. Belokonov, 'Proval nastupleniia nemtsev', l. 35.
9. General Konrad's claim that the Germans took the Goitkh pass on 16 October is false: Konrad and Rümmler, *Kampf um dem Kaukasus*, 38–40. The Germans never took the pass.
10. Lanz, *Gebirgsjäger*, 163.
11. Belokonov, 'Proval nastupleniia nemtsev', ll. 39–42.
12. Konrad and Rümmler, *Kampf um dem Kaukasus*, 39.
13. 49th Mountain Corps, 'Zahlenmässige Übersicht'; Tieke, *The Caucasus and the Oil*, 212, 219.
14. 49th Mountain Corps (no date), BA-MA, RH 24-49/232.
15. The reinforcements consisted of the 353rd Rifle Division, the 83rd 'Mountain' Division, the 63rd Cavalry Division, the 8th and 9th Guards Divisions, the 10th, 107th, and 165th Rifle Brigades, the 83rd Marine Brigade, the 26th NKVD Regiment, and the 323rd Marine Battalion: Belokonov, 'Proval nastupleniia nemtsev', ll. 30, 38, 67; Grechko, *Bitva za Kavkaz* (1971), 162, 163.
16. Lanz, *Gebirgsjäger*, 163; Tieke, *The Caucasus and the Oil*, 215.

17. Konrad and Rümmler, *Kampf um dem Kaukasus*, 43, 44; Tieke, *The Caucasus and the Oil*, 215, 216.
18. Belokonov, 'Proval nastupleniia nemtsev', l. 68.
19. Grechko, *Bitva za Kavkaz* (1971), 155.
20. Belokonov, 'Proval nastupleniia nemtsev', ll. 20, 63.
21. Grechko, *Bitva za Kavkaz* (1971), 154, 155.
22. Belokonov, 'Proval nastupleniia nemtsev', l. 53.
23. Ibid., ll. 51, 53, 59, 61.
24. Ibid., l. 66.
25. Konrad and Rümmler, *Kampf um dem Kaukasus*, 39; A. Luchinskii, '83-ia Internatsional'naia', in G. Akopian, *V boiiakh za Tuapse*, http://budetinteresno.narod.ru/kraeved/tuapse_war_11.htm (accessed on 1 September 2016).
26. Both of these Soviet formations redeemed themselves when they later offered stubborn defence to the Lanz Division, although the Soviet forces considerably outnumbered Germans in that region by that time.
27. Belokonov, 'Proval nastupleniia nemtsev', ll. 39–42.
28. Konrad and Rümmler, *Kampf um dem Kaukasus*, 45.
29. Belokonov, 'Proval nastupleniia nemtsev', l. 67.
30. Luchinskii, '83-ia Internatsional'naia'.
31. Belokonov, 'Proval nastupleniia nemtsev', l. 72.
32. Ibid., ll. 68, 72.
33. General Ivan Petrov to the Military Council of the TCF (October 1942), TsAMO, f. 47, op. 1063, d. 31, l. 138.
34. The temperature in the Tuapse region hovered around 0 °C during the worst weather: Tieke, *The Caucasus and the Oil*, 216.
35. Linets and Ianush, *Oborona Severnogo Kavkaza*, 313.
36. Konrad and Rümmler, *Kampf um dem Kaukasus*, 37, 40; Lanz, *Gebirgsjäger*, 163; Tieke, *The Caucasus and the Oil*, 200.
37. Luchinskii, '83-ia Internatsional'naia'; Batyrov, Grebeniuk and Matveev, eds., *Bitva za Kavkaz*, 140, 141.
38. Belokonov, 'Proval nastupleniia nemtsev', l. 72.
39. '*Poka grom ne grianet, muzhik ne perekrestitsia.*'
40. Gusev, *El'brus v ogne*, 204, 205; Gneushev and Poput'ko, *Taina Marukhskogo lednika* (1971), 331.
41. Moskalenko, *Na iugo-zapadnom napravlenii*, II:436.
42. Ivan Konev, *Zapiski komanduiushchego frontom* (Moscow: Nauka, 1972), 293.
43. General V. Korovikov, head of Operations Section of the 4th Ukrainian Front, and Colonel Levshuk, head of the Section for Utilising War Experience, 'Karpatskaia operatsiia 4-go Ukrainskogo Fronta' (no date) (hereafter cited as 'Karpatskaia operatsiia'), TsAMO, f. 244, op. 3000, d. 723, l. 80. Marshal Andrei Grechko plagiarised this study and published it as his own book: A. Grechko, *Cherez Karpaty* (Moscow: MO SSSR, 1972).
44. Konev, *Zapiski komanduiushchego frontom*, 304.
45. Moskalenko, *Na iugo-zapadnom napravlenii*, II:432; Korovikov and Levshuk, 'Karpatskaia operatsiia', ll. 67, 68.
46. Konev, *Zapiski komanduiushchego frontom*, 301–5; Moskalenko, *Na iugo-zapadnom napravlenii*, II:439.
47. Moskalenko, *Na iugo-zapadnom napravlenii*, II:432, 434, 475; Konev, *Zapiski komanduiushchego frontom*, 304, 310.
48. Konev, *Zapiski komanduiushchego frontom*, 304.
49. Korovikov and Levshuk, 'Karpatskaia operatsiia', ll. 8, 9.

50. Ibid., ll. 8, 9, 22, 193.
51. Konev, *Zapiski komanduiushchego frontom*, 307.
52. Korovikov and Levshuk, 'Karpatskaia operatsiia', l. 28; Konev, *Zapiski komanduiushchego frontom*, 332.
53. The 2nd and 8th Air Armies.
54. Moskalenko, *Na iugo-zapadnom napravlenii*, II:432, 436, 438, 442.
55. Ibid., II:434.
56. Ivan Petrov, commander of the 4th Ukrainian Front, and Lev Mekhlis, member of the Military Council of the 4th Ukrainian Front, 'Instruktsiia voiskam, deistvuiushchim v gorno-lesistioi mestnosti' (26 August 1944) (hereafter cited as 'Instruktsiia voiskam'), TsAMO, f. 244, op. 3000, d. 561, l. 58.
57. Ibid., ll. 52–82; Petrov and Mekhlis, 'Organizatsionnye ukazaniia po podgotovke voisk k deistviiam v gorakh' (11 August 1944) (hereafter cited as 'Organizatsionnye ukazaniia'), TsAMO, f. 244, op. 3000, d. 561, ll. 10–16.
58. Petrov and Mekhlis, 'Instruktsiia voiskam', ll. 56–58; Korovikov and Levshuk, 'Karpatskaia operatsiia', ll. 68–69.
59. Petrov and Mekhlis, 'Organizatsionnye ukazaniia', ll. 10–13.
60. Petrov and Mekhlis, 'Instruktsiia voiskam', l. 56.
61. Petrov and Mekhlis, 'Organizatsionnye ukazaniia', ll. 12, 14.
62. Ibid., ll. 13–15.
63. Petrov and Mekhlis, 'Instruktsiia voiskam,' l. 52.
64. Korovikov and Levshuk, 'Karpatskaia operatsiia', ll. 67–72, 77.
65. A. Vedenin, 'V nastuplenii – gornye strelki', in B. Venkov, ed., *V boiiakh za Karpaty* (Uzhgorod: Karpaty, 1975), 304.
66. Rakhmiel Sitnitskii in Drabkin, ed., *Vytashchit' s togo sveta*, 381; Vedenin, 'V nastuplenii – gornye strelki', 305.
67. Grechko, *Cherez Karpaty*, 69.
68. Andrei Grechko, 'Cherez Glavnyi karpatskii khrebet', in Venkov, ed., *V boiiakh za Karpaty*, 199; Korovikov and Levshuk, 'Karpatskaia operatsiia', l. 21.
69. The reinforcements included the 75th, 357th, and 544th Infantry Divisions: Moskalenko, *Na iugo-zapadnom napravlenii*, II:449, 457, 463.
70. Konev, *Zapiski komanduiushchego frontom*, 315, 323.
71. Moskalenko, *Na iugo-zapadnom napravlenii*, II:472, 473.
72. Lieutenant-Colonel Smirnov, head of Section for Utilising War Experience at the 1st Guards Army, 'Vedenie ognia v gorakh iz pekhotnogo oruzhiia' (18 October 1944), TsAMO, f. 244, op. 3000, d. 718, ll. 1, 2.
73. V. Korovikov, 'Preodolevaia soprotivlenie vraga', in Venkov, ed., *V boiiakh za Karpaty*, 206, 207.
74. Moskalenko, *Na iugo-zapadnom napravlenii*, II:438, 472; Korovikov and Levshuk, 'Karpatskaia operatsiia', ll. 155, 156; Moskalenko, *Na iugo-zapadnom napravlenii*, II:478.
75. Korovikov and Levshuk, 'Karpatskaia operatsiia', ll. 106, 127, 200, 203.
76. Vedenin, 'V nastuplenii – gornye strelki', 307; Korovikov and Levshuk, 'Karpatskaia operatsiia', ll. 195, 199.
77. Moskalenko, *Na iugo-zapadnom napravlenii*, II:484; Krivosheev, ed., *Rossiia i SSSR v voinakh XX veka*, 298.
78. Korovikov and Levshuk, 'Karpatskaia operatsiia', ll. 211, 212, 215.
79. Moskalenko, *Na iugo-zapadnom napravlenii*, II:472, 473.
80. Korovikov and Levshuk, 'Karpatskaia operatsiia', ll. 92, 201; General A. Batiunia, chief of staff of the 1st Guards Army, 'Boevoe donesenie No. 001853' (20 September 1944), TsAMO, f. 292, op. 6850, d. 434, l. 310.

81. Korovikov and Levshuk, 'Karpatskaia operatsiia', ll. 93–95; Grechko, *Cherez Karpaty*, 208, 209.
82. Konev, *Zapiski komanduiushchego frontom*, 325, 339, 343.
83. Ibid., 337, 339.
84. Korovikov and Levshuk, 'Karpatskaia operatsiia', l. 21; Moskalenko, *Na iugo-zapadnom napravlenii*, II:457.
85. Korovikov, 'Preodolevaia soprotivlenie vraga', 208; Konev, *Zapiski komanduiushchego frontom*, 339.
86. Korovikov and Levshuk, 'Karpatskaia operatsiia', l. 190; Krivosheev, ed., *Rossiia i SSSR v voinakh XX veka*, 299. The data of the 1st Ukrainian Front probably exclude the casualties sustained by the reinforcements it received after the beginning of the operation.
87. Moskalenko, *Na iugo-zapadnom napravlenii*, II:485.
88. Konev, *Zapiski komanduiushchego frontom*, 345; Moskalenko, *Na iugo-zapadnom napravlenii*, II:475.
89. The reinforcements that the 38th Army received after the offensive had begun consisted of three rifle divisions, two tank corps and two tank brigades, an anti-tank artillery brigade, several other artillery brigades, and a Czechoslovak airborne brigade flown to Slovakia on 18 September: Konev, *Zapiski komanduiushchego frontom*, 310, 311; Moskalenko, *Na iugo-zapadnom napravlenii*, II:473.
90. Moskalenko mentions 'up to twelve' German divisions against his army throughout the battle of the Beskids: the 68th, 75th, 78th, 208th, 357th, 359th, and 545th Infantry Divisions; the 1st, 8th, and 24th Tank Divisions; the 101st Jäger Division; and units of the 544th and '1st Ski-Jäger' Divisions (Moskalenko, *Na iugo-zapadnom napravlenii*, II:475). However, the 78th Infantry Division that he claims was present in the Beskids had already been destroyed during Operation Bagration, far away from the Beskids, and only some units of the 101st Jäger Division and the 1st Tank Division faced the 38th Army, while others opposed the 1st Guards Army and the 18th Army. A contemporary Soviet military study shows that by 26 September the Germans had, against the 38th Army, only the 68th, 75th, 208th, and 545th Infantry Divisions; the 8th and 24th Tank Divisions; 'five infantry regiments of other divisions, several independent battalions ... and more than seventy artillery and mortar batteries': Grechko, *Cherez Karpaty*, 194, 246. It is likely that even this study inflated the enemy forces, as Soviet generals usually did when they assessed the opposition.
91. The 1st Guards Army consisted, eventually, of the 30th, 141st, 155th, 167th, 226th, 237th, 271st, and 276th Rifle Divisions; the 129th Guards Rifle Division; the 242nd Mountain and 318th 'Mountain' Divisions; and the 128th Guards Mountain Division: Grechko, *Cherez Karpaty*, Map 5.
92. These were the 96th, 168th, 254th, and 357th Infantry Divisions; the 97th and 101th Jäger Divisions; and units of the 1st Tank Division: ibid., 194.
93. Konev, *Zapiski komanduiushchego frontom*, 345.
94. Zolotarev and Sevost'ianov, eds., *Velikaia Otechestvennaia voina*, IV:326.
95. '*Gladko bylo na bumage, da zabyli pro ovragi, a po nim khodit'*.' The original verse was published in the journal *Poliarnaia zvezda* in 1857.
96. Konev, *Zapiski komanduiushchego frontom*, 346.
97. Mezentsev, 'Itogovyi doklad', ll. 188–193; Bozhenko, 'Iz opyta boev na perevalakh GKKh' (25 November 1942), TsAMO, f. 1524, op. 1, d. 9, ll. 162–165; Zav'ialov, 'Oborona Glavnogo Kavkazskogo Khrebta', ll. 1–17v; Lieutenant-Colonel Konstantin Belokonov, 'Proval nastupleniia nemtsev na Tuapsinskom napravlenii' (no date), TsAMO, f. 47, op. 1063, d. 144, ll. 11–76.

10 Disdain for Military Professionalism as a Component of the Universal Stalinist Paradigm

1. '*Tiazhelo v uchen'i – legko v pokhode!*', in G. P. Meshcheriakov, ed., *A. V. Suvorov. Dokumenty* (Moscow: Voennoe izdatel'stvo Voennogo ministerstva SSSR, 1952), III:351.
2. '*Ne bogi gorshki obzhigaiut.*' Literally, 'One does not need a divine spark to make clay pots.'
3. Suvenirov, *Tragediia RKKA*, 24.
4. Hannah Arendt, *Origins of Totalitarianism* (New York: Harcourt Brace Jovanovich, 1976), 339.
5. '*Geroem stanovitsia liuboi*': Iurii Rubtsov, *Alter ego Stalina* (Moscow: Zvonnitsa, 1999), 114.
6. Suvenirov, *Tragediia RKKA*, 52.
7. Ibid., 69.
8. Zolotarev, ed., *Tainy i uroki*, 224.
9. Zolotarev and Sevost'ianov, eds., *Velikaia Otechestvennaia voina*, I:81, 82.
10. Glantz, *Stumbling Colossus*, 109.
11. Zolotarev and Sevost'ianov, eds., *Velikaia Otechestvennaia voina*, I:80.
12. Ibid., I:81.
13. Ibid., I:81, 82, 192.
14. Ibid., I:81, 82, 88.
15. Clausewitz, *On War*, 122.
16. Vasilii Briukhov, *Pravda tankovogo asa* (Moscow: EKSMO, 2013), 34; Aleksei Tonkonogov and Stepan Shebalin in Vladimir Pershanin, ed., *My pol-Evropy po-plastunski propakhali* (Moscow: Iauza-Eksmo, 2010), 133, 189.
17. Dmitrii Pikulenko, Fedor Lapshin and Stepan Shebalin in Pershanin, ed., *My pol-Evropy po-plastunski propakhali*, 12, 13, 78, 189.
18. V. Shevchenko, ibid., 212.
19. Boris Nazarov in Drabkin, ed., *Glavnoe – vybit' u nikh tanki*, 129.
20. V. Shevchenko in Pershanin, ed., *Stalingradskaia miasorubka*, 211.
21. Ivan Mel'nikov in Pershanin, *My pol-Evropy po-plastunski propakhali*, 385, 386; Apel', *Dokhodiaga*, 18–20.
22. Mikhail Chernomordik in Drabkin, ed., *Glavnoe – vybit' u nikh tanki*, 268, 269.
23. Apel', *Dokhodiaga*, 20. See also Boris Rapoport in Artem Drabkin, ed., *Ia – bomber* (Moscow: Iauza-Eksmo, 2011), 469. See also Grigorii Krivosheev in Drabkin, ed., *My dralis' na istrebiteliakh*, 341.
24. Aleksei Isaev, *Mify i pravda o Stalingrade* (Moscow: Eksmo, 2013), 201, 202.
25. J. Stalin, 'Prikaz ob ispol'zovanii tankistov po spetsial'nosti' (13 December 1942), in Artem Drabkin, ed. *Ia dralsia na T-34* (Moscow: Iauza-Eksmo, 2010), 558.
26. Aleksandr Rogachev in Drabkin, ed., *Glavnoe – vybit' u nikh tanki*, 307, 308. See also Fedor Lapshin and Stepan Shebalin in Pershanin, ed., *My pol-Evropy po-plastunski propakhali*, 78, 220; P. Solov'ev, in Pershanin, ed., *Stalingradskaia miasorubka*, 175; Vladimir Logachev in Drabkin, ed., *Vstavai, strana ogromnaia*, 135.
27. Vasilii Ustimenko in Pershanin, ed., *My pol-Evropy po-plastunski propakhali*, 443.
28. Nikolai Zheleznov in Drabkin, ed., *Ia dralsia na T-34*, 241; Mikhail Baitman in Drabkin, ed., *My khodili za liniiu fronta*, 283; Nikolai Vinokur in Drabkin, ed., *Vytashchit' s togo sveta*, 123.

29. Fedor Lapshin and Aleksandr Gordeev in Pershanin, ed., *My pol-Evropy po-plastunski propakhali*, 115, 581.
30. Aleksei Tonkonogov, Vasilii Ustimenko and Aleksandr Gordeev, ibid., 133, 440, 581.
31. Vasilii Ustimenko, ibid., 439–42.
32. Aleksandr Gordeev, ibid., 555; Stepan Bondarenko in Drabkin, ed., *Vstavai, strana ogromnaia*, 250.
33. Briukhov, *Pravda tankovogo asa*, 35.
34. Kliment Voroshilov in Zolotarev, ed., *Tainy i uroki*, 433; Headquarters of the 8th Army (April 1940), ibid., 389, 390.
35. Genrikh Kats in Drabkin, ed., *My khodili za liniiu fronta*, 246.
36. Ivan Mel'nikov in Pershanin, ed., *My pol-Evropy po-plastunski propakhali*, 387.
37. Nikolai Iaganov in Drabkin, ed., *My khodili za liniiu fronta*, 204.
38. Mstislav Ivanov, Ivan Kobets, Nikolai Khvatkin, Vladimir Bukhenko, Genrikh Kats and Mikhail Baitman, ibid., 11, 33, 51, 102, 222, 286.
39. Nikolai Chernov, ibid., 192.
40. Mstislav Ivanov, Ivan Kobets, Nikolai Khvatkin, Vladimir Bukhenko, Vladimir Voitsekhovich, Genrikh Kats, Aleksandr Solov'ev, and Mikhail Baitman, ibid., 14, 61, 104–9, 119, 225, 247, 261, 283.
41. Nikolai Khvatkin, Vladimir Bukhenko, Nikolai Iaganov, Aleksandr Solov'ev, and Sigizmund Andrievskii, ibid., 100, 115, 209, 260, 277.
42. Mstislav Ivanov and Mikhail Baitman, ibid., 12, 283, 290; Ivan Proskurov in Kul'kov and Rzheshevskii, eds., *Zimniaia voina*, II:210.
43. Vladimir Zemakov in Drabkin, ed., *Glavnoe – vybit' u nikh tanki*, 204.
44. Zolotarev and Sevost'ianov, eds., *Velikaia Otechestvennaia voina*, I:84; David Glantz, *A History of Soviet Airborne Forces* (Portland, OR: Frank Cass, 1994), 43, 44.
45. Vasilii Poleev in Pershanin, ed., *My pol-Evropy po-plastunski propakhali*, 315; Matvei Likhterman in Drabkin, ed., *Vstavai, strana ogromnaia*, 18.
46. Glantz, *A History of Soviet Airborne Forces*, 276; Matvei Likhterman in Drabkin, ed., *Vstavai, strana ogromnaia*, 16, 24–8.
47. Glantz, *A History of Soviet Airborne Forces*, 286.
48. Matvei Likhterman in Drabkin, ed., *Vstavai, strana ogromnaia*, 24, 25, 29; Glantz, *A History of Soviet Airborne Forces*, 274.
49. Glantz, *Stumbling Colossus*, 160.
50. Nikolai Shishkin in Drabkin, ed., *Glavnoe – vybit' u nikh tanki*, 217.
51. Moisei Dorman and Mikhail Chernomordik, ibid., 161, 268.
52. Moisei Dorman, ibid., 161, 162.
53. Aleksandr Rogachev, ibid., 320.
54. Nikolai Malygin in Pershanin, ed., *My pol-Evropy po-plastunski propakhali*, 608; Matvei Likhterman in Drabkin, ed., *Vstavai, strana ogromnaia*, 14; Moisei Dorman and Mikhail Chernomordik in Drabkin, ed., *Glavnoe – vybit' u nikh tanki*, 166, 180, 269, 278, 295.
55. Vitalii Ul'ianov in Drabkin, *Glavnoe – vybit' u nikh tanki*, 30, 31. See also Mikhail Borisov, ibid., 98; Mikhail Shister in Drabkin, ed., *Ia dralsia na T-34*, 418; Dmitrii Pikulenko in Pershanin, ed., *My pol-Evropy po-plastunski propakhali*, 10; Matvei Likhterman in Drabkin, ed., *Vstavai, strana ogromnaia*, 6.
56. Iiurii Novikov in Drabkin, ed., *Vstavai, strana ogromnaia*, 151.
57. Solonin, *Iiun' 41-go*, 8; Krivosheev, *Rossiia i SSSR v voinakh XX veka*, 472.
58. Mark Solonin, *Drugaia khronologiia katastrofy 1941* (Moscow: Iauza-Eksmo, 2011), 18.

59. Aleksandr Bondar' and Ivan Maslov in Drabkin, ed., *Ia dralsia na T-34*, 51, 70, 392.
60. Aleksei Isaev, *Chudo prigranichnogo srazheniia* (Moscow: Eksmo, 2013), 32–7; Zolotarev and Sevost'ianov, eds., *Velikaia Otechestvennaia voina*, I:86–8; Vasilii Briukhov and Konstantin Shits in Drabkin, ed., *Ia dralsia na T-34*, 165, 453.
61. Vasilii Briukhov in Drabkin, ed., *Ia dralsia na T-34*, 164, 165. See also Pavel Kuleshov and Ion Degen, ibid., 259, 353.
62. A. Zhuravlev in Pershanin, ed., *Stalingradskaia miasorubka*, 10.
63. Glantz, *Stumbling Colossus*, 135.
64. A. Zhuravlev in Pershanin, ed., *Stalingradskaia miasorubka*, 10; Dmitrii Pikulenko in Pershanin, ed., *My pol-Evropy po-plastunski propakhali*, 10–12; Iurii Polianovskii and Pavel Kuleshov in Drabkin, ed., *Ia dralsia na T-34*, 91, 259.
65. Krivosheev, *Rossiia i SSSR v voinakh XX veka*, 468.
66. Briukhov, *Pravda tankovogo asa*, 54.
67. Glantz, *Stumbling Colossus*, 133, 135, 139; J. Stalin, 'Prikaz Stavki' (22 January 1942), 'Prikaz Stavki' (5 June 1942), and 'Prikaz o boevom primenenii tankovykh i mekhanizirovannykh chastei' (16 October 1942), in Drabkin, ed., *Ia dralsia na T-34*, 535, 541, 546, 547.
68. Glantz, *Stumbling Colossus*, 127, 142.
69. Drabkin, ed., *Ia dralsia na T-34*, 52.
70. P. Pospelov et al., eds., *Istoriia Velikoi Otechestvennoi voiny Sovetskogo Soiuza* (Moscow: IML, 1961–5), I:476. See also Glantz, *Stumbling Colossus*, 135; Semen Ariia, Aleksandr Fadin and Petr Kirichenko in Drabkin, ed., *Ia dralsia na T-34*, 82, 86, 113, 143.
71. Drabkin, ed., *Ia dralsia na T-34*, 59.
72. Glantz, *Stumbling Colossus*, 145.
73. Briukhov, *Pravda tankovogo asa*, 54; Iiurii Polianovskii in Drabkin, ed., *Ia dralsia na T-34*, 91.
74. Aleksandr Burtsev in Drabkin, ed., *Ia dralsia na T-34*, 152.
75. Isaev, *Chudo prigranichnogo srazheniia,* 683; Zolotarev and Sevost'ianov, eds., *Velikaia Otechestvennaia voina*, I:88; Glantz, *Stumbling Colossus*, 118, 134.
76. Glantz, *Stumbling Colossus*, 135; Solonin, *Iiun' 41-go*, 308.
77. Isaev, *Chudo prigranichnogo srazheniia,* 530, 562, 584.
78. Konstantin Shits in Drabkin, ed., *Ia dralsia na T-34*, 454; Isaev, *Mify i pravda o Stalingrade*, 67.
79. Vasilii Briukhov and Nikolai Aleksandrov in Drabkin, ed., *Ia dralsia na T-34*, 165, 514.
80. Aleksandr Bondar', ibid., 71.
81. Dmitrii Pikulenko in Pershanin, ed., *My pol-Evropy po-plastunski propakhali*, 17.
82. Krivosheev, *Rossiia i SSSR v voinakh XX veka*, 468.
83. Solonin, *Iiun' 41-go*, 8, 341.
84. Isaev, *Mify i pravda o Stalingrade*, 42, 67–70.
85. Petr Kirichenko, Aleksandr Burtsev, Arsentii Rod'kin, Ivan Nikonov, and Aleksandr Shlemotov in Drabkin, ed., *Ia dralsia na T-34*, 146, 151, 215, 307, 438.
86. Ion Degen, ibid., 357.
87. Stalin, 'Prikaz o boevom primenenii', 549.
88. Briukhov, *Pravda tankovogo asa*, 214.
89. Solonin, *'Uprezhdaiushchii udar' Stalina*, 68.
90. Elena Miliutina and Aleksei Maksimenko in Drabkin, ed., *Ia – bomber*, 8, 376; A. Pekarsh and Vitalii Klimenko in Drabkin, ed., *My dralis' na istrebiteliakh*, 7, 16.

91. A. Pekarsh, Nikolai Dudnik, Nikolai Golodnikov, and Petr Rassadkin in Drabkin, ed., *My dralis' na istrebiteliakh*, 7, 49, 168–71, 248; Lev Mekhlis in Kul'kov and Rzheshevskii, eds., *Zimniaia voina*, II:96.
92. A. Pekarsh in Drabkin, ed., *My dralis' na istrebiteliakh*, 8.
93. A. Pekarsh, Nikolai Dudnik, and Stepan Mikoian, ibid., 7, 49, 98.
94. Headquarters of the 8th Army (April 1940) in Zolotarev, ed., *Tainy i uroki*, 391; Filipp Gorelenko in Kul'kov and Rzheshevskii, eds., *Zimniaia voina*, II:89; Ivan Kopets, ibid., II:115, 116.
95. Grigorii Kravchenko in Kul'kov and Rzheshevskii, eds., *Zimniaia voina*, II:95.
96. Solonin, *Drugaia khronologiia katastrofy*, 310.
97. Ibid., 158, 159; Pospelov, *Istoriia Velikoi Otechectvennoi voiny*, I:476; Zolotarev and Sevost'ianov, eds., *Velikaia Otechestvennaia voina*, I:88; Nikolai Golodnikov in Drabkin, ed., *My dralis' na istrebiteliakh*, 171.
98. Sergei Gorelov in Drabkin, ed., *My dralis' na istrebiteliakh*, 312.
99. Nikolai Smol'skii, Ivan Kabakov, Andrei Kalinichenko, and Vladimir Pshenko in Drabkin, ed., *Ia – bomber*, 56, 166, 174, 507; Vitalii Klimenko, Aleksandr Shvarev, Stepan Mikoian, Viktor Sinaiskii, Nikolai Golodnikov, Aleksandr Khaila, Vasilii Kanishchev, and Vladimir Tikhomirov in Drabkin, ed., *My dralis' na istrebiteliakh*, 28, 37, 59, 97, 156, 172, 291, 377, 533, 554.
100. Solonin, *Drugaia khronologiia katastrofy*, 315.
101. Ibid., 289, 293.
102. Aleksandr Anosov in Drabkin, ed., *Ia – bomber*, 195; Semen Bukchin in Drabkin, ed., *My dralis' na istrebiteliakh*, 363.
103. Aleksandr Shvarev and Semen Bukchin in Drabkin, ed., *My dralis' na istrebiteliakh*, 71, 363.
104. Vasilii Kanishchev, ibid., 378.
105. Andrei Kalinichenko in Drabkin, ed., *Ia – bomber*, 175.
106. Aleksandr Anosov, ibid., 197.
107. Stepan Mikoian and Ivan Kozhemiako in Drabkin, ed., *My dralis' na istrebiteliakh*, 106, 401–3; Victor Kaliadin in Drabkin, ed., *Ia – bomber*, 335.
108. Aleksandr Shvarev, Nikolai Golodnikov, and Konstantin Zvonarev in Drabkin, ed., *My dralis' na istrebiteliakh*, 87, 173, 697.
109. Artem Drabkin, ed., *Ia dralsia na Il-2* (Moscow: Iauza-Eksmo, 2011), II:248.
110. Andrei Kalinichenko in Drabkin, ed., *Ia – bomber*, 175.
111. Anatolii Lilin, Nikolai Smol'skii, Vladimir Ermakov, Vladimir Temerov, and Nikolai Butorin, ibid., 25, 35, 55, 74, 129, 144, 149, 150.
112. Nikolai Dudnik and Sergei Gorelov in Drabkin, ed., *My dralis' na istrebiteliakh*, 49, 317.
113. Krivosheev, *Rossiia i SSSR v voinakh XX veka*, 468; Solonin, *Iiun' 41-go*, 8. On the Southwestern Front, the Red Air Force enjoyed a five-fold numerical superiority over the Luftwaffe at the beginning of Operation Barbarossa: ibid., 161.
114. Aleksandr Anosov, Boris Rapoport, Nikolai Belousov, Nikolai Gunbin, and Mikhail Borisov in Drabkin, ed., *Ia – bomber*, 224, 460, 654, 630, 675.
115. Semen Bukchin in Drabkin, ed., *My dralis' na istrebiteliakh*, 363; Dmitrii Shaglin, Dmitrii Vaulin, and Nikolai Belousov in Drabkin, ed., *Ia – bomber*, 113, 548, 641; Petr Katsevman in Drabkin, ed., *Ia dralsia na Il-2*, II:23.
116. Aleksandr Riazanov in Drabkin, ed., *My dralis' na istrebiteliakh*, 578.
117. Naum Kravets in Drabkin, ed., *Ia – bomber*, 100.
118. Vladimir Tikhomirov in Drabkin, ed., *My dralis' na istrebiteliakh*, 535.
119. Stepan Mikoian, Nikolai Golodnikov, Sergei Gorelov, Ivan Kozhemiako, and Vladimir Tikhomirov, ibid., 100, 178, 322, 477, 478, 533; Andrei Kalinichenko

and Boris Rapoport in Drabkin, ed., *Ia – bomber*, 176, 468; Petr Katsevman, Vladimir Titovich, and Boris Buchin in Drabkin, ed., *Ia dralsia na Il-2*, II:25, 81–4, 254.

120. Stepan Mikoian and Nikolai Golodnikov in Drabkin, ed., *My dralis' na istrebiteliakh*, 108, 172; Boris Rapoport in Drabkin, ed., *Ia – bomber*, 176, 471.
121. Nikolai Golodnikov in Drabkin, ed., *My dralis' na istrebiteliakh*, 194.
122. Nikolai Golodnikov, ibid., 192, 199. See also Aleksandr Shvarev, Petr Rassadkin, Vitalii Rybalko, Semen Bukchin, and Leonid Maslov, ibid., 79, 255, 283, 366, 513.
123. Aleksandr Khaila and Ivan Kozhemiako in Drabkin, ed., *My dralis' na istrebiteliakh*, 296, 297, 454, 460.
124. Solonin, *Iiun' 41-go*, 8, 12.
125. Iurii Novikov in Drabkin, ed., *Vstavai, strana ogromnaia*, 153; Mikhail Chernomordik in Drabkin, ed., *Glavnoe – vybit' u nikh tanki*, 294.
126. Solonin, *Iiun' 41-go*, 355–8.
127. Ministerstvo oborony Rossiiskoi Federatsii (Ministry of Defence of the Russian Federation) (13 November 2014), 'V Federatsii al'pinizma Rossii proshlo soveshchanie, posviashchennoe voprosam podgotovki voennosluzhashchikh i sotrudnikov spetspodrazdelenii k deistviiam v gorakh', http://mil.ru/et/news/more.htm?id=11999815@egNews&_print=true (accessed on 8 May 2017).

BIBLIOGRAPHY

Archives

Bundesarchiv-Militärarchiv (BA-MA), Germany.
Gosudarstvennyi arkhiv Rossiiskoi Federatsii (GARF) (State Archive of the Russian Federation).
Rossiiskii gosudarstvennyi arkhiv sotsial'no-politicheskoi istorii (RGASPI) (Russian State Archive of Socio-Political History).
Rossiiskii gosudarstvennyi voenno-istoricheskii arkhiv (RGVIA) (Russian State Military Historical Archive).
Rossiiskii gosudarstvennyi voennyi arkhiv (RGVA) (Russian State Military Archive).
Tsentral'nyi arkhiv Ministerstva oborony Rossiiskoi Federatsii (TsAMO) (Central Archives of the Ministry of Defence of the Russian Federation).

Document Collections, Memoirs, and Contemporary Sources

Abalakov, Evgenii. *Na vysochaishikh vershinakh Sovetskogo Soiuza*. Moscow: AN SSSR, 1962.
Abalakov, Vitalii. *Osnovy al'pinizma*. Moscow: FiS, 1941.
Abalakov, V., A. Get'e and D. Gushchin. *Vysokogornye uchebnye pokhody i ekspeditsii*. Moscow: Fizkul'tura i turizm, 1937.
Abramov, Vasilii. *Na ratnykh dorogakh*. Moscow: MO SSSR, 1962.
Antonov-Saratovskii, V. 'Na vysshuiu stupen'', *Na sushe i na more* 11 (1930), 2.
'Turizm, partiia i gosudarstvo', *Na sushe i na more* 1 (1930), 1–2.
Apel', Iurii. *Dokhodiaga*. Moscow: Rosspen, 2009.
Arem'ev, G. 'OPT v Kabardino-Balkarii', *Na sushe i na more* 12 (1929), 15.

Aristov, O. and Iu. Korobkov. 'Po tropam iuzhnoi Kirgizii', *Na sushe i na more* 17 (1933), 8–10.
Badanin, B. *Na boevykh rubezhakh Kavkaza*. Moscow: MO SSSR, 1962.
Barkhash, L. 'Distsiplina sredi turistov', *Na sushe i na more* 11 (1930), 15–16.
'Vnimanie, samodeiatelnye turisty', *Na sushe i na more* 1 (1935), 4.
Batyrov, U., S. Grebeniuk and V. Matveev, eds. *Bitva za Kavkaz*. Moscow: Triada, 2002.
Bauer, Josef Martin. *Unternehmen 'Elbrus'*. Munich: Herbig, 1976.
Blume, Helmut. *Zum Kaukasus 1941–1942. Aus dem Tagebuch und Briefen eines jungen Artilleristen*. Tübingen: Narr Francke Attempto, 1993.
Bogdanovich, M. *Pokhody Suvorova v Italii i Shveitsarii*. St Petersburg: Voennaia tipografiia, 1846.
Bonch-Bruevich, Mikhail. *Poteria nami Galitsii v 1915 g*. Moscow: 20-ia gosudarstvennaia tipografiia, 1920.
Briukhov, Vasilii. *Pravda tankovogo asa*. Moscow: EKSMO, 2013.
Brusilov, Aleksei. *Moi vospominaniia*. Moscow: Rosspen, 2001.
Budylin. 'Ratsiia na Elbruse', *Na sushe i na more* 22–4 (1932), 26.
Cherepov, I. *Al'pinizm*. Moscow: Fizkul'tura i sport, 1940.
Gornolyzhnaia podgotovka. Moscow: Voenizdat, 1941.
Gorno-lyzhnyi sport. Moscow: Fizkul'tura i sport, 1940.
'Kak sokhranit' turistskoe snariazhenie', *Na sushe i na more* 15 (1933), 15.
'Kreplenie lyzhnika-turista', *Na sushe i na more* 31–2 (1932), 14.
ed. *Nastavlenie dlia gorno-strelkovykh chastei germanskoi armii*. Moscow: Voenizdat, 1941.
ed. *Pamiatka boitsa lyzhnika-al'pinista*. Uchebnaia gornolyzhnaia baza Upraforma Zakavkazskogo Fronta, December 1942.
Clausewitz, Carl von. *On War*. Princeton: Princeton University Press, 1984.
Shveitsarskii pokhod Suvorova. Moscow: Voennoe izdatel'stvo, 1939.
De-Lazari, A. 'Kul'turnaia revoliutsiia i turizm', *Na sushe i na more* 3 (1930), 14–15.
Demin, M. 'Molodye turisty-bezbozhniki', *Na sushe i na more* 3 (1930), 21.
Drabkin, Artem, ed. *Glavnoe – vybit' u nikh tanki*. Moscow: Iauza-Eksmo, 2011.
ed. *Ia – bomber*. Moscow: Iauza-Eksmo, 2011.
ed. *Ia dralsia na Il-2*. Moscow: Iauza-Eksmo, 2011.
ed. *Ia dralsia na T-34*. Moscow: Iauza-Eksmo, 2010.
ed. *My dralis' na istrebiteliakh*. Moscow: Iauza-Eksmo, 2014.
ed. *My khodili za liniiu fronta*. Moscow: Iauza-Eksmo, 2011.
ed. *Vstavai, strana ogromnaia*. Moscow: Iauza-Eksmo, 2010.
ed. *Vytashchit' s togo sveta*. Moscow: Iauza-Eksmo, 2012.
Dzerdzeevskii, B. 'Prognoz pogody zimoi', *Na sushe i na more* 2 (1941), 12.
Fadeev, R. *60 let Kavkazskoi voiny*. Moscow: Gosudarstvennaia publichnaia istoricheskaia biblioteka Rossii, 2007.

Fuks, Egor. *Istoriia rossiisko-avstriiskoi kampanii 1799 g.* St Petersburg: Voennaia tipografiia General'nogo Shtaba, 1825–6.

Furst, K. 'Turizm za granitsei', *Na sushe i na more* 9 (1930), 20.

General'nyi shtab Krasnoi Armii [General Staff of the Red Army]. *Nastavlenie dlia deistvii voisk RKKA v gorakh*. Moscow: NKO SSSR, 1936.

Gioev, Mikhail. *Bitva za Kavkaz: razdum'ia frontovogo ofitsera*. Vladikavkaz: Ir, 2007.

Glavnoe upravlenie sviazi [Main Signals Directorate]. *Spravochnik po voiskovym i tankovym radiostantsiiam*. Moscow: Voennoe izdatel'stvo NKO, 1943.

Gordin, Iakov, ed. *Osada Kavkaza*. St Petersburg: Zvezda, 2000.

ed. *Darginskaia tragediia*. St Petersburg: Zvezda, 2001.

'Gornomu turizmu – boevye tempy', *Na sushe i na more* 16 (1932), 2.

'Gornye lageri', *Na sushe i na more* 4 (1936), 2.

Grechko, Andrei. *Bitva za Kavkaz*. Moscow: MO SSSR, 1969.

Bitva za Kavkaz. Moscow: MO SSSR, 1971.

Grigor'ev, K. 'Turizm za granitsei', *Na sushe i na more* 3 (1930), 19.

'Voennyi turizm na zapade', *Na sushe i na more* 4 (1931), 18–20.

Gurvich, L. 'Izvlechem bol'shevistskii urok', *Na sushe i na more* 31–2 (1932), 15.

'Turizm i oborona', *Na sushe i na more* 13 (1932), 10.

Gusev, Aleksandr. *El'brus v ogne*. Moscow: MO SSSR, 1980.

'Slovo znamenostsam', *Turist* 3 (1967), 3.

Gushchin, D. 'Kak byl vziat pik Stalina', *Na sushe i na more* 18 (1933), 5–7.

'Shkola al'pinizma', *Na sushe i na more* 8 (1935), 13.

Gutman, L., S. Khodakevich and I. Antonovich. *Tekhnika al'pinizma*. Moscow: Fizkul'tura i sport, 1939.

Uchebnoe posobie dlia nachinaiushchikh al'pinistov. Moscow: Fizkul'tura i sport, 1939.

Halder, Franz. *The Halder Diaries: The Private War Journals of Colonel General Franz Halder*. Boulder: Westview Press, 1976.

Hillgruber, Andreas, ed. *Kriegstagebuch des Oberkommandos der Wehrmacht*. Munich: Bernard & Graefe, 1982.

Hubatsch, Walter, ed. *Hitlers Weisungen für die Kriegsfürung, 1939–1945*. Munich: Deutscher Taschenbuch Verlag, 1965.

Ialukhin, N., I. Dolgikh and G. Mukhoedov, eds. *Shturm Belukhi*. Novosibirsk: Zapadno-Sibirskoe Kraevoe Izdatel'stvo, 1936.

Iampol'skii V. et al., eds. *Organy gosudarstvennoi bezopasnosti SSSR v Velikoi Otechestvennoi voine*. Moscow: Rus', 2003.

Ianin, S. 'Kursy v gorakh', *Na sushe i na more* 1 (1935), 7.

Iatsenko, V. *V gorakh Pamira*. Moscow: Izdatel'stvo geograficheskoi literatury, 1950.

'Instruktory po turizmu', *Na sushe i na more* 5 (1941), 2.

Kal'pus, B. 'Turizm v RKKA', *Na sushe i na more* 2 (1936), 13.
Kamenev, S. 'Turizm i oborona', *Na sushe i na more* 11 (1929), 9.
Kechiev. 'Boevye deistviia v Al'pakh', *Na sushe i na more* 4 (1941), 13–14.
'V gorakh Albanii', *Na sushe i na more* 2 (1941), 14.
Kizel', Vladimir. *Gory zovut*. Moscow: Lokis, 2005.
Klement'ev, Vasilii. *Boevye deistviia gornykh voisk*. Moscow: Voenizdat, 1940.
Cherez lednikovye perevaly Kavkaza: voenno-turistskii pokhod. Moscow: Fizkul'tura i turizm, 1931.
Konev, Ivan. *Zapiski komanduiushchego frontom*. Moscow: Nauka, 1972.
Konrad, Rudolf and E. Wolf Rümmler. *Kampf um dem Kaukasus*. Munich: Copress, 1954.
Koritskii, N. 'Voenizatsiia turizma', *Na sushe i na more* 3 (1930), 2.
Kotovich, O. 'Pobezhdat' gory bez avarii', *Na sushe i na more* 5 (1941), 8.
'Krepi oboronu SSSR', *Na sushe i na more* 22 (1930), 1–2.
Krylenko, N. 'Al'pinizm na novom etape', *Na sushe i na more* 4 (1936), 4–6.
Po neissledovannomy Pamiru. Moscow: Gosudarstvennoe izdatel'stvo geograficheskoi literatury, 1980.
ed. *V lednikakh: vysokogornye pokhody komandirov RKKA v 1934 g*. Moscow: Gosudarstvennoe voennoe izdatel'stvo, 1935.
Kudinov, B. 'Radiostantsiia v gorakh', *Na sushe i na more* 8 (1935), 14.
Kuhn, Franz von. 'Gornaia voina', *Voennyi sbornik* 133 (1880).
Kul'kov, E. and O. Rzheshevskii, eds. *Zimniaia voina, 1939–1940*. Moscow: Nauka, 1998.
Kurchev, N. *Gory v nashikh serdsakh*. St Petersburg: Professiia, 2001.
Kuznetsov, I. 'Iz istorii turizma', *Na sushe i na more* 5 (1941), 20.
Lanz, Hubert. *Gebirgsjäger*. Bad Nauheim: Hans-Hennig Podzun, 1954.
Lenin, Vladimir. *Polnoe sobranie sochinenii*. Moscow: Izdatel'stvo politicheskoi literatury, 1967.
Mashuk, L. 'Uchet i obmen opytom leta', *Na sushe i na more* 21 (1931), 1–2.
'Materialy dlia istorii Shipki', *Voennyi sbornik* 135(1) (1880).
'Materialy dlia istorii Shipki', *Voennyi sbornik* 135(2) (1880).
Meshcheriakov, G. P., ed. *A. V. Suvorov. Dokumenty*. Moscow: Voennoe izdatel'stvo Voennogo ministerstva SSSR, 1952.
Ministerstvo oborony Rossiiskoi Federatsii [Ministry of Defence of the Russian Federation] (13 November 2014), 'V Federatsii al'pinizma Rossii proshlo soveshchanie, posviashchennoe voprosam podgotovki voennosluzhashchikh i sotrudnikov spetspodrazdelenii k deistviiam v gorakh', http://mil.ru/et/news/more.htm?id=11999815@egNews&_print=true (accessed on 8 May 2017).
Moskalenko, Kirill. *Na iugo-zapadnom napravlenii, 1943–1945*. Moscow: Nauka, 1973.
Mozokhin, O., ed. *Politbiuro i delo Beriia*. Moscow: Kuchkovo pole, 2012.

Narodnyi Komissariat Oborony [People's Commissariat of Defence]. *Polevoi ustav RKKA PU-39*. Moscow: Gosudarstvennoe Voennoe Izdatel'stvo NKO SSSR, 1941.
Vremennyi Polevoi Ustav RKKA PU-36. Moscow: Gosudarstvennoe Voennoe Izdatel'stvo NKO SSSR, 1937.
Nemirovich-Danchenko, V. *God voiny: dnevnik russkago korrespondenta*. St Petersburg: Novoe vremia, 1878.
Nesterov, A. 'Turizm na sluzhbe oborone SSSR', *Na sushe i na more* 4 (1933), 3–4.
Nikolaev, S. 'Gornye massovki i uchebnye pokhody', *Na sushe i na more* 10 (1933), 14.
Noskov, P. 'Boevye zadachi lodochnogo turizma', *Na sushe i na more* 5 (1930), 3.
'Novaia popytka podniat'sia na Belukhu', *Na sushe i na more* 25 (1931), 9.
Obzor voennykh deistvii na Kavkaze v 1845 godu. Tbilisi: Shtab otdel'nago kavkazskago korpusa, 1846.
'Ot redaktsii', *Na sushe i na more* 1 (1930), 1.
Pankratov, S. 'Turizm i oborona', *Na sushe i na more* 5 (1932), 2–3.
Perlin, V. 'Krasnaia zvezda na El'bruse', *Na sushe i na more* 17 (1933), 5–6.
'Na loshadiakh cherez Shari-Vtsek,' *Na sushe i na more* 21 (1930), 6–7.
'Shkola al'pinista i boitsa', *Na sushe i na more* 18 (1931), 2–3.
'Turizm i Krasnaia armiia', *Na sushe i na more* 4 (1931), 1–2.
'Turizm v Krasnoi armii', *Na sushe i na more* 10 (1931), cover.
ed. *Turizm v Krasnoi armii*. Moscow: Fizkul'tura i turizm, 1930.
Pershanin, Vladimir, ed. *My pol-Evropy po-plastunski propakhali*. Moscow: Iauza-Eksmo, 2010.
ed. *Stalingradskaia miasorubka*. Moscow: Iauza-Eksmo, 2012.
Pobol', N. and P. Polian. *Stalinskie deportatsii*. Moscow: Demokratiia, 2005.
Pogrebetskii, M. 'Kak byl vziat Khan-Tengri', *Na sushe i na more* 7 (1932), 4–5.
'Kak byl vziat Khan-Tengri', *Na sushe i na more* 9 (1932), 8–9.
'Tekhnika gorovoskhozhdeniia', *Na sushe i na more* 17 (1932), 14–15.
Tri goda bor'by za Khan-Tengri. Kharkov: Ukrains'kyi robitnyk, 1935.
'Pokhod zakavkazskoi pekhotnoi shkoly', *Na sushe i na more* 22 (1930), 10.
Pokrovskii, N. 'Turizm i oborona', *Na sushe i na more* 1 (1941), 4–5.
'Poriadok utverzhdeniia marshrutov', *Na sushe i na more* 6 (1933), 14.
'Proletarskii turizm – na sluzhbu oborone strany', *Na sushe i na more* 4 (1933), 8–10.
Pshenianik, Georgii. *Krakh plana 'Edel'veis'*. Moscow: Tsentrpoligraf, 2013.
Rakovskii, A. 'Kak my stroili priiut OPT', *Na sushe i na more* 11 (1929).
Reding-Biberegg, Rudolf von. *Pokhod Suvorova cherez Shveitsariiu*. St Petersburg: T-vo khudozhestvennoi pechati, 1902.
Rikhter, Zinaida. *Shturm El'brusa: vtoraia al'piniada RKKA*. Moscow: Molodaia gvardiia, 1935.
Savel'ev, V. 'Gotovim gornykh strelkov', *Na sushe i na more* 5 (1941), 2.

Sbornik materialov po russko-turetskoi voine 1877–1878 gg. na Balkanskom poluostrove. St Petersburg: Izdanie Voenno-Istoricheskoi Komissii Glavnago Shtaba, 1898.
Sebin, V., ed. *Pamiat' i skorb'*. Petrozavodsk: Administration of Pitkiaranty, 1999.
Sediakin, A. 'Turizm i al'pinizm v Krasnoi armii', *Na sushe i na more* 4 (1935), 5.
Semanov, S., ed. *Aleksandr Vasil'evich Suvorov*. Moscow: Russkii mir, 2000.
Semenovskii, Vasilii. *Al'pinizm*. Moscow: FiS, 1936.
Shantsev, V. et al., eds. *Butovskii poligon, 1937–1938 gg*. Moscow: Al'zo, 2002.
Shapovalov, V., ed. *Bitva za Kavkaz v dokumentakh i materialakh*. Stavropol: SGU, 2003.
Shebalin, D., ed. *Nastavlenie dlia deistvii voisk v gorakh*. Moscow: NKO SSSR, 1940.
Shpeer, Al'bert. *Vospominaniia*. Smolensk: Rusich, 1997.
'Sotsialisticheskoe stroitel'stvo i turizm', *Na sushe i na more* 2 (1930), 1–2.
Sudoplatov, Pavel. *Spetsoperatsii*. Moscow: Olma-Press, 1999.
Tiulenev, Ivan. *Cherez tri voiny*. Moscow: MO SSSR, 1960.
Krakh operatsii 'Edelveis'. Ordzhonikidze: Ir, 1975.
Traskovich, F. 'Za rost obshchestva i razvitie samodeiatel'nogo turizma', *Na sushe i na more* 6 (1935), 2.
Tsentral'nyi Sovet OPTE. *Spasatel'naia rabota v gorakh*. Moscow: Put' Oktiabria, 1936.
'Turistskii den'', *Na sushe i na more* 4 (1933), 2.
'Turizm v Krasnoznamennoi Kavkazskoi', *Na sushe i na more* 19 (1930), cover.
V.P. 'Kak vesti dnevnik', *Na sushe i na more* 11 (1930), 15.
Vorob'ev, V. 'Kavkaz pod bokom', *Na sushe i na more* 1 (1932), 15.
'Na kruton pod'eme', *Na sushe i na more* 20 (1931), 4–5.
'Tekhnika gornogo turizma dybom', *Na sushe i na more* 15 (1932), 13.
Voroshilov, K. 'Prikaz Narkoma Soiuza SSR', *Na sushe i na more* 1 (1935), 2.
'Vsem otdeleniiam OPTE', *Na sushe i na more* 15 (1930), 1.
Vyrypaev, Nikolai. *Shest' mesiatsev na Shipke*. St Petersburg: Chtenie dlia soldat, 1884.
'Za massovyi turizm v Krasnoi armii', *Na sushe i na more* 12 (1930), 8.
Zhemchuzhnikov, A. 'Turist – na gornye lyzhi', *Na sushe i na more* 2–3 (1933), 7.
Zhigulin, V. 'Nositeli znachkov', *Na sushe i na more* 5 (1941), 18.
Zolotarev, V., ed. *Tainy i uroki zimnei voiny, 1939–1940*. St Petersburg: Poligon, 2002.

Secondary Sources

Achkasov, V., et al. *Russko-turetskaia voina 1877–1878*. Moscow: Voenizdat, 1977.

Akopian, G. *V boiiakh za Tuapse*, http://budetinteresno.narod.ru/kraeved/tuapse_war_11.htm (accessed on 8 May 2017).

Al'binin, V. 'Pomnish granatu i zapisku v nei . . . ', *Turist* 8 (1976), 31.

Andreev, German. 'Istoriia spasatel'noi sluzhby SSSR – Rossii', http://alpklubspb.ru/ass/46.htm (accessed on 8 May 2017).

Arendt, Hannah. *Origins of Totalitarianism*. New York: Harcourt Brace Jovanovich, 1976.

Aretov, Nikolai, ed. *Purva radost e za mene. Emotsionalnoto sudurzhanie na bulgarskata natsionalna identichnost: istoricheski koreni i suvremenni izmereniia*. Sofia: Kralitsa Mab, 2012.

Basov, A., et al. *Narodnyi podvig v bitve za Kavkaz*. Moscow: Institut Istorii AN SSSR, 1981.

Batyrov, U., ed. *Materialy mezhdunarodnoi nauchnoi konferentsii, posviashchennoi 60-letiiu bitvy za Kavkaz*. Vladikavkaz: Iriston, 2003.

Bekishvili, V. 'Oborona kavkazskikh perevalov', PhD dissertation, Tbilisi, 1977.

Beskrovnyi, A. and A. Preobrazhenskii, eds. *Aleksandr Vasil'evich Suvorov*. Moscow: Nauka, 1980.

Bezugol'nyi, A. *Narody Kavkaza i Krasnaia armiia*. Moscow: Veche, 2007.

Bobrov, M. M. *Front nad oblakami*. St Petersburg: Sankt-Peterburgskii gumanitarnyi universitet profsoiuzov, 2005.

Buchner, Alex. *Gebirgsjäger an allen Fronten*. Berg am See: Kurt Vowinckel, 1984.

Kampf im Gebirge. Munich: Schild, 1957.

Bugai, Nikolai and Askarbi Gonov, *Kavkaz: narody v eshelonakh*. Moscow: INSAN, 1998.

Cooke, Philip and Ben Shepherd, eds. *European Resistance in the Second World War*. Barnsley: Pen & Sword, 2013.

Dobkovich, V. *Turizm v SSSR*. Leningrad: Vsesoiuznoe obshchestvo po rasprostraneniiu politicheskikh i nauchnykh znanii, 1954.

Dolzhenko, G. *Istoriia turizma v dorevoliutsionnoi Rossii i SSSR*. Rostov-on-Don: Izdatel'stvo Rostovskogo Universiteta, 1988.

Dolzhenko, G. and Iu. Putrik. *Istoriia turizma v Rossiiskoi imperii, Sovetskom Soiuze i Rossiiskoi Federatsii*. Moscow and Rostov-on-Don: MarT, 2010.

Erickson, Edward. *Ordered to Die*. Westport, CT: Greenwood Press, 2001.

Gashchuk, A. and V. Vukolov. *Turizm v vooruzhennykh silakh SSSR*. Moscow: Voenizdat, 1983.

Gerua, I., ed. *Opisanie russko-turetskoi voiny 1877–1878 gg*. St Petersburg: Voennaia tipografiia, 1912.

Glantz, David. *A History of Soviet Airborne Forces*. Portland, OR: Frank Cass, 1994.

Stumbling Colossus: The Red Army on the Eve of World War. Lawrence: University of Kansas, 1998.

Gneushev, V. and A. Poput'ko. *Taina Marukhskogo lednika*. Moscow: Sovetskaia Rossiia, 1966.

Taina Marukhskogo lednika. Moscow: Sovetskaia Rossiia, 1971.

Govorukhin, Stanislav. *Belyi vzryv*. Film, 1969.

Grechko, A. *Cherez Karpaty*. Moscow: MO SSSR, 1972.

Grechko, Andrei et al., eds. *Istoriia vtoroi mirovoi voiny 1939–1945*. Moscow: MO SSSR, 1975.

Hoffmann, Joachim. *Kaukasien 1942/1943. Das deutsche Heer und die Orientvölker der Sowjetunion*. Freiburg: Rombach Verlag KG, 1991.

Ibragimbeili, Khadzhi Murat. *Krakh 'Edel'veisa' i blizhnii vostok*. Moscow: Nauka, 1977.

Il'ina, I. *Obshchestvennye organizatsii Rossii v 1920-e gody*. Moscow: IRI RAN, 2000.

Isaev, Aleksei. *Chudo prigranichnogo srazheniia*. Moscow: Eksmo, 2013.

Mify i pravda o Stalingrade. Moscow: Eksmo, 2013.

Kaltenegger, Ronald. *Gebirgsjäger im Kaukasus*. Graz: Leopold Stocker Verlag, 1995.

Kersnovskii, A. *Istoriia russkoi armii*. Moscow: Golos, 1993.

Khadzhi-Murad, Donogo. 'Arakanskii sindrom', http://muhajir.netai.net/yaseen/arkans.htm (accessed on 8 May 2017).

Korsun, Nikolai. *Sarykamyshskaia operatsiia*. Moscow: Voenizdat, 1937.

Koval'chuk, V. et al., eds. *Dobrovol'nye obshchestva v Petrograde-Leningrade v 1917–1937 gg*. Leningrad: Nauka, 1989.

Krivosheev, Grigorii, ed. *Rossiia i SSSR v voinakh XX veka*. Moscow: OLMA Press, 2001.

Linets, S. and S. Ianush. *Oborona Severnogo Kavkaza v gody Velikoi Otechestvennoi voiny*. Moscow: Ileksa, 2010.

Lota, V. I. *Sorvat' 'Edelveis'*. Moscow: Kuchkovo pole, 2010.

Lukirskii, S., ed. *Taktika v trudakh voennykh klassikov*. Moscow: Gosudarstvennoe voennoe izdatel'stvo, 1926.

Medvenskii, N. I. *Boevye operatsii na perevalakh Abkhazii v khode bitvy za Kavkaz 1942–1943 gg*. Sukhum, 2012.

Meyer, Hermann Frank. *Blutiges Edelweiss: Die 1. Gebirgs-Division im Zweiten Weltkrieg*. Berlin: Ch. Links, 2008.

Miliutin, Dmitrii. *Istoriia voiny 1799 goda mezhdu Rossiei i Frantsiei*. St Petersburg: Imperatorskaia Akademiia Nauk, 1857.

Moshchanskii, Il'ia. *Oborona Kavkaza*. Moscow: Veche, 2009.

Stoiat' nasmert'! Moscow: Veche, 2010.

N.R. 'Sarykamysh', *Voina i revoliutsiia* 3 (1927), 158–71.

Opryshko, O. *Zaoblachnyi front Priel'brus'ia*. Moscow: MO SSSR, 1976.

Orlov, Igor' and Elena Iurchikova. *Massovyi turizm v stalinskoi povsednevnosti*. Moscow: Rosspen, 2010.

Pospelov, P. et al., eds. *Istoriia Velikoi Otechestvennoi voiny Sovetskogo Soiuza.* Moscow: IML, 1961–5.

Prochko, I. *Istoriia razvitiia artillerii.* Moscow: Poligon, 1994.

Rubtsov, Iurii. *Alter ego Stalina.* Moscow: Zvonnitsa, 1999.

Sankt-Peterburg Alpine Club. 'Al'pinisty severnoi stolitsy', http://alpklubspb.ru/ass/a155-3.htm (accessed on 8 May 2016).

Shunkov, V. *Oruzhie Krasnoi armii.* Minsk: Kharvest, 1999.

Oruzhie Vermakhta. Minsk: Kharvest, 1999.

Simonov, Evgenii. 'Geroi El'brusa', *Turist* 3 (1967), 3.

Skorodumov, D. 'Plan Shveitsarskogo pokhoda Suvorova', *Voenno-istoricheskii zhurnal* 2 (1941), 65.

Solonin, Mark. *Drugaia khronologiia katastrofy 1941.* Moscow: Iauza-Eksmo, 2011.

Iiun' 41-go: okonchatel'nyi diagnoz. Moscow: Iauza-Eksmo, 2014.

'Uprezhdaiushchii udar' Stalina. Moscow: Iauza-Katalog, 2014.

Statiev, Alexander. 'The Nature of Anti-Soviet Armed Resistance, 1942–1944: The North Caucasus, the Kalmyk Autonomous Republic, and Crimea', *Kritika: Explorations in Russian and Eurasian History* 6/2 (2005), 285–318.

'Penal Units in the Red Army', *Europe-Asia Studies* 62(5) (July 2010), 721–47.

'Romanian Naval Doctrine and Its Tests in the Second World War', *War in History* 15(2) (2008), 191–210.

Stoehr, Ingo. *German Literature of the Twentieth Century.* Rochester: Camden House, 2001.

Sukhomlin, A., ed. *Suvorovskii sbornik.* Moscow: AN SSSR, 1951.

Surin, A. V., et al. *Istoriki razmyshliaiut.* Moscow: Universitetskii gumanitarnyi litsei, 1999.

Suvenirov, Oleg. *Tragediia RKKA, 1937–1938.* Moscow: Terra, 1998.

Tereshkin, Aleksei. *Istoriia otechestvennogo voennogo al'pinizma.* Documentary film, 2012.

Tieke, Wilhelm. *The Caucasus and the Oil.* Winnipeg: J. J. Fedorowicz, 1995.

Tunstall, Graydon. *Blood on the Snow.* Lawrence: University Press of Kansas, 2010.

Usyskin, Grigorii. *Ocherki istorii rossiiskogo turizma.* St Petersburg: Gerda, 2000.

Uziel, Daniel. *The Propaganda Warriors.* Oxford: Peter Lang, 2008.

Venkov, B., ed. *V boiiakh za Karpaty.* Uzhgorod: Karpaty, 1975.

Zav'ialov, A. and T. Kaliadin. *Bitva za Kavkaz.* Moscow: MO SSSR, 1957.

Zolotarev, V. and G. Sevost'ianov, eds. *Velikaia Otechestvennaia voina, 1941–1945.* Moscow: Nauka, 1998.

INDEX